Study Guide

Anderson's Business Law and the Legal Environment

21st EDITION

Twomey & Jennings

SOUTH-WESTERN
CENGAGE Learning

Australia • Brazil • Japan • Korea • Mexico • Singapore • Spain • United Kingdom • United States

SOUTH-WESTERN
CENGAGE Learning™

ISBN-13: 978-0-324-82978-5
ISBN-10: 0-324-82978-7

South-Western Cengage Learning
5191 Natorp Boulevard
Mason, OH 45040
USA

Cengage Learning is a leading provider of customized learning solutions with office locations around the globe, including Singapore, the United Kingdom, Australia, Mexico, Brazil, and Japan. Locate your local office at: **international.cengage.com/region**.

Cengage Learning products are represented in Canada by Nelson Education, Ltd.

For your course and learning solutions, visit **www.cengage.com**.

Purchase any of our products at your local college store or at our preferred online store **www.cengagebrain.com**.

For product information and technology assistance, contact us at **Cengage Learning Academic Resource Center, 1-800-423-0563**.

For permission to use material from this text or product, submit all requests online at **www.cengage.com/permissions**. Further permissions questions can be emailed to **permissionrequest@cengage.com**.

READ IMPORTANT LICENSE INFORMATION

Printed in the United States of America
2 3 4 5 6   19 18 17 16 15

CONTENTS

CHAPTER 1
THE NATURE AND SOURCES OF LAW

MAKE THE CONNECTION

SUMMARY

Law provides rights and imposes duties. One such right is the right of privacy, which affords protection against unreasonable searches of our property and intrusion into or disclosure of our private affairs.

Law consists of the pattern of rules established by society to govern conduct and relationships. These rules can be expressed as constitutional provisions, statutes, administrative regulations, and case decisions. Law can be classified as substantive or procedural, and it can be described in terms of its historical origins, by the subject to which it relates, or in terms of law or equity.

The sources of law include constitutions, federal and state statutes, administrative regulations, ordinances, and uniform laws generally codified by the states in their statutes. The courts are also a source of law through their adherence to case precedent under the doctrine of *stare decisis* and through their development of time-honored principles called the common law.

LEARNING OUTCOMES
After studying this chapter, you should be able to

A. NATURE OF LAW AND LEGAL RIGHTS
LO.1   Discuss the nature of law and legal rights

B. SOURCES OF LAW
LO.2   List the sources of law

C. UNIFORM STATE LAWS
LO.3   Explain uniform state laws

D. CLASSIFICATIONS OF LAW
LO.4   Describe the classifications of law

CHAPTER OUTLINE

A. NATURE OF LAW AND LEGAL RIGHTS

Law consists of the principles that govern conduct and that can be enforced in court or by administrative agencies.

1. LEGAL RIGHTS

GENERAL RULES. ▶ A right is the legal power to require someone else to do or not to do something.   ▶ A duty is the legal obligation to do or not to do something.
STUDY HINT.   Rights flow from the federal and state constitutions, statutes, and local ordinances.

1

2. INDIVIDUAL RIGHTS

The U.S. Constitution grants certain fundamental rights to persons, and these rights cannot be altered or eliminated by any statutes, ordinances, or judicial decisions.

3. THE RIGHT OF PRIVACY

GENERAL RULE. ▶Americans enjoy a fundamental right of privacy. ▶ The right of privacy guarantees:
(1) the right to be protected from unreasonable governmental searches and seizures; and (2) the right to be free from intrusions by the government and others into one's private affairs.
STUDY HINTS. ▶ The right to privacy is recognized by the U.S. Constitution, many state constitutions, and by certain federal and state statutes. ▶ The constitutional right to privacy may be violated when government law enforcement officers allow a non-governmental third party, such as the media, to accompany them on a criminal search. ▶ If your home or business is illegally searched, then any evidence obtained during the unlawful search is not admissible as evidence in a criminal trial due to the Fourth Amendment.
▶**LEARNING OUTCOME EXAMPLE.** See *Wilson v Layne*, p. 5.

4. PRIVACY AND TECHNOLOGY

GENERAL RULE. Even though technology may enable others to invade one's privacy, a person's reasonable expectation of privacy still governs his or her privacy rights.
STUDY HINT. Electronic violation of a person's right of privacy may be both a crime and a breach of a person's right to privacy.
▶**LEARNING OUTCOME EXAMPLE.** See E-Commerce and Cyberlaw, p. 10.

B. SOURCES OF LAW

GENERAL RULE. Important sources of the law include:

➤ *Constitutional law*: law created by the U.S. Constitution and state constitutions. This type of law typically creates the structure of the government and its relationship to the people governed.

➤ *Statutory law*: law created by Congress, state legislatures, and local governments, such as cities. Statutory laws adopted by local governments are called ordinances.

➤ *Administrative regulations*: law (rules) created by federal and state administrative agencies.

➤ *Case law*: law created by courts. ▶ Courts may adopt a precedent, that is a rule of law which is adopted for the first time. Under the doctrine of stare decisis, other courts in the same jurisdiction in future, similar cases, typically follow this rule. However, courts may refuse to apply a precedent when they feel that it is wrong, outdated, or for other good reasons. ▶ In some cases, courts may resolve a legal dispute by applying time-honored rules of law that are called common law.

➤ *Other laws*: treaties by the United States and orders of the president of the United States and other government officials.

STUDY HINTS. ▶ Laws sometimes conflict with each other. When this occurs, there are two priorities that generally determine which law prevails. ▶ One priority ranks laws in the following order: (1) federal law; (2) state law; and (3) local law. ▶ A second priority ranks laws within the federal or state legal systems in the following order: (1) constitutional law, (2) statutory law, (3) administrative law, and (4) case law.

►**LEARNING OUTCOME EXAMPLE.** See the **For Example** discussion of landlords developing rules for tenants on everything from parking to laundry room use on p. 7.

C. UNIFORM STATE LAWS

► Uniform state laws are statutes that have been drafted by the National Conference of Commissioners on Uniform State Laws (NCCUSL), and they are proposed for adoption by state legislatures. ► Example: Uniform Commercial Code (UCC) that regulates various areas of commercial transactions.
►**LEARNING OUTCOME EXAMPLE.** See the list and explanation of uniform laws on pp. 8 and 9.

D. CLASSIFICATIONS OF LAW

GENERAL RULE.   Law is classified in many ways. Important classifications include:

> *Legal rights and procedures*: ► Substantive law creates and defines the legal rights and liabilities of persons.   Example: right not to have another person wrongfully injure your reputation. ► Procedural law specifies the steps that must be followed to enforce a person's substantive legal rights and liabilities. Example: statutes that limit the time within which you can sue another person.

> *Origin of the law*: English common law (basis for early American law); Roman (civil) law; law merchant.

> *Subject matter of the law*: Examples include law of contracts, property law, and tort law.

> *Nature of relief sought (law and equity)*: ► Principles that are used to resolve civil lawsuits may be classified by the relief sought. ► Principles of law are used if a party seeks monetary damages. ► Rules of equity are used if a party seeks a remedy other than damages (money), such as a court order that directs a party to perform a contract. Equitable principles are more flexible than principles of law and provide a remedy in accordance with equity and justice. Equitable relief is denied unless a party will suffer a loss that cannot be adequately remedied by damages.

STUDY HINTS.   ► A particular law may fall within two or more classifications. ► Example: The legal rule that a person may recover damages from others who negligently injure the person may be classified as substantive law, common law, tort law, and a principle of law.

►**LEARNING OUTCOME EXAMPLES.** See further discussion of law, equity, and substantive law on pp. 8 and 9; See the Sports & Entertainment Law discussion of steroids in baseball on p. 9; See footnote 8 with the discussion of the Jennifer Lopez/Marc Anthony suit on p. 10.

4

CONCEPT REVIEW AND APPLICATIONS

Matching Exercise

Select the term or phrase that best matches a definition or statement stated below. Each term or phrase is the best match for only one statement or definition. Not all terms and phrases will necessarily be used.

administrative	equity	right
regulations	law	*stare decisis*
case law	precedent	statutory law
common law	private law	substantive law
constitution	procedural law	
duty	right of privacy	

_____ 1. Classification of law that defines the steps required to enforce legal rights and obligations.

_____ 2. Law that is created by federal and state administrative agencies.

_____ 3. Classification of law that defines legal rights and obligations.

_____ 4. Legal obligation to perform or to refrain from performing an act.

_____ 5. Body of law that is created by Congress and state legislatures.

_____ 6. Rule of law adopted by a court for the first time.

_____ 7. Law that is created by courts.

_____ 8. Rule generally requiring that precedents be followed in future, similar cases.

_____ 9. Individual's entitlement to be free from unreasonable intrusion by others.

True/False

Write **T** if the statement is true, write **F** if it is false.

_____ 1. Religious principles are part of the law.

_____ 2. The U.S. Constitution grants individuals certain basic rights.

_____ 3. A statute cannot alter a person's right if the U.S. Constitution protects the right.

_____ 4. The U.S. Constitution does not grant individuals the right of privacy. Only statutes in some states grant the right of privacy.

_____ 5. A court may forbid the use of evidence in a criminal trial if that evidence was obtained by violating the defendant's right of privacy.

_____ 6. The government has the legal right to prohibit persons from engaging in any private conduct that it chooses to forbid.

_____ 7. States are legally required to enact all uniform state laws that are proposed by the National Conference of Commissioners on Uniform State Law.

_____ 8. Money damages are not an equitable remedy.

Multiple Choice

_____ 1. Awesome Television aired a show entitled "Do It Yourself." This program instructed the viewing audience on how to manufacture certain illegal drugs and where to buy the necessary ingredients. Awesome Television was notified that it was being charged with violation of a regulation of the FCC, a federal agency. What type of law was Awesome Television charged with violating?
   a. Constitutional law.
   b. Statutory law.
   c. Administrative law.
   d. Case law.

_____ 2. A state supreme court adopted a principle of law, which stated that a skier may sue a ski area for negligence even if the skier was skiing out of bounds (constitutional rights are not involved). This state's legislature later enacted a law, which stated that a skier could *not* hold a ski area liable if the skier was skiing out of bounds. Under these facts:
   a. The principle of law adopted by the state supreme court is statutory law.
   b. The principle of law adopted by the state supreme court is case law.
   c. The principle of law enacted by the state legislature is statutory law.
   d. b and c.

_____ 3. Which of the following is an example of administrative law?
   a. The state legislature passes a statute requiring businesses with more than 10 employees to offer a maternity leave program for the employees.
   b. In resolving a legal controversy between two parties, a state supreme court adopts a rule of law that an agreement is not valid unless there is both a valid offer and acceptance.
   c. The president of the United States issues an executive order restricting exports to a hostile nation.
   d. The Department of Motor Vehicles changes the fee for renewing a driver's license.

_____ 4. Ray Inc. was sued by a government agency for violating federal antidiscrimination law. At its trial in a lower federal trial court, Ray asserted that the law in question was unconstitutional. However, in a previous case involving other parties, the U.S. Supreme Court held, for the first time, that this law was constitutional. Under these facts:
   a. The prior decision of the Supreme Court is a precedent.
   b. Under the doctrine of *stare decisis*, the trial court in Ray's case is generally bound to follow the Supreme Court's prior decision and to find the law to be constitutional.
   c. Under the doctrine of *stare decisis*, the trial court in Ray's case is generally not bound to follow the Supreme Court's prior decision and it may find the law to be unconstitutional.
   d. a and b.

_____ 5. Roger and Teresa owned competing grocery stores. Roger told a group of Teresa's customers that she had previously been convicted of selling spoiled meat. Teresa claimed this statement was false, and she sued Roger for $50,000 for defamation (i.e., the wrongful injury to Teresa' reputation). Roger asserted two defenses: (1) What he said was true and, therefore, he did not commit this wrong; and (2) Teresa failed to sue him in accordance with laws that dictate how a person must file a lawsuit against another person. Under these facts:
   a. Defense (1) is based on procedural law.
   b. Defense (2) is based on procedural law.
   c. Defense (2) is based on substantive law.
   d. a and c.

_____ 6. In most states, the highest state court is the:
   a. The small claims court.
   b. The state general trial court.
   c. The state supreme court.
   d. The state appellate court.

Case Problem

Answer the following problem, briefly explaining your answer.

Trenton Antiques contracted to sell a painting to Janis for $500. The painting is a rare portrait that cannot be replaced. Trenton later refused to perform this contract and Janis sued. In this lawsuit, Janis requested the court to issue an order of requiring Trenton to perform the contract. Under these facts:

1. Will principles of law or equity determine whether Janis is awarded the relief that she requested?
2. What, if anything, must Janis establish in order to be awarded the relief that she has requested?

_____

_____

_____

Internet Exercise

Using the Internet, locate the U.S. Constitution and its amendments. Once you have read this material, answer the following questions:

1. Identify the web site where you located the U.S. Constitution.
2. Do any of the amendments to the U.S. Constitution *expressly* grant individuals the right of privacy?
3. Identify one or more of the amendments to the U.S. Constitution that may be *interpreted* as establishing the right of privacy?

_____

_____

_____

CHAPTER 2
THE COURT SYSTEM AND DISPUTE RESOLUTION

MAKE THE CONNECTION

SUMMARY

Courts have been created to hear and resolve legal disputes. A court's specific power is defined by its jurisdiction. Courts of original jurisdiction are trial courts, and courts that review the decisions of trial courts are appellate courts. Trial courts may have general jurisdiction to hear a wide range of civil and criminal matters, or they may be courts of limited jurisdiction—such as a probate court or the Tax Court—with the subject matter of their cases restricted to certain areas.

The courts in the United States are organized into two different systems: the state and federal court systems. There are three levels of courts, for the most part, in each system, with trial courts, appellate courts, and a supreme court in each. The federal courts are federal district courts, federal courts of appeals, and the U.S. Supreme Court. In the states, there may be specialized courts, such as municipal, justice, and small claims courts, for trial courts. Within the courts of original jurisdiction, there are rules for procedures in all matters brought before them. A civil case begins with the filing of a complaint by a plaintiff, which is then answered by a defendant. The parties may be represented by their attorneys. Discovery is the pretrial process used by the parties to find out the evidence in the case. The parties can use depositions, interrogatories, and document requests to uncover relevant information.

The case is managed by a judge and may be tried to a jury selected through the process of *voir dire*, with the parties permitted to challenge jurors on the basis of cause or through the use of their peremptory challenges. The trial begins following discovery and involves opening statements and the presentation of evidence, including the direct examination and cross-examination of witnesses. Once a judgment is entered, the party who has won can collect the judgment through garnishment and a writ of execution.

Alternatives to litigation for dispute resolution are available, including arbitration, mediation, MedArb, reference to a third party, association tribunals, summary jury trials, rent-a-judge plans, minitrials, judicial triage, and the use of ombudsmen. Court dockets are relieved and cases consolidated using judicial triage, a process in which courts hear the cases involving the most serious medical issues and health conditions first. Triage is a blending of the judicial and alternative dispute resolution mechanisms.

LEARNING OUTCOMES
After studying this chapter, you should be able to

A. THE COURT SYSTEM
LO.1   Explain the federal and state court systems

B. COURT PROCEDURE
LO.2   Describe court procedures

C. ALTERNATIVE DISPUTE RESOLUTION (ADR)
LO.3   List the forms of alternative dispute resolution and distinguish among them

CHAPTER OUTLINE

A. THE COURT SYSTEM

A court is a tribunal established by a government to decide controversies, provide a remedy for persons who have been wronged, punish wrongdoers, and prevent wrongs.

1. THE TYPES OF COURTS

GENERAL RULES. ▶ Jurisdiction is the power to hear and decide cases. ▶ Courts have subject matter jurisdiction to decide only certain types of cases (lawsuits). ▶ Courts may have:

(a) *Original or appellate jurisdiction*: original jurisdiction is the power to decide cases for the first time, whereas appellate jurisdiction is the power to review decisions of lower courts to determine if a lower court made a reversible error.

(b) *General or limited jurisdiction*: general jurisdiction is the power to decide most types of cases, whereas limited jurisdiction is the power to decide only certain types of cases.

(c) *Criminal or civil jurisdiction*: criminal courts can decide cases involving crimes, whereas civil courts can decide cases involving private wrongs and other civil disputes.

STUDY HINTS. ▶ Courts with original jurisdiction are trial courts, and they render the initial judgment in civil and criminal cases. ▶ A reversible error usually occurs when a lower court: (1) applies the wrong law in resolving the case; or (2) incorrectly interprets or applies the law in resolving a case.

2. THE FEDERAL COURT SYSTEM

The federal court system consists of the following three levels of courts:

(a) *Federal district courts*: ▶ Federal district courts have original jurisdiction to decide most cases filed in federal court including: (1) civil suits in which the U.S. is a party; (2) actions involving any federal law, such as the U.S. Constitution, federal statutes or administrative rules, or U.S. treaties; and (3) cases between parties who are residents of different states if $75,000 or more is involved. ▶ Other federal courts with limited jurisdiction include federal bankruptcy court, Tax Court, U.S. Court of International Trade, and U.S. Claims Court.

(b) *U.S. courts of appeals*: ▶ U.S. courts of appeals have only appellate jurisdiction. ▶ These courts review judgments of federal district courts in their respective circuits. The decision of a U.S. court of appeals is final unless the Supreme Court hears an appeal of the case.

(c) *U.S. Supreme Court*: ▶ The Supreme Court is the highest federal court. ▶ The Supreme Court has original jurisdiction over cases involving ambassadors, public ministers or consuls, and for cases in which two states are involved. ▶ The Supreme Court has appellate jurisdiction over all cases brought in federal court and certain cases appealed from state supreme courts. Through the process of granting a *writ of certiorari*, the Court has the discretion to decide whether to hear an appeal

(d) ▶ **LEARNING OUTCOME EXAMPLE.** See Figure 2-1 on textbook p. 19 and accompanying text.

3. **STATE COURT SYSTEMS**

The typical state court system consists of the following types of courts:

(a) *General trial court*: Most states have trial courts with general jurisdiction of criminal/civil cases.

(b) *Specialty courts*: States may *have courts with l*imited jurisdiction, such as juvenile courts, probate courts, and f*amily law courts.*

(c) *City, municipal and justice courts*: Cities and counties may also have courts.

(d) *Small claims courts*: Most states have small claims courts that hear small civil cases.

(e) *State appellate courts*: These state courts hear appeals from state general trial courts.

(f) *State supreme court*: The highest court in most states is called the state supreme court, which generally has appellate jurisdiction. The decision of a state supreme court is typically final unless it involves a federal law, treaty, or the U.S. Constitution.

(g) **LEARNING OUTCOME EXAMPLE.** See Figure 2-3 on textbook p. 21 and accompanying text.

B. **COURT PROCEDURE**

4. **PARTICIPANTS IN THE COURT SYSTEM**

► The plaintiff is the party who commences a civil lawsuit and the prosecutor is the party who brings a criminal case on behalf of the government. The defendant is the party against whom a civil or criminal suit is brought. ► The judge is the primary court officer, and the jury is a body of citizens who are appointed by a court to decide the facts and render a verdict in a case.

5. **WHICH LAW APPLIES – CONFLICTS OF LAW**

► Conflict of laws is the principle that determines whether a court should apply the law of its own state or the law of another jurisdiction. ► If contracting parties do not state which law controls, then the trend is that the state law that has the most significant contacts with the transaction governs a contract.

6. **INITIAL STEPS IN A LAWSUIT**

A civil lawsuit typically involves the following beginning steps:

(a) Filing a complaint, which is a pleading that describes the wrongful conduct allegedly committed by the defendant, along with a request for relief, such as money damages.

(b) The defendant must be served with process, which notifies the defendant of the lawsuit.

(c) The defendant must file an appropriate response, which may be: an answer (response to the allegations stated in the complaint; a counterclaim (the defendant's claim for relief against the plaintiff), or other preliminary motions.

(d) ► Discovery is the process by which either party can find out from the other party most information relating to a lawsuit. ► Types of discovery include: a deposition (the taking of testimony of a witness or party outside of court); interrogatories (written questions served on a party); and written requests for production of documents.

(e) A party may request a summary judgment if there are no important factual issues and the party is entitled to win as a matter of law.

(f) If a case goes to trial, the parties may want to designate whom they intend to call as an expert witness, meaning a witness who has a certain expertise and who will give his or her opinion at trial.

(g) ► LEARNING OUTCOME EXAMPLE. See the discussion of steps in litigation that begins on textbook p. 23.

7. **THE TRIAL**

    (a) *Selecting a jury.* When there is a jury trial, the first step is selection of the jury. Jurors are selected from a jury pool through the process of *voir dire*, which is an examination to decide if prospective jurors are biased in favor of either party and whether they are otherwise suitable to be jurors.

    (b) *Opening statements, presentation of evidence, motion for directed verdict, and summation.*

    (c) *Jury instructions and verdict.* After the parties' summation, the court gives the jurors instructions on the law to apply in rendering its verdict. Once the jury gives its verdict, the court typically enters a judgment that conforms to the verdict. If the jury is deadlocked and cannot reach a verdict, the court will declare a mistrial, thereby dismissing the case, which may then be brought again.

    (d) *Motion for mistrial; motion for new trial; motion for judgment n.o.v.* (e) ▶ **LEARNING OUTCOME EXAMPLE.** See the **For Example** discussion of the Martha Stewart *voir dire* example on textbook p. 25.

8. **POSTTRIAL PROCEDURES**

    (a) *Recovery of costs/attorney fees.* Generally, the winning party is awarded certain costs incurred in a civil lawsuit. A party may recover attorney fees if recovery is authorized by statute or a contract authorizes such recovery.

    (b) *Execution of judgment.* If a party fails to pay a judgment, the judgment may be collected by a sheriff selling the losing party's nonexempt property pursuant to a writ of execution, or by the winning party obtaining wages or debts owed to the losing party pursuant to a writ of garnishment.

C. **ALTERNATIVE DISPUTE RESOLUTION (ADR)**

    LEARNING OUTCOME EXAMPLES. See the discussion of other forms of ADR, mediation, minitrials, rent-a-judge, MedArb, judicial triage, and referral to a third party that begins on textbook p. 28.

9. **ARBITRATION**

    GENERAL RULES. ▶ Arbitration is typically a voluntary process by which parties agree to submit a dispute to disinterested persons called "arbitrators." ▶ The parties' agreement determines whether a particular dispute must be submitted to arbitration. ▶ The arbitrator's decision generally is final, i.e., it is legally binding on the parties. ▶ The decision can be set aside by a court only if it is the result of fraud, arbitrary (grossly unreasonable) conduct by the arbitrator, or serious procedural mistakes.
    LIMITATION. Laws may require mandatory arbitration of some disputes. In this situation, the decision can be appealed and a party is entitled to a new trial (trial *de novo*).
    LEARNING OUTCOME EXAMPLE. See the discussion of arbitration that begins on textbook p. 29.

10. **MEDIATION**

    Mediation is a process whereby a neutral party (mediator) delivers settlement proposals from one party to the second party, and the mediator may also make suggestions for settlement of the dispute. The mediator's suggestions are not legally binding on the parties.

11. **MEDARB**

    This new form of ADR allows an arbitrator to also act as a mediator in the same matter.

12. REFERENCE TO A THIRD PERSON

GENERAL RULES. ▶ Parties may voluntarily refer determination of a fact, such as the value of a fire loss, to an impartial third party or committee. ▶ The parties usually agree that the decision will be final.

LEARNING OUTCOME EXAMPLE. See the discussion of employee and employer referrals of disputes to a designated board or committee on textbook p. 31.

13. ASSOCIATION TRIBUNALS

An association tribunal is a panel that resolves disputes between association members or between an association member and a consumer. The decision binds the association member, not the consumer.

14. SUMMARY JURY TRIAL

A summary jury trial is a pretend trial that is held before a jury; the decision is *not* binding.

15. RENT-A-JUDGE

Parties may hire a judge to try a case; the decision is binding unless reversed on appeal.

16. MINITRIAL

Parties submit a disputed issue to a person, such as a retired judge, for determination.

17. JUDICIAL TRIAGE

Courts may examine cases from a time perspective, first hearing those cases that must not be delayed.

18. CONTRACT PROVISIONS

Contracts often require that parties use one of the foregoing procedures.

19. DISPOSITION OF COMPLAINTS AND OMBUDSMEN

An ombudsman receives complaints and makes recommendations for improvement. An ombudsman reviews, but does not legally decide, complaints.

CONCEPT REVIEW AND APPLICATIONS

Matching Exercise

Select the term or phrase that best matches a definition or statement stated below. Each term or phrase is the best match for only one statement or definition. Not all terms and phrases will necessarily be used.

admissibility
affirm
answer
appeal
appellate jurisdiction
arbitration
association tribunal
attorney-client privilege
complaint
counterclaim
court
cross-examination
defendant
demurrer
deposition
direct examination
directed verdict
discovery
en banc
execution
expert witness

federal district courts
garnishment
general jurisdiction
impeach
instructions
interrogatories
judge
judgment n.o.v.
judicial triage
jurisdiction
jury
limited jurisdiction
mediation
minitrial
mistrial
motion for summary
judgment
motion to dismiss
ombudsman
opening statements
original jurisdiction

plaintiff
pleadings
process
prosecutor
recross-examination
redirect examination
reference to a third person
remand
rent-a-judge plan
requests for production of
documents
reverse
reversible error
small claims courts
special jurisdiction
subject matter jurisdiction
summary jury trial
summations
trial *de novo*
voir dire examination
writ of *certiorari*

_____ 1. Pleading stating a defendant's response to a plaintiff's complaint.

_____ 2. Jurisdiction that allows a court to hear and decide a case for the first time.

_____ 3. Legal notice of a lawsuit that is served on a defendant.

_____ 4. Pleading states a defendant's claim against a plaintiff and the defendant's demand for relief.

_____ 5. The party who files a civil lawsuit against another.

_____ 6. Pleading stating a plaintiff's claim against a defendant and the plaintiff's demand for relief.

_____ 7. Jurisdiction that allows a court to review the judgment of a lower court.

_____ 8. Procedure to enforce money judgment by which the winning party may obtain wages or debts that are owed by a third person or employer to the losing party.

_____ 9. Power of a court to hear and decide only a particular type of case.

_____10. Action that appellate courts take when setting aside verdicts or judgments of lower courts.

True/False

Write **T** if the statement is true, write **F** if it is false.

____ 1. If a statute requires arbitration of a dispute, then the arbitration decision is generally not final and a party may obtain a court trial on all of the issues (a trial *de novo*).

____ 2. Parties are legally prohibited from hiring a private judge or referee to hear and decide a dispute that they have with one another.

____ 3. *Voir dire* examination is the process by which jurors are selected.

____ 4. A court will not shorten a lawsuit by granting a summary judgment if there are important, disputed factual issues regarding a claim or defense.

____ 5. In civil cases, a party can generally use discovery procedures to find out information from the other party that relates to the lawsuit.

____ 6. The testimony and opinions of experts cannot be admitted as evidence at a trial.

____ 7. Direct examination is questioning a witness by the attorney who called the witness to testify.

____ 8. In a jury trial, the jury generally resolves questions of fact and the judge resolves questions of law.

____ 9. Ombudsmen do not generally have the power to legally hear and decide complaints.

____ 10. The winning party in a civil lawsuit is generally awarded recovery of his or her costs in the action.

Multiple Choice

____ 1. Carol stole inventory from Acme Corp., her employer. Eventually, Carol was apprehended. Under these facts:
   a. Acme may sue Carol for money damages in criminal court.
   b. The state may prosecute Carol for theft in civil court.
   c. Acme may sue Carol for money damages in civil court, and the state may prosecute Carol for theft in criminal court.
   d. Acme may sue Carol for money damages in criminal court, and the state may prosecute Carol for theft in civil court.

____ 2. Kevin intends to sue his employer in federal court for violation of federal antidiscrimination laws. Under these facts, the federal trial court that will first hear and decide this case is the:
   a. Federal district court.
   b. U.S. court of appeals.
   c. U.S. Supreme Court.
   d. Tax Court.

_____ 3. Tim, a resident of Iowa, is suing Rod, a resident of New York, for $90,000. Tim is suing for breach of contract (state law). Would a federal district court have jurisdiction to decide this case?
   a. Yes. Federal district courts have jurisdiction to decide all lawsuits.
   b. Yes. A federal district court would have jurisdiction because Tim and Rod are residents of different states and the lawsuit involves $75,000 or more.
   c. No. Federal district courts do not have jurisdiction unless federal law is involved.
   d. No. Federal district courts do not have jurisdiction unless $100,000 or more is involved.

_____ 4. Lawrence wants to sue his former landlord in order to recover his security deposit that the landlord has wrongfully failed to return. Under these facts:
   a. Lawrence will commence the lawsuit by filing a judgment with the clerk of the court.
   b. Lawrence will commence the lawsuit by filing a complaint with the clerk of the court.
   c. The landlord is automatically subject to the power of the court upon the filing of a complaint. Nothing is required to be served on the landlord to subject him to the power of the court.
   d. b and c.

_____ 5. Patti and Daryl are involved in an automobile accident. Patti properly commences a lawsuit against Daryl and process is served on Daryl. Daryl does not believe that he is liable to Patti. Also, Daryl believes that Patti is actually liable to him due to this accident. In this case, Daryl should:
   a. File an answer denying the incorrect allegations stated in Patti's complaint.
   b. File a counterclaim asserting Daryl's claim against Patti and requesting appropriate relief.
   c. Do nothing.
   d. a and b.

_____ 6. Rosa sued T&S Co. for breach of contract. Based on substantial factual evidence, the jury returned a $5,000 verdict in favor of Rosa, and the judge entered judgment in her favor for this amount. If T&S Co. appeals this judgment to the court of appeals, the court of appeals:
   a. May set aside or modify the judgment if the lower court made serious errors of law.
   b. Will not review the record of the proceedings of the lower court.
   c. Will have the witnesses testify again.
   d. Will conduct a new trial.

_____ 7. Arco Construction and Joe entered into a contract whereby Arco agreed to construct a building for Joe. A contract dispute has now arisen regarding Arco's work. The contract states that all disputes relating to the contract must be submitted to arbitration. In this case:
   a. Joe need not submit this dispute to arbitration. If he desires, he can file a lawsuit.
   b. Joe must submit the dispute to arbitration. He gave up his right to file suit.
   c. If an arbitration is held, the arbitrator's decision is not legally binding on the parties.
   d. b and c.

_____ 8. Carol leased a shop from Rentco Inc. The parties had a disagreement and they agreed to submit their dispute to binding arbitration. Under these facts:
   a. The parties have no right to appeal the arbitrator's award (decision) to a court.
   b. The parties may appeal the arbitrator's award to a court.
   c. If the arbitrator's award is appealed, the court will set the award aside if, for any reason, the court disagrees with the award.
   d. b and c.

_____ 9. Don had a dispute with Ace involving a $500 claim. State law required arbitration of all civil disputes under $5,000. In arbitration, Don was awarded $300. Under these facts:
   a. The award is not legally binding because mandatory arbitration is unconstitutional.
   b. The award is final. Don has no right to appeal the award.
   c. The award is not final. Don may appeal the award to court and receive a trial *de novo*.
   d. The award is not final. Don may appeal the award, but there will not be a new trial.

_____ 10. Tex bought a new car from Lansing Co., a new car dealer. Tex alleges that the car is defective. The parties want to use an alternate means of dispute resolution to help resolve this matter. In this case:
   a. The parties can refer the dispute to a third person, and the parties can determine whether the third party's decision is legally binding on Tex and Lansing Co.
   b. In many states, the parties can use an association tribunal operated by new car dealers, but the tribunal's decision is legally binding on only the Lansing Co.
   c. The parties cannot use any form of ADR because it is illegal to do so.
   d. a and b.

Case Problem

Answer the following problem, briefly explaining your answer.

Roger was negligently injured by Diane. Roger is preparing to file a lawsuit against Diane in state court for $25,000 damages as compensation for the private wrong that Diane committed against him.

The state in question has these courts: (a) state supreme court that has appellate jurisdiction; (b) state district court that has original jurisdiction of all cases involving private wrongs; and (c) small claims court that has original jurisdiction of cases relating to private wrongs that involve $5,000 in damages or less. In this case:
1. Is Roger legally entitled to bring his lawsuit in any court that he chooses?
2. Which court has the power to hear and decide this lawsuit for the first time?
3. Will Roger bring his lawsuit in a civil court or a criminal court?

_____

_____

_____

Internet Exercise

Using the Internet, locate the web site for the National Center for State Courts. Using the information available on this web site, answer the following questions:

1. Identify the total number of civil cases that were reported as being filed in state courts of general jurisdiction.
2. Identify the main state court website for the state in which you attend school.
3. Should states maintain web sites that make it easier for individuals to sue one another? Discuss the pros and cons of the states providing such information.

_____

_____

_____

CHAPTER 3
BUSINESS ETHICS, SOCIAL FORCES, AND THE LAW

MAKE THE CONNECTION

SUMMARY
Business ethics is the application of values and standards to business conduct and decisions. These values originate in various sources from positive (codified) law to natural law to stakeholder values. Business ethics is important because trust is a critical component of good business relationships and free enterprise. A business with values will enjoy the additional competitive advantage of a good reputation and, over the long term, better earnings. When businesses make decisions that violate basic ethical standards, they set into motion social forces and cause the area of abuse to be regulated, resulting in additional costs and restrictions for business. Voluntary value choices by businesses position them for a competitive advantage.

The categories of ethical values in business are truthfulness and integrity, promise keeping, loyalty and avoiding conflicts of interest, fairness, doing no harm, and maintaining confidentiality.

Resolution of ethical dilemmas is possible through the use of various models that require a businessperson to examine the impact of a decision before it is made. These models include stakeholder analysis, the Blanchard and Peale test, the frontpage-of-the-newspaper test, the Laura Nash model, and the Wall Street Journal model.

LEARNING OUTCOMES
After studying this chapter, you should be able to

A. WHAT IS BUSINESS ETHICS?
LO.1   Define business ethics

B. WHY IS BUSINESS ETHICS IMPORTANT?
LO.2   Discuss why ethics are important in business

C. HOW TO RECOGNIZE AND RESOLVE ETHICAL DILEMMAS
LO.3   Describe how to recognize and resolve ethical dilemmas

CHAPTER OUTLINE

A. WHAT IS BUSINESS ETHICS?

GENERAL RULE.   Ethics is a branch of philosophy dealing with values that relate to the nature of human conduct and the moral goodness or rightness of the motives and actions of people. Business ethics seeks to balance the goal of making profits with the values of individuals and society.
LEARNING OUTCOME EXAMPLE. See the discussion of the definition, balancing the goal of profits with the values of individuals and society, on textbook p. 40.

1. **THE LAW AS THE STANDARD FOR BUSINESS ETHICS**

   GENERAL RULE. One set of moral standards is based on: What does positive (or codified) law require? Under this standard, any behavior is ethical if it does not break the law.
   LIMITATION. The issue of fairness is not necessarily addressed under this standard.
   STUDY HINT. Moral standards come from different sources, and there is no universal agreement on what moral standards are appropriate.

2. **THE NOTION OF UNIVERSAL STANDARDS FOR BUSINESS ETHICS**

   GENERAL RULE. The natural law theory holds that behavioral standards exist universally and they cannot be changed or modified by positive law.
   STUDY HINT. ▶ Those who believe in the natural law theory feel that higher standards of behavior than those required by codified laws must be followed even if those higher standards violate the codified law. Thus, proponents of the natural law theory feel that civil disobedience may sometimes be justified. ▶ Example: Although slavery was legally permissible in the U.S. in the early 1800s, civil disobedience would have been justified to help slaves escape under the natural law principle of individual freedom.

3. **THE STANDARD OF SITUATIONAL BUSINESS ETHICS OR MORAL RELATIVISM**

   GENERAL RULE. Situational ethics or moral relativism is a flexible standard of behavior that allows an examination of circumstances and motivation before deciding whether conduct is "right" or "wrong."
   STUDY HINTS. ▶ The issue in situational ethics is not whether a wrong was committed, but whether the motivation and circumstances excuse or justify the actions. ▶U.S. companies when evaluating the morality of their international operations often use moral relativism.

4. **THE BUSINESS STAKEHOLDER STANDARD OF BEHAVIOR**

   GENERAL RULE. Under the business stakeholder standard of behavior, a business must consider the interests of the various stakeholders, i.e., those with interests in the business, to resolve ethical dilemmas.
   STUDY HINTS. ▶ Stakeholders might include: (1) shareholders, who have an interest in the business's maximizing earnings and dividends; (2) members of the community where the business is located, who have an interest in preserving jobs; and (3) employees, who have an interest in job security. ▶ Views differ along the continuum of extremes of the belief that the business's sole responsibility is to make as much money as legally possible to the belief that the business exists to solve social problems. Many businesses operate by trying to respond to all stakeholders and to balance conflicting interests.

B. **WHY IS BUSINESS ETHICS IMPORTANT?**

   ➢ Values are an important part of business success.

   ➢ Regardless of a business's views on social responsibility, complying with the law and being fair in business transactions are widely shared concerns.

   ➢ **LEARNING OUTCOME EXAMPLES.** See "The Importance of Trust" on textbook p. 44; see "Business Ethics and Financial Performance" on textbook p. 45; see "The Importance of a Good Reputation" on textbook p. 46.

5. **THE IMPORTANCE OF TRUST**

Business investment, purchases and sales, hiring of employees, and growth are based on trust. Although courts provide remedies for breaches of agreements, it is the reliance on promises, not the reliance on litigation, which results in good business relationships.

6. **BUSINESS ETHICS AND FINANCIAL PERFORMANCE**

Studies show that companies with high standards for product quality, employee welfare, and customer service are more likely to succeed over the long term than those companies making poor ethical choices.

7. **THE IMPORTANCE OF A GOOD REPUTATION**

A breach of ethics can be costly to a business through: (1) drops in earnings, (2) payment of fines, and (3) loss of customer trust that may impact the business for years.

8. **BUSINESS ETHICS AND BUSINESS REGULATION: PUBLIC POLICY, LAW, AND ETHICS**

➢ Legislation and governmental regulation are responses to business activities that are unfair or abusive. Businesses may act voluntarily to treat customers, employees, and shareholders fairly and may thus avoid costly and intrusive legislation and regulation by government.

➢ Businesses that ignore society's views and desire for change speed the transition from businesses' value choices to enforceable law. Societal values that lead to change have one or more of these underlying goals:

(a) *Protection of the state*

GENERAL RULE. The need to protect the federal and state governments has given rise to many laws. Examples: treason laws; tax laws; federal law that requires a person to give his or her social security number in order to obtain a government benefit (which helps prevent false claims).
STUDY HINT. If the need to protect the state conflicts with the need to protect a person (and individual freedoms), then the law attempts to balance these social forces.

(b) *Protection of the person*

GENERAL RULES. ► Many laws have been adopted to protect the health, safety, personal rights (such as the right to privacy), civil rights, and economic interests of individuals. ► Examples: criminal laws; tort law; laws that generally prohibit discrimination in connection with voting, employment, education, governmental assistance programs, and hotel accommodations.
STUDY HINT. One act can be both: (1) a crime for which the wrongdoer may be imprisoned; and (2) a civil wrong (tort) for which an injured person may receive damages.

(c) *Protection of public health, safety, and morals*

Examples: health regulations that require food and restaurant inspections; motor vehicle laws that regulate speed limits and require car occupants to wear seat belts; obscenity laws.

(d) *Protection of property: its use and title*

> **GENERAL RULE.** Those who have title to property may use the property as they see fit.
>
> **LIMITATION.** Even ownership has restrictions imposed by law, such as zoning, nuisance, and environmental protection restrictions.
>
> **STUDY HINT.** ► Types of property that may be protected include real property, personal property, and intangible or intellectual property. ► Examples of laws protecting property: civil law that permits an owner to exclude others from coming upon his or her private, real property; criminal law that punishes a thief who wrongfully takes another's personal property; civil law that allows recovery of lost royalties because of another's infringement of one's copyrighted intellectual property.

(e) *Protection of personal rights*

> **GENERAL RULE.** ► Many constitutional and statutory principles are intended to protect the freedom of persons to choose how to act. ► Examples: constitutional rights of freedom of speech, religion, and press; in many states, right of a patient (or guardian) to refuse life-support treatment.
>
> **LIMITATION.** ► Like other social forces that protect individual freedoms, the freedom of personal action is balanced against and limited by the need to protect society from harmful conduct and the need to prevent unreasonable interference with the rights of others. ► Example of balancing: freedom of speech does not permit one to wrongfully injure another's reputation.

(f) *Enforcement of individual intent*

> **GENERAL RULE.** In connection with voluntary transactions, such as the making of a contract or will, the law generally enforces the intent of the parties.
>
> **LIMITATIONS.** ► Parties' intentions are not enforced if they are not stated in the legally required manner, e.g., an oral contract or will is unenforceable if it violates a legal requirement that it be written. ► The intent of parties will not be enforced if the intended action is illegal.

(g) *Protection from exploitation, fraud, and oppression*

> Examples: laws that allow minors (persons under the legal age) to set aside contracts; securities laws; antidiscrimination laws; food processing and labeling laws.

(h) *Furtherance of trade*

> Examples: laws that establish a currency; laws that permit and regulate instruments, such as checks and promissory notes; antitrust laws that promote competition.

(i) *Protection of creditors and rehabilitation of debtors*

> **GENERAL RULES.** ► Creditors are protected by laws that make contracts binding and statutes that make it fraudulent for a debtor to conceal property from a creditor. ► The social force of rehabilitation of debtors is furthered by bankruptcy law that allows debtors to escape liability for certain debts and thereby achieve a new economic life.
>
> **STUDY HINT.** Debtors are no longer imprisoned for not paying debts.

(j) *Stability and flexibility*

GENERAL RULES. ► Stability is important in business dealings. Also, the desire for stability causes courts to follow existing decisions (precedents) unless there is a significant reason to change. ► Virtually all laws can be changed. ► A law may be changed because the reason for the law no longer exists or because society's sense of what is just has changed.

LIMITATION. The social forces of stability and flexibility often conflict.

STUDY HINTS. ► If no law or former decision directly resolves a question, then courts commonly resolve the issue by making a logical extension of the reasoning stated in other similar cases. ► It is relatively easy to change statutes; it is difficult to change constitutions. ► Flexibility is often accomplished by (1) creating exceptions to a law or (2) stating legal duties in general terms (such as the reasonable person standard). ► The social force that seeks to maximize protection of the person will often determine whether or not a law should be changed.

C. HOW TO RECOGNIZE AND RESOLVE ETHICAL DILEMMAS

9. CATEGORIES OF ETHICAL BEHAVIOR

Business managers often find themselves confronted with the difficult task of deciding what is ethically right or wrong in a particular situation. A majority of large companies provide employees with some form of ethical training, identifying categories of conduct that may or may not be an ethical breach.

(a) *Integrity and truthfulness*

Integrity is the adherence to one's values and principles despite the costs and consequences.

(b) *Promise-keeping*

Most business undertakings are based upon promises, some legally enforceable and others not. The strategic question is whether a firm should make promises that will realize little profit for the firm. In the long run, a firm's reputation is largely determined on the degree to which it keeps its promises.

(c) *Loyalty - avoiding conflicts of interest*

Employees owe a duty of loyalty to their employers, and conduct that compromises this loyalty is a conflict of interest. Some firms have a zero tolerance for conduct that may create a conflict, such as a complete ban on employees' accepting any gifts whatsoever from suppliers or clients.

(d) *Fairness*

One way to decide what is fair is to evaluate this issue from both parties' perspective.

(e) *Doing no harm*

A basic rule of business is that you should not do anything that you know will harm others.

(f) *Maintaining confidentiality*

Employees owe a duty of confidentiality to their employers.

10. RESOLVING ETHICAL DILEMMAS

In addition to the section on stakeholders, other models for solving ethical dilemmas include:

(a) *Blanchard and Peale three-part test*

Ethical breaches may be evaluated by asking three questions: (1) Is it legal? (2) Is it balanced? (3) How does it make me feel?

(b) *Front-page-of-the-newspaper test*

This test simply asks: "Would you want your spouse, children, and friends read about a proposed action on the front page of your local newspaper?" If not, then the proposed action is unethical.

(c) *Laura Nash model*

This model asks a series of questions, examining a dilemma from all perspectives.

(d) **Wall Street Journal** *model*

The "three-C model", once stated in The Wall Street Journal, suggests the following simple approach for resolving ethical dilemmas: (1) Will this conduct comply with the law? (2) What contribution does this conduct make to the shareholders, community, and employees? (3) What are the consequences of this conduct?

CONCEPT REVIEW AND APPLICATIONS

Matching Exercise

Select the term or phrase that best matches a definition or statement stated below. Each term or phrase is the best match for only one statement or definition. Not all terms and phrases will necessarily be used.

business ethics	integrity	primum non nocere
civil disobedience	moral relativism	situational ethics
conflict of interest	natural law	stakeholder analysis
ethics	positive law	stakeholders

_____ 1. Branch of philosophy that focuses on values relating to human conduct and the moral goodness of human motives and actions.

_____ 2. The act of remaining faithful to one's values and principles notwithstanding the consequences.

_____ 3. Different constituencies of a business, often holding conflicting goals for the business.

_____ 4. Undertaking by a person that may violate a duty of loyalty that the person owes to another.

_____ 5. Law that is enacted and codified by the government.

_____ 6. Ethical process that seeks to balance the goal of realizing profits when doing business with the moral values of individuals and society.

_____ 7. The act of violating governmental laws in order to promote higher standards of natural law.

_____ 8. Flexible standard of ethics that allows an examination of circumstances and motivation before attaching a label of "right" or "wrong" to the conduct.

_____ 9. Theory that higher standards of behavior than those required by codified law must be followed even if these standards are contrary to the written law.

True/False

Write **T** if the statement is true, write **F** if it is false.

_____ 1. Social forces significantly affect both the ethics and laws of society.

_____ 2. A conflict of interest may arise if a purchasing agent for a company accepts baseball tickets from one of the company's suppliers.

_____ 3. The ethical values of society may change over time.

_____ 4. The law requires a person to conform his or her conduct to all ethical values of good and bad.

_____ 5. Important, fundamental ethical values frequently give rise to and are incorporated into various laws.

_____ 6. One way for business to avoid increased government regulation is for business to voluntarily conform its conduct to the ethical values of society.

_____ 7. Capitalism succeeds because of trust.

_____ 8. Laws are intended to further only individual freedoms; laws are not intended to protect the federal or state governments.

_____ 9. The social force of protection of the person includes a desire to protect the economic interests of persons as well as their physical safety.

_____ 10. The freedom of personal action is not unlimited; this freedom cannot be exercised in such a manner that it unreasonably interferes with the rights of others or important interests of society.

Multiple Choice

_____ 1. A state is considering adopting a law that requires its police officers to take mandatory drug tests. The testing is intended to protect the state by assuring that police officers can safely carry out their duties. But, the testing will intrude upon the privacy of the officers tested. In this case:
   a. Protection of the state is not a proper social force to consider.
   b. Protection of personal rights (here the right to privacy) is not a proper social force to consider.
   c. It is proper for the state to consider both protection of the state and protection of personal rights, and to create a law that seeks to balance or synthesize these social forces.
   d. a and b.

_____ 2. Two Forks Village is considering adopting a law that prohibits selling pornographic books within the city. This law is intended to protect the public morals. Ken, who sells this type of book, objects to this law, maintaining that it will impair his freedom of personal action. In this case:
   a. Protecting public morals is not a social force that may be considered.
   b. Protecting personal rights is a social force that may be considered.
   c. The law in question should not be adopted because it is ethically wrong to adopt a law if doing so will limit anyone's personal rights.
   d. The law in question must be adopted because protection of public interests always prevails over protection of personal rights.

_____ 3. Stan has lost his job and he cannot pay his debts.
   a. In order to further debtor rehabilitation, bankruptcy laws have been adopted that may allow Stan to escape liability for certain unpaid debts.
   b. The law does not provide a procedure whereby Stan can escape liability for his debts.
   c. Under these facts, Stan will be imprisoned if he fails to pay his debts.
   d. b and c.

_____ 4. Assume that a state law generally allows a person to create a trust for the benefit of another and to give his or her property to such trust. However, this law does not permit a person to do so if the person is acting with the intent to defraud his or her creditors. Under these facts:
   a. This law furthers only the social force of enforcement of individual intent.
   b. This law furthers only the social force of protection of creditors.
   c. This law furthers only the social force of freedom of personal rights.
   d. This law represents a synthesis (combination) of the social forces of enforcement of individual intent, protection of creditors, and protection of personal rights.

_____ 5. Acme Food Corp. decided to sell to third world countries all of its out-of-date canned food products. While it is illegal to sell these products in the United States, it is not illegal to sell them elsewhere. Although these products are not very pleasing to taste, they are still edible. The Acme board of directors' reasoned that if their decision were publicized in local newspapers, they could personally justify their decision and, therefore, this course of action is ethically proper. What ethical model did the directors use to arrive at their decision?
   a. Stakeholders' model.
   b. Blanchard and Peale three-part test.
   c. The front-page-of-the-newspaper test.
   d. Laura Nash model.

Case Problems

Answer the following problems, briefly explaining your answers.

1. Assume that a state's law permits an employer to fire an employee at will (an employee who is not hired for a definite time) for any reason provided the firing does not involve discrimination. In order to better protect employees, the state in question has proposed changing this law and adopting a law that requires employers to have a sufficient legal reason before discharging an employee.
   a. What social forces would be furthered if the state adopts the new law?
   b. What social forces would be furthered if the state does not adopt the new law?

_____

_____

_____

2. State _X_ presently forbids all gambling. State _X_ is considering adopting a law to permit limited gambling. This law will generate tax revenues for the state, and it will allow persons to spend their money in the manner they choose, thereby enhancing their freedom of choice. But, adoption of this law will cause an increase in crime and it will allow exploitation of persons who are habitual gamblers.
   a. What social forces would be furthered if the state adopts the new law permitting limited gambling?
   b. What social forces would be furthered if the state does not adopt this new law?

_____

_____

_____

Internet Exercise

Using the Internet, locate the code of ethics of a particular business, or business or professional association. Then, answer the following questions:

1. Identify the web site where the code of ethics is posted.
2. Analyze why this business or association may have adopted this code of ethics.
3. What types of ethical behavior does this code of ethics encourage?

_____

_____

_____

CPA REVIEW

The following questions were given on CPA examinations. The answers for these questions are the unofficial answers prepared by the American Institute of Certified Public Accountants, Inc. (AICPA). All material is reproduced with permission of the AICPA.

_____ 1. Which of the following actions by a CPA most likely violates the profession's ethical standards?
   a. Arranging with a financial institution to collect notes issued by a client in payment of fees due.
   b. Compiling the financial statements of a client that employed the CPA's spouse as a bookkeeper.
   c. Retaining client records after the client has demanded their return.
   d. Purchasing a segment of an insurance company's business that performs actuarial services for employee benefit plan.

_____ 2. A CPA owes a duty to:
   a. Provide for a successor CPA in the event death or disability prevents completion of an audit.
   b. Advise a client of errors contained in a previously filed tax return.
   c. Disclose client fraud to third parties.
   d. Perform an audit according to GAAP so that fraud will be uncovered.

_____ 3. A violation of the profession's ethical standards most likely would have occurred when a CPA:
   a. Issued an unqualified opinion on the 1992 financial statements when fees for the 1991 audit were unpaid.
   b. Recommended a controller's position description with candidate specifications to an audit client.
   c. Purchased a CPA firm's practice of monthly write-ups for a percentage of fees to be received over a three-year period.
   d. Made arrangements with a financial institution to collect notes issued by a client in payment of fees due for the current year's audit.

_____ 4. A violation of the profession's ethical standards least likely would have occurred when a CPA:
   a. Purchased another CPA's accounting practice and based the price on a percentage of the fees accruing from clients over a three-year period.
   b. Received a percentage of the amounts invested by the CPA's audit clients in a tax shelter with the clients' knowledge and approval.
   c. Had a public accounting practice and also was president and sole stockholder of a corporation that engaged in data processing services for the public.
   d. Formed an association-not a partnership with two other sole practitioners and called the association "Adams, Betts and Associates."

_____ 5. According to the profession's ethical standards, an auditor would be considered independent in which of the following instances?
   a. The auditor is the officially appointed stock transfer agent of a client.
   b. The auditor's checking account that is fully insured by a federal agency is held at a client financial institution.
   c. The client owes the auditor fees for more than two years prior to the issuance of the audit report.
   d. The client is the only tenant in a commercial building owned by the auditor.

_____ 6. According to the profession's ethical standards, a CPA would be considered independent in which of the following instances?
   a. A client leases part of an office building from the CPA, resulting in a material indirect financial interest to the CPA.
   b. The CPA has a material direct financial interest in a client, but transfers the interest into a blind trust.
   c. The CPA owns an office building and the mortgage on the building is guaranteed by a client.
   d. The CPA belongs to a country club client in which membership requires the acquisition of a pro rata share of equity.

_____ 7. In which of the following situations would a CPA's independence be considered to be impaired?
   I   The CPA maintains a checking account that is fully insured by a government deposit insurance agency at an audit-client financial institution.
   II.   The CPA has a direct financial interest in an audit client, but the interest is maintained in a blind trust.
   III   The CPA owns a commercial building and leases it to an audit client. The rental income is material to the CPA.

   a. I and II.
   b. II and III.
   c. I and III.
   d. I, II, and III.

_____ 8. Which of the following statements best explains why the CPA profession has found it essential to promulgate ethical standards and to establish means for ensuring their observance?
   a. A distinguishing mark of a profession is its acceptance of responsibility to the public.
   b. A requirement for a profession is to establish ethical standards that stress primary responsibility to clients and colleagues.
   c. Ethical standards that emphasize excellence in performance over material rewards establish a reputation for competence and character.
   d. Vigorous enforcement of an established code of ethics is the best way to prevent unscrupulous acts.

CHAPTER 4
THE CONSTITUTION AS THE FOUNDATION OF THE LEGAL ENVIRONMENT

MAKE THE CONNECTION

SUMMARY

The U.S. Constitution created the structure of our national government and gave it certain powers. It also placed limitations on those powers. It created a federal system with a tripartite division of government and a bicameral national legislature.

The national government possesses some governmental powers exclusively, while both the states and the federal government share other powers. In areas of conflict, federal law is supreme.

The U.S. Constitution is not a detailed document. It takes its meaning from the way it is interpreted. In recent years, liberal interpretation has expanded the powers of the federal government. Among the powers of the federal government that directly affect business are the power to regulate commerce; the power to tax and to borrow, spend, and coin money; and the power to own and operate businesses.

Among the limitations on government that are most important to business are the requirements of due process and the requirement of equal protection of the law. In addition, government is limited by the rights given to individuals such as freedom of speech, freedom of religion, and equal protection. The equal protection concept of the U.S. Constitution prohibits both the federal government and the state governments from treating one person differently from another unless there is a legitimate reason for doing so and unless the basis of classification is reasonable.

LEARNING OUTCOMES
After studying this chapter, you should be able to

A. THE U.S. CONSTITUTION AND THE FEDERAL SYSTEM
LO.1   Describe the U.S. Constitution and the Federal System

B. THE U.S. CONSTITUTION AND THE STATES
LO.2   Explain the relationship between the U.S. Constitution and the States

C. INTERPRETING AND AMENDING THE CONSTITUTION
LO.3   Discuss interpreting and amending the Constitution

D. FEDERAL POWERS
LO.4   List and describe the significant federal powers

E. CONSTITUTIONAL LIMITATIONS ON GOVERNMENT
LO.5   Discuss constitutional limitations on governmental power

CHAPTER OUTLINE

A. THE U.S. CONSTITUTION AND THE FEDERAL SYSTEM

The United States has a federal system of government. This means that a central government (the federal government) regulates matters of national concern and states regulate matters of local concern.

1. WHAT A CONSTITUTION IS

The U.S. Constitution establishes the structure of the government. It also establishes the fundamental powers of the federal and state governments and limitations upon those powers.

2. THE BRANCHES OF GOVERNMENT

GENERAL RULE. The Constitution created a tripartite (three-part) federal government comprised of a legislative branch (Congress) to make laws, an executive branch (President) to execute the laws, and a judicial branch (federal courts) to interpret the laws.
STUDY HINT. Congress is a bicameral (two-house) body (Senate and House of Representatives).

B. THE U.S. CONSTITUTION AND THE STATES

3. DELEGATED AND SHARED POWERS

➢ *Delegated powers*: Certain powers ("delegated powers") were given by the states to the federal government. These powers are stated in the U.S. Constitution.

➢ *Shared powers*: ▶ The federal government has the exclusive right to exercise certain delegated powers. Example: power to make war. ▶ Other delegated powers are shared with states, meaning that states can also exercise these powers. Example: power to tax.

➢ **LEARNING OUTCOME EXAMPLE.** See Figure 4-1 on textbook p. 68 for an illustration of the delegation of powers.

4. OTHER POWERS

➢ *State police power*: Subject to certain limits, states have the "police power" to adopt laws that are necessary to protect the health, welfare, safety, and morals of people.

➢ *Prohibited powers*: The Constitution prohibits federal and state governments from doing certain acts, e.g., making *ex post facto* laws (laws that make criminal an act that has already been done).

5. FEDERAL SUPREMACY

GENERAL RULES. ▶ The Constitution embraces the concept of federal supremacy, which makes federal law supreme over state law. If a federal law conflicts with a state law, the federal law prevails. ▪ A state law is invalid if: (1) the state law directly conflicts with federal law; or (2) the state law relates to a subject that Congress has preempted (i.e., has taken over.)

STUDY HINTS. ▶ A subject is preempted if Congress expressly or by implication indicates an intent to exclusively regulate the subject. ▶ A failure by Congress to regulate a subject may indicate an intent to preempt the subject, particularly if uniform national regulation of the subject is needed.

C. INTERPRETING AND AMENDING THE CONSTITUTION

6. CONFLICTING THEORIES

  ➢ *Bedrock view*: The Constitution states fundamental rules for all time. The bedrock view embraces strict constructionist interpretation of the Constitution, i.e. the Constitution should be interpreted narrowly, giving the federal government only limited power.

  ➢ *Living document view*: The Constitution states only goals and objectives. The Constitution is intended to change to meet the needs of society, and it is interpreted broadly to give the federal government expansive power.

7. AMENDING THE CONSTITUTION

GENERAL RULE. The Constitution's meaning and its protections have been amended (changed): (1) expressly through constitutional amendment; (2) by judicial interpretation; and (3) by practice.

STUDY HINTS. ▶ Article V states rules for express constitutional amendments. ▶ There have been few express amendments; most constitutional changes have resulted from judicial interpretation.

8. THE LIVING CONSTITUTION

During the past century the Supreme Court has generally followed the living document view. Consequently, the Constitution has been liberally interpreted resulting in the following:

  ➢ *Strong government*: The federal government has been permitted to become a strong government.

  ➢ *Strong president*: The U.S. President is strong and is actively involved in the lawmaking process.

  ➢ *Eclipse of the states*: The federal government has the greatest power to regulate business.

  ➢ *Administrative agencies*: Agencies exercise immense power in regulating business.

D. FEDERAL POWERS

The federal government has only the powers delegated to it by the Constitution.

9. THE POWER TO REGULATE COMMERCE

> *The commerce power becomes a general welfare power*: Article I, Section 8, Clause 3, known as the "commerce clause," gives the federal government the power to regulate interstate commerce.

> *The commerce clause today*: Interstate commerce is interpreted very broadly. It includes virtually all business and labor activities; it is not limited to goods or activities that directly cross state lines.

> *The commerce power as a limitation on states*: Although a state may regulate interstate commerce, it cannot do so if: (1) regulation is preempted by the federal government; (2) state law conflicts with   federal law; (3) state law discriminates against interstate commerce (e.g., tax is imposed on only interstate commerce); or (4) state law imposes an unreasonable burden on interstate commerce (i.e., burden on interstate commerce outweighs the need for the state law).

10. THE FINANCIAL POWERS

GENERAL RULE.   The federal government has the power to tax, borrow, spend, and make money.

LIMITATIONS.   ▶ In general, federal and state taxes are subject to an implied limitation that they can be levied only to accomplish a public purpose. ▶ State taxes must be apportioned, meaning that a state cannot tax income that is earned by a business or individual in other states. ▶ A state can tax a business on its income only if the business has sufficient "minimum contacts" with the state.

STUDY HINT.   State governments can tax, borrow, and spend, although state law frequently limits the amount of state borrowing.

E. CONSTITUTIONAL LIMITATIONS ON GOVERNMENT

GENERAL RULE.   Some of the most important constitutional limitations on government are constitutional provisions that guarantee fundamental individual rights.

LIMITATION.   Constitutional limits, such as due process, only apply to government action. These limits do not apply to conduct by private parties; statutes and administrative rules limit private conduct.

LEARNING OUTCOME EXAMPLES. See the discussion of the Bill of Rights on textbook p. 79; see the discussion of the Fourth Amendment on textbook p. 79; see the discussion of due process on textbook p. 77; see the **For Example** discussion of a student taking a grade grievance beyond a faculty member's decision on textbook p. 77.

11. DUE PROCESS

GENERAL RULES. ► The Fifth and Fourteenth Amendments to the Constitution prohibit the federal and state governments, respectively, from depriving any person of life, liberty, or property without due process of law. ► The "due process clause": (1) prohibits unreasonable government procedures and laws; and (2) guarantees certain fundamental individual rights and interests. ► Examples of due process guarantees: right to reasonable notice and an opportunity to be heard; right not to be sued in a state unless one has reasonable contacts with the state in question; students' right not to be expelled without having their side heard.

LIMITATION. Due process does not nullify a law merely because the law is of debatable value.

STUDY HINTS. ► In general, if the government proposes to take an action that will substantially interfere with a person's fundamental personal or property rights, due process guarantees that person a right to notice and an opportunity to defend his or her rights. ► Due process is often provided by expedited, quasi-judicial proceedings.

12. EQUAL PROTECTION OF THE LAW

GENERAL RULE. Broadly speaking, the equal protection clause prohibits the federal and state governments from discriminating against persons because they are members of a particular class.

LIMITATIONS. ► The equal protection clause does not always require equal treatment for everyone. ► A law may treat classes of persons or businesses differently if the law is reasonably related to and furthers a sufficiently important, legitimate government purpose.

STUDY HINTS ► The justification needed to uphold a discriminatory action by the government depends on the basis used for deciding how to treat different people, e.g., is the government treating people differently because of their race (compelling justification needed) or merely because of their income (only rational justification needed). ► Examples of *invalid* laws (classifications) absent a sufficient justification: (1) laws that discriminate on the basis of race, religion, or national origin; and (2) laws that are not rationally or reasonably related to accomplishing a legitimate government interest. ► A rational basis does not exist if the action is arbitrary or capricious.

13. PRIVILEGES AND IMMUNITIES

► The Constitution generally prohibits a state from treating residents and nonresidents of the state differently. ► Example: Residents and nonresidents generally have the same right to do business, practice a profession, and own property in a state.

14. PROTECTION OF THE PERSON

► The Supreme Court has expanded the constitutional protection of many individual rights, including rights not expressly stated in the Constitution. ► The Constitution protects only living persons.

15. THE BILL OF RIGHTS AND BUSINESS AS A PERSON

The first 10 Amendments which are known as the Bill of Rights accord various protections for both natural persons and business entities, such as corporations.

CONCEPT REVIEW AND APPLICATIONS

Matching Exercise

Select the term or phrase that best matches a definition or statement stated below. Each term or phrase is the best match for only one statement or definition. Not all terms and phrases will necessarily be used.

bedrock view
bicameral
commerce clause
constitution
delegated powers
due process clause
ex post facto laws

executive branch
federal system
judicial branch
legislative branch
living-document view
police power
preemption

privileges and immunities
 clause
quasi-judicial proceedings
shared powers
tripartite

_____ 1. Belief that the Constitution states fundamental principles that apply for all time and that the Constitution should be strictly interpreted.

_____ 2. Written document that generally sets forth the structure and powers of a government.

_____ 3. Belief that the Constitution states only objectives, that the Constitution must evolve to meet society's needs, and that the Constitution should be liberally interpreted.

_____ 4. Constitutional provision that generally entitles both citizens and non-citizens of a state equal rights to contract, own property, and engage in business in that state.

_____ 5. Constitutional provision that grants the federal government the power to regulate both interstate commerce and foreign commerce.

_____ 6. Constitutional provision that generally guarantees protection against the loss of property or rights without the chance to be heard.

_____ 7. Government in which a central government governs matters of national concern, and states govern matters of local concern.

_____ 8. The power of states to generally adopt laws and regulate activities within their respective borders in order to promote and protect the health, safety, welfare, and morals of the people.

_____ 9. Doctrine granting Congress the exclusive power to regulate an activity or subject matter.

_____10. Law that retroactively makes criminal an act that has already been done.

True/False

Write T if the statement is true, write F if it is false.

_____ 1.   The United States has a parliamentary system of government.

_____ 2.   Congress is comprised of two houses, the House of Representatives and the Supreme Court.

_____ 3.   Federal judges are appointed by the President with the approval of the Senate and generally serve for life.

_____ 4.   The federal government possesses only the powers delegated to it by the U.S. Constitution.

_____ 5.   Subject to certain limits, a matter may be regulated by both the federal government and a state.

_____ 6.   If a federal statute and a state statute conflict, the concept of federal supremacy generally provides that the state statute is superior and cancels the federal statute.

_____ 7.   A state cannot regulate an activity or subject matter that has been preempted by Congress.

_____ 8.   The silence of Congress and its failure to regulate a subject may indicate an intent by Congress to preempt that subject thereby preventing state regulation of that subject.

_____ 9.   During the past 100 years, the Supreme Court generally followed the bedrock view and strictly interpreted the Constitution.

_____10.   Most changes to the Constitution result from judicial interpretation, not express amendment.

Multiple Choice

_____ 1.   Some people have suggested that the federal government needs to more closely regulate the Internet. If the federal government decided to do this, then:
   a.   The executive branch would adopt and carry out needed laws, and the judicial branch would enforce the laws against violators.
   b.   The legislative branch would adopt and carry out needed laws, and the judicial branch would enforce the laws against violators.
   c.   The legislative branch would adopt needed laws, the executive branch would carry out the laws, and the judicial branch would enforce the laws against violators.
   d.   The judicial branch would adopt, carry out, and enforce needed laws.

_____ 2.   Assume Congress enacted a law prohibiting open-pit uranium mines. State _X_ then passed a law allowing mining companies to operate open-pit uranium mines within the state. Under these facts:
   a.   The state law is unconstitutional - it violates federal supremacy.
   b.   The state law is unconstitutional - it seeks to regulate interstate commerce.

  c. The state law is constitutional - the state has the police power to regulate this activity.

  d. The state law is constitutional - the federal government cannot regulate this activity.

_____ 3. Wood Inc. manufactures and sells furniture in interstate commerce. Wood's manufacturing plant is located in Chicago, Illinois. Under these facts, select the correct answer.

  a. The federal government has the power to regulate Wood's business.

  b. Subject to certain limits, Illinois has the power to regulate Wood's business conducted in Illinois.

  c. Illinois does not have the power to regulate any aspect of Wood's business; states do not have the power to regulate any matters that the federal government regulates.

  d. a and b.

_____ 4. Federal law generally requires that certain private employers must pay time and a half for hours worked in excess of 40 hours per week. Assume that a state law directly conflicts with this federal law by requiring payment of time and a half for only those hours worked in excess of 60 hours per week. Under these facts, select the correct answer.

  a. Federal law controls.

  b. State law controls.

  c. Neither federal nor state law controls; conflicting federal and state laws cancel each other.

  d. Neither federal nor state law controls; government cannot regulate private businesses.

_____ 5. Cargo Storage is in the business of storing toxic wastes. For 10 years, Cargo has stored low-level toxic wastes in steel drums. The state just adopted a new criminal law that makes the past or future storage of low-level toxic wastes in steel drums a felony. Under these facts:

  a. As applied to both Cargo's past and future activities, the law is an unconstitutional *ex post facto* law.

  b. As applied only to Cargo's future activities, the law is an unconstitutional *ex post facto* law.

  c. As applied only to Cargo's past activities, the law is an unconstitutional *ex post facto* law.

  d. As applied to both Cargo's past and future storage activities, the law is constitutional.

_____ 6. Jackson Manufacturing operates a steel fabrication plant in New Jersey. Jackson is subject to various federal tax laws. New Jersey has recently passed a state law that assesses a new tax on certain manufacturing firms, such as Jackson Manufacturing, in order to help pay for state environmental clean-up operations. Jackson opposes this state law, arguing that the state lacks the power to assess this tax. Under these facts:

  e. The state law is valid. The power to tax businesses is shared by the federal and state governments, and both may tax a business.

  a. The state law is valid. The power of states to tax businesses is not subject to any limits.

  b. The state law is invalid. The power to tax rests solely with the federal government.

  f. The state law is invalid. While the power to tax is shared by the federal and state governments, states cannot use tax if the federal government has already done so.

_____ 7. A state legislature enacted a law requiring adult bookstores to be located 2000 feet or more away from any school, but the law does not impose the same restriction on other businesses. The purpose of the law is to protect school children from exposure to pornographic materials. Ginger bought a building to use as an adult bookstore, but now she cannot use it for this purpose. Under these facts:
   a. This statute is unconstitutional. It violates Ginger's guarantee of equal protection because other types of businesses are not subject to this restriction.
   b. This statute is unconstitutional. Any law that discriminates against any person or company violates the constitutional guarantee of equal protection.
   c. This statute is constitutional. The law bears a rational (reasonable) relationship to a legitimate governmental interest.
   d. a and b.

_____ 8. State health agents found evidence of illegal drug sales during a warrantless inspection of Acme Pharmacy, Inc. Criminal charges were filed against Acme. The Fourth Amendment of the U.S. Constitution expressly requires the government to have a warrant before conducting a search. However, the U.S. Supreme Court has interpreted the Constitution as not requiring a warrant in this situation. Did the state violate Acme's constitutional rights?
   a. Yes. The state violated the express terms of the Constitution.
   b. No. The Constitution does not protect business entities.
   c. No. The Constitution has been amended by interpretation and the state did not violate the Constitution, as interpreted.
   d. b and c.

_____ 9. Roscoe owns three restaurants in one southern state. The restaurants primarily cater to local customers, but occasionally, travelers from other states stop in to have a meal. Roscoe refuses to pay the minimum wage required by federal law, arguing that he is not engaged in interstate commerce and, therefore, he is exempt from federal law. Is Roscoe engaged in interstate commerce?
   a. No. Roscoe does not sell goods across state lines.
   b. No. Roscoe does not have businesses in more than one state.
   c. No. Roscoe's business does not substantially affect interstate commerce.
   d. Yes. Roscoe's business activities fall within the broad meaning given to "interstate commerce."

_____ 10. One of the primary cash crops grown in State X is apples. In order to protect its in-state apple producers, the legislature of State X enacted a law forbidding the sale of any apples grown outside the state. Without this law, many smaller in-state apple producers may be driven out of business. Under these facts:
   a. This law is constitutional. State X is properly exercising its police power.
   b. This law is unconstitutional. State X cannot regulate any aspect of interstate commerce.
   c. This law is unconstitutional. State X is discriminating against interstate commerce.
   d. b and c.

Case Problem

Answer the following problem, briefly explaining your answer.

Amex Corp.'s manufacturing plant is located in Missouri. Amex Corp. sells its goods in several states, and it conducts a significant portion of its business in Colorado. Under these facts:

1. Is Amex Corp. engaging in interstate commerce?
2. Does the federal government have the right to regulate Amex Corp.'s business?
3. In general, does Colorado have the constitutional power to regulate business conducted by Amex Corp. in Colorado?
4. What restrictions will apply if Colorado regulates Amex Corp.'s business activities?

_____

_____

_____

Internet Exercise

Assume Congress passed the following laws: (1) a law making it a crime to sell 3Dchemical; and (2) a law making it a crime to say profane words in public. Kim, a chemical dealer, sold 3Dchemical to a rancher in State X and, on several occasions, she said profane words in public. Kim was prosecuted for violating both laws. She argues, however, that the federal government did not have the power to enact these laws. The government argues that it had the power to enact these laws because the regulated activities are interstate commerce.

1. Using the Internet, identify a recent U.S. Supreme Court decision that deals with the main issue in this case.
2. Applying this decision, did the federal government have the power to enact either or both of these laws?

_____

_____

_____

_____

CHAPTER 5
GOVERNMENT REGULATION OF COMPETITION AND PRICES

MAKE THE CONNECTION

SUMMARY

Regulation by government has occurred primarily to protect one group from the improper conduct of another group. The police power is the basis for government regulation. Regulation is passed when the free enterprise system fails to control abuses, as with the recent passage of investment banking regulations. Unfair methods of competition are prohibited.

Prices have been regulated both by prohibiting setting the exact price or a maximum price and discrimination in pricing. Price discrimination between buyers is prohibited when the effect of such discrimination could tend to create a monopoly or lessen competition. Price discrimination occurs when the prices charged different buyers are different despite the same marginal costs. However, resale price maintenance is not illegal per se if the control is for purposes of providing customer service.

The Sherman Antitrust Act prohibits conspiracies in restraint of trade and the monopolization of trade. The Clayton Act prohibits mergers or the acquisition of the assets of another corporation when this conduct would tend to lessen competition or create a monopoly. The Justice Department requires premerger notification for proposed mergers. Violation of the federal antitrust statutes subjects the wrongdoer to criminal prosecution and possible civil liability that can include treble damages.

LEARNING OUTCOMES
After studying this chapter, you should be able to

A. POWER TO REGULATE BUSINESS
LO.1   State the extent to which government can regulate business.

B. REGULATION OF MARKETS AND COMPETITION
LO.2   Explain what laws regulate the markets and protect competition.

C. POWER TO PROTECT BUSINESS
LO.3   Discuss the powers and remedies available to protect business competition.

CHAPTER OUTLINE

A. POWER TO REGULATE BUSINESS

➤ The Constitution empowers the federal government to regulate virtually all aspects of interstate commerce.

➤ The Constitution gives the government the powers to not only regulate business, but also the power to regulate business competition and prices.

➢ Subject to the federal government's power to regulate business, each state may exercise its police powers to regulate all aspects of business conducted within its boundaries. Local governments may exercise police powers to the extent permitted by the state.

1. REGULATION, FREE ENTERPRISE, AND DEREGULATION

GENERAL RULE. ▶ The noted economist Milton Friedman writes that government regulation of business interferes with the free enterprise system. Friedman suggests that in a free marketplace there would be no government regulation of business for the marketplace would implement needed protections. ▶ There has been some deregulation in certain industries.

LIMITATION. ▶ Deregulation has sometimes caused undesirable results and regulation has been reinstated. ▶ Example: Deregulation of the banking and savings industries contributed to various unsound lending practices, prompting adoption of new regulations, such as the Financial Institutions Reform, Recovery, & Enforcement Act (FIRREA).

▶**LEARNING OUTCOME EXAMPLE.** See the **For Example** discussion of the subprime mortgage market on textbook p. 88

2. REGULATION OF PRODUCTION, DISTRIBUTION, AND FINANCING

GENERAL RULES. ▶ The federal government can regulate all types of interstate activities involving transportation, production of goods, financing, and communication. ▶ Examples: The federal government can regulate standards for foods and drugs, the quantity of goods that a firm may produce, and the sales price for goods. ▶ By virtue of its police powers, a state can also generally regulate intrastate activities (that is, activities that occur within the state).

STUDY HINTS ▶ The power to regulate includes the power to regulate the quality of goods and the power to require parties to acquire a license in order to deal in certain goods. ▶ The ability of business to finance its operations is impacted by the federal government's regulation of the national currency and the Federal Reserve banking system.

3. REGULATION OF UNFAIR COMPETITION

GENERAL RULES. ▶ The Federal Trade Commission Act declares illegal all "unfair methods of competition … and unfair or deceptive acts or practices" and the Federal Trade Commission (FTC) enforces this Act. The FTC has prohibited a wide range of activities, such as boycotting, obtaining and using confidential information of others, and false and deceptive advertising. ▶ States also commonly forbid various forms of unfair competition.

STUDY HINTS. ▶ An act may be unfair competition because it is harmful to competitors or consumers. ▶ Unfair competition is regulated by statutes and administrative regulations.

B. REGULATION OF MARKETS AND COMPETITION

The federal and state governments can regulate prices and interest rates and may impose rent controls.

4. REGULATION OF PRICES

(a) *Prohibition on price fixing*

► An agreement between competitors to fix a minimum or maximum price for goods or services, known as horizontal price fixing, is a per se (automatic) violation of Section 1 of the Sherman Act. ► **LEARNING OUTCOME EXAMPLES.** See the Ethics & the Law discussion of Marsh & McLennan on textbook p. 93; see the *Kahn* oil case on price controls, textbook p. 94; see the *Leegin* case on resale price maintenance, textbook p. 90;

(b) *Prohibited price discrimination*

GENERAL RULE. The Clayton and Robinson-Patman Acts prohibit price discrimination in interstate or foreign commerce if the discrimination may substantially lessen competition or may create a monopoly.

STUDY HINTS. ► Price discrimination is charging different customers different prices for the same goods. ► Discriminatory pricing disguised as advertising allowances or other valuable benefits that are given to some, but not all, buyers may violate federal antitrust law. ► Bona fide volume discounts that account for different marginal costs for selling to different buyers are legal. ►**LEARNING OUTCOME EXAMPLE.** See the *Utah Pie* case on predatory pricing, textbook p. 91.

(c) *Permitted price discrimination*

Price discrimination is allowed if different prices are justified by a: (1) difference in grade, quality, or quantity of goods sold; (2) difference in the cost of goods, such as different transportation costs; (3) closeout sale of goods; (4) good faith attempt by a seller to meet the competition in a particular competitive market by lowering the price charged in that market; or (5) deterioration of goods.

5. PREVENTION OF MONOPOLIES AND COMBINATIONS

(a) *The Sherman Act*

➢ *Prohibited conduct*:

► *Section 1 of the Sherman Antitrust Act*: This section forbids a conspiracy or agreement by two or more persons to unreasonably restrain trade (i.e., to unreasonably limit competition), which includes agreements to fix prices. Because a violation of Section 1 requires an agreement by two or more parties, an agreement between a corporation and its employees or officers does not to violate this law. ► Horizontal price fixing (agreement between competitors) and vertical price fixing (e.g., agreement between a manufacturer and retailer on the resale price of a good) are both prohibited. ► Tying arrangements (i.e., a seller refuses to sell one product to a buyer unless the buyer also purchases a second product from the seller) are generally forbidden.

► *Section 2 of the Sherman Antitrust Act*: This section prohibits an unlawful monopolization or attempt to monopolize an industry by one or more persons or companies.

➢ *Scope of the Act*: The Act applies to most persons engaging in interstate commerce, including sellers and professionals, and to most activities, including manufacturing and production.

(b) *Monopolization*

> **GENERAL RULES.** ► Section 1 of the Sherman Act applies only if there is an agreement between two or more parties to restrain trade, i.e., to limit competition. ► An illegal monopolization or attempt to monopolize may be committed by one party acting alone.
>
> **LIMITATIONS.** ► Significant market power alone is not sufficient to prove illegal monopolization conduct. ► To establish illegal monopolization conduct, it is necessary to prove that the alleged wrongdoer purposefully set out to gain or maintain a monopoly. (See *U.S. v. Microsoft*). ► The Sherman Act does not forbid large businesses, simply because they are big, or domination of a market by a company because of its superior product or business judgment.
>
> **STUDY HINTS.** ► To decide whether a party has engaged in illegal monopolization behavior, the courts look at the party's "market power" in terms of both geography and the market for a particular product. ► Market power is the ability to control price and to exclude competitors.

(c) *Tying*

> ► In general, tying arrangements are a violation of the Sherman Act. ► Tying is the practice of requiring a buyer to purchase one product from the seller in order to be allowed to purchase a second, different product from the same seller. ► **LEARNING OUTCOME EXAMPLE.** See the Sports & Entertainment Law feature on tying, textbook p. 95

(d) *Business Combinations*

> **GENERAL RULES.** ► The Clayton Act forbids a company from acquiring an interest in the assets, ownership, or control of another firm if doing so will substantially lessen competition or may create a monopoly. Before large firms can merge, they must first give a premerger notification to the FTC so this agency can block improper mergers before they are completed. ► If necessary, a court may enter a divestiture order that requires a party to give up a prohibited interest in another company or its assets.
>
> **STUDY HINTS.** ► The federal government and four-fifths of states regulate takeovers (i.e., mergers or consolidations of two companies). ► However, a state's regulation of corporate takeovers generally apply only to takeover activities that occur within the state's jurisdiction.

C. POWER TO PROTECT BUSINESS

By statute or court decision, certain industries are exempt from antitrust laws, such as associations of exporters, farm cooperatives, and labor unions. Agreements between competitors that do not directly or indirectly involve price fixing are generally evaluated under the rule of reason and not the per se rule.

6. REMEDIES FOR ANTICOMPETITIVE BEHAVIOR

> **GENERAL RULES.** ► Violation of the Sherman Act includes: (1) imprisonment of individuals for up to ten years; (2) fines of up to $100 million for companies and $1 million for individuals; (3) civil suit by persons harmed for treble damages (three times actual damages suffered); and (4) a state may file a class action on behalf of its citizens (*parens patriae* action).
>
> **LEARNING OUTCOME EXAMPLE.** See Section 6 for a list of the penalties and remedies on textbook p. 97

CONCEPT REVIEW AND APPLICATIONS

Matching Exercise

Select the term or phrase that best matches a definition or statement stated below. Each term or phrase is the best match for only one statement or definition. Not all terms and phrases will necessarily be used.

Clayton Act   Sherman Antitrust Act
divestiture order   takeover laws
market power   treble damages
price discrimination   tying
Robinson-Patman Act

_____ 1. The sales practice of requiring a buyer to purchase one product in order to be able to purchase a second product offered by the seller.

_____ 2. Federal law that generally forbids price discrimination and that also regulates business combinations that may substantially lessen competition or tend to create a monopoly.

_____ 3. A company's possession of a significant percentage of a given market that enables the company to control or influence prices and to exclude some competitors.

_____ 4. Federal law that prohibits price discrimination that may substantially lessen competition.

_____ 5. Federal law that prohibits monopolies and agreements that unreasonably restrain trade.

_____ 6. Court decree compelling a party to give up a prohibited interest in a company.

_____ 7. Three times the actual damages suffered.

_____ 8. Federal and state laws regulating acquisition of ownership of one company by another company.

_____ 9.. A seller's pricing practice that charges different prices to different buyers for commodities that are similar in grade and quality.

True/False

Write T if the statement is true, write F if it is false.

_____ 1. A state may generally regulate business within its boundaries provided that the state's regulations do not impose an unreasonable burden on interstate commerce.

_____ 2. A state cannot regulate or restrict takeovers of corporations within the state because the federal government has preempted this entire field.

_____ 3. The federal government has completely deregulated most industries within the United States.

_____ 4. Milton Freeman, a famous economist, has written that government regulation of business interferes with the free enterprise system.

_____ 5. Deregulation of certain industries has sometimes produced negative, undesirable results.

_____ 6. A per se violation of federal antitrust laws means that an action automatically violates the law regardless of the factual background in a particular case.

_____ 7. In general, both the federal and state governments may regulate the prices charged for goods or services.

_____ 8. Subject to certain exceptions, price discrimination is unlawful in connection with interstate commerce.

_____ 9. A manufacturer cannot charge different customers different prices for the same goods even if the different prices can be justified by a difference in the cost of shipping the goods to the customers.

_____ 10. The Sherman Antitrust Act only applies to conduct by sellers or buyers of goods; it does not apply to professionals or others who merely render services.

Multiple Choice

_____ 1. The federal government has the power to adopt which of the following business regulations?
   a. Regulation that requires automobile manufacturers to install dual front seat air bags in every new automobile that is sold in the United States.
   b. Regulation that forbids the interstate sale of vitamins unless they satisfy certain quality standards.
   c. Regulation that regulates accountants and financial reporting of publicly-held companies.
   d. All of the above.

_____ 2. Select the correct answer.
   a. States cannot regulate antitrust matters; this area has been preempted by the federal government.
   b. Federal antitrust laws and state takeover laws are separate regulations from one another.
   c. States can regulate corporate takeovers that occur within their jurisdiction.
   d. b and c.

_____ 3. Heifer Co. and other meat producers agree to fix the prices that they charge for their competitive meat products that are sold in interstate commerce. Under these facts:
   a. Heifer Co. may be liable for three times the actual damages caused by its price fixing.
   b. Heifer Co. may be subject to fines of up to $10 billion.
   c. Individuals who are guilty of this price fixing may be fined, but they cannot be imprisoned.
   d. No one can be sued, fined, or imprisoned for their conduct in this case because price fixing is generally legal under the Sherman Antitrust Act.

_____ 4. LubeTech manufactures 1Lube, a universal lubricant that works on all engines and moving parts, in any temperature, and in all conditions. 1Lube is also cheaper than comparable lubricants. Because of 1Lube, LubeTech controls 80 percent of the lubricant market. Has LubeTech violated federal antitrust law?
   a. Yes. LubeTech controls more than 70 percent of the lubricant market.
   b. Yes. LubeTech has an illegal monopoly.
   c. No.
   d. a and b.

_____ 5. Which law provides that no corporation shall acquire the assets of another corporation if the effect of such acquisition may substantially lessen competition?
   a. Section 1 of the Sherman Act.
   b. Section 2 of the Sherman Act.
   c. Robinson-Patman Act.
   d. Clayton Act.

_____ 6. CompuTron makes the Micro Data Unit (MiDU), the hottest new data storage system that dominates the personal computer market. In order to maximize its profits, CompuTron will not sell its MiDU unless the buyer also purchases 20 Computron disks. These disks are good, but disks made by other manufacturers work just as well in the MiDU. Has CompuTron violated federal antitrust law?
   a. Yes, this is illegal price fixing.
   b. Yes, this is an illegal tying arrangement.
   c. Yes, this is an illegal boycott.
   d. No.

_____ 7. Which of the following agreements may violate the Sherman Antitrust Act?
   a. Members of Union Local 412 agree that the base wage that they charge will be $10 per hour.
   b. Members of the Iowa Farmer's Cooperative agree on a uniform, reasonable price for which the Cooperative will store corn.
   c. Ten manufacturers of sheet metal agree on a uniform price that they will charge for their product.
   d. a and c.

_____ 8. Palisade Co. and Eagle Inc. both engage in interstate commerce and they are two of the largest makers of medical equipment in the U.S. Both firms are formed under the laws of State X. All shareholders of Eagle Inc. reside in State X, and its corporate offices and plants are also in State X. Palisade Corp. is proposing taking over and merging with Eagle Inc. Under these facts:
   a. The proposed merger of Palisade and Eagle may violate the Clayton Act if the effect of the merger is to substantially lessen competition or may tend to create a monopoly.
   b. State X cannot regulate any activity relating to this proposed takeover even if it   occurs within State X because only the federal government can regulate corporate takeovers.
   c. Palisade may have to file a premerger notification with the FTC before merging with Eagle.
   d. a and c.

_____ 9. Reality+ has created a virtual-reality game that dominates the video market. Reality+ has recently entered the video rental market. In order to gain market share in the rental market and to hurt its competition, Reality+ refuses to sell its virtual-reality game to any competitors. Has Reality+ violated *Section 1 of the Sherman Act*?
   a. Yes, Reality+'s conduct is an unreasonable restraint of trade.
   b. Yes, Reality+'s conduct is an illegal tying arrangement.
   c. Yes, Reality+'s conduct is an illegal boycott.
   d. No, a single company, acting alone, cannot generally violate Section 1 of the Sherman Act.

_____ 10. Perfecto, a major apparel manufacturer, wanted to get an order from the Grant Department Store chain. Perfecto got the contract by selling its clothes to Grant for 40 percent less than it sold the same goods to other stores in the same market. As a result, Grant enjoyed a major competitive advantage over other area stores. Under these facts:
   a. Perfecto engaged in illegal price discrimination in violation of federal antitrust law.
   b. Perfecto engaged in illegal price-fixing in violation of federal antitrust law.
   c. Perfecto engaged in legal price discrimination in compliance with federal antitrust law.
   d. Perfecto acted legally because its conduct is not subject to federal antitrust law.

Case Problem

Answer the following problem, briefly explaining your answer.

Compu Co. manufactures computers, and it sells its computers to retail stores throughout the U.S. Compu is considering various pricing plans. Would the following plans be unlawful under federal antitrust laws?

Plan A: Compu will sell its X computer to its best customers for $1,800. It will sell the same computer to less-favored customers for $3,000. This pricing plan will substantially lessen competition.
Plan B: Compu will sell its Z computer to stores in one competitive market for $800, but it will sell the same computer to stores in a different market for $600. The lower price is charged in the second market in order to match the price that a competitor charges for a comparable computer in that market.

_____

_____

_____

_____

Internet Exercise

The City of Joy, a large metropolis, uses a few private physicians to provide medical care for poor persons. The city pays these physicians only $20 per hour, and it has refused to increase their wages. These independent physicians, who do not belong to a union, agreed among themselves to boycott the city and refused to provide any further services until the city agreed to pay each of them $50 per hour.

The city claims that the physicians' action is an illegal boycott and illegal price-fixing in violation of federal antitrust law. The physicians claim their conduct is not illegal because they do not possess any market power.

1. Using the Internet, locate the U.S. Supreme Court's decision in *FTC v. Superior Court Trial Lawyers Assn.*, and identify the web site where you found this case.
2. Evaluate the legality of the physicians' conduct and the validity of their defense by referring to the decision in *FTC v. Superior Court Trial Lawyers Assn.*

CHAPTER 6
ADMINISTRATIVE AGENCIES

MAKE THE CONNECTION

SUMMARY

The administrative agency is unique because it combines the three functions that are kept separate under our traditional governmental system: legislative, executive, and judicial. By virtue of legislative power, an agency adopts regulations that have the force of law, although agency members are not elected by those subject to the regulations. By virtue of the executive power, an agency carries out and enforces the regulations, makes investigations, and requires the production of documents. By virtue of the judicial power, an agency acts as a court to determine whether a violation of any regulation has occurred. To some extent, an agency is restricted by constitutional limitations in inspecting premises and requiring the production of papers. These limitations, however, have a very narrow application in agency actions. When an agency acts as a judge, a jury trial is not required, nor must ordinary courtroom procedures be followed. Typically, an agency gives notice to the person claimed to be acting improperly, and a hearing is then held before the agency. When the agency has determined that there has been a violation, it may order that the violation stop. Under some statutes, the agency may go further and impose a penalty on the violator.

An appeal to a court may be taken from any decision of an agency by a person harmed by the decision. Only a person with a legally recognized interest can appeal from the agency ruling. No appeal can be made until every step available before the agency has been taken; that is, the administrative remedy must first be exhausted. An agency's actions can be reversed by a court if the agency exceeded its authority, the decision is not based in law or fact, the decision is arbitrary and capricious, or, finally, the agency violated procedural steps.

Protection from secret government is provided by Sunshine laws that afford the right to know what most administrative agency records contain; by the requirement that most agency meetings be open to the public; by the invitation to the public to take part in rulemaking; and by publicity given, through publication in the Federal Register and trade publications, to the guidelines followed by the agency and the regulations it has adopted.

LEARNING OUTCOMES
After studying this chapter, you should be able to

A. NATURE OF THE ADMINISTRATIVE AGENCY

LO.1   Describe the nature and purpose of administrative agencies

B. LEGISLATIVE POWER OF THE AGENCY

LO.2   Discuss the legislative or rulemaking power of administrative agencies

C. EXECUTIVE POWER OF THE AGENCY

LO.3   Explain the executive or enforcement function of administrative agencies

D. JUDICIAL POWER OF THE AGENCY

LO.4   Discuss the judicial power of administrative agencies including the rule on exhaustion of administrative remedies

CHAPTER OUTLINE

A. NATURE OF THE ADMINISTRATIVE AGENCY

► Administrative agencies are governmental bodies that generally are created by Congress and state legislatures to administer and carry out legislation. ► Example: Federal Trade Commission (FTC).

1. PURPOSE OF ADMINISTRATIVE AGENCIES

► Federal and state agencies govern large segments of the economy. ► Examples: Environmental Protection Agency: environment; Securities and Exchange Commission: interstate sales of securities; state employment agencies: workers' compensation. ► Agencies are governed by administrative law.

2. UNIQUENESS OF ADMINISTRATIVE AGENCIES

GENERAL RULES. ► Administrative agencies are usually run by appointed officials. ► Important administrative agencies commonly exercise legislative, executive, and judicial powers.

STUDY HINTS. ► Courts generally recognize that it is both fair and constitutional for an agency to exercise a combination of the foregoing powers. ► But to better assure impartial administrative action, some agencies have separated their various functions. Example: Judicial function of the FTC is now performed by administrative law judges.

3. OPEN OPERATION OF ADMINISTRATIVE AGENCIES

The federal Administrative Procedure Act (APA) and similar state statutes govern the procedures of many agencies. Procedures that enable the public to be informed of agency matters include:

➢ *Open records*: ► The Freedom of Information Act (FOIA) generally makes information contained in federal agency records available to the public upon request. Similar state laws also generally make state agency records available. These federal and state laws are liberally construed, and a person claiming an exemption from disclosure has the burden to establish the exemption. ► Limitations on disclosure: (1) a party can find out only information that relates to a legitimate concern; (2) FOIA allows inspection of only governmental records; (3) FOIA exempts certain commercial and financial information that is not ordinarily made public; and (4) state laws often exempt information that would constitute an invasion of privacy. The Electronic Freedom of Information Act Amendments of 1996 extends the public availability of information to electronically stored data.

➢ *Open meetings*: ► The Sunshine Act of 1976, known as the "open meeting law," requires that meetings of most important federal agencies be open to the public. ► The Sunshine Act applies to those meetings involving "deliberations" of the agency or those that "result in the joint conduct or disposition of official agency business." ► Many states have similar statutes.

➢ *Public announcement of agency guidelines*: The APA generally requires that each federal agency publish its rules, principles, and procedures.

B. LEGISLATIVE POWER OF THE AGENCY

4. AGENCY'S REGULATIONS AS LAW

GENERAL RULES.   ▶ Agencies make law by adopting regulations. ▶ An agency may adopt regulations within the sphere of its authority. This power includes the right to: (1) regulate new technologies that develop within an agency's realm of authority; and (2) establish policies regarding regulated matters if such policies are not already defined by statute.

LIMITATIONS.   ▶ The modern approach is to view an agency as having all powers necessary to carry out its duties. ▶ An agency rule or action is invalid if: (1) it exceeds the scope of the statute that created the agency; or (2) it exceeds standards established for the agency.

STUDY HINTS.   ▶ An unlawful administrative regulation can be challenged by anyone affected by it. ▶ In general, courts will not review the *policy* decisions of administrative agencies.

5. AGENCY ADOPTION OF REGULATIONS

➢ Before an agency may act, Congress must give it jurisdiction to do so.

➢ The FTC and other agencies may hold public hearings to gather nonbinding input from industry.

➢ The Federal Register Act requires that proposed administrative regulations be published in the *Federal Register*.

➢ The public has 30 days to comment on proposed federal regulations (the "public comment period").

➢ Following public comment, an agency may promulgate, (adopt), modify, or withdraw a proposed regulation. For example, a federal agency recently adopted a new regulation that requires automobile manufacturers to install advanced air bags in cars starting in September 2003.

➢ **LEARNING OUTCOME EXAMPLES.** See the *State Farm* case on textbook p. 110; see the *San Diego Air Sports* case on textbook p. 111; see the National Do-Not-Call case on textbook p. 118.

C. EXECUTIVE POWER OF THE AGENCY

6. ENFORCEMENT OR EXECUTION OF THE LAW

GENERAL RULE.   Contemporary administrative agencies can investigate, call witnesses, require production of documents, and bring legal actions to enforce compliance with regulations, statutes, and judicial decisions within the scope of their jurisdiction.

STUDY HINT.   An agency can investigate to determine: (1) if there is a need for additional regulations; (2) whether its rules or other relevant laws have been violated; (3) facts relating to an alleged violation; and (4) whether a party is complying with a final order issued by the agency.

LEARNING OUTCOME EXAMPLE. See the *CBS* case on p. 125.

7. CONSTITUTIONAL LIMITATIONS ON ADMINISTRATIVE INVESTIGATION

GENERAL RULE. In general, the constitutional protections against unreasonable searches and seizures and involuntary self-incrimination apply to agency investigations.

LIMITATION. A search warrant is not needed by an administrative agency in order to: (1) administratively search highly regulated businesses; (2) inspect premises if a violation endangers health or safety; or (3) inspect areas that are visible from a public place or from the air.

STUDY HINTS. ▶ The protection against unreasonable searches and seizures does not apply to subpoenas that require a person to produce papers or to testify. ▶ The guarantee against involuntary self-incrimination does not entitle a corporate officer to refuse to produce records of the *corporation*. ▶ An agency generally can require a business to prove that it is in compliance with agency regulations.

D. JUDICIAL POWER OF THE AGENCY

8. THE AGENCY AS A SPECIALIZED COURT

▶ Although agencies are not courts, they may be given the power to conduct a hearing in order to determine whether a party has violated relevant laws and agency regulations, and the courts recognize the validity of this exercise of judicial power. ▶ Due process generally requires that a person be given notice and a hearing before an administrative agency takes an action against the person. Procedures followed generally include:

(a) *Beginning enforcement - preliminary steps*

▶ An action commonly begins with a written complaint that alleges a violation of an agency rule. This complaint may be filed by another agency or by a private party. ▶ The alleged wrongdoer is served with the complaint and may dispute the complaint in a written answer.

(b) *The Administrative hearing*

▶ The hearing is conducted by an administrative law judge (ALJ). ▶ Notice must be given to all affected parties, and an agency must generally hold a hearing at which all interested parties may be heard. Example: A civil service employee is entitled to a hearing prior to being discharged.

▶ However, an agency may reach a tentative decision without a hearing, provided the agency conducts a hearing if an interested party objects to the agency's decision. ▶ There is no right to a jury trial in administrative hearings.

(c) *Streamlined procedure: consent decrees*

▶ Actions may be settled by informal procedures, such as consent decrees, stipulations, or voluntary agreements. ▶ The Administrative Dispute Resolution Act of 1990 authorizes federal agencies to use means of dispute resolution other than the procedures outlined in (a) and (b) above.

(d) *Form of administrative decision*

When agencies make a decision, they usually file an opinion summarizing the facts and basis for its decision. In some situations, such opinions are legally required.

9. PUNISHMENT AND ENFORCEMENT POWERS OF AGENCIES

Agencies can enforce the law by issuing cease-and-desist orders and assessing penalties.

10. **EXHAUSTION OF ADMINISTRATIVE REMEDIES**

In most cases, a party cannot appeal an agency action to the courts until all agency procedures are completed and the agency has made its final decision.

11. **APPEAL FROM ADMINISTRATIVE ACTION AND FINALITY OF ADMINISTRATIVE DETERMINATION**

GENERAL RULES. ▶ Statutes typically state to what court the appeal of an administrative decision must be taken. In general, only persons directly affected by an agency action or persons authorized by statute can appeal an agency decision to the courts. ▶ A court may review and set aside an administrative decision because: (1) the agency violated required procedural law or misapplied the law in arriving at its decision; (2) the agency exceeded its jurisdiction; or (3) the agency acted arbitrarily and capriciously. ▶ For example, the Supreme Court struck down a federal administrative regulation that forbid the disclosure of alcohol content on beer labels because the regulation violated the First Amendment.

LIMITATIONS. ▶ Courts do not reverse agency decisions regarding questions of fact or mixed questions of law and fact if there is substantial evidence to support the agency's decision. ▶ Courts typically uphold agency decisions relating to technical matters.

LEARNING OUTCOME EXAMPLE. See the *Mainstream Marketing* case on textbook p. 118.

12. **LIABILITY OF THE AGENCY**

An agency and its officials are not liable for losses caused by actions that were taken in good faith.

CONCEPT REVIEW AND APPLICATIONS

Matching Exercise

Select the term or phrase that best matches a definition or statement stated below. Each term or phrase is the best match for only one statement or definition. Not all terms and phrases will necessarily be used.

administrative agency	Federal Register Act
administrative law	Federal Register
Administrative Procedure Act	Freedom of Information Act
cease-and-desist order	informal settlements
consent decrees	open meeting law
exhaustion of administrative remedies	

_____ 1. Order directing a person or company to discontinue certain conduct.

_____ 2. Federal law that generally permits public inspection of federal agency records.

_____ 3. Governmental body typically created by Congress or a state legislature to implement legislation and to regulate a particular segment of the economy or society.

_____ 4. Judicial or administrative order voluntarily agreed to by an administrative agency and a party against whom an administrative action has been filed.

_____ 5. Publication that provides public notice of federal agency rules, principles, and procedures.

_____ 6. Requirement that an administrative agency makes a final decision before the parties may file a lawsuit.

_____ 7. Body of law that generally governs administrative agencies.

_____ 8. Federal law that generally establishes procedures for federal administrative agencies.

_____ 9. Law that requires advance public notice of an agency meeting and public access to the meeting.

True/False

Write **T** if the statement is true, write **F** if it is false.

_____ 1.   Administrative agencies are generally created by courts to carry out judicial orders.

_____ 2.   Administrative agencies do not have the power to make laws. The power to make laws can only be exercised by Congress or state legislatures.

_____ 3.   Administrative agencies are typically run by officials who are elected by the public.

_____ 4.   An agency claiming that it is exempt from the disclosure requirements of the Freedom of Information Act has the burden to prove such exemption.

_____ 5.   The Sunshine Act of 1976 requires federal agencies to open their meetings to the public only if the agencies voluntarily choose to do so.

_____ 6.   An agency can adopt a regulation only if doing so is within the agency's scope of authority.

_____ 7.   In general, agencies do not have the power to require businesses to prove that they are in compliance with the agencies' regulations.

_____ 8.   An agency cannot exercise its judicial powers to determine a party's rights in a matter if the agency previously conducted an investigation of the same matter.

_____ 9.   In general, an administrative agency can make a *final* determination of a person's rights without first conducting a hearing.

_____10.   In an agency hearing, a person accused of violating an agency regulation is entitled to a jury trial.

Multiple Choice

_____ 1. Congress is considering adopting new regulations of leveraged buy-outs and mergers of American companies. Congress is also debating whether it can create a new federal administrative agency to administer these laws and what powers this agency may exercise. Under these facts:
a. Congress cannot create an agency; only the President can create agencies.
b. Congress can create an agency, but it can only authorize the agency to enforce federal statutes. Congress cannot authorize the agency to exercise legislative or judicial powers.
c. Congress can create an agency, and Congress can generally authorize the agency to exercise legislative, executive, and judicial powers.
d. Congress can create an agency. The agency will automatically have the power to do anything it wants, and it will not be subject to any constitutional limits regarding what it can do.

_____ 2. The Federal Trade Commission (FTC) conducted an investigation and public hearing regarding misleading advertising by razor manufacturers. Cutting Edge, a razor manufacturer, was investigated and it filed a request under the Freedom of Information Act (FOIA) to inspect certain records relating to this matter. Pursuant to its FOIA request:
a. Cutting Edge is generally entitled to inspect FTC records of the public hearing.
b. Cutting Edge may require other razor manufacturers to disclose their proposed advertising campaigns to Cutting Edge for its examination.
c. Cutting Edge is generally entitled to compel other razor manufacturers to allow Cutting Edge to inspect their financial records relating to the advertising campaigns in question.
d. a and b.

_____ 3. To avoid problems that can arise from secret activities of government, the following federal legislation has been enacted to provide for public knowledge of administrative agency activities:
a. The Freedom of Information Act, which requires certain agency records to be open to the public.
b. The Sunshine Act, which requires most meetings of major agencies to be open to the public.
c. The APA generally requires federal agencies to publish their rules principles, and procedures.
d. All of the above.

_____ 4. Terri owns a lawn service and she used a certain chemical fertilizer in her business in violation of a new regulation adopted by the Environmental Protection Agency (EPA), a federal agency. This regulation was published 90 days previously in the *Federal Register*. Statutes provide that violators of this regulation are subject to fines. Terri did not know that this regulation had been adopted. After an appropriate administrative hearing:
a. Terri can be fined for violating this regulation.
b. Terri cannot be fined for violating this regulation because publication of a federal agency regulation in the *Federal Register* does not provide sufficient public notice of a regulation.
c. Terri cannot be fined for violating this regulation because a federal agency regulation does not become effective until one year after publication in the *Federal Register*.
d. Terri cannot be fined for violating this regulation because federal agencies do not have the power to impose fines for violations of agency regulations.

_____ 5. The Equal Employment Opportunity Commission (EEOC) is investigating a complaint against J&J Distributors. In this situation, the EEOC may:
   a. Require employees and former applicants of J&J to appear as witnesses.
   b. Require witnesses to produce relevant records.
   c. File a complaint against J&J if the EEOC investigation shows that J&J violated employment laws.
   d. All of the above.

_____ 6. The EPA can investigate which of the following matters?
   a. Whether Toxic Co. has been illegally dumping toxic wastes in violation of EPA regulations.
   b. Whether Petro Inc. has been complying with an EPA order to stop polluting a river.
   c. Whether the current national clean air standards need to be revised.
   d. All of the above.

_____ 7. An agent from the Bureau of Alcohol, Tobacco, and Firearms was flying over a gun shop and he saw people loading suspicious-looking firearms into a truck at a business next door. After the agent landed, he entered the gun shop and, without a warrant, conducted a search of its premises. He also got a warrant and searched the business next door. After investigating, the Bureau brought charges against the gun shop and the business next door to it. Under these facts, which action could the Bureau successfully defend against charges that the action was an unreasonable search and seizure?
   a. The entry and search of the gun shop.
   b. The search by air of the business next to the gun shop.
   c. The subpoena of the businesses' records related to the investigation.
   d. All of the above.

_____ 8. Susan is vice president of S & S Inc., a stock brokerage firm. The firm is required by federal securities law to keep records of all stock trades. By subpoena, the Securities and Exchange Commission (SEC) orders Susan to produce the *firm's* records for an administrative inspection. Susan is afraid that the records may expose illegal conduct on her part. Under these facts:
   a. Susan must produce the records.
   b. Susan can refuse to produce the records because forcing her to turn over the records would violate her constitutional protection against unreasonable searches and seizures.
   c. Susan can refuse to produce the records because forcing her to turn over the records would violate her constitutional protection against involuntary self-incrimination.
   d. Susan can refuse to produce the records; agencies cannot investigate suspected wrongdoing.

_____ 9. David has been getting headaches from the fumes he breathes while working at the Brighton Paint Factory. He filed a written complaint with the Occupational Safety and Health Administration (OSHA) charging that the factory has inadequate ventilation. Under typical administrative procedure:
   a. David's complaint cannot be investigated, since he is a private individual and any complaints can be filed only by an agency itself.
   b. Due process generally requires that Brighton be notified of the charges and that it be given a chance to present its case at some type of hearing.
   c. Due process generally guarantees Brighton a right to trial by jury.
   d. Due process requirements are generally fulfilled if Brighton receives a copy of the written complaint and it files an answer. No hearing is necessary.

_____ 10. Which of the following is not ordinarily within the power of an administrative agency?
   a. The power to impose a civil penalty.
   b. The power to impose criminal penalties and to imprison parties who violate its regulations.
   c. The power to issue a binding order for a regulated business to stop a practice the agency finds improper.
   d. The power to require a regulated business to file a detailed statement showing it is acting within agency guidelines.

Case Problems

Answer the following problems, briefly explaining your answers.

1. The EPA is given broad authority by Congress to regulate all matters necessary to protect the purity of water in the U.S. Assume that the EPA proposes to adopt: (1) a new environmental policy characterizing contaminated storm water runoff as a serious threat to clean water; and (2) a new regulation requiring cities and companies to install devices to control contaminated storm water runoff.

   a. Can the EPA establish the new policy regarding contaminated storm water runoff?
   b. Under the modern view, to what extent can the EPA adopt rules and is the proposed rule permissible?
   c. Must the EPA hold public hearings regarding this proposed regulation?

   _____

   _____

   _____

2. Medco manufactures and sells a certain type of vitamin. A number of individuals and state health agencies allege that the vitamin violates regulations of the Food and Drug Administration (FDA), a federal agency. The FDA can fine Medco if the vitamin violates FDA regulations.

   a. Is Medco entitled to notice and a hearing before the FDA imposes a fine?
   b. What preliminary steps may occur in an administrative action in this case?
   c. In an administrative action, is Medco entitled to have a jury determine the case?
   d. What informal procedures can the parties use to resolve this matter?

   _____

   _____

   _____

3. The State Health Agency has commenced an administrative action against Sue to suspend her license as a beautician due to certain violations of state health regulations. The administrative hearing is in process. If Sue loses at the hearing, there is an internal agency appeals procedure available.

   a. If Sue loses at the first hearing, can she immediately appeal the decision to a court?
   b. Can Sue appeal a final administrative decision to a court? Can Beauty Co., an unrelated party, appeal the decision?
   c. If Sue is found to have violated this regulation, how can the Agency enforce its decision?

_____

_____

_____

Internet Exercise

On-the-Move Co. manufactures a four-wheeled vehicle known as a "golf cart." Presently, On-the-Move's carts have a maximum speed of 15 miles per hour, and they are used for traversing golf courses. Henry, president of On-the-Move, has noticed that an increasing number of prospective buyers want to buy these carts for traveling about their retirement communities, but only if the vehicles' maximum speed is 25 miles per hour. Henry has asked you to determine whether increasing the maximum speed of the carts will subject the carts to regulation by the National Highway Traffic Safety Administration (NHTRA). Using the Internet, locate the web site for the (*Code of*) *Federal Register* (CFR) and answer the following questions:

1. What section of the CFR is directly applicable to this case?
2. Are On-the-Move's present (slower) carts subject to NHTRA regulations?
3. Would On-the-Move's new (faster) carts be subject to NHTRA regulations?

_____

_____

_____

CHAPTER 7
THE LEGAL ENVIRONMENT OF INTERNATIONAL TRADE

MAKE THE CONNECTION

SUMMARY

The World Trade Organization, a multilateral treaty subscribed to by the United States and most of the industrialized countries of the world, is based on the principle of trade without discrimination. The United Nations Convention on Contracts for the International Sale of Goods provides uniform rules for international sales contracts between parties in contracting nations. The European Union is a regional trading group that includes most of western Europe. The North American Free Trade Agreement involves Mexico, Canada, and the U.S. and eliminates all tariffs between the three countries over a 15-year period.

U.S. firms may choose to do business abroad by making export sales or contracting with a foreign distributor to take title to their goods and sell them abroad. U.S. firms may also license their technology or trademarks for foreign use. An agency arrangement or the organization of a foreign subsidiary may be required to participate effectively in foreign markets. This results in subjecting the U.S. firm to taxation in the host country. However, tax treaties commonly eliminate double taxation.

The Export Administration Act is the principal statute imposing export controls on goods and technical data.

In choosing the form for doing business abroad, U.S. firms must be careful not to violate the antitrust laws of host countries. Anticompetitive foreign transactions may have an adverse impact on competition in U.S. domestic markets. U.S. antitrust laws have a broad extraterritorial reach. U.S. courts apply a "jurisdictional rule of reason," weighing the interests of the United States against the interests of the foreign country involved in making a decision on whether to hear a case. Illegal conduct may occur in U.S. securities markets. U.S. enforcement efforts sometimes run into foreign countries' secrecy and blocking laws that hinder effective enforcement.

Antidumping laws offer relief for domestic firms threatened by unfair foreign competition. In addition, economic programs exist to assist industries, communities, and workers injured by import competition. The Foreign Corrupt Practices Act restricts U.S. firms doing business abroad from paying public officials "commissions" for getting business contracts from the foreign governments.

LEARNING OUTCOMES
After studying this chapter, you should be able to

A. GENERAL PRINCIPLES
LO.1   Explain which country's law will govern an international contract should a dispute arise.

LO.2   Identify seven major international organizations, conferences, and treaties that affect the multinational markets for goods, services, and investments.

LO.3   List the forms of business organizations for doing business abroad.

B. GOVERNMENTAL REGULATION
LO.4   Explain the tariff barriers and nontariff barriers to the free movements of goods across borders.

LO.5   Explain U.S. law regarding payment to foreign government officials as a means of obtaining business contracts with other governments, and compare U.S. law to laws and treaties applicable to most First World nations.

CHAPTER OUTLINE

A. GENERAL PRINCIPLES

1. THE LEGAL BACKGROUND

➤ *What law applies*: Laws of different countries frequently vary. Consequently, international contracts often contain a choice of law clause whereby the parties determine which country's law to apply in case of a dispute. Otherwise, an international treaty may determine which law controls.

➤ *The arbitration alternative*: To avoid lawsuits, parties may contractually agree to arbitrate disputes according to stated rules, and the arbitration is often required to be held in a neutral country.

➤ *Conflicting ideologies*: Different values give rise to different laws in various countries.

➤ *Financing international trade*: There is no international currency. Thus, parties generally agree in *their contract on the curren*cy to be used for payment, and letters of credits are often required.

➤ *LEARNING OUTCOME EXAMPLE.* See the choice of law example where the U.S. Court required the Lipcons to "honor their bargains" and vindicate their claims in an English Court on textbook p. 127.

2. INTERNATIONAL TRADE ORGANIZATIONS, CONFERENCES, AND TREATIES

The following organizations, conferences, and treaties significantly regulate international trade:

➤ *GATT (General Agreement on Tariffs and Trade) 1994 and WTO (World Trade Organization)*: ▶ GATT provides protection of domestic industries through tariffs and promotes nondiscriminatory trade among its members through its most favored nation clause. ▶ The WTO administers the GATT. ▶ The 1994 GATT has been signed by 126 countries, including the U.S.

➤ *CISG (United Nations Convention on Contracts for the International Sale of Goods)*: ▶ CISG states rules for international sales contracts between parties in countries that have adopted it. ▶ Unlike the UCC, parties may opt out of coverage by the CISG, and the CISG does not apply to sales of goods for personal, family or household purposes.

➤ *UNCTAD (United Nations Conference on Trade and Development)*: This Conference aids developing countries by creating preferences for manufactured goods from third world countries.

➤ *EU (European Union), formerly EEC (European Economic Community)*: ▶ EU is an organization of European countries that focuses on monetary and political union for member nations. ▶ EU goals are: (1) unified monetary policies; (2) common foreign and security policies; and (3) cooperation in justice.

➤ *NAFTA (North American Free Trade Agreement)*: This agreement, effective in January 1994, is between the U.S., Mexico, and Canada. It eventually eliminates all tariffs between these countries.

➤ *Regional trading groups*: Developing countries have created many regional trading groups.

➤ *IMF (International Monetary Fund) - World Bank*: ▶ IMF established a complex lending system to expand and stabilize international trade after World War II. ▶ IMF members hold "special drawing rights" by which they can borrow money to enable them to stabilize their currencies.

> *OPEC (Organization of Petroleum Exporting Countries)*: This group is a cartel of oil producing countries whose main goals are to: (1) raise taxes and royalties for the benefit of member countries; and (2) take control of oil production and exploration from major oil companies.

3. FORMS OF BUSINESS ORGANIZATIONS

Foreign trade is carried out in many ways. Important methods of conducting such trade include:

> *Export sales*: U.S. company sells and exports goods directly to customers in a foreign country without maintaining a physical presence in that country.

> *Agency arrangements*: ▶ U.S. manufacturer appoints a person or firm to make contracts for the manufacturer in a foreign country. ▶ Appointing an agent subjects the U.S. firm to foreign taxation.

> *Foreign distributorships*: A seller transfers title to goods to a foreign distributor for resale.

> *Licensing*: U.S. firm licenses a foreign company to use its technology to make a product abroad.

> *Wholly owned subsidiaries*: ▶ U.S. company owns and does business through a separate company in a foreign country. ▶ Sales to a foreign subsidiary at less than fair value may allow the IRS to reallocate the parent company's income, increasing the parent company's liability for U.S. taxes.

> *Joint ventures*: ▶ Traditionally, a joint venture entails U.S. and foreign firms contractually agreeing to work together with each party providing separate services/value in order to achieve a common business goal. ▶ In China, there may be a contract joint venture as described above or an equity joint venture whereby each firm owns part of the joint venture business.

B. GOVERNMENTAL REGULATION

4. EXPORT REGULATIONS

GENERAL RULES. ▶ The Export Administration Act (EAA) controls the export of goods and technical data from the United States. ▶ Under 1996 regulations, not all exported products require a license. ▶ Whether an export license is required depends on the type of product and its proposed destination. ▶ Expert assistance about export licensing is available through the U.S. Department of Commerce and through licensed foreign-freight forwarders. ▶ Persons who violate the EAA may be subject to criminal and civil penalties

LIMITATION. Special restrictions may apply to exports of strategic commodities, commodities in short supply, and certain unpublished technical data to certain countries.

5. PROTECTION OF INTELLECTUAL PROPERTY RIGHTS

> *Counterfeit goods*: ▶ Importation of counterfeit goods (goods bearing counterfeit trademarks) and goods that infringe on U.S. patents violate U.S. law. ▶ Intellectual property (trademarks, copyrights, and patents) are also protected by various international treaties, including the Madrid System of International Registration of Marks that provides for registration of marks in over 60 countries.

> *Gray market goods*: ▶ Federal law forbids importing gray market goods into the U.S. without the written consent of the affected U.S. firm. ▶ Gray market goods bear the trademark of a U.S. firm but the goods were made in a foreign country by: (1) a foreign firm under license by the U.S. firm; or (2) an affiliate of the U.S. firm, but the goods are different from goods made in the U.S.

6. ANTITRUST

GENERAL RULES. ► Under the "effects doctrine," U.S. courts may apply American antitrust laws to business conducted outside of the U.S. if there is a direct, substantial, and foreseeable effect on U.S. commerce. ► If this effect is found, U.S. courts will then apply the "jurisdictional rule of reason" and will balance U.S. interests with those of a foreign country to decide which law controls.

LIMITATION. Defenses against U.S. antitrust laws: (1) act of state doctrine (court will not judge act of a foreign government that is done in its own jurisdiction); (2) sovereign compliance doctrine (no liability if act is *compelled* by a foreign government); (3) sovereign immunity doctrine (a party cannot sue a foreign country for its *governmental* acts, but one can sue a foreign country for its *commercial* conduct).

STUDY HINT. Foreign antitrust laws frequently differ from U.S. antitrust laws.

7. SECURITIES & TAX FRAUD REGULATION IN AN INTERNATIONAL ENVIRONMENT

GENERAL RULE. U.S. securities laws apply to fraudulent sales of securities if: (1) a U.S. citizen living in the U.S. suffers a loss, regardless of where the sale occurred; or (2) a U.S. citizen living abroad suffers a loss *and* the sale occurred in the U.S.

LIMITATION. Enforcement of U.S. securities laws may be hampered by: (1) secrecy laws (foreign laws forbid disclosure of bank records and bank customer names); and (2) blocking laws (foreign laws forbid disclosure of documents pursuant to orders issued by foreign officials).

8. BARRIERS TO TRADE

➢ *Tariff barriers*: Tariffs (import or export taxes on goods) make imported goods more expensive.

➢ *Nontariff barriers*: ► Quotas restrict the amount of imported goods that may come into a foreign country. ► Complex foreign customs procedures may hinder the sale of imported goods.

➢ *Export controls as instruments of foreign policy*: Export controls may be used to carry out foreign policy by limiting trade with a country. ►*LEARNING OUTCOME EXAMPLES.* See the *Sabritas* case on the applicability of tariff barriers on textbook p. 142; see the U.S. embargo on all Brazilian shrimp example because of Brazil's failure to require turtle excluder devices on its shrimp boats textbook p. 143.

9. RELIEF MECHANISMS FOR ECONOMIC INJURY CAUSED BY FOREIGN TRADE

American law provides some economic relief for losses caused by foreign competition including:

➢ *Antidumping laws and export subsidies*: The dumping of foreign goods in the United States (selling foreign goods in U.S. for less than fair value) is forbidden. If dumping occurs and a U.S. industry is hurt, additional duties may be imposed on the foreign goods.

➢ *Relief from import injuries*: ► The Trade Act of 1974 offers government help to communities, firms, and employees hurt by foreign competition. Assistance includes readjustment allowances and job training. ► This Act authorizes duties or quotas on foreign goods hurting U.S. workers.

➢ *Retaliation and relief against foreign unfair trade restrictions*: The Omnibus Trade and Competitiveness Act of 1988 allows economic retaliation against unreasonable, unjustifiable, or discriminatory trade acts by a foreign country ("Section 301 authority").

10. EXPROPRIATION

Expropriation (that is, nationalization of assets by a foreign country) is a business risk for U.S. firms doing business abroad. Firms may reduce this risk by employing political scientists to assess the risks of expropriation and by obtaining insurance from private firms or the U.S. government.

11. THE FOREIGN CORRUPT PRACTICES ACT

GENERAL RULE. This U.S. law forbids any offer, payment, or gift to foreign officials or third parties to influence trading decisions. But, payments to low-level officials to expedite routine services are allowed. ►**LEARNING OUTCOME EXAMPLE.** See the Ethics & the Law discussion of the tax deductions for "useful expenditures" (bribes) claimed by Siemens AG, textbook p. 147.

CONCEPT REVIEW AND APPLICATIONS

Matching Exercise

Select the term or phrase that best matches a definition or statement stated below. Each term or phrase is the best match for only one statement or definition. Not all terms and phrases will necessarily be used.

act-of-state doctrine	export sale	principal
agent	franchising	secrecy laws
blocking laws	freight forwarders	sovereign compliance doctrine
choice-of-law clause	gray market goods	
comity	intellectual property rights	sovereign immunity doctrine
Dispute Settlement Body (DSB)	joint venture	special drawing rights (SDRs)
distributor	jurisdictional rule of reason	tariff
dumping	letter of credit	
effects doctrine	licensing	
	most-favored-nation clause	

_____ 1. Doctrine provides that courts will not judge acts of a foreign government done within its jurisdiction.

_____ 2. Provision in international treaties that generally forbids trade discrimination against member countries.

_____ 3. Doctrine holding that U.S. antitrust laws do not apply to conduct occurring outside of the United States unless there is a direct, substantial, and foreseeable effect on U.S. commerce.

_____ 4. Foreign laws that forbid disclosure of banking information, including names of bank customers.

_____ 5. Doctrine that forbids suing a foreign government due to its governmental actions.

_____ 6. Foreign laws that forbid disclosure of documents pursuant to orders issued by other countries.

_____ 7. Direct sale to customers in a foreign country.

_____ 8. Sale of foreign goods in the U.S. at less than fair value.

_____ 9. Trademark, copyright and patent rights that are protected by law.

_____ 10. Doctrine creating a defense to antitrust liability if an action is compelled by a foreign country.

True/False

Write **T** if the statement is true, write **F** if it is false.

_____ 1. Foreign secrecy and blocking laws make enforcement of U.S. securities laws more difficult.

_____ 2. A distributor takes title to U.S. goods and resells them in a foreign country.

_____ 3. A U.S. firm may be subject to foreign taxation if it appoints a foreign agent to do business for it in a foreign country.

_____ 4. Licensing allows foreign businesses to manufacture goods using the technology of U.S. firms.

_____ 5. It is not a violation of U.S. law to import gray market goods into the U.S.

_____ 6. Sovereign immunity doctrine holds that a country cannot be sued for its *commercial* activities.

_____ 7. Foreign antitrust laws are frequently different from U.S. antitrust laws.

_____ 8. In general, U.S. antitrust law does not apply to conduct occurring outside of the U.S. if the conduct does not affect commerce within the U.S.

_____ 9. The Single European Act removed trade barriers for U.S. firms doing business in Europe.

_____ 10. U.S. securities laws protect an American citizen from a fraudulent sale of securities only if the American citizen lives in the U.S. and the transaction occurs within the U.S.

Multiple Choice

_____ 1. Micro-Tech, a U.S. firm, made a contract to buy transistors from a Japanese firm. A disagreement arose between the firms regarding the time in which payment had to be made without interest charges. Assume the laws of the U.S. and Japan differ on this point. Under these facts:
   a. If the parties specified in their contract whether U.S. or Japanese law applies to their contract, that contract provision would govern.
   b. A choice of law contractual clause could govern as to whether U.S. or Japanese law applies.
   c. If the parties failed to specify in their contract which law applies in case of conflict, a treaty between the U.S. and Japan could govern.
   d. All of the above.

____ 2. Xy-Cor, a U.S. firm, entered a sales contract with MTR, a German firm. In their contract, the firms agreed to arbitrate any disputes arising under their contract in France with an arbitrator fluent in German and English. The parties specified that in case of a dispute, full discovery would be available and that any decision of the arbitrator would be final and binding on both parties. Under these facts:

  a. The parties cannot specify that arbitration take place in France. Arbitration must take place in the country of one of the parties to the contract.

  b. The parties can specify that their arbitrator be fluent in both German and English.

  c. Full discovery is ordinarily available to the parties to an arbitration, even if they do not specify in their contract that they want full discovery available.

  d. The decision of the arbitrator would not be final and binding if the parties had not specified this in their contract.

____ 3. Uniform rules to govern international sales contracts between ratifying nations are found in:

  a. The GATT.

  b. The WTO.

  c. The CISG.

  d. The UCC.

____ 4. Freedom Corporation, a U.S. manufacturer of steel products, has recently lost several important U.S. customers to foreign competitors that have been selling the same products for significantly less than Freedom Corporation. Freedom contacted the International Trade Administration and International Trade Commission ("Commerce") to request that Commerce investigate whether the foreign competitors are violating U.S. or international antidumping laws and to take appropriate remedial action. Under these facts:

  a. Commerce may take remedial action against the foreign competitors if they are selling their steel products in the U.S. for less than fair value.

  b. Commerce may take remedial action against the foreign competitors if they are injuring U.S. firms, whether or not they are selling their steel products in the U.S. for less than fair value.

  c. Commerce may take remedial action against the foreign competitors if their governments are subsidizing the sale of steel products in the U.S. for less than fair value.

  d. a and c.

____ 5. The European Union is made up of:

  a. European Council, European Commission, European Parliament, and European Court of Justice (including the lower Court of First Instance).

  b. European Council, World Court, and International Monetary Fund.

  c. European Commission, European Parliament, European Economic Cooperative, and World Court.

  d. European Court of Justice, European Congress, and European Executive Commission.

____ 6. Tymes Corporation is considering marketing its products internationally, but it does not want to be subject to foreign taxation, to manage a foreign operation, or to transfer its technology rights to anyone else. What way of doing business abroad would best meet Tymes' objectives?

  a. Appointing an agent to represent Tymes in the foreign market.

  b. Licensing.

  c. Franchising.

  d. Export sales.

_____ 7. QTC Inc. found that jackets bearing its well-known trademark, but not made by QTC, were being sold in discount stores in the United States. The jackets did not meet the standards of QTC, and they were sold for considerably less than the normal price of QTC jackets. QTC began losing sales of its jackets because of these foreign-made counterfeit jackets. What remedies are available to QTC?

    a. Triple damages from the counterfeiters.

    b. Seizure and destruction of the counterfeit jackets.

    c. Both a and b.

    d. None of the above. The manufacture of goods at a lower quality and price, bearing a trademark of another manufacturer, is a fair method of competition.

_____ 8. Which of the following is not a defense to the application of U.S. antitrust laws outside of the United States?

    a. The act of state doctrine.

    b. The expropriation doctrine.

    c. The sovereign compliance doctrine.

    d. The sovereign immunity doctrine.

_____ 9. The American Shoe Company has suffered severe economic losses due to competition from imported foreign shoes. The Company fears that it will be forced to lay off its workforce or to shut down entirely. What relief may be available under the Trade Act of 1974?

    a. The U.S. may impose duties or quotas on foreign shoes.

    b. The U.S. may provide readjustment allowances for workers who lose their jobs.

    c. The U.S. may provide job training for workers who lose their jobs.

    d. All of the above.

_____ 10. Kristen Jones is vice president of sales for Arnold Appliance Corporation. She wishes to expedite a sale of household appliances to a customer in a foreign country. Which of the following actions may Kristen take without violating the Foreign Corrupt Practices Act?

    a. Kristen may bribe a high government official in order to gain the official's approval.

    b. Kristen may make valuable gifts to high government officials in order to gain their approval.

    c. Kristen may pay low-level government officials to expedite routine paperwork.

    d. Kristen may not make any kind of payment to any government official.

CASE PROBLEM

Answer the following problem, briefly explaining your answer.

The BYTE Corp. designs computer parts and develops technical data that can be used for a variety of commercial or military uses. BYTE Corp. wants to export certain computer parts and technology to a firm in Mongolia.
1. What U.S. law primarily controls BYTE Corp.'s exportation of the computer parts and technology?
2. How can BYTE Corp. determine if a license is needed to export the computer parts to Mongolia?
3. What type of sanctions could BYTE Corp. face if it falsifies information on a license application to export the computer parts and technology to the firm in Mongolia?

_____

_____

_____

Internet Exercise

Thread-Bare Corp. manufactures a line of athletic clothing, using a secret, waterproof fabric that Thread-Bare has developed. Thread-Bare managers are considering shifting the company's fabrication operations to Mexico in order to take advantage of lower unskilled labor costs. These managers are concerned, however, that Mexican law may require them to employ all Mexican workers, and limit the company's right to import materials necessary to make the company's products. Under these facts:
1. What international treaty applies to Thread-Bare's proposed Mexican operation?
2. Does this treaty address Thread-Bare's concerns? Explain.

_____

_____

_____

CHAPTER 8
CRIMES

MAKE THE CONNECTION

SUMMARY

When a person does not live up to the standards set by law, this punishable conduct, called *crime,* may be common law or statutory in origin. Crimes are classified as *felonies,* which generally carry greater sentences and more long-term consequences, and *misdemeanors.*

Employers and corporations may be criminally responsible for their acts and the acts of their employees. The federal sentencing guidelines provide parameters for sentences for federal crimes and allow judges to consider whether the fact that a business promotes compliance with the law is a reason to reduce a sentence.

White-collar crimes include those relating to financial fraud. Sarbanes-Oxley reforms increased the penalties for financial fraud and added fraudulent financial statement certification as a crime. Other white-collar crimes include bribery, extortion, blackmail, and corrupt influence in politics and in business. Also included as white-collar crimes are counterfeiting, forgery, perjury, making false claims against the government, obtaining goods or money by false pretenses, using bad checks, false financial reporting, and embezzlement. The common law crimes include those that involve injury to person and/or property, such as arson and murder.

Statutes have expanded the area of criminal law to meet situations in which computers are involved. Both federal and state statutes make the unauthorized taking of information from a computer a crime. The diversion of deliveries of goods and the transfer of funds, the theft of software, and the raiding of computers are made crimes to some extent by federal laws. Newer federal statutes that apply to computers are the Economic Espionage Act, which prohibits downloading or copying information via computer to give to a competitor, and the Digital Millennium Copyright Act that prohibits circumventing or designing programs to circumvent encryption devices.

Criminal procedure is dictated by the Fourth, Fifth, and Sixth Amendments. The Fourth Amendment protects against unreasonable searches, the Fifth Amendment protects against self-incrimination and provides due process, and the Sixth Amendment guarantees a speedy trial.

LEARNING OUTCOMES
After studying this chapter, you should be able to

A. GENERAL PRINCIPLES
LO.1   Discuss the nature and classification of crimes.

LO.2   Describe the basis of criminal liability.

LO.3 Identify who is responsible for criminal acts
LO.4 Explain the penalties for crimes and the sentencing for corporate crimes.

B. WHITE-COLLAR CRIMES
LO.5 List examples of white-collar crimes and their elements.

LO.6 Describe the common law crimes.

C. CRIMINAL LAW AND THE COMPUTER
LO.7 Discuss crimes related to computers.

D. CRIMINAL PROCEDURE RIGHTS FOR BUSINESSES
LO.8 Describe the rights of businesses charged with crimes and the constitutional protections afforded.

CHAPTER OUTLINE

A. GENERAL PRINCIPLES

A crime is conduct that is prohibited and punished by a government.

1. NATURE AND CLASSIFICATION OF CRIMES

GENERAL RULE. Crimes are classified by: (1) source (common law or statutes); or (2) seriousness – misdemeanor (offense punishable by less than 1 year in jail) or felony (more serious crimes).
STUDY HINT. A crime that is a misdemeanor in one state may be a felony in another state.

2. BASIS OF CRIMINAL LIABILITY

GENERAL RULE. A crime consists of (1) an act or omission (2) and a mental state (usually, all that is required is that a person voluntarily committed the wrong).
LIMITATION. For certain crimes, a particular mental state or a specific intent must be present.
STUDY HINT. Harm or knowledge that an act/omission is against the law is not necessary.
▶ **LEARNING OUTCOME EXAMPLES.** See the **For Example** discussion of dumping waste and intent on textbook p. 156; see *U.S. v Erickson* on textbook p. 157.

3. RESPONSIBILITY FOR CRIMINAL ACTS

➤ *Corporate liability*: Modern trend is to hold corporations criminally liable for their agents' crimes.

➤ *Officers and agents of corporations*: Managers of companies who authorize employees to commit crimes may be held criminally liable for such crimes.

➤ *Forfeiture as a penalty for crime*: Property that is used to commit a crime or gained through commission of a crime may be forfeited, i.e., the government may confiscate such property.

➤ *Penalties for business and white-collar crimes*: ▶Fine for a business often is computed to be a percentage of the firm's earnings. ▶Officer and director sentences may be affected by whether they tried to prevent business crime. ▶ Federal (U.S.) Sentencing Guidelines permit a judge to consider whether a guilty firm had a crime prevention program in deciding the firm's length of probation.

➤ *Sarbanes-Oxley reforms to criminal penalties*: This Act includes the White-Collar Crime Penalty Enhancement Act of 2002 that substantially increases criminal penalties.

➤ *Learning outcome examples.* See *U.S. v Park* on textbook p. 158; see Thinking Things Through on textbook p. 162.

4. INDEMNIFICATION OF CRIME VICTIMS

GENERAL RULE. For most crimes, the criminal pays a fine to the government, not to the victim.

LIMITATIONS. ► Some criminal laws allow indemnification (payment) to victims for damages they suffer as a result of specified criminal acts. ► Victims of a criminal act typically can sue the criminal in a civil action for damages suffered. ►Innocent persons wrongly convicted of a crime usually are entitled to indemnification from the state.

B. WHITE-COLLAR CRIMES

White-collar crimes are business crimes that do not involve the use or threat of physical force.

5. CONSPIRACIES

► A conspiracy is an agreement between two or more persons to commit an unlawful act.
► **LEARNING OUTCOME EXAMPLE.** See the Sports & Entertainment Law discussion of the NBA referee on textbook p. 171.

6. CRIMES RELATED TO PRODUCTION, COMPETITION, AND MARKETING

The transmission of fraudulent information or transportation of prohibited goods in interstate commerce, as well as violations of federal securities laws, are typically federal crimes.

7. MONEY LAUNDERING

► The federal Money Laundering Control Act (MLCA) forbids the knowing and willful participation in any financial transaction that is intended to conceal or disguise the source of unlawful funds (money laundering). ► Pursuant to the USA Patriot Act, these prohibitions apply to all financial transactions, even small businesses such as automobile dealers, currency dealers, and travel agencies.

8. RACKETEERING (Racketeer Influenced and Corrupt Organizations Act)

➢ *RICO*: RICO punishes racketeering activities (2 or more unlawful racketeering acts within 10 years).
➢ *Criminal and civil applications*: RICO authorizes criminal penalties against violators, and also authorizes victims of racketeering to recovery treble (triple) damages from wrongdoers.
➢ *Expanding usage*: RICO civil actions have been brought against numerous bona fide parties.

9. BRIBERY

►Bribery is giving money or other value to wrongfully influence a the judgment of another person, such as a public official, in favor of the giver. ► The giving and receiving of bribes are both crimes.

10. COMMERCIAL BRIBERY

► Commercial bribery occurs when a person secretly gives value, such as money, to an employee in order to influence the employee's conduct in connection with his or her employer's business.

11. EXTORTION AND BLACKMAIL

➢ *Extortion*: ► Traditionally: Illegal demand made by a public official appearing to act in an official capacity. ► Modern laws: Extortion occurs if anyone obtains anything by making an illegal threat.
➢ *Blackmail*: Same as extortion, except the crime is committed by a person who is not a public official.

12. CORRUPT INFLUENCE

> *Improper political influence*: Government official accepts gifts, money, or other value from persons who have an interest in obtaining favorable governmental action.
> *Foreign Corrupt Practices Act*: ▶ The FCPA forbids making payments or gifts of anything valuable with the intent to corrupt foreign officials. ▶ Grease or facilitation payments are legal.

13. COUNTERFEITING

It is a crime to make, pass, or possess (with intent to pass) counterfeit coins, money, or securities.

14. FORGERY

Forgery is signing another's name to or altering a legal instrument creating a liability against another.

15. PERJURY

▶ Perjury is knowingly giving false testimony in a judicial proceeding after swearing to tell the truth. ▶ Giving a false answer on a governmental form may also be perjury.

16. FALSE CLAIMS AND PRETENSES

▶ Knowingly making a false statement or claim to an insurance company or to a governmental agency may be a crime. ▶ In most states, obtaining money or goods by false pretenses is a crime. ▶Unauthorized obtaining money from an ATM or lying on a bank loan application are federal crimes.

17. BAD CHECKS

▶ It is a crime to use or pass a check, knowing that the account will have insufficient funds to pay the check. ▶ The required intent to defraud is presumed if a check is not paid within a certain time.

18. CREDIT CARD CRIMES

▶ It is a crime to use a canceled or counterfeit credit card, or to steal or improperly use the credit card of another. ▶ It is forgery to sign another's signature on a credit card charge slip without authorization.

19. EMBEZZLEMENT

Embezzlement is fraudulent conversion of property or money by a person to whom it is entrusted.

20. OBSTRUCTION OF JUSTICE: SARBANES-OXLEY

The federal Sarbanes-Oxley Act makes it a felony for anyone to alter, destroy, conceal, etc. with the intent to impede or otherwise hinder any investigation by any federal agency.

21. CORPORATE FRAUD: SARBANES-OXLEY

This Act created a new type of mail and wire fraud, which is committed when a corporate officer certifies a corporate financial statement that contains false material information.

22. THE COMMON LAW CRIMES

Common law crimes that involve the threat or use of force, physical injury, or property damage include larceny, robbery, burglary, arson, and riots and civil disorders.

C. CRIMINAL LAW AND THE COMPUTER

23. WHAT IS A COMPUTER CRIME?

▶ A computer crime is a crime that requires knowledge of computers. ▶ **LEARNING OUTCOME EXAMPLE.** See the E-Commerce & Cyberlaw discussion of cyber-bullying on textbook p. 175.

24. THE COMPUTER AS VICTIM

The theft or intentional destruction of hardware or software is a crime under traditional criminal law.

25. UNAUTHORIZED USE OF COMPUTERS

The unauthorized use of another's computer may or may not be a crime under state law.

26. COMPUTER RAIDING

Unauthorized use of secret data stored in a computer is theft of trade secrets or "computer trespass."

27. DIVERTED DELIVERY BY COMPUTER

Unlawfully diverting goods or money by use of a computer is larceny, theft, or embezzlement.

28. ECONOMIC ESPIONAGE BY COMPUTER

The Economic Espionage Act (EEA) makes it a felony to use any means to steal a trade secret.

29. ELECTRONIC FUND TRANSFER CRIMES

Under the federal Electronic Fund Transfers Act, it is a crime: (1) to use a counterfeit or wrongfully obtained device (e.g., a credit card) to obtain money or goods through an electronic fund transfer system; or (2) to ship or receive such forbidden devices or wrongfully obtained goods.

30. CIRCUMVENTING COPYRIGHT PROTECTION DEVICES VIA COMPUTER

The Digital Millennium Copyright Act makes it a crime to circumvent or create programs to circumvent encryption devices that copyright holders place on copyrighted material to prevent unauthorized copying.

31. SPAMMING

States are beginning to enact statutes that make spamming (sending unsolicited e-mail) a crime.

D. CRIMINAL PROCEDURE RIGHTS FOR BUSINESSES

32. FOURTH AMENDMENT RIGHTS FOR BUSINESSES

▶ Government officers must have a search warrant to search a business, unless an exception applies. ▶ **LEARNING OUTCOME EXAMPLE.** See the *Dow* case on textbook p. 178.

33. FIFTH AMENDMENT SELF-INCRIMINATION RIGHTS FOR BUSINESSES

▶ Individuals, but not corporations, have a right to refuse to say or do things that may incriminate them. ▶ **LEARNING OUTCOME EXAMPLE.** See the *Dickerson* case on textbook p. 180.

34. DUE PROCESS RIGHTS FOR BUSINESSES

Individuals and businesses have the right to be heard, question witnesses, and present evidence a crime.

CONCEPT REVIEW AND APPLICATIONS

Matching Exercise

Select the term or phrase that best matches a definition or statement stated below. Each term or phrase is the best match for only one statement or definition. Not all terms and phrases will necessarily be used.

blackmail	Federal Sentencing Guidelines	Penalty Enhancement Act of 2002
computer crime	felonies	predicate act
conspiracy	Fifth Amendment	Racketeer Influenced and Corrupt Organizations (RICO) Act
crime	Foreign Corrupt Practices Act (FCPA)	
due process		
Economic Espionage Act (EEA)	forgery	search warrant
embezzlement	Fourth Amendment	Sixth Amendment
extortion	grease payment	uttering
facilitation payments	*Miranda* warnings	white-collar crime
	misdemeanors	

_____ 1. Class of minor crimes that are punishable by less than one year in prison.

_____ 2. Broad category of business crimes that do not use or threaten the use of force.

_____ 3. Crime of issuing or delivering a forged instrument to another party.

_____ 4. Federal law that forbids bribing foreign officials.

_____ 5. Federal law that makes it a felony to copy, download, transmit, or in any way transfer proprietary files, documents, and information from a computer to an unauthorized person.

_____ 6. Judicial authorization for a search of property where there is the expectation of privacy.

_____ 7. Crime that is committed when two or more persons agree to commit another crime.

_____ 8. Crime involving fraudulent taking of money or property by a party to whom it was entrusted.

_____ 9. Federal law for prosecuting racketeering that permits victims to sue for treble damages.

_____ 10. Class of serious crimes that are punishable by imprisonment for greater than one year or by death.

True/False

Write **T** if the statement is true, write **F** if it is false.

_____ 1. Government officers do not need a search warrant in order to inspect property in "plain view."

_____ 2. A required element for a crime is that the criminal party voluntarily commit the prohibited act.

_____ 3. A person cannot commit a crime if the person does not know that his or her conduct is criminal.

_____ 4. The Digital Millennium Copyright Act allows a person to thwart encryption devices that copyright holders place on copyrighted material if the person has purchased the copyrighted item in question.

_____ 5. The Fourth Amendment prohibits all government searches of businesses.

_____ 6. The Fifth Amendment protects natural persons, but not corporations, from having to provide information that may render them criminally liable.

_____ 7. _Traditionally_, a criminal is required to pay fines to the government and not to the crime victim.

_____ 8. The Economic Espionage Act makes a felony for American companies to sell their patents or trade secrets to a foreign citizen or company.

_____ 9. A court can generally order a criminal to forfeit (give up) property that was used to commit a crime.

_____ 10. Federal sentencing guidelines allow a court to consider the efforts of business managers to prevent criminal wrongdoing when the court is sentencing such managers for business crimes.

Multiple Choice

_____ 1. Over a period of four years, Allen knowingly and willfully engaged in numerous transactions that entailed the fraudulent sale of worthless swampland to elderly persons who lived in various parts of the United States. Mrs. Hinton unsuspectingly bought some of this worthless land from Allen, and she paid him $10,000 for the property. Under these facts:
a. Allen can only be criminally prosecuted for violation of RICO.
b. Allen can only be civilly sued by the government for violation of RICO.
c. Allen can be criminally prosecuted for violation of RICO and he can be civilly sued by Mrs. Hinton for $10,000 for violation of RICO.
d. Allen can be criminally prosecuted for violation of RICO and he can be civilly sued by Mrs. Hinton for $30,000 for violation of RICO.

76

_____ 2. Jackson Electrical employees were repairing power lines when one of its "cherry pickers" came into contact with a power line, electrocuting a worker. Prior to this accident, the employees had complained to Jackson supervisors that operation of this equipment so near to the power lines was unsafe and exposed them a significant risk of injury. The supervisors talked this over with Jackson and they all agreed: "We can always replace one of these employees if necessary, but we can't replace the client for whom we are doing this work." The supervisors then ordered the employees to continue to work (the crime of criminal negligence). Who can be prosecuted for this crime?
   a. Only the supervisors.
   b. Only the supervisors and Jackson.
   c. Only Jackson Electrical.
   d. The supervisors, Jackson, and Jackson Electrical.

_____ 3. Toni and Rob agreed that they would hijack and steal a truck that was transporting equipment. Toni bought a gun, and she and Rob went to a truck stop to wait for the truck. Before the truck arrived, the police arrived to investigate what Toni and Rob were doing, preventing them from stealing the truck and its cargo. Under these facts, what crimes, if any, did Toni and Rob commit?
   a. Embezzlement.
   b. Obstruction of justice.
   c. Conspiracy.
   d. a and c.

_____ 4. May was suspected of selling stolen goods in interstate commerce. FBI agents got a warrant to search her office. During the search, the FBI found papers evidencing her crime. Two days later, the FBI found some stolen goods when they conducted a warrantless search of May's car. A week later, an FBI agent was walking on a public sidewalk outside May's offices when he saw more stolen goods that May disposed of in a public dumpster. What evidence can be used against May?
   a. The papers seized at May's office.
   b. The stolen goods seized from May's car.
   c. The stolen goods seized from the public dumpster.
   d. a and c.

_____ 5. Under *traditional rules*, in which case is the crime of *extortion* committed?
   a. Sheriff Ross demands that Ruth pay him $10,000 or he will arrest her.
   b. Ida offers to pay Judge Rye $500 if Judge Rye will dismiss a driving complaint against her.
   c. Nanny, a private person, demands that Mayor Traynor pay Nanny $5,000 or she will publicly reveal evidence of certain immoral conduct by the mayor.
   d. Fargo Securities fraudulently sold stock in violation of U.S. securities laws.

_____ 6. Which of the following is the crime of *corrupt influence*?
   a. A city council member lies while testifying during her divorce hearing.
   b. A mayor counterfeits money.
   c. A congresswoman accepts $10,000 from a developer in return for voting in favor of a bill that the developer wants passed.
   d. A state senator sells illegal drugs.

_____ 7. In which case does Barbie commit the crime of *forgery*?
a. Without permission, Barbie took a blank check belonging to Kim. Barbie then filled the check out, signed Kim's name, and cashed the check.
b. Without permission, Barbie took a credit card belonging to Sarah. Barbie bought goods, charged the bill to Sarah's card, and Barbie signed Sarah's name to the charge card slip.
c. Without permission, Barbie printed and passed fake $20 bills.
d. a and b.

_____ 8. In which case did Kelly probably commit a crime?
a. Kelly cashed a personal check for $50. Unknown to Kelly, she had insufficient funds in her account and the check was not paid. When informed that her bank refused payment, Kelly immediately paid the check.
b. Kelly used her credit card to purchase goods for $500, not knowing that this exceeded her approved credit limit. She paid this excess with her next monthly payment.
c. Kelly used her credit card even though she knew it had been canceled.
d. b and c.

_____ 9. Russ used a computer network to break into Grant Inc.'s computer and direct delivery of a shipment of goods to Russ' warehouse. Russ' acts were discovered and he was arrested. Under these facts:
a. Russ can be prosecuted for diverted delivery by computer.
b. Russ cannot be prosecuted for diverted delivery by computer because he never physically touched the bank's computer.
c. The government may forfeit Russ' computer network.
d. a and c.

_____ 10. Ben, an employee, systematically took tools from his employer when he was left to lock up his employer's store. Ben was arrested one night while taking tools. What crime has Ben committed?
a. Larceny.
b. Burglary.
c. Embezzlement.
d. Swindle.

Case Problem

Answer the following problem, briefly explaining your answer.

Over a period of five years, Drake knowingly and willfully engaged in a pattern of criminal activity that entailed repeated fraudulent sales of worthless swampland to elderly persons. Drake advertised this land by mailing fraudulent brochures to persons in many states. Drake also paid money to government officials in order to obtain their approval of these land sales. Mrs. Hinton unsuspectingly bought some of this worthless land from Drake, and she paid him $10,000 for the property.

1. What white collar crimes did Drake commit?
2. What criminal penalties may be imposed against Drake?
3. What remedies does Mrs. Hinton have against Drake?

_____

_____

_____

Internet Exercise

Leo worked for Motorworks U.S.A., an American firm that manufactures an engine that uses water as its fuel. The engine's design and the process by which it converts water to fuel are secrets known to only a few Motorworks' engineers and executives. This secret information gives Motorworks a commercial advantage over its competitors. When Leo quit working for Motorworks, he hacked Motorworks' computers and downloaded this secret information. He also took photos of the various stages of manufacture of this engine. Leo agreed to sell the data and photographs to White Corp., a Swiss firm, doing business in the United States.

1. Locate the Economic Espionage Act of 1996 (the "Act") on the Internet.
2. Did Leo violate the Act? If so, what punishment may levied against him under the Act?
3. Did White Corp. violate the Act? If so, what punishment may be levied against White Corp. under the Act?

_____

_____

_____

CHAPTER 9
TORTS

MAKE THE CONNECTION

SUMMARY

A *tort* is a civil wrong that affords recovery for damages that result. The three forms of torts are intentional torts, negligence, and strict liability. A tort differs from a crime in the nature of its remedy. Fines and imprisonment result from criminal violations, whereas money damages are paid to those who are damaged by conduct that constitutes a tort. An action may be both a crime and a tort, but the tort remedy is civil in nature.

Selected intentional torts are false imprisonment, defamation, product disparagement, contract interference or tortious interference, and trespass. False imprisonment is the detention of another without his or her permission. False imprisonment is often called the *shopkeeper's tort* because store owners detain suspected shoplifters. Many states provide a privilege to store owners if they detain shoplifting suspects based on reasonable cause and in a reasonable manner. Defamation is slander (oral) or libel (written) and consists of false statements about another that damage the person's reputation or integrity. Truth is an absolute defense to defamation, and there are some privileges that protect against defamation, such as those for witnesses at trial and for members of Congress during debates on the floor. There is a developing privilege for employers when they give references for former employees. Invasion of privacy is intrusion into private affairs; public disclosure of private facts; or appropriation of someone's name, image, or likeness for commercial purposes.

To establish the tort of negligence, one must show that there has been a breach of duty in the form of a violation of a statute or professional competency standards or of behavior that does not rise to the level of that of a reasonable person. That breach of duty must have caused the foreseeable injuries to the plaintiff, and the plaintiff must be able to quantify the damages that resulted. Possible defenses to negligence include contributory negligence, comparative negligence, and assumption of risk.

Strict liability is absolute liability with few defenses.

LEARNING OUTCOMES
After studying this chapter, you should be able to

A. GENERAL PRINCIPLES
LO.1   Explain the difference between torts and crimes

B. INTENTIONAL TORTS
LO.2   Distinguish between an assault and a battery
LO.3   Explain the three different torts of invasion of privacy
LO.4   Explain the torts of defamation and defenses

C. NEGLIGENCE
LO.5   Explain the elements of negligence and defenses

D. STRICT LIABILITY
LO.6   Explain the tort of strict liability and why very few defenses are available

CHAPTER OUTLINE

A. GENERAL PRINCIPLES

1. WHAT IS A TORT?

▶ A tort is a wrongful interference against a person or property for which a person may recover civil remedies. ▶ A tort is not the same as a crime or a breach of contract.

2. TORT AND CRIME DISTINGUISHED

GENERAL RULE. A crime arises from a violation of a public duty, whereas a tort arises from a violation of a private duty that is owed to a particular person.
STUDY HINTS. ▶ An act that is a crime can also be a tort if the act causes an injury or loss to a particular person. ▶ Example: An employee's theft of his or her employer's property that was entrusted to the employee is the crime of embezzlement and it is also the tort of trespass to personal property.
LEARNING OUTCOME EXAMPLES. ▶ See the discussion on wrongs that are a violation of a private duty as torts, and wrongs that are a violation of a public duty of crimes, textbook p. 188.
▶ See the discussion on wrongs that are a violation of a private duty as torts, and wrongs that are a violation of a public duty of crimes, textbook p. 188.

3. TYPES OF TORTS

There are three types of torts: (1) intentional torts (torts involve intentional conduct); (2) negligence (torts involve carelessness); and (3) strict liability (torts impose liability without requiring any intention to harm or negligence).

B. INTENTIONAL TORTS

4. ASSAULT

GENERAL RULE. An assault is intentional conduct by one person that places another in reasonable apprehension of imminent harm provided that the first person has the present ability to carry out the threat of harm.
LEARNING OUTCOME EXAMPLE. See the "kick your butt" threat example of an assault on textbook p. 189.

5. BATTERY

GENERAL RULE. A battery is the unlawful offensive touching of another person without that person's consent.
STUDY HINT. A battery requires physical contact; an assault does not.

6. FALSE IMPRISONMENT

GENERAL RULE. False imprisonment is the detention of a person without that person's consent.
LIMITATION. All states have a shopkeeper's privilege that allows a merchant, who has a reasonable suspicion to suspect a person of shoplifting, to detain that person for a reasonable time and in a reasonable manner without committing false imprisonment.

7. INTENTIONAL INFLICTION OF EMOTIONAL DISTRESS

Intentional infliction of emotional distress is the intentional causing of severe emotional harm to another through the use of outrageous actions.

8. INVASION OF PRIVACY

GENERAL RULE. The tort of invasion of privacy actually includes three separate torts: (1) intrusion into the plaintiff's private affairs (such as putting a hidden microphone in a person's office); (2) public disclosure of private facts; and (3) appropriation of another's name, likeness, or image for commercial advantage, known as invasion of the "right of publicity."
►**LEARNING OUTCOME EXAMPLE.** See the discussion of the intrusion into a person' private affairs, public disclosure of private facts, and right to publicity torts beginning on textbook p. 192.

9. DEFAMATION

GENERAL RULES. Defamation is words/conduct that wrongfully harms another person's reputation.
LIMITATIONS. ► Defenses to defamation include: (1) truth; (2) absolute privilege, meaning a person, such as a legislator or other public officer, has a complete defense to liability for false statements that are made while carrying out his or her duties; and (3) qualified privilege, which means that a party, such as the media, is protected from liability for defamation provided that the false statement is made without malice and the statement is retracted or corrected when it is brought to the party's attention. ►Numerous states by statute now grant a qualified privilege to employers regarding job references. ►A qualified privilege also generally exists with respect to communications that are made to protect the interests of a private employer, particularly when the statements relate to actual or suspected wrongdoing.
STUDY HINT. Slander is spoken defamation, and libel is defamation that is made in a writing, photo, film, or similar form of communication.
►**LEARNING OUTCOME EXAMPLES.** See the discussion of slander, libel, and trade libel beginning on textbook p. 193. ► See the discussion of the requirement of the enhanced element of malice for cases in which the victim is a public figure, textbook p. 193. ► See the defense of privilege raised in the *Clemens* case on textbook p. 194.

10. PRODUCT DISPARAGEMENT

GENERAL RULE. Product disparagement is the making of a false statement about another's business or product.
LIMITATION. Truthful comparative advertising is not product disparagement.

11. WRONGFUL INTERFERENCE WITH CONTRACTS

GENERAL RULE. The tort of intentional interference with contract is the intentional and unjustified interference with the performance of a contract between other two or more other parties.
STUDY HINTS. ► This tort is sometimes known as contract interference, tortious interference with contracts, or tortious interference. ► A necessary element of this tort is intentionally causing another person to terminate an existing contract that the person has with someone else.

82

12. TRESPASS

GENERAL RULE. A trespass is an unauthorized action with respect to land or personal property.

STUDY HINT. A trespass can take several forms including: (1) trespass to land involving the intentional, unauthorized interference with the possession or enjoyment by others of their real property; or (2) trespass to personal property, also known as conversion, which entails the intentional, unauthorized interference with the possession or enjoyment by others of their personal property.

C. NEGLIGENCE

13. ELEMENTS OF NEGLIGENCE

The elements required to establish liability for negligence are: (1) duty; (2) a voluntary act that breaches the duty; (3) causation; and (4) damages that are caused by the defendant's breach of duty.

➢ *Duty*: ▶ There is a general duty for all persons to act in every situation as an ordinary and reasonably prudent person would act. ▶ Malpractice is the failure by professionals to exercise the degree of care and skill that is exercised by others in their profession under similar circumstances.

➢ *Breach of a duty*: ▶ A breach occurs when a person fails to fulfill a duty imposed by law or by the reasonable person standard. ▶ A breach must result from a *voluntary* act or failure to act (omission).

➢ *Causation*: ▶ A defendant's breach must be the legal ("but for") cause of the plaintiff's harm. ▶ Courts typically find causation if a plaintiff's harm is a foreseeable consequence of a wrongful act. ▶ A person may be liable for failing to stop a third party who commits a foreseeable wrong against the plaintiff. Example: landlord fails to provide proper security, enabling someone to assault a tenant.

➢ *Damages*: ▶ A plaintiff may recover damages (money) to compensate the plaintiff for both economic losses (lost wages, medical expenses, etc.) and noneconomic losses (physical and mental pain and suffering, etc.). ▶ A plaintiff may sometimes recover punitive damages if the defendant acted recklessly or intentionally harmed the plaintiff. ▶ The constitutionality of punitive damage awards is determined by comparing the amount awarded with (1) how bad the defendant's conduct is; (2) the harm suffered by the plaintiff; and (3) the civil penalties that are authorized in comparable cases. ▶ On appeal, the appellate court can make its own determination of the appropriate amount of punitive damages and it is not bound by the jury's determination.

➢ **LEARNING OUTCOME EXAMPLE.** See the discussion of the elements of negligence: duty, breach of duty, and causation and damages beginning on textbook p. 197.

14. DEFENSES TO NEGLIGENCE

➢ *Contributory negligence*: ▶ Contributory negligence means a plaintiff's own negligence is a partial cause of his or her injuries. ▶ At common law, a plaintiff's contributory negligence (no matter how slight) bars the plaintiff from recovering anything. ▶ Example: Joe and Coni are in an accident, and Coni suffers $1,000 damages. Coni's damages are 90 percent caused by Joe's negligence and 10 percent caused by Coni's own negligence. Coni recovers nothing under contributory negligence.

➢ ***Comparative negligence***: ► Today, many states do not follow the common law contributory negligence doctrine. ► In some of these states, a court ignores the plaintiff's negligence if it is slight and the defendant's negligence is gross. In most of these states, courts apply a comparative negligence concept whereby damages are reduced to the extent they are caused by the plaintiff's fault. ► Example: In the example above, Coni would recover $900 under comparative negligence. ► In most states, recovery is barred if the plaintiff was more than 50 percent responsible for the harm suffered.

➢ ***Assumption of risk***: ► Assumption of risk means a plaintiff voluntarily exposes himself or herself to a known danger. ► At common law, assumption of risk bars any recovery. ►Express assumption of risk arises when a person signs a written exculpatory agreement, e.g., a written release. ►Implied primary assumption of risk arises when a person impliedly consents to release a defendant from possible liability that may result from a specific, known risk, e.g., person agrees to box with another.

➢ **LEARNING OUTCOME EXAMPLE.**See the discussion of the defenses of contributory negligence, comparative negligence, assumption of risk, and immunity beginning on textbook p. 200.

D. STRICT LIABILITY

15. WHAT IS STRICT LIABILITY?

GENERAL RULE. Strict liability is absolute liability that is imposed in certain cases, such as doing an ultrahazardous act.
LEARNING OUTCOME EXAMPLE. See the dynamite excavation example, holding the contractor liable for any damages with no defenses because of the hazardous activity, textbook p. 204.

16. IMPOSING STRICT LIABILITY

Strict liability is imposed most often when required by statute or in connection with products liability.

CONCEPT REVIEW AND APPLICATIONS

Matching Exercise

Select the term or phrase that best matches a definition or statement stated below. Each term or phrase is the best match for only one statement or definition. Not all terms and phrases will necessarily be used.

absolute privilege	intentional torts	shopkeeper's privilege
contract interference	invasion of privacy	slander of title
contributory negligence,	libel	slander
defamation	malpractice,	strict liability
false imprisonment	negligence	tort
intentional infliction of	product disparagement	trade libel
emotional distress	qualified privilege	trespass

_____ 1. Tort that occurs when a third party wrongfully and intentionally causes the termination of an existing contract between two other parties

_____ 2. Defamation of another person that is communicated orally.

_____ 3. Wrongful, intentional detainment of another person.

_____ 4. Negligent or improper performance of a legal duty by a professional.

_____ 5. Defamation of another person that is communicated by written word or visual communication.

_____ 6. Intentional or reckless making of false statements regarding a seller's title to property.

_____ 7. A complete defense against the tort of defamation.

_____ 8. False statements regarding the quality of a business' goods that cause damage to the business.

_____ 9. Violation of a private duty that causes harm to another person or another's property.

_____ 10. Failure to act as a reasonably prudent person would act under similar circumstances.

True/False

Write **T** if the statement is true, write **F** if it is false.

_____ 1. One wrongful act may be both a crime and a tort.

_____ 2. A person is not entitled to recover for every injury or loss that is caused by another person.

_____ 3. Strict liability may be imposed only if a party intentionally or negligently harms another.

_____ 4. A required element for all torts is that the defendant intends to cause harm to the plaintiff.

_____ 5. Under tort law, one owes a duty to society to conform his or her conduct to a required standard.

_____ 6. Traditionally, under the common law, contributory negligence by a plaintiff bars recovery of any damages.

_____ 7. The U.S. government has immunity from being sued for harm caused by the negligence of federal employees.

_____ 8. In order to prove negligence, it is generally required for the plaintiff to prove that the defendant's breach of duty was both the factual cause and proximate cause of the plaintiff's loss.

_____ 9. The media enjoy a qualified privilege for communicating false statements regarding others and this privilege may protect them from inadvertently publishing false statements about others.

_____ 10. Companies can now make commercial use of the name or likeness of celebrities without first obtaining the celebrities' permission to do so because most states do not recognize the tort of invasion of the right to publicity.

Multiple Choice Questions

_____ 1. One afternoon, Carrie slipped on grapes that had fallen on the floor in the produce department of Acme Groceries, injuring herself. Acme inspected the floor once in the morning and once at closing for spilled produce, even though it knew that produce was dropped on the floor more often. Is Acme liable for negligence?
   a. No, Acme owed no duty to Carrie.
   b. No, Acme did not breach its duty to Carrie.
   c. No, Acme's conduct was not the cause of Carrie's injuries.
   d. Yes, Acme was negligent and is liable to Carrie.

_____ 2. John and Ken went to a baseball game at their college. They sat high up in the stands behind first base even though they knew that foul balls often landed in this area. In the third inning, a foul ball struck John in the head, causing him serious injuries. John sued the college for negligence. In all likelihood, is the college liable to John?
   a. Yes, the college was negligent in allowing spectators to watch the baseball game.
   b. Yes, the college is liable under strict liability because baseball is an ultrahazardous activity.
   c. No, John assumed the risk that foul balls would sometimes land in the stands.
   d. No, colleges owe no duty to protect students from unreasonable risks of harm.

_____ 3. Maria and Barb were competing for head cheerleader. With the intent to cause emotional harm to Maria, Barb repeatedly made terrible, harassing, and obscene phone calls to Maria. Maria was so frightened by the calls that she suffered a nervous breakdown requiring her to be hospitalized. Under these facts:
   a. Maria can sue Barb for the tort of battery.
   b. Maria can sue Barb for the tort of intentional infliction of emotional distress.
   c. Maria can sue Barb for the tort of slander of title.
   d. Maria can sue Barb for malpractice.

_____ 4. Ken is a famous politician who is running for public office. In which situation can Ken sue for the tort of invasion of privacy?
   a. The *Evening Star*, a magazine, hid a camera in the ceiling of Ken's bedroom in order to get some exclusive photos of Ken's personal life.
   b. The *Daily News* published a story about Ken's recent behavior at a local, public nightclub.
   c. Without Ken's permission, Armco Inc. used Ken's picture to advertise its deodorant products.
   d. a and c.

_____ 5. Joe wanted to buy a car from EZ Sales on credit. EZ contacted TriCo Credit Co. from whom EZ obtained credit information regarding prospective customers. Based on information from reliable sources, TriCo in good faith furnished a written report stating that Joe was delinquent on several bills. Unknown to TriCo, this information was wrong. As a result of this report, EZ refused to sell the car to Joe. Under these facts:

    a. TriCo is liable to Joe for defamation by libel.

    b. TriCo is liable to Joe for defamation by slander.

    c. TriCo is not liable for defamation because it has a qualified privilege that protects it from liability in this situation.

    d. TriCo is not liable for defamation because defamation does not apply to business transactions.

_____ 6. Joe was angry with a clerk and, standing a foot away from the clerk, Joe drew his arm back with a clenched fist and stated, "I am going to punch your lights out." What tort did Joe commit?

    a. Defamation.

    b. False imprisonment.

    c. Battery.

    d. Assault.

_____ 7. Select the correct answer.

    a. Alex stole Jose's automobile. In this case, Alex committed the tort of trespass to personal property.

    b. An ABC Store security guard had reasonable grounds to believe that Ben stole some goods and the security guard detained Ben for a few minutes to ask him some questions. In fact, Ben was innocent. In this case, the security guard committed the tort of false imprisonment.

    c. Lenny wrongfully tried to hit Shawn with his fist but missed. However, Shawn fell off the chair he was sitting on in order to dodge the hit and broke his arm as a result. In this case, Shawn cannot sue Lenny for assault because Lenny did not touch Shawn.

    d. a and b.

_____ 8. Rene owned a word processing company. One day, Rene intentionally planted a virus in software of a competitive firm with the intent to destroy the information stored in the competitor's computer system. The virus soon destroyed nearly all of the information that had been stored in the competitor's computer system. Under these facts:

    a. The competitor can sue Rene for only actual damages.

    b. The competitor can sue Rene for only punitive damages.

    c. The competitor can sue Rene for actual and punitive damages.

    d. The competitor cannot sue Rene for damages. Rene's conduct is a crime, not a tort.

_____ 9. Alejondro suffered a broken finger when using a jackhammer that was improperly designed and manufactured by Ram Set Inc. Alejondro will fully recover from his injuries. Ram Set Inc. did not know that its jackhammers were dangerous, but it failed to adequately test them to assure their safety as a reasonable manufacturer would do. Under these facts:

    a. Alejondro may sue Ram Set for negligence.

    b. Alejondro may sue Ram Set for product liability.

    c. Alejondro may sue Ram Set for battery.

    d. a and b.

Case Problems

Answer the following problems, briefly explaining your answers.

1. One rainy day, Lily was driving to work. The speed limit was 45 m.p.h. Lily was driving 45 m.p.h. as were some other drivers. But, a reasonable person would have been driving only 30 m.p.h. Paul negligently rode his bike onto the road. Due to the speed Lily was driving, she could not stop and her car struck Paul. Paul suffered $5,000 damages, which were caused 80 percent by Lily's conduct and 20 percent by Paul's conduct.
   a. What duty did Lily owe to Paul?
   b. Was Lily negligent?
   c. If Lily was negligent, how much could Paul recover under common law contributory negligence rules?
   d. If Lily was negligent, how much could Paul recover under the comparative negligence doctrine?

_____

_____

_____

_____

2. Maxco sold food products to restaurants. In connection with its business, Maxco: (a) falsely told a food magazine that Juan's Cafe, a cafe that had canceled a contract with Maxco, served spoiled food, causing Juan's to lose money; customers; and (b) paid $25,000 to Queen's Cafes, a restaurant chain, in order to maliciously induce Queen's Cafes to breach a contract with a Maxco competitor and to instead buy its food from Maxco. What torts did Maxco commit?

_____

_____

Internet Exercise

Using the Internet, locate a website that defines and discusses state "veggie libel laws." After doing so, answer the following questions:

1. Define what constitutes state "veggie libel laws." Identify the web page where these laws are discussed.
2. Discuss the pros and cons of state "veggie libel laws."

_____

_____

_____

_____

CHAPTER 10
INTELLECTUAL PROPERTY RIGHTS
AND THE INTERNET

MAKE THE CONNECTION

SUMMARY

Property rights in trademarks, copyrights, and patents are acquired as provided primarily in federal statutes. A trademark or service mark is any word, symbol, design, or combination of these used to identify a product (in the case of a trademark) or a service (in the case of a service mark). Terms will fall into one of four categories: (1) generic, (2) descriptive, (3) suggestive, or (4) arbitrary or fanciful. Generic terms are never registrable. However, if a descriptive term has acquired a secondary meaning, it is registrable. Suggestive and arbitrary or fanciful marks are registrable as well. If there is likelihood of confusion, a court will enjoin the second user from using a particular mark.

A copyright is the exclusive right given by federal statute to the creator of a literary or an artistic work to use, reproduce, or display the work for the life of the creator and 70 years after the creator's death.

A patent gives the inventor an exclusive right for 20 years from the date of application to make, use, and sell an invention that is new and useful but not obvious to those in the business to which the invention is related. Trade secrets that give an owner an advantage over competitors are protected under state law for an unlimited period so long as they are not made public.

Protection of computer programs and the design of computer chips and mask works is commonly obtained, subject to certain limitations, by complying with federal statutes, by using the law of trade secrets, and by requiring restrictive licensing agreements. Many software developers pursue all of these means to protect their proprietary interests in their programs.

LEARNING OUTCOMES
After studying this chapter, you should be able to

A. TRADEMARKS AND SERVICE MARKS
LO.1   Explain the spectrum of distinctiveness used to classify trademarks and explain why distinctiveness is important.
LO.2   Explain how personal names can acquire trademark protection.
LO.3   List the remedies available for improper use of trademarks.

B. COPYRIGHTS
LO.4   Explain what is and is not copyrightable; explain the fair use defense.

C. PATENTS
LO.5   Explain the "new and not obvious" requirement necessary to obtain a patent.

D. SECRET BUSINESS INFORMATION
LO.6   List and explain the defensive measures employers take to preserve confidential business information.

E. PROTECTION OF COMPUTER SOFTWARE AND MASK WORKS
LO.7   Explain the extent of protection provided owners of software.

CHAPTER OUTLINE

A. TRADEMARKS AND SERVICE MARKS

1. INTRODUCTION

GENERAL RULES. ▶ A trademark is a word, name, symbol, or combination of these that identifies the manufacturer of a product. A service mark is the same thing, except it identifies the provider of a service. ▶ Registration on the federal Principal Register entitles a person to exclusive use of a mark.

LIMITATION. Validity of a trademark registration may be challenged within five years.

STUDY HINT. Subject to certain limits, an advance registration of a mark may be made for up to three years prior to actual use of the mark by filing an application certifying a bona fide "intent-to-use."

2. INTERNATIONAL REGISTRATION

The U.S. and more than 60 other countries signed Madrid System of International Registration of Marks that allows U.S. firms to protect product and service marks in all these countries by filing one form in the U.S.

3. REGISTRABLE MARKS

GENERAL RULES. ▶ A mark may be registered if it distinguishes a person's product or service from products or services of competitors. ▶ Arbitrary, fanciful, or suggestive marks are presumed to be distinctive and to merit protection. ▶ Generic terms that merely describe a class of products or services cannot be registered. Examples: "motor oil"; "airline." ▶ Descriptive or geographical terms, and surnames cannot be registered unless they acquire a secondary meaning. Examples: descriptive mark: "anti-knock gasoline"; geographic mark: "California wine"; surname: "Lucas' Pizza."

LIMITATION. ▶ Descriptive or geographical terms, and surnames may be protected if they acquire a secondary meaning, i.e., through long usage the public identifies the mark with a particular product or service of a specific provider. Example: "Best Western" Motels. ▶ Functional marks that merely use words in their ordinary sense are not protected. Example: "You have mail" to tell a party he has e-mail.

STUDY HINTS. ▶ Arbitrary or fanciful names are names that have no other meaning. Example: "7-Up." ▶ Suggestive terms indirectly hint as to the nature of a product. Example: "Duracell" battery.

LEARNING OUTCOME EXAMPLES. See the Kodak example, a coined most distinctive mark, textbook p. 213; see the Sports Illustrated example, a descriptive mark with acquired distinctiveness; see the *Harley Davidson* case where H.O.G. was found to be generic and not distinctive at all; see the Paul Frank example on textbook p. 214.

4. REMEDIES FOR IMPROPER USE OF MARKS

GENERAL RULES. ▶ The owner of a mark may obtain a court order (injunction) to prevent the improper use or duplication of a mark if such use may likely confuse the public regarding the source of a product. ▶The owner of an infringed-upon mark may also recover lost profits, other actual losses, and, in the case of intentional infringement, treble damages.

LEARNING OUTCOME EXAMPLE. See the remedies applied in the *Venture Tape* case, injunctive relief, lost profits, and attorney's fees.

5. ABANDONMENT OF EXCLUSIVE RIGHT TO MARK

▶ If the owner of a mark permits widespread use of the mark to describe a general class of products, the exclusive right to the mark may be lost. Examples: "cellophane"; "aspirin." ▶Nonuse of a mark for three consecutive years creates is prima facie evidence of abandonment.

6. TRADE DRESS PROTECTION

▶ Trade dress is the total appearance of a product, including its packaging, label, shape, and size. Trade dress may also include physical structures associated with a particular product or service, such as the distinctive shape of a fast food chain sign. ▶ Trade dress may qualify as a protected trademark or service mark if it is distinctive and identifies the source of a specific product or service.

7. LIMITED LANHAM ACT PROTECTION OF PRODUCT DESIGN

A product's design may be protected by the Lanham Act only if it has acquired a secondary meaning.

8. PREVENTION OF DILUTION OF FAMOUS MARKS

▶ Federal Trademark Act of 1995 forbids the incompatible commercial use of a famous mark or tradename that dilutes the distinctive quality of the mark. ▶ Example: "Cadillac Toilets." ▶ If marks are not identical, the famous mark must show actual dilution, i.e., actual financial loss, in order to recover.

9. INTERNET DOMAIN NAMES AND TRADEMARK RIGHTS

▶ An Internet domain name is the address by which an Internet resource is identified and found by a Wed browser. ▶ Any unused domain name can be registered on a first come first serve basis so long as it differs from registered names by at least one character. ▶ Domain names are trademarks and are protected from cybersquatters, i.e., persons who register and set up domain names that are the same as or confusingly similar to existing trademarks or famous persons. ▶ A safe harbor shelters parties from liability when they have reasonable grounds to believe that use of a domain name was fair use or legal.

B. COPYRIGHTS

A copyright is the exclusive right to use an original expression that is preserved in a tangible form.

10. DURATION OF COPYRIGHT

GENERAL RULE. A copyright gives the creator of the work the exclusive right to use or reproduce a literary, artistic, audiovisual, or musical work or computer program for the creator's life plus 70 years.

LIMITATION. If a work is a "work made for hire," meaning that a person was hired specifically to create the copyrighted work, then the business employing the creator may register the copyright and is entitled to protection for 120 years from creation or 95 years from publication, whichever is less.

11. COPYRIGHT NOTICE

▶ Prior to 1989, the author of an original work secured his or her copyright protection by (1) placing the word "copyright" or the symbol © on the work together with other information and (2) registering the copyright with the Copyright office. ▶ Under current law, placing notice of copyright on a work is strongly suggested, but is no longer required in order to be protected.

12. WHAT IS COPYRIGHTABLE?

GENERAL RULES. ▶ Requirements: original, independently created, and some minimal creativity. ▶ Many expressions can be copyrighted, including writings, books, musical compositions, architectural works, paintings, photographs, audio and video recordings, compilations of facts and data, and computer programs.
LEARNING OUTCOME EXAMPLE. See the Darden example of a denial of a copyright because of lack of creativity, textbook p. 222.

13. COPYRIGHT OWNERSHIP AND THE INTERNET

Unless otherwise agreed, when a freelancer is employed offsite for a fixed fee by a firm to develop software, the freelancer owns the software and the employing firm only has a license to use the software.

14. RIGHTS OF COPYRIGHT HOLDERS

▶ A copyright owner has the exclusive right to: (1) reproduce or copy a work; (2) rent, sell, license, or dispose of a work; (3) perform or display a work publicly; and (4) prepare further works based on a copyrighted work. ▶ Copyright law sets statutory rates to be paid when a copyrighted work is used.

15. LIMITATION ON EXCLUSIVE CHARACTER OF COPYRIGHT

GENERAL RULE. "Fair use" permits the limited use of copyrighted matters for purposes of comment, criticism, parody, teaching, research, or news reporting.▶**LEARNING OUTCOME EXAMPLE.** See the *Wind Done Gone* example of fair use parody.

16. SECONDARY LIABILITY FOR INFRINGEMENT

Liability arises for distributing a device with the intent people will use it to infringe others' copyrights.

17. DIGITAL MILENNIUM COPYRIGHT ACT

Forbids manufacture, import, or sale of devices to prevent circumvent encryption of copyrighted works.

C. PATENTS

A patent is the exclusive right to own and use an invention or design.

18. TYPES, DURATION, AND NOTICE

▶ Devices, processes, and inventions that embody new, useful, and nonobvious scientific principles, technologies, or processes can be patented. ▶ Three types of patents are: (1) utility patents used for most new products and processes; valid for 20 years; (2) plant patents for new types of asexually reproduced plants; valid for 20 years; and (3) design patents for new, original, ornamental designs for manufactured goods; valid for 14 years. ▶ Patents are presumed valid but may be invalidated by a showing of prior art.

19. PATENTABILITY

GENERAL RULE. To acquire patent protection, an invention must be novel, nonobvious, and useful.
LEARNING OUTCOME EXAMPLES. ▶ See the DNA "not obvious" example on textbook p. 226.
▶See the mounted chain saw "obvious" example on textbook p. 226.

20. PATENTABLE BUSINESS METHODS

Business methods that state steps to perform a business process with a useful result may be patented.

21. INFRINGEMENT

▶A patent owner patent has the exclusive right to make, use, and sell the invention. ▶Violation of this exclusive right is infringement and may entitle the patent owner to obtain an injunction to prevent this violation and to monetary damages.

D. SECRET BUSINESS INFORMATION

22. TRADE SECRETS

▶ A trade secret is secret business information that gives its owner a competitive advantage over others. ▶ Trade secrets may include a special formula, recipe, method of production or operation, or a compilation of data, such as market statistics or customer lists.

23. LOSS OF PROTECTION

GENERAL RULE. A trade secret is no longer protected if it is disclosed to the public, unless the secret is only disclosed in a restrictive manner to persons who know of its confidential nature.
STUDY HINT. Unpatented goods may be "reverse engineered" after unrestricted public sale.

24. DEFENSIVE MEASURES

GENERAL RULE. In order to protect trade secrets, Employers should allow employees access to trade secrets only on a "need-to-know" basis and should have employees sign nondisclosure agreements.
LEARNING OUTCOME EXAMPLE. See the discussion on signing and enforcing nondisclosure agreements on textbook p. 231.

25. CRIMINAL SANCTIONS

The Industrial Espionage Act of 1996 makes it a crime to copy, steal, or purchase trade secrets.

E. PROTECTION OF COMPUTER SOFTWARE AND MASK WORKS

26. COPYRIGHT PROTECTION OF COMPUTER PROGRAMS

▶ In general, computer programs may be copyrighted. ▶ The Computer Software Copyright Act protects copyrighted programs from infringement. ▶ Infringement is determined by examining the similarity of significant steps of programs, instead of just comparing the number of similar steps.

27. PATENT PROTECTION OF PROGRAMS

GENERAL RULE. In appropriate cases, computer programs may be patented.

LEARNING OUTCOME EXAMPLE. See the *Apple Computer* example on textbook p. 232.

28. TRADE SECRETS

Trade secret laws are sometimes used to protect computer programs.

29. RESTRICTIVE LICENSING

Creators of software often restrict use of software by limiting reverse engineering and relicensing.

30. SEMICONDUCTOR CHIP PROTECTION

The Semiconductor Chip Protection Act gives an owner of a mask work exclusive rights for ten years.

CONCEPT REVIEW AND APPLICATIONS

Matching Exercise

Select the term or phrase that best matches a definition or statement stated below. Each term or phrase is the best match for only one statement or definition. Not all terms and phrases will necessarily be used.

acquired distinctiveness   prior art   trade dress
copyright   secondary meaning   trade secret
cybersquatters   semiconductor chip   trademark
distinctiveness   product
mask work   service mark

_____ 1. Private information that gives its owner a business advantage and which is protected by state law.

_____ 2. Proof that another's invention is not entitled to patent protection because, as a whole, it would have been obvious to a person of ordinary skill in the art when the invention was patented.

_____ 3. Degree to which a name or mark may identify the source of a product, service, or other item.

_____ 4. Stencil that controls the etching process by which transistors are attached to semiconductor chips.

_____ 5. A product's total image.

_____ 6. Small square base with transistors that enables a computer to function according to a program.

_____ 7. Exclusive right to use a mark that identifies a service.

_____ 8. Exclusive right to use or reproduce a literary, artistic, musical, or audiovisual work.

_____ 9. Exclusive right to use a mark that identifies a product.

_____ 10. Intellectual property term that indicates that certain words have acquired a special meaning in the mind of the public sufficient to identify the source of a product, service, or item.

True/False

Write **T** if the statement is true, write **F** if it is false.

_____ 1. In general, a competitor is legally entitled to "reverse engineer" or copy a product if the product is sold to the public and the product has not been copyrighted or patented.

_____ 2. Trademarks may be protected for up to three years prior to the time that they are actually used.

_____ 3. A descriptive mark may be registered as a trademark if it acquires a secondary meaning.

_____ 4. In general, generic terms can be validly registered as trademarks or service marks.

_____ 5. A patent that has been issued by the U.S. Patent and Trademark Office may be invalidated if a party can prove in litigation that the patented invention would be obvious to a person of ordinary skill in the art.

_____ 6. In some cases, registration of a mark will not prevent its use by another party for a different, noncompetitive product or service that is sold in a different market.

_____ 7. A copyright provides protection for the creator's life plus an additional 100 years.

_____ 8. In general, mere ideas and concepts cannot be copyrighted or patented.

_____ 9. A trade secret may be disclosed without losing its legal protection if it is restrictively disclosed to another person who is aware of its secret nature.

_____ 10. A utility or functional patent grants a patent owner the exclusive right to use and sell the patented item for 20 years.

Multiple Choice

_____ 1. Carl invented a new eating instrument for people who like to eat fast: a five-pronged fork. (Normal forks have only four prongs). Under these facts, can Carl patent his new fork?
   a. Yes, it is novel.
   b. Yes, it is useful.
   c. Yes, it is both novel and useful.
   d. No, it is an obvious derivative of an existing product, the four-pronged fork.

_____ 2. Which of the following items CANNOT be copyrighted?
   a. A new book.
   b. A new idea for a movie.
   c. A new photograph.
   d. A new architectural drawing.

_____ 3. Ken invented a new type of mathematical calculator that he called "Wiser Guyser." Under these facts, the name "Wiser Guyser":
   a. Can be protected by registration for a patent.
   b. Can be protected by registration for a copyright.
   c. Can be protected by registration for a trademark.
   d. Cannot be protected.

_____ 4. Select the correct answer.
   a. Federal law does not provide any protection for software.
   b. Software may be copyrighted.
   c. Software may sometimes be patented.
   d. b and c.

_____ 5. Which of the following names can be registered for trademark protection?
   a. "Motor oil," the name of a product that is used to lubricate engines.
   b. "Hot sauce," the name for a spicy food additive.
   c. "DuraBond," the name for a new type of glue.
   d. "Southern food," the name for food from the southern part of the United States.

_____ 6. In 2003, Hillary Thompson began selling enormous pieces of sourball candy called "Thompson's Giant Sour Ball Candies." By 2011, Hillary's candies had become nationally known, and people thought only of her candy when they heard the words "Thompson's Giant Sour Ball Candies." Is the name for this candy entitled to trademark protection?
   a. No, the name is merely descriptive.
   b. No, the name is merely Hillary's surname.
   c. No, the name is merely generic.
   d. Yes, the name has acquired a secondary meaning.

_____ 7. Selma wrote a computer program and copyrighted it under U.S. copyright law. Selma allowed a German firm to review the program, but the German firm stated that they were not interested in the program. Unknown to Selma, the German firm duplicated the program and is selling it in Germany. Germany has signed the Berne convention. Under these facts:
   a. Selma cannot enforce her copyright against the German firm.
   b. Selma can enforce her copyright against the German firm only if it agrees to be sued.
   c. Selma can enforce her copyright against the German firm under the Berne convention.
   d. a and b.

_____ 8. For many years, Wowee Corp. manufactured and sold high-quality toy slot cars known as "Wowee Toys." Wowee registered this trademark ten years ago. One year ago, Waui Enterprises, a travel agency, commenced business and started marketing cruise packages called "Waui Cruises." Has Waui Enterprises violated Wowee Corp.'s trademark?
   a. No, because the mark "Wowee Toys" was not properly registrable.
   b. No, because Waui Enterprises can challenge the validity of the registration of this mark.
   c. No, because the mark "Waui Cruises" is not the same or deceptively similar to "WoweeToys."
   d. Yes.

_____ 9. Jesse created a fictional tale about the life of a squirrel that became king of the animal world. He did not write it down, but instead told it neighborhood children. His tale was so popular with little children that he then wrote it down. Under these facts:
   a. Jesse cannot copyright the idea for his tale.
   b. Jesse can copyright the idea for his tale.
   c. Jesse can copyright the written version of his tale.
   d. b and c.

_____ 10. Over a five-year period, Jackson Corp. spent considerable time and money to develop a private list of 200,000 area homeowners. This list tracks home values, year of construction, and last home-repair project. This list has proven invaluable for marketing its home-improvement services. Under these facts, Jackson Corp. should protect this information as a:
   a. Patent
   b. Trade secret
   c. Trademark
   d. Service mark

Case Problem

Answer the following problem, briefly explaining your answer.

Baxco Corp. makes and sells several products, and it wants to register the products' names on the Principal Register in order to obtain federal trademark protection. Baxco wants to register: (1) "Xeri-fun," the name of a new candy; (2) "Appalachian Whiskey," the name of an alcoholic product that Baxco has sold for many years and a name that the public associates only with Baxco's product; and (3) "soft-serve ice cream," the name of Baxco's machine-dispensed ice cream. (Soft-serve ice cream is a type of ice cream that includes any ice cream that is dispensed from a machine. Numerous companies throughout the U.S. sell their own "soft-serve ice cream.")

1. Is Baxco entitled to register the foregoing marks?
2. If Baxco properly registers a mark, what can Baxco do if another party intentionally uses or infringes upon the registered mark?

_____

_____

_____

_____

Internet Exercise

Beth wrote a fictional story about life on a distant star. Her tale was so popular with her friends that she considered filing a copyright registration for her story. Under these facts:

1. Is Beth entitled to copyright her fictional story? Explain.
2. Using the Internet, determine what Beth must do to register her fictional story.

_____

_____

_____

_____

CHAPTER 11
CYBERLAW

MAKE THE CONNECTION

SUMMARY

The term *cyberlaw* seems to indicate a new body of law that exists or is being created to manage all of the legal issues of the cybereconomy, cyberspace, and cybertechnology. Even though some new criminal statutes have been enacted to address specific types of computer crimes, the law, with its great flexibility, has been able to easily adapt to address many of the legal issues that affect the new economy in cyberspace.

Six existing areas of law apply to cyberspace: tort issues, contract issues, intellectual property issues, criminal violations, constitutional restraints and protections, and securities law issues.

In tort law, the issues that arise on the Internet relate to privacy and defamation. In contracts, the issues center on formation and signatures, as well as the need for diligence in handling fraud and misrepresentation in the course of formation of contracts. Infringement and fair use are the key topics of intellectual property law that arise through the Internet. Although some peculiar issues such as linking Web sites and copyrighted materials or the types of domain names that may be used exist, the laws to address these new ways of possible infringement of others' intellectual property rights are in place. Criminal violations remain centered on the crimes of trespass and theft. Computers are either used to commit crimes or become the object of crimes, and both old criminal statutes and new ones protect property from harm, even on the Internet. The Constitution still applies to questions of jurisdiction and taxation. The standards of fairness still apply, and courts simply face the issue of whether a company is present because the Internet is available in every state and country. Finally, securities fraud is securities fraud whether committed face-to-face, by paper, by phone, or by chat room.

LEARNING OUTCOMES
After studying this chapter, you should be able to

A. INTRODUCTION TO CYBERLAW
LO1   Identify the privacy rights of employees and obligations of employees with regard to the Internet, their e-mails, and servers.

B. TORT ISSUES IN CYBERSPACE
LO.2   Discuss the issue of defamation on the Web.

C. CONTRACT ISSUES IN CYBERSPACE
LO.3   Explain the obligations of service providers to reveal identity and content.
LO.4   Discuss the constitutional law issues that have resulted from cyberspace.

D. INTELLECTUAL PROPERTY ISSUES IN CYBERSPACE
LO.5   Describe the intellectual property issues in cyberspace.

E. CRIMINAL LAW ISSUES IN CYBERSPACE

F. CONSTITUTIONAL RESTRAINTS AND PROTECTIONS IN CYBERSPACE
LO.6   Explain the concerns and legal issues blogging raises.

G. SECURITIES LAW ISSUES IN CYBERSPACE

CHAPTER OUTLINE

A. INTRODUCTION TO CYBERLAW

1. WHAT IS CYBERLAW?

Cyberlaw is an informal term that refers to new legislation and case law that is directed to legal issues associated with cyberspace and also areas of traditional law that are relevant to this mode of communication.

2. WHAT ARE THE ISSUES IN CYBERLAW?

Legal issues relating to cyberspace can be broken down into: tort issues, contract issues; intellectual property issues; criminal law issues; constitutional restraints and protections; and securities law issues.

B. TORT ISSUES IN CYBERSPACE

3. EMPLOYER/EMPLOYEE PRIVACY ISSUES IN CYBERLAW

GENERAL RULES. ▶ As a general proposition, employers may be held legally responsible for the contents of employee e-mails and other electronic communications (at least to the extent that it is work-related). ▶ Employers generally have the right to regulate an employee's use of computers, the Internet, and other communication devices at work. Employers also generally have the right to monitor an employee's e-mail and Internet usage at work, an employee's live communications at work, such as tweeting or texting, an employee's communications made via an employer-furnished computer or server, and when an employee agrees to such monitoring. ▶ An employer can examine information that job applicants or employees publicly post online, such as information posted on Facebook or YouTube.

LIMITATIONS: ▶ An employer should, at the time of a job interview, inform a job applicant that it may examine information that is publicly available via the Internet. ▶ In order to minimize claims of invasion of privacy, an employer should inform employees that it may monitor their all of their communications at work and obtain their consent for doing so.

LEARNING OUTCOME EXAMPLES. See the Standard & Poor's example on textbook p. 244; see E-Commerce & Cyberlaw, "Ten Commandments for Avoiding Workplace Exposure," on textbook p. 248; see *Quon v Arch Wireless Operating Co., Inc.,* on textbook p. 247; see the Ethics & the Law discussion of the blogger who kissed and told, textbook p. 251.

4. WEB USER INFORMATION AND PRIVACY

GENERAL RULE. ▶ Cyberspace is sometimes used to commit the tort of invasion of privacy. ▶ In order to prove the tort of intrusion into private affairs or public disclosure of private facts, the plaintiff must prove that (1) the defendant revealed private information about the plaintiff, (2) the information is presumed private, and (3) the information is entitled to privacy protection. ▶ While the law is somewhat unsettled, Web sites generally should allow their visitors the opportunity to refuse to have their information disclosed or sold.

LIMITATIONS. ▶ When relevant to lawsuits for defamation or other wrongs, courts may allow plaintiffs to obtain from ISPs the identity of their customers. ▶ At least one court has held that the unauthorized planting of "cookies" on another's computer is wrongful. ▶ There are a number of federal and state laws that protect the privacy of specific types of communications, such as financial information and information regarding children.

LEARNING OUTCOME EXAMPLE. See, *Sony Music Entertainment Inc. v Does 1– 40* on textbook p. 249.

5. APPROPRIATION IN CYBERSPACE

► It is the tort of appropriation (one form of invasion of privacy) for a business to use someone else's image, likeness, or name for commercial advantage. This common law tort applies to such usage in cyberspace. ► Example: SuperPrivateCop.com uses the image of the Attorney General of the United States in a web advertisement for its private detective services.

6. DEFAMATION IN CYBERSPACE

► A party commits the tort of defamation if he or she posts an untrue statement about another on a blog or otherwise communicates such statement to a third party via the Internet. ► **LEARNING OUTCOME EXAMPLES.** See the John Mackey example on textbook p. 251; see the Delta and Starbucks examples on textbook p. 251.

C. CONTRACT ISSUES IN CYBERSPACE

7. FORMATION OF CONTRACTS IN CYBERSPACE

► General rules of contract law govern the formation of contracts via the Internet. ► Forty-six states and the District of Columbia have enacted the Uniform Electronic Transactions Act (UETA) for regulating electronic transactions.

8. MISREPRESENTATION AND FRAUD IN CYBERSPACE

GENERAL RULES. ► General tort rules relating to misrepresentation and fraud apply to transactions conducted in cyberspace, as do consumer-related business regulations. ► Examples: It is fraud to intentionally lie about an object that is being auctioned on the Internet. It is a violation of federal law for firms not to tell purchasers when the firms cannot ship ordered products.
STUDY HINTS. ► It is fraud for companies that operate search engines to misrepresent the capabilities of their products. ► Misrepresentation and fraud are defenses to contracts and entitle a misled party to rescind (terminate) the contract and/or to sue for damages. ► Identity theft is a pervasive problem in cyberspace and many companies have voluntarily taken steps to provide secure sites to minimize the risk of this type of fraud.

D. INTELLECTUAL PROPERTY ISSUES IN CYBERSPACE

► Federal intellectual property laws relating to such matters as trademarks, copyrights, and patents are applicable to conduct in cyberspace. For example, the Federal Trademark Dilution Act forbids a party from using another party's trademark in such a manner that it diminishes the value or stature of the mark. ► New laws and regulations relating to intellectual property in cyberspace include:

(1) The Digital Millennium Copyright Act (DMCA): This Act makes it clear that unauthorized linking to a copyrighted site can be infringement. The DMCA also makes it a federal crime to circumvent or create programs to circumvent encryption devices that copyright owners have placed on copyrighted material in order to prevent unauthorized copying.

(2) Uniform Domain Name Dispute Resolution Policy: This regulation mandates arbitration if there is a dispute between two parties regarding the right to use a domain name for a website.

(3) **LEARNING OUTCOME EXAMPLE.** See *Sony Music Entertainment Inc. v Does* on textbook p. 249.

E. CRIMINAL LAW ISSUES IN CYBERSPACE

9. NATURE AND TYPES OF CYBERSPACE CRIMES

GENERAL RULES. ▶ Computer crime is criminal activity that is conducted using computers and/or cyberspace. ▶ Computer crimes may be prosecuted under traditional criminal statutes and increasingly under new criminal laws that specifically address criminal wrongdoing in cyberspace.

STUDY HINTS. ▶ Improperly rerouting users from sites that they seek to other sites may be a crime. ▶ Computers may be tools of a crime (stealing another's identity), the target of a crime (theft of a computer), or incidental to a crime (used in connection with money-laundering). ▶New types of criminal wrongdoing in cyberspace include (a) phishing (sending e-mail that appears to be from a party's bank and other account sources in order to get the party's private financial information); (b) pharming (process that secretly redirects a party to another website in order to obtain the party's financial information); and evil twins phenomenon (false Wi-Fi network used to obtain party's financial information and passwords).

10. CRIMINAL PROCEDURE AND RIGHTS IN CYBERSPACE

▶ The Fourth Amendment to the U.S. Constitution applies to searches of computers. ▶ **LEARNING OUTCOME EXAMPLE.** See *U.S. v King* on textbook p. 256.

F. CONSTITUTIONAL RESTRAINTS AND PROTECTIONS IN CYBERSPACE

11. FIRST AMENDMENT RIGHTS IN CYBERSPACE

▶ Communications on the Internet are protected by the First Amendment of the U.S. Constitution. ▶ Example: The U.S. Supreme Court declared unconstitutional the Child Pornography Prevention Act because it violated the First Amendment rights of companies and individuals in connection with communicating pornography.

12. COMMERCE CLAUSE ISSUES IN CYBERSPACE

GENERAL RULES. ▶ The federal government can regulate the Internet because it involves interstate commerce. ▶ The federal Internet Tax Freedom Act (ITFA) was recently renewed and this Act prohibits states and local governments from taxing Internet access.

LIMITATIONS: ▶ The ITFA does not prohibit sales taxes being assessed on Internet transactions so long as the sales transactions have a sufficient relationship to the state imposing the tax. ▶ As with other types of interstate sales, states must apportion among themselves the tax revenue generated from Internet transactions.

STUDY HINT. In order to impose a sales tax on an Internet transaction, the seller must have some physical presence in the state or must engage in doing business there.

13. DUE PROCESS ISSUES IN CYBERSPACE

Due process requires that a party being sued have a "nexus" (sufficient connection) with a state before it can be sued in that state. An unresolved question is whether doing business via the Internet establishes such a connection.

G. SECURITIES LAW ISSUES IN CYBERSPACE

GENERAL RULE. Federal securities laws, such as insider-trading laws, apply to conduct in cyberspace that relates to the securities of businesses, whether or not the businesses engage in business in cyberspace.

STUDY HINT. "Pump-and-dump" is a practice whereby someone releases false positive statements on the Internet in order to cause a company's stock price to increase, and then the person sells their stock in that company before the market learns that these statements were false. This activity is unlawful. ▶ **LEARNING OUTCOME EXAMPLE.** See the AOL example on booking ad revenues on textbook p. 259.

CONCEPT REVIEW AND APPLICATIONS

Matching Exercise

Select the term or phrase that best matches a definition or statement stated below. Each term or phrase is the best match for only one statement or definition. Not all terms and phrases will necessarily be used.

appropriation	E-sign	misrepresentation
contract	fair use	pump-and-dump
cybercrime	identity theft	search engines
cyberlaw	infringement	tort
cyberspace	intellectual property rights	warrants
defamation	invasion of privacy	

_____ 1. Electronic signature made using the Internet.

_____ 2. Wrongful injury to the reputation of another.

_____ 3. Wrongful use of another person's credit information, social security number, or other type of identification in order to obtain cash, goods, or credit without permission.

_____ 4. Court order permitting law enforcement agents to search for evidence of a crime.

_____ 5. Principle of intellectual property law that allows the limited use of copyrighted material for teaching, research, and news reporting.

_____ 6. Category of tort that involves a person's wrongful intrusion of another's reasonable expectation of privacy.

_____ 7. Legislation and case law dealing with legal issues associated with cyberspace and related communications.

_____ 8. Form of invasion of privacy that entails the taking of another's image, likeness, or name for commercial advantage.

Multiple Choice

Write **T** if the statement is true, write **F** if it is false.

_____ 1. Conduct on the Internet is subject to traditional rules of law as well as new statutes and case law relating to cyberspace activities.

_____ 2. Communications sent via the Internet are not protected by the U.S. Constitution.

_____ 3. Phishing and pharming are criminal uses of computers by which unscrupulous individuals obtain private financial information of innocent parties.

_____ 4. Employers do not have a right to look at employees' e-mail even if it is communicated via the employers' e-mail system.

_____ 5. Computer crime refers to special crimes that can be committed only by use of a computer.

_____ 6. The Fourth Amendment prohibits the government from conducting unreasonable searches of a person's computer.

_____ 7. Due process requires that a party being sued have a "nexus" with a state before it can be sued in that state.

_____ 8. An employee does not generally have a protectable right to privacy regarding information that is stored on a computer that belongs to the employer and operates using the employer's server.

_____ 9. Federal securities law may apply to stock transactions conducted via the Internet.

_____10. Federal intellectual property law does not apply to the Web.

Multiple Choice

_____ 1. Carl advertised his 2001 automobile for sale on the Internet. In his advertisement, he stated that the car had 75,000 miles, which was false. As Carl knew, the car had 175,000 miles. Frank reasonably believed Carl's statement that the car had only 75,000 miles and contracted to buy it from Carl. Under these facts:
   a. Carl committed fraud.
   b. Carl did not commit fraud because his statements were made only on the Internet and Frank is bound to the contract.
   c. Frank can rescind the contract to purchase the car.
   d. a and c.

_____ 2. Terence went online and stated in a public Internet chat room that Margo, a former girlfriend, had a sexually transmitted disease. As Terence knew, this statement was false. Under these facts, Terence committed:
   a. The tort of invasion of privacy.
   b. The tort of defamation.
   c. The tort of trespass.
   d. No tort since Terence did not know who would read his false statement.

_____ 3. In which case did Grace probably commit a crime?
   a. Grace used her computer and the World Wide Web to make an unauthorized transfer of $50,000 from Acme's bank account into her personal bank account.
   b. Grace used her computer to hack into Direct Book's web site to obtain the numbers of credit cards belonging to others. Grace then used these numbers to purchase items.
   c. a and b.
   d. Grace did not commit any crimes.

_____ 4. Selma developed new computer software and copyrighted it under U.S. copyright law. Data Corporation bought a copy Selma's software and without authorization it began to resell this software via its Web site on the Internet. Under these facts:
   a. Data Corporation did not commit any wrongs since it purchased the original software.
   b. Data Corporation did not commit any wrongs since software cannot be copyrighted.
   c. Data Corporation did not commit any wrongs since it sold the software only via the Internet.
   d. Data Corporation committed copyright infringement.

_____ 5. Ginger is an employee at Do-It-Right Corporation. In which of the following situations, did Do-It-Right commit the tort of invasion of privacy?
   a. Do-It-Right monitored Ginger's e-mail that she sent and received via Do-It-Right's e-mail system. Do-It-Right had previously informed Ginger and its other employees that it reserved the right to monitor their e-mail at work.
   b. Do-It-Right monitored Ginger's text messaging that she sent during working hours using a device furnished by Do-It-Right. Do-It-Right had previously informed Ginger and its other employees that it reserved the right to monitor their communications made at work.
   c. Do-It-Right monitored Ginger's e-mail that she sent and received via her personal computer at her home. Ginger had not consented to this monitoring.
   d. a and b.

_____ 6. Acme Inc. developed a Web site called the PEPSI Drug Site, a site that provided information to teenagers on how to manufacture drug paraphernalia. Under these facts, Acme may have violated:
   a. The Digital Millennium Copyright Act.
   b. The Electronic Signatures in Global and National Commerce Act.
   c. The Federal Trademark Dilution Act.
   d. The Electronic Communications Privacy Act of 1986.

_____ 7. The City of Hope Police Department suspected that Jasmine had been engaging in the sale of stolen goods. The police, however, did not have sufficient evidence to establish probable cause and therefore search Jasmine's computer for proof of this crime. Nonetheless, the police gained access to her home one day and searched the data files on her computer for evidence of criminal wrongdoing. Under these facts, the police violated:
   a. The First Amendment.
   b. The Fourth Amendment.
   c. The Eleventh Amendment.
   d. No constitutional provisions since the protections of the U.S. Constitution do not apply to computers.

Case Problem

Answer the following case problem, explaining your answer.

Cara is an attorney and she was hired to prepare a registration statement (disclosure document) in connection with the interstate offering of stock in "You're-Being-Connected-Right-Now.com," an Internet company. Cara knowingly misstated important information in the statement regarding the risks that were associated with this company in return for a $50,000 bonus paid by You're-Being-Connected-Right-Now.com management. Management did not want Cara to fully disclose the risks so that investors would not be scared away. Lilly bought stock in the company based on the information in the statement and, as a result, she suffered large financial losses.

Analyze what claims, if any, Lilly may have against Cara, the attorney.

_____

_____

_____

_____

Internet Exercise

1. Using the Internet, find and identify the name of the electronic system that exists to receive and process digital applications and digital deposits of copyrighted works for electronic registration via the Internet.

2. Identify the federal government web site where the foregoing system is discussed in detail.

_____

_____

_____

_____

CHAPTER 12
NATURE AND CLASSES OF CONTRACTS: CONTRACTING ON THE INTERNET

MAKE THE CONNECTION

SUMMARY

A contract is a binding agreement between two or more parties. A contract arises when an offer is accepted with contractual intent (the intent to make a binding agreement).

Contracts may be classified in a number of ways according to form, the way in which they were created, validity, and obligations. With respect to form, a contract may be either informal or formal, such as those under seal or those appearing on the records of courts. Contracts may be classified by the way they were created as those that are expressed by words— written or oral—and those that are implied or deduced from conduct. The question of validity requires distinguishing between contracts that are valid, those that are voidable, and those that are not contracts at all but are merely void agreements. Contracts can be distinguished on the basis of the obligations created as executed contracts, in which everything has beenperformed, and executory contracts, in which something remains to be done. The bilateral contract is formed by exchanging a promise for a promise, so each party has the obligation of thereafter rendering the promised performance. In the unilateral contract, which is the doing of an act in exchange for a promise, no further performance is required of the offeree who performed the act.

In certain situations, the law regards it as unjust for a person to receive a benefit and not pay for it. In such a case, the law of quasi contracts allows the performing person to recover the reasonable value of the benefit conferred on the benefited person even though no contract between them requires any payment. Unjust enrichment, which a quasi contract is designed to prevent, sometimes arises when there was never any contract between the persons involved or when there was a contract, but for some reason it was avoided or held to be merely a void agreement.

LEARNING OUTCOMES

After studying this chapter, you should be able to

A. NATURE OF CONTRACTS

LO.1   Explain the meaning and importance of privity of a contract.

LO.2   Describe the way in which a contract arises.

B. CLASSES OF CONTRACTS

LO.3   Distinguish between bilateral and unilateral contracts.

LO.4   Explain the reasoning behind quasi-contract recovery.

C. CONTRACTING ON THE INTERNET

LO.5   Explain how Internet contracts involve the same types of issues as offline contracts.

CHAPTER OUTLINE

A. NATURE OF CONTRACTS

1. DEFINITION OF A CONTRACT

GENERAL RULE.   A contract is a legally binding agreement. Stated another way, "a contract is a promise or a set of promises for the breach of which the law gives a remedy, or the performance of which the law in some way recognizes as a duty." (Restatement, Contracts, 2d)
STUDY HINT.   The essence of a contract is that (1) by mutual agreement (2) parties create obligations that can be legally enforced.

2. ELEMENTS OF A CONTRACT

Elements of a valid contract are: (1) an agreement; (2) competent parties; (3) genuine assent to the contract; (4) consideration given by each party; (5) legal purpose; and (6) proper form of contract.

3. SUBJECT MATTER OF CONTRACTS

A contract may relate to virtually any type of transaction. Contracts may relate to performance of a service, sale or transfer of ownership of property, or a combination of such transactions.

4. PARTIES TO A CONTRACT

GENERAL RULES. ▶ Parties to a contract may be persons, partnerships, corporations, or governments. ▶ There may be more than two parties to a contract (e.g., a credit card transaction).
▶ With some exceptions, only the parties making a contract have rights or duties under the contract.
STUDY HINTS.   Parties may have special names, e.g., promisor (party makes a promise) and promisee (party to whom a promise is made).
LEARNING OUTCOME EXAMPLE. See the example of the subcontractor, RPR & Associates, who worked on a project but could not sue the owner for payment, textbook p. 269

5. HOW A CONTRACT ARISES

GENERAL RULES.   ▶ A contract is created by an agreement. ▶ An agreement is made when an offeror makes an offer, and the offeree accepts the offer by making an acceptance.
STUDY HINTS.   ▶ A contract cannot be made without both an offer and an acceptance. ▶ An offer may be made to a particular person or an offer may be made to the public. ▶ Example of a public offer: an owner's offer to pay a reward to anyone who returns the owner's lost pet.

6. INTENT TO MAKE A BINDING AGREEMENT

GENERAL RULE.   Formation of a contract requires that both the offeror and the offeree intend to enter into a legally binding agreement.
LIMITATIONS.   A contract is not created by: (1) a preliminary agreement; (2) an agreement that states parties' future plans but does not obligate them to perform such plans; or (3) statements that merely indicate the parties' desire to do something without actually obligating them to do it.

7. FREEDOM OF CONTRACT

Subject to certain limits, parties may make any agreement they choose.

B. CLASSES OF CONTRACTS

A contract may be classified by: (1) the form of the contract; (2) how the contract was created; (3) the validity or binding nature of the contract or agreement; (4) the extent to which the contract has been performed; or (5) how the offer to contract may be accepted.

8. FORMAL AND INFORMAL CONTRACTS

GENERAL RULE. Classified according to its form, a contract may be either a:

➤ *Formal contract*: A formal contract is a: (1) contract under seal (seal or equivalent mark is made on or attached to an agreement); (2) contract of record (agreement recorded with a court, such as an agreement to forfeit a bond if a party does not appear at a trial, or an agreement made with an administrative agency); or (3) negotiable instrument (contract that satisfies certain commercial law requirements, such as a check); or

➤ *Informal (simple) contract*: any contract other than a formal contract.

STUDY HINT. Formal and informal contracts are both legally enforceable.

9. EXPRESS AND IMPLIED CONTRACTS

GENERAL RULE. Classified according to how a contract is created, a contract may be either an:

➤ *Express contract*: agreement is formed by the oral or written words of the parties; or
➤ *Implied (implied in fact) contract*: agreement is formed by the conduct of the parties.

LIMITATIONS. ► An implied contract cannot arise if an express contract relating to the subject matter in question already exists. ► An implied contractual duty to pay does not generally arise if a person receives a service or goods from a family member and the service or goods were intended as a gift. Example: son gratuitously brings meals to and takes care of his elderly father.

STUDY HINTS. ► Express and implied contracts are both legally enforceable, and they have the same basic legal effect. ► An implied contract arises if a person does a service for another party with an expectation of payment, and the other party accepts the service knowing that payment is expected.

10. VALID AND VOIDABLE CONTRACTS AND VOID AGREEMENTS

GENERAL RULE. Classified according to its validity, a contract or agreement is either a:

➤ *Valid contract*: legally binding contract that is made in accordance with all legal requirements;
➤ *Voidable contract*: contract that may be set aside by a party because of circumstances surrounding the making of the contract or because a party lacked contractual capacity (examples: a contract made by a party as the result of fraudulent conduct by the other contracting party or a minor's contract to buy a camera or clothing; or
➤ *Void agreement*: agreement that is of no legal effect; frequently an illegal agreement.

STUDY HINT. A void agreement cannot be made valid by a later ratification (approval).

11. EXECUTED AND EXECUTORY CONTRACTS

Classified according to the degree that it has been performed, a contract is either an:

➤ *Executed contract*: contract that has been fully performed; or
➤ *Executory contract*: contract that has not been fully performed by all parties.

12. BILATERAL AND UNILATERAL CONTRACTS

GENERAL RULE. Classified according to how an offeree can accept an offer, a contract is a:

> *Bilateral contract*: contract is formed by an offeree's accepting an offer by making the requested promise; or

> *Unilateral contract*: contract is formed by an offeree's accepting an offer by actually doing the requested act.

LIMITATION. An offeree cannot accept an offer for a unilateral contract by promising to do an act; an offer for a unilateral contract can be accepted only by performing the requested act.

STUDY HINTS. ► Whether an offer is for a bilateral or unilateral contract is determined by the offeror's intent; focus on what the offeror is demanding in return for his or her promise. ► Two types of bilateral contracts are: (1) an option contract which grants a person the legal right (but not obligation) to accept an existing offer; and (2) a right of first refusal contract which grants a party a right to accept an offer if and when the offer is made.

LEARNING OUTCOME EXAMPLES. See the example of the Nantucket painters on textbook p. 276; see the *AON Risk Services* case where an insurance agent won his case based on a unilateral contract theory, textbook p. 273.

13. QUASI CONTRACTS

GENERAL RULES. ► Quasi contract is a contract implied by law (i.e., by a court) to prevent unjust enrichment. ► Elements generally required to establish quasi contract are: (1) plaintiff gave a nongratuitous benefit (good or service) to the defendant; (2) the defendant has knowledge of the actual benefit conferred; and (3) it would be unfair to allow the defendant to keep the benefit without paying for it. ► Quasi contract requires a party to pay the reasonable value for the benefit received (or in some jurisdictions the reasonable value of the work).

LIMITATIONS. ► Quasi contract does not require a party to reimburse the other party for all expenses or losses that the other party may have incurred. ► In general, quasi contract does *not* permit recovery:

> simply because a benefit is given to another person (unjust enrichment must be proven);

> when a party seeks to recover unexpected expenses that are required in order to perform a contract;

> when a party seeks to recover a greater amount than is required to be paid by an existing express contract; or

> the value of goods or services that are given as a gift.

STUDY HINTS. ► Quasi contract may require payment for a benefit even though there is not a valid express or implied contract that requires payment. ► Recovery under quasi contract does not require proof that the defendant did anything wrong. ► When appropriate, quasi-contractual relief may be given if: (1) a benefit is given by mistake; (2) a benefit is given (but not paid for) in expectation of the making of a contract which is never made; or (3) a benefit is given (but not paid for) pursuant to a voidable or void contract that is subsequently set aside.

LEARNING OUTCOME EXAMPLE. See the example whereby Cher had to pay a home designer for certain work even though there was no contract, textbook p. 275.

C. CONTRACTING ON THE INTERNET

GENERAL RULES. ▶ E-commerce transactions are largely governed by intellectual law, privacy laws, the common law of contracts, and UCC Article 2 relating to the sales of goods. ▶ Federal and state deceptive advertising laws apply to E-commerce as well as statutes specifically enacted to regulate Internet-related activities.

STUDY HINT. The federal Electronic Signatures in Global and National Commerce Act (E-Sign) and the Uniform Electronic Transactions Act (UETA) generally validate both electronic and paper contracts.

LEARNING OUTCOME EXAMPLE. See the eBay example on textbook p. 279.

CONCEPT REVIEW AND APPLICATIONS

Matching Exercise

Select the term or phrase that best matches a definition or statement stated below. Each term or phrase is the best match for only one statement or definition. Not all terms and phrases will necessarily be used.

bilateral contract	obligee	quantum meruit
contract	obligor	quasi contract
contracts under seal	offeree	recognizance
executed contract	offeror	right of first refusal
executory contract	option contract	unilateral contract
express contract	privity	valid contract
formal contracts	privity of contract	void agreement
implied contract	promisee	voidable contract
informal contract	promisor	

_____*bilateral*_____ 1. Contract that is formed by an offeree's accepting an offer by promising to do a requested act.

_____*implied*_____ 2. Contract that is created by the conduct of the parties.

_____*voidable*_____ 3. Contract that may be avoided by a party because it was not properly formed.

_____*Quasi-contract*____ 4. Contract implied in law in order to avoid unjust enrichment.

_____*Offeror*_____ 5. Party who makes an offer.

_____*void agreement*____ 6. Agreement that is of no legal effect.

_____*express*_____ 7. Contract that is created by a written or oral agreement.

_____*formal contract*____ 8. Legally binding contract that cannot be set aside by a party.
Valid agreement

Unilateral   9.   Contract that can be formed only when the offer is accepted by the offeree's performance of a requested act

Privity   10.   Relationship between two parties who have entered into a contract with one another.

True/False

Write **T** if the statement is true, write **F** if it is false.

T 1.   In some cases, a party may have a duty under quasi contract to pay for benefits received even though the party never contractually agreed to pay for such benefits.

T 2.   Contracts may relate to virtually any type of legal transaction, including performing services.

F 3.   An offeree can accept an offer for a bilateral contract by promising to perform the requested act. However, a contract is not legally formed until both the offeror and offeree complete performance of their respective promises.

T 4.   An agreement that does not actually obligate the parties to do anything is not a binding contract.

T 5.   In general, an agreement is not a legally binding contract unless the parties sufficiently indicate an intent to be legally bound by the terms of the agreement.

T 6.   The Electronic Signatures in Global and National Commerce Act and the Uniform Electronic Transactions Act generally provide that electronic contracts are as valid as paper contracts.

F 7.   Individuals and corporations can make contracts, but government agencies cannot.

T 8.   A right of first refusal contract gives a party the right to accept an offer only if a second party subsequently decides to make the offer.

F 9.   An offeree can accept an offer for a _unilateral contract_ by merely promising to do the act requested by the offeror.

T 10.   An option contract is a contract that gives one party the right or choice to accept an existing offer within a stated period of time.

Multiple Choice

_____ 1. Bruce and Seller were negotiating Bruce's proposed purchase of a grocery store from Seller. In which situation did the parties manifest the necessary intent to enter into a legally binding contract for the sale of the store?
   a. Bruce and Seller signed a complete, definite agreement whereby Bruce agreed to buy the store from Seller and Seller agreed to sell the store to Bruce upon the terms stated in the agreement.
   b. Bruce and Seller signed a preliminary agreement whereby they indicated their intention to continue to negotiate terms for the sale of the store.
   c. Bruce and Seller signed an agreement whereby Bruce indicated his desire to buy the store from Seller and Seller indicated his desire to sell the store to Bruce upon terms that the parties would later agree upon.
   d. a and c.

_____ 2. An implied contract is created in which of the following situations?
   a. Abe voluntarily helped to paint his parents' fence.
   b. Bob and Pamela entered into a complete, written contract for the sale of Bob's car to Pamela.
   c. Rosa and Nan made an oral contract whereby Nan agreed to clean Rosa's home for $70.
   d. Kim requested Pete's Pest Control to fumigate her home, and Pete's did as requested. There was no express contract, but Pete's expected payment and Kim was aware of this expectation.

_____ 3. Select the correct answer regarding quasi contract?
   a. Quasi contract relief is not available unless parties have entered into a legally enforceable contract.
   b. Quasi contract relief is available even though parties have not entered into a legally enforceable contract.
   c. Quasi contract relief is available whenever one party receives a benefit from someone else.
   d. b and c.

_____ 4. Jackie offered to pay Glen $500 in consideration for Glen's complete trimming of all trees located on Jackie's property. This offer is an offer for a unilateral contract. Under these facts:
   a. Glen can accept the offer by promising to trim the trees.
   b. Glen can accept the offer by completely trimming the trees.
   c. Glen can accept the offer by promising to trim the trees or by completely trimming the trees.
   d. Glen cannot accept the offer; offers for unilateral contracts are illegal.

_____ 5. Diane and Rick entered into a signed, written contract whereby Diane promised to sell a motel to Rick for $200,000 and Rick promised to pay Diane $200,000 for the motel. Rick then paid the $200,000 purchase price to Diane, but Diane has not conveyed title to the motel to Rick. Under these facts:
   a. This contract is a formal contract.
   b. This contract is an executed contract.
   c. This contract is a bilateral contract.
   d. There is no contract until Diane conveys title to the motel to Rick.

114

_____ 6. Larry owned an apartment building and he rented one apartment to Rhonda. Larry contracted with Ace Painters to have Rhonda's apartment painted. Ace painted Rhonda's unit, but Larry refused to pay Ace. Under these facts:
a. Larry has a contractual obligation to pay Ace for painting Rhonda's apartment.
b. Rhonda has a contractual obligation to pay Ace for painting her apartment.
c. Rhonda has a quasi-contractual obligation to pay Ace for painting her apartment.
d. a and c.

_____ 7. Dick offered to sell his car to Jacqueline for $2,000 and she accepted the offer by promising to pay the requested price. Both parties were competent to make a contract, and they drew up the contract in the proper form. Under these facts, this contract is:
a. Valid.
b. Voidable.
c. Void.
d. Unenforceable.

_____ 8. Kirk offered to sell his video store to Edward for $50,000 and Edward accepted. Both parties were competent and the contract was in proper form. However, Kirk fraudulently lied about the past profits of the business. Under these facts, the contract is:
a. Valid.
b. Voidable.
c. Void.
d. Unenforceable.

_____ 9. In a signed writing, Patty offered to sell her business to Carol for $50,000. In this same writing, Patty promised not to revoke this offer for 30 days in exchange for $500 paid by Carol. Under these facts:
a. The parties have entered into a legally enforceable quasi contract.
b. The parties have entered into a legally enforceable right of first refusal.
c. The parties have entered into a legally enforceable option contract.
d. The parties have entered into a legally unenforceable future agreement.

_____ 10. Which of the following agreements is a formal contract?
a. A contract to sell an office building.
b. An invitation to a formal wedding reception.
c. A defendant's agreement to pay a $5,000 fine, which agreement is recorded with a court.
d. A notarized will.

Case Problem

Answer the following question, briefly explaining your answer.

Dan drove his car to Ty's Garage and requested Ty's to fix the radio. Before leaving, Dan noticed a mechanic getting ready to work on his car's engine. Dan overheard the mechanic say that he was going to overhaul the engine. Dan did not say anything to correct this mistake. When Dan returned, Ty's had overhauled the engine. The reasonable value of this work was $500. Ty's demanded $750, which included damages for Ty's lost profits. Under these facts:
1. Should Dan be required by quasi contract to pay for the engine overhaul?
2. If Dan is required to pay, how much must Dan pay?

_____

_____

_____

_____

Internet Exercise

Barbara is negotiating to sell her personal collection of silver war medals to a U.S. firm that specializes in purchasing and reselling war memorabilia. Can Barbara and the U.S. firm validly contract utilizing electronic documents sent via the Internet? Under these facts:
1. Search the Internet and locate the federal Electronic Signatures in Global and National Commerce Act (E-Sign) and identify the web site where you located it.
2. Refer to E-sign and explain whether it validates electronic signatures by consumers, such as Barbara, as well as businesses and, if so, if it generally requires that any special disclosures be made to consumers.

_____

_____

_____

_____

CHAPTER 13
FORMATION OF CONTRACTS:
OFFER AND ACCEPTANCE

MAKE THE CONNECTION

SUMMARY

Because a contract arises when an offer is accepted, it is necessary to find that there was an offer and that it was accepted. If either element is missing, there is no contract.

An offer does not exist unless the offeror has contractual intent. This intent is lacking if the statement of the person is merely an invitation to negotiate, a statement of intention, or an agreement to agree at a later date. Newspaper ads, price quotations, and catalog prices are ordinarily merely invitations to negotiate and cannot be accepted.

An offer must be definite. If an offer is indefinite, its acceptance will not create a contract because it will be held that the resulting agreement is too vague to enforce. In some cases, an offer that is by itself too indefinite is made definite because some writing or standard is incorporated by reference and made part of the offer. In some cases the offer is made definite by implying terms that were not stated. In other cases, the indefinite part of an offer is ignored when that part can be divided or separated from the balance of the offer.

Assuming that there is in fact an offer that is made with contractual intent and that it is sufficiently definite, it still does not have the legal effect of an offer unless it is communicated to the offeree by or at the direction of the offeror.

In some cases, there was an offer but it was terminated before it was accepted. By definition, an attempted acceptance made after the offer has been terminated has no effect. The offeror may revoke the ordinary offer at any time. All that is required is the showing of the intent to revoke and the communication of that intent to the offeree. The offeror's power to revoke is barred by the existence of an option contract under common law or a firm offer under the Uniform Commercial Code. An offer is also terminated by the express rejection of the offer or by the making of a counteroffer, by the lapse of the time stated in the offer or of a reasonable time when none is stated, by the death or disability of either party, or by a change of law that makes illegal a contract based on the particular offer.

When the offer is accepted, a contract arises. Only the offeree can accept an offer, and the acceptance must be of the offer exactly as made without any qualification or change. Ordinarily, the offeree may accept or reject as the offeree chooses.

The acceptance is any manifestation of intent to agree to the terms of the offer. Ordinarily, silence or failure to act does not constitute acceptance. The recipient of unordered goods and tickets may dispose of the goods or use the goods without such action constituting an acceptance. An acceptance does not exist until the words or conduct demonstrating assent to the offer is communicated to the offeror. Acceptance by mail takes effect at the time and place when and where the letter is mailed or the fax is transmitted.

In an auction sale, the auctioneer asking for bids makes an invitation to negotiate. A person making a bid is making an offer, and the acceptance of the highest bid by the auctioneer is an acceptance of that offer and gives rise to a contract. When the auction sale is without reserve, the auctioneer must accept the highest bid. If the auction is not expressly without reserve, the auctioneer may refuse to accept any of the bids.

LEARNING OUTCOMES
After studying this chapter, you should be able to

A. REQUIREMENTS OF AN OFFER
LO.1   Decide whether an offer contains definite and certain terms.

B. TERMINATION OF AN OFFER
LO.2   Explain the exceptions the law makes to the requirement of definiteness.
LO.3   Explain all the ways an offer can be terminated.

C. ACCEPTANCE OF AN OFFER
LO.4   Explain what constitutes the acceptance of an offer.
LO.5   Explain the implications of failing to read a clickwrap agreement.

CHAPTER OUTLINE

A. REQUIREMENTS OF AN OFFER

▶ One element of a contract is a valid agreement. An agreement is comprised of a valid offer made by an offeror and a valid acceptance made by an offeree. ▶ An offer is a promise that is given in exchange for (1) an act, (2) forbearance (refraining from doing an act one can legally do), or (3) a return promise.

1. CONTRACTUAL INTENTION

GENERAL RULES.   ▶ A requirement for a valid offer is that the offeror objectively (outwardly) express the intent to be bound by the offer if the offeree accepts it. ▶ These expressions do *not* typically indicate the required intent and they are not offers: (1) social invitations; (2) statements made in fun or excitement; (3) invitations to negotiate, such as advertisements to sell, circulars, catalogs, invitations for bids, and price quotes; (4) agreements to make a contract in the future or to contract upon terms that will be agreed upon later.
LIMITATION.   A price quotation may be an offer due to a trade custom or due to prior dealings between the parties in which they viewed a price quotation as being an offer.

2. DEFINITENESS

GENERAL RULES.   ▶ An offer must be definite and certain. To be definite and certain an offer must indicate the important terms of the proposed contract. ▶ An offer is sufficiently definite if necessary terms: (1) are stated in writings that are referred to or incorporated into the contract; (2) can be determined by reference to prior dealings between the parties or trade customs; or (3) are implied by law or the parties' conduct. ▶ Output and requirements contracts are sufficiently definite.
LIMITATIONS.   ▶ An offer may be sufficiently definite even if it contains a vague term or provides that the term shall be agreed upon in the future, if the term is not important. ▶ An offer is sufficiently definite if it states an objective standard or formula by which terms can be determined. Example: "blue book" price for a car. ▶ If a divisible contract is partially indefinite, a court may enforce the definite portion and not enforce the indefinite portion.
STUDY HINTS.   ▶ An offer generally is invalid and cannot form a contract if material terms: (1) are missing; (2) are so vague that their meaning cannot be determined; or (3) are left to be agreed upon later. ▶An agreement to use one's "best efforts" to do something may be sufficiently definite.

LEARNING OUTCOME EXAMPLES. See the *Plankenhorn* case for the meaning of a "damn good job" on textbook p. 286; see the legal impact of a party's statement that the contract "was going to be signed" in the *Hewitt* example on textbook p. 286; see the *Delphi* case on requirements contracts, textbook p. 290.

3. COMMUNICATION OF OFFER TO OFFEREE

GENERAL RULE. An offer must be communicated to the offeree.

STUDY HINT. ▶ A unilateral contract is not formed by a party doing an act if the party did not know of the offer at the time the act was performed. ▶ Example: Lisa returned a ring, not knowing that a reward was offered for return of the ring. In this case, a contract is not formed.

B. TERMINATION OF OFFER

An offer may be terminated in several ways. An offer cannot be accepted after it has been terminated.

4. REVOCATION OF OFFER BY OFFEROR

GENERAL RULES. ▶ An offeror can revoke an offer at any time before the offer has been accepted. ▶ A revocation may result from the words or conduct of the offeror that clearly indicate the offeror's intent to terminate the offer.

LIMITATIONS. An offeror's right to revoke an offer may be limited by: (1) an option contract (binding promise to keep an offer open); or (2) a firm offer (signed, written promise by a merchant not to revoke an offer to buy or sell goods).

STUDY HINTS. ▶ In most states a revocation is not effective until received. ▶ A subcontractor cannot revoke a bid that has been detrimentally relied upon by a general contractor.

5. COUNTEROFFER BY OFFEREE

GENERAL RULES. ▶ A counteroffer is a manifestation by an offeree that an offer is not acceptable and that the offeree is offering to contract on terms that are different from those stated in the offer. ▶ A counteroffer terminates the original offer, and it constitutes a new offer. ▶ A contract is formed if the original offeror accepts a counteroffer.

STUDY HINT. An attempted "acceptance" (conditional acceptance) that states terms in addition to those stated in the offer or that changes any terms of the offer is actually a counteroffer.

6. REJECTION OF OFFER BY OFFEREE

A rejection is an offeree's expression that an offer is unacceptable. A rejection terminates an offer.

7. LAPSE OF TIME

An offer that is not accepted automatically terminates upon: (1) expiration of the time stated in the offer; or (2) if no time is stated in the offer, within a reasonable time after the offer is made.

8. DEATH OR DISABILITY OF EITHER PARTY

An offer is terminated if either party dies or becomes mentally incompetent before the offer is accepted.

9. SUBSEQUENT ILLEGALITY

An offer is terminated if the contract's subject matter becomes illegal before the offer is accepted.

C. ACCEPTANCE OF OFFER

10. WHAT CONSTITUTES AN ACCEPTANCE?

GENERAL RULE.   An acceptance is a clear expression that the offeree agrees to be bound by the terms of the offer.

LEARNING OUTCOME EXAMPLES. See the *Sadeghi* example where acceptance of an offer created a binding contract, textbook p. 295; see the *Keryakos Textiles* case on the impact of a counteroffer, textbook p. 296.

11. PRIVILEGE OF OFFEREE

GENERAL RULE.   Ordinarily, an offeree is not legally required to accept an offer.

STUDY HINT.   In general, an offeree can reject an offer even if the two parties have previously engaged in business with one another.

12. EFFECT OF ACCEPTANCE

GENERAL RULE.   Acceptance of an offer creates a contract if all other contract elements are present.

STUDY HINT.   Once a contract is made, one party cannot unilaterally terminate or change it.

13. NATURE OF ACCEPTANCE

GENERAL RULES.   ▶ An acceptance is a definite, unconditional expression of intent by an offeree to agree to the terms of the offer. ▶ At common law, an acceptance must accept all terms of the offer without changing or adding any terms.

STUDY HINTS.   ▶ An acceptance may be made by words or conduct. ▶ An offeree's intent is determined by the offeree's objective (outward) intent, not by subjective or secret intentions.

14. WHO MAY ACCEPT?

An offer can be accepted by only: (1) the person to whom the offer is made; or (2) a member of a class to whom the offer is made.

15. MANNER AND TIME OF ACCEPTANCE

GENERAL RULE.   If an offeror states a required, exclusive manner for acceptance, the offeree must accept in this manner. Failure to accept in the required manner renders an acceptance ineffective.

LIMITATION.   Failure to accept in a manner stated by the offeror does not invalidate an acceptance if: (1) the manner of acceptance stated by the offeror was a suggestion, not a requirement; or (2) the offeror acts as if a contract has been formed.

STUDY HINTS.   ▶ A failure to respond to an unsolicited offer and a failure to return unordered goods received in the mail do not constitute acceptances. ▶ Silence is usually not a valid acceptance. ▶ A party to an existing contract cannot modify the contract without the other contracting party's acceptance of such modification. ▶*Clickwrap* agreements, i.e., contracts formed by agreeing to contract on a website, are generally valid if sufficient disclosure of terms is made and the party clicking acceptance should reasonably understand that a contract is being made.

LEARNING OUTCOME EXAMPLE. See the *Feldman* case as an example of an enforceable clickwrap agreement containing notice and manifested assent, textbook p. 297.

16. COMMUNICATION OF ACCEPTANCE

GENERAL RULES. ▶ An acceptance of a bilateral contract offer must be communicated in order to form a contract. ▶ The UCC and the modern trend is that an acceptance can be communicated in any manner and using any method of communication that is reasonable. Thus, an acceptance generally can be sent by mail unless the offeror requires otherwise. ▶ Under the "mailbox rule," an acceptance is effective when it is properly mailed. Example: Tim deposits an acceptance in the mail on May 1, and it is received by the offeror on May 8. The acceptance was effective on May 1.

LIMITATION. A specific method for communicating an acceptance may be expressly required by an offeror.

STUDY HINTS. ▶ An offer can be accepted by telephone unless a written writing is required by the offeror or by law. ▶ A telephoned acceptance is effective when and where the acceptance is communicated. ▶ Although the law is still unsettled, it is likely that acceptances by e-mail, fax, or other electronic memos are governed by the same rules that apply to acceptances sent by mail or telephone.

17. AUCTION SALES

GENERAL RULES. ▶ Placing goods for sale at an auction is merely an invitation to negotiate. ▶ A bid at an auction is an offer. A contract is formed only when the auctioneer accepts the bid.

STUDY HINT. An auctioneer can refuse to sell any item unless the sale is conducted "without reserve." If an auction is without reserve, property must be sold to the highest bidder.

CONCEPT REVIEW AND APPLICATIONS

Matching Exercise

Select the term or phrase that best matches a definition or statement stated below. Each term or phrase is the best match for only one statement or definition. Not all terms and phrases will necessarily be used.

acceptance   offer

counteroffer   output contract

divisible contract   requirements contract

firm offer

_____ 1. Merchant's signed, written offer to buy or sell goods that promises that the offer will not be revoked for a period of time, not to exceed three months.

_____ 2. Offeree's expression that both rejects an offer and constitutes an offer by the offeree to contract upon different terms.

_____ 3. Contract by a buyer to purchase goods necessary to meet the good faith needs of the buyer.

_____ 4. Offeree's agreement to the terms of an offer.

output contract 5. Contract to sell the entire production of a seller to a buyer.

Divisible 6. Agreement consisting of two or more parts, each calling for corresponding performances of each part by the parties.

_____ 7. Offeror's proposal to enter into a contract regarding a specific subject matter.

True/False

Write **T** if the statement is true, write **F** if it is false.

T 1. An acceptance made by telephone is effective when and where it is spoken into the telephone.

T 2. Absent special circumstances, price quotations are typically invitations to negotiate, not offers.

F 3. An agreement to sell land on terms to be agreed upon by the seller and buyer at a later date is sufficiently definite to be a contract.

T 4. An offer is sufficiently definite if the important terms of the proposed contract are stated in the offer or would be implied from the parties' conduct.

T 5. An offer to hire a lawyer to provide all legal services that a client may require during a specified period of time in consideration for a stated fee may be sufficiently definite to form a contract.

F 6. An offer is not required to be communicated to the offeree.

F 7. In general, an offeror cannot revoke an offer without first allowing the offeree a reasonable time within which to accept the offer.

T 8. An acceptance is not effective if it is made in a manner that is different from the exclusive manner of acceptance clearly required by the offeror.

T 9. An acceptance may form a contract even if it contains a vague term if that term is not essential to the parties' agreement.

T 10. An offeree cannot accept an offer after the offer has been revoked or rejected.

Multiple Choice

_____ 1. Which action manifests the necessary contractual intent to constitute a valid offer?
   a. Carlos offers to take Mandy to the movies on a date.
   b. In response to Homeowner's request, Contractor submits a detailed, signed bid to Homeowner to do certain described remodeling work for $5,000.
   c. Central City posts a notice inviting contractors to submit bids to construct a new city hall.
   d. Henry distributes circulars stating that he will shampoo carpeting for $10 per room.

123

_____ 2. Which proposal is too indefinite to be a valid offer?
   a. Red proposes to sell a company to Melanie for a price to be mutually agreed upon in 30 days.
   b. Luis proposes to sell ten ounces of gold to Tony at a price equal to the closing bid price stated by the Bank of New York on January 1, 2011.
   c. Farmer proposes to sell his entire 2010 apple crop to Co-op for $5 per bushel.
   d. Wholesaler signs a written proposal to sell Buyer ten items of equipment for $2,000 cash. The proposal refers to and incorporates another writing that identifies the equipment.

_____ 3. In which case is Alex legally entitled to revoke his offer?
   a. Alex offers to sell a business to Will. Alex promises not to revoke the offer for 24 hours in consideration for $100 paid by Will. One hour later and before Will had accepted, Alex revokes his offer, and he offers to return the $100 to Will.
   b. Alex (a subcontractor) submits a bid to Contractor for certain work to be done on a project for which Contractor intends to bid. Contractor detrimentally relies on Alex's bid in connection with bidding for the project. Alex then revokes his bid.
   c. In a signed writing, Alex (a merchant) offers to sell Liz a car and promises not to revoke the offer for 48 hours. One hour later and before Liz accepts, Alex revokes his offer.
   d. Alex offers to sell his condo to Ben. Before Ben accepts, Alex revokes his offer.

_____ 4. Select the correct answer.
   a. Ike offered to sell a patent to Ken. Before Ken accepted the offer, Ike died. In this case, Ike's offer was not terminated, and Ken can still accept the offer.
   b. R&R Co. offered to sell some chemicals to Lex. Before Lex accepted the offer, Congress passed a law making the sale of the chemicals illegal. In this case, the offer was terminated.
   c. Tom offered to sell a business to Jack. The offer stated that the offer would lapse on September 1. On September 2, Jack accepted the offer. In this case, a contract was formed.
   d. Vicky offered to sell a TV to Carl. Carl replied, "No, the price is too high." Then Carl reconsidered, and he accepted the offer. In this case, a contract was formed.

_____ 5. Seller offered to sell certain land to Joe for $90,000. Which of the following expressions by Joe would *not* be a valid acceptance of the offer?
   a. In writing Joe stated: "I accept the offer, provided that Seller must deliver good title to the land." (You may assume that applicable state law would imply this new term.)
   b. In writing Joe stated: "I accept the offer provided that the price is reduced to $89,000."
   c. In writing Joe stated: "I accept the offer. Also, I would appreciate a tour of the property."
   d. In writing Joe stated: "I accept the offer. Also, I request that I be given a copy of the signed documents for my files."

_____ 6. In which case does Tara effectively accept the offer in question?
   a. Plantco mailed Tara a box of tulip bulbs with an offer to sell the bulbs to her. Tara did not order the bulbs and she did not accept Plantco's offer. But, Tara did not return the bulbs.
   b. Sam offered to sell a car to Tara. The offer stated that Tara's failure to reject the offer within 24 hours would be an acceptance. Tara was silent, and she did not expressly reject the offer.
   c. Bob mailed an offer to sell a motorcycle to Tara. Immediately upon receiving the offer, Tara mailed back a definite, unconditional acceptance of the offer.
   d. All of the above.

_____ 7. On April 1, Gina mailed Oscar an offer to buy his home. Oscar received the offer on April 5. On April 6, Oscar deposited a properly addressed, stamped acceptance in the mail. Gina received the acceptance on April 10. On April 8, Gina changed her mind, and she personally delivered a written revocation of the offer to Oscar. In most states:

    a. A contract was formed on April 5.

    b. A contract was formed on April 6.

    c. A contract was formed on April 10.

    d. A contract was not formed.

Case Problems

Answer the following problems, briefly explaining your answers.

1. Seller advertised land for sale. In response, Bart delivered a signed, written purchase offer to Seller. The offer appeared to be sincere and it stated all of the contract terms. Unknown to Seller, Bart did not actually intend to buy the land unless he first obtained certain financing. Seller accepted Bart's offer. (a) Was Seller's advertisement an offer? (b) Did Bart manifest a sufficient contractual intent to be bound by his purchase offer? (c) What was the effect of Seller's acceptance?

_____

_____

_____

2. Fawn offered to sell a carpet-cleaning franchise to Missy. Fawn mailed the offer to Missy via first-class U.S. mail. The offer was silent regarding the required manner of acceptance. (a) Can Missy accept the offer by remaining silent, or must she communicate an acceptance to Fawn? (b) Under modern rules, how can Missy communicate an acceptance of the offer? (c) When will Fawn's offer lapse? (d) If Missy sends an acceptance via first-class U.S. mail, when will the acceptance be effective?

_____

_____

_____

3. Henry, an auctioneer, conducted an auction of certain goods. The auction was a standard auction; it was *not* conducted without reserve. At the auction the following occurred:

    a. Henry invited bids for a table. Felix bid $25 for the table, and Henry accepted the bid. Was Henry's invitation for bids an offer to sell? Was a contract formed?

    b. Henry invited bids for an antique chair. Rene's $300 bid was the highest bid. However, Henry was not satisfied with this bid, and he refused to sell the chair to Rene. Was Henry legally required to sell the chair to Rene?

_____

_____

_____

Internet Exercise

1. Using the Internet, locate and identify a company's advertisement page for its product.
2. Does this advertisement page constitute a valid contractual offer? Explain.

_____

_____

_____

CPA REVIEW

The following questions were given on past CPA examinations. The answers for these questions are the unofficial answers prepared by the American Institute of Certified Public Accountants, Inc. (AICPA). All material is reproduced with permission of the AICPA.

_____ 1. On February 12, Harris sent Fresno a written offer to purchase Fresno's land. The offer included the following provision: "Acceptance of this offer must be by registered or certified mail, received by Harris no later than February 18 by 5:00 p.m. CST." On February 18, Fresno sent Harris a letter accepting the offer by private overnight delivery service. Harris received the letter on February 19. Which of the following statements is correct?
   a. A contract was formed on February 19.
   b. Fresno's letter constituted a counteroffer.
   c. Fresno's use of the overnight delivery service was an effective form of acceptance.
   d. A contract was formed on February 18 regardless of when Harris actually received Fresno's letter.

_____ 2. On June 15, Peters orally offered to sell a used lawn mower to Mason for $125. Peters specified that Mason had until June 20 to accept the offer. On June 16, Peters received an offer to purchase the lawn mower for $150 from Bronson, Mason's neighbor. Peters accepted Bronson's offer. On June 17, Mason saw Bronson using the lawn mower and was told the mower had been sold to Bronson. Mason immediately wrote to Peters to accept the June 15 offer. Which of the following statements are correct?
   a. Mason's acceptance would be effective when received by Peters.
   b. Mason's acceptance would be effective when mailed.
   c. Peters' offer had been revoked and Mason's acceptance was ineffective.
   d. Peters was obligated to keep the June 15 offer open until June 20.

_____ 3. Kraft Corp. published circulars containing price quotes and a description of products, which it would like to sell. Rice, a prospective customer, demands the right to purchase one of the products at the quoted price. Which of the following statements are correct under general contract law?
   a. Kraft must sell the product which Rice demands at the quoted price.
   b. Rice has accepted Kraft's firm offer to sell.
   c. Kraft has made an offer.
   d. Rice has made an offer.

_____ 4. Carson Corp., a retail chain, asked Alto Construction to fix a broken window at one of Carson's stores. Alto offered to make the repairs within three days at a price to be agreed on after the work was completed. A contract based on Alto's offer would fail because of indefiniteness as to the

    a. Price involved.

    b. Nature of the subject matter.

    c. Parties to the contract.

    d. Time for performance.

_____ 5. Nix sent Castor a letter offering to employ Castor as controller of Nix's automobile dealership. Castor received the letter on February 1 9. The letter provided that Castor would have until February 23 to consider the offer and, in the meantime, Nix would not withdraw it. On February 20, Nix, after reconsidering the offer to Castor, decided to offer the job to Vick, who accepted immediately. That same day, Nix called Castor and revoked the offer. Castor told Nix that an acceptance of Nix's offer was mailed on February 19. Under the circumstances,

    a. Nix's offer was irrevocable until February 23.

    b. No contract was formed between Nix and Castor because Nix revoked the offer before Nix received Castor's acceptance.

    c. Castor's acceptance was effective when mailed.

    d. Any revocation of the offer would have to be in writing because Nix's offer was in writing.

_____ 6. Opal offered, in writing, to sell Larkin a parcel of land for $300,000. If Opal dies, the offer will

    a. Terminate prior to Larkin's acceptance only if Larkin received notice of Opal's death.

    b. Remain open for a reasonable period of time after Opal's death.

    c. Automatically terminate despite Larkin's prior acceptance.

    d. Automatically terminate prior to Larkin's acceptance.

_____ 7. On September 10, Harris, Inc., a new car dealer, placed a newspaper advertisement stating that Harris would sell 10 cars at its showroom for a special discount only on September 12, 13, and 14. On September 12, King called Harris and expressed an interest in buying one of the advertised cars. King was told that five of the cars had been sold and to come to the showroom as soon as possible. On September 13, Harris made a televised announcement that the sale would end at 10:00 PM that night. King went to Harris' showroom on September 14 and demanded the right to buy a car at the special discount. Harris had sold the 10 cars and refused King's demand. King sued Harris for breach of contract. Harris' best defense to King's suit would be that Harris'

    a. Offer was unenforceable.

    b. Advertisement was not an offer.

    c. Television announcement revoked the offer.

    d. Offer had not been accepted.

CHAPTER 14
CAPACITY AND GENUINE ASSENT

MAKE THE CONNECTION

SUMMARY

An agreement that otherwise appears to be a contract may not be binding because one of the parties lacks contractual capacity. In such a case, the contract is ordinarily voidable at the election of the party who lacks contractual capacity. In some cases, the contract is void. Ordinarily, contractual incapacity is the inability, for mental or physical reasons, to understand that a contract is being made and to understand its general terms and nature. This is typically the case when it is claimed that incapacity exists because of insanity, intoxication, or drug use. The incapacity of minors arises because society discriminates in favor of that class to protect them from unwise contracts.

The age of majority is 18. Minors can disaffirm most contracts. If a minor received anything from the other party, the minor, on avoiding the contract, must return what had been received from the other party if the minor still has it.

When a minor disaffirms a contract for a necessary, the minor must pay the reasonable value of any benefit received.

Minors only are liable for their contracts. Parents of a minor are not liable on the minor's contracts merely because they are the parents. Frequently, an adult enters into the contract as a coparty of the minor and is then liable without regard to whether the minor has avoided the contract.

The contract of an insane person is voidable to much the same extent as the contract of a minor. An important distinction is that if a guardian has been appointed for the insane person, a contract made by the insane person is void, not merely voidable.

An intoxicated person lacks contractual capacity if the intoxication is such that the person does not understand that a contract is being made.

The consent of a party to an agreement is not genuine or voluntary in certain cases of mistake, deception, or pressure. When this occurs, what appears to be a contract can be avoided by the victim of such circumstances or conduct.

As to mistake, it is necessary to distinguish between unilateral mistakes that are unknown to the other contracting party and those that are known. Mistakes that are unknown to the other party usually do not affect the binding character of the agreement. A unilateral mistake of which the other contracting party has knowledge or has reason to know makes the contract avoidable by the victim of the mistake.

The deception situation may be one of negligent misrepresentation or fraud. The law ordinarily does not attach any significance to nondisclosure. Contrary to this rule, there is a duty to volunteer information when a confidential relationship exists between the possessor of the knowledge and the other contracting party.

When concealment goes beyond mere silence and consists of actively taking steps to hide the truth, the conduct may be classified as fraud. A statement of opinion or value cannot ordinarily be the basis for fraud liability.

The voluntary character of a contract may be lacking because the agreement had been obtained by pressure. This may range from undue influence through the array of threats of extreme economic loss (called *economic duress*) to the threat of physical force that would cause serious personal injury or damage to property (called *physical duress*). When the voluntary character of an agreement has been destroyed by deception, or pressure, the victim may avoid or rescind the contract or may obtain money damages from the wrongdoer.

LEARNING OUTCOMES
After studying this chapter, you should be able to

A. CONTRACTUAL CAPACITY
LO.1   Define contractual capacity.
LO.2   Explain the extent and effect of avoidance of a contract by a minor.

B. MISTAKE
LO.3   Distinguish unilateral mistakes and mutual mistakes.

C. DECEPTION
LO.4   Explain the difference between intentional misrepresentation, negligent misrepresentation and puffery.

D. PRESSURE
LO.5   Explain the difference between undue influence and duress.

CHAPTER OUTLINE

A. CONTRACTUAL CAPACITY

The law generally presumes that everyone has the capacity to contract. But if a party does lack the capacity to do so, then a contract is usually voidable and the incapacitated party may avoid the contract.

1. CONTRACTUAL CAPACITY DEFINED

GENERAL RULES. ▶ Contractual capacity is the ability to understand that a contract is being made and to understand its essential terms. ▶ A person may lack capacity due to: (1) status incapacity, i.e., the person is a member of a group that is legally viewed as lacking capacity; or (2) factual incapacity, i.e., the person is in fact unable to understand the nature and terms of the contract. ▶ Examples: status incapacity: a minor; factual incapacity: a mentally incompetent person.
STUDY HINT.   With the exception of minors, virtually all classes of individuals, such as married women and aliens, now have the capacity to enter into contracts.
LEARNING OUTCOME EXAMPLE. See the example where Jacqueline, age 22, did not understand parts of a storage contract, textbook p. 308.

2. MINORS

In most states, a minor is a person under the age of 18. A contract made by a minor is generally voidable, and the minor can elect to disaffirm (avoid) the contract subject to the following rules:

➢ *Minor's power to avoid contracts*: ▶ Disaffirmance may be express or implied. Example of implied disaffirmance: a minor refuses to perform a contract. ▶ A minor may disaffirm while he or she is a minor, or within a reasonable time after reaching majority. ▶ In most states, a minor can disaffirm even if the minor misrepresented his or her age to the other party.

➢ *Restitution by minor after avoidance*: ▶ A minor must return benefits only to the extent the minor still has them. ▶ Traditionally: minor is not liable for depreciation to or loss of property received from adult. ▶ Trend: minor is liable if guilty of gross negligence or intentional tort.

➢ *Recovery of property by minor on avoidance*: Upon disaffirmance, the other party must repay all money paid by a minor and return all property given by a minor (or pay its fair value).

➢ *Contracts for necessaries*: ▶ Necessaries are food, clothing, shelter, and other things required for the proper care of a minor. They now also generally include expenses necessary for the health, and education of the minor, and services required to enable a minor to obtain employment have also been held to be necessaries. ▶ Minors can avoid contracts for necessaries, but under quasi contract minors must pay the reasonable value for necessaries.

➢ *Ratification of voidable contract*: ▶ Ratification is a definite expression of an intent to be bound by a contract. ▶ A minor can ratify only after attaining his or her majority. ▶ Ratification may result from words or conduct, but some states require it to be written. ▶ A failure to disaffirm a contract within a reasonable time after attaining majority is an implied ratification. ▶ Making payments after attaining one's majority may be a ratification if payments are made with the intent to ratify. ▶ A contract cannot be avoided after it has been ratified.

➢ *Contracts that minors cannot avoid*: ▶ In many states, statutes do not permit a minor to avoid contracts for education loans, medical care, bank accounts, insurance or stock. ▶ In many states, a minor cannot avoid a contract if a court approved it or if it was made in business.

➢ *Liability of third person for minor's contract*: ▶ Parents are not liable for a minor's contracts unless the minor is contracting for the parents, or the contract involves necessaries and the parents have abandoned the minor. ▶ At common law, a parent is liable for medical expenses provided to a minor child. ▶ A person who cosigns a contract with a minor remains liable on the contract even if the minor disaffirms the contract.

➢ LEARNING OUTCOME EXAMPLE. See the *Prince George's Hospital* case where a minor had to pay for medical necessaries, textbook p. 311.

3. MENTALLY INCOMPETENT PERSONS

GENERAL RULES. ▶ An incompetent is a person who is mentally impaired. ▶ An incompetent who cannot understand the legal nature of a contract and its essential terms lacks contractual capacity, and a contract made by this person is generally voidable. ▶ A contract is void if made by an incompetent after a guardian has been appointed to administer the affairs of the incompetent.

LIMITATIONS. ▶ A contract is not voidable if an incompetent understands a contract is being made and the incompetent understands the general nature of the transaction. ▶ A mentally incompetent person or that person's estate is liable for the reasonable value of any necessaries furnished to the incompetent person.

STUDY HINTS. ▶ Incompetency may result from any physical condition or psychological disorder. ▶ An incompetent can ratify a contract once his or her disability is overcome.

4. INTOXICATED PERSONS

A person lacks contractual capacity if due to intoxication he or she cannot understand that a contract is being made. Under these circumstances, the contract is voidable and it can be rescinded.

B. MISTAKE

5. UNILATERAL MISTAKE

GENERAL RULE. A unilateral mistake (one party's mistake) does not make a contract voidable.
LIMITATION. A contract can be rescinded if one party knows or has reason to know of the other party's unilateral mistake of fact.
LEARNING OUTCOME EXAMPLE. See the *Shurgard Storage* case where the "other party" should have known of the unilateral mistake, textbook p. 315.

6. MUTUAL MISTAKE

GENERAL RULE. A contract is void if both parties are mistaken regarding a material matter of fact or law.
LIMITATION. In most cases, a contract's validity is not affected by mistakes regarding expectations or matters of judgment, such as the suitability of a machine for a particular job.
LEARNING OUTCOME EXAMPLE. See the example of the mutual mistake of fact regarding the fertility of a cow on textbook p. 315.

7. MISTAKE IN THE TRANSCRIPTION OR PRINTING OF THE CONTRACT: REFORMATION

GENERAL RULES. ▶ When parties reach an oral agreement but inaccurately write down the terms of their agreement, the parties may request a court to rewrite their contract so that it correctly states the terms of their agreement. ▶ Reformation of contract is the remedy requested to effect the foregoing change.
LIMITATION. The party requesting reformation of contract has the burden to prove by clear and convincing evidence that a mistake was made.

C. DECEPTION

8. INTENTIONAL MISREPRESENTATION

If a party is induced into making a contract by the other party's intentional misrepresentation of material fact, then the deceived party may rescind the contract.

9. FRAUD

GENERAL RULES. ▶ The elements of fraud are: (1) a false statement of fact; (2) made by a party who knows it is false or who has no basis to believe it to be true; (3) with the intent that the other party rely on the statement; (4) the other party does rely on the statement; (5) causing harm to the relying party. ▶ Broadly speaking, fraud cannot be based on statements regarding: (1) an opinion; (2) mere sales talk, i.e., puffing ("this car is the best car ever made"); (3) an item's value; (4) a matter of law; or (5) predictions of the future. ▶ Under common law, a defrauded party may (1) rescind the contract or (2) perform the contract and sue for his or her damages, i.e., the money lost because of the facts were misstated.

LIMITATION. False statements of opinion may also be grounds for liability if the speaker knows facts that clearly make such opinions unbelievable.

STUDY HINT. Fraud cannot occur without actual reliance on a misrepresentation.

LEARNING OUTCOME EXAMPLE. See the example of the purchase of the used Honda where the misrepresentation was found to be fraud not puffery on textbook p. 317.

10. NEGLIGENT MISREPRESENTATION

A contract is voidable if a contracting party negligently (unintentionally) misstates a material fact to the other contracting party who reasonably relies on such misstatement.

11. NONDISCLOSURE

In general, a party has no duty to voluntarily disclose information to the other party. However, a failure to conform to the following duties may render a contract voidable:

➢ *Unknown defect or condition*: A party must disclose facts relating to important defects or other negative matters if these facts are unknown to and cannot be readily discovered by the other party.

➢ *Confidential relationship*: If the contracting parties are in a confidential relationship (a relationship of trust and confidence, such as an attorney-client or parent-child relationship), the party in the position of trust must disclose all important facts to the other party.

➢ *Active concealment*: A party cannot actively hide an important fact from the other party.

D. PRESSURE

12. UNDUE INFLUENCE

GENERAL RULES. ▶ Undue influence is: (1) domination by one party of another contracting party; (2) that deprives the weaker party of his or her free will; (3) resulting in an unfair contract. ▶ Undue influence is presumed if parties are in a confidential relationship and the dominant party benefits from the contract. To overcome this presumption, the dominant party must prove that the contract was fair.

LIMITATION. Nagging and normal persuasion are not undue influence.

LEARNING OUTCOME EXAMPLE. See the *Fisher v. Schefers* undue influence litigation, textbook p. 322.

13. DURESS

GENERAL RULES. ▶ Duress is: (1) a wrongful threat or wrongful act by a contracting party; (2) that deprives the other party of his or her free will; (3) forcing the other party to make a contract. ▶ Duress may be: (1) physical duress (threat of harm to a contracting party or family member); or (2) economic duress (threat of wrongful act that will cause serious financial harm, e.g., breach a contract).

LIMITATION. Hard bargaining or threatening to sue to collect a valid debt is not duress.

LEARNING OUTCOME EXAMPLE. See the Katahdin bicycle example on economic duress, textbook p. 323.

CONCEPT REVIEW AND APPLICATIONS

Matching Exercise

Select the term or phrase that best matches a definition or statement stated below. Each term or phrase is the best match for only one statement or definition. Not all terms and phrases will necessarily be used.

confidential relationship
contractual capacity
duress
economic duress
fraud

necessaries
physical duress
reform (contract)
status quo ante
undue influence

contractual capacity 1. Ability to understand that a contract is being made and to understand its general meaning.

confidential relat 2. Original positions of the parties. *status quo ante*

3. Relationship in which one person places complete trust in and relies upon another person.

necessaries 4. Basic necessities of life, such as food, clothing, and shelter.

economic duress 5. Wrongful threat of financial loss.

physical duress 6. Wrongful threat of physical harm to person or property.

duress 7. In general, a wrongful threat or act that deprives a party of his or her free will thereby causing the party to make a contract.

reform 8. Remedy whereby a court corrects a written contract that incorrectly states the parties' agreement.

fraud 9. Intentional misrepresentation of fact reasonably relied upon by another party to his or her harm.

undue influence 10. Domination by one contracting party of the other contracting party that deprives the weaker party of his or her free will causing the weaker party to enter into an unfair contract.

True/False

Write **T** if the statement is true, write **F** if it is false.

_F_ 1. A negligent (unintentional) misrepresentation of material fact made by one contracting party to the other contracting party does not render the contract voidable.

T 2. In general, a minor who misrepresents his or her age can disaffirm a contract. However, in some states misrepresentation of age will make the minor liable for damages caused to the other party.

F 3. A minor cannot avoid a contract if the minor cannot return all of the contract benefits that the minor received from the other party.

T 4. A party who previously lacked contractual capacity cannot avoid a contract if the party has already ratified the contract.

T 5. Seller contracted to sell land to Buyer. Unknown to the parties, there was a typographical error in the contract that incorrectly stated the legal description (boundaries) of the land. In this situation, a court will correct the mistake and will enforce the contract as corrected.

F 6. An incompetent can rescind a contract even if the incompetent understood that he or she was making a contract and the incompetent understood the essential elements of the contract.

T 7. In most cases, a party cannot rescind a contract merely because the party did not read or fully understand the terms of a contract.

F 8. A contract is voidable whenever one party persuades another party to make a one-sided contract.

T 9. There is a modern trend that requires a party to disclose an important latent (hidden) defect that is unknown to, and cannot be reasonably discovered by, the other contracting party.

T 10. A statement that a person intends to do an act may be fraud if the person does not actually intend to do the act.

Multiple Choice

_____ 1. Mindy purchased a stereo when she 16 years old. Mindy has used the stereo for a year, and she now wants to avoid the contract. (For purposes of this question, you may assume that 18 is the age of majority.) Under these facts:
a. Mindy can disaffirm the contract, but she must do so before she turns 18.
b. Mindy can disaffirm the contract, but she must pay for any depreciation to the stereo.
c. Mindy can disaffirm the contract, and the seller must repay all money paid by Mindy.
d. Mindy cannot under any circumstance disaffirm the contract.

_____ 2. While Ken was a minor and living on his own without any support from his parents, Ken made the contracts described below. Select the correct answer regarding these contracts.
a. Ken contracted to buy a motorcycle that he used for pleasure. In this case, the motorcycle is a necessary and Ken can disaffirm the contract.
b. Ken contracted to lease an apartment. In this case, the apartment is a necessary and Ken cannot disaffirm the contract.
c. Ken contracted to buy a raincoat. In this case, the coat is a necessary and Ken can disaffirm the contract, but he must pay the reasonable value for the coat under quasi contract.
d. Ken contracted to buy a TV. In this case, the TV is a necessary and Ken cannot disaffirm the contract.

134

_____ 3. Molly was a minor and living on her own without any support from her parents when she entered into the contracts described below. In some states, statutes would prohibit Molly from avoiding which of these contracts?
   a. Contract for an educational loan that she used to pay her tuition to vocational school.
   b. Contract for car insurance.
   c. Contract for medical services that were needed when Molly contracted pneumonia.
   d. All of the above.

_____ 4. In which case did the party in question have the contractual capacity to make a valid contract?
   a. Reggie was judicially declared incompetent and a guardian was appointed to handle his personal and legal affairs. Reggie then contracted to buy a house.
   b. Irving contracted to buy a TV. Due to dementia, Irving could neither understand that the contract was a legal obligation nor understand the basic terms of the contract.
   c. Gary contracted to buy a iPhone. Gary had been drinking, and he was intoxicated. Gary understood that he was making a contract and he understood the terms of the contract.
   d. Yin, 17 years old, contracted to buy a mountain bike.

_____ 5. Traditionally, which contract is voidable or void due to mistake?
   a. Subcontractor submitted a $10,000 bid to Contractor. Contractor did not know that Subcontractor had made a mistake and that the bid should have been $11,000. Contractor accepted the bid thereby forming a contract, and Contractor detrimentally relied on the bid.
   b. Holly contracted to sell a cabin to Rob. Both parties mistakenly believed that the cabin still existed. In fact, a fire had destroyed the cabin the previous night.
   c. Seller contracted to sell some land to Buyer. Seller and Buyer both mistakenly thought that the land would be in the path of new developments, but they were wrong.
   d. Wayne contracted to sell his business to Betsy. Wayne and Betsy both expected that the business would make a profit after Betsy purchased the business, but they were wrong.

_____ 6. Which contract is probably voidable due to fraud?
   a. Seller intentionally misrepresented to Buyer that a car being sold was a 1977 Mustang when it was actually a 1978 Mustang. However, Buyer did not rely on this misstatement because Buyer knew that the car was a 1978 Mustang.
   b. Kate contracted to sell her car to Sue. During negotiations, Kate told Sue that, in her opinion, the car was worth at least $4,000. In fact, the value of the car was only $2,500.
   c. Ali contracted to sell a store to Buyer. During negotiations, Ali intentionally lied to Buyer about the store's past profits stating that the profits were greater than they actually were, and Buyer reasonably relied on Ali's statement.
   d. a and c.

_____ 7. Select the correct answer.
   a. Robin and Tim, her son, are in a confidential relationship and Robin does whatever Tim says to do. Robin contracted to sell some corporate stock to Tim for an unfairly low price because Tim demanded that she do so. In this case, this contract can be avoided due to undue influence.
   b. Employer persuaded Ron to agree to an employment contract that paid a salary of $50,000, not $70,000 as Ron wanted. In this case, this contract can be avoided due to duress.
   c. Rex threatened to injure Ina's child unless Ina lent $10,000 to Rex. Due to these threats, Ina felt compelled to agree to loan the money to Rex. This contract is voidable due to duress.
   d. a and c.

Case Problems

Answer the following problems, briefly explaining your answers.

1. When Nancy was 16 years old, she bought a pedigree dog on credit for $200. While Nancy was a minor she made numerous payments, paying off the entire contract price. The dog has now contracted a serious illness. Nancy has just turned 18, and she is trying to decide what to do with the dog.

    (a) Did Nancy ratify the contract by paying the contract price while she was a minor?
    (b) Can Nancy avoid the contract? If so, what must Nancy return, and what is she is entitled to be repaid?
    (c) If Nancy keeps the dog for another year to breed it, can she avoid the contract at that time?

    _____

    _____

    _____

    _____

2. Lon is selling his home that has a severely damaged foundation. This damage is obvious. The home also has asbestos inside its walls, but this condition cannot be discovered without tearing the walls apart.

    (a) Under traditional rules, does Lon have a duty to volunteer information to prospective buyers regarding the obviously damaged foundation?
    (b) Can Lon plaster over the damaged foundation in order to hide the damage?
    (c) Under modern rules, does Lon have a duty to disclose the asbestos condition to prospective buyers?

    _____

    _____

    _____

3. Seller contracted to sell an airplane to Buyer. Seller intentionally misrepresented to Buyer that the plane did not have any mechanical problems. In fact, the plane had serious defects that rendered the plane unsafe to operate. Buyer was unaware of these defects, and Buyer was induced into making this contract due to Buyer's reliance on Seller's misrepresentation.

    (a) Did Seller commit fraud?
    (b) Is the contract between Seller and Buyer voidable?

    _____

    _____

    _____

    _____

Internet Exercise

Using the Internet, locate and print out a company's order form for one of its products.

1. Identify the web site where you located the order form.
2. Does the order form include a representation regarding the age or capacity of the person placing the order? Would it be wise to include such a term in the order form? Explain.

_____

_____

_____

_____

CPA REVIEW

The following questions were given on past CPA examinations. The answers for these questions are the unofficial answers prepared by the American Institute of Certified Public Accountants, Inc. (AICPA). All material is reproduced with permission of the AICPA.

_____ 1. On May 1, 1985, Mint, a 16-year old, purchased a sail boat from Sly Boats. Mint used the boat for six months at which time he advertised it for sale. Which of the following statements is correct?
   a. The sale of the boat to Mint was void, thereby requiring Mint to return the boat and Sly to return the money received.
   b. The sale of the boat to Mint may be avoided by Sly at its option.
   c. Mint's use of the boat for six months after the sale on May 1 constituted a ratification of that contract.
   d. Mint may disaffirm the May 1 contract at any time prior to reaching majority.

_____ 2. Payne entered into a written agreement to sell a parcel of land to Stevens. At the time the agreement was executed, Payne had consumed alcoholic beverages. Payne's ability to understand the nature and terms of the contract was not impaired. Stevens did not believe that Payne was intoxicated. The contract is
   a. Void as a matter of law.
   b. Legally binding on both parties.
   c. Voidable at Payne's option.
   d. Voidable at Stevens' option.

_____ 3. To prevail in a common law action for fraud in the inducement, a plaintiff must prove that the
   a. Defendant was an expert with regard to the misrepresentations.
   b. Defendant made the misrepresentations with knowledge of their falsity and with an intention to deceive.
   c. Misrepresentations were in writing.
   d. Plaintiff was in a fiduciary relationship with the defendant.

_____ 4. Which of the following, if intentionally misstated by a seller to a buyer, would be considered a fraudulent inducement to make a contract?
   a. Nonexpert opinion.
   b. Appraised value.
   c. Prediction.
   d. Immaterial fact.

_____ 5. Miller negotiated the sale of Miller's liquor store to Jackson. Jackson asked to see the prior year's financial statements. Using the store's checkbook, Miller prepared a balance sheet and profit and loss statement as well as he could. Miller told Jackson to have an accountant examine Miller's records because Miller was not an accountant. Jackson failed to do so and purchased the store in reliance on Miller's financial statements. Jackson later learned that the financial statements included several errors that resulted in a material overstatement of assets and net income. Miller was not aware that the errors existed. Jackson sued Miller, claiming Miller misrepresented the store's financial condition and that Jackson relied on the financial statements in making the decision to acquire the store. Which of the following statements is correct?
   a. Jackson will prevail if the errors in the financial statements were material.
   b. Jackson will not prevail because Jackson's reliance on the financial statement was not reasonable.
   c. Money damages is the only remedy available to Jackson if, in fact, Miller has committed a misrepresentation.
   d. Jackson would be entitled to rescind the purchase even if the errors in the financial statements were not material.

_____ 6. Paco Corp., a building contractor, offered to sell Preston several pieces of used construction equipment. Preston was engaged in the business of buying and selling equipment. Paco's written offer had been prepared by a secretary who typed the total price as $10,900, rather than $109,000, which was the approximate fair market value of the equipment. Preston, on receipt of the offer, immediately accepted it. Paco learned of the error in the offer and refused to deliver the equipment to Preston unless Preston agreed to pay $109,000. Preston has sued Paco for breach of contract. Which of the following statements is correct?
   a. Paco will not be liable because there has been a mutual mistake of fact.
   b. Paco will be able to rescind the contract because Preston should have known that the price was erroneous.
   c. Preston will prevail because Paco is a merchant.
   d. The contract between Paco and Preston is void because the price set forth in the offer is substantially less than the equipment's fair market value.

_____ 7. Maco, Inc. and Kent contracted for Kent to provide Maco certain consulting services at an hourly rate of $20. Kent's normal hourly rate was $90 per hour, the fair market value of the services. Kent agreed to the $20 rate because Kent was having serious financial problems. At the time the agreement was negotiated, Maco was aware of Kent's financial condition and refused to pay more than $20 per hour for Kent's services. Kent has now sued to rescind the contract with Maco, claiming duress by Maco during the negotiations. Under the circumstances, Kent will
   a. Win, because Maco refused to pay the fair market value of Kent's services.
   b. Win, because Maco was aware of Kent's serious financial problems.
   c. Lose, because Maco's actions did not constitute duress.

CHAPTER 15
CONSIDERATION

MAKE THE CONNECTION

SUMMARY

A promise is not binding if there is no consideration for the promise. Consideration is what the promisor requires as the price for his promise. That price may be doing an act, refraining from the doing of an act, or merely promising to do or to refrain. In a bilateral contract, it is necessary to find that the promise of each party is supported by consideration. If either promise is not so supported, it is not binding, and the agreement of the parties in not a contract. Consequently, the agreement cannot be enforced. When a promise is the consideration, it must be a binding promise. The binding character of a promise is not affected by the circumstance that there is a condition precedent to the performance promised. A promise to do what one is already obligated to do is not consideration, although some exceptions are made. Such exceptions include the rendering of a partial performance or a modified performance accepted as a good-faith adjustment to a changed situation, a compromise and release of claims, a part-payment check, and a compromise of creditors. Because consideration is the price that is given to obtain the promise, past benefits conferred on the promisor cannot be consideration.

A promise to refrain from doing an act can be consideration. A promise to refrain from suing or asserting a particular claim can be consideration. When consideration is forbearance to assert a claim, it is immaterial whether the claim is valid as long as the claim has been asserted in the good-faith belief that it was valid.

When the promisor obtains the consideration specified for the promise, the law is not ordinarily concerned with the value or adequacy of that consideration.

Under the doctrine of promissory estoppel a court may enforce a promise lacking consideration where it is the only way to avoid injustice.

LEARNING OUTCOMES
After studying this chapter, you should be able to

A. GENERAL PRINCIPLES—CONSIDERATION
LO.1   Explain what constitutes consideration.

B. SPECIAL SITUATIONS
LO.2   Distinguish between a "preexisting legal obligation" and "past consideration".
LO.3   Explain why promises based on moral obligations lack consideration.

C. EXCEPTIONS TO THE LAWS OF CONSIDERATION
LO.4   List the exceptions to the requirement of consideration.
LO.5   Explain the "fundamental idea" underlying promissory estoppel

CHAPTER OUTLINE

A. GENERAL PRINCIPLES

Consideration is a required element for a contract. In general, an agreement is not a legally binding contract and it will not be enforced unless each party to the agreement gives consideration.

139

1. CONSIDERATION DEFINED AND EXPLAINED

GENERAL RULES. ▶ Consideration is what a contracting party demands and receives in exchange for undertaking a legal obligation. ▶ Consideration in a bilateral contract is the promise by the offeror and the promise by the offeree. ▶ Consideration in a unilateral contract is the offeror's promise and the offeree's actual performance of a requested act or actual forbearance from doing an act. ▶ A promise or an agreement is not binding if it is not supported by consideration.
▶ A person can refuse to perform a promise or an agreement without being liable unless the promise or agreement is made pursuant to a contract that is supported by consideration.
STUDY HINTS. ▶ A party gives consideration if the party: (1) undertakes a new legal obligation; and (2) the obligation is undertaken pursuant to an agreed exchange for the other party's promise, act, or forbearance. ▶ In some states, consideration is defined as a benefit received by the promisor or a detriment undertaken by the promisee.
▶ **LEARNING OUTCOME EXAMPLES.** See the "bargained for exchange" example involving Beth and Kerry, textbook p. 332; see the "benefit-detriment" approach to consideration example, textbook p. 332.

2. GIFTS

GENERAL RULE. A promise to make a gift is not binding because consideration is not given for the promise.
LIMITATIONS. ▶ Once a gift has been made, the donor cannot take it back. ▶ A charitable subscription, e.g., a pledge to a church, is enforceable if the charity has relied upon the subscription.

3. ADEQUACY OF CONSIDERATION

GENERAL RULES. ▶ Courts do not examine the adequacy of considerations exchanged. ▶ A contract is enforceable even if the considerations exchanged are not of equal value.
LIMITATION. A significant difference between the considerations exchanged by the parties may indicate that the contract is the result of fraud, mistake, undue influence, or duress.

4. FORBEARANCE AS CONSIDERATION

GENERAL RULE. ▶ Forbearance from doing, or a promise to forbear from doing, an act that one is legally entitled to do is consideration. ▶ Examples: (1) promise not to sue for breach of contract or for damages relating to a disputed debt; (2) promise not to sue for injuries caused by another person; (3) insurance releases; (4) promise not to assert a good faith legal claim; (5) an employee's promise not to compete against his or her employer after the employment has ended.
LIMITATION. A promise not to assert a claim is consideration only if the claim is valid or is made in good faith. A promise not to assert a bad faith claim that has no merit is not consideration.

5. ILLUSORY PROMISES

GENERAL RULES. ▶ A promise is consideration only if it actually imposes a legal obligation on a party. ▶ An illusory promise is not consideration. ▶ An illusory promise is a promise that imposes no actual duty on the promisor.
LIMITATION. A promise that imposes a legal obligation is consideration even if: (1) the obligation is conditioned on the occurrence of an event; or (2) the agreement can be canceled by giving notice.
STUDY HINT. ▶ Frequently, an illusory promise is a promise to do something only if the promisor decides in the future that he or she wishes to do it. ▶ Example: " I promise to buy your car next week if I still want to buy it at that time."

B. SPECIAL SITUATIONS

6. PREEXISTING LEGAL OBLIGATION

GENERAL RULES. ► Promising to do an act that one has a legal duty to do is not consideration. ► A person may have a preexisting duty to do an act as a result of: (1) statutes (criminal or civil); (2) general rules of law (e.g., tort law); (3) duties relating to holding a government position (e.g., duties of elected officials or police officers); or (4) an existing contract between the parties.

LIMITATION. A party *does* give consideration if a party promises to perform a preexisting duty *and* also promises to do something else that the party is not legally required to do.

STUDY HINTS. ► Consideration generally requires that a party undertake a new legal obligation. ► A new legal obligation is undertaken if: (1) a person promises to do or does an act that he or she is not legally required to do; or (2) a person promises to forbear (refrain) from doing or actually forbears from doing an act that he or she is legally entitled to do. ► Everyone has many legal obligations to do certain things and to refrain from doing certain things. Promising to perform or performing such preexisting duties is not consideration.

► **LEARNING OUTCOME EXAMPLE.** See the preexisting duty example involving Officer Rogers on textbook p. 336.

Common situations that involve the question of preexisting legal obligations include the following:

(a) *Completion of contract (and contract modification)*

GENERAL RULES. ► In general, a promise by a contracting party to complete a contract that the party already has a duty to complete is not consideration. ► A contract modification is effective only if both parties give consideration pursuant to the modification agreement. ► Consideration is given if a party agrees to complete an existing contract *and* the party also agrees to do something that is not required. Example: For an extra $300, Painter agrees to paint a house, as required, and also agrees to paint a barn, a new obligation.

LIMITATIONS. ► There is a trend to enforce a good faith price adjustment despite the lack of consideration if unusual, unforeseen events cause the parties to voluntarily adjust the price. ► Under the UCC, a good faith modification of a contract to sell goods does not need consideration to be binding.

(b) *Compromise and release of claims*

➤ A creditor's agreement to accept a debtor's partial payment of an liquidated (undisputed) debt in return for a release of the debtor from the balance of the debt is not supported by consideration. The creditor may accept the payment and still sue for the balance of the debt.

➤ An agreement to pay and to accept a certain amount as complete satisfaction of an unliquidated debt or claim is supported by consideration and legally binds the parties.

(c) *Part-payment checks*

A creditor's cashing of a check that is part payment of a disputed debt constitutes a release of the debtor from the balance of the debt if the check states that it constitutes payment in full. In some states the same result may occur even if the debt is undisputed.

(d) *Composition of creditors*

An agreement by creditors to accept part payment as payment in full is supported by consideration and is binding if the agreement is made pursuant to a composition of creditors.

7. PAST CONSIDERATION

▶ A promise (or act or forbearance) is consideration only if it is undertaken pursuant to an agreed exchange. In other words, to be consideration a promise must be made because it is the price demanded for the other party's promise. ▶ Consequently, past consideration (benefit voluntarily given in the past) cannot be consideration, and a later promise to pay for this benefit is not binding. ▶ **LEARNING OUTCOME EXAMPLE.** See the example involving Fred O'Neal where he found out the past consideration is no consideration rule, textbook p. 338.

8. MORAL OBLIGATION

▶ In most states, a promise to do something is not consideration and is not legally enforceable if it is merely made out of a sense of moral obligation and it is not made in exchange for something of value. ▶ **LEARNING OUTCOME EXAMPLE.** See the example of the gratuitous deeds of Tom Synder on textbook p. 336.

C. EXCEPTIONS TO THE LAWS OF CONSIDERATION

9. EXCEPTIONS TO CONSIDERATION

Consideration is not required in the following situations:

➢ *Charitable subscriptions*: Pledges to charities are generally binding regardless of consideration.

➢ *Uniform Commercial Code*: The following do not require consideration: (1) a firm offer (i.e., a merchant's signed, written promise not to revoke an offer to buy or sell goods); (2) a good faith modification of a contract to sell goods; and (3) a written waiver of a claim for damages for breach of a commercial contract.

Promissory estoppel: ▶ Promissory estoppel permits enforcement of a promise if: (1) a promisor should expect that a promise will induce the promisee to substantially rely on the promise; (2) the promise does induce such reliance; and (3) injustice can only be avoided by enforcing the promise. ▶ *Promissory estoppel* does not apply unless a promisee actually relies on the promise. ▶ If promissory estoppel applies, a promise is enforced even if the promisee did not give consideration. ▶ **LEARNING OUTCOME EXAMPLE.** See the *Chaplake Holdings* case where the court enforced Chrysler's promise in order to correct an injustice, textbook p. 341.

CONCEPT REVIEW AND APPLICATIONS

Matching Exercise

Select the term or phrase that best matches a definition or statement stated below. Each term or phrase is the best match for only one statement or definition. Not all terms and phrases will necessarily be used.

cancellation provision

composition of creditors

consideration

forbearance

illusory promise

past consideration

promissory estoppel

_____ 1. Contract term that allows a contracting party to terminate the agreement under stated circumstances.

_____ 2. Benefit previously given as a voluntary gesture and not because the benefit was the price demanded for another's promise or act.

_____ 3. Price that is demanded and received in exchange for a promise, act, or forbearance by another.

_____ 4. Doctrine that permits enforcement of a promise if a promisor should reasonably expect that the promise will induce the promisee to substantially rely on the promise, and the promise does induce reliance in such a manner that injustice can only be avoided by enforcing the promise.

_____ 5. Refraining from doing (i.e., not doing) an act.

_____ 6. Agreement among creditors that each shall accept a part payment as full payment in consideration of the other creditors doing the same.

_____ 7. Promise that does not impose any legal duty.

True/False

Write **T** if the statement is true, write **F** if it is false.

_____ 1. An agreement is not legally binding unless each party to the agreement gives consideration.

_____ 2. A contracting party gives consideration if the party is required to perform a new legal obligation and this is true even if the benefit from this performance is to be given to a third person and not directly to the other contracting party.

_____ 3. A promise to make a gift is legally binding.

_____ 4. If a person agrees to pay more for something than it is worth, then the agreement is not a contract and it is not legally binding because the consideration is not adequate.

_____ 5.   A promise cannot be consideration if it is conditioned upon the occurrence of another event.

_____ 6.   A promise to do something only if the promisor decides that he or she wants to do it is an illusory promise and it is not consideration.

_____ 7.   There is a trend to uphold a reasonable, good faith price adjustment even though consideration is not given for the adjustment if extraordinary unforeseeable events justify the adjustment.

_____ 8.   Consideration is not required to modify a contract for the sale of goods.

_____ 9.   The release of a good faith claim is not consideration if the claim ultimately proves to be invalid.

_____ 10. A charitable subscription (pledge) cannot be legally enforced if the charity doesn't give consideration for the subscription.

Multiple Choice

_____ 1.   Which agreement is sufficiently supported by consideration to be a contract?
   a.   Alex and Wendy entered into an agreement whereby Alex promised to name Wendy as the beneficiary under his life insurance policy. Wendy did not promise or do anything in return.
   b.   Rick promised to pay $500 to Diane because she had been a good friend and voluntarily took care of him during a recent illness.
   c.   Ann agreed to pay $400 to Rod in exchange for Rod's promise to transfer title to his car to Ann's son.
   d.   Hal agreed to pay $500 to Juan because Hal felt morally obligated to pay this sum because Juan had voluntarily tutored Hal the previous semester.

_____ 2.   Which promise by Penny is consideration?
   a.   On March 1, Penny signed a lease agreement. Pursuant to this agreement Penny promised to rent a house on March 20 if, at that time, she still wanted to rent the house.
   b.   Penny signed an agreement whereby she promised to buy a parcel of land from Seller. However, Penny's promise was conditioned on the zoning board's agreeing to rezone the land.
   c.   Penny signed an agreement whereby Penny promised to lease a car. However, Penny can terminate the agreement by giving six months' prior written notice.
   d.   b and c.

_____ 3.   Which promise by Traci is consideration?
   a.   In exchange for Jack's promise to pay Traci $1,000, Traci (a police officer) promised to find and arrest the person who had vandalized Jack's store.
   b.   In exchange for Kim's promise to pay Traci $500, Traci promised to refrain from publishing an article that would slander Kim (a tort).
   c.   In exchange for Beth's promise to pay Traci $200, Traci promised not to breach an existing contract between Beth and Traci.
   d.   In exchange for Emilio's promise to pay Traci $1,000, Traci promised to refrain from using illegal drugs, and she also promised to enroll herself in a drug rehabilitation program.

     4. Rob contracted to build a garage for Tim. The contract required Rob to pay for all materials and labor. Later, Tim promised to pay Rob an additional $1,000. Under *traditional* rules, Tim's promise to pay the additional $1,000 is legally binding if it is given for:

     a. Rob's promise to complete the original contract with Tim.

     b. Rob's promise to complete the original contract, if labor costs are higher than Rob expected.

     c. Rob's promise to complete the original contract with Tim and his promise to construct a shed that Rob was not obligated to build.

     d. Rob's promise not to breach the original contract with Tim.

     5. In which situation is the creditor entitled to sue for the unpaid balance of the debt?

     a. Alice owed Otis $500. The debt was not disputed. Alice and Otis orally agreed that Alice would pay $200 in exchange for Otis' promise to release Alice from the balance of the debt.

     b. Dan hired May to paint his home for $1,000. There was an honest dispute about whether the work was done properly. Pursuant to a compromise agreement, Dan paid $800 as payment in full.

     c. Angie contractually agreed to pay Harry $300 for a tune-up of her car. There is an honest dispute regarding the amount owed because the car still frequently stalls. Angie gave Harry a $150 check that stated that it was payment in full. Harry endorsed and cashed the check.

     d. Pursuant to a composition of creditors, Oscar (a creditor) agreed to accept $500 as payment in full of a $1,000 debt, and Debtor paid the $500 to Oscar.

     6. Which agreement is sufficiently supported by consideration to be a contract?

     a. Randy and Alice were in an auto accident, and there is an honest dispute regarding who was at fault. Randy agreed to pay Alice $500 in exchange for her promise not to sue him.

     b. At the time Sue was hired as general manager, she agreed not to compete against Employer after her employment ended.

     c. Jody suffered a self-inflicted injury, but she falsely blamed Stu for the injury. Stu agreed to pay $1,000 to Jody in exchange for Jody's promise not to sue Stu for her injury.

     d. a and b.

     7. Which promise or agreement is generally *not* binding?

     a. Lynn promised to donate $100 to a charity that operates a shelter for abused children. The charity relied upon Lynn's promise, but promised nothing in return.

     b. Seller and Buyer agreed to modify a land sale contract by reducing the acreage that Seller was obligated to convey. However, the price was not reduced and Seller gave no consideration for this contract modification.

     c. Seller and Buyer in good faith agreed to modify a contract for the sale of a car by reducing the price from $400 to $350. Buyer gave no consideration for this contract modification.

     d. b and c.

Case Problems

Answer the following problems, briefly explaining your answers.

1. Aries Inc. took the following actions regarding its employees: (a) Aries agreed to pay Randy a $5,000 bonus for extra services that Randy voluntarily performed the previous year; (b) Aries agreed to pay Fred a $1,000 bonus in exchange for his promise not to breach an existing contract with Aries; and (c) Aries refused to perform a one-year contract with Hill because Aries had contractually agreed to pay Hill $30,000 pursuant to this contract, but his services were only worth $15,000.
    a) Is the agreement with Randy legally binding? (b) Is the agreement with Fred legally binding? (c) Is Aries entitled to refuse to perform its contract with Hill because the consideration it is receiving is inadequate?

_____

_____

_____

2. Lad lived in Virginia. Ratco, a California firm, repeatedly called Lad and promised that Ratco would hire Lad if he ever lived in California. (Note: Lad and Ratco never entered into an employment contract, and Lad never gave consideration for Ratco's promise to hire him.) With Ratco's encouragement and in reasonable reliance on Ratco's promises, Lad quit his job, sold his home, and moved his family to California. When Lad arrived in California, Ratco refused to hire him. Is Ratco's promise to hire Lad enforceable under promissory estoppel?

_____

_____

_____

_____

Internet Exercise

Tom, manager of Tom's Used Autos, offered to sell a car to Lilly for $4,500. Lilly replied that she had to first discuss this offer with her husband. Tom orally promised to keep the offer open for 24 hours. Lilly returned two hours later, and Tom told her that the price was now $4,700. Lilly protested, but finally agreed to pay the $4,700. After contracting, the parties discovered that the car's engine needed $300 worth of repairs, whereupon Lilly and Tom agreed to modify the contract to reduce the price to $4,400.

1. Using the Internet locate and identify the sections of UCC Article 2 that govern this case.
2. Was Tom's original offer an enforceable firm offer? Was Tom entitled to revoke his offer when he did?
3. Is the parties' agreement to modify the contract enforceable even though Lilly did not give consideration?

_____

_____

_____

_____

CPA REVIEW

The following questions were given on CPA examinations. The answers for these questions are the unofficial answers prepared by the American Institute of Certified Public Accountants, Inc. (AICPA). All material is reproduced with permission of the AICPA.

_____ 1. In determining whether the consideration requirement has been satisfied to form a contract, the courts will be required to decide whether the consideration
   a. Was bargained for.
   b. Was fair and adequate.
   c. Has sufficient economic value.
   d. Conforms to the subjective intent of the parties.

_____ 2. For there to be consideration for a contract, there must be
   a. A bargained-for detriment to the promisor(ee) or a benefit to the promisee(or).
   b. A manifestation of mutual assent.
   c. Genuineness of assent.
   d. Substantially equal economic benefits to both parties.

_____ 3. In which of the following situations does the first promise serve as valid consideration for the second promise?
   a. A police officer's promise to catch a thief for a victim's promise to pay a reward.
   b. A builder's promise to complete a contract for a purchaser's promise to extend the time for completion.
   c. A debtor's promise to pay $500 for a creditor's promise to forgive the balance a $600 liquidated (undisputed) debt.
   d. A debtor's promise to pay $500 for a creditor's promise to forgive the balance of a $600 disputed debt.

_____ 4. Kay, an art collector, promised Hammer, an art student, that if Hammer could obtain certain rare artifacts within two weeks, Kay would pay for Hammer's postgraduate education. At considerable effort and expense, Hammer obtained the specified artifacts within the two-week period. When Hammer requested payment, Kay refused. Kay claimed that there was no consideration for the promise. Hammer would prevail against Kay based on
   a. Unilateral contract.
   b. Unjust enrichment.
   c. Public policy.
   d. Quasi contract.

_____ 5. Dye sent Hill a written offer to sell a tract of land located in Newtown for $60,000. The parties were engaged in a separate dispute. The offer stated that it would be irrevocable for 60 days if Hill would promise to refrain from suing Dye during this time. Hill promptly delivered a promise not to sue during the term of the offer and to forego suit if Hill accepted the offer. Dye subsequently decided that the possible suit by Hill was groundless and therefore phoned Hill and revoked the offer 15 days after making it. Hill mailed an acceptance on the 20th day. Dye did not reply. Under the circumstances,
   a. Dye's offer was supported by consideration and was not revocable when accepted.
   b. Dye's written offer would be irrevocable even without consideration.
   c. Dye's silence was an acceptance of Hill's promise.
   d. Dye's revocation, not being in writing, was invalid.

_____ 6. Grove is seeking to avoid performing a promise to pay Brook $1,500. Grove is relying on lack of consideration on Brook's part. Grove will prevail if he can establish that
   a. Prior to Grove's promise, Brook had already performed the requested act.
   b. Brook's only claim of consideration was the relinquishment of a legal right.
   c. Brook's asserted consideration is only worth $400.
   d. The consideration to be performed by Brook will be performed by a third party.

_____ 7. Which of the following requires consideration in order to be binding on the parties?
   a. A written promise signed by a merchant to keep an offer to sell goods open for 10 days.
   b. Material modification of a sale of goods contract under the UCC.
   c. Ratification of a contract by a person after reaching the age of majority.
   d. Material modification of a contract involving the sale of real estate.

_____ 8. Which of the following will be legally binding despite lack of consideration?
   a. An employer's promise to make a cash payment to a deceased employee's family in recognition of the employee's many years of service.
   b. A promise to donate money to a charity on which the charity relied in incurring large expenditures.
   c. A modification of a signed contract to purchase a parcel of land.
   d. A merchant's oral promise to keep an offer open for 60 days.

CHAPTER 16
LEGALITY AND PUBLIC POLICY

MAKE THE CONNECTION

SUMMARY

When an agreement is illegal, it is ordinarily void and no contract arises from it. Courts will not allow one party to an illegal agreement to bring suit against the other party. There are some exceptions to this, such as when the parties are not equally guilty or when the law's purpose in making the agreement illegal is to protect the person who is bringing suit. When possible, an agreement will be interpreted as being lawful. Even when a particular provision is held unlawful, the balance of the agreement may be saved so that the net result is a contract minus the clause that was held illegal.

The term *illegality* embraces situations in unconscionable contract clauses in which the courts hold that contract provisions are unenforceable because they are too harsh or oppressive to one of the parties to a transaction. If the clause is part of a standard form contract drafted by the party having superior bargaining power and is presented on a take-it-or-leave-it basis (a contract of adhesion) and the substantive terms of the clause itself are unduly oppressive, the clause will be found to be unconscionable and not enforced.

Whether a contract is contrary to public policy may be difficult to determine because public policy is not precisely defined. That which is harmful to the public welfare or general good is contrary to public policy. Contracts condemned as contrary to public policy include those designed to deprive the weaker party of a benefit that the lawmaker desired to provide, agreements injuring public service, and wagers and private lotteries. Statutes commonly make the wager illegal as a form of gambling. The private lottery is any plan under which, for a consideration, a person has a chance to win a prize.

Illegality may consist of the violation of a statute or administrative regulation adopted to regulate business. An agreement not to compete may be illegal as a restraint of trade except when reasonable in its terms and when it is incidental to the sale of a business or to a contract of employment.

The charging by a lender of a higher rate of interest than allowed by law is usury. Courts must examine transactions carefully to see whether a usurious loan is disguised as a legitimate transaction.

LEARNING OUTCOMES
After studying this chapter, you should be able to

A. GENERAL PRINCIPLES
LO.1   Explain the general contract principles on "illegality."
LO.2   Explain the implied obligation on all parties of good faith and fair dealing.

B. AGREEMENTS AFFECTING PUBLIC WELFARE
LO.3   Understand that it is only in unusual situations that a contract provision will be unenforceable because it is unconscionable.

C. REGULATION OF BUSINESS
LO.4   Explain the rationale for requiring licenses to carry on as a business, trade, or profession
LO.5   Distinguish between noncompete clauses after the sale of a business and noncompete clauses in employment contracts

CHAPTER OUTLINE

A. GENERAL PRINCIPLES

Crime or tort

An agreement is illegal if its formation or performance: (1) is a crime or tort; (2) violates public policy; or (3) is unconscionable.

1. EFFECT OF ILLEGALITY

GENERAL RULES. ▶ Illegal agreements are generally void. ▶ In most cases, parties to an illegal agreement are denied remedies of any nature. A court will not require parties to perform an illegal agreement, and a court will not award damages because a party fails to perform.
STUDY HINT. Typically, a party to an illegal agreement may keep a benefit received pursuant to the agreement, and a court will not make the party pay for or return the benefit.
▶**LEARNING OUTCOME EXAMPLE.** See the unenforceable illegal lease to nonprofessionals example on textbook p. 348.

2. EXCEPTIONS TO EFFECT OF ILLEGALITY

GENERAL RULE. A party to an illegal agreement may obtain an appropriate judicial remedy if:
(1) the law that is violated is intended to protect that party; or (2) one party is not *in pari delicto*, in other words, one party is not as guilty as the other party.
STUDY HINT. An agreement that is legal on its face may be declared to be illegal if it is entered into for an illegal purpose.

3. PARTIAL ILLEGALITY

GENERAL RULE. If a contract contains legal and illegal promises and the promises can be severed from one another, then the legal promises can be enforced but the illegal promises are void.
STUDY HINT. If a contract can be interpreted to be legal or illegal, then a court will ordinarily adopt the interpretation that makes the contract legal.

4. CRIMES AND CIVIL WRONGS

▶ Agreements that require a party to commit a crime or a tort are illegal and void. ▶ **LEARNING OUTCOME EXAMPLE.** See the example where a contract to manufacture and sell illegal slot machines is void, textbook p. 350.

5. GOOD FAITH AND FAIRNESS

GENERAL RULE. In every contract, the law requires parties to act fairly and in good faith.
STUDY HINT. A contracting party may be entitled to an appropriate legal or equitable remedy if the other contracting party fails to live up to these minimum standards of behavior.
LEARNING OUTCOME EXAMPLE. See the example of the Vermont landlord who deprived a tenant of her rights under a lease, textbook p. 350.

6. UNCONSCIONABLE CLAUSES

GENERAL RULES. ▶ An unconscionable agreement or clause is unenforceable. ▶ A test for unconscionability that is used in some states requires both procedural unconscionability (i.e., unfair circumstances surrounding the making of the agreement) and substantive unconscionability (i.e., the terms of the agreement are unfair or oppressive to one party). ▶ A second test used by some courts consider whether the doctrine of adhesion and whether a contract term is oppressive.
LIMITATION. A contract is not unconscionable simply because a party makes a bad bargain.
STUDY HINTS. ▶ A contract of adhesion is one that is made on a take-it-or-leave-it basis. ▶ If only a contractual term is improper, courts may enforce the contract but not the improper clause.
LEARNING OUTCOME EXAMPLE. See the *Kramper Family Farm* example where the court refused to consider whether the contract was fair or unfair, wise or foolish, textbook p. 350.

B. AGREEMENTS AFFECTING PUBLIC WELFARE

7. AGREEMENTS CONTRARY TO PUBLIC POLICY

GENERAL RULES. ▶ Public policy creates standards of conduct necessary to protect the government, the legal system, and fundamental social values, interests, and institutions, such as marriage. ▶ An agreement or a term in an agreement is unenforceable if it violates an important public policy. ▶ The Supreme Court has found that provisions in employment contracts that require arbitration of employee claims against employers generally are enforceable and do not violate public policy.
LIMITATION. ▶ An agreement may violate public policy and be unenforceable even if it does not involve a crime or tort, or violate a statute. ▶ Example: unreasonable covenant not to compete. ▶ An arbitration provision in an employment contract may be unenforceable if it is so one-sided in favor of the employer so as to be unconscionable.
STUDY HINTS. ▶ By implication, statutes may establish public policy. Thus, an agreement that violates a statute, which creates a public policy, may be void even if the statute does not expressly state this consequence. ▶ Agreements that eliminate a statutory benefit or protection are often unenforceable because they violate public policy. ▶ Whether a contract is invalidated for public policy reasons often involves balancing the interests of society with the contracting parties' interests.

8. GAMBLING, WAGERS, AND LOTTERIES

GENERAL RULES. ▶ Gambling contracts, wagers, and lotteries are generally illegal. ▶ Elements of a wager or lottery are: (1) for a chance; (2) to win a prize; (3) one pays consideration.
LIMITATIONS. ▶ In many states, government-sponsored lotteries are legal. ▶ In some (but not all) states, bingo games, lotteries, and raffles are legal if the proceeds go to charity.
STUDY HINTS. ▶ Promotional giveaways and games that give prizes for guessing an answer are legal if one is not required to buy anything in order to win. ▶ Bets on sporting events are illegal.

C. REGULATION OF BUSINESS

9. EFFECT OF VIOLATION

GENERAL RULE. A contract is void if it violates a statute or administrative rule that expressly states that the contract is void, or if violation of the statute or rule violates an important public policy.
LIMITATION. Some courts void a contract only if a law expressly requires this.

10. STATUTORY REGULATION OF CONTRACTS

Statutes often require certain types of contracts to include specified contractual terms. This is especially the case in connection with consumer contracts.

11. LICENSED CALLINGS OR DEALINGS

GENERAL RULE. A contract is void if performance of the contract requires a party to violate a licensing statute that is intended to guard against unqualified work.
LIMITATION. A contract may be valid and can be enforced if the contract only requires violation of a statute that is intended to only raise money for the government.
STUDY HINTS. ▶ Example of void agreement: party is not licensed to practice law or medicine or to be a real estate broker. ▶ Example of valid contract: party does not have a required license to do landscaping work and the license is merely required in order to raise money for the government.

12. CONTRACTS IN RESTRAINT OF TRADE

Contracts that *unreasonably* restrain (diminish) trade (competition) are illegal and void.

13. AGREEMENTS NOT TO COMPETE

GENERAL RULE. ▶ An agreement not to compete is legal if: (1) it relates to a sale of a business or employment; (2) it is necessary to protect the other party; and (3) it is for a reasonable time and area. ▶ Example: When Joan was hired as president of XYZ Co., she agreed that she would not compete against XYZ Co. in the city where XYZ Co. was located for one year after she quit.
STUDY HINT. If an agreement is unreasonable, some (but not all) courts will enforce the agreement for a reasonable time and area (the "blue pencil rule").
▶**LEARNING OUTCOME EXAMPLES.** See the example where the California court enforced a 5 year noncompete clause against the seller of a business, textbook p. 356; see the example involving Julie Murray's noncompete clause and why it was modified from 24 months to one year, textbook p. 357.

14. USURIOUS AGREEMENTS

GENERAL RULES. ▶ Usury is the charging of a greater rate of interest that is permitted by statute. ▶ Most states limit the rate of interest that may be charged for certain loans.
STUDY HINT. Interest includes any fees that are charged by a lender that exceed the reasonable expenses for making the loan.

CONCEPT REVIEW AND APPLICATIONS

Matching Exercise

Select the term or phrase that best matches a definition or statement stated below. Each term or phrase is the best match for only one statement or definition. Not all terms and phrases will necessarily be used.

contract of adhesion

good faith

in pari delicto

lotteries

public policy

usury

_____*lotteries*_____ 1. Scheme by which a consideration is given for a chance to win a prize; it consists of three elements: (1) there must be a payment of money or something of value for an opportunity to win, (2) a prize must be available, and (3) the prize must be offered by lot or chance.

_____*public policy*_____ 2. Standard or policy that furthers or protects fundamental public and social values or interests.

_____*contract of adhesion*_____ 3. Contract offered by a dominant party to a party with inferior bargaining power on a take-it-or-leave it basis.

_____*good faith*_____ 4. Under the UCC, a standard of conduct that requires a merchant who is buying or selling goods to act honestly and to follow reasonable business standards of fair dealing.

_____*in pari delicto*_____ 5. Equally wrong or equally at fault.

_____*usury*_____ 6. Lending money at a rate of interest greater than that permitted by law.

True/False

Write **T** if the statement is true, write **F** if it is false.

__F__ 1. If a contract includes an unconscionable clause, a court must void the entire agreement.

__F__ 2. A contract that only requires commission of a tort is generally legal and enforceable.

__T__ 3. Procedural unconscionability relates to the fairness of the circumstances surrounding the making of a contract.

__T__ 4. Unconscionable agreements are illegal and void.

F 5. A contract of adhesion is one that is made between two parties who have relatively equal bargaining power.

T 6. An agreement may violate public policy even if the agreement does not require a party to commit a crime or tort, or require a party to violate a statute.

T 7. All states now prohibit the noncompetition covenants in connection with the making of an employment contract.

T 8. Agreements to acquire a monopoly or to fix prices are unreasonable trade restraints and are void.

F 9. A covenant not to compete is illegal even if it is made in connection with the sale of a business, it is necessary to protect the buyer of the business, and it is for a reasonable time and area.

F 10. For purposes of determining whether a lender has committed usury, interest includes both the stated interest and all reasonable expenses incurred by the lender to make the loan and which are charged to the borrower..

Multiple Choice

1. Chemco and Glen entered into an illegal agreement whereby Glen agreed to wrongfully acquire and copy a competitor's new chemical formula in consideration for $10,000. Performance of the agreement would be a crime. If Chemco paid the $10,000 to Glen, but Glen failed to perform:
   a. A court would not require Glen to perform the agreement.
   b. A court would make Glen repay the $10,000 to Chemco.
   c. A court would make Glen pay for any damages Chemco suffered due to his failure to perform.
   d. All of the above.

2. Select the correct answer.
   a. J&J hired Mona, age 13, in violation of child labor laws. These laws protect children, such as Mona. If Mona works but she is not paid, Mona cannot obtain any judicial relief.
   b. Merchant agreed to give a car to the contest entrant whose name was selected. It was not necessary to purchase anything in order to enter the contest. This agreement is an unenforceable gambling transaction.
   c. Sonny made one contract to perform two services. One service is legal, the other service is illegal. Separate considerations are stated for each service. The illegal service does not taint or affect the legal service. Under these facts, the entire contract is unenforceable.
   d. a and b.

3. U-Store-It, Inc. contracted to store certain goods for Philip. Performance of this contract requires violation of a business regulation that is created by a civil (noncriminal) statute. The statute does not state whether offending contracts are valid or void. In most states:
   a. The contract is void. Violation of any business regulation renders a contract illegal and void.
   b. The contract is void if the statute offends an important public policy.
   c. The contract is valid. Violating a statute does not render a contract void.
   d. The contract is valid. Violating a statute does not render a contract void unless there is a crime involved.

_____ 4. Neal was hired as general manager for a food distributor doing business in Pork City, U.S.A. Neal managed all important customer accounts, and he was responsible for developing the company's sales strategy. When hired, Neal agreed not to compete in the food distribution business after he quit. (Pork City is located in a state that has not specifically prohibited covenants not to compete in connection with employment contracts). Under these facts, Neal's agreement would probably be:

a. Valid, if it prohibited Neal from competing in Pork City for one year after he quit.
b. Valid, if it prohibited Neal from competing anywhere in the state in which Pork City was located for ten years after he quit.
c. Valid regardless of its terms. All agreements not to compete are valid.
d. Void regardless of its terms. All agreements not to compete are illegal and void.

Case Problem

Answer the following problem, briefly explaining your answer.

Todd agreed to employ Mara as general contractor to make structural modifications to a residence. A person is legally required to be licensed to be a general contractor. To assure the competency of general contractors and to protect the public from unqualified work, this license requires extensive experience and successful completion of a comprehensive exam. Mara does not have the required license.

1. What is the purpose of the required statute?
2. Is the agreement between Todd and Mara valid or void?
3. If Mara performs the agreement but Todd fails to pay, can Mara enforce the agreement against Todd?

_____

_____

_____

_____

Internet Exercise

Kim is Director of the U.S. Department of Freeways. Kim makes the final decision for awarding federal road construction contracts. Kim is concerned that she may have had conflicts of interest relating to two recent government contracts that she approved. These contracts involved the following: (1) a contract between the government and Jack Co., who paid Kim $5,000 as a "special thank you" for the contract; and (2) a contract between the government and Farris Inc., a company that is owned by her best friend, Farris.

1. Using the Internet, locate and read 18 U.S.C. §201 and evaluate the legality of Kim's conduct in connection with these two contracts and whether these contracts are valid or void.
2. What could Kim have done differently to avoid a conflict of interest or appearance of conflict of interest?

_____

_____

_____

CPA REVIEW

The following questions were given on CPA examinations. The answers for these questions are the unofficial answers prepared by the American Institute of Certified Public Accountants, Inc. (AICPA). All material is reproduced with permission of the AICPA.

_____ 1. Which of the following is unenforceable because the subject matter is illegal?
   a. A contingent fee charged by an attorney to represent a plaintiff in a negligence action.
   b. An arbitration clause in a supply contract.
   c. A restrictive covenant in an employment contract prohibiting a former employee from using the employer's trade secrets.
   d. An employer's promise not to press embezzlement charges against an employee who agrees to make restitution.

_____ 2. Tell, an Ohio real estate broker, misrepresented to Allen that Tell was licensed in Michigan under Michigan's statute regulating real estate brokers. Allen signed a standard form listing contract agreeing to pay Tell a 6% commission for selling Allen's home in Michigan. Tell sold Allen's home. Under circumstances, Allen is
   a. Not liable to Tell for any amount because Allen signed a standard form contract.
   b. Not liable to Tell for any amount because Tell violated the Michigan licensing requirements.
   c. Liable to Tell only for the value of services under a quasi-contract theory.
   d. Liable to Tell for the full commission under a promissory estoppel theory.

_____ 3. Samm, a plumber, entered into a contract for $75,000 with Orr, Inc., to perform certain plumbing services in a building owned by Orr. After Samm had satisfactorily performed the work, Orr discovered that Samm had violated the state licensing statute by failing to obtain a plumbing license. The licensing statute was enacted merely to raise revenue for the state. An independent appraisal of Samm's work indicated that the building's fair market value increased by $70,000 as a result of Samm's work. The cost of the materials which Samm supplied was $35,000. If Samm sues Orr, Samm is entitled to
   a. $0
   b. $35,000
   c. $70,000
   d. $75,000

_____ 4. Todd is a licensed real estate broker in Ohio. One of Todd's largest clients, Sun Corp., contracted in writing with Todd to find a purchaser for its plant in New York and agreed to pay him a 6% commission if he were successful. Todd located a buyer who purchased the plant. Unknown to Todd, New York has a real estate broker's licensing statute which is regulatory in nature, intended to protect the public against unqualified persons. Todd violated the licensing statute by failing to obtain a New York license. If Sun refuses to pay Todd any commission and Todd brings an action against Sun, he will be entitled to recover
   a. Nothing.
   b. A fee based on the actual hours spent.
   c. The commission agreed upon.
   d. Out of pocket expenses only.

_____ 5. Parr is the vice-president of research of Lynx, Inc. When hired, Parr signed an employment contract prohibiting Parr from competing with Lynx during and after employment. While employed, Parr acquired knowledge of many of Lynx's trade secrets. If Parr wishes to compete with Lynx and Lynx refuses to give Parr permission, which of the following statements is correct?
   a. Parr has the right to compete with Lynx upon resigning from Lynx.
   b. Parr has the right to compete with Lynx only if fired from Lynx.
   c. In determining whether Parr may compete with Lynx, the court should not consider Parr's ability to obtain other employment.
   d. In determining whether Parr may compete with Lynx, the court should consider, among other factors, whether the agreement is necessary to protect Lynx's legitimate business interests.

_____ 6. Wert, an employee of Salam Corp., signed an agreement not to compete with Salam during and after being employed with Salam. Wert is the director of research and has knowledge of many of Salam's trade secrets. If Wert's employment with Salam is terminated and Wert wishes to compete with Salam, which of the following statements is not correct?
   a. The agreement is only enforceable if Wert voluntarily terminates his employment with Salam.
   b. The agreement must be necessary to protect Salam's legitimate interests in order to be enforceable.
   c. The geographic area covered by the agreement must be reasonable in order to be enforceable.
   d. The court will consider Wert's ability to obtain other employment against Salam's right to protect its business.

_____ 7. Parr is a CPA licensed to practice in State A. Parr entered into a contract with Jet, Inc., to perform an audit in State B for $50,000 (including expenses). After Parr had satisfactorily performed the audit, Jet discovered that Parr had violated State B's licensing statute by failing to obtain a CPA license in State B. Parr incurred $10,000 in expenses in connection with the audit. Jet refuses to pay any fee to Parr, arguing that it could have engaged a local CPA licensed in State B to perform the same services for $35,000 (including expenses). If Parr sues Jet based on breach of contract, Parr will be entitled to recover a maximum of
   a. $0
   b. $10,000
   c. $35,000
   d. $50,000

CHAPTER 17
WRITING, ELECTRONIC FORMS, AND
INTERPRETATION OF CONTRACTS

MAKE THE CONNECTION

SUMMARY

An oral agreement may be a contract unless it is the intention of the parties that they should not be bound by the agreement without a writing executed by them. Certain contracts must be evidenced by a writing, however, or else they cannot be enforced. The statutes that declare this exception are called *statutes of frauds*. Statutes of frauds commonly require that a contract be evidenced by writing in the case of (1) an agreement that cannot be performed within one year after the contract is made, (2) an agreement to sell any interest in land, (3) a promise to answer for the debt or default of another, (4) a promise by the executor or administrator of a decedent's estate to pay a claim against the estate from personal funds, (5) a promise made in consideration of marriage, and (6) a contract for the sale of goods for a purchase price of $500 or more.

To evidence a contract to satisfy a statute of frauds, there must be a writing of all essential terms. The writing must be signed by the defendant against whom suit is brought for enforcement of the contract.

If the applicable statute of frauds is not satisfied, the oral contract cannot be enforced. To avoid unjust enrichment, a plaintiff barred from enforcing an oral contract may in most cases recover from the other contracting party the reasonable value of the benefits conferred by the plaintiff on the defendant.

When there is a written contract, the question arises whether that writing is the exclusive statement of the parties' agreement. If the writing is the complete and final statement of the contract, parol evidence as to matters agreed to before or at the time the writing was signed is not admissible to contradict the writing. This is called the *parol evidence rule*. In any case, the parol evidence rule does not bar parol evidence when (1) the writing is ambiguous, (2) the writing is not a true statement of the agreement of the parties because of fraud, duress, or mistake, or (3) the existence, modification, or illegality of a contract is in controversy.

Because a contract is based on the agreement of the parties, courts must determine the intent of the parties manifested in the contract. The intent that is to be enforced is the intent as it reasonably appears to a third person. This objective intent is followed.

In interpreting a contract, ordinary words are to be given their ordinary meanings. If trade or technical terms have been used, they are interpreted according to their technical meanings. The court must consider the whole contract and not read a particular part out of context. When different writings are executed as part of the same transaction, or one writing refers to or incorporates another, all of the writings are to be read together as the contract of the parties.

When provisions of a contract are contradictory, the court will try to reconcile or eliminate the conflict. If this cannot be done, the conclusion may be that there is no contract because the conflict makes the agreement indefinite as to a material matter. In some cases, conflict is solved by considering the form of conflicting terms. Handwriting prevails over typing and a printed form, and typing prevails over a printed form. Ambiguity will be eliminated in some cases by the admission of parol evidence or by interpreting the provision strictly against the party preparing the contract, particularly when that party has significantly greater bargaining power.

159

LEARNING OUTCOMES
After studying this chapter, you should be able to

A. STATUTE OF FRAUDS
LO.1   Explain when a contract must be evidenced by a writing.
LO.2   Explain the effect of noncompliance with the statute of frauds.

B. PAROL EVIDENCE RULE
LO.3   Explain the parol evidence rule and the exceptions to this rule.

C. RULES OF CONSTRUCTION AND INTERPRETATION
LO.4   Understand the basic rule of contract construction that a contract is enforced according to its terms
LO.5   State the rules for interpreting ambiguous terms in a contract

CHAPTER OUTLINE

A.   STATUTE OF FRAUDS

1.   VALIDITY OF ORAL CONTRACTS

GENERAL RULE.   Broadly speaking, oral contracts are valid and courts will enforce oral contracts.

STUDY HINT.   It is sound business practice to stipulate at the beginning of negotiations that no one is bound until all parties sign a written contract.

2.   CONTRACTS THAT MUST BE EVIDENCED BY A WRITING

The following contracts are required by the statute of frauds to be evidenced by a writing to be enforceable:

(a) *Agreement that cannot be performed within one year after the contract is made*

GENERAL RULES.   ▶ A writing must evidence a contract that cannot be fully performed within one year from the date it is made. The one-year period begins the day after a contract is made (not when the work is to begin) and concludes the day performance will be completed. ▶There is no part performance exception for an oral contract that is not performable within one year.

LIMITATION.   A writing is not required if: (1) it is reasonably possible that a contract may be fully performed in less than one year; or (2) either party may terminate the contract at will, i.e., either party may terminate the contract whenever they desire to do so.

STUDY HINTS.   ▶ A writing is not excused merely because a breach of contract by a party may terminate the contract. ▶ Ordinarily, a contract for an unstated duration need not be in writing since it is usually possible to perform this type of contract in less than one year.
▶ An extension of a written contract that is not required to be in writing may be oral even though the contract requires all modifications to be in writing.

Promise to answer debt   over 1-year, sale ≥$500   161
Concerning marriage, Sale of lands
executor assumes debt

(b) Agreement to sell or a sale of an interest in land

GENERAL RULES. ▶ Contracts for the sale or transfer of any interest in land must be evidenced by a sufficient writing to be enforceable. Included in this category are: (1) contracts for the sale of land or buildings affixed to the land; (2) mortgages; and (3) option to purchase real property. ▶ Leases of real estate for more than one year must be evidenced by a writing, whereas oral leases of real estate for a term of less than one year are enforceable in some states.

LIMITATION. An oral land sale contract can be enforced in an action for specific performance if the buyer has taken possession of the property and made valuable improvements, the value of which is difficult to determine, or the buyer has taken possession and paid part of the purchase price.

(c) Promise to answer for the debt or default of another

GENERAL RULE. A promise to pay a debt or to perform an obligation of another party if that party fails to do so is required to be evidenced by a sufficient writing to be enforceable.

LIMITATIONS. ▶ If the main purpose for promising to pay another's debt is to benefit the party making the promise and not the debtor, a writing is not needed. Example: Dee owes Robert $800, but Dee cannot repay this debt. To enable Dee to repay him this debt, Robert orally promises Bank that if it lends Dee the $800 and she fails to repay the loan, then Robert will repay the loan to Bank. ▶ A promise to personally pay for a good or service that the other contracting party will merely deliver to a third party is not a promise to answer for the debt of another.

STUDY HINT. The most common type of promise that is subject to this statute is a guarantee whereby one promises to pay a debtor's obligation if the debtor fails to do so.

(d) Promise by the executor or administrator of a decedent's estate to pay a claim against the estate from personal funds

GENERAL RULE. A promise by a personal representative (an executor or administrator) to personally pay a debt of an estate must be evidenced by a writing to be enforceable.

LIMITATION. An oral promise by a personal representative that *the estate* will do something does not fall within this rule, and the oral promise may be enforced.

STUDY HINT. Ordinarily, an executor is not personally liable to pay an estate's debts.

(e) Promise made in consideration of marriage

A promise made in consideration for a person's promise to marry, or for actually marrying, another person is required by statute to be evidenced by a sufficient writing.

(f) Sale of goods

UCC Article 2 requires contracts for the sale of goods for a price of $500 or more to be evidenced by a writing.

(g) Promissory estoppel

The statute of frauds may not be applied if the party seeking to get around the statute of frauds is able to prove an enhanced promissory estoppel.

3. NOTE OR MEMORANDUM (REQUIRED WRITING)

GENERAL RULES. ▶ At common law, a writing must: (1) state the material contract terms (including price, subject matter, quantity, and parties); and (2) be signed by the party sought to be charged (i.e., the party who is asserting the statute of frauds as a defense for not performing a contract). ▶ More than one writing may be considered if they refer to one another or are sufficiently related to each other.

LIMITATIONS. ▶ Some states require the authorization of an agent to be written if the contract to be signed by the agent is required to be in writing. ▶ Under the Electronic Signatures in Global and National Commerce Act of 2000, electronically signed contracts cannot be denied legal effect because of the form of signature or because they are delivered electronically. ▶ Trusts, wills, and similar estate documents cannot be electronically signed.

STUDY HINTS. ▶ Any writing may suffice; a complete written contract signed by both parties is not needed. ▶ The writing may be letters, signed minutes of meetings, or other comparable writings. ▶ Any signature, initials, or symbol suffices if the party intends to use it as his or her signature. ▶ An electronic signature is any electronic sound, symbol or process that is associated with a contract and is executed with the intent to sign the contract.

4. EFFECT OF NONCOMPLIANCE

GENERAL RULE. An oral agreement that does not comply with a statute of frauds is voidable (in a few states, void) and cannot be judicially enforced if the defendant raises this defense.

LIMITATIONS. ▶ Parties may voluntarily perform an oral contract even though a writing was required. ▶ The statute of frauds cannot be used to rescind a fully performed oral contract. ▶ Only a party to the contract can raise the defense of the statute of frauds.

STUDY HINTS. ▶ If a contract is unenforceable, quasi contract entitles a party to recover the reasonable value for contract benefits that the party has given if the other party has not paid for such benefits. ▶ Violating the statute of frauds renders a contract voidable even if all other elements for a valid contract are present and no fraud actually occurred.

▶**LEARNING OUTCOME EXAMPLE.** See the example in which an oral contract cannot be enforced because it is not in writing, but the plaintiff may recover the reasonable value of the services rendered, textbook p. 377.

B. PAROL EVIDENCE RULE

5. EXCLUSION OF PAROL EVIDENCE (RULE FOR COMPLETE CONTRACTS)

GENERAL RULE. The parol evidence rule provides that the terms of a final, complete written contract cannot be added to, modified, or contradicted by evidence of oral statements or writings that were made before, or at the same time, the written contract was made.

LIMITATION. ▶ If a writing is intended to be a final statement of only part of a contract (an "incomplete contract"), then the parol evidence rule permits proof of prior matters to establish terms that are not expressly stated in the written contract and that are not otherwise implied by law into the contract. ▶ Example: Sam sold a TV to Julie pursuant to a written contract. The writing only stated the parties' agreement regarding price. In this situation, Julie can prove that during negotiations Sam orally promised to service the TV without charge for one year.

STUDY HINT. ▶ The parol evidence rule prohibits changing or adding terms even if parties previously agreed to other terms. ▶ Example: Seller and Buyer sign a final, complete written contract for the sale of a business. The contract clearly states that the business does not include a particular computer owned by Seller. In this case, the parol evidence rule would not allow Buyer to prove that Seller orally stated during negotiations that the business included the computer.

►LEARNING OUTCOME EXAMPLE. See the example in which the tenant is not allowed to call a witness to testify about a prior oral agreement that would add to and alter the written lease, textbook p. 379.

6. WHEN THE PAROL EVIDENCE RULE DOES NOT APPLY

The parol evidence rule does not prevent the use of parol evidence to:

> ➤ Explain the meaning of an ambiguous term, or to prove a special trade meaning for a word;

> ➤ Prove a trade usage or course of performance in connection with a contract for the sale of goods;

> ➤ Prove the existence of a contract defense, such as fraud, mistake, accident, or illegality; or

> ➤ Prove a contract modification that was agreed to *after* the making of the written contract.

C. RULES OF CONSTRUCTION AND INTERPRETATION

1. INTENTION OF THE PARTIES

A court seeks to determine what parties intended contract terms to mean so that it can enforce the contract in the manner intended by the parties. A court must enforce a contract according to the meaning the parties intended.

> ➤ *Meaning of words*: ► Prior dealings between parties may be used to interpret the meaning of words. ► Rules that are used by courts to interpret words include the following: (1) ordinary words are given their ordinary meaning; (2) technical words used in a technical setting are given their technical meaning; and (3) common meanings for words are typically used unless the parties clearly intended words to mean something else.

> ➤ *Incorporation by reference*: ► If a contract refers to and states that it incorporates (includes) another writing, this indicates an intent that the writing is a part of the contract. ► This rule applies only if the contract adequately describes the document or portion of it that is to be incorporated. ► LEARNING OUTCOME EXAMPLE. See the example of the interpretation of the word "costs" on textbook p. 381.

8. WHOLE CONTRACT

A contract should be interpreted as a whole, and every word should be given effect if it is reasonable to do so.

9. CONTRADICTORY AND AMBIGUOUS TERMS

GENERAL RULES. ► A contract is ambiguous if the parties' intent is unclear and the contract is capable of more than one reasonable interpretation. ► If a contract contains terms that conflict with one another or it contains ambiguous terms, then the following rules are used to interpret the contract:

> ➤ Handwritten terms prevail over conflicting typed terms.

➤ Typed terms prevail over conflicting terms that are preprinted in a form contract. Figures that are written as words prevail over conflicting figures that are written as numbers. A contract is strictly construed against the party who wrote it. In other words, if a term can reasonably be interpreted in two ways, a court will adopt the interpretation that favors the party who did not write the contract.

LIMITATIONS. ▶ A term is not ambiguous merely because parties disagree about its meaning, and a contract is not ambiguous just because it does not address a matter. ▶ A contract may be unenforceable if it remains ambiguous regarding an important term *after* applying all appropriate rules of interpretation.

10. IMPLIED TERMS

If a contract is silent regarding a matter, a court may imply the following terms:

➤ *Duration of contract*: A contract that does not have an expressly stated duration will continue for a reasonable time.

➤ *Details of performance*: Certain terms relating to the parties' performances may be implied if not stated. Examples: (1) parties must perform within a reasonable time; and (2) services are to be done using such skill as is necessary to properly do the work.

➤ *Good faith*: A duty of good faith and fair dealing is implied by law into all contracts. Good faith requires a party: (1) to act honestly; (2) to cooperate in carrying out a contract; and (3) not to unreasonably interfere with the other party's right to perform a contract.

11. CONDUCT AND CUSTOM

GENERAL RULE. A contract may be interpreted using evidence of: (1) repeated performances by one party in carrying out the contract in question if these performances have been accepted by the other party; or (2) trade or industry customs that relate to the contract in question.

LIMITATION. Trade customs cannot negate clear, express terms of a contract.

STUDY HINT. Repeated performances in carrying out a contract that are inconsistent with the terms of a contract may establish that the parties have modified the contract.

12. AVOIDANCE OF HARDSHIP

GENERAL RULE. A contract is binding even if it benefits one party more than another party.

LIMITATION. A court will interpret an ambiguous contract in a way necessary to avoid: (1) an unfair hardship to a weaker party; or (2) a forfeiture, i.e., an arbitrary loss of money or property.

STUDY HINT. To avoid a hardship, courts may sometimes imply an appropriate term.

CONCEPT REVIEW AND APPLICATIONS

Matching Exercise

Select the term or phrase that best matches a definition or statement stated below. Each term or phrase is the best match for only one statement or definition. Not all terms and phrases will necessarily be used.

administrator

ambiguous term

decedent

executor

good faith

incorporation by reference

parol evidence rule

personal representative

statute of frauds

suretyship

usages of trade

_____Statute of Frauds_____ 1. Rule of law that requires a contract to be evidenced by a sufficient writing in order to be judicially enforceable.

_____parol evidence_____ 2. Rule of law that prohibits altering a final, complete written contract by proving evidence of oral statements that were made prior to or at the same time the written contract was made.

_____duration_____ 3. Legal commitment to pay the debt or be liable for the default of another.

_____ambiguous term_____ 4. Contractual term that may reasonably have more than one meaning.

_____in. by_____ 5. Legal process by which an additional document or statement is made a part of the main body of a contract.

_____personal rep._____ 6. Administrator or executor who legally represents and manages the estate of a deceased person.

True/False

Write **T** if the statement is true, write **F** if it is false.

___F__ 1. All oral contracts are unenforceable.

___T__ 2. The parol evidence rule is intended to prevent false assertions that parties orally agreed to certain terms.

___T__ 3. The parol evidence rule generally forbids using evidence of prior oral agreements to modify or contradict a final and complete written contract.

___T__ 4. In general, a personal guarantee to pay another person's debt must be evidenced by a writing to be enforceable.

___ 5. A party may use parol evidence to prove that a final and complete written contract is voidable due to fraud, mistake, duress, or undue influence.

___ 6. The statute of frauds (at common law) generally requires that a writing state all of the material terms of the contract.

___ 7. Only formal written contracts signed by all of the contracting parties can satisfy the writing requirement of the statute of frauds.

___ 8. Trade customs and usages of trades generally override clear, express contract terms.

___ 9. A party may usually recover the reasonable value of benefits that have been given pursuant to a contract that is unenforceable under the statute of frauds if the other party has not paid for such benefits.

___ 10. The statute of frauds does not entitle a party to rescind a fully performed oral contract even if the contract was required to be evidenced by a writing to be enforceable.

Multiple Choice

___ 1. On March 1, Julie orally contracted to work for Employer from April 1 through March 30 of the following year. Under these facts:
a. The contract violates the statute of frauds because it cannot be performed within one year from the date the contract was made.
b. The contract violates the statute of frauds because all employment contracts must be written.
c. The contract does not violate the statute of frauds because it can be performed within one year from when the work begins.
d. The contract does not violate the statute of frauds because it may be terminated at any time.

___ 2. Which of the following oral contracts is voidable?
a. Biff orally contracts to sell an apartment house to Marty.
b. Sue orally contracts to grant Finance Co. a mortgage on Sue's home.
c. Lin orally contracts to sell some land to Ashley.
d. All of the above.

___ 3. Phil orally contracts to sell a parcel of land to Amanda. Amanda takes possession of the land, and she also makes valuable improvements, the value of which is hard to determine. This contract is:
a. Enforceable because the statute of frauds does not apply to land sale contracts.
b. Enforceable due to Amanda's part performance.
c. Voidable and cannot be enforced because the contract violates the statute of frauds.
d. Void and cannot be enforced because the contract violates the statute of frauds.

_____ 4. Which oral promise violates the statute of frauds?
   a. Pete promises Lender that, if Lender loans $5,000 to Pete's father and Pete's father does not repay the loan, then Pete will repay the loan.
   b. Mom promises Son that if Son borrows money for college and Son is unable to repay this loan, Mom will repay the loan.
   c. Personal representative promises Attorney that an estate will pay Attorney $150 per hour for services rendered to the estate.
   d. a and c.

_____ 5. Which oral contract violates the statute of frauds?
   a. Dad and Jose make an oral contract whereby Dad promises to make Jose general manager of a company in exchange for Jose's promise to marry Dad's daughter.
   b. Tom orally contracts to buy a TV for $400.
   c. Osa orally contracts to buy a car for $10,000.
   d. a and c.

_____ 6. Select the correct answer.
   a. Seller sold Buyer a TV. The contract is a printed form. A printed term states that Seller will repair the TV for one year. A specially typed term that the parties incorporated into the contract instead states that Seller will repair the TV for two years. In this case, the one-year term controls.
   b. A contract states a price "Ten Dollars ($11.00)." In this case, the buyer must pay $11.
   c. In a sales contract for a car, a handwritten term requires Seller to service the car for one year, but a typed term requires Seller to service the car for only three months. In this case, Seller is required to service the car for only three months.
   d. Landlord prepared a lease contract with Tenant. The lease states that Landlord will pay for "utilities." Landlord intended this to mean only electricity. Tenant thought it meant electricity and gas. In this case "utilities" will probably be interpreted to mean electricity and gas.

_____ 7. Select the correct answer.
   a. Ann agreed to supply Diner with 250 pounds of carrots per month. A duration for the contract is not stated. In this case, the contract is invalid because its duration is not stated.
   b. Vick agreed to build a fence for Kim. Time for completion of the fence is not stated. In this case, it is implied that Vick must complete the work within a reasonable time.
   c. Al contracted to install a lawn sprinkler system for Ellen. The quality of the work was not specified. In this case, the law will generally imply that Al must perform the work in a reasonably competent manner.
   d. b and c.

_____ 8. Subcontractor agreed to supply and install 200 "standard toilets" in an apartment house being built by Contractor. Which of the following matters can be considered in interpreting this term?
   a. In the construction industry, which includes both Subcontractor and Contractor, there is an understanding that "standard toilets" means a certain type and quality of toilet.
   b. Pursuant to this contract Plumber has supplied and installed, and Contractor has accepted, 100 toilets of identical type and quality.
   c. a and b.
   d. None of the above.

Case Problem

Answer the following problem, briefly explaining your answer.

Sid bought a computer pursuant to a final and complete written contract signed by Sid and the seller. The contract states that the price is $2,000, payable on delivery. The contract also guarantees the computer to be free of "serious defects," an ambiguous term. Can Sid use parol evidence to prove: (1) the meaning of the term "serious defects"; (2) that prior to signing the written contract, the parties had orally agreed that payment was to be 30 days after delivery; (3) that the written contract was subsequently modified to change the price to $1,900?

_____

_____

_____

_____

Internet Exercise

Using the Internet, locate the decision in *Zaitsev v. Salomon Brothers, Inc.* that was rendered by the U.S. Court of Appeals for the Second Circuit.
1. Do you agree with the court's decision regarding the contract's enforceability under the statute of frauds?
2. As a matter of business strategy, what should Mr. Zaitsev have done differently in order to avoid this suit?

_____

_____

_____

_____

CPA REVIEW

The following questions were given on CPA examinations. The answers for these questions are the unofficial answers prepared by the American Institute of Certified Public Accountants, Inc. (AICPA). All material is reproduced with permission of the AICPA.

_____ 1. On April 3, 1985, Fier entered into an oral employment contract with Reich, whereby Reich was hired as a sales manager for a term of one year. Although Fier and Reich did not agree to a definite starting date, Fier indicated that Reich could begin employment that same day or any time prior to April 15, 1985. Reich began working on April 10. On June 15, 1985, Reich was fired without cause. If Reich sues for breach of the employment contract and Fier asserts the statute of frauds as a defense, Reich will
   a. Prevail since the contract was capable of being performed within one year.
   b. Prevail since the UCC statute of frauds applies.
   c. Lose since the contract was not in writing and signed by Fier.
   d. Lose since Reich did not begin employment until April 10.

___ 2. Nolan agreed orally with Train to sell Train a house for $100,000. Train sent Nolan a signed agreement and a down payment of $10,000. Nolan did not sign the agreement, but allowed Train to move into the house. Before closing, Nolan refused to go through with the sale. Train sued Nolan to compel specific performance. Under the provisions of the Statute of Frauds,
   a. Train will win because Train signed the agreement and Nolan did not object.
   b. Train will win because Train made a down payment and took possession.
   c. Nolan will win because Nolan did not sign the agreement.
   d. Nolan will win because the house was worth more than $500.

___ 3. Payne borrowed $500 from Onest Bank. At the time the loan was made to Payne, Gem orally agreed with Onest that Gem would repay the loan if Payne failed to do so. Gem received no personal benefit as a result of the loan to Payne. Under the circumstances,
   a. Gem is secondarily liable to repay the loan.
   b. Both Gem and Payne are primarily liable to repay the loan.
   c. Gem is free from liability concerning the loan.
   d. Gem is primarily liable to repay the loan.

___ 4. Able hired Carr to restore Able's antique car for $800. The terms of their oral agreement provided that Carr was to complete the work within 18 months. Actually, the work could be completed within one year. The agreement is
   a. Unenforceable because it covers services with a value in excess of $500.
   b. Unenforceable because it covers a time period in excess of one year.
   c. Enforceable because personal service contracts are exempt from the Statute of Frauds.
   d. Enforceable because the work could be completed within one year.

___ 5. King sent Foster, a real estate developer, a signed offer to sell a specified parcel of land to Foster for $200,000. King, an engineer, had inherited the land. On the same day that King's letter was received, Foster telephoned King and accepted the offer. Which of the following statements is correct under the Statute of Frauds?
   a. No contract was formed because Foster did not sign the offer.
   b. No contract was formed because King is not a merchant and, therefore, King's letter is not binding on Foster.
   c. A contract was formed although it would be enforceable only against King.
   d. A contract is formed and is enforceable against King and Foster.

___ 6. Which of the following offers of proof are inadmissible under the parol evidence rule when a written contract is intended as the complete agreement of the parties?
   I. Proof of the existence of a subsequent oral modification of the contract.
   II. Proof of the existence of a prior oral agreement that contradicts the written contract.

   a. I only.
   b. II only.
   c. Both I and II.
   d. Neither I nor II.

CHAPTER 18
THIRD PERSONS AND CONTRACTS

MAKE THE CONNECTION

SUMMARY

Ordinarily, only the parties to contracts have rights and duties with respect to such contracts. Exceptions are made in the case of third-party beneficiary contracts and assignments.

When a contract shows a clear intent to benefit a third person or class of persons, those persons are called *intended third-party beneficiaries*, and they may sue for breach of the contract. A third-party beneficiary is subject to any limitation or restriction found in the contract. A third-party beneficiary loses all rights when the original contract is terminated by operation of law or if the contract reserves the right to change the beneficiary and such a change is made.

In contrast, an incidental beneficiary benefits from the performance of a contract, but the conferring of this benefit was not intended by the contracting parties. An incidental beneficiary cannot sue on the contract.

An assignment is a transfer of a right; the assignor transfers a right to the assignee. In the absence of a local statute, there are no formal requirements for an assignment. Any words manifesting the intent to transfer are sufficient to constitute an assignment. No consideration is required. Any right to money may be assigned, whether the assignor is entitled to the money at the time of the assignment or will be entitled or expects to be entitled at some time in the future.

A right to a performance may be assigned except when (1) it would increase the burden of performance, (2) the contract involves the performance of personal services, or (3) the transaction is based on extending credit.

When a valid assignment is made, the assignee has the same rights—and only the same rights—as the assignor. The assignee is also subject to the same defenses and setoffs as the assignor had been.

The performance of duties under a contract may be delegated to another person except when a personal element of skill or judgment of the original contracting party is involved. The intent to delegate duties may be expressly stated. The intent may also be found in an "assignment" of "the contract" unless the circumstances make it clear that only the right to money was intended to be transferred. The fact that there has been a delegation of duties does not release the assignor from responsibility for performance. The assignor is liable for breach of the contract if the assignee does not properly perform the delegated duties. In the absence of an effective delegation or the formation of a third-party beneficiary contract, an assignee of rights is not liable to the obligee of the contract for its performance by the assignor.

Notice is not required to effect an assignment. When notice of the assignment is given to the obligor together with a demand that future payments be made to the assignee, the obligor cannot discharge liability by payment to the assignor.

When an assignment is made for a consideration, the assignor makes implied warranties that the right assigned is valid and that the assignor owns that right and will not interfere with its enforcement by the assignee.

LEARNING OUTCOMES
After studying this chapter, you should be able to

A. THIRD-PARTY BENEFICIARY CONTRACTS
LO.1 Explain the two types of intended third-party beneficiaries.
LO.2 Explain why an incidental beneficiary does not have the right to sue as a third-party beneficiary.

B. ASSIGNMENTS
LO.3 Define an assignment.
LO.4 Explain the general rule that a person entitled to receive money under a contract may generally assign that right to another person.
LO.5 List the nonassignable rights to performance.

CHAPTER OUTLINE

A. THIRD-PARTY BENEFICIARY CONTRACTS
In general, only contracting parties can enforce a contract. However, subject to certain limitations, a third party who is a third-party beneficiary may sue on and enforce a third-party beneficiary contract.

1. DEFINITION

GENERAL RULE.   In general, a third party is an intended third-party beneficiary if: (1) a contract directly benefits the third party and (2) the benefit satisfies an obligation owing by one contracting party to the third party or a contracting party intends to give the benefit as a gift to the third party.
LIMITATIONS.   ▶ A third party is a third-party beneficiary only if the contracting parties made a contract with the intent to directly benefit the third party. ▶ Express contractual statements that third parties cannot enforce a contract or that third parties are not third-party beneficiaries prevents creation of third-party beneficiaries. ▶ A person has the burden to prove that he or she is a third-party beneficiary.
STUDY HINTS.   ▶ The most important factor is whether the contracting parties expressly or by implication intended a person to be a third-party beneficiary. ▶ A third-party beneficiary may be specifically named in the contract or the contract may designate a specific class of persons for whose benefit the contract is made.
▶**LEARNING OUTCOME EXAMPLES.** See the Sameway Laundry example that illustrates how the "intended creditor beneficiary" can sue the buyer, textbook p. 393; see the text discussion explaining that a life insurance contract is an "intended" donee third-party beneficiary contract, textbook p. 393.

2. MODIFICATION OR TERMINATION OF INTENDED THIRD-PARTY BENEFICIARY CONTRACT

GENERAL RULE.   Contracting parties cannot modify or terminate a third-party beneficiary contract without the consent of the intended third-party beneficiary.
LIMITATIONS.   ▶ Contracting parties can modify or rescind a contract or they can change beneficiaries without a third-party beneficiary's consent if the right to do so is expressly stated in the contract. ▶ Rights of a third-party beneficiary are extinguished if the contract is terminated by operation of the law. Example: a necessary party to a contract dies, thereby terminating the contract.

3. LIMITATIONS ON INTENDED THIRD-PARTY BENEFICIARY

GENERAL RULE. An intended third-party beneficiary has only the same right to enforce a contract as do the original contracting parties.

STUDY HINT. A beneficiary's rights are subject to all contractual terms and defenses.

4. INCIDENTAL BENEFICIARIES

► An incidental beneficiary cannot enforce a contract. ► A third party is an incidental beneficiary if the contracting parties do not intend to directly benefit the third party ► **LEARNING OUTCOME EXAMPLE.** See the *Ensil* case in which the owner had no standing to sue as an incidental beneficiary, textbook p. 395.

B. ASSIGNMENTS

GENERAL RULES. ► An assignment transfers a contract right from one contracting party (the assignor) to a third party (the assignee). ► In general, an assignee can sue on and enforce an assigned right.

LIMITATIONS. ► The assignee's right to enforce a contract is subject to all contract defenses. ► An assignment does not relieve an assignor of his or her contractual duties.

5. DEFINITIONS

► An assignment is a transfer of legal rights. ► An assignor is a party who transfers legal rights to another party. ► An assignee is a party to whom legal rights are transferred. ► **LEARNING OUTCOME EXAMPLE.** See the Hunington *Beach Board* example that discusses the assignee's direct rights against the obligor, textbook p. 396.

6. FORM OF ASSIGNMENT

GENERAL RULES. ► An assignment can be oral or written. ► Consideration is not required to make an assignment. ► Any words clearly showing an intent to transfer a right may be an assignment.

LIMITATION. Statutes often require certain assignments to be in writing.

7. NOTICE OF ASSIGNMENT

GENERAL RULES. ► An assignment is effective when it is made. In other words, an assignee has a legal claim to an assigned right when an assignment is made, and notice of assignment is not required. ► If a right to money (or any other right) is assigned and the party owing the money (the obligor) is informed of the assignment and told to pay the assignee, then payment to the assignee is legally required. Payment to the assignor does not satisfy the duty to pay the assignee.

LIMITATION. If a right to money is assigned but the obligor is not told of the assignment or is not told to pay the assignee, then payment to the assignor reduces the amount of the obligation.

8. ASSIGNMENT OF RIGHT TO MONEY

GENERAL RULES. ► A party can assign a right to receive money that is due under a contract. The modern rule and the rule under the UCC permit an assignment of a right to money (i.e., an assignment of an account receivable) even if a contract prohibits such assignment. ► The modern rule is that a party can assign a right to receive money in the future even though the money has not yet been earned. ► An assignment is proper if the contract expressly authorizes the assignment.

LIMITATION. At common law, an assignment is invalid if the contract expressly prohibits the assignment.

▶**LEARNING OUTCOME EXAMPLE.** See the example of an automobile dealer assigning a customer's credit contract to a finance company in order to raise cash to buy more inventory, textbook p. 399.

9. NONASSIGNABLE RIGHTS

GENERAL RULE. In general, a party can assign a right to receive a service from another party.
LIMITATION. A party cannot assign a right to receive a performance if the transfer would affect or alter a duty or the rights of the obligor. An assignment may not be permitted in the following situations:

> *Assignment increasing burden of performance*: A party cannot assign a right if doing so may significantly increase the burden or risk to the other party.

> *Personal services*: ▶ In general, contracts for personal services cannot be assigned. ▶ A party cannot assign a right to have an act done to a person's personal satisfaction. This would change the nature of the duty of the other party.

> *Credit transaction*: The right to buy on credit or the right to borrow money cannot be assigned.

10. RIGHTS OF ASSIGNEE

GENERAL RULES. ▶ An assignee stands in the shoes of the assignor. In other words, an assignee has only the same right to enforce a contract as the assignor had. ▶ A condition, contractual defense, or set-off that can be asserted against the assignor can also be asserted against the assignee.
LIMITATION. Contracts often state that defenses cannot be asserted against an assignee. This provision is typically valid, but laws may restrict this limitation in certain consumer contracts.

11. CONTINUING LIABILITY OF ASSIGNOR

GENERAL RULE. When an entire contract is assigned, the assignee becomes the party primarily obligated to perform the assignor's contractual obligations.
LIMITATION. Unless otherwise agreed by the contracting parties, an assignment does not excuse an assignor from assuring that the assignee performs the assignor's contractual duties. If the assignee fails to perform any such duties, then the assignor remains legally bound to perform all such obligations.
STUDY HINT. One way for an assignor to avoid continuing responsibilities under an assigned contract is to have the assignment made pursuant to a novation. In a novation, the assignor, assignee, and the other contracting party agree that the assignor is released from liability under the original contract.

12. LIABILITY OF ASSIGNEE

GENERAL RULES. ▶ Ordinarily, an assignee is not liable for a breach of the contract by an assignor. ▶ An assignment that is made "subject to" a claim means that the other claim has a right to be paid before the assignee. It does NOT mean that the assignee is obligated to pay this claim.
LIMITATION. Sometimes, federal and state consumer protection laws may make an assignee of a consumer debt liable for the assignor's misconduct.

13. WARRANTIES OF ASSIGNOR

If an assignment is made for consideration, the assignor warrants to the assignee that: (1) the assignor owns the assigned right; (2) the assigned right is valid, that is, it is not subject to any defenses; and (3) the assignor will not interfere with the assignee's rights.

14. DELEGATION OF DUTIES

GENERAL RULES. ▶ A delegation of duties is a transfer of duties by a contracting party to a third party who is to perform such duties. ▶ In general, a party may delegate a standardized, nonpersonal contractual duty thereby authorizing a third party to perform the duty. ▶ A party who delegates a duty ordinarily remains liable to the other contracting party for the proper performance of the delegated work.

LIMITATION. A party cannot delegate a duty without the consent of the other contracting party if the duty is personal in nature and it is important that the original party performs.

STUDY HINT. Unless otherwise indicated by the circumstances, the UCC provides that a general assignment of "the contract" or comparable language both assigns contract rights and delegates contract duties. This modern rule is followed by the UCC.

CONCEPT REVIEW AND APPLICATIONS

Matching Exercise

Select the term or phrase that best matches a definition or statement stated below. Each term or phrase is the best match for only one statement or definition. Not all terms and phrases will necessarily be used

assignee
assignment
assignor
cause of action
claim
debtor
delegation of duties
delegation
duties
implied warranty
intended beneficiary
novation
obligee
obligor
rights
third-party beneficiary

_____ 1. Third party to whom a contract right is assigned.

_____ 2. Third party who may benefit from a contract between others although the contracting parties did not intend to contract for the benefit of the third party.

_____ 3. Transfer of a contract right to a third party.

_____ 4. Transfer of contract duties to a third party.

_____ 5. Third party whom contracting parties intend to directly benefit by entering into a contract.

_____ 6. Contracting party who has an obligation to perform a duty.

_____ 7. Legal obligation to do or not to do an act.

_____ 8. Contracting party who has the right to receive a performance from the other contracting party.

_____ 9. Contracting party who assigns a contract right to a third party.

True/False

Write **T** if the statement is true, write **F** if it is false.

_____ 1. A third-party beneficiary contract may expressly reserve the right of the original contracting parties to change third-party beneficiaries whenever the contracting parties choose to do so.

_____ 2. In most cases, contracting parties can modify or terminate a third-party beneficiary contract without obtaining the consent of an intended beneficiary if the contract is silent on this matter.

_____ 3. The intention of contracting parties determines whether a third party is an intended beneficiary.

_____ 4. An intended beneficiary can enforce a contract only in accordance with the terms of the contract.

_____ 5. If contracting parties know that a contract will benefit a third party, then this fact, by itself, conclusively establishes that the third party is an intended third-party beneficiary.

_____ 6. If a contractor contracted with a university to build a gymnasium for physical education classes, students at the university would be only incidental beneficiaries of the contract.

_____ 7. If an assignor assigns his or her rights under a contract, then the assignment terminates the assignor's duty to perform any obligations under the contract.

_____ 8. The modern trend allows a party to assign a right to receive money under a contract even if the contract prohibits the assignment.

_____ 9. One cannot assign a right to be insured because the assignment may increase the risk to the insurer.

_____ 10. An employer can generally assign the right to receive the services of an employee.

Multiple Choice

_____ 1. Select the third party who is an intended beneficiary who can enforce the contract in question.
   a. Loan Co. lent Alice $5,000 to pay bills. The loan contract states that the parties do not intend for any of Alice's creditors to be third-party beneficiaries. Third party is a creditor of Alice.
   b. Ned contracted with Rock Insurance Co. whereby the insurance company agreed to pay $25,000 to Ned's sister (third party) upon Ned's death.
   c. Samantha contracts to sell her car to Tom for $6,000. The contract requires Tom to pay the $6,000 directly to Last Chance Bank (third party) to whom Samantha owes $6,000.
   d. b and c.

_____ 2. Bank contracted to lend Terra Corp. $100 million to build a residential development. Terra is considering building the development in one of several locations. One location is near land owned by Ted. The value of Ted's land will increase if Terra builds near his land. Under these facts:
   a. Ted is an intended third party beneficiary of the contract between Bank and Terra.
   b. Ted is an incidental beneficiary of the contract between Bank and Terra.
   c. Ted can enforce the contract between Bank and Terra.
   d. Bank and Terra cannot modify the loan contract without Ted's consent.

_____ 3. Cody owed Don $1,000. Don orally told Cody and Sylvia: "I transfer to Sylvia my right to be repaid the $500; Cody pay Sylvia the $1,000." Sylvia did not give Don anything in exchange for Don's right to receive this money. (You may assume that there are no special statutes in this case relating to the manner in which the assignment must be made.) Under these facts:
   a. The assignment by Don is invalid because Don did not use the word "assign."
   b. The assignment by Don is invalid because the assignment is oral.
   c. The assignment by Don is invalid because Sylvia did not give any consideration.
   d. The assignment by Don to Sylvia is valid.

_____ 4. Which right can be assigned without the consent of the other contracting party? (The agreements in question do not expressly prohibit assignments.)
   a. Donna agreed to pay $2,000 to Bret. Bret wants to assign the right to receive this money.
   b. Painter agreed to paint a portrait of Keri, and Painter guaranteed personal satisfaction. Keri wants to assign to her sister the right to have a portrait painted to her personal satisfaction.
   c. D&D agreed to lend $5,000 to Fred. Fred wants to assign to Dee the right to borrow the $5,000.
   d. Central Airlines has an employment contract with Captain Buck, a pilot. Central Airlines wants to assign its right to Captain Buck's services to Air Asia, another airline.

_____ 5. Art sold a truck to Lucky on credit for $20,000. Art breached the contract with Lucky, and Lucky can claim a $5,000 set-off against Art. Art validly assigned to Stella all of Art's rights to receive money from Lucky. Lucky was informed of the assignment and was told to pay Stella. Lucky refuses to pay anything. Under these facts, how much can Stella collect from Lucky?
   a. $0
   b. $5,000
   c. $15,000
   d. $20,000

Case Problem

Answer the following problem, briefly explaining your answer.

Erecto Construction Co. contracted to build an office building for Owner. Without Owner's consent, Erecto delegated its duty to do the excavation work to Gopher Inc., a subcontractor. The excavation work is standard, nonpersonal work that does not require any special skill. Gopher failed to do the work properly.

1. Was Erecto legally entitled to delegate its duty to do the excavation work to Gopher without first obtaining Owner's consent?
2. Is Erecto liable to Owner because Gopher failed to properly do the work?

_____

_____

_____

_____

Hannah and Lynn are the partners in a newly formed partnership. If one of the partners dies, the partnership agreement requires the other partner to buy the deceased partner's interest. Also, the partnership has purchased a car on credit from Ace Finance, and it is leasing a building from Carla.

1. Search the Internet for, and identify, three types of insurance that the parties may need in this case.
2. Will there be any intended beneficiaries under these contracts of insurance? If so, who should they be?

_____

_____

_____

_____

CPA REVIEW

The following questions were given on CPA examinations. The answers for these questions are the unofficial answers prepared by the American Institute of Certified Public Accountants, Inc. (AICPA). All material is reproduced with permission of the AICPA.

_____ 1. Ace contracted with Big City to train and employ handicapped, unemployed veterans residing in Big City. Ace breached the contract and Bell, a resident of Big City who is a handicapped, unemployed veteran, sues Ace for damages. Under the circumstances, Bell will
   a. Lose, because Bell is merely an incidental beneficiary of the contract.
   b. Win, because Bell is a third-party beneficiary entitled to enforce the contract.
   c. Lose, because Big City did not assign its contract rights to Bell.
   d. Win, because the intent of the contract was to confer a benefit on all handicapped, unemployed veterans residing in Big City.

_____ 2. Barr entered into a contract with Gray that required Gray to construct a warehouse on land owned by Barr. The contract specifically provided for Gray to use Apex Corp. pipe fittings for all the plumbing. Gray failed to use Apex pipe fittings. Apex had learned of the contract between Barr and Gray and, in anticipation of receiving an order from Gray, manufactured additional pipe fittings. Apex is
a. Entitled to money damages due to Gray's breach of contract.
b. Entitled to money damages since it changed its position to its detriment by relying on the contract.
c. Not entitled to money damages since it is merely a donee beneficiary.
d. Not entitled to money damages since it is merely an incidental beneficiary.

_____ 3. Long purchased a life insurance policy with Tempo Life Insurance Co. The policy named Long's daughter as beneficiary. Six months after the policy was issued, Long died of a heart attack. Long had failed to disclose on the insurance application a known pre-existing heart condition that caused the heart attack. Tempo refused to pay the death benefit to Long's daughter. If Long's daughter sues, Tempo will
a. Win, because Long's daughter is an incidental beneficiary.
b. Win, because of Long's failure to disclose the pre-existing heart condition.
c. Lose, because Long's death was from natural causes.
d. Lose, because Long's daughter is a third-party donee beneficiary.

_____ 4. Wilcox Co. contracted with Ace Painters, Inc. for Ace to paint Wilcox' s warehouse. Ace, without advising Wilcox, assigned the contract to Pure Painting Corp. Pure failed to paint Wilcox's warehouse in accordance with the contract specifications. The contract between Ace and Wilcox was silent with regard to a party's right to assign it. Which of the following statements is correct?
a. Ace remained liable to Wilcox despite the fact that Ace assigned the contract to Pure.
b. Ace would not be liable to Wilcox if Ace had notified Wilcox of the assignment.
c. Ace's duty to paint Wilcox's warehouse was nondelegable.
d. Ace's delegation of the duty to paint Wilcox's warehouse was a breach of the contract.

_____ 5. On February 1, Burns contracted in writing with Nagel to sell Nagel a used car. The contract provided that Bunns was to deliver the car on February 15 and Nagel was to pay the $800 purchase price not later than March 15. On February 21, Burns assigned the contract to Ross for $600. Nagel was not notified of the assignment. Which of the following statements is correct?
a. By making the assignment, Burns impliedly warranted Nagel would pay the full purchase price.
b. The assignment to Ross is invalid because Nagel was not notified.
c. Ross will not be subject to any contract defenses Nagel could have raised against Bunns.
d. By making the assignment, Burns impliedly warranted a lack of knowledge of any fact impairing the value of the assignment.

_____ 6. Egan contracted with Barton to buy Barton's business. The contract provided that Egan would pay the business debts Barton owed Ness and that the balance of the purchase price would be paid to Barton over a 10 year period. The contract also required Egan to take out a decreasing term life insurance policy naming Barton and Ness as beneficiaries to ensure that the amounts owed Barton and Ness would be paid if Egan died.

Barton's contract rights were assigned to Vim, and Egan was notified of the assignment. Despite the assignment, Egan continued making payments to Barton. Egan died before completing payment and Vim sued Barton for the insurance proceeds and the other payments on the purchase price received by Barton after the assignment. To which of the following is Vim entitled?

	Payments on purchase price	Insurance proceeds
a.	No	Yes
b.	No	No
c.	Yes	Yes
d.	Yes	No

_____ 7. One of the criteria for a valid assignment of a sales contract to a third party is that the assignment must
a. Not materially increase the other party's risk or duty.
b. Not be revocable by the assignor.
c. Be supported by adequate consideration from the assignee.
d. Be in writing and signed by the assignor.

CHAPTER 19
DISCHARGE OF CONTRACTS

MAKE THE CONNECTION

SUMMARY

A party's duty to perform under a contract can be affected by a condition precedent, which must occur before a party has an obligation to perform; a condition subsequent, that is, a condition or event that relieves the duty to thereafter perform; and concurrent conditions, which require mutual and often simultaneous performance.

Most contracts are discharged by performance. An offer to perform is called a *tender of performance*. If a tender of performance is wrongfully refused, the duty of the tenderer to perform is terminated. When the performance called for by the contract is the payment of money, it must be legal tender that is offered. In actual practice, it is common to pay and to accept payment by checks or other commercial paper.

When the debtor owes the creditor on several accounts and makes a payment, the debtor may specify which account is to be credited with the payment. If the debtor fails to specify, the creditor may choose which account to credit.

When a contract does not state when it is to be performed, it must be performed within a reasonable time. If time for performance is stated in the contract, the contract must be performed at the time specified if such time is essential (is of the essence). Ordinarily, a contract must be performed exactly in the manner specified by the contract. A less-than-perfect performance is allowed if it is a substantial performance and if damages are allowed the other party.

A contract cannot be discharged by unilateral action unless authorized by the contract itself or by statute, as in the case of consumer protection rescission.

Because a contract arises from an agreement, it may also be terminated by an agreement. A contract may also be discharged by the substitution of a new contract for the original contract; by a novation, or making a new contract with a new party; by accord and satisfaction; by release; or by waiver.

A contract is discharged when it is impossible to perform. Impossibility may result from the destruction of the subject matter of the contract, the adoption of a new law that prohibits performance, the death or disability of a party whose personal action was required for performance of the contract, or the act of the other party to the contract. Some courts will also hold that a contract is discharged when its performance is commercially impracticable or there is frustration of purpose. Temporary impossibility, such as a labor strike or bad weather, has no effect on a contract. It is common, though, to include protective clauses that excuse delay caused by temporary impossibility.

A contract may be discharged by operation of law. This occurs when (1) the liability arising from the contract is discharged by bankruptcy, (2) suit on the contract is barred by the applicable statute of limitations, or (3) a time limitation stated in the contract is exceeded.

LEARNING OUTCOMES
After studying this chapter, you should be able to

A. CONDITIONS RELATING TO PERFORMANCE
LO.1   List the three types of conditions that affect a party's duty to perform

B. DISCHARGE BY PERFORMANCE
LO.2   Explain the on-time performance rule

C. DISCHARGE BY ACTION OF PARTIES
LO.3   Explain four ways a contract can be discharged by agreement of the parties

D. DISCHARGE BY EXTERNAL CAUSES
LO.4   State the effect on a contract of the death or disability of one of the contracting parties
LO.5   Explain when impossibility or impracticability may discharge a contract

CHAPTER OUTLINE

A. CONDITIONS RELATING TO PERFORMANCE

1. CLASSIFICATIONS OF CONDITIONS

GENERAL RULE.   A condition is an event, the happening or nonhappening of which creates a duty to act or terminates a duty to act. A condition may be a:

➤ *Condition precedent*: event that must occur *before* a party has a legal duty to perform;

➤ *Condition subsequent*: event that *terminates* an *existing legal duty* to perform; or

➤ *Concurrent condition*s: event that must occur at the *same time* that another event occurs;

Duties may be subject to a variety of conditions. Examples of conditions include:

➤ *Condition precedent*: Buyer's duty to purchase a house is "subject to" (i.e., conditioned upon) Buyers being able to obtain appropriate financing.

➤ *Condition concurrent*: Buyer's payment for goods is required when Seller delivers the goods.

➤ *Condition subsequent*: Insured's failure to give Insurance Company a required notice of a fire loss terminates Insurance Company's obligation to pay for the loss.

STUDY HINTS.   ▶ Parties' duties under a bilateral contract are typically conditions concurrent, i.e., parties must perform at the same time. ▶ If a contracting party's duty is subject to a condition that is not met, then the party is discharged from such duty, the party is not required to perform that duty and the failure to perform is not a breach of contract. ▶ Conditions are often indicated by words such as "if," "provided that," "when," and other words of similar import. ▶LEARNING OUTCOME EXAMPLES. See the "pay-if-paid" condition-precedent example on textbook p. 411; see the TV anchor's "failed urinalysis test" condition-subsequent example on textbook p. 412.

B. DISCHARGE BY PERFORMANCE

➤ If a party's contractual duties are discharged, this means: (1) the duties no longer exist; (2) the party is not required to perform such duties if they have not already been performed; and (3) the party can enforce the contract against the other party unless the other party has also been discharged.

➤ A discharge may result from: (1) adequate performance of contract duties (or in some cases a refusal by the other party to accept a tender of performance); (2) action by the parties; or (3) outside events.

2. NORMAL DISCHARGE OF CONTRACTS

Most contracts are discharged by the parties' performance of their contractual duties, such as doing a required act or making a required payment, or by expiration of the time stated in the contract.

3. NATURE OF PERFORMANCE

(a) *Tender (of performance)*

► A tender is an offer to perform. ► A party's refusal to accept the other party's *tender to do an act* generally discharges the other party's duty to perform that act. ► A valid *tender of payment* requires that the obligor offer to pay the entire amount owed on the date due.

(b) *Payment*

➤ Payments must be applied in the manner stated by a debtor. If a debtor does not specify how payments are to be applied, a creditor can apply payments to any legal debt that is presently owing.

➤ Payment by check is only conditional payment. A debt is not discharged until the check is paid. If a check is not paid, the creditor can sue on either the original debt or on the check.

4. TIME OF PERFORMANCE

GENERAL RULES. ► A common issue is whether a party has performed in a sufficiently timely fashion to entitle that party to enforce the contract. ► If time for performance is not stated, the law implies a duty to perform in a reasonable time. ► If time for performance is stated, a party should perform within the time stated. Nonetheless, late performance is sufficient to entitle one to enforce a contract if: (1) performance is done in a reasonable time; and (2) time is not of the essence. ► A party may waive a provision that time is of the essence.
LIMITATIONS. ► If time is of the essence, i.e., timely performance is essential, a party can enforce a contract only if the party performs his or her duties within the time stated.
STUDY HINTS. ► Typically, time is of the essence only when this is expressly stated in the contract. ► Factors that affect whether time is of the essence: (1) the contract expressly states that time is of the essence; (2) the nature of the subject matter of the contract; and (3) there will be no significant change in value of the subject matter of the contract if performance is slightly delayed.

5.   ADEQUACY OF PERFORMANCE

(a) *Substantial performance*

GENERAL RULES.   ▶ Another common issue is whether a party has sufficiently performed to entitle that party to enforce a contract. ▶ In most cases, the rule of substantial performance enables a party to enforce a contract if the party in good faith substantially performs his or her duties. (Note: A party must pay for "cost of completion" damages caused by his or her failure to perfectly perform.)

LIMITATION.   The cost of completion damages rule does not apply in a substantial completion case if the cost would be unreasonably great compared to the actual harm suffered. In this situation, the breaching party must pay only for the decrease in value caused by the breach.

STUDY HINTS.   ▶ Substantial performance means: (1) a party's performance is nearly equivalent to what was required; and (2) the benefits derived from the performance can be used by the other party for their intended purposes. ▶ Whether a breach is intentional or not is one factor that is considered in deciding whether substantial performance was rendered.

(b) *Fault of complaining party*
A party cannot complain about a performance that complies with terms dictated by that party.

(c) *Satisfaction of promisee or third person*

GENERAL RULES.   ▶ If a party promises to perform to the personal satisfaction of the other party regarding a matter of personal taste, then most courts hold that performance is not adequate (and the duty is not discharged) unless the other party is actually satisfied. ▶ If a contract requires that a mechanical or impersonal performance be done to the satisfaction of the other party and that performance can be objectively evaluated, then most courts hold that a performance is adequate (and the duty is discharged) if a reasonable person would be satisfied. **LIMITATION.**   Most courts, require that a person in good faith be dissatisfied, i.e., a party cannot falsely assert that he or she is dissatisfied with the other party's performance.

▶**LEARNING OUTCOME EXAMPLES.** See the "mailed payment" example on textbook p. 414; see the "time is of the essence" example on p. 415.

C. DISCHARGE BY ACTION OF PARTIES

6.   DISCHARGE BY UNILATERAL ACTION

GENERAL RULE.   In general, a party cannot unilaterally (i.e., on one's own) cancel a contract.

LIMITATIONS.   ▶ A contract may allow one party to cancel the contract. ▶ A contract that does not have a fixed duration may be ended by a party at any time. ▶ The Consumer Credit Protection Act allows a debtor three business days to rescind a contract that imposes a lien on the debtor's home. ▶ FTC rules give a buyer three business days to rescind a home solicitation sale for more than $25.

7. DISCHARGE BY AGREEMENT

GENERAL RULE. A contract may be discharged by: (1) original contract terms (for example, a contract states that it ends on a certain date); (2) mutual cancellation (parties agree to end a contract); (3) mutual rescission (parties agree to terminate a contract and to return each other to their original positions); (4) the contracting parties' substitute a new contract between themselves in place of their original contract; (5) novation (a contract is replaced by a new contract between one of the original contracting parties and a new party); (6) accord and satisfaction (parties accept a new performance in place of a performance that is required by the contract, but which is now subject to a dispute between the parties); (7) release; or (8) waiver.

LIMITATION. An accord is not valid unless it fulfills all requirements for a contract. If an accord is not performed (i.e., no satisfaction occurs), the original obligation is not discharged and it may be enforced.

STUDY HINTS. ► An accord is an agreement by parties to accept a new performance in place of an existing, but disputed, obligation. ► A satisfaction is the performance of accord.

D. DISCHARGE BY EXTERNAL CAUSES

8. DISCHARGE BY IMPOSSIBILITY

GENERAL RULES. ► A contract is discharged if performance is made impossible by external causes such as: (1) destruction of a particular subject matter that is essential for performance of the contract; (2) a change in law that makes performance illegal; or (3) the death of a party who is to perform a service involving a special skill. ► A party is also discharged if performance is made impossible due to the other party's wrongful act or failure to act in good faith. ► Example: Manufacturer cannot build a product for Buyer because Buyer wrongfully failed to cooperate in supplying necessary specifications for the product.

LIMITATIONS. ► A contract is not discharged because: (1) a party is personally unable to perform (for example, a contractor cannot afford to hire necessary workers to build a house that he contracted to build); (2) performance is merely more difficult or costly than expected; (3) a law changes, but the change only makes performance more difficult or less profitable than expected; (4) a party accepted the risk that performance might be impossible; or (5) a party dies, if the party's duty is only to pay money or to sell property. ► Delays caused by riots, strikes, or material shortages do not discharge a contract.

►**LEARNING OUTCOME EXAMPLE.** See the Subway Sandwich Shops example on textbook p. 421; see the *Specialty Tire* impracticability case on textbook p. 422; see the Ryder Cup frustration-of-purpose example on textbook p. 423.

9. DEVELOPING DOCTRINES

GENERAL RULES. ► The doctrine of commercial impracticability may discharge a contract or contractual duty when an unforeseen event makes it unreasonably expensive for a party to perform the contract or contractual duty. ► Under the doctrine of frustration of purpose, a contract or contractual duty may be discharged if an unforeseen event destroys the value and purpose for the contract for one of the parties.

LIMITATIONS. ► A contract is not discharged merely because it is unprofitable or more expensive to perform. ► An event does not discharge a contract if a party assumed the risk that the event would occur. ► Common law did not recognize the doctrines of commercial impracticability or frustration of purpose. ►These defenses generally are not available due to an event that was foreseeable at the time of contracting.

10. TEMPORARY IMPOSSIBILITY

GENERAL RULE. ► According to most courts, an event that makes performance only temporarily impossible temporarily excuses performance. ► Unless otherwise agreed, acts of God, such as floods, do not excuse performance of a contract.

LIMITATIONS. Contracts often contain a "weather clause" that expressly excuses nonperformance that is caused by weather conditions or expressly denies any special rights due to weather conditions.

11. DISCHARGE BY OPERATION OF LAW

A contract (or a party's duty) is discharged by: (1) a material, wrongful alteration of a contract by the other party; (2) destruction of a written contract by the other party with the intent to discharge it; (3) a discharge in bankruptcy of the party; (4) a running of the statute of limitations (i.e., the statutory time within which to bring a suit on a contract has expired); or (5) expiration of a contractually agreed-upon time within which a suit was required to be brought to enforce the contract.

CONCEPT REVIEW AND APPLICATIONS

Matching Exercise

Select the term or phrase that best matches a definition or statement stated below. Each term or phrase is the best match for only one statement or definition. Not all terms and phrases will necessarily be used.

accord and satisfaction	rescission
bankruptcy	statute of limitations
condition precedent	substantial performance
condition subsequent	substitution
condition	tender
operation of law	waiver

_____ 1. Law that limits the time within which a suit may be brought to enforce a legal right.

_____ 2. Event identified in a contract, which if it occurs or does not occur, may affect the rights of the parties.

_____ 3. Agreement to accept an alternative performance in place of a disputed contractual obligation together with completion of the alternative performance.

_____ 4. Doctrine authorizing a party to enforce a contract if the party has almost completely performed his or her contractual obligations.

_____ 5. Event or act, which is identified in a contract, that must be met before any rights arise under the contract.

_____ 6. Offer to perform a contractual duty.

_____ 7. Termination of a contract and return of the parties to the position they were in prior to contracting.

_____ 8. Release or giving up of a known right or objection.

_____ 9. Contracting parties' replacement of an existing contract between them with a substitute contract between the same parties.

True/False

Write **T** if the statement is true, write **F** if it is false.

_____ 1. A valid tender of payment only requires an offer to pay the contract price, and it need not include an offer to pay interest or costs that are also due.

_____ 2. If a party's tender of payment is refused, this refusal discharges the party's duty to pay.

_____ 3. If a party's tender to do an act is wrongfully refused by the other contracting party, this refusal generally discharges the party's duty to perform that act.

_____ 4. If payment is made by check, the debt is not discharged until final payment of the check is made.

_____ 5. If Buyer enters into an option contract to buy property that requires Buyer to accept by June 1 and time is of the essence, then an acceptance made on June 2 would not be effective.

_____ 6. Under the rule of substantial performance, if a buyer's duty to purchase a house is subject to a condition precedent that the buyer be able to obtain a $25,000 loan, then this condition would be satisfied if the buyer can obtain a loan for $24,000.

_____ 7. In applying the rule of substantial performance to large construction contracts, if damages are small, then courts tend to ignore the fact that a party's failure to completely perform was intentional.

_____ 8. Under the Consumer Credit Protection Act, a consumer generally has three business days within which to cancel a contract that grants a lien against the consumer's home.

_____ 9. A contract may be discharged if both parties agree to cancel or rescind the contract.

_____ 10. If a person enters into a contract and he or she subsequently files for and receives a discharge in bankruptcy, then the person's duties under the contract are typically discharged.

188

Multiple Choice

_____ 1. Penelope agreed to reupholster Flynn's couch and chair by May 1. The contract does not state that time is of the essence, and timely performance is not vital to this contract. Penelope completed the work on May 7, a reasonable time under the circumstances. Under these facts:
   a. Time is not of the essence in this contract. Penelope can enforce the contract.
   b. Time is not of the essence in this contract. Penelope cannot enforce the contract.
   c. Time is of the essence in this contract. Penelope cannot enforce the contract.
   d. Time is of the essence in this contract. Penelope can enforce the contract.

_____ 2. JR contracted to renovate an historical home for June for $100,000. The renovations were completed as required, except JR unintentionally failed to refinish one oak banister. It will cost $250 to have someone else do this refinishing. Under these facts, JR is entitled to recover:
   a. $0. JR failed to completely perform his duties. Thus, JR cannot enforce the contract.
   b. $99,750. JR substantially performed his duties. Thus, JR can enforce the contract. June must pay the contract price, less damages caused by JR's imperfect performance.
   c. $100,000. JR substantially performed his duties. Thus, JR is entitled to the full contract price.
   d. Only such amount, if any, that June may decide to pay JR.

_____ 3. Ken contracted to set up ordinary accounting books for Paul's business, and Ken guaranteed Paul's satisfaction. Ken set up the books in accordance with generally accepted accounting principles, and a reasonable person would be satisfied. However, Paul refuses to pay because he is not actually satisfied with the books. Under these facts, most courts would hold that:
   a. Ken cannot enforce the contract because Paul is not actually satisfied with the books.
   b. Ken cannot enforce the contract because personal satisfaction contracts are illegal.
   c. Ken can enforce the contract because a reasonable person would be satisfied with the books.
   d. Ken can enforce the contract because promises to perform to another person's personal satisfaction are ignored by courts.

_____ 4. Patty contracted to buy a car from Cars-4-U for $5,000. A dispute arose regarding the amount that Patty must pay because the car failed to satisfy certain warranties. Patty and Cars-4-U entered into an accord whereby Patty agreed to pay, and Cars-4-U agreed to accept, $3,000 as payment in full of the $5,000 disputed debt. Under these facts:
   a. The $5,000 debt was discharged when Patty and Cars-4-U made the accord.
   b. The $5,000 debt is not discharged until Patty pays the $3,000, i.e., a satisfaction occurs.
   c. The $5,000 debt is not discharged even if Patty pays the $3,000 to Cars-4-U.
   d. The $5,000 debt is not discharged until Patty pays the entire $5,000 to Cars-4-U.

_____ 5. Select the contract that is discharged pursuant to the doctrine of impossibility.
   a. Acme Corp. contracted to sell a heart medicine to Wholesaler. The contract was legal when made. Prior to performance, the FDA unforeseeably declared the sale of this medicine illegal.
   b. XYZ contracted to sell a standard Sony stereo to Bob. Prior to performance, XYZ's stereos were destroyed by fire. XYZ can obtain the required stereo elsewhere to deliver to Bob.
   c. Larry contracted to buy a house. Prior to either party's performing, Larry died.
   d. Papco Inc. contracted to overhaul an airplane for Beefsteak Airlines. Papco cannot perform the contract on time due to a shortage of necessary materials.

____ 6. NASA contracted to hire Pete as a scientist. The contract stated that NASA did not have a duty to hire Pete unless he first passed a security check. Pete failed the check. Under these facts.
  a. NASA's duty to hire Pete was subject to a condition precedent.
  b. NASA's duty to hire Pete was subject to a condition concurrent.
  c. NASA's duty to hire Pete was subject to a condition subsequent.
  d. NASA will be liable for breach of contract if it does not hire Pete.

____ 7. Depending on the particular contract, a condition may be:
  a. An event or performance that must occur before a contracting party has a duty to perform.
  b. An event or performance that may suspend a contracting party's duty to perform.
  c. An event or performance that may discharge a contracting party's duty to perform.
  d. All of the above.

____ 8. Julie contracted to buy a duplex from Nat. The contract stated that Julie's duty to purchase the property is conditioned upon her first being able to obtain $400,000 financing. Julie was unable to obtain the financing. Under these facts, must Julie purchase the duplex?
  a. Yes. Julie contracted to buy the property.
  b. Yes. Conditions are not permitted in real estate sales contracts and, therefore, Julie had a contractual obligation to buy the property.
  c. No. A contract never was formed because Julie never had a legal obligation to do anything.
  d. No. The failure of the financing condition discharged Julie's contractual obligation to purchase the property.

____ 9. Roberto's insurance required him to give notice of a loss within seven days. On July 4, Roberto's business was vandalized, but he did not report this loss until August 10. Under these facts:
  a. The notice requirement is a condition precedent to the insurer's duty to pay.
  b. The notice requirement is a condition subsequent of the insurer's duty to pay.
  c. Once Roberto gave notice, the insurer had a duty to pay.
  d. b and c.

____ 10. Jason agreed to purchase lumber inventory from Paul Bunyan Lumber for $5,000 cash. The law implies that Jason's duty to pay is a condition concurrent to Paul Bunyan's duty to deliver the lumber. Under these facts:
  a. Jason must pay for the lumber before it is delivered.
  b. Jason must pay for the lumber at the time it is delivered.
  c. Jason must pay for the lumber within 10 days after it is delivered.
  d. Jason does not have to pay for the lumber.

Case Problem

Answer the following problem, briefly explaining your answer.

Roger contracted to buy a silver mining company. After contracting, the price of silver fell sharply making it unprofitable to mine silver. Prior to contracting, Roger was aware that the price of silver could fall sharply which would negatively affect the value of the mining company, and Roger assumed this risk.

1. In general, when is a contract discharged under the doctrine of commercial impracticability?
2. In general, when is a contract discharged under the doctrine of frustration of purpose?
3. Is Roger's contract to purchase the silver mining company discharged under either of these doctrines?

_____

_____

_____

_____

Internet Exercise

Janice contracted with the U.S. Department of Wildlife to track and then tag 200 "stealth birds" (an endangered species). The contract provided for $50,000 compensation to be paid to Janice, and the contract stated that the federal agency could terminate the contract in accordance with 48 CFR 49 et. seq. (Code of Federal Regulations). After Janice had tagged 100 birds, she was given notice that funding for the project had been canceled and the contract was being terminated. Under these facts:

1. Did the government agency have the unilateral right to terminate this contract?
2. Using the Internet, locate the relevant federal regulations and briefly explain how the federal agency will proceed in discharging the contract.

_____

_____

_____

_____

CPA REVIEW

The following questions were given on CPA examinations. The answers for these questions are the unofficial answers prepared by the American Institute of Certified Public Accountants, Inc. (AICPA). All material is reproduced with permission of the AICPA.

_____ 1. To cancel a contract and to restore the parties to their original positions before the contract, the parties should execute a
   a. Novation
   b. Release
   c. Rescission
   d. Revocation

_____ 2. Under a personal services contract, which of the following circumstances will cause the discharge of a party's duties?
   a. Death of the party who is to receive the services.
   b. Cost of performing the services has doubled.
   c. Bankruptcy of the party who is to receive the services.
   d. Illegality of the services to be performed.

_____ 3. On June 1, 1986, Nord Corp. engaged Milo & Co., CPAs, to perform certain management advisory services for nine months for a $45,000 fee. The terms of their oral agreement required Milo to commence performance any time before October 1, 1986. On June 30, 1987, after Milo completed the work to Nord's satisfaction, Nord paid Milo $30,000 by check. Nord conspicuously marked on the check that it constituted payment in full for all services rendered. Nord has refused to pay the remaining $15,000 arguing that, although it believes the $45,000 fee is reasonable, it had received bids of $30,000 and $38,000 from other firms to perform the same services as Milo. Milo endorsed and deposited the check. If Milo commences an action against Nord for the remaining $15,000, Milo will be entitled to recover
   a. $0 because there has been an enforceable accord and satisfaction.
   b. $0 because the statute of frauds has not been satisfied.
   c. $8,000 because $38,000 was the highest other bid.
   d. $15,000 because it is the balance due under the agreement.

_____ 4. Which of the following statements correctly applies to a typical statute of limitations?
   a. The statute requires that a legal action for breach of contract be commenced within a certain period of time after the breach occurs.
   b. The statute provides that only the party against whom enforcement of a contract is sought must have signed the contract.
   c. The statute limits the right of a party to recover damages for misrepresentation unless the false statements were intentionally made.
   d. The statute prohibits the admission into evidence of proof of oral statements about the meaning of a written contract.

_____ 5. Castle borrowed $5,000 from Nelson and executed and delivered to Nelson a promissory note for $5,000 due on April 30. On April 1 Castle offered, and Nelson accepted, $4,000 in full satisfaction of the note. On May 15, Nelson demanded that Castle pay the $1,000 balance on the note. Castle refused. If Nelson sued for the $1,000 balance Castle would

   a. Win, because the acceptance by Nelson of the $4,000 constituted an accord and satisfaction.

   b. Win, because the debt was unliquidated.

   c. Lose, because the amount of the note was not in dispute.

   d. Lose, because no consideration was given to Nelson in exchange for accepting only $4,000.

_____ 6. Parc hired Glaze to remodel and furnish an office suite. Glaze submitted plans that Parc approved. After completing all the necessary construction and painting, Glaze purchased minor accessories that Parc rejected because they did not conform to the plans. Parc refused to allow Glaze to complete the project and refused to pay Glaze any part of the contract price. Glaze sued for the value of the work performed. Which of the following statements is correct?

   a. Glaze will lose because Glaze breached the contract by not completing performance.

   b. Glaze will win because Glaze substantially performed and Parc prevented complete performance.

   c. Glaze will lose because Glaze materially breached the contract by buying the accessories.

   d. laze will win because Parc committed anticipatory breach.

_____ 7. Dell owed Stark $9,000. As the result of an unrelated transaction, Stark owed Ball that same amount. The three parties signed an agreement that Dell would pay Ball instead of Stark, and Stark would be discharged from all liability. The agreement among the parties is

   a. A novation.

   b. An executed accord and satisfaction.

   c. Voidable at Ball's option.

   d. Unenforceable for lack of consideration.

_____ 8. In September 1988, Cobb Company contracted with Thrifty Oil Company for the delivery of 100,000 gallons of heating oil at the price of 75¢ per gallon at regular specified intervals during the forthcoming winter. Due to an unseasonably warm winter, Cobb took delivery on only 70,000 gallons. In a suit against Cobb for breach of contract, Thrifty will

   a. Lose, because Cobb acted in good faith.

   b. Lose, because both parties are merchants and the UCC recognizes commercial impracticability.

   c. Win, because this is a requirements contract.

   d. Win, because the change of circumstances could have been contemplated by the parties.

CHAPTER 20
BREACH OF CONTRACT AND REMEDIES

MAKE THE CONNECTION

SUMMARY

When a party fails to perform a contract or performs improperly, the other contracting party may sue for damages caused by the breach. What may be recovered by the aggrieved person is stated in terms of being direct or consequential damages. Direct damages are those that ordinarily will result from the breach. Direct damages may be recovered on proof of causation and amount. Consequential damages can be recovered only if, in addition to proving causation and amount, it is shown that they were reasonably within the contemplation of the contracting parties as a probable result of a breach of the contract. The right to recover consequential damages is lost if the aggrieved party could reasonably have taken steps to avoid such damages. In other words, the aggrieved person has a duty to mitigate or reduce damages by reasonable means.

In any case, the damages recoverable for breach of contract may be limited to a specific amount by a liquidated damages clause.

In a limited number of situations, an aggrieved party may bring an action for specific performance to compel the other contracting party to perform the acts called for by the contract. Specific performance by the seller is always obtainable for the breach of a contract to sell land or real estate on the theory that such property has a unique value. With respect to other contracts, specific performance will not be ordered unless it is shown that there was some unique element present so that the aggrieved person would suffer a damage that could not be compensated for by the payment of money damages.

The aggrieved person also has the option of rescinding the contract if (1) the breach has been made concerning a material term and (2) the aggrieved party returns everything to the way it was before the contract was made.

Although there has been a breach of the contract, the effect of this breach is nullified if the aggrieved person by word or conduct waives the right to object to the breach. Conversely, an aggrieved party may accept a defective performance without thereby waiving a claim for breach if the party makes a reservation of rights. A reservation of rights can be made by stating that the defective performance is accepted "without prejudice," "under protest," or "with reservation of rights."

LEARNING OUTCOMES
After studying this chapter, you should be able to

A. WHAT CONSTITUTES A BREACH OF CONTRACT
LO.1 Explain what constitutes a breach of contract and an anticipatory breach of contract

B. WAIVER OF BREACH
LO.2 Describe the effect of a waiver of a breach

C. REMEDIES FOR BREACH OF CONTRACT
LO.3 Explain the range of remedies available for breach of contract

193

D. CONTRACT PROVISIONS AFFECTING REMEDIES AND DAMAGES
LO.4 Explain when liquidated damages clauses are valid and invalid
LO.5 State when liability-limiting clauses and releases are valid

CHAPTER OUTLINE

A. WHAT CONSTITUTES A BREACH OF CONTRACT?

1. DEFINITION OF BREACH

▶ A **BREACH** of contract is a failure to perform contractual duties. A party is entitled to contractual remedies if the other party breaches a contract. ▶ LEARNING OUTCOME EXAMPLE. See the illustration of a painting contractor's failure to properly paint a house, textbook p. 434.

2. ANTICIPATORY BREACH

GENERAL RULE. An anticipatory repudiation (i.e., a disavowal of a contract) occurs when a contracting party clearly indicates, before performance is required, that he or she will not perform the contract when the time for performance arrives.
LIMITATION. A contracting party can retract an anticipatory repudiation if the other party has not relied on the repudiation. If the other party has relied on the anticipatory repudiation, however, then the party making the repudiation cannot retract it.
STUDY HINTS. ▶ An anticipatory repudiation may result from: (1) an express statement or (2) conduct that makes it impossible for the other party to perform the contract. ▶ An anticipatory repudiation may be treated as a breach prior to the time that performance is actually due.
LEARNING OUTCOME EXAMPLE. See the *Tips* case in which damages are assessed for anticipatory repudiation of a contract, textbook p. 434.

B. WAIVER OF BREACH

3. CURE OF BREACH BY WAIVER

GENERAL RULE. A party may waive a breach of contract by the other party. Example: Buyer is required to pay May 1, but Buyer pays May 2. Seller accepts payment, telling Buyer it's OK.
STUDY HINT. A party who waives a breach: (1) gives up the right to damages or remedies regarding such breach; and (2) cannot use the breach as a reason for not performing the contract.
LEARNING OUTCOME EXAMPLE. See the application of the waiver doctrine as applied in the Massey example on textbook p. 438.

4. EXISTENCE AND SCOPE OF WAIVER

GENERAL RULE. ▶ A waiver may be express or implied. ▶ Example of implied waiver: accepting a defective performance without objection and without reserving one's rights to sue for breach.
LIMITATION. ▶ A waiver applies only to the specific matter waived. ▶ A party is entitled to require the other party to strictly perform all other contractual obligations and all future obligations.
▶ If a contract states that it cannot be modified by a waiver, then waivers do not modify it and the original contract terms can be enforced regarding future performances.

5. RESERVATION OF RIGHTS

GENERAL RULE.   A party retains the right to recover damages caused by another's breach if the party expressly reserves the right to damages at the time the party accepts a defective performance.

STUDY HINT.   A "reservation of rights" (to damages) is indicated by an acceptance stating that a defective performance is accepted "without prejudice" to a claim for damages or "under protest."

C. REMEDIES FOR BREACH OF CONTRACT

6. REMEDIES UPON ANTICIPATORY REPUDIATION

If a party makes an anticipatory repudiation, the other party has the following options: (1) do nothing, wait until the time for performance, and then sue if performance is not made; or (2) treat the repudiation as a definite breach and sue immediately; or (3) treat the repudiation as an offer to cancel the contract and accept the offer, thereby terminating the contract.

7. REMEDIES IN GENERAL AND THE MEASURE OF DAMAGES

► Courts may provide a quasi-contractual or restitution remedy in certain situations when a contract is unenforceable but one of the parties has performed. ► Ordinarily, when there is a breach of contract the court will award monetary damages to compensate the wronged party. ► When damages are inadequate, a court may award an equitable remedy, such as specific performance. ►A party must make restitution (return) money received in expectation of a contract being made if the contract is never actually formed and the party has done nothing pursuant to the anticipated contract.

► LEARNING OUTCOME EXAMPLE. See Figure 20.1, "What Follows the Breach," on textbook p. 439.

8. MONETARY DAMAGES

A contracting party is entitled to damages if the other party breaches a contract. In general, damages are the sum of money necessary to put a party in the same or equivalent financial position the party would have been in had the contract been performed. Important rules include:

> *Measure of damages*: ► A party can recover compensatory damages for any actual loss that the party can prove with reasonable certainty. ► Compensatory damages may include direct damages and consequential damages. ► In most breach of contract cases, a party cannot recover punitive damages, that is damages that are awarded solely to punish a wrongdoer. A party cannot recover damages for annoyance, emotional upset, or for uncertain, speculative losses. ► If no actual loss occurred, a court may award nominal (token) damages, such as $1.

> *Direct and consequential damages*: ► Direct (general) damages are those that naturally flow from a breach and include incidental damages (out-of-pocket expenses) caused by the breach. Direct damages are losses that anyone would have suffered from this breach. ► Consequential damages occur due to the particular circumstances of the injured party. A party can recover consequential damages only if a person in the position of the breaching party could have reasonably foreseen that the injured party might suffer this type of loss if the contract is breached.

> *Mitigation of damages*: ▶ A nonbreaching party has a duty to mitigate damages, i.e., to take reasonable steps to minimize damages. ▶ A party cannot recover damages that the party could have reasonably avoided. A party does not have a duty to mitigate damages if: (1) there is no reasonable way to minimize damages; or (2) the cost of mitigation is unreasonably great.

> *LEARNING OUTCOME EXAMPLE.* See the *Spenser Adams* example involving a range of monetary damages on textbook p. 441.

9. RESCISSION

GENERAL RULES. ▶ A party may rescind a contract if the other party commits a material breach. If necessary, a party may file an action to obtain a judicial rescission of the contract. ▶ A rescinding party: (1) must return the other party to the position that the other party was in prior to contracting (i.e., the party must return all contract benefits received); and (2) is entitled under quasi contract to recover the reasonable value of money paid or other benefits already given to the other party.

LIMITATION. A party cannot rescind if the other party cannot be returned to his or her precontracting position.

STUDY HINT. A breach is material if it deprives the other party of the basic benefit that the party was to receive under the contract.

LEARNING OUTCOME EXAMPLE. See the *Pedro Morena* example involving rescission of a contract on textbook p. 442.

10. ACTION FOR SPECIFIC PERFORMANCE

GENERAL RULE. A party may obtain specific performance (i.e., an order compelling performance of a contract) if: (1) a subject matter is unique; and (2) damages are inadequate to remedy the harm.

LIMITATION. When the plaintiff's damages can be measured, specific performance is denied.

STUDY HINTS. ▶ A party can generally obtain specific performance of contracts to buy: (1) land; (2) stock representing a controlling interest in a close corporation (i.e., a nonpublic corporation with few shareholders) if there is no established value for the stock; or (3) goods that are unique or cannot be purchased elsewhere. ▶ Typically, a party cannot obtain specific performance of personal service contracts or employment contracts.

LEARNING OUTCOME EXAMPLE. See the rare Revolutionary War musket example of specific performance textbook p. 443.

11. ACTION FOR AN INJUNCTION

If a party threatens to commit an act that would cause a material breach of a contract, a court may issue an injunction (court order) that prohibits the party from doing the threatened act.

12. REFORMATION OF CONTRACT BY A COURT

▶ If a written contract does not accurately state the terms of the parties' agreement, then either party may request a court to reform, i.e., to correct the errors, so that the writing does correctly state the contractual terms. ▶ A court may reform a court when one party makes a unilateral mistake that is so significant that enforcing the contract would be unreasonable.

D. CONTRACT PROVISIONS AFFECTING REMEDIES AND DAMAGES

13. LIMITATION OF REMEDIES

► In general, a contract may limit the remedies that a nonbreaching party may obtain. ► Example: Troy purchases a new truck from ABC Truck Sales and the contract limits Troy's remedies to having ABC repair or replace the truck if it is defective.

14. LIQUIDATED DAMAGES

GENERAL RULE. A contract may state the amount of damages to be paid if the contract is breached. This amount is "liquidated damages." Upon a party's breach, the other party will recover this amount of damages whether actual damages are more or less than the liquidated amount.

LIMITATIONS. ► Liquidated damages are valid only if: (1) the amount of actual damages is difficult or impossible to foresee; and (2) the liquidated amount is a reasonable forecast of probable damages. ► If a liquidated damage is unreasonably large, it is called a penalty and the liquidated damage clause is void. In this event, the injured party can recover only his or her actual damages.

LEARNING OUTCOME EXAMPLE. See the Dow Corning faulty breast implants settlement agreement example in which liquidated damages of a $100 per day late payment were found to be unenforceable penalty provision, textbook p. 445.

15. ATTORNEYS' FEES

GENERAL RULE. Under the "American rule," the parties to a breach of contract lawsuit generally must pay their own attorneys' fees unless recovery of such fees is authorized (1) by the contract in question or (2) by a statute.

LIMITATION. Even if recovery of attorneys' fees is authorized, the court has the equitable discretion to limit or eliminate the recovery of attorneys' case because of the facts of the particular case.

16. LIMITATION OF LIABILITY CLAUSES

GENERAL RULE. In general, an exculpatory that eliminates a party's liability for damages caused by a breach of contract or a limitation of liability clause that limits the amount for which a contracting party may be held liable are valid and enforceable.

LIMITATION. An exculpatory clause may be invalid if the clause completely eliminates the liability of a party for his or her gross negligence or intentional act.

STUDY HINTS. ► Release forms signed by participants in sporting activities are generally valid. ► Exculpatory clauses are typically upheld if agreed to by businesses with equal bargaining power.

LEARNING OUTCOME EXAMPLE. See the example in which the city of Newton successfully raised a signed exculpatory release as a defense in a high school cheerleading injury case, textbook p. 448.

CONCEPT REVIEW AND APPLICATIONS

Matching Exercise

Select the term or phrase that best matches a definition or statement stated below. Each term or phrase is the best match for only one statement or definition. Not all terms and phrases will necessarily be used.

anticipatory breach
anticipatory repudiation
breach
compensatory damages
consequential damages
direct damages
exculpatory clause

injunction
limitation-of-liability
clause
liquidated damages
liquidated damages clause
nominal damages
punitive damages

remedies
reservation of rights
specific performance
valid
waiver

_____ 1.   Loss that is the natural result of a breach.

_____ 2.   Damages awarded to punish a party.

_____ 3.   Remedy that prohibits a party from doing an act that would constitute a breach of contract.

_____ 4.   Contractually agreed-upon damages to be paid if a party breaches a contract.

_____ 5.   Contract provision stating that a party shall not be liable for damages caused by a breach.

_____ 6.   Unreasonably large liquidated damage amount that is unrelated to potential damages that may result from a breach.

_____ 7.   Loss occurring because of the particular circumstances of the injured party.

_____ 8.   Express or implied acceptance of a defective performance by the other party.

_____ 9.   Damages awarded to compensate a party for actual losses suffered.

_____ 10. Equitable remedy requiring performance of a contract.

True/False

Write **T** if the statement is true, write **F** if it is false.

_____ 1.   A contracting party's wrongful act that makes performance of a contract impossible may constitute an anticipatory repudiation.

_____ 2.   An anticipatory repudiation cannot be taken back even if no one has relied on the repudiation.

_____ 3.   In general, a party cannot waive a breach unless the waiver is stated in a signed writing.

_____ 4.   An example of a contractual limitation of remedy that is generally valid is a clause that limits a buyer's remedy to having a seller repair or replace a defective good._____ 5.   A party may accept a defective performance by the other party and still be entitled to sue for damages if the party reserves a right to damages at the time the performance is accepted.

_____ 6.   If a party commits an anticipatory repudiation, the other party cannot sue for breach of contract until the time for performance has passed.

_____ 7.   A party cannot recover damages if the damages are speculative and uncertain.

_____ 8.   A party cannot get consequential damages unless that type of loss was reasonably foreseeable.

_____ 9.   One party breached a contract and the other party suffered $1,000 damages. If $500 of the damages were reasonably avoidable but the injured party failed to take the necessary steps to avoid these damages, then the injured party can recover no damages whatsoever.

_____10.   A party is not required to expend an unreasonable sum of money to mitigate damages.

_____11.   A court may refuse to award specific performance if specific performance will cause the breaching party an unreasonable hardship.

_____13.

Multiple Choice

_____ 1.   Gill contracted to sell pasta to Cafe each week. Gill agreed to deliver the pasta every Monday. One week, Gill breached the contract when he did not deliver the pasta until Wednesday. Cafe waived the breach resulting from this one late delivery. Under these facts:
   a. Cafe can cancel the contract due to the one late delivery.
   b. Cafe can sue Gill for damages due to the one late delivery.
   c. Cafe cannot cancel the contract or sue Gill for damages due to the one late delivery.
   d. In the future, Cafe cannot enforce the original contract term requiring delivery on Monday.

_____ 2.   R&R Pesticide Co. agreed to spray Farmer's fields on July 1. On May 1, R&R told Farmer that there was a 50 percent chance that it might not be able to perform the contract. Under these facts:
   a. R&R has committed an anticipatory repudiation.
   b. R&R has not committed an anticipatory repudiation.
   c. Farmer is entitled to cancel the contract on May 1.
   d. a and c.

_____ 3.   Beth agreed to repair a computer for AAA Tax Service. Beth unintentionally breached the contract. As a result of Beth's breach, the computer suffered $250 damage, and AAA lost profits of $5,000 because it could not complete certain tax returns without the computer. The lost profits were reasonably foreseeable, although Beth never actually thought about them. Mitigation was not possible. Under these facts, can AAA recover any damages from Beth?
   a. AAA cannot recover any damages. Beth did not agree to pay for losses caused by a breach.
   b. AAA can recover only $250 direct damages.
   c. AAA can recover $250 direct damages and $5,000 consequential damages.
   d. AAA can recover $250 direct damages, $5,000 consequential damages, and $5,000 punitive damages.

_____ 4.   Lori contracted to buy a tract of land from Ken. Lori has not paid the purchase price, but Ken has conveyed title to Lori. Prior to taking possession, Lori discovered that Ken fraudulently stated to her that the property was 100 acres when in fact it was only 75 acres. Under these facts:
   a. Lori can rescind the contract and she can sue for all of her compensatory damages.
   b. Lori can rescind the contract, but she must return title to the land to Ken.
   c. Lori can rescind the contract and she can retain title to the land.
   d. Lori cannot rescind the contract.

_____ 5. Juan can obtain specific performance of which contract?
   a. Seller contracted to sell Juan a farm. Seller wrongfully refuses to convey title.
   b. Juan bought a bull. Seller wrongfully failed to deliver the bull. The bull is a unique, hybrid bull that is to be used for breeding and it cannot be replaced. Damages cannot be measured.
   c. Juan hired Tex to be a ranch foreman. Tex wrongfully refuses to perform.
   d. a and b.

Case Problem

Answer the following problem, briefly explaining your answer.

Mica Co. agreed to build a commercial storage building by September 1 for Pack Rat Storage. It was hard to predict Pack Rat's losses if the building was not completed on time. The parties estimated that Pack Rat would lose $200 in storage fees per day if the building was not completed on time. Thus, the contract required Mica to pay liquidated damages of $200 per day if the work was completed late. Mica finished ten days late. Pack Rat actually lost $1,800 due to the breach.

1. Is the liquidated damage amount stated in the contract between Mica Co. and Pack Rat Storage valid, or is it an invalid penalty?
2. How much in damages can Pack Rat Storage recover from Mica Co.?

_____

_____

_____

_____

Internet Exercise

1. Find and read the recent U.S. Supreme Court decision in *BMW of North America, Inc. v. Gore*.
2. In this case, what was the basis for the award of punitive damages - was it for breach of contract or fraud?
3. What three factors must be considered when deciding whether a punitive damage award is excessive or not?

_____

_____

_____

_____

CPA REVIEW

The following questions were given on CPA examinations. The answers for these questions are the unofficial answers prepared by the American Institute of Certified Public Accountants, Inc. (AICPA). All material is reproduced with permission of the AICPA.

___ 1. Ames Construction Co. contracted to build a warehouse for White Corp. The construction specifications required Ames to use Ace lighting fixtures. Inadvertently, Ames installed Perfection lighting fixtures, which are of slightly lesser quality than Ace fixtures, but in all other respects meet White's needs. Which of the following statements is correct?
  a. White's recovery will be limited to monetary damages because Ames' breach of the construction contract was not material.
  b. White will not be able to recover any damages from Ames because the breach was inadvertent.
  c. Ames did not breach the construction contract because the Perfection fixtures were substantially as good as the Ace fixtures.
  d. Ames must install Ace fixtures or White will not be obligated to accept the warehouse.

___ 2. Which of the following remedies is available to a party who has entered into a contract in reliance upon the other contracting party's innocent misrepresentation as to material facts?

	Compensatory damages	Punitive damages	Rescission
a.	No	No	No
b.	Yes	No	Yes
c.	No	No	Yes
d.	Yes	Yes	No

___ 3. Under the UCC Sales Article, a plaintiff who proves fraud in the formation of a contract may
  a. Elect to rescind the contract and need not return the consideration received from the other party.
  b. Be entitled to rescind the contract and sue for damages resulting from the fraud.
  c. Be entitled to punitive damages provided physical injuries resulted from the fraud.
  d. Rescind the contract even if there was no reliance on the fraudulent statement.

___ 4. Kaye contracted to sell Hodges a building for $310,000. The contract required Hodges to pay the entire amount at closing. Kaye refused to close the sale of the building. Hodges sued Kaye. To what relief is Hodges entitled?
  a. Punitive damages and compensatory damages.
  b. Specific performance and compensatory damages.
  c. Consequential damages or punitive damages.
  d. Compensatory damages or specific performance.

_____ 5. In general, a clause in a real estate contract entitling the seller to retain the purchaser's down payment as liquidated damages if the purchaser fails to close the transaction, is enforceable
   a. In all cases, when the parties have a signed contract.
   b. If the amount of the down payment bears a reasonable relationship to the probable loss.
   c. As a penalty, if the purchaser intentionally defaults.
   d. Only when the seller cannot compel specific performance.

_____ 6. Foster Co. and Rice executed a contract by which Foster was to sell a warehouse to Rice for $270,000. The contract required Rice to pay the entire $270,000 at the closing. Foster has refused to close the sale of the warehouse to Rice. If Rice commences lawsuit against Foster, what relief would Rice likely be entitled to?
   a. Specific performance or compensatory damages.
   b. Specific performance and compensatory damages.
   c. Compensatory damages or punitive damages.
   d. Compensatory damages and punitive damages.

CHAPTER 21
PERSONAL PROPERTY
AND BAILMENTS

MAKE THE CONNECTION

SUMMARY

Personal property consists of whole or fractional ownership rights in things that are tangible and movable, as well as rights in things that are intangible.

Personal property may be acquired by purchase. Personal property may also be acquired by gift when the donor has present intent to make a gift and delivers possession to the donee or makes a constructive delivery. Personal property may be acquired by occupation and under some statutes may be acquired by finding. The state may acquire property by escheat.

All rights in a particular object of property can be held by one individual, in which case it is said to be held *in severalty*. Ownership rights may be held concurrently by two or more individuals, in which case it is said to be held in cotenancy. The major forms of cotenancy are (1) tenancy in common, (2) joint tenancy, (3) tenancy by entirety, and (4) community property.

A bailment is the relationship that exists when tangible personal property is delivered by the bailor into the possession of the bailee under an agreement, express or implied, that the identical property will be returned or delivered in accordance with the agreement. No title is transferred by a bailment. The bailee has the right of possession. When a person comes into the possession of the personal property of another without the owner's consent, the law classifies the relationship as a constructive bailment.

Bailments may be classified in terms of benefit—that is, for the (1) sole benefit of the bailor, (2) sole benefit of the bailee, or (3) benefit of both parties (mutual benefit bailment). Some courts state the standard of care required of a bailee in terms of the class of bailment. Thus, if the bailment is for the sole benefit of the bailor, the bailee is required to exercise only slight care and is liable for gross negligence only. When the bailment is for the sole benefit of the bailee, the bailee is liable for the slightest negligence. When the bailment is for the mutual benefit of the parties, as in a commercial bailment, the bailee is liable for ordinary negligence. An ordinary bailee may limit liability except for willful misconduct or where prohibited by law.

A bailee must perform the bailee's part of the contract. The bailee has a lien on the bailed property until they have paid for storage or repair charges.

In a mutual benefit bailment, the bailor is under a duty to furnish goods reasonably fit for the purposes contemplated by the parties. The bailor may be held liable for damages or injury caused by the defective condition of the bailed property.

LEARNING OUTCOMES
After studying this chapter, you should be able to

A. PERSONAL PROPERTY
LO.1   Explain how title to personal property is acquired
LO.2   List and explain the various types of gifts

LO.3 Explain the legal theory whereby an owner can recover his or her property from the wrongful exclusionary retention of another

B. BAILMENTS

LO.4 Identify the elements necessary to create a bailment
LO.5 Explain the standard of care a bailee is required to exercise over bailed property

CHAPTER OUTLINE

A. PERSONAL PROPERTY

1. PERSONAL PROPERTY IN CONTEXT

GENERAL RULES. ▶ Personal property includes: (1) rights in tangible, movable property; (2) choses in action (legal claims and debts); and (3) intangible rights, such as copyrights, patents, and trademarks. ▶ Personal property does not include rights in real property (i.e., land, things embedded in land, such as gasoline tanks, and things attached to the land, such as buildings).
STUDY HINTS. ▶ In a legal sense, the term "property" includes land, objects and things, as well as a person's right in any of the foregoing items. ▶ A person may own the entire interest or only a partial interest in property.

2. TITLE TO PERSONAL PROPERTY

GENERAL RULE. A person may acquire title to personal property by purchase, gift, finding of lost property, occupation, and escheat.
STUDY HINT. A person cannot title to a stolen item from a thief. Upon locating a stolen item, the owner may recover the item from the thief or from a third party that purchased the item from the thief.
▶**LEARNING OUTCOME EXAMPLE.** See the example of Steam Engine No. 952 where the museum had possession and control of the locomotive for over 50 years but could not overcome the lender's good title, textbook p. 470.

3. GIFTS

A gift of property is a: (1) passing of title; (2) made with the intent to pass title; (3) without receiving money or value in consideration for the passing of title. Types of gifts include:

➤ *Inter vivos gifts*: ▶ An inter vivos gift is made if a donor: (1) expresses the intent to convey all rights to property at the present time; and (2) delivers the property to the donee, or makes symbolic (constructive) delivery of the property by delivering the means to control the property or a symbol of ownership, such as keys or documents of title. ▶ Depositing money into a joint bank account with an adult donee with the intent to make a gift constitutes a gift of the money deposited.

➤ *Gifts causa mortis*: ▶ A gift causa mortis is a conditional gift made by a donor who believes that he or she will soon die, and it is made with the intent that a donee will own the property if the donor dies. ▶ A gift causa mortis fails and the intended donee acquires no rights if: (1) the donor does not die; (2) the donee dies first; or (3) the donor takes back the gift before death.

➢ *Gifts and transfers to minors*: ▶ Several Uniform Acts allow property to be given or transferred to a minor by delivering the property to a custodian. The custodian may use the property for the minor's benefit, education, maintenance, and support. ▶ Under these Uniform Acts, a minor is usually entitled to possession of the property at age 21. ▶ A gift cannot be revoked once it is made in accordance with these Uniform Acts.

➢ *Conditional gifts*: ▶ A conditional gift transfers rights only when certain stated conditions are met. A gift may be subject to a condition precedent or a condition subsequent. ▶ Marriage engagement gifts are conditional gifts. Most states allow the party who gave an engagement ring to recover it, regardless who called off the marriage.

➢ *Anatomical gifts*: ▶ Anatomical gifts are gifts of organs or body parts. ▶ The Uniform Anatomical Gift Act allows anatomical gifts to be made by persons who are 18 or older, or by certain members of a decedent's family.

4. FINDING OF LOST PROPERTY

GENERAL RULES. ▶ Lost property is property that an owner has misplaced without intending to give up ownership. ▶ A person who finds lost property does not acquire title to the property. At most, a finder of lost property is entitled to possession of the property until it is claimed by the owner.

LIMITATIONS. ▶ Lost property that is found in a public place must be turned over to the manager of the place if it appears that the property was intentionally placed there by its owner. ▶ In some states, a finder of lost property may sell or keep the property if the true owner does not claim it.

5. OCCUPATION OF PERSONAL PROPERTY

GENERAL RULE. Subject to possible statutory limitations, the first person to find and take possession of abandoned property (i.e., property voluntarily left behind or given up) or to take control of a wild animal becomes the owner of the abandoned property or wild animal.

LIMITATIONS. ▶ Property left behind due to an emergency is not abandoned property. ▶ The owner of tangible or intangible personal property that is lost and found by another person who refuses to return it may bring an action for conversion in order to regain possession of such property.

▶**LEARNING OUTCOME EXAMPLE.** See the example of the real estate agent who recovered her computerized client investment list from a former employer under the legal theory called "conversion," textbook p. 465.

6. ESCHEAT

Escheat statutes typically provide that a state owns personal property that is not claimed by anyone. Many states have adopted the Uniform Unclaimed Property Act, which addresses this situation.

7. MULTIPLE OWNERSHIP OF PERSONAL PROPERTY

(a) TENANCY IN COMMON

GENERAL RULE. Tenants in common own undivided fractional interests in the same property. An owner may transfer an interest during life or upon death without terminating a tenancy in common.

LIMITATION. Partition (division) of tenancy in common property results in each owner's acquiring complete ownership of a specific portion of the property.

(b) JOINT TENANCY

GENERAL RULE. Joint tenants jointly own property with a right of survivorship.

LIMITATION. To create a joint tenancy, many states require that an instrument state that the co-owners are acquiring title "with right of survivorship."

STUDY HINTS. ▶ If a joint tenant dies, surviving owners acquire the deceased owner's interest. ▶ If a joint tenant transfers the interest to a third party, the new owners become tenants in common.

(c) TENANCY BY ENTIRETY

GENERAL RULES. ▶ At common law, transfer of property to a husband and wife created a tenancy by entirety. If a spouse died, the surviving spouse got the decedent's interest in the property. ▶ A creditor of *both* spouses can execute on (take and sell) property that is held by the entirety.

LIMITATIONS. ▶ A spouse cannot unilaterally transfer his or her interest. ▶ Creditors of only one spouse cannot claim property. ▶ Divorce converts tenancy by entirety into tenancy in common.

8. COMMUNITY PROPERTY

In certain states, most property acquired by either spouse during marriage is community property.

B. BAILMENTS

9. DEFINITION

A bailment is a relationship whereby personal property is delivered by a party (bailor) to another party (bailee), and the property must be returned or delivered in the manner agreed to by the parties.

10. ELEMENTS OF BAILMENT

GENERAL RULES. ▶ Elements of a bailment are: (1) an agreement; and (2) delivery and acceptance of bailed property. ▶ A bailment agreement typically is a contract. The agreement may be express or implied, and it may be oral or written. ▶ A bailment is made when bailed property is delivered to the bailee, and the bailee accepts the property subject to the terms of the bailment agreement.

LIMITATION. Acceptance requires knowledge that goods are in one's possession and control. Without this knowledge there is no bailment.

▶**LEARNING OUTCOME EXAMPLE.** See the Roosevelt University example in which there could be no bailment created because there was no agreement or acceptance of delivery, textbook p. 470.

11. NATURE OF THE PARTIES' INTERESTS

➢ *Bailor's interest*: ▶ A bailor only needs to have a right to possession of bailed goods in order to have the rights of a bailor, including the right to return of bailed goods and the right to sue for damages for wrongful injury to bailed goods. ▶ A bailor does not need to actually own bailed goods in order to have the rights of a bailor.

➢ *Bailee's interest*: ▶ A bailee has only the right to possess and use bailed goods to the extent that such rights are given by the bailment agreement. A bailee does not receive title to bailed goods. ▶ A bailee does not have the right to sell bailed goods unless the bailee is the bailor's authorized agent. ▶ In most cases, a bailee's wrongful sale of bailed goods does not transfer title to a third party purchaser, and the bailor can recover the goods from the third party buyer.

12. CLASSIFICATION OF ORDINARY BAILMENTS

➢ *Gratuitous bailment*: bailment made without expectation of compensation or value.

➢ *Bailment for sole benefit of bailor*: bailee receives no benefits. Example: Denise asks a friend to hold her purse while she makes a phone *call*.

➢ *Bailment for sole benefit of bailee*: bailor receives no benefits. Example: Iris borrowed Li's hedge clippers.

➢ *Mutual benefit bailment*: both parties derive a benefit. Example: Pat left her car with Zeno's Garage for repairs.

➢ *Constructive bailment*: a party comes into possession of property without the owner's consent and, under the circumstances, the possessor of the property has a duty to return it to the owner.

13. RENTING OF SPACE DISTINGUISHED

A bailment is not created if a person stores personal property in: (1) a locker or other space, and (2) the person keeps the exclusive right to use and control that locker or other space.

14. DUTIES AND RIGHTS OF THE BAILEE

▶ In a bailment for the sole benefit of bailor, the bailee's duty is to exercise slight care. Thus, the bailee is liable only for its gross negligence. ▶ In a bailment for the sole benefit of bailee, the duty of care for the bailee is to exercise great care. The bailee is liable for damages caused by even slight negligence. ▶ In a mutual benefit bailment, the bailee must exercise reasonable care and is liable for its ordinary negligence.

15. BREACH OF DUTY OF CARE: BURDEN OF PROOF

In a suit by a bailor, the bailor must prove that bailed goods were not returned or were damaged due to the bailee's fault. This burden is initially met if a bailor proves that goods were delivered, but were not returned or were damaged. If this is proven, the bailor may recover damages unless a bailee proves that the loss or damage was not caused by the bailee's lack of care or unauthorized use of the goods.

16. LIABILITY FOR DEFECTS IN BAILED PROPERTY

▶ In a mutual benefit bailment, a bailor has a duty to provide a good that is reasonably fit for the purposes contemplated by the parties. ▶ If a bailor receives some benefit under the bailment, then the bailor must warn the bailee of known dangers and also reasonably investigate to discover defects. ▶ In a bailment for the sole benefit of bailee, a bailor has a duty to warn a bailee of known dangers.

17. CONTRACT MODIFICATION OF LIABILITY

A bailee can generally limit liability for negligence (not willful wrongs) if: (1) the bailment does not involve a public interest (i.e., a fundamental service or good needed by most persons is not involved); (2) statutes do not forbid disclaimers of liability; (3) the limitation is part of the contract; and (4) the bailor has notice of the limitation at the time of contracting.

CONCEPT REVIEW AND APPLICATIONS

Matching Exercise

Select the term or phrase that best matches a definition or statement stated below. Each term or phrase is the best match for only one statement or definition. Not all terms and phrases will necessarily be used.

bailee	constructive delivery	joint tenancy
bailee's lien	cotenancy	personal property
bailment	donee	prima facie
bailments for mutual benefit	donor	real property
bailor	escheat	severalty
choses in action	gift	symbolic delivery
community property	gift causa mortis	tenancy by entirety
constructive bailment	gratuitous bailments	tenancy by the entireties
	inter vivos gift	tenancy in common

_____ 1. Gift that is made in contemplation of death and that is conditioned upon the death of the donor.

_____ 2. Transfer of ownership of unclaimed property to the state.

_____ 3. In some states, most property that is acquired by a husband or wife during marriage.

_____ 4. Present gift of property.

_____ 5. Broad category of property that includes land and things permanently affixed to or part of land.

_____ 6. Type of co-ownership; each owner owns an undivided interest in the same property and there is no right of survivorship.

_____ 7. Gift that is effective only if certain stated conditions are satisfied. Broad category of property that includes all property rights except rights in real property.

_____ 8. Type of co-ownership; if a co-owner dies, the other co-owners acquire the decedent's interest.

_____ 9. Property that an owner has misplaced without intending to give up ownership.

True/False

Write **T** if the statement is true, write **F** if it is false.

_____ 1. A bailment cannot be implied from the conduct of parties; a bailment must be expressly made.

_____ 2. A bailee only receives possession of bailed goods; a bailee does not receive title to bailed goods.

_____ 3. In many states, in order to create a joint tenancy, title must be taken by the parties specifically stating that they are taking title "with right of survivorship."

_____ 4. Ordinary bailees are generally prohibited by law from limiting their liability for harm that is caused to bailed property.

_____ 5. If X and Y own property as tenants in common and X dies, then X's interest in the property will pass to X's heirs. In this event, X's heirs and Y will own the property as tenants in common.

_____ 6. If A and B own property by joint tenancy and A transfers her interest in the property to C, then B and C will own the property as joint tenants.

_____ 7. If a party finds lost personal property that belongs to someone else, the finder possesses the property as a bailee pursuant to a constructive bailment.

_____ 8.   Persons over the age of 18 may now legally make an anatomical gift.

_____ 9.   A third party who in good faith buys an item of personal property from a thief acquires good title to the property if the third party did not know the property was stolen and paid value for it.

_____ 10. Community property is now followed in all states.

Multiple Choice

_____ 1.   Select the correct answer.
   a. Rose rents a locker at Airport and she puts a bag in the locker. Rose keeps the locker key. In this case, the bag has been delivered to and accepted by Airport, and Airport is a bailee.
   b. Hill rents a boat to Dan. The boat is located at a lake 30 miles away. Hill gives Dan keys to the boat. Dan drives to the lake and takes possession of the boat. In this case, the boat has been delivered to and accepted by Dan, and Dan is a bailee.
   c. Unknown to Lon, Jake left a bike at Lon's house. In this case, the bike has been delivered to and accepted by Lon, and Lon is a bailee.
   d. b and c.

_____ 2.   In accordance with an applicable Uniform Act, Jean made a completed gift of some corporate stock to her 17-year-old daughter. Jean was named as the custodian of the stock. Under these facts:
   a. Jean cannot spend income from the stock to pay for her daughter's college tuition.
   b. Jean can spend income from the stock to pay for Jean's personal credit card bills.
   c. In most cases, Jean's daughter would be entitled to receive the stock when she turns 21.
   d. Jean can revoke the gift of the stock whenever she wants, reclaiming the stock as her own.

_____ 3.   George found a "lost" diamond bracelet in the wall safe in his hotel room (a public place). Which answer best describes George's rights to the bracelet?
   a. George owns the bracelet. A person automatically owns lost property that he or she finds.
   b. Pursuant to the doctrine of escheat, George automatically owns the bracelet.
   c. George may keep the bracelet until the owner reclaims it.
   d. George must turn the bracelet over to the hotel for safekeeping for the bracelet's true owner.

_____ 4.   Thief stole Mary's iPod, and Thief sold the iPod to Gordon for $300. Gordon did not know that the iPod was stolen, and he paid the $300 purchase price to Thief. Under these facts:
   a. Gordon did not acquire title to the iPod even though he bought it for value and in good faith.
   b. Gordon acquired valid title to the iPod because he bought it for value and he was unaware that the iPod was stolen.
   c. Mary cannot recover the iPod from Gordon.
   d. The iPod is an example of abandoned property.

_____ 5.   Quinn rented a paint spray gun from U-Rent-Um Rentals for $25 per day. This bailment is a:
   a. Bailment for the sole benefit of the bailor.
   b. Bailment for the sole benefit of the bailee.
   c. Mutual benefit bailment.
   d. Gratuitous bailment.

_____ 6. Brighton parked his car in a public garage and walked away, keeping the keys to the car. Sarah gave her keys to a parking valet, who parked Sarah's car and kept the keys until she returned. Under these facts, who created a bailment?
a. Only Brighton.
b. Only Sarah.
c. Both Brighton and Sarah.
d. Neither Brighton nor Sarah.

Case Problem

Answer the following problem, briefly explaining your answer.

Jethro was diagnosed as having advanced brain cancer and the doctors believed that he had only a few days to live. He told Sally May, his girlfriend, that he wanted her to have his car when he died. Sally May immediately took possession of the car. As it turns out, the doctors misdiagnosed Jethro's condition and he rapidly recovered. Several weeks later, Jethro was struck by a hit-and-run driver and he died shortly afterwards. Who is entitled to the car - Sally May or Jethro's estate?

_____

_____

_____

Internet Exercise

1. Using the Internet, identify three firms that are offering to enter into bailment contracts with customers.
2. For each firm, analyze (a) for whose benefit the bailment would be and (b) the duty that the bailor would owe to the bailee.

_____

_____

CPA REVIEW

The following questions were given on CPA examinations. The answers for these questions are the unofficial answers prepared by the American Institute of Certified Public Accountants, Inc. (AICPA). All material is reproduced with permission of the AICPA.

_____ 1. Which of the following requirements must be met to create a bailment?

I. Delivery of personal property to the intended bailee.
II. Possession by the intended bailee.
III. An absolute duty on the intended bailee to return or dispose of the property according to the bailor's directions.

a. I and II only.
b. I and III only.
c. II and III only.
d. I, II, and III.

CHAPTER 22
LEGAL ASPECTS OF SUPPLY CHAIN MANAGEMENT

MAKE THE CONNECTION

SUMMARY

A warehouse stores the goods of others for compensation and has the rights and duties of a bailee in an ordinary mutual benefit bailment. A warehouse issues a warehouse receipt to the depositor of the goods. This receipt is a document of title that ordinarily entitles the person in possession of the receipt to receive the goods. The warehouse receipt can be bought, sold, or used as security to obtain a loan. A nonnegotiable warehouse receipt states that the goods received will be delivered to a specified person. A negotiable warehouse receipt states that the goods will be delivered "to the bearer" or "to the order of " a named person. If a negotiable warehouse receipt is duly negotiated, the transferee may acquire rights superior to those of the transferor. A warehouse may limit its liability for loss or damage to goods resulting from its own negligence to an agreed valuation of the property stated in the warehouse receipt, provided the depositor is given the right to store the goods without the limitation at a higher storage rate.

A common carrier of goods is in the business of transporting goods received from the general public. It issues to the shipper a bill of lading or an airbill. Both of these are documents of title and provide rights similar to those provided by a warehouse receipt. A common carrier is absolutely liable for any loss or damage to the goods unless the carrier can show that the loss was caused solely by an act of God, an act of a public enemy, an act of a public authority, an act of the shipper, or the inherent nature of the goods. The carrier may limit its liability in the same manner as a warehouse.

A factor is a special type of bailee who has possession of the owner's property for the purpose of sale. The factor, or consignee, receives a commission on the sale.

A hotelkeeper is in the business of providing living accommodations to transient persons called guests. Subject to exceptions, at common law, hotelkeepers were absolutely liable for loss or damage to their guests' property. Most states, however, provide a method of limiting this liability. A hotelkeeper has a lien on the property of the guest for the agreed charges.

LEARNING OUTCOMES
After studying this chapter, you should be able to

A. WAREHOUSERS
LO.1 Identify and explain all of the features of a negotiable warehouse receipt

B. COMMON CARRIERS
LO.2 List and explain the differences between the three types of motor carriers of goods
LO.3 Explain a common carrier's liability for loss or damage to goods

C. FACTORS AND CONSIGNMENTS
LO.4 Identify and explain the role of each of the persons or business entities involved in the sale of goods on consignment

D. HOTELKEEPERS
LO.5 Describe a hotelkeeper's liability for loss of a guest's property

CHAPTER OUTLINE

A. WAREHOUSES

1. DEFINITIONS

▶ *Warehouse*: a party who engages in the business of storing goods for others for compensation.
▶ *Public warehouse*: a warehouse that stores goods for the public without discrimination.

2. RIGHTS AND DUTIES OF WAREHOUSES

GENERAL RULES. ▶ Rights and duties of warehouses are governed in a majority of states by revised Article 7 of the UCC. ▶ A warehouse is treated as a bailee in a mutual benefit bailment. Thus, a warehouse is liable only for negligent loss or damage to goods. ▶ A warehouse has a specific lien on goods in its possession for charges relating to those goods; goods may be sold to obtain payment.
LIMITATIONS. ▶ Unless otherwise agreed, a lien attaches to only those goods for which charges are owed. ▶ Goods must be returned if charges and expenses are paid prior to sale of the goods.

3. WAREHOUSE RECEIPTS

GENERAL RULE. A warehouse receipt is a writing issued by a warehouse (issuer) acknowledging receipt of goods for storage from a customer (depositor). A receipt states the terms of the contract.
STUDY HINTS. ▶ Warehouse receipts do not need to be in any particular form. ▶ Warehouse receipts are one type of document of title, i.e., a document evidencing a person's right to goods.
▶ **LEARNING OUTCOME EXAMPLES.** See the example of the bona fide purchase of a warehouse receipt of 4,000 pairs of ice skates on textbook p. 483; see textbook Figure 22-1.

4. RIGHTS OF HOLDERS OF WAREHOUSE RECEIPTS

➢ *Nonnegotiable warehouse receipts*: ▶ A warehouse receipt is a nonnegotiable warehouse receipt if it requires delivery of goods to a named person, and the words "bearer" or "order" are not used. Example: "Deliver goods to Jim Hood." ▶ A transferee of a nonnegotiable warehouse receipt receives only the same right and title to goods as the transferor of the warehouse receipt had. ▶ The rights of a transferee of a nonnegotiable warehouse receipt may be defeated by a person who in good faith buys the goods from the transferor of the warehouse receipt.

➢ *Negotiable warehouse receipts*: ▶ A receipt is a negotiable warehouse receipt if it requires delivery of goods to "bearer" or "to the order of" a named person. Example: "Deliver goods to the order of Jim Hood." ▶ A party receives good title to a negotiable receipt and the goods it represents if: (1) the party takes the receipt by negotiation; or (2) the receipt is duly negotiated to that person. The rights of a person to whom a receipt is duly negotiated are superior to those of almost everyone, except the original owner of goods if the goods were stolen from the owner. ▶ *Negotiation* means: (1) delivery of a receipt to the holder (buyer) if goods are to be delivered to "bearer"; or (2) proper indorsement of a receipt and delivery of the receipt if goods are to be delivered "to the order of" a person. ▶ *Duly negotiated* means: a holder takes a receipt: (1) in good faith; (2) in the ordinary course of business; (3) without notice of any defenses; and (4) the holder pays value for the receipt.

> *Warranties*: A person who transfers any document of title for value by implication makes guarantees.

5. FIELD WAREHOUSING

Field warehousing: goods are stored on an owner's premises; a warehouse controls the storage area.

6. LIMITATION OF LIABILITY OF WAREHOUSES

GENERAL RULE. A warehouse can limit its liability if: (1) for a higher fee, a customer has the right to store goods without limited liability; and (2) a limit is stated for each item or unit of weight.

STUDY HINT. A limitation of liability is not effective if the customer is not informed of it at the time of contracting.

B. COMMON CARRIERS

7. DEFINITIONS

> *Basic definitions*: ▶ *Carrier*: party who agrees to transport goods, regardless of the method of shipment. ▶ *Consignor*: party who delivers goods to a carrier for shipment (i.e., a consignor is the shipper). ▶ *Consignee*: party to whom goods are shipped.

> *Types of carriers*: ▶ *Common carrier*: carrier willing to transport goods for compensation for any member of the public without discrimination. ▶ *Contract carrier*: carrier only transporting goods pursuant to individual contracts. ▶ *Private carrier*: carrier owned and operated by the shipper.

> *Controlling law*: ▶ Common carriers: common carrier law. ▶ Contract carriers: bailment law. ▶ Private carriers: employment law.

> Learning outcome example. See the *Fortunoff* case and distinctions made between "common" and "contract" carriers, textbook p. 486.

8. BILLS OF LADING

> *Definitions*: ▶ *Bill of lading*: document of title issued by a carrier for goods to be shipped by land. ▶ *Airbill*: document issued for goods to be shipped by air. ▶ *Nonnegotiable (straight) bill of lading*: goods are shipped to a named person; the words "bearer" or "order" are not used. ▶ *Negotiable bill of lading*: goods are shipped to "bearer" or "to the order of" a named person.
> *Law*: ▶ Intrastate shipment: UCC. ▶ Interstate shipment: Federal Bills of Lading Act.
> *Rules*: Rules regarding the transfer of bills of lading, rights of transferees of bills, and warranties are determined by the same rules previously discussed for warehouse receipts. (see Section 4 above)

9. RIGHTS OF COMMON CARRIER

GENERAL RULE. A common carrier can: (1) adopt reasonable business rules; (2) determine rates in order to earn a fair return (subject to government regulations); (3) charge a demurrage; and (4) have a specific lien on goods for shipment fees, demurrage charges, and expenses for preserving and selling goods.

LIMITATIONS. ▶ A lien only attaches to the goods that are shipped under the contract for which charges are owing. ▶ A lien is lost to the extent goods are delivered to the consignee.

10. DUTIES OF COMMON CARRIER

GENERAL RULES. ► A common carrier must: (1) accept and ship goods for all persons to the extent it can do so; (2) furnish proper storage and shipping facilities; (3) load and unload goods (unless otherwise agreed); and (4) ship and deliver goods in accordance with shipment contracts. ► Delivery under negotiable bill of lading: carrier must not deliver without first getting a properly indorsed bill of lading. ► Delivery under straight bill: carrier may deliver goods to consignee without getting bill.

LIMITATION. A common carrier is not obligated to carry goods if: (1) the goods are not appropriate for transportation; or (2) the carrier does not have the necessary facilities for shipment.

11. LIABILITIES OF COMMON CARRIER

➤ *Liability for delay*: A carrier is liable for damages caused by its failure to deliver in a reasonable time. But, a shipper bears the risk for losses caused by ordinary delays associated with shipping.

Limitation of liability: Subject to certain limits, a carrier can generally limit its liability.

➤ *Notice of claim:* The bill or laws may require notice within a set time in order to claim damages. *Liability C.O.D. (cash-on-delivery) shipment*: Common carrier must not deliver goods without first receiving payment and if it improperly does so, then it is liable to the shipper for damages.

➤ *Liability for rejected goods*: A carrier is liable only for its negligence once delivery is offered, but refused. But, absolute liability is reinstated once new shipping instructions are received.

➤

➤ *Liability during shipment*: In general, a common carrier has absolute liability for any damage or loss to goods, but it does not have liability for losses that are caused by or result from: (1) act of God (natural phenomenon); (2) act of public enemy; (3) act of government official; (4) act of shipper (improper packaging); or (5) inherent nature of goods (such as perishable food).

➤ **LEARNING OUTCOME EXAMPLE.** See the *Great West Casualty* case applying the Carmack Amendment rule on carrier liability, textbook p. 490.

➤

C. FACTORS AND CONSIGNMENTS

12. DEFINITIONS

► *Factor*: special bailee (consignee) who sells bailed (consigned) goods. ► *Selling on consignment*: entrusting goods to another who is to sell the goods. ► *Consignor*: owner who consigns goods.

► *Consignee*: person to whom goods are consigned. ► *Commission:* compensation paid to a factor.

► **LEARNING OUTCOME EXAMPLE.** See the Rolly Tasker Sails example involving breach of a consignment agreement on textbook p. 493.

13. EFFECT OF FACTOR TRANSACTION

An authorized sale of consigned goods by a factor passes title to the goods to the buyer unless the consignor did not own the goods. In certain cases, a factor's creditors may take consigned goods.

D. HOTELKEEPERS

14. DEFINITIONS

▶ *Hotelkeeper*: operator of a hotel or motel, or other person who regularly offers temporary accommodations to guests. ▶ *Guest*: transient person who stays overnight. A guest is not a person visiting a guest or a person who stays overnight with a guest without a hotelkeeper's knowledge.

15. DURATION OF GUEST RELATIONSHIP

A hotelkeeper-guest relationship begins when a guest is received by a hotelkeeper, and it ends when the guest leaves (with baggage) or the guest arranges for permanent lodging with the hotelkeeper.

16. HOTELKEEPER'S LIABILITY FOR GUEST'S PROPERTY

▶ A hotelkeeper is a bailee regarding property actually given to the hotelkeeper. ▶ At common law, a hotelkeeper had absolute liability for loss of guest's property, subject to the same exceptions that apply to common carriers. ▶ By statute, most states now allow hotelkeepers to limit their liability. ▶ **LEARNING OUTCOME EXAMPLE.** See the *Paraskevaides v Four Seasons Washington* case for a discussion of the common law rule on liability for loss of a guest's property and application of a statutory exemption, textbook p. 495.

17. HOTELKEEPER'S LIEN

A hotelkeeper has a lien on a guest's baggage for room charges. To obtain payment, baggage may be sold. A lien is lost if: (1) charges are paid; or (2) baggage is unconditionally returned to a guest.

18. BOARDERS OR LODGERS

A boarder takes lodging on a permanent basis. A hotelkeeper is liable for negligent damage to a boarder's property. A hotelkeeper has no lien unless given this right by contract or statute.

CONCEPT REVIEW AND APPLICATIONS

Matching Exercise

Select the term or phrase that best matches a definition or statement stated below. Each term or phrase is the best match for only one statement or definition. Not all terms and phrases will necessarily be used.

airbill	document of title	nonnegotiable warehouse
bill of lading	factorage	receipt
carrier	factor	private carrier
commission merchant	field warehousing	public warehouses
commission	guest	selling on consignment
common carrier	hotelkeeper	specific lien
consignee	issuer	straight bill of lading
consignor	negotiable bill of lading	warehouse receipt
contract carrier	negotiable warehouse	warehouse
conversion	receipt	
depositor	nonnegotiable bill of lading	

_____ 1. Warehousing arrangement whereby goods are stored in a separate area on an owner's premises, and a warehouse is given exclusive control of this area.

_____ 2. Document of title issued by a carrier when it receives goods to be shipped by ai transportation.

_____ 3. Transient person who stays overnight at an establishment operated by a hotelkeeper.

_____ 4. Party who stores goods for compensation for members of the public without discrimination.

_____ 5. Carrier that holds itself out as being willing to provide transportation for compensation for any member of the public without discrimination.

_____ 6. Broad category of bailments that involves a strong public interest.

_____ 7. Special bailee who sells consigned goods that belong to another party.

_____ 8. Bill of lading shipping goods to the "bearer" or "to the order of" a named person.

_____ 9. Bill of lading shipping goods to a person without using the words "bearer" or "to the order of."

_____ 10. Carrier that transports goods for compensation under individual contracts, and the carrier does not hold it out as being willing to provide transportation for all members of the public.

True/False

Write **T** if the statement is true, write **F** if it is false.

____ 1. In general, a warehouse is absolutely liable for any damage or loss to stored goods.

____ 2. Unless otherwise expressly stated, a warehouse has a lien on stored goods to secure payment of only the storage charges and expenses that relate to the goods being stored.

____ 3. A warehouse receipt typically is a receipt for stored goods, a memorandum of the storage contract, and a document of title.

____ 4. To negotiate a negotiable warehouse receipt that requires delivery to the "bearer," the transferor of the receipt must first indorse the receipt and then deliver the receipt to the transferee.

____ 5. Assume that a thief steals a stereo, the thief receives a negotiable warehouse receipt when he stores the stereo, and the receipt is negotiated to a third party who takes it by due negotiation. In this situation, the original owner of the stereo still has the superior right to the stereo.

____ 6. In general, a common carrier has no duty to load or unload goods that are delivered to it for shipment.

____ 7. In general, a warehouse cannot limit its liability unless it first allows a customer the opportunity to pay a higher fee for storing the goods without a limitation of liability.

____ 8. If a factor sells stolen goods for a thief/consignor, the factor may be liable to the owner of the goods for damages due to conversion even if the factor did not know that the goods were stolen.

_____ 9. At common law, a hotelkeeper did not have a lien on the baggage of a boarder.

_____ 10. A common carrier is only required to ship goods for those parties that it may choose to serve.

Multiple Choice

_____ 1. Charles owned tools that he stored with Ace Warehouse. Ace issued Charles a *nonnegotiable* warehouse receipt for the tools. Charles sold the tools to Zeke who bought them for value, and Zeke took possession of the tools in good faith. Later, Charles sold the warehouse receipt to Alice who bought it for value and in good faith. Who has the superior right to the tools?
   a. Charles
   b. Zeke
   c. Alice
   d. Zeke and Alice have equal rights to the tools.

_____ 2. Irving stored furniture with We-Store-Um, a warehouse. We-Store-Um issued Irving a warehouse receipt that directs the furniture to be delivered to the "bearer." Irving negotiated the warehouse receipt to Steve who took it by due negotiation. The next day, We-Store-Um delivered the furniture to Irving without first receiving the warehouse receipt. Under these facts:
   a. The warehouse receipt is a nonnegotiable warehouse receipt.
   b. The warehouse receipt is a negotiable warehouse receipt.
   c. We-Store-Um was legally entitled to deliver the furniture to Irving. We-Store-Um is not liable to Steve for damages he may suffer because the furniture was delivered to Irving.
   d. a and c.

_____ 3. Keep-On-Trucking, a common carrier, contracted to ship equipment for Judd Fabricators. The equipment was damaged during shipment. Subject to certain exceptions, Keep-On-Trucking is:
   a. Liable for the damage only if the damage was due to its intentional wrongdoing.
   b. Liable for the damage only if the damage was due to its negligence.
   c. Absolutely liable for the damage even if it was not due to Keep-On-Trucking's fault.
   d. Not liable for the damage; the risk of loss or damage is always borne by the shipper.

_____ 4. In which case is Conn Carrier, a common carrier, liable for the damage or loss in question?
   a. Goods being transported by Conn were stolen by a thief.
   b. Goods being transported by Conn were destroyed by an unforeseeable earthquake.
   c. Goods being transported by Conn were damaged due to improper packaging by the shipper.
   d. Goods being transported by Conn were confiscated by government health officials.

_____ 5. Daisy checked into the Palms Motel for an overnight stay. Daisy left a cashmere coat in her room. While Daisy was having dinner, her coat was taken from her room. Under these facts:
   a. At common law, the Palms has absolute liability for the loss of the coat.
   b. At common law, the Palms is liable for the lost coat only if the loss was due to its negligence
   c. In most states today, statutes would prohibit the Palms from limiting its liability for the coat.
   d. a and c.

_____ 6. What is a warehouse's standard of care for stored goods?
   a. A warehouse is strictly liable for any loss or damage to stored goods.
   b. A warehouse is liable for loss or damage that results from the slightest negligence on the part of the warehouse.
   c. A warehouse is liable for loss or damage that results from ordinary negligence on the part of the warehouse.
   d. A warehouse is liable for loss or damage only if it results from gross negligence on the part of the warehouse.

_____ 7. Which of the following is NOT a document of title?
   a. A nonnegotiable bill of lading.
   b. A negotiable bill of lading.
   c. A negotiable warehouse receipt.
   d. A negotiable promissory note.

_____ 8. A person who for value negotiates a warehouse receipt for stored goods does NOT warrant that:
   a. The goods are fit for the ordinary purposes for which they are intended.
   b. The person owns the goods.
   c. The warehouse receipt is genuine.
   d. a and b.

_____ 9. AirOne Airlines issued Carla a negotiable bill of lading "to the order of Carla Rodriguez" for goods that she was shipping. What must Carla do in order to negotiate this bill of a lading to Harold, a customer?
   a. Carla must only deliver the bill of lading to Harold.
   b. Carla must indorse the bill of lading and deliver it to Harold.
   c. Carla must deliver the bill of lading to AirOne Airlines who must then cancel the bill of lading and issue a new one to Harold.
   d. Carla cannot negotiate the bill of lading to Carla. She must take delivery of the goods.

Case Problem

Answer the following problem, briefly explaining your answer.

Bob, Joe, and Sam separately registered as guests at the Essex Motel. All three guests wrongfully failed to pay their respective room charges, and the Essex refused to return their baggage. Bob then paid the charge for his room. At Joe's request, the Essex returned Joe's baggage even though he had not paid.

1. What rights does the Essex have with regard to Sam's baggage?
2. What rights does the Essex have with regard to Joe's baggage?
3. Must the Essex return Bob's baggage to him?

_____

_____

_____

_____

Internet Exercise

Lawrence owned a business that transported passengers by bus from his home town across the state border to a location where gambling was legal. One day, Sally bought a ticket and bordered Lawrence's bus, carrying a single suitcase. The ticket given Sally stated that Lawrence's liability was limited to $250 for lost luggage unless the passenger wanted to pay a higher tariff for greater coverage. Sally did not read this term of the ticket. When the bus arrived at the destination, everyone exited including Lawrence and Sally. Sally, however, forgot her suitcase and it disappeared from the bus. The suitcase contained $1,000 in quarters.

1. Using the Internet, locate and identify the federal regulation that regulates limitations of liability by interstate common carriers.
2. For how much can Lawrence be held liable in this case?

_____

_____

_____

_____

CPA REVIEW

The following questions were given on CPA examinations. The answers for these questions are the unofficial answers prepared by the American Institute of Certified Public Accountants, Inc. (AICPA). All material is reproduced with permission of the AICPA.

____ 1. Bond Corp. issued a negotiable warehouse receipt to Grey for goods stored in Bond's warehouse. Grey's goods were lost due to Bond's failure to exercise such care as a reasonably careful person would under like circumstances. The state in which this transaction occurred follows the UCC rule with respect to a warehouseman's liability for lost goods. The warehouse receipt is silent on this point. Under the circumstances, Bond is
a. Liable because it was negligent.
b. Liable because it is strictly liable for any loss.
c. Not liable unless Grey can establish that Bond was grossly negligent.
d. Not liable because the warehouse receipt was negotiable.

____ 2. Klep burglarized the premises of Apple Sales Co. He stole several negotiable warehouse receipts which were deliverable to the order of Apple. Klep indorsed Apple's name on the instruments and transferred them to Margo Wholesalers, a bona Fide purchaser for value. As between Apple and Margo,

    a. Apple will prevail since the warehouseman must be notified before any negotiation is effective.

    b. Apple will prevail since the thief's indorsement prevents a due negotiation.

    c. Margo will prevail since it has taken a negotiable warehouse receipt as a bona fide purchaser for value.

    d. Margo will prevail since the warehouse receipt was converted to a bearer instrument by Klep's indorsement.

____ 3. Unless otherwise agreed, which of the following warranties will not be conferred by a person negotiating a negotiable warehouse receipt for value to his immediatepurchaser?

    a. The document is genuine.

    b. Transferor is without knowledge of any fact which would impair its validity or worth.

    c. The goods represented by the warehouse receipt are of merchantable quality.

    d. Negotiation by the transferor is rightful and fully effective with respect to the title to the document.

____ 4. The procedure necessary to negotiate a document of title depends principally on whether the document is

    a. An order document or a bearer document.

    b. Issued by a bailee or a consignee.

    c. A receipt for goods stored or goods already shipped.

    d. A bill of lading or a warehouse receipt.

CHAPTER 23
NATURE AND FORM OF SALES

MAKE THE CONNECTION

SUMMARY

Contracts for services and real estate are governed by the common law. Contracts for the sale of goods are governed by Article 2 of the UCC. *Goods* are defined as anything movable at the time they are identified as the subject of the transaction. Goods physically existing and owned by the seller at the time of the transaction are *existing goods*.

A *sale of goods* is the transfer of title to tangible personal property for a price. A *bailment* is a transfer of possession but not title and is therefore not a sale. A *gift* is not a sale because no price is paid for the gift. A contract for services is an ordinary contract and is not governed by the UCC. If a contract calls for both the rendering of services and the supplying of goods, the contract is classified according to its dominant element.

The common law contract rules for intent to contract apply to the formation of contracts under the UCC. However, several formation rules under the UCC differ from common law contract rules. A merchant's firm offer is irrevocable without the payment of consideration. The UCC rules on additional terms in an acceptance permit the formation of a contract despite the changes. These proposals for new terms are not considered counteroffers under the UCC. The terms that are included are determined by detailed rules. If the transaction is between nonmerchants, a contract is formed without the additional terms, which the original offeror is free to accept or reject. If the transaction is between merchants, the additional terms become part of the contract if those terms do not materially alter the offer and no objection is made to them. There is no distinction between merchant and nonmerchant for additional terms under Revised Article 2 and the terms issues is left to the courts.

The same defenses available to formation under common law are incorporated in Article 2. In addition, the UCC recognizes unconscionability as a defense to formation.

The UCC does not require the parties to agree on every aspect of contract performance for the contract to be valid. Provisions in Article 2 will govern the parties' relationship in the event their agreement does not cover all terms. The price term may be expressly fixed by the parties. The parties may make no provision as to price, or they may indicate how the price should be determined later. In output or requirements contracts, the quantity that is to be sold or purchased is not specified, but such contracts are nevertheless valid. A salescontract can be modified even though the modification is not supported by consideration. The parol evidence rule applies to a sale of goods in much the same manner as to ordinary contracts. However, the UCC permits the introduction of evidence of course of dealing and usage of trade for clarification of contract terms and performance.

The UCC's statute of frauds provides that a sales contract for $500 ($5,000 under Revised Article 2) or more must be evidenced by a record. The UCC's merchant's confirmation memorandum allows two merchants to be bound to an otherwise oral agreement by a memo or letter signed by only one party that standswithout objection for 10 days. Several exceptions to the UCC statute of frauds exist: when the goods are specially made or procured for the buyer and are nonresellable in the seller's ordinary market; when the buyer has received and accepted the goods; when the buyer has made either full or partial payment; andwhen the party against whom enforcement is sought admits in court pleadings or testimony that a contract for sale was made.

Uniform rules for international sales are applicable to contracts for sales between parties in countries that have ratified the CISG. Under the CISG, a contract for the sale of goods need not be in any particular form and can be proven by any means.

Article 2A of the UCC regulates consumer leases, commercial leases, finance leases, nonfinance leases, and subleases of tangible movable goods. A lease subject to Article 2A must be in writing if the lease payments will total $1,000 or more.

LEARNING OUTCOMES
After studying this chapter, you should be able to

A. NATURE AND LEGALITY
LO.1   Define a sale of goods and explain when UCC Article 2 applies to contracts
LO.2   Distinguish between an actual sale of goods and other types of transactions in goods
LO.3   Describe how contracts are formed under Article 2, and list the differences in formation standards between the UCC and common law

B. FORM OF SALES CONTRACT
LO.4   Explain when a contract for the sale of goods must be in writing
LO.5   List and explain the exceptions to the requirement that certain contracts be in writing

C. UNIFORM LAW FOR INTERNATIONAL SALES
LO.6   Discuss the purpose of the United Nations Convention on Contracts for the International Sale of Goods

CHAPTER OUTLINE

A. NATURE OF SALES

A sale of goods is a (1) present transfer of title (2) to tangible movable property (3) that is made for a price. The price paid for goods may be money, property, or performance of a service by a buyer. UCC Article 2 governs contracts for the sale of goods.

1. SUBJECT MATTER OF SALES

GENERAL RULES.   ▶ "Goods" include tangible personal property that is movable at the time it is identified to a contract. ▶ Goods may be new or used. ▶ Goods do not include: (1) investment securities (stocks or bonds); (2) choses in action (promissory notes); or (3) real estate (land and permanent buildings).
STUDY HINT.   A party can contract to sell existing goods (goods existing and owned by a seller at time of contracting) or future goods (goods not owned by the seller or goods not yet existing).
▶**LEARNING OUTCOME EXAMPLE.** See *Wall Street Network, Ltd. v New York Times Company,* on textbook p. 506.

2. SALE DISTINGUISHED FROM OTHER TRANSACTIONS

GENERAL RULE. A "sale" requires a transfer of title. A sale does not include a: (1) bailment or lease of goods; (2) gift; or (3) contract for services.

STUDY HINT. ► If the seller is required to both sell goods and render a service, the contract is classified by its dominant element. Therefore, if the sale of goods is the dominant aspect of the contract and the service is merely incidental, it is a sales contract. ► Example: A&A Appliances contracts to sell a stove to Joan for $500. The price includes $450 for the stove, and $50 for delivery and installation of the stove. This contract is a sales contract because sale of the stove is the dominant element.

3. FORMATION OF SALES CONTRACTS

(a) *Necessary detail for formation*: A sales contract may be formed even if one or more terms is not stated, so long as the parties intend to enter into a contract.

(b) *The Merchant versus nonmerchant parties*: Article 2 governs sales of goods by merchants and nonmerchants. Sometimes, though, certain rules apply only to merchants and some apply only to transactions between merchants.

(c) *Offer*: ► A merchant cannot revoke a "firm offer" if: (1) in a signed writing; (2) the merchant promised not to revoke the offer to buy or sell goods. ► A firm offer is irrevocable for the time stated, not to exceed three months. If no time is stated, it is irrevocable for a reasonable time. ► A firm offer is irrevocable even if consideration is not given for the promise not to revoke.

(d) *Acceptance*:

➢ *Manner*: Unless otherwise clearly stated by an offeror, an offer may be accepted in anymanner and using any means of communication that is reasonable under the circumstances.

➢ *Timing*: The mailbox rule for determining when an acceptance is effective applies if the acceptance is sent in a reasonable manner.

➢ *Language*: An acceptance may form a contract even if its terms vary from the terms of the offer:

➢ *Acceptance varies from terms of offer*: Under the original Article 2, the following rules apply.

➢ *Acceptance with additional terms (in general)*: A definite, unconditional statement of acceptance is generally a valid acceptance and forms a contract even though the acceptance states a new term that is in addition to the terms stated in the offer. An additional term in an acceptance does not necessarily create a rejection or counteroffer.

➢ *Acceptance with additional terms (nonmerchants)*: If a valid acceptance has an additional term and either party is not a merchant, a contract is formed and it is comprised solely of the terms stated in the offer. The additional term is not part of the contract unless the offeror agrees to it.

➢ *Acceptance with additional terms (merchants)*: ► If a valid acceptance has an additional term and both parties are merchants, then: (1) a contract is formed and (2) the new term is part of the contract unless: (a) the offer limits acceptance to the offer's terms; (b) the term materially alters the contract; or (c) the offeror objects to the term within a reasonable time. ► A term is not a material change if it is a common business term and it does not significantly alter the parties' duties. Example: typical contract term that charges interest on late payments.

➤ *Acceptance with conflicting terms*: If an acceptance contains terms that conflict with terms of the offer but the parties nonetheless intend to contract (e.g., the parties perform the intended contract), then Article 2 recognizes that a contract is formed. In this case, the contract consists of terms upon which the offer and acceptance agree, coupled with other terms implied by law.

➤ *Revised Article 2*: The effect of revised §2-207 is to leave the issues of what is or is not included in a contract to the courts.

➤ *Learning outcome examples*: See the **For Example** discussion of Joe and Susan's X-box transaction on textbook p. 509; see the *Greenbriar* basket case on textbook p. 517.

(e) *Defenses to formation*: ▶ (1) Unconscionability: A sales contract is not enforceable if it is grossly unfair, i.e., unconscionable. (2) Illegality: ▶ A sale is illegal if the subject matter is illegal, the contract states that the subject matter is to be used in an illegal manner, or a seller helps a buyer to make illegal use of goods. ▶ In general, no remedies are available for breach of an illegal contract.

4. TERMS IN THE FORMED CONTRACT

(a) *Price*: The contract price is: (1) the price expressly agreed upon; or (2) if no price is stated, the price is a reasonable price (which is often determined by industry custom or market price).

(b) *Output and requirement contracts*: ▶ Parties can contract to buy and sell a quantity of goods measured by a seller's production (an output contract), or by a buyer's needs (a requirements contract). ▶ Limits: (1) parties must act in good faith; and (2) the amount offered or requested cannot be unreasonably different from contract estimates or from prior output or requirements.

(c) *Indefinite duration term*: If a contract requires periodic deliveries of goods but a fixed term is not stated, the contract continues for a reasonable time. Either party may terminate such a contract by giving written notice of termination.

(d) *Changes in terms*: A good faith contract modification is valid even without consideration.

(e) *Contradicting terms: parol evidence rule*. ▶ A final and exclusive written contract can be explained using parol evidence (prior oral statements), but parol evidence cannot be used to add to or contradict the terms of the written contract. ▶ If a writing is a final statement of only part of a contract, parol evidence may also be used to prove consistent, additional terms.

(f) *Interpreting contract terms: course of dealing and usage of trade.* Evidence of course of dealing (series of prior dealings between the same parties) and usage of trade (practice of doing business regularly followed in a trade) may be used to: (1) explain the meaning of contract terms; and (2) supply missing terms.

5. BULK TRANSFERS

▶ UCC Article 6 was created to deal with bulk sales of goods. ▶ A substantial number of states have repealed this portion of the UCC.

B. FORM OF SALES CONTRACT

6. AMOUNT

Sales contracts for $500 or more are required by the statute of frauds to be evidenced by a writing.

7. NATURE OF THE WRITING REQUIRED

GENERAL RULES. ► The statute of frauds requires that a writing: (1) indicate that parties have made a contract; (2) state the quantity of goods; and (3) be signed by the party who is using the statute of frauds as a defense (the defendant). ► If both parties are merchants, the writing requirement is met if: (1) one merchant signs a sufficient "confirmation memorandum"; (2) the confirmation is sent to the other merchant; and (3) the other merchant does not object in writing within 10 days.

STUDY HINTS. ► A writing can satisfy the statute of frauds even if it is not made for that purpose and it is not a formal written contract. ► Two or more writings may comprise the needed writing.

LEARNING OUTCOME EXAMPLE. See the *Basquiat* case on textbook p. 516.

8. EFFECT OF NONCOMPLIANCE (WITH THE STATUTE OF FRAUDS)

Noncompliance renders a contract unenforceable, but parties can voluntarily perform the contract.

9. EXCEPTIONS TO REQUIREMENT OF A WRITING

(a) *Specially manufactured goods*: An oral contract for specially made goods is enforceable if: (1) goods are not suitable for resale; and (2) before the buyer disavows the contract, the seller has made a substantial beginning either in making the goods or in committing to obtain the goods.

(b) *Other exceptions*: ► An oral contract is enforceable *to the extent that*: (1) goods are delivered to and received and accepted by a buyer; (2) the price is paid and accepted by a seller; or (3) the party who refuses to perform admits in judicial proceedings or pleadings that a contract was made. ► Part payment for a single item makes the contract enforceable. ► Payment for less than all items purchased makes the contract enforceable for only the items for which payment is made. ► **LEARNING OUTCOME EXAMPLE**. See the **For Example** discussion of Wayne and the baseball jackets on textbook p. 519.

10. NONCODE REQUIREMENTS

Federal and state laws may impose additional requirements regarding consumer sales contracts.

11. BILL OF SALE

A bill of sale is a writing evidencing a sale or transfer of title; it is not a contract.

C. UNIFORM LAW FOR INTERNATIONAL SALES

United Nations Convention on Contracts for the International Sale of Goods (CISG) governs sales contracts made between a party in the U.S. and a party in a country that has adopted this convention.

12. SCOPE OF THE CISG

► CISG does not apply to: (1) sales contracts that exclude its application; (2) contracts for goods purchased for personal, family, or household use; (3) service contracts; or (4) liability for death or personal injury caused by goods. ► The CISG is similar in many respects to Article 2 of the UCC.

D. LEASES OF GOODS

Article 2A of the UCC governs leases of tangible movable goods. A lease is "a transfer of the right to possession and use of goods for a term in return for consideration."

13. TYPES OF LEASES

Article 2A governs all leases and subleases of goods including the following types of lease:

➢ *Consumer lease*: (1) lease of goods (2) made by a merchant lessor (lessor is regularly engaged in the business of selling or leasing goods of that kind) (3) to a natural person (not a corporation)(4) for personal, family, or household use (5) and total payments under the lease are $25,000 or less.

➢ *Commercial (nonconsumer) lease*: any lease of goods that is not a consumer lease.

➢ *Finance lease*: lease of goods whereby (1) lessee (not the lessor) selects the goods, (2) lessor then acquires or leases the goods from a supplier on terms that are acceptable to the lessee, and (3) the lessee then leases or subleases the goods from the lessor.

14. FORM OF LEASE CONTRACT

A lease of goods must be evidenced by a writing to be enforceable if the total lease payments are $1,000 or more. A writing must (1) describe the goods, (2) state the term of the lease, (3) indicate that a lease has been made, and (4) be signed by the party against whom the lease is being enforced.

15. WARRANTIES

GENERAL RULE. With one limitation (under a finance lease), a lessor of goods makes the same express or implied warranties to a lessee as a seller of goods makes to a buyer (unless warranties are properly disclaimed or modified).

LIMITATION. Under a finance lease, warranties made by a supplier to a lessor are passed through to the lessee who enforces them directly against the supplier. The lessor under a finance lease makes no implied warranties and is liable for only express warranties (if any) made by the lessor to the lessee.

16. DEFAULT

The lease agreement and Article 2A determine whether a party is in default. If a lessee defaults, the lessor can recover any rent due, future rent, and incidental damages.

CONCEPT REVIEW AND APPLICATIONS

Matching Exercise

Select the term or phrase that best matches a definition or statement stated below. Each term or phrase is the best match for only one statement or definition. Not all terms and phrases will necessarily be used.

acceptance	cost plus	mirror image rule
Article 2	course of dealing	nonconsumer lease
bailee	existing goods	offer
bailment	finance lease	output contract
battle of the forms	firm offer	parol evidence rule
bill of sale	future goods	requirements contract
commercial lease	gift	statute of frauds
consumer lease	goods	unconscionable
Contracts for the	lease	usage of trade
International Sale of	mailbox rule	
Goods (CISG)	merchants	

_____ 1. Writing that merely evidences the making of a sale or a transfer of title to a buyer.

_____ 2. Goods that are physically existing and owned by a seller at the time a sales contract is made.

_____ 3. Goods that do not exist, or are not owned by a seller, at the time a sales contract is made.

_____ 4. Gratuitous (free) transfer of title to property.

_____ 5. International convention (treaty) that governs many international sales of goods.

_____ 6. Merchant's signed, written offer to buy or sell goods which promises that the offer will not be revoked for a certain period of time, not to exceed three months.

_____ 7. Lease of goods by a natural person primarily for personal, family, or household use.

_____ 8. Transfer of the right to possession or use of goods for a term in return for consideration.

_____ 9. Property that is movable at the time that it is identified to a contract.

_____10. Lease of goods by which a lessee selects the goods and a lessor then obtains the goods from a supplier.

True/False

Write **T** if the statement is true, write **F** if it is false.

_____ 1. The writing requirement of the statute of frauds regarding sales contracts is satisfied only if there is a formal written contract that is signed by both the seller and the buyer.

_____ 2. Under a requirements contract, a seller must meet all of the buyer's requirements even if the quantity demanded is unreasonably different from the buyer's prior requirements.

_____ 3. A good faith modification of a sales contract is invalid unless it is supported by consideration.

_____ 4. A party may enter into a contract to sell future goods.

_____ 5. Under Article 2, if both parties to a contract are merchants, an additional term that is stated in an acceptance does not become part of the contract if it would materially change the contract or the offeror objects to the term within a reasonable time.

_____ 6. If a contract requires a seller to convey title to a good and to perform a service, then the contract is always viewed as being a sale of goods that is governed by Article 2 of the UCC.

_____ 7. A sales contract cannot be formed if one or more terms is not stated.

_____ 8. A merchant can revoke a firm offer unless the party to whom the offer is made gives the merchant consideration for the firm offer.

_____ 9. If a seller states an exclusive manner of acceptance, then the offer must be accepted in that manner.

_____ 10. If an acceptance states a term that conflicts with a term in the offer for the sale of goods but the buyer and seller perform the intended contract, Article 2 will recognize the creation of a contract.

Multiple Choice

_____ 1. Which contract is a sales contract that is governed by Article 2 of the UCC?
   a. Floors Inc., a carpet manufacturer, contracts to sell a shipment of carpeting to Retailer.
   b. Earl contracts to sell his farm to Mindy.
   c. Wayne contracts to sell 500 shares of Acme Inc. stock to Claire.
   d. Bob contracts to sell a promissory note to Amanda.

_____ 2. Which agreement is a sales contract that is governed by Article 2 of the UCC?
   a. Dr. Hanson agrees to donate some Walt Whitman books to the college library.
   b. Terri contracts to buy a portable, pre-made storage shed. The total price is $10,000, which includes $500 for the seller's labor that is required to assemble the shed.
   c. Vicky contracts to pay Ted $3,000 to paint Vicky's house. The price includes $2,500 for labor and $500 for paint and other supplies.
   d. Zodiac Rentals rents a saw to Carl.

_____ 3. Braxon Co., a merchant, offered to buy a tool from S& Inc., a merchant. The offer was silent regarding the time for delivery of the tool. S&S sent Braxon a definite, unconditional acceptance that stated that S&S would deliver the tool within 14 days after the date of acceptance. This additional delivery term was common in the industry, and it would not surprise or cause hardship to Braxon. Braxon did not object to this additional term. Under these facts, under Article 2:
   a. A contract was not formed because the acceptance stated a term that was not in the offer.
   b. A contract would be formed only if Braxon agreed to the delivery term in the acceptance.
   c. A contract was formed, and the additional delivery term is part of the contract.
   d. A contract was formed, but the additional delivery term is not part of the contract.

_____ 4. Gold Producer agreed to sell 50 ounces of gold to Gold Wholesaler. Both parties are merchants who regularly engage in the gold industry. The parties definitely intended to contract, but the parties intentionally did not state the price to be paid. Under these facts:
   a. The agreement is invalid because it fails to state the price to be paid.
   b. The agreement is a valid contract; Wholesaler must pay a reasonable price.
   c. The agreement is a valid contract; Wholesaler can pay whatever price it chooses to pay.
   d. The agreement is a valid contract; Wholesaler must pay the price Producer requests.

_____ 5. Wren Equipment Sales Co. bought a crane from Equipment Manufacturer pursuant to a final written contract. The contract ambiguously states that Manufacturer will "reasonably train" Wren's employees to use the crane. The contract also states that Manufacturer will store the crane with a public storage company for 30 days, but it does not state who will pay the storage costs. Prior to signing the contract, Manufacturer had orally promised to store the crane for 60 days. (Mistake is not involved in this question.) Under these facts:
   a. Parol evidence can be used to prove the meaning of the ambiguous term "reasonably train."
   b. Parol evidence can be used to change the terms of the contract by proving Manufacturer's promise to store the crane for 60 days.
   c. A usage of trade can be used to prove who must pay the storage fees.
   d. a and c.

_____ 6. Which contract is unenforceable because it violates the statute of frauds?
   a. A&M orally contracted to buy a shipment of sugar from Refinery for $2,000. A&M immediately sent Refinery a signed, written confirmation that stated all of the contract terms. Refinery received the confirmation, and Refinery never objected to the confirmation.
   b. Seller sold Buyer a truck for $5,000. Both parties signed a writing confirming their agreement and the contract terms. The writing, however, does not state the contract price.
   c. Judy made an oral contract to buy cosmetics for $800.
   d. Rod made an oral contract to buy a stereo for $300.

_____ 7. Which contract is enforceable?
   a. Peter orally contracted to sell a shipment of nuts to Bill for $1,000. Peter delivered the nuts to Bill, who received and accepted the nuts.
   b. Jarvis orally contracted to sell a car to Buyer for $5,000. Buyer paid Jarvis $3,500 of the purchase price. Jarvis accepted this payment.
   c. Cy orally contracted to sell a horse to Buyer for $1,000. Cy now refuses to perform the contract because it is oral. At trial, Cy admitted making the contract.
   d. All of the above.

_____ 8. Which agreement is a commercial finance lease that is governed by Article 2A of the UCC?
   a. Cindy agreed to buy a TV for her bar and grill restaurant.
   b. Tom agreed to lease an office building for his business.
   c. Pat agreed to lease an automobile for his personal use. Pat selected the automobile from Lessor's existing fleet of lease automobiles.
   d. JD agreed to lease portable carpet cleaning equipment from Lessor. JD selected the equipment and Lessor then purchased the equipment from Supplier on terms that were satisfactory to JD.

_____ 9. Which lease is *unenforceable?*
   a. James orally agreed to lease a computer for total lease payments of $500.
   b. Katherine orally agreed to lease a truck for total lease payments of $4,000.
   c. Jack orally agreed to lease a plane for total lease payments of $15,000. Jack sent the lessor asigned letter confirming the lease, describing the plane, and stating the lease term. Jack nowrefuses to perform the lease.
   d. All of the above.

_____ 10. Jackson Co. leased a crane from R&R Rental Co. for two years. After 18 months, Jackson Co. defaulted on the lease. Jackson Co. failed to pay $900 past rent, and it also failed to pay the remaining $1,800 future rent under the lease. R&R retook the crane, but it was unable to rent the crane to anyone else. R&R incurred a $200 shipping expense and a $300 storage expense due to Jackson Co.'s default. In this case, what damages can R&R recover from Jackson Co.?

    a. $0
    b. $900
    c. $2,700
    d. $3,200

Case Problem

Answer the following problems, briefly explaining your answers.

Barney, a consumer, sent a purchase order for a table saw to Tonko Manufacturers. The order was silent regarding how disputes between the parties would be settled. Tonko sent back a definite, unconditional acceptance that contained an additional term which stated that disputes must be submitted to arbitration. Barney received the acceptance, but he never agreed or objected to the additional term.

1. Did Tonko's acceptance form a contract between Barney and Tonko?
2. If a contract was formed, was the additional term in the acceptance part of the contract?

_____

_____

_____

_____

_____

Internet Exercise

Ameri Inc., a U.S. firm, exports tennis racquets. Ameri Inc. orally contracted to sell one shipment of racquets to Cannes Co., a wholesaler located in a France, and another shipment to Kiev Inc., a Russian firm. Ameri Inc. also contracted to sell to Felipe, a Spanish citizen, a racquet for his personal use.

1. Locate the text of the CISG on the Internet.
2. Does the CISG govern the contracts between Ameri Inc. and Cannes Co., Kiev Inc., and or Felipe? Explain.
3. Is the contract between Ameri Inc. And Cannes Co. legally enforceable?

_____

_____

_____

CPA REVIEW

The following questions were given on CPA examinations. The answers for these questions are the unofficial answers prepared by the American Institute of Certified Public Accountants, Inc. (AICPA). All material is reproduced with permission of the AICPA.

___ 1. Under the Sales Article of the UCC, which of the following statements is correct?
   a. The obligations of the parties to the contract must be performed in good faith.
   b. Merchants and nonmerchants are treated alike.
   c. The contract must involve the sale of goods for a price of more than $500.
   d. None of the provisions of the UCC may be disclaimed by agreement.

___ 2. Bean ordered 40 beige refrigerators at list price from Tish Co. Immediately upon receipt of Bean's order, Tish sent Bean an acceptance which was received by Bean. The acceptance indicated that shipment would be made within ten days. On the tenth day Tish discovered that all of its supply of beige refrigerators had been sold. Instead it shipped 40 white refrigerators, stating clearly on the invoice that the shipment was sent only as an accommodation. Which of the following is correct?
   a. Bean's order is a unilateral offer, and can only be accepted by Tish's shipment of the goods ordered.
   b. Tish's shipment of white refrigerators is a counteroffer, thus no contract exists between Bean and Tish.
   c. Tish's note of accommodation cancels the contract between Tish and Bean.
   d. Tish's shipment of white refrigerators constitutes a breach of contract.

___ 3. An oral agreement concerning the sale of goods entered into without consideration is binding if the agreement
   a. Is a firm offer made by a merchant who promises to hold the offer open for 30 days.
   b. Is a waiver of the non-breaching party's rights arising out of a breach of the contract.
   c. Contradicts the terms of a subsequent written contract that is intended as the complete and exclusive agreement of the parties.
   d. Modifies the price in an existing, enforceable contract from $525 to $475.

___ 4. Baker and Able signed a contract which required Able to purchase 600 books from Baker at 90¢ per book. Subsequently, Able, in good faith, requested that the price of the books be reduced to 80¢ per book. Baker orally agreed to reduce the price to 80¢. Under the circumstances, the oral agreement is
   a. Unenforceable, because Able failed to give consideration, but proof of it will be otherwise admissible into evidence.
   b. Unenforceable, due to the statute of frauds, and proof of it will be inadmissible into evidence.
   c. Enforceable, but proof of it will be inadmissible into evidence.
   d. Enforceable, and proof of it will be admissible into evidence.

___ 5. To satisfy the UCC Statute of Frauds, a written agreement for the sale of goods must
   a. Contain payment terms.
   b. Be signed by both buyer and seller.
   c. Indicate that a contract for sale has been made.
   d. Refer to the time and place of delivery.

___ 6. Jefferson Hardware ordered three hundred Ram hammers from Ajax Hardware. Ajax accepted the order in writing. On the final date allowed for delivery, Ajax discovered it did not have enough Ram hammers to fill the order. Instead, Ajax sent three hundred Strong hammers. Ajax stated on the invoice that the shipment was sent only as an accommodation. Which of the following statements is correct?

    a.   Ajax's note of accommodation cancels the contract between Jefferson and Ajax.

    b.   Jefferson's order can only be accepted by Ajax's shipment of the goods ordered.

    c.   Ajax's shipment of Strong hammers is a breach of contract.

    d.   Ajax' s shipment of Strong hammers is a counteroffer and no contract exists between Jefferson and Ajax.

___ 7. Cookie Co. offered to sell Distrib Markets 20,000 pounds of cookies at $1.00 per pound, subject to certain specified terms for delivery. Distrib replied in writing as follows: "We accept your offer for 20,000 pounds of cookies at $1.00 per pound, weighing scale to have valid city certificate." Under the UCC

    a.   A contract was formed between the parties.

    b.   A contract will be formed only if Cookie agrees to the weighing scale requirement.

    c.   No contract was formed because Distrib included the weighing scale requirement in its reply.

    d.   No contract was formed because Distrib' s reply was a counteroffer.

CHAPTER 24
TITLE AND RISK OF LOSS

MAKE THE CONNECTION

SUMMARY

All along the supply chain of a business are issues of risk and title that are often complicated by additional questions about damage to goods in transit, the claims of creditors to goods that are in process under a contract, and insurance. Unless the parties specifically agree otherwise, the solution to these problems depends on the nature of the transaction between the seller and the buyer.

The first issue to be addressed in answering questions of risk, title, and loss is whether the goods are identified. Existing goods are identified at the time the contract is entered into. Future goods, or goods not yet owned by the seller or not yet in existence (as in goods to be manufactured by the seller), are identified when they are shipped, marked, or otherwise designated for the buyer. Without identification, title and risk of loss cannot pass from buyer to seller, nor can the buyer hold an insurable interest.

Once identification has occurred, the issue of title, and hence creditor's rights, can be addressed. If there are identified goods but there is no document of title associated with the goods, then title to the goods passes from the seller to the buyer at the time of the contract.

Sellers can have their goods covered by a document of title. The most common types of documents of title are bills of lading and warehouse receipts. These documents of title, if properly transferred, transfer title to both the document and the underlying goods.

While the seller has no obligation under UCC Article 2 to deliver the goods to the buyer, the parties can agree on delivery as part of their contract. Several common delivery terms are used in supply chain management. *FOB* is "free on board," and its meaning depends on the location that follows the term. *FOB place of shipment* requires the seller to deliver the goods to the carrier. In an FOB place of shipment contract, title to the goods passes from the seller to the buyer when the goods are delivered to the carrier. *FOB place of destination* requires the seller to get the goods to the buyer or a location specified by the buyer and tender the goods there. *FAS* is "free alongside ship," which means free on board for shipment by sea. *CF* is "cost and freight" and requires the seller to deliver the goods to the carrier and make a contract for their shipment. *CIF* is "cost, insurance, and freight" and requires the seller to deliver the goods to the carrier, make a contract for shipment, and purchase insurance for the goods in transit. *COD* means "cash on delivery" and requires the buyer to pay for the goods before taking possession of them.

Ordinarily, sellers cannot pass any title greater than that which they possess. In some cases, however, the law permits a greater title to be transferred even though the transferor may hold voidable title or be in possession of the goods only as in a bailment. These exceptions protect good-faith purchasers.

Risk of loss is an issue for buyers, sellers, and insurers. When risk of loss passes from seller to buyer is controlled, again, by the terms of the contract. In a contract in which there is no agreement on delivery, the risk of loss passes to the buyer upon receipt of the goods if the seller is a merchant and upon tender if the seller is a nonmerchant. Under Revised Article 2, the risk of loss in nonshipment contracts always passes upon receipt, regardless of whether the contract involves a merchant or nonmerchant. If there is an agreement for delivery and the contract provides for shipment only, or FOB place of shipment, then risk of loss passes from seller to buyer when the goods are delivered to the carrier. If the contract provides for

235

delivery to a particular location, or FOB place of destination, then the risk of loss passes from the seller to the buyer when the goods are tendered to the buyer.

Some types of arrangements, such as sales on approval, sales or returns, and consignments or factor arrangements, have specific rules for passage of title and risk of loss. Also, if there is a breach of the contract and the seller ships goods different from those ordered, the breach prevents the risk of loss from passing from the seller to the buyer.

LEARNING OUTCOMES
After studying this chapter, you should be able to

A. IDENTIFYING TYPES OF POTENTIAL PROBLEMS AND TRANSACTIONS
LO.1   Explain when title and risk of loss pass with respect to goods

B. DETERMINING RIGHTS: IDENTIFICATION OF GOODS
LO.2   Determine who bears the risk of loss when goods are damaged or destroyed

C. DETERMINING RIGHTS: PASSAGE OF TITLE
LO.3   Explain why it is important to know when risk of loss and title pass in transactions for the sale of goods

D. DETERMINING RIGHTS: RISK OF LOSS
LO.4   Describe the passage of title and risk in special situations, such as a bailment, sale or return, or a sale on approval
E. DETERMINING RIGHTS: SPECIAL SITUATIONS
LO.5   Classify the various circumstances in which title can be passed to a bona fide purchaser

CHAPTER OUTLINE

A. IDENTIFYING TYPES OF POTENTIAL PROBLEMS AND TRANSACTIONS

1. DAMAGE TO GOODS

Risk of loss rules determine whether a seller or buyer bears a loss caused by a casualty to goods.

2. CREDITORS' CLAIMS

Rules regarding title to goods often determine the rights of creditors to goods.

3. INSURANCE

Insurable interest rules determine whether an insurer must pay for a loss to goods.

B. DETERMINING RIGHTS: IDENTIFICATION OF GOODS

Rights regarding insurable interest, title, and risk of loss often depend on the type of goods sold.

4. EXISTING GOODS

Existing goods exist and are owned by the seller at the time of contracting.

5. FUTURE GOODS

GENERAL RULES. ► Future goods either do not exist at time of contracting or the seller does not own them at this time. ► Goods are identified when specific goods are designated as being for a specific buyer.

STUDY HINT. Goods are identified if specific, existing goods are described in the contract, or specific goods are identified as being for a particular buyer by being marked, shipped, or segregated.

6. FUNGIBLE GOODS

► Fungible goods are goods that are indistinguishable from each other. ► Example: pieces of coal.

7. EFFECT OF IDENTIFICATION

► A buyer has an insurable interest in goods once they are identified to the contract. ► Title and risk of loss cannot pass to a buyer until the goods are identified.

C. DETERMINING RIGHTS: PASSAGE OF TITLE

► Parties' rights may be affected by a seller's delivery duties. ► A seller may have to: (1) deliver documents of title to a buyer; (2) deliver goods at the seller's business; (3) deliver goods to a carrier for shipment to a buyer (place of shipment contract); or (4) deliver goods to a buyer at the destination (place of destination contract).

8. PASSAGE OF TITLE USING DOCUMENTS OF TITLE

GENERAL RULES. ► A document of title is a written or electronic record that in business dealings legally evidences that a person in possession or control of the record has the right to receive, hold and dispose of the record and the goods that the record covers. ► Unless otherwise agreed, (1) if goods are identified at the time of contracting and (2) the seller is required to deliver a document of title (i.e., a warehouse receipt or bill of lading) to the buyer, then these rules apply:

➢ *Insurable interest*: ► A seller has an insurable interest in goods if the seller has title to, or a security interest in, the goods. ► A buyer has an insurable interest at the time of contracting.

➢ *Title*: Title to goods passes when the seller delivers the document of title to the buyer.

➢ *Risk of loss*: Risk of loss generally passes to a buyer when a seller delivers the document of title.

STUDY HINTS. ► A document of title enables parties to transfer title to goods without actually moving the goods. ► The primary types of documents of title are warehouse receipts and bills of lading. ► Basic concepts relating to documents of title include the following:

(a) *Warehouse Receipts*

► A warehouse receipt is a writing issued by a warehouser acknowledging receipt of goods for storage from a customer (depositor). The receipt states the terms of the contract. ►Because a warehouse receipt is a document of title, it can be bought, sold, and used as collateral for a loan.

(b) *Bills of Lading*

- ▶ A bill of lading is a document of title issued by a carrier for goods to be shipped by land.
- ▶ A bill of lading is both a receipt for goods and a memorandum of the parties' contract.

9. PASSAGE OF TITLE IN NONSHIPMENT CONTRACTS (SELLER HAS POSSESSION OF GOODS)

GENERAL RULE.   Unless otherwise agreed, (1) if goods are identified at time of contracting, (2) there are no documents of title, and (3) the goods are not to be shipped, then the following rules apply:

➢ *Insurable interest*: ▶ A seller has an insurable interest in goods if the seller has title to or a security interest in the goods. ▶ A buyer has an insurable interest at the time of contracting.

➢ *Title*: Title to goods passes to the buyer at the time of contracting.

STUDY HINT.   A seller and buyer may both have an insurable interest in goods at the same time.

10. PASSAGE OF TITLE IN WAREHOUSE ARRANGEMENTS (SELLER DOES NOT HAVE POSSESSION OF GOODS)

➢ Document of title: When goods are sold, the goods are in a warehouse or the possession of a third party, and a document of title covers the goods, then title passes from the seller to the buyer when the buyer receives the document of title.

➢ No document of title: When goods are sold, the goods are in a warehouse or the possession of a third party and there is no document of title, then title passes from the seller to the buyer when paperwork required for the third party or warehouse to turn over the goods and the goods are available for the buyer.

11. PASSAGE OF TITLE IN BAILMENTS AND OTHER FORMS OF POSSESSION

In general, a buyer of goods receives only the title (if any) held by the seller. Situations involving this issue include the following:

(a) *Stolen property*: ▶ A buyer of stolen goods does not receive title to the goods and the original owner is entitled to the return of such goods. ▶ LEARNING OUTCOME EXAMPLE. See *Northern Insurance Company of New York v 1996 Sea Ray Model 370DA Yacht* on textbook p. 537.

(b) *Estoppel*: ▶ Wrongful or misleading conduct by an owner of goods that would unfairly cause a buyer a loss may estop (prevent) the owner from asserting ownership to goods. ▶ Example: Charlie puts the title to his motorcycle in the name of his friend Chris in order to hide this asset from his wife who is divorcing him. Under these facts, Chris has the power to transfer title to the motorcycle.

(c) *Authorization:*: A person who is authorized to sell an item by its owner may pass good title to it.

(d) *Voidable title*: ▶ A seller has voidable title to goods if the seller: (1) bought goods and paid with a "bad" check; (2) bought goods in a cash sale, but failed to pay; or (3) acquired title by fraud. ▶ A good faith buyer for value acquires good title to goods if the seller had voidable title.

(e) ***Bailments or sale by entrustee***: ► A merchant who regularly sells goods of the kind in question and to whom a good is entrusted, has the power to transfer the owner's title to a buyer in the ordinary course of business. Example: Carla left her CD player to be repaired with Ace Electronics, a merchant that regularly buys and sells used CD players. Ace could transfer Carla's title to a good faith buyer. ► Except as noted above, any other person to whom a good is merely entrusted, such as a repair shop or a friend who is permitted to temporarily use the good, does not have the power to transfer title to the good. ► **LEARNING OUTCOME EXAMPLE.** See Thinking Things Through, *Tempur-Pedic Intern., Inc. v Waste to Charity, Inc.*, on textbook p. 538.

12. DELIVERY AND SHIPMENT TERMS

➤ ***FOB Place of shipment*** : ► FOB ("Free on Board") place of shipment means the seller's duty is to deliver goods to the carrier for delivery. ► Title passes to the buyer when conforming goods are duly delivered to the carrier for shipment.

➤ ***FOB Place of destination*** : ► FOB place of destination means the seller's duty is to tender(offer) delivery of goods to the buyer at the destination. ► Title passes when this duty is fulfilled.

➤ ***FAS***: FAS acts the same as FOB for shipment contracts utilizing boats.

➤ ***CF, CIF, and COD***: ► CF means the contract price includes both the cost of the goods and the expense of shipping. ► CIF means the price also includes the cost of insuring the goods during shipment. ► COD means cash on delivery.

13. PASSAGE OF TITLE IN SHIPMENT CONTRACTS

➤ ***FOB place of shipment contract***: title passes to a buyer when goods are delivered to a carrier for shipment. ► LEARNING OUTCOME EXAMPLE. See *Lite-On Peripherals, Inc. v Burlington Air Express, Inc.* on textbook p. 542.

➤ ***FOB place of destination contract***: title passes when goods are tendered or made available to the buyer at the destination.

D. DETERMINING RIGHTS: RISK OF LOSS

14. RISK OF LOSS IN NONSHIPMENT CONTRACTS

► In a nonshipment contract that does not involve a document of title, passing of risk of loss depends on whether the seller is a merchant. ► If a seller is a merchant, risk of loss passes when the buyer takes physical possession of the goods. ► If the seller is a nonmerchant, risk of loss passes when delivery to the buyer is tendered.

15. RISK OF LOSS IN SHIPMENT CONTRACTS

► In an FOB place of shipment contract, the risk of loss passes to a buyer when the goods are delivered to the carrier for shipment. ► In an FOB place of destination contract, the risk of loss passes when the goods are tendered or made available to the buyer at the destination.

16. DAMAGE TO OR DESTRUCTION OF GOODS

> *Damage to identified goods before risk of loss passes*: ▶ A contract for the sale of goods is terminated if: (1) goods essential to the contract are identified at time of contracting; (2) risk of loss has not passed to the buyer; and (3) the goods are destroyed without fault of either party. In this event, there is no breach of contract by either party. ▶ If a partial loss occurs, a buyer may inspect the goods and either: (1) cancel the contract; or (2) accept the goods with an appropriate reduction in price.

> *Damage to identified goods after risk of loss passes*: If a casualty occurs and a buyer has the risk of loss, the contract is not avoided; the buyer must pay the contract price for the goods, and the buyer must bear any financial loss resulting from the casualty.

> *Damage to unidentified goods*: In general, casualty to unidentified goods does not affect a sales contract, and both parties must still perform. The seller bears the loss to unidentified goods.

> **LEARNING OUTCOME EXAMPLES.** See the **For Example** discussion of Gunnell's Jewelry on textbook p. 537; see the For Example discussion of a home gymnasium that is purchased from TV on textbook p. 546.

17. EFFECT OF SELLER'S BREACH IN RISK OF LOSS

▶ A seller generally bears the risk of loss if the seller breaches, giving a buyer a right to reject goods.
▶ **LEARNING OUTCOME EXAMPLE.** See *King Jewelry Inc. v Federal Express Corporation* on textbook p. 545.

E. DETERMINING RIGHTS: SPECIAL SITUATIONS

18. RETURNABLE GOODS TRANSACTIONS

GENERAL RULE. Parties may enter into transactions whereby they agree that goods can be returned even though the goods meet all contract specifications. These transactions may be a:

> *Sale on approval*: ▶ In a sale on approval, a sale does not occur until a buyer accepts the goods, i.e., a buyer clearly indicates that the buyer regards the goods as his or her own property. Approval may be (1) express words, (2) conduct, or (3) lapse of time. ▶ Testing goods in a permitted manner is not an approval. Failure to return goods within the time agreed is an approval. ▶ Title and risk of loss do not pass to a buyer until the buyer approves goods. ▶ A seller bears the risk of loss and expense for return of goods. ▶ A buyer's creditors cannot reach goods prior to a buyer's approval of goods.

> *Sale or return*: ▶ A sale or return is a sale with an option for a buyer to return goods. ▶ Goods may be returned when agreed, or within a reasonable time if no time is stated. Goods must be returned in their original condition. ▶ The general rules regarding insurable interest, title, and risk of loss apply to a sale or return contract. ▶ A buyer bears the expense and risk of loss in returning goods.

19. CONSIGNMENTS AND FACTORS

▶ A consignment is a transaction whereby an owner of goods (consignor) delivers them to a seller (consignee) to be sold for the owner's benefit. ▶ Title is not transferred by the owner to the consignee. ▶ A consignment is treated as a sale or return. Thus, a consignee's creditors usually can take possession of consigned goods if necessary to satisfy a claim against the consignee unless the consignor files an appropriate notice in accordance with Article 9 of the UCC.

20. SELF-SERVICE STORES

Most courts hold that a contract is not made, and title does not pass until a buyer pays for the goods.

21. AUCTION SALES

Title to a good passes when an auctioneer's hammer signifies that a good or lot is sold to a bidder.

CONCEPT REVIEW AND APPLICATIONS

Matching Exercise

Select the term or phrase that best matches a definition or statement stated below. Each term or phrase is the best match for only one statement or definition. Not all terms and phrases will necessarily be used.

bills of lading	existing goods	insurable interest
CF	factor	risk of loss
CIF	FAS	sale on approval
COD	FOB place of destination	sale or return
consignee	FOB place of shipment	tender
consignment	fungible goods	voidable title
consignor	future goods	warehouse receipt
document of title	identification	
estoppel	identified	

_____ 1. Transaction that permits a party to return goods if the party does not approve of the goods.

_____ 2. Owner of goods who transfers them to another to sell on the owner's behalf.

_____ 3. Goods that when mixed together are indistinguishable from one another.

_____ 4. Document of title that is given to the depositor when goods are delivered for storage in a warehouse.

_____ 5. Transaction that permits a merchant to return goods that it has purchased.

_____ 6. Goods that do not exist, or are not owned by a seller, at the time of contracting.

_____ 7. Defective title to goods that is acquired by a person who pays for the goods with a "bad" check, who fails to pay the cash purchase price for the goods, or who obtains the goods by fraud.

_____ 8.   Transfer of possession of property to a party coupled with an authorization to sell the property.

_____ 9.   A document of title issued by a carrier for goods to be shipped.

_____ 10. Party who is supposed to sell consigned goods on behalf of the owner.

True/False

Write T if the statement is true, write F if it is false.

_____ 1.   Seller owns an existing inventory of shovels, and Seller contracts to sell one unspecified shovel from this inventory. In this situation, the shovel sold is an identified good.

_____ 2.   If a buyer purchases goods from a thief, then the buyer receives only void (no) title, and the owner of the goods may recover the goods from the buyer.

_____ 3.   Creditors of a consignee can never reach and execute on consigned goods because title to the consigned goods belongs to the consignor

_____ 4.   In an auction sale, title does not pass to a buyer until the buyer has in fact paid the price.

_____ 5.   Future goods become identified when the goods are, shipped, marked, or otherwise clearly indicated by the seller as being the goods to be delivered to the buyer under the sales contract.

_____ 6.   Seller sold existing, identified furniture to Buyer. If Seller must deliver a document of title to Buyer, then title and risk of loss do not pass to Buyer until the document of title is delivered.

_____ 7.   In general, a seller's breach of contract has no effect on who bears the risk of loss.

_____ 8.   If an agreement is unclear on the point, a transaction that allows a buyer to return conforming goods is interpreted as being a sale on approval if a consumer intends the goods for personal use, but it is a sale or return if the goods are intended to be resold by a merchant.

_____ 9.   In a sale or return contract, the expense and risk of loss of returning goods is borne by the seller.

_____ 10. A buyer's creditors do not have any rights to goods received by the buyer pursuant to a sale on approval before the buyer approves of the goods.

Multiple Choice

_____ 1.   On May 1, John contracted to buy an existing, identified filing cabinet from Seller, a merchant. Documents of title were not involved. Delivery was required to be made at Seller's business. On June 1, Seller tendered delivery of the filing cabinet to John, but John did not take the filing cabinet. On July 1, John took physical possession of the filing cabinet. Under these facts:
   a.   John had an insurable interest in the filing cabinet on May 1.
   b.   Title to the filing cabinet passed to John on June 1.
   c.   Risk of loss passed to John on July 1.
   d.   a and c.

_____ 2. Select the right answer. (The damage to the goods in question was not the fault of either party.)
   a. Walt contracted to buy a one-of-a-kind statue from Seller. The statue was identified and existing at time of contracting. Before risk of loss passed to Walt, the statue was destroyed. In this case, the contract is not avoided, and Seller is in breach if Seller fails to perform.
   b. Seller contracted to sell a desk to Bill. After risk of loss had passed to Bill, the desk was destroyed. In this case, the contract is avoided, and Bill is not required to pay for the desk.
   c. Seller contracted to sell an unidentified G.E. oven to Lisa. Before risk of loss passed, Seller's inventory of ovens was destroyed. In this case, the contract is not avoided, Seller bears the loss, and Seller is liable for breach if an appropriate oven is not delivered to Lisa.
   d. b and c.

_____ 3. Amanda received a hair dryer from Seller pursuant to a sale on approval agreement. The agreement allows Amanda to test the dryer for 14 days, and she may return it at any time during this period if she is not satisfied. Amanda received the dryer on June 1. Amanda tested the dryer for a few days, and shipped it back to Seller on June 9. During return shipment, the dryer was damaged. Under these facts:
   a. Title and risk of loss passed to Amanda on June 1.
   b. Title and risk of loss never passed to Amanda.
   c. Amanda must pay for the return shipment of the dryer.
   d. Amanda was not entitled to return the dryer because she used it; Fran must pay for the dryer.

_____ 4. Nicki sold a iPod to Jasper. Jasper paid Nicki with a "bad" check, and Jasper's bank refused to pay the check due to insufficient funds. Prior to Nicki's rescinding the sale, Jasper took the iPod and sold it to Gary for value. Gary was unaware of the transaction between Nicki and Jasper. Under these facts:
   a. Gary received only voidable title to the iPod.
   b. Gary received valid or good title to the iPod.
   c. Nicki cannot recover the iPod from Gary.
   d. b and c.

Case Problem

Did Buyer receive Owner's title to the goods in question? Briefly explain your answer.

1. Owner delivered her lawn mower to AAA Lawn Mowers, a merchant who regularly bought and sold used mowers. AAA was supposed to repair the mower. Instead, AAA sold the mower to Buyer in the ordinary course of business. Buyer paid for the mower, and Buyer did not know that the mower belonged to Owner.

1. Owner delivered her car to Wet N' Wild, a retail car wash. Wet N' Wild did not normally buy or sell cars. Without Owner's permission, Wet N' Wild sold Owner's car to Buyer for $8,000, a fair price. Buyer did not know that the car belonged to Owner, or that the sale was improper.

_____

_____

_____

Internet Exercise

On March 15, Senmore Co. contracted to sell a shipment of eyeglasses to Beacon Corp. The eyeglasses were future goods, not yet identified. Senmore is located in Miami, and Beacon is located in Baltimore. The contract requires the goods to be shipped "FOB Miami." On April 15, Senmore duly delivered the eyeglasses to a carrier for shipment to Beacon. On May 1, the shipment was delivered to Beacon at the destination. The glasses were crushed during shipment. Under these facts:

1. Using the Internet, locate and identify the sections of UCC Article 7 that apply in this case.
2. Explain who bears the risk of loss for the glasses and whether that party has an insurable interest in the goods.

_____

_____

_____

CPA REVIEW

The following questions were given on CPA examinations. The answers for these questions are the unofficial answers prepared by the American Institute of Certified Public Accountants, Inc. (AICPA). All material is reproduced with permission of the AICPA.

____ 1. Quick Corp. agreed to purchase 200 typewriters from Union Suppliers, Inc. Union is a wholesaler of appliances and Quick is an appliance retailer. The contract required Union to ship the typewriters to Quick by common carrier, "F.O.B. Union Suppliers, Inc. Loading Dock." Which of the parties bears the risk of loss during shipment?
   a. Union, because the risk of loss passes only when Quick receives the typewriters.
   b. Union, because both parties are merchants.
   c. Quick, because title to the typewriters passed to Quick at the time of shipment.
   d. Quick, because the risk of loss passes when the typewriters are delivered to the carrier.

Questions 2 and 3 are based on the following:

On May 2, Lace Corp., an appliance wholesaler, offered to sell appliances worth $3,000 to Parco, Inc., a household appliances retailer. The offer was signed by Lace's president, and provided that it would not be withdrawn before June 1. It also included the shipping terms: "FOB- Parco's warehouse." On May 29, Parco mailed an acceptance of Lace's offer. Lace received the acceptance June 2.

____ 2. Risk of loss for the appliances will pass to Parco when they are
  a. Identified to the contract.
  b. Shipped by Lace.
  c. Tendered at Parco's warehouse.
  d. Accepted by Parco.

____ 3. If Lace inadvertently ships the wrong appliances to Parco and Parco rejects them two days after receipt, title to the goods will
  a. Pass to Parco when they are identified to the contract.
  b. Pass to Parco when they are shipped.
  c. Remain with Parco until the goods are returned to Lace.
  d. Revert to Lace when they are rejected by Parco.

____ 4. Lazur Corp. agreed to purchase 100 radios from Wizard Suppliers, Inc. Wizard is a wholesaler of small home appliances and Lazur is an appliance retailer. The contract required Wizard to ship the radios to Lazur by common carrier, "F.O.B. Wizard Suppliers, Inc. Loading Dock." Risk of loss for the radios during shipment to Lazur would be on
  a. Lazur, because the risk of loss passes when the radios are delivered to the carrier.
  b. Wizard, because the risk of loss passes only when Lazur receives the radios.
  c. Wizard, because it is a shipment contract.
  d. Lazur, because title to the radios passes to Lazur at the time of shipment.

____ 5. Which of the following factors is most important in deciding who bears the risk of loss between merchants when goods are destroyed during shipment?
  a. The agreement of the parties.
  b. Whether the goods are perishable.
  c. Who has title at the time of the loss.
  d. The terms of applicable insurance policies.

____ 6. On Monday, Wolfe paid Aston Co., a furniture retailer, $500 for a table. On Thursday, Aston notified Wolfe that the table was ready to be picked up. On Saturday, while Aston was still in possession of the table, it was destroyed in a fire. Who bears the loss of the table?
  a. Wolfe, because Wolfe had title to the table at the time of loss.
  b. Aston, unless Wolfe is a merchant.
  c. Wolfe, unless Aston breached the contract.
  d. Aston, because Wolfe had not yet taken possession of the table.

___ 7. Lazur Corp. entered into a contract with Baker Suppliers, Inc. to purchase a used word processor from Baker. Lazur is engaged in the business of selling new and used word processors to the general public. The contract required Baker to ship the goods to Lazur by common carrier pursuant to the following provision in the contract: "F.O.B.-Baker Suppliers, Inc. loading dock." Baker also represented in the contract that the word processor had been used for only 10 hours by its previous owner. The contract included the provision that the word processor was being sold "as is" and this provision was in a larger and different type style than the remainder of the contract. Assume that during shipment to Lazur the word processor was seriously damaged when the carrier's truck was involved in an accident. When the carrier attempted to deliver the word processor, Lazur rejected it and has refused to pay Baker the purchase price. Under the UCC Sales Article,

    a.   Lazur rightfully rejected the damaged computer.

    b.   The risk of loss for the computer was on Lazur during shipment.

    c.   At the time of the accident, risk of loss for the computer was on Baker because title to the computer had not yet passed to Lazur.

    d.   Lazur will not be liable to Baker for the purchase price of the computer   because of the F.O.B. provision in the contract.

CHAPTER 25
PRODUCT LIABILITY: WARRANTIES AND TORTS

MAKE THE CONNECTION

SUMMARY

Five theories protect parties from loss caused by nonconforming goods: (1) express warranty, (2) implied warranty, (3) negligence, (4) fraud, and (5) strict tort liability.

Theories of product liability are not mutually exclusive. A given set of facts may give rise to liability under two or more theories.

The requirement of privity of contract (that is, the parties to the sales contract for warranty liability) has been widely rejected. The law is moving toward the conclusion that persons harmed because of an improper product may recover from anyone who is in any way responsible. The requirement of privity has beenabolished by most states, and remote buyers as well as their families, members of their households, and guests are covered under the UCC warranties.

Warranties may be express or implied. The types of implied warranties are the warranty of title, the implied warranty of merchantability, and the implied warranty of fitness for a particular purpose. The warranty of title provides that the transfer is lawful, the title is good, and there are no infringement issues. Under Revised Article 2, the warranty of title also protects the buyer against unreasonable litigation. The warranty of merchantability is given by merchants and warrants that the goods are of average quality and will do what those types of goods commonly can do. The implied warranty of fitness for a particular purpose is given in those circumstances in which the buyer relies on the seller's expertise and the seller is aware of that reliance and offers a recommendation on the types of goods.

Express warranties arise from statements of fact and promises of performance made by the seller to the buyer that become a part of the basis for the buyer contracting. Express warranties arise from samples, models, and descriptions.

Warranties may be disclaimed by agreement of the parties provided the disclaimer is not unconscionable. Merchants can have oral disclaimers, but for consumers, warranty disclaimers must be in a record and must be conspicuous. Also for consumers, certain language must be used to disclaim each type of warranty.However, for both merchants and nonmerchants, the use of terms such as "as is" or "with all faults" can disclaim both the warranty of merchantability and the implied warranty of fitness for a particular purpose (although for consumers, there must still be a record and the language must be conspicuous).

The warranties of merchantability and fitness exist under the CISG. However, disclaimers under the CISG need not mention merchantability, nor must such disclaimers be conspicuous.

The strict tort liability plaintiff must show that there was a defect in the product at the time it left the control of the defendant. No negligence need be established on the part of the defendant, nor is the plaintiff's contributory negligence a defense. If negligence is established, however, knowledge by the seller can result in punitive damages. The defendant may show that the injured party assumed the risk.

LEARNING OUTCOMES
After studying this chapter, you should be able to

A. GENERAL PRINCIPLES
LO.1 List the theories of product liability

LO.2 Identify who may sue and who may be sued when a defective product causesharm

B. EXPRESS WARRANTIES
LO.3 Define and give examples of an express warranty

C. IMPLIED WARRANTIES
LO.4 List and explain the types of implied warranties

LO.5 Explain warranty protections under federal law

LO.6 State what constitutes a breach of warranty

D. DISCLAIMER OF WARRANTIES
LO.7 Describe the extent and manner in which implied warranties may be disclaimed under the UCC and the CISG

E. OTHER THEORIES OF PRODUCT LIABILITY

CHAPTER OUTLINE

A. GENERAL PRINCIPLES

1. THEORIES OF LIABILITY

Potential theories of products liability include: (1) express warranty; (2) implied warranty; (3) negligence; (4) fraud; and (5) strict tort liability.

2. NATURE OF HARM

GENERAL RULES. ▶ Types of harm: (1) personal injuries; (2) property damage; and (3) economic or commercial loss. ▶ One can usually sue for any type of harm that is caused. For example, under the modern view, courts permit a consumer to sue for purely economic losses even if the consumer was not in privity of contract with the defendant.

STUDY HINT. Economic losses include lost profits and damage to the purchased good itself.

3. WHO IS LIABLE IN PRODUCT LIABILITY

➤ *Who can Recover Under UCC Warranties* ▶ In most states, a buyer, a member of a buyer's family or household, or a buyer's guest may sue for personal injuries that are suffered due to a breach of warranty. ▶ Under the modern view, other third parties (including bystanders, customers, and employees) who suffer foreseeable physical harm can sue for product liability without proving privity of contract. A few states still will not allow parties to sue only for economic losses unless there is privity of contract.

➤ *Who is Liable Under UCC Warranties* ▶ A seller, wholesaler, or manufacturer of a good or component part can generally be sued for product liability. ▶ If privity of contract is required to sue, many courts find this requirement met if a plaintiff had direct dealings with a defendant.

B. EXPRESS WARRANTIES

4. DEFINITION OF EXPRESS WARRANTY

▶ An express warranty is a (1) statement of fact or promise regarding the quality or performance of a good (2) that is a basis of the bargain (i.e., it is presumed to be part of the contract). ▶ Under the UCC dealing with warranties, an "immediate buyer" is the party who contracted directly with the seller and a "remote purchaser" is the party that buys or leases goods from the immediate buyer or someone in the normal chain of distribution. ▶ LEARNING OUTCOME EXAMPLE: See *La Trace v Webster* on textbook p. 561.

5. FORM OF EXPRESS WARRANTY

No special words are needed; an express warranty may be written, oral, or arise due to a seller's conduct. Express warranties may arise from statements made in negotiations, ads, labels, etc.

6. SELLER'S OPINION OR STATEMENT OF VALUE

GENERAL RULE. Statements of value, opinions, and sales talk do not create express warranties.
LIMITATION. An expert seller's opinion that is relied upon by a buyer may create a warranty.

7. WARRANTY OF CONFORMITY TO DESCRIPTION, SAMPLE, OR MODEL

An express warranty may be created by a description of goods (labels), or by showing a buyer a sample (specimen of actual goods to be furnished) or a model (example of what goods will be like).

8. FEDERAL REGULATION OF EXPRESS WARRANTIES

Federal law regulates express warranties made in sales of consumer goods for $10 or more. This law requires that express warranties be labeled as either full or limited, and meet these requirements:

➢ *Full warranties*: ▶ Seller must fix or replace a defective good within a reasonable time, without cost to a buyer. If this cannot be done, a buyer has the choice to request a refund or a free replacement. ▶ A full warranty is valid for its stated period regardless of a change of ownership. ▶ Implied warranty cannot be limited to a term shorter than term of a full warranty.

➢ *Limited warranties*: Any express warranty that gives less protection than is given by a full warranty.

➢ *The Consumer Product Safety Improvement Act (CPSIA)*: This federal legislation forbids lead in products for children under the age of 12.

9. EFFECT OF BREACH OF EXPRESS WARRANTY

A seller is liable for all harm caused by a breach of an express warranty even if the seller was not negligent and the seller did not know that a good failed to satisfy the express warranty.

C. IMPLIED WARRANTIES

10. DEFINITION OF IMPLIED WARRANTY

An implied warranty is one implied by law. It automatically arises when a sales contract is made.

11. IMPLIED WARRANTIES OF SELLERS

➤ *Warranty of title*: ▶ Most sellers warrant: (1) a buyer will receive good title; and (2) the seller has the right to transfer title. ▶ Title is not warranted if: (1) a contract disclaims this warranty; or
(2) goods are sold by a sheriff, a creditor enforcing a lien, or an administrator of an estate.

➤ *Warranty against encumbrances*: Every seller warrants that, when delivered, goods will not be subject to a security interest that the buyer did not know about when the contract was made.

➤ *Warranty of fitness for a particular purpose*: This warranty arises if: (1) a seller has reason to know a buyer has an unusual purpose for a good, and that the buyer is relying on the seller to select an appropriate good; and (2) the buyer actually relies on the seller to select the good.

➤ **LEARNING OUTCOME EXAMPLES**: See *Oheka Management, Inc. v Home Theater Interiors* on textbook p. 563; see *Mitchell v T.G.I. Friday's* on textbook p. 565.

12. ADDITIONAL IMPLIED WARRANTIES OF MERCHANT SELLERS

➤ *Warranty against infringement*: Merchant sellers warrant against patent/trademark infringement.

➤ *Warranty of merchantability or fitness for normal use*: ▶ Merchant sellers impliedly warrant that goods are merchantable, i.e., goods will perform ordinary tasks in a safe manner. ▶ This warranty requires goods to be fit for the ordinary purposes for which they are sold, but goods do not have to be the best or perfect. ▶ Sellers may breach this warranty without being negligent.

13. IMPLIED WARRANTIES IN PARTICULAR SALES

➤ *Sale on buyer's specifications*: Ordinary warranties apply except: (1) no warranty of fitness for a particular purpose can arise; and (2) a seller is not liable for a loss caused by a design defect.

➤ *Sale of secondhand (used) goods*: The warranty of merchantability typically applies to used goods, although the fitness required for used goods is less than for new goods.

➤ *Sale of food or drink*: The fitness (merchantability) of food is determined by one of two tests: (1) *reasonable expectations test*: an unintended substance in food, whether natural or foreign, renders food unfit if an ordinary person would not expect to find the substance in the food; or (2) *foreign substance-natural substance test*: food is fit if an unintended substance is natural, such as a pit in a prune; it is unfit if the substance is foreign, such as a stone in pea soup.

14. NECESSITY OF DEFECT

▶ Generally, liability for breach of the implied warranty of merchantability requires proof that there was a defect in the product, that this defect made the product not fit for its normal use, and that this caused the buyer's harm. ▶ Defects may be (a) a manufacturing defect, (b) a design defect, (c) inadequate instructions on use of the product, or (d) inadequate warning against dangers regarding use of the product. ▶ Proof of a defect is not needed to prove a breach of express warranty.

15. WARRANTIES IN THE INTERNATIONAL SALE OF GOODS

Warranties of merchantability and fitness for particular purpose may apply, but can be disclaimed.

D. DISCLAIMER OF WARRANTIES

16. VALIDITY OF DISCLAIMER

> *Disclaimers*: ▶ A seller and buyer may agree to disclaim (eliminate) any or all express or implied warranties. ▶ Disclaimers of the warranty of merchantability: (1) may be oral or written; (2) must use the word "merchantability"; and (3) must be conspicuous, if written. ▶ Disclaimers of the warranty of fitness for a particular purpose must be (1) written and (2) conspicuous.

> *Unconscionability*: ▶ In general, disclaimers permitted by Article 2 are not unconscionable. ▶ In some states, however, disclaimers may be invalid due to public policy or consumer laws.

17. PARTICULAR LANGUAGE FOR DISCLAIMERS

▶ The implied warranties of merchantability and fitness for a particular purpose may be excluded by a general disclaimer such as "as is" or "with all faults," but an oral disclaimer must be brought to the buyer's attention. (Revised Article 2 provides that the foregoing rule only applies to merchants and it sets out a new rule regarding consumer purchasers). ▶ Disclaimers do not prohibit suits for fraud, negligence, or strict tort liability.

18. EXCLUSION OF WARRANTIES BY EXAMINATION OF GOODS

If a buyer examines (or refuses to examine) a good, sample, or model before contracting, *no implied warranties* are made regarding matters the buyer should have discovered by examining the good. (Revised Article 2 provides that this rule applies only if the seller demands that the buyer inspect during the contracting process.)

19. POSTSALE DISCLAIMER

A disclaimer is invalid if it is not communicated to a buyer until after a sales contract is made.

E. OTHER THEORIES OF PRODUCT LIABILITY

20. NEGLIGENCE

A negligent seller or manufacturer may be sued by a person who is injured by a defective product, and privity of contract is not required.

21. FRAUD

A party defrauded in connection with the purchase of a product may sue for the tort of fraud.

22. STRICT TORT LIABILITY

▶ A manufacturer of a good or component part, a distributor, or a retailer has strict tort liability for injuries suffered by anyone due to a defective, unreasonably dangerous product; privity of contract is not required. ▶ Strict tort liability is not absolute liability; this liability is imposed only if a product is defective. ▶ Assumption of risk by an injured party is a defense; contributory negligence is not.

23. CUMULATIVE THEORIES OF LIABILITY

▶ In some cases, a plaintiff may be able to sue on two or more theories of product liability.
▶ LEARNING OUTCOME EXAMPLES: See *Austin v Will-Burt Company* on textbook p. 570; see the **For Example** discussion of the use of the term "Vehicle Warranty" in the "Conspicuousness" section on textbook p. 567; see the "Ethics & the Law" discussion of lead paint and toys on textbook p. 571.

CONCEPT REVIEW AND APPLICATIONS

Matching Exercise

Select the term or phrase that best matches a definition or statement stated below. Each term or phrase is the best match for only one statement or definition. Not all terms and phrases will necessarily be used.

Consumer Product Safety Improvement Act (CPSIA)

express warranty

full warranty

implied warranty of fitness for a particular purpose

implied warranty of merchantability

limited warranty

negligence

privity of contract

privity

strict tort liability

warranties

warranty against encumbrances

warranty of title

_____ 1. Broad category of warranties that automatically arise when a sales contract is made.

_____ 2. Implied warranty that a good is fit for the ordinary purposes for which the good is sold.

_____ 3. Broad category of warranties that arise due to the words or conduct of a seller.

_____ 4. Theory of product liability that imposes liability upon the manufacturer, seller, or distributor of goods for harm caused by a defective good.

_____ 5. Under federal law, a classification of express warranty in a sale of consumer goods that, among other things, obligates a seller to fix or replace a defective product within a reasonable period of time without cost to a buyer.

_____ 6. Warranty that a buyer will receive good title and that the seller has the right to transfer title.

_____ 7. Relationship between two parties who contract with one another.

_____ 8. Warranty that a good is not subject to a lien that the buyer is unaware of at the time of contracting.

_____ 9. Implied warranty that a good can perform an unusual use that is intended by a buyer.

_____ 10. Under federal law, a classification of express warranty in a sale of consumer goods that provides less protection than would be provided by a full warranty.

True/False

Write **T** if the statement is true, write **F** if it is false.

_____ 1. In general, a disclaimer does not eliminate liability for fraud, negligence, or strict tort liability.

_____ 2. In most states, only a buyer can sue for personal injuries caused by a breach of warranty.

_____ 3. A buyer who is injured by a defective and unreasonably dangerous good may be able to sue the seller and/or the manufacturer of the good.

_____ 4. Statements of fact made by a seller in advertisements or catalogs cannot create an express warranty.

_____ 5. Statements of value and opinions do not ordinarily create express warranties.

_____ 6. A warranty made after a sale is not binding unless the buyer paid consideration for the warranty.

_____ 7. If an express warranty conflicts with a warranty of merchantability, the express warranty prevails.

_____ 8. A seller cannot be held liable for breach of an express warranty unless the seller was negligent in making the good or the seller knew the warranty was false.

_____ 9. A description of goods does not create an express warranty unless it is stated in the contract.

_____ 10. Seller showed Buyer a sample of wheat that Seller offered to sell to Buyer. In this case, Seller's conduct created an express warranty that Buyer's wheat would be the same as the sample.

Multiple Choice

_____ 1. In which situation does Seller make an express warranty?
   a. During negotiations, Seller gave Byron a brochure regarding a ring that Byron was considering purchasing. The brochure stated that the ring was sterling silver.
   b. During negotiations for the sale of a drill, Seller stated to Buyer: "This drill is the best little drill on the market today." Seller did not say or do anything else.
   c. During negotiations for the sale of a chair to be specially manufactured, Seller showed Buyer a model of what the chair would be like. Seller did not say or do anything else.
   d. a and c.

_____ 2. Carson Co. sold Tami a watch for $25 for her personal use. In connection with the sale, Carson made a "Full Warranty," guaranteeing the watch against any defects for one year. In this case:
   a. If during the warranty period the watch fails due to a defect, then Carson must repair the watch. However, Carson can charge Tami a reasonable fee for repairing the watch.
   b. If during the warranty period the watch fails due to a defect and Carson fails to fix or replace the watch within a reasonable time, then Tami can demand a refund or a new watch.
   c. If Tami sells the watch to Gina, Gina will not have any right to enforce the warranty.

      d. Carson is entitled to disclaim all implied warranties.

___ 3. Select the correct statement.
      a. K&L foreclosed a lien on a debtor's goods. K&L held a sale of the goods. Prior to sale, buyers were told that only the debtor's interest, if any, was being sold. As it turns out, the debtor had defective title to the goods. In this case, K&L breached the warranty of title.
      b. Kit sold an engine to Buyer. Unknown to the parties, Kit did not have title to the engine. In this case, Kit breached the warranty of title.
      c. John sold a car to Sam. Unknown to Sam, the car was subject to a lien. Prior to delivery, John had the lien removed. In this case, John breached the warranty against encumbrances.
      d. All of the above are correct.

___ 4. In which case is the implied warranty of fitness for a particular purpose breached?
      a. Manufacturer sold an egg incubator to a zoo. At time of contracting, Manufacturer knew the zoo needed an incubator for hatching ostrich eggs (an unusual purpose), and that the zoo was relying on Manufacturer to select an appropriate incubator. (The zoo did in fact rely on Manufacturer.) The incubator delivered did not hatch ostrich eggs; it baked them.
      b. Buyer needed a paint that could withstand unusual, prolonged heat. Buyer developed a paint formula and furnished Manufacturer with specifications for the paint. The paint was made in accordance with the specifications, but it failed to perform the unusual task.
      c. Seller sold Buyer a lawn mower. Unknown to Seller, Buyer intended to use the mower to cut three-foot-tall salt marsh grass, an unusual purpose. The mower failed to cut this grass.
      d. a and b.

___ 5. The implied warranty of merchantability is breached in which case?
      a. Juanita (a nonmerchant) sold Buyer a new toaster that Juanita had received as a gift. The toaster cannot toast bread.
      b. Seller (a merchant) sold an ordinary private airplane to Buyer. The airplane operates safely and it is fit for ordinary private use. However, the plane cannot perform acrobatic stunts.
      c. Manufacturer, a merchant, sold a portable plastic pool to Buyer. The pool leaks badly, and it cannot be repaired. However, Manufacturer was not negligent in making the pool.
      d. All of the above.

___ 6. M&M Cafe sold JoJo a guacamole taco. The taco had a piece of avocado pit in it. Although guacamole is made from avocados which have pits, an ordinary person would not reasonably expect to find a piece of an avocado pit in a guacamole taco. Under these facts:
      a. M&M did not breach the warranty of merchantability; the UCC does not apply to food sales.
      b. Under the natural substance-foreign substance test, the taco is fit (merchantable).
      c. Under the reasonable expectations test, the taco is fit (merchantable).
      d. b and c.

___ 7. Seller (a used car dealer) sold Buyer a 2004 truck. Seller expressly warranted that the truck was a 2005 truck. Prior to contracting, Seller demanded that Buyer inspect the truck, but Buyer refused. An inspection would have revealed that the engine hoses were cracked, rendering the truck unfit to drive. An inspection would not have revealed the true model year of the truck. *After* the contract was made, Seller disclaimed all warranties. Under these facts:
      a. Buyer can sue for breach of the express warranty regarding the model year of the truck.

b. Buyer can sue for breach of the warranty of merchantability due to the cracked hoses.
c. Buyer cannot sue Seller for breach of any express or implied warranties because Seller disclaimed all warranties.
d. a and b.

Case Problems

Answer the following problems, briefly explaining your answers.

1. Aqua Boats manufactured a boat and sold it to Crest Sales Co. Aqua disclaimed all warranties. Crest sold the boat to Gary for family use. Crest expressly warranted that the boat's hull was shatterproof. While Gary and his wife were boating one day, the boat struck a small rock. The rock shattered the boat's hull, causing the boat to sink. Not only did the boat not satisfy the warranties made by Crest, but the boat was also defective and unreasonably dangerous. Gary and his wife suffered personal injuries, they lost personal property on the boat, and the boat itself was lost.
(a) Who can sue Crest for breach of warranty? (b) Can Gary and his wife both sue for strict tort liability? (c) Do Aqua and Crest both have strict tort liability?

_____

_____

_____

_____

2. Vision Inc., a maker of commercial microscopes, plans to sell a new microscope. Vision is concerned about potential liability for implied warranties. Vision asks you: (a) Can Vision disclaim the warranties of merchantability and fitness for a particular purpose, or are disclaimers unconscionable? (b) Can Vision disclaim the warranty of merchantability by burying a disclaimer in the contract, using the same size, type, and color of print that is used for other terms? (c) If Vision's contracts conspicuously state that microscopes are sold "AS IS," what effect would this term have on implied warranties?

_____

_____

_____

_____

Internet Exercise

1. Time to go shopping on the Internet! Using the Internet, find two identical products that are offered for sale. One product should include an express warranty, and one product should not. Alternatively, find a seller who is offering to sell the same product, both with or without an extended warranty.

2. Compare the difference in prices between the goods that have the greater and lesser warranty protection. Analyze what additional protection is provided if you purchase the product with the more extensive express warranty. Is the difference in cost worth the extra protection?

_____

_____

_____

CPA REVIEW

The following questions were given on CPA examinations. The answers for these questions are the unofficial answers prepared by the American Institute of Certified Public Accountants, Inc. (AICPA). All material is reproduced with permission of the AICPA.

____ 1. Under the Sales Article of the UCC, which of the following statements is correctregarding the warranty of merchantability arising when there has been a sale of goods by a merchant seller?
a. The warranty must be in writing.
b. The warranty arises when the buyer relies on the seller's skill in selecting the goods purchased.
c. The warranty cannot be disclaimed.
d. The warranty arises as a matter of law when the seller ordinarily sells the goods purchased.

____ 2. High sues the manufacturer, wholesaler, and retailer for bodily injuries caused by a power saw High purchased. Which of the following statements is correct under strict liability theory?
a. Contributory negligence on High's part will always be a bar to recovery.
b. The manufacturer will avoid liability if it can show it followed the custom of the industry.
c. Privity will be a bar to recovery insofar as the wholesaler is concerned if the wholesaler did not have a reasonable opportunity to inspect.
d. High may recover even if he cannot show any negligence was involved.

____ 3. Vick bought a used boat from Ocean Marina that disclaimed "any and all warranties" in connection with the sale. Ocean was unaware the boat had been stolen from Kidd. Vick surrendered it to Kidd when confronted with proof of the theft. Vick sued Ocean. Who is likely to prevail and why?
a. Vick, because the implied warranty of title has been breached.
b. Vick, because a merchant cannot disclaim implied warranties.
c. Ocean, because of the disclaimer of warranties.
d. Ocean, because Vick surrendered the boat to Kidd.

____ 4. With respect to the sale of goods, the warranty of title
a. Applies only if the seller is a merchant.
b. Applies only if it is in writing and signed by the seller.
c. Provides that the seller deliver the goods free from any lien of which the buyer lacked knowledge when the contract was made.
d. Provides that the seller cannot disclaim the warranty if the sale is made to a bona fide urchaser for value.

_____ 5. Under the UCC Sales Article, an action for breach of the implied warranty of merchantability by a party who sustains personal injuries may be successful against the seller of the product only when
   a. The seller is a merchant of the product involved.
   b. An action based on negligence can also be successfully maintained.
   c. The injured party is in privity of contract with the seller.
   d. An action based on strict liability in tort can also be successfully maintained.

_____ 6. Lazur Corp. entered into a contract with Baker Suppliers, Inc. to purchase a used word processor from Baker. Lazur is engaged in the business of selling new and used word processors to the general public. The contract required Baker to ship the goods to Lazur by common carrier pursuant to the following provision in the contract: "F.O.B.-Baker Suppliers, Inc. loading dock." Baker also represented in the contract that the word processor had been used for only 10 hours by its previous owner. The contract included the provision that the word processor was being sold "as is" and this provision was in a larger and different type style than the remainder of the contract. With regard to the contract between Lazur and Baker.
   a. An implied warranty of merchantability does not arise unless both Lazur and Baker are merchants.
   b. The "as is" provision effectively disclaims the implied warranty of title.
   c. No express warranties are created by the contract.
   d. The "as is" provision would not prevent Baker from being liable for a breach of any express warranties created by the contract.

_____ 7. On May 2, Handy Hardware sent Ram Industries a signed purchase order that stated, in part, as follows: "Ship for May 8 delivery 300 Model A-X socket sets at current dealer price. Terms 2/10/net 30." Ram received Handy's purchase order on May 4. On May 5, Ram discovered that it had only 200 Model A-X socket sets and 100 Model W-Z socket sets in stock. Ram shipped the Model A-X and Model W-Z sets to Handy without any explanation concerning the shipment. The socket sets were received by Handy on May 8. Assuming a contract exists between Handy and Ram, which of the following implied warranties would result?

   I.   Implied warranty of merchantability.
   II. Implied warranty of fitness for a particular purpose.
   III. Implied warranty of title.

   a. I only.
   b. III only.
   c. I and III only.
   d. I, II and III

CHAPTER 26
OBLIGATIONS AND PERFORMANCE

MAKE THE CONNECTION

SUMMARY

Every sales contract imposes an obligation of good faith in its performance. Good faith means honesty in fact in the conduct or transaction concerned. For merchants, the UCC imposes the additional requirement of observing "reasonable commercial standards of fair dealing in the trade."

In the case of a cash sale where no transportation of the goods is required, both the buyer and the seller may demand concurrent performance.

A buyer's or a seller's refusal to perform a contract is called a *repudiation*. A repudiation made in advance of the time for performance is called an *anticipatory repudiation* and is a breach of the contract. If either party to a contract feels insecure about the performance of the other, that party may demand by a record adequate assurance of performance. If that assurance is not given, the demanding party may treat the contract as repudiated.

The seller has a duty to deliver the goods in accordance with the terms of the contract. This duty does not require physical transportation; it requires that the seller permit the transfer of possession of the goods to the buyer.

With the exception of COD contracts, the buyer has the right to inspect the goods upon tender or delivery. Inspection includes the right to open cartons and conduct tests. If the buyer's inspection reveals that the seller has tendered nonconforming goods, the buyer may reject them. Subject to certain limitations, the seller may then offer to replace the goods or cure the problems the buyer has noted.

The buyer has a duty to accept goods that conform to the contract, and refusal to do so is a breach of contract. The buyer is deemed to have accepted goods either expressly or by implication through conduct inconsistent with rejection or by lapse of time. The buyer must pay for accepted goods in accordance with the terms of the contract. The buyer can reject goods in commercial units, accept the goods and collect damages for their problems, or reject the full contract shipment. The buyer must give notice of rejection to the seller and cannot do anything with the goods that would be inconsistent with the seller's ownership rights. The buyer should await instructions from the seller on what to do with the goods.

Even following acceptance, the buyer may revoke that acceptance if the problems with the goods substantially impair their value and the problems were either not easily discoverable or the buyer kept the goods based on the seller's promises to repair them and make them whole. Upon revocation of acceptance, the buyer should await instructions from the seller on what steps to take.

Performance can be excused on the grounds of commercial impracticability, but the seller must show objective difficulties that have created more than cost increases.

LEARNING OUTCOMES
After studying this chapter, you should be able to:

A. GENERAL PRINCIPLES
LO.1 List the steps that can be taken when a party to a sales contract feels insecure about the other party's performance

B. DUTIES OF THE PARTIES
LO.2 Explain the obligations of the seller and the buyer in a sales contract

LO.3 Identify the types of actions and conduct that constitute acceptance

LO.4 Explain the excuses that exist for nonperformance by one party

CHAPTER OUTLINE

A. GENERAL PRINCIPLES

1. OBLIGATION OF GOOD FAITH

➢ Every party has an implied duty to act in good faith in performing and enforcing a sales contract.

➢ Good faith requires nonmerchants to act honestly. Good faith requires merchants to act honestly and to also observe reasonable business standards of fair dealing.

2. TIME REQUIREMENTS OF OBLIGATIONS

GENERAL RULE. ▶ Unless otherwise agreed, if a sale is for cash and it does not involve movement of goods, a buyer and seller must perform at the same time; i.e., a buyer must pay at the time goods are delivered. ▶ Example: Ferris contracted to buy a TV for $400 cash, and delivery is to be made at Seller's place of business. In this case, Ferris must pay the $400 when he takes the TV.

STUDY HINT.   If a seller and buyer are obligated to perform at the same time but one fails to perform, then the other party may withhold performance without breaching the contract.

3. REPUDIATION OF THE CONTRACT

GENERAL RULES. ▶ A repudiation occurs if a seller or buyer clearly expresses an intent not to perform a contract at the time of performance. ▶ An anticipatory repudiation occurs if, prior to the time performance is required, a party's words or actions clearly indicate that the party is unwilling to perform a contract. ▶ Example: Roger contracted to sell his car to Molly on June 1. On May 1, Roger told Molly that he refused to sell his car to her and that he had instead sold the car to Tom. This is an anticipatory repudiation.

STUDY HINTS.   ▶ If a party fails to perform because the party incorrectly believes that the other party has committed a repudiation or anticipatory repudiation, then the nonperforming party is in breach of contract. ▶ Revised Article 2 requires repudiation to be stated in a "record."

4. ADEQUATE ASSURANCE OF PERFORMANCE

➢ *Right to demand adequate assurance of performance*: If a contracting party is reasonably insecure regarding whether the other party will perform, the insecure party may make written demand on the other party for an adequate assurance of proper performance.

➢ *Form of assurance*: ▶ The party on whom a demand for assurance is made must give "such assurance of due performance as is adequate under the circumstances of the particular case." ▶ The UCC does not specify a particular form for assurances of performance. Therefore, what constitutes an adequate assurance depends on the facts of each case. Example: A statement by a large, international oil company that it will perform a $50,000 contract may be an adequate assurance, whereas such a statement by a financially troubled small company may be insufficient.

➢ *Failure to give assurance*: If a contracting party wrongfully fails to give an adequate assurance of performance within 30 days, then the other party may: (1) treat such failure as a repudiation of the contract; (2) sue for damages for breach of contract; and (3) buy alternative goods from a third party.

➢ **LEARNING OUTCOME EXAMPLE**. See *Magic Valley Foods, Inc. v Sun Valley Potatoes, Inc.* on textbook p. 583.

B. DUTIES OF THE PARTIES

5. SELLER'S DUTY TO DELIVER

A seller has a duty to deliver goods (i.e., transfer possession of goods) to the buyer in accordance with the terms of the sales contract. *Unless otherwise agreed*, specific duties include the following:

(a) *Place, time, and manner of delivery*

GENERAL RULE. Delivery is required (1) within a reasonable time after contracting (2) at the seller's place of business or, if there is no business, at the seller's residence.

LIMITATIONS. ▶ If a contract is for the sale of identified goods and, at the time of contracting, the parties know the goods are in a particular place, then that place is the place of delivery. ▶ If an agreed method of delivery is unavailable or commercially impracticable, the seller must utilize and the buyer must accept a reasonable, alternative method of delivery if one is available.

STUDY HINT. The obligation of parties to use a reasonable, alternative method of delivery is most often incurred in connection with transportation strikes, embargoes, or boycotts.

(b) *Quantity delivered*

In general, a buyer can demand that all goods be delivered at the same time, and a buyer can refuse an improper partial delivery of goods.

6. BUYER'S DUTY UPON RECEIPT OF GOODS

(a) *Right to examine goods*

▶ In general, a buyer may inspect goods prior to paying the contract price. ▶ But, if goods are shipped C.O.D., a buyer must pay for the goods before inspecting them.

(b) *Right to refuse or return goods*

GENERAL RULES. ▶ A buyer has a right to reject goods that do not conform to the contract. A minor nonconformity of any sort is sufficient to justify rejection of the goods. ▶ Rejection means the buyer refuses to take and keep the goods as his or her own property. ▶ To reject goods, the buyer must: (1) give the seller notice of rejection within a reasonable time after delivery; (2) the notice must identify any defect that the seller can cure (correct); and (3) the buyer must hold the goods for the seller without using them.

STUDY HINTS. ▶ If any goods in a shipment are nonconforming, a buyer may: (1) reject all of the goods; (2) accept all of the goods; or (3) accept any commercial unit and reject the remaining goods. ▶ A commercial unit is a good or collection of goods that is viewed as a whole unit for purposes of sale and whose value or usefulness is seriously lessened if divided into smaller units.

(c) *Cure of defective tender or delivery*

GENERAL RULE. Broadly speaking, a buyer may reject (i.e., refuse to take or accept) goods that do not perfectly conform to contract requirements.

LIMITATION. A buyer cannot reject goods if a seller exercises its "right to cure" by tending conforming goods. A seller has the following right to cure:

➢ *Contract time not expired*: A seller can cure if: (1) the seller gives timely notice of an intent to cure; and (2) the seller tenders conforming goods within the original time for performance.

➢ *Contract time expired*: After the original time to perform has expired, a seller has an additional reasonable time within which to cure if: (1) the seller reasonably believed that the goods delivered were acceptable; and (2) the seller gives timely notice of an intent to cure.

➢ *Revised Article 2*: Seller's right of cure means a buyer must give notice of rejection and the reason for that rejection, if the seller has the right, but not necessarily the intent, to cure.

7. BUYER'S DUTY TO ACCEPT GOODS

▶ A buyer must accept and pay for goods that conform to the contract. ▶ LEARNING OUTCOME EXAMPLE. See *Weil v Murray* on textbook p. 586.

(a) *What constitutes acceptance of goods*

GENERAL RULE. A buyer accepts goods if: (1) a buyer expressly states that goods conform to contract requirements contract requirements, or that a buyer will keep goods even though they do not conform; (2) a buyer fails to effectively reject goods; for example, a buyer waits too long to reject after inspecting the goods; or (3) a buyer does any act that is inconsistent with a rejection.

STUDY HINTS. ▶ Examples of acceptance: (1) buyer resells the goods; (2) buyer continues to use the goods for a substantial time without attempting to reject them; or (3) buyer significantly alters the goods. ▶ If a buyer accepts goods, the buyer must generally pay the contract price for the goods. However, the buyer may still recover damages if the goods do not conform to contract requirements.

LEARNING OUTCOME EXAMPLES. See *Jackson Hole Traders, Inc. v Joseph* on textbook p. 588; see Thinking Things Through on textbook p. 589.

(b) *Revocation of acceptance*

GENERAL RULES. A buyer can revoke an acceptance of goods if (1) they are nonconforming, (2) the nonconformity substantially impairs the value of the goods to the buyer, and (3) the buyer accepted the goods (a) knowing they were nonconforming because the buyer reasonably assumed the seller would cure the nonconformity, which did not occur, or (b) not knowing that the goods were nonconforming because either the defects were hard to detect or the seller assured the buyer that the goods conformed.

STUDY HINTS. ► Substantial impairment means significant injury to the value of goods, not minor defects. ► Revocation of acceptance is a buyer's retraction of an acceptance of goods.

(c) *Notification of revocation of acceptance*

The buyer must give notice of revocation of acceptance to the seller within a reasonable time after the buyer discovers or should have discovered the nonconformity and before the condition of the goods substantially changes (unless the change is due to the nonconformity).

(d) *Buyer's responsibilities upon revocation of acceptance*

Following revocation, the buyer must hold the goods for the seller, and await instructions for their disposition. If the seller does not give proper instructions for disposing of the goods, the buyer may keep them as security for any down payments made.

8. BUYER'S DUTY TO PAY

➤ *Time of payment*: ► In general, a buyer must pay the price for goods that the buyer accepts and payment is due when goods are properly delivered to a buyer. ► But, a contract may require advance payment, or it may allow a buyer to buy on credit, thereby postponing the time for payment.

➤ *Form of payment*: ► A buyer may offer payment by check (or by a promissory note) if this is a generally accepted manner of payment. But, a buyer must pay in cash if the seller demands this. If a seller demands cash, then the seller must give the buyer a reasonable extension of time within which to obtain the required cash. ► If payment is made by check and the check is not paid by the buyer's bank, the purchase price remains unpaid.

9. WHEN DUTIES ARE EXCUSED

► Under the doctrine of commercial impracticability, a party is excused from performing a contractual duty when: (1) performance becomes unreasonably costly or difficult to perform (2) due to an unforeseen event that the parties assumed would not occur. ► LEARNING OUTCOME EXAMPLE. See *Ecology Services, Inc. v GranTurk Equipment* on textbook p. 590.

CONCEPT REVIEW AND APPLICATIONS

Matching Exercise

Select the term or phrase that best matches a definition or statement stated below. Each term or phrase is the best match for only one statement or definition. Not all terms and phrases will necessarily be used.

acceptance

anticipatory repudiation

commercial impracticability

commercial units

good faith

repudiation

right to cure

seasonable

substantial impairment

_____ 1. Clear declaration made prior to time for performance that a party will not perform a contract.

_____ 2. Wrongful failure to perform a contract at the time performance is required.

_____ 3. Buyer agrees to take goods as his or her own.

_____ 4. Timely.

_____ 5. Units that are generally viewed as being a whole.

_____ 6. Duty to act honestly and, for merchants, to also follow business standards of fair dealing.

_____ 7. Defense that may excuse a party from his or her duty to perform a sales contract.

_____ 8. Seller right to correct an improper performance by delivering conforming goods to abuyer.

True/False

Write **T** if the statement is true, write **F** if it is false.

_____ 1. Good faith requires a nonmerchant to act honestly.

_____ 2. In a cash sale not involving movement of goods, a buyer's duty to pay and a seller's duty to deliver goods are concurrent, i.e., payment and delivery must be performed at the same time.

_____ 3. Ken and Renee made a contract. Ken mistakenly believed that Renee had breached the contract and, therefore, he refused to perform his obligations under the contract. In this case, Ken has not committed a repudiation and he has not breached the contract.

_____ 4. If a contracting party repudiates a contract, the other party is excused from having to perform the contract but the other party is not entitled to sue the repudiating party for damages.

_____ 5. If a contracting party repudiates a contract before the time for performance, the other party can treat the anticipatory repudiation as a repudiation of the contract and may sue for breach of contract.

_____ 6. If a contracting party reasonably feels insecure about the likelihood that the other party will perform, the insecure party can make written demand for an adequate assurance of performance.

_____ 7. If a contracting party fails to give an adequate assurance of performance when properly requested to do so, the other party may treat such failure as a repudiation of the contract.

_____ 8. If a contract requires shipment by railroad but this transportation is unavailable due to a strike, the contract is automatically canceled even if reasonable, alternative transportation is available.

_____ 9. A seller may make a curative tender by tendering goods that meet contract requirements, or by tendering substitute goods that the seller believes are an acceptable alternative.

_____ 10. A buyer is generally entitled to examine goods prior to payment unless goods are shipped C.O.D.

Multiple Choice

_____ 1. Foodco, a merchant, and Jan made a contract whereby Foodco granted Jan the right to sell Foodco's products in a certain region. However, the contract states that Foodco may allow others to also sell in this region if Foodco determines that additional sales representatives are needed. The contract is silent regarding good faith. Under these facts:
   a. Foodco must act in good faith since the UCC implies this duty. Good faith requires Foodco to act honestly, and to also observe reasonable business standards of fair dealing.
   b. Foodco must act in good faith since the UCC implies this duty. Good faith only requires Foodco to act honestly.
   c. Foodco must act in good faith since the UCC implies this duty. Good faith prohibits Foodco from exercising any contract right that may be detrimental to Jan.
   d. Foodco is under no duty to act in good faith since the contract is silent on this matter.

_____ 2. Decor Inc. contracted to sell wallpaper to Karen. The wallpaper is located at Decor's place of business. The contract is silent regarding time and place of delivery. Under these facts:
   a. Decor is obligated to deliver the wallpaper to Karen at her home.
   b. Decor is obligated to deliver the wallpaper to Karen at Decor's place of business.
   c. Decor is obligated to have the wallpaper ready for delivery only at such time Decor chooses.
   d. Decor is obligated to have the wallpaper ready for delivery whenever Karen demands delivery.

____ 3. On May 1 (the required delivery date), Seller delivered goods that Seller reasonably believed were acceptable. The next day, Seller was told that the goods were nonconforming. Seller immediately gave notice that the improper performance would be cured. Under these facts:
   a. Seller cannot cure. A seller cannot cure an improper performance.
   b. Seller cannot cure. A seller can cure only if a cure is done within the original contract time.
   c. Seller can cure if Seller tenders conforming goods to the buyer within a reasonable time.
   d. Seller can cure whenever Seller chooses to do so.

____ 4. In which case did Buyer accept the goods in question?
   a. Buyer bought a tractor. During inspection Buyer learned that the tractor was nonconforming. After using the tractor for nine months, Buyer told Seller that the tractor was unacceptable.
   b. Buyer bought an electric barbecue. When Buyer first attempted to use the barbecue, it did not work properly. Buyer immediately told Seller that the barbecue was unacceptable.
   c. Buyer bought a computer. When the computer was delivered, Buyer discovered that the computer was nonconforming. Nonetheless, Buyer modified numerous significant internal components of the computer. Later, Buyer told Seller that the computer was unacceptable.
   d. a and c.

Case Problem

Answer the following problem, briefly explaining your answer.

Grace purchased an organ from Mistro Music Store. Mistro warranted that the organ was solid oak. At the time of delivery, Grace noticed that the organ was pine, stained with an oak finish. She protested to the Mistro manager and he told her: "Calm down. This is just a silly clerical mistake. Keep this one for now, and we will shortly send out the solid oak piano you ordered." After a month of broken promises, Grace is still without a piano.

Can Grace reject or revoke her acceptance of the piano? Explain your answer.

_____

_____

_____

_____

Internet Exercise

You are on the Internet again, and this time you were shopping for Art. On his behalf, you contracted to buy a sofa for $500. Art is to take delivery at Seller's place of business where the sofa is located. Art has inspected and accepted the sofa. Based on your research of UCC Article 2, answer the following questions, identifying the controlling section of UCC Article 2:

1. When must Art pay for the sofa?
2. What form of payment may Art tender?

_____

_____

_____

_____

CPA REVIEW

The following questions were given on CPA examinations. The answers for these questions are the unofficial answers prepared by the American Institute of Certified Public Accountants, Inc. (AICPA). All material is reproduced with permission of the AICPA.

____ 1. Smith contracted in writing to sell Peters a used personal computer for $600. The contract did not specifically address the time for payment, place of delivery, or Peters' right to inspect the computer. Which of the following statements is correct?
   a. Smith is obligated to deliver the computer to Peters' home.
   b. Peters is entitled to inspect the computer before paying for it.
   c. Peters may not pay for the computer using a personal check unless Smith agrees.
   d. Smith is not entitled to payment until 30 days after Peters receives the computer.

____ 2. Under the Sales Article of the UCC, which of the following events will release the buyer from all its obligations under a sales contract?
   a. Destruction of the goods after risk of loss passed to the buyer.
   b. Impracticability of delivery under the terms of the contract.
   c. Anticipatory repudiation by the buyer that is retracted before the seller cancels the contract.
   d. Refusal of the seller to give written assurance of performance when reasonably demanded by the buyer.

____ 3. Lazur Corp. agreed to purchase 100 radios from Wizard Suppliers, Inc. Wizard is a wholesaler of small home appliances and Lazur is an appliance retailer. The contract required Wizard to ship the radios to Lazur by common carrier, "F.O.B. Wizard Suppliers, Inc. Loading Dock." Under the UCC Sales Article
   a. Title to the radios passes to Lazur at the time they are delivered to the carrier, even if the goods are nonconforming.
   b. Lazur must inspect the radios at the time of delivery or waive any defects and the right to sue for breach of contract.
   c. Wizard must pay the freight expense associated with the shipment of the radios to Lazur.
   d. Lazur would have the right to reject any shipment if Wizard fails to notify Lazur that the goods have been shipped.

___ 4. Lazur Corp. entered into a contract with Baker Suppliers, Inc. to purchase a used word processor from Baker. Lazur is engaged in the business of selling new and used word processors to the general public. The contract required Baker to ship the goods to Lazur by common carrier pursuant to the following provision in the contract: "F.O.B.-Baker Suppliers, Inc. loading dock." Baker also represented in the contract that the word processor had been used for only 10 hours by its previous owner. The contract included the provision that the word processor was being sold "as is" and this provision was in a larger and different type style than the remainder of the contract. (A)ssume that the contract between Lazur and Baker is otherwise silent. Under the UCC Sales Article,

   a. Lazur must pay Baker the purchase price before Baker is required to ship the word processor to Lazur.
   b. Baker does not warrant that it owns the word processor.
   c. Lazur will be entitled to inspect the word processor before it accepts or pays for it.
   d. Title to the word processor passes to Lazur when it takes physical   possession.

___ 5. Yost Corp., a computer manufacturer, contracted to sell its computers to Ivor Corp., a computer retailer. The contract specified that delivery was to be made by truck to Ivor's warehouse. Instead, Yost shipped the computers by rail. When Ivor claimed that Yost did not comply with the contract, Yost told Ivor that there had been a trucker's strike when the goods were shipped. Ivor refused to pay for the computers. Under these circumstances, Ivor

   a. Is obligated to pay for the computers because Yost made a valid substituted performance.
   b. Is obligated to pay for the computers because title to them passed to Ivor when Ivor received them.
   c. May return the computers and avoid paying for them because of the way Yost delivered them.
   d. May return the computers and avoid paying for them because the contract was void under the theory of commercial impracticability.

___ 6. On March 7, 2009, Wax Corp. contracted with Noll Wholesalers to supply Noll with specific electrical parts. Delivery was called for on June 3, 2009. On May 2, 2009, Wax notified Noll that it would not perform and that Noll should look elsewhere. Wax had received a larger and more lucrative contract on April 21, 2009, and its capacity was such that it could not fulfill both orders. The facts

   a. Will prevent Wax from retracting its repudiation of the Noll contract.
   b. Are not sufficient to clearly establish an anticipatory repudiation.
   c. Will permit Noll to sue only after June 3, 2009, the latest performance date.
   d. Will permit Noll to sue immediately after May 2, 2009, even though the performance called for under the contract was not due until June 3, 2009.

___ 7. If a contract for the sale of goods includes a C. & F. shipping term and the seller has fulfilled all of its obligations, the

   a. Title to the goods will pass to the buyer when the goods are received by the buyer at the place of destination.
   b. Risk of loss will pass to the buyer upon delivery of the goods to the carrier.
   c. Buyer retains the right to inspect the goods prior to making payment.
   d. Seller must obtain an insurance policy at its own expense for the buyer's benefit.

CHAPTER 27
REMEDIES FOR BREACH OF SALES CONTRACTS

MAKE THE CONNECTION

SUMMARY

The law provides a number of remedies for the breach of a sales contract. Remedies based on UCC theories generally are subject to a four-year statute of limitations, with Revised UCC adding an extension of one additional year (making it five years) in cases in which the breach is discovered in year four. If the remedy sought is based on a non-UCC theory, a tort or contract statute of limitations established by state statute will apply.

Remedies of the seller may include (1) a lien on the goods until the seller is paid, (2) the right to resell the goods, (3) the right to cancel the sales contract, (4) the right to recover the goods from the carrier and the buyer, and (5) the right to bring an action for damages or, in some cases, for the purchase price. The seller may also have remedies because of secured transactions. Remedies of the buyer may include (1) the rejection of nonconforming goods, (2) the revocation of acceptance, (3) an action for damages for nondelivery of conforming goods, (4) an action for breach of warranty, (5) the cancellation of the sales contract, (6) the right to resell the goods, (7) the right to bring an action for conversion, recovery of goods, or specific performance, and (8) the right to sue for damages and cancel if the seller has made a material breach of the contract.

The parties may modify their remedies by a contractual provision for liquidated damages, for limitations on statutory remedies, or for waiver of defenses. When consumers are involved, this freedom of contract is to some extent limited for their protection.

Under the CISG, the seller may require the buyer to pay the price, take delivery, and perform obligations under the contract, or the seller may avoid the contract if there is a fundamental breach. A buyer may reject goods under the CISG only if there is a fundamental breach of contract. The buyer may also reduce the price of nonconforming goods.

LEARNING OUTCOMES
After studying this chapter, you should be able to

A. STATUTE OF LIMITATIONS

B. REMEDIES OF THE SELLER
LO.1   List the remedies of the seller when the buyer breaches a sales contract

C. REMEDIES OF THE BUYER
LO.2   List the remedies of the buyer when the seller breaches a sales contract

D. CONTRACT PROVISIONS ON REMEDIES
LO.3   Determine the validity of clauses limiting damages

E. REMEDIES IN THE INTERNATIONAL SALE OF GOODS

CHAPTER OUTLINE

A. STATUTE OF LIMITATIONS

1. TIME LIMITS FOR SUITS UNDER THE UCC

► An action for breach of contract must be filed within four years after a cause of action arises. A cause of action arises: (1) for a breach of warranty for *future performance* when the performance begins; and (2) for a breach for nonpayment by a buyer at the time the buyer fails to pay. ► Revised Article 2 in effect extends the time to five years in those cases in which a breach is discovered in year four.

2. TIME LIMITS FOR OTHER SUITS

Actions for strict tort liability, fraud, or negligence are subject to tort statute of limitations.

B. REMEDIES OF THE SELLER

Seller's remedies include: (1) stopping or withholding delivery; (2) canceling the contract; (3) suing for incidental damages; and (4) suing for the purchase price or for damages caused by a breach.

3. SELLER'S LIEN

A seller has a lien on goods, entitling the seller to keep possession of the goods until the buyer pays.

4. SELLER'S REMEDY OF STOPPING SHIPMENT

► When a seller learns a buyer is insolvent, the seller may refuse to deliver unless the buyer pays cash. ► Generally, a seller may reclaim (retake) goods that have been delivered to an insolvent buyer: (1) for 10 days after delivery; or (2) for longer than 10 days if the buyer, in writing, lied to the seller about the buyer's insolvency within 3 months preceding delivery. ► Revised Article 2 eliminates the 10-day time limit and also eliminates the distinctions on sizes of shipments and rights. ► LEARNING OUTCOME EXAMPLE. See the **For Example** discussion of the Whirlpool refrigerators on textbook p. 601.

5. RESALE BY SELLER

GENERAL RULES. ► If a buyer breaches, a seller may resell goods by public or private sale. ► If goods are resold, damages are the contract price minus resale price.
LIMITATION. In general, a buyer must be given reasonable notice of a sale.
STUDY HINTS. ► If a seller resells goods, the seller may not sue for the contract price. ► If a seller makes a profit on the resale of goods, the seller is entitled to retain the profit.

6. CANCELLATION BY SELLER

GENERAL RULES. ► If a buyer commits a material breach of contract, the seller may cancel the contract unless the seller sues for the purchase price. ► Cancellation of a contract terminates unperformed duties of both parties, but it does not affect a seller's right to recover damages.
STUDY HINT. The right to cancel a contract is in addition to a seller's other remedies.

7. SELLER'S ACTION FOR DAMAGES UNDER THE MARKET PRICE FORMULA

If a buyer fails to pay for accepted goods, a seller may choose to sue for contract price minus market price.

8. SELLER'S ACTION FOR LOST PROFITS

If the market price formula does not adequately compensate the seller for a loss, then the seller may recover his or her lost profits.

9. OTHER TYPES OF DAMAGES

In addition to other damages, a seller can recover incidental damages caused by a buyer. These damages are out-of-pocket expenses, such as expenses for inspection, towing, storage, and transportation.

10. SELLER'S ACTION FOR THE PURCHASE PRICE

If a buyer fails to pay for accepted goods or for specially manufactured goods that cannot be resold, then the seller can recover the purchase price.

11. SELLER'S NONSALE REMEDIES (IN ADDITION TO ARTICLE 2 REMEDIES)

▶ When a buyer breaches, a seller may have additional, noncode remedies. ▶ Example: seller and buyer entered into a *secured transaction*, whereby the seller can retake goods if a buyer fails to pay.

C. REMEDIES OF THE BUYER

12. REJECTION OF IMPROPER TENDER

▶ In general, a buyer may reject goods and sue for remedies if a seller fails to perfectly perform.
▶ LEARNING OUTCOME EXAMPLE. See *Furlong v Alpha Chi Omega Sorority* on textbook p. 606.

13. REVOCATION OF ACCEPTANCE

A buyer can revoke an acceptance of goods if a nonconformity substantially impairs the value of the goods to the buyer. The buyer may then sue for his or her remedies.

14. BUYER'S ACTION FOR DAMAGES FOR NONDELIVERY - MARKET PRICE RECOVERY

If goods are not delivered (or a buyer refuses nonconforming goods), a buyer can sue for damages equal to the market price for the goods less the contract price.

15. BUYER'S ACTION FOR DAMAGES FOR NONDELIVERY - COVER PRICE RECOVERY

GENERAL RULE.   If goods are not delivered (or a buyer refuses nonconforming goods), a buyer may "cover," i.e., buy comparable replacement goods. In this case, damages = cover price - contract price.
STUDY HINT.   A buyer is not required to cover.
LEARNING OUTCOME EXAMPLE. See *Billy Cain Ford Lincoln Mercury, Inc. v Kaminski* on textbook p. 605.

16. OTHER TYPES OF DAMAGES

▶ In addition to other damages, a buyer may also recover (1) incidental damages and (2) consequential damages, i.e., losses that occur due to the particular needs of the buyer. ▶ Examples of consequential damages: lost profits; property damage; personal injuries.

17. ACTION FOR BREACH OF WARRANTY

GENERAL RULE. If a seller breaches but the buyer accepts the goods, damages are: (1) *breach of warranty*: value of goods had they conformed to warranties minus actual value; or *other breaches*: actual damages (typically, contract price less actual value).

LIMITATION. A buyer must give due notice of any breach or the buyer cannot sue for the breach.

STUDY HINT. A buyer may deduct damages from the unpaid portion of the purchase price.

18. CANCELLATION BY BUYER

▶ A buyer may cancel if a seller breaches, unless the buyer accepts and keeps the goods. ▶ Cancellation ends a buyer's duty to take and pay for goods; it does not affect a buyer's rights to remedies. ▶A buyer who cancels can recover damages, any money paid, and the value of property traded in.

19. BUYER'S RESALE OF GOODS

On rejection or revocation of acceptance, a buyer has a security interest in goods held by the buyer to secure repayment of money paid and expenses incurred; a buyer may resell goods if necessary.

20. ACTION FOR SPECIFIC PERFORMANCE

▶ A buyer may obtain specific performance of a contract if: (1) unique goods are not delivered; or
(2) in other proper cases, such as when essential, irreplaceable goods are not delivered. ▶ A rise in the market price for goods, standing alone, will not justify awarding specific performance. ▶ Revised Article 2 allows the buyer or seller to obtain specific performance, and it is enforceable as a contract provision in nonconsumer contracts.

21. NONSALE REMEDIES OF THE BUYER (IN ADDITION TO ARTICLE 2 REMEDIES)

▶ A buyer may sue under tort law for fraud, negligence, or strict tort liability. ▶ A defrauded buyer can cancel the sales contract *and* sue the seller for damages.

D. CONTRACT PROVISIONS ON REMEDIES

22. LIMITATION OF DAMAGES

➢ *Liquidated damages*: Liquidated damages (fixed damages) are valid if reasonable in light of: (1) actual damages; (2) difficulty in estimating damages; and (3) impracticality of other remedies.

> *Exclusion of damages*: ▶ A contract can limit damages if a limit is conscionable. ▶ It is primafacie unconscionable to limit damages for personal injuries caused by defective consumer goods.

> ➤ **LEARNING OUTCOME EXAMPLES**. See *Rodriguez v Learjet, Inc.* on textbook p. 608; see the E-Commerce & Cyberlaw discussion of software damages on textbook p. 611.

23. DOWN PAYMENTS AND DEPOSITS

A buyer's deposit must be returned *to the extent it exceeds* (1) liquidated damages or (2) if liquidated damages are not stated, the lesser of 20 percent of the price or $500 (unless actual losses are more).

24. LIMITATION OF REMEDIES

▶ Parties may limit remedies that are available for a breach. ▶ Example: A buyer's remedies for a nonconforming product may be limited to requesting the seller to repair or replace the product.

25. WAIVER OF DEFENSES

▶ A buyer cannot use a breach of contract defense against a seller (or assignee) if (1) a contract has a waiver of defense clause stating that defenses are waived or (2) a buyer impliedly waives defenses. ▶ LEARNING OUTCOME EXAMPLE. See the Thinking Things Through discussion of the Harley purchase on textbook p. 610.

26. PRESERVATION OF DEFENSES

In certain consumer transactions, FTC rules require contracts to have a notice preserving the right of consumers to assert defenses against a party acquiring the contract; many states have similar laws.

E. REMEDIES IN THE INTERNATIONAL SALE OF GOODS

27. REMEDIES OF THE SELLER

A seller's remedies include requiring a buyer to pay the price or declaring the sales contract void.

28. REMEDIES OF THE BUYER

A buyer may reject goods only if a seller commits a fundamental (material) breach of the contract.

CONCEPT REVIEW AND APPLICATIONS

Matching Exercise

Select the term or phrase that best matches a definition or statement stated below. Each term or phrase is the best match for only one statement or definition. Not all terms and phrases will necessarily be used.

breach	liquidated damages
consequential damages	secured transaction
incidental damages	statute of limitations

_____ 1. Out-of-pocket expenses incurred by a party due to the other party's breach of contract.

_____ 2. Stipulated amount of damages to be paid if a party breaches a contract.

_____ 3. Time within which a lawsuit must be filed.

_____ 4. Transaction that allows a seller to retake goods (collateral) if a buyer fails to pay a debt.

_____ 5. Damages that arise due to the particular needs of a party, such as the buyer in a sales contract.

_____ 6. Nonperformance of contractual duties.

True/False

Write **T** if the statement is true, write **F** if it is false.

_____ 1. A breach of contract suit must be commenced within two years after the cause of action arises.

_____ 2. A nonbreaching party's cancellation of a contract terminates the party's right to sue for damages.

_____ 3. A buyer cannot reject goods unless a nonconformity substantially impairs the value of the goods to the buyer.

_____ 4. In general, a seller may stop a shipment of goods if they were sold on credit and the buyer is insolvent.

_____ 5. In certain situations, a seller may reclaim goods from an insolvent buyer.

_____ 6. If a seller breaches a contract, the buyer can sell goods in the buyer's possession if this is necessary in order for the buyer to recover payments that the buyer has made to the seller.

_____ 7. If a seller refuses to deliver goods, a buyer is always entitled to specific performance.

_____ 8. The UCC forbids liquidation of damage clauses in sales contracts.

_____ 9. A contract term that excludes recovery of damages is generally valid if the clause is not unconscionable and the contract does not involve consumers.

_____10. In general, it is unconscionable for a sales contract to limit damages for personal injuries that are caused by nonconforming consumer goods.

Multiple Choice

_____ 1. Seller sold his personal motorcycle to Buyer for $5,000. Prior to delivery or payment, Buyer breached the contract and refused to take the cycle. After the breach, Seller properly held a public sale and sold the cycle for $4,500. Seller had to pay a $500 commission to the auctioneer who conducted the sale. Under these facts, Seller can recover how much in damages?
   a. $0
   b. $500
   c. $1,000
   d. $5,000

_____ 2. Select the correct answer.
   a. AAA Appliances sold an oven to Beth for $600. Beth refused the oven and breached the contract. AAA would have made a profit of $300 on the sale. At the time the oven was tendered to Beth, the oven's market price was $500. In this case, AAA can recover $300 in damages.
   b. Ike sold his personal record collection to Brie for $500. Brie refused the records and breached the contract. The market price of the records was $200 at the time they were tendered to Brie. Ike did not resell the records. In this case, Ike can recover $300 in damages.
   c. Seller sold a set of encyclopedias to Buyer for $1,000. Buyer accepted the encyclopedias, but Buyer refuses to pay. In this case, Seller can recover the $1,000 purchase price.
   d. All of the above.

_____ 3. Mary bought and paid for a sewing machine. Mary accepted the machine, unaware that the machine was nonconforming. Soon afterwards, the machine's engine seized due to the nonconformity, and the machine was rendered worthless. Seller failed to cure. Under these facts:
   a. Mary cannot revoke her acceptance because she accepted the sewing machine.
   b. Mary can revoke her acceptance.
   c. If Mary revokes her acceptance, she may sue for damages under the market price formula.
   d. b and c.

_____ 4. Ralph bought a power sander from Seller for $500. _Prior to paying_, Ralph properly rejected the sander due to Seller's breach. An identical sander can be purchased elsewhere for $550. The market price of the sander at the time Ralph learned of the breach was $600. Under these facts:
   a. If Ralph buys the replacement sander, Ralph can recover $50 in damages.
   b. If Ralph buys the replacement sander, Ralph cannot recover any damages.
   c. If Ralph does not buy the replacement sander, Ralph can recover $600 in damages.
   d. If Ralph does not buy the replacement sander, Ralph cannot recover any damages.

Case Problem

Answer the following problem, briefly explaining your answer.

During a promotional sale, Alicia bought a used car from Seller for $10,000. Seller warranted that the car had no defects. The car would have been worth $11,000 had it complied with Seller's warranty. In fact, the car's transmission was defective, a breach of warranty. As a result, the actual value of the car was only $9,000. Alicia spent $200 for a rental car when the transmission of the car she purchased failed and she could not drive the car. Alicia has accepted the car, and she intends to keep the car.

(1) Is Alicia required to give Seller notice of the breach? (2) What are the consequences if Alicia does not give notice of the breach? (3) If Seller refuses to cure the breach (i.e., Seller refuses to replace or repair the transmission), how much in damages can Alicia recover? (4) Is Alicia entitled to cancel the contract?

_____

_____

_____

_____

Internet Exercise

Shopping for goods on the Internet can pose hidden risks for the unwary shopper. For instance, are the remedies of a buyer limited? Your task is to locate three different vehicles with a sales price under $10,000 that are offered for sale by a dealer, and to then analyze the advertised terms regarding the buyer's remedies. For each vehicle, you must then: (1) identify the web site where it is advertised; (2) the terms regarding remedies; and (3) what risks, if any, that these remedy terms may pose for a buyer.

_____

_____

_____

_____

CPA REVIEW

The following questions were given on past CPA examinations. The answers for these questions are the unofficial answers prepared by the American Institute of Certified Public Accountants, Inc. (AICPA). All material is reproduced with permission of the AICPA.

____ 1. Under the UCC Sales Article, which of the following legal remedies would a buyer not have when a seller fails to transfer and deliver goods identified to the contract?
   a. Suit for specific performance.
   b. Suit for punitive damages.
   c. Purchase substitute goods (cover).
   d. Recover the identified goods (capture).

___ 2. Cara Fabricating Co. and Taso Corp. agreed orally that Taso would custom manufacture a compressor for Cara at a price of $120,000. After Taso completed the work at a cost of $90,000, Cara notified Taso that the compressor was no longer needed. Taso is holding the compressor and has requested payment from Cara. Taso has been unable to resell the compressor for any price. Taso incurred storage fees of $2,000. If Cara refuses to pay Taso and Taso sues Cara, the most Taso will be entitled to recover is
   a. $92,000
   b. $105,000
   c. $120,000
   d. $122,000

Questions 3 and 4 are based on the following information:

On April 5, 1987, Anker, Inc., furnished Bold Corp. with Anker's financial statements dated March 31, 1987. The financial statements contained misrepresentations which indicated that Anker was solvent when in fact it was insolvent. Based on Anker's financial statements, Bold agreed to sell Anker 90 computers, "F.O.B.-Bold's loading dock." On April 14, Anker received 60 of the computers. The remaining 30 computers are in the possession of the common carrier and in transit to Anker.

___ 3. If on April 28, Bold discovered that Anker was insolvent, then with respect to the computers delivered to Anker on April 14, Bold may
   a. Reclaim the computers upon making a demand.
   b. Reclaim the computers irrespective of the rights of any subsequent third party.
   c. Not reclaim the computers since ten days have elapsed from its delivery.
   d. Not reclaim the computers since it is entitled to recover the price of the computers.

___ 4. With respect to the remaining 30 computers in transit, which of the following statements is correct if Anker refuses to pay Bold in cash and Anker is not in possession of a negotiable document of title covering the computers?
   a. Bold may stop delivery of the computers to Anker since their contract is void due to Anker's furnishing of the false financial statements.
   b. Bold may stop delivery of the computers to Anker despite the fact that title had passed to Anker.
   c. Bold must deliver the computers to Anker on credit since Anker has not breached the contract.
   d. Bold must deliver the computers to Anker since the risk of loss had passed to Anker.

___ 5. On February 15, Mazur Corp. contracted to sell 1,000 bushels of wheat to Good Bread, Inc. at $6.00 per bushel with delivery to be made on June 23. On June 1, Good advised Mazur that it would not accept or pay for the wheat. On June 2, Mazur sold the wheat to another customer at the market price of $5.00 per bushel. Mazur had advised Good that it intended to resell the wheat. Which of the following statements is correct?
   a. Mazur can successfully sue Good for the difference between the resale price and the contract price.
   b. Mazur can resell the wheat only after June 23.
   c. Good can retract its anticipatory breach at any time before June 23.
   d. Good can successfully sue Mazur for specific performance.

___ 6. Lazur Corp. entered into a contract with Baker Suppliers, Inc. to purchase a used word processor from Baker. Lazur is engaged in the business of selling new and used word processors to the general public. The contract required Baker to ship the goods to Lazur by common carrier pursuant to the following provision in the contract: "F.O.B.-Baker Suppliers, Inc. loading dock." Baker also represented in the contract that the word processor had been used for only 10 hours by its previous owner. The contract included the provision that the word processor was being sold "as is" and this provision was in a larger and different type style than the remainder of the contract. For this item only, assume that Lazur refused to accept the word processor even though it was in all respects conforming to the contract and that the contract is otherwise silent. Under the UCC Sales Article,

a. Baker can successfully sue for specific performance and make Lazur accept and pay for the word processor.

b. Baker may resell the word processor to another buyer.

c. Baker must sue for the difference between the market value of the word processor and the contract price plus its incidental damages.

d. Baker cannot successfully sue for consequential damages unless it attempts to resell the word processor.

___ 7. Cain and Zen Corp. orally agreed that Zen would specially manufacture a machine for Cain at a price of $40,000. After Zen completed the work at a cost of $30,000, Cain notified Zen that it no longer needed the machine. Zen is holding the machine for Cain and has requested payment from Cain. Despite making reasonable efforts, Zen has been unable to resell the machine for any price. Zen has incurred warehouse fees of $500 for storing the machine. If Cain refuses to pay Zen and Zen sues Cain, the most Zen will be entitled to recover is

a. $0

b. $30,500

c. $40,000

d. $40,500

CHAPTER 28
KINDS OF INSTRUMENTS, PARTIES, AND EGOTIABILITY

MAKE THE CONNECTION

SUMMARY

An instrument or piece of commercial paper is a transferable, signed promise or order to pay a specified sum of money that is evidenced by a record. An instrument is negotiable when it contains the terms required by the UCC.

Negotiable instruments have two categories: (1) promises to pay and (2) orders to pay. Checks and drafts are orders to pay. Notes and certificates of deposits are promises to pay. In addition to ordinary checks, there are cashier's checks and teller's checks. A bank money order is a check even though it bears the words *money order*.

The original parties to a note are the maker and the payee. The original parties to a draft are the drawer, the drawee, and the payee. The term *party* may refer to a natural person or to an artificial person, such as a corporation. Indorsers and accommodation parties are considered secondary obligors.

The requirements of negotiability are that the instrument (1) be evidenced by a record, (2) be signed (authenticated) by the maker or the drawer, and (3) contain a promise or order (4) of an unconditional character (5) to pay in money (6) a sum certain (7) on demand or at a definite time (8) to order or bearer. A check may be negotiable without being payable to order or bearer.

If an instrument meets the requirements of negotiability, the parties have the rights and protections of Article 3. If it does not meet the requirements of negotiability, the rights of the parties are governed under contract law.

LEARNING OUTCOMES
After studying this chapter, you should be able to:

A. TYPES OF NEGOTIABLE INSTRUMENTS AND PARTIES
LO.1   Explain the importance and function of negotiable instruments
LO.2   Name the parties to negotiable instruments

B. NEGOTIABILITY
LO.3   Describe the concept of negotiability and distinguish it from assignability
LO.3   List the requirements for a negotiable instrument

CHAPTER OUTLINE

A. TYPES OF NEGOTIABLE INSTRUMENTS AND PARTIES

GENERAL RULE. Negotiable instruments, (also known as commercial paper and sometimes referred to as "paper" in this study guide) are important because certain transferees of negotiable instruments, known as "holders in due course," may acquire a greater right to demand payment from a debtor than would an assignee of a contract.
STUDY HINT. ▶ *Negotiable instrument example*: Beth signed a negotiable promissory note to pay for goods, and Seller failed to deliver the goods. If Seller transferred the note to Rod (a holder in due course), Beth must pay Rod. ▶ *Contract example*: Bill signed a contract promising to pay for goods, and Seller failed to deliver the goods to Bill. Bill is not obligated to pay even if Seller assigned the contract to a third party.

1. DEFINITION

➢ A negotiable instrument is an unconditional promise or order to pay a fixed sum of money that is payable to bearer or order, is payable on demand or at a definite time and does not state any other undertaking or instruction in addition to the payment of money. signed, written promise or order to pay a specific sum of money. Written or electronic promissory notes are now permissible.

➢ Instruments are negotiable when they contain the terms required by the UCC.

2. KINDS OF INSTRUMENTS

➢ *Promissory notes*: ▶ Unconditional written, signed promises to pay a sum certain in money on demand or at a definite time to order or bearer. ▶ Parties: maker and payee.

➢ *Certificates of deposit*: ▶ Promissory notes issued by a bank, which acknowledge receipt of money and state a promise to pay the certificates when they become due. ▶ Parties: maker (bank), payee.

➢ *Drafts*: ▶ Unconditional written orders by one party directing another to pay a sum certain in money on demand or at a definite time to order or bearer. ▶ Parties: drawer, drawee, and payee.

➢ *Checks*: ▶ Special types of draft whereby a depositor (drawer) orders a bank or credit union (drawee) to pay the amount of the check to a payee on demand. ▶ A check's distinguishing features are that it is drawn on a bank or credit union as drawee and (2) is payable on demand. ▶ Four special types of checks are cashier's checks, teller's checks, traveler's checks, and money orders.

3. PARTIES TO INSTRUMENTS

➢ *Maker*: Party who creates and originally signs a promissory note. Example: Mary signs and issues a negotiable promissory note promising to pay $100 to Ellie. Mary is a maker.

➢ *Drawer*: Party who creates and originally signs a draft or check. Example: Dave signs his check ordering his bank to pay $100 to Paul. Dave is a drawer.

> *Drawee*: Party ordered by a drawer to pay a draft or check. Example: Dave issues his check ordering his bank, ABC Bank, to pay $100 to Paul. ABC Bank is a drawee.

> *Payee*: Party originally named on the face of an instrument as the party to receive payment. Example: Dave issues his check ordering ABC Bank to pay $100 to Paul. Paul is a payee.

> *Acceptor*: Drawee who, in writing on a draft, agrees to pay the draft. Example: Dave issues a check ordering ABC Bank to pay $100 to Paul and, in writing on the check, ABC Bank agreed to pay. ABC Bank is an acceptor.

> *Secondary obligor*: ► A secondary obligor (formerly known as an accommodation party) is a party   (1) who is not an original party to an instrument and (2) who voluntarily allows his or her name to be added to the instrument (3) in order to strengthen its collectability. ► Revised Article 3 also classifies drawers and indorsers as secondary obligors. ► A secondary obligor has liability to pay an instrument under certain circumstances.

B. NEGOTIABILITY

4. DEFINITION OF NEGOTIABILITY

GENERAL RULE. If an instrument meets the definition of negotiability, it is a negotiable instrument and a transferee can be a holder in due course, taking it free of many defenses that can avoid a right to be paid. If paper is nonnegotiable, a transferee has only rights of an assignee of a contract.
STUDY HINTS.   ► Negotiability is determined when an instrument is issued or completed. ► The instrument itself must satisfy all negotiability requirements. ► Negotiability is the characteristic that distinguishes negotiable instruments from ordinary contracts.

5. REQUIREMENTS OF NEGOTIABILITY

> In general, a negotiable instrument must:

  (1) be evidenced by a record (writing);
  (2) be authenticated (signed in case of tangible instruments) by the maker or drawer;
  (3) contain a promise or order;
  (4) of an unconditional nature;
  (5) to pay in money;
  (6) a sum certain;
  (7) on demand or at a definite time;
  (8) to order or bearer (words of negotiability).

►In addition, the instrument must be issued by the maker or drawer (or their authorized agent) and delivered to the payee with the intent to create a legal obligation. ► LEARNING OUTCOME EXAMPLE: See *Smith v Vaughn* on textbook p. 631.

► Important negotiability rules include:

> *Record*: ► A record includes any writing or electronic record. ► Parol evidence rule forbids proving a prior oral agreement in order to change a final, complete, written instrument.

> *Signed by the maker or drawer*: ► Paper must be signed by a maker or drawer. ► An agent can sign for a principal, and the agent generally is not liable on the paper. ► If an agent signs paper without disclosing a principal's identity and the agent's representative capacity, the agent may be liable. ► An agent is not liable on a check drawn on a principal's bank account, even if the agent's representative capacity is not stated. ► If the instrument does not show the representative capacity of the signer or it fails to identify the represented person, the representative is liable to (1) any holder in due course who subsequently takes the instrument and (2) any other holder or transferee of the instrument unless the representative proves that the original parties did not intend the representative to be bound.

> *Promise or order to pay*: ► A promissory note must contain a promise to pay money; a draft or check must contain an order to pay money. ► An IOU is not a negotiable instrument.

> *Unconditional promise or order*: ► A promise or order to pay must be unconditional; it cannot depend on an event not certain to occur. Examples of conditional promises: promise to pay if party performs a contract; promise to pay is subject to terms of another contract. ► A drawer's notation to charge an instrument to a certain account is allowed. Example: check states "charge petty cash." ► *The issuer of a negotiable* instrument is not required to be personally obligated to pay; that is, the paper may be payable out of a trust, estate, partnership, or unincorporated association.

> *Payment in money*: Paper must be payable in money. Money is defined broadly.

> *Sum certain*: ► Negotiable instruments must state the precise amount to be paid. ► Instruments can state a separate *interest rate to be charged after maturity, and they can require payment of collection costs and attorney fees. ► In most states, the sum payable under a negotiable instrument is certain even if it calls for the payment of a floating or a variable interest rate.

> *Time of payment*: ► A negotiable instrument must be payable on demand or at a definite time. ► *Payable on demand*: payable "on demand," "at sight," "upon presentation," or if no time for payment is stated. ► *Payable at definite time*: payable on or before a stated or readily ascertainable date. ► A negotiable instrument can properly include these terms: (1) acceleration clause; (2) holder may extend time for payment; (3) maker or acceptor may extend time for payment to a later, definite date; and (4) payment may be extended to a later, definite date automatically after a specified event. ► Undated instruments are valid. ► The date on demand paper controls the time for payment, and paper is not due before the date stated.

> *Words of Negotiability: Payable to order or bearer*: ► Negotiable instruments other than checks must be payable to "order" or "bearer", which are known as "words of negotiability." ► *Order paper*: drawn "to the order of *X*" or "to *X* or order"; after indorsement if indorsement states the next party to be paid. ► *Bearer paper*: drawn "pay to bearer," "pay to the order of *X* or bearer," or "pay to cash"; after indorsement if last endorsement is a blank indorsement; no payee is identified. ► LEARNING OUTCOME EXAMPLES: See *New Mexico v Herrera* on textbook p. 633; see *Sirius LC v Erickson* on textbook p. 632 to see the effects of negotiability.

6. FACTORS NOT AFFECTING NEGOTIABILITY

An instrument may be negotiable even if: (1) the date of execution is omitted, (2) the instrument is antedated or postdated, or (3) a debtor is required to give or maintain collateral.

7. **AMBIGUOUS LANGUAGE**

   ► Words control over conflicting numbers. ► Handwriting prevails over conflicting typewritten or printed terms. ► Typewritten terms prevail over conflicting preprinted terms.

8. **STATUTE OF LIMITATIONS**

   There is a three-year period for most suits on negotiable instruments, and a six-year period for actions on certificates of deposit and accepted drafts.

CONCEPT REVIEW AND APPLICATIONS

Matching Exercise

Select the term or phrase that best matches a definition or statement stated below. Each term or phrase is the best match for only one statement or definition. Not all terms and phrases will necessarily be used.

acceptor	definite time	order paper
accommodation party	draft, or bill of exchange	party
ambiguous	drawee	payable to order
bearer	drawer	payee
bearer paper	maker	postdating
cashier's check	money	promissory note
certificate of deposit (CD)	money order	representative capacity
check	negotiability	sum certain
collateral	negotiable instrument	teller's check
commercial paper	nonnegotiable instrument	traveler's check

_____ 1. Unconditional signed, written order by one person ordering another party to pay on demand or at a definite time a sum certain in money to order or to bearer.

_____ 2. Special type of draft that orders a drawee bank to pay the draft on demand.

_____ 3. Type of draft issued by a bank or nonbank.

_____ 4. Drawee who agrees to pay a draft by writing such agreement on the draft.

_____ 5. Unconditional signed, written promise to pay on demand or at a definite time a sum certain in money to order or to bearer.

_____ 6. Party whom a drawer orders to pay a draft or check.

_____ 7. Party who voluntarily signs a draft in order to strengthen the likelihood of payment.

_____ 8. Instrument originally made payable to the order of a named person, or an instrument that is specially indorsed to a named indorsee.

_____ 9. Party who originally signs and issues a draft or check.

_____ 10. Instrument issued to bearer or to cash, or one that is indorsed in blank.

True/False

Write **T** if the statement is true, write **F** if it is false.

_____ 1. Subject to certain limits, a transferee of a negotiable instrument may acquire a greater right to payment than an assignee of a contract right would acquire.

_____ 2. A draft or check has two original parties: a maker and a payee.

_____ 3. Chris borrowed $10,000 from Mazin and he gave Mazin an unsigned promissory note requiring Chris to repay this sum in stated installments together with stated interest of 18% per annum. Under these facts, the promissory note is a negotiable instrument.

_____ 4. An IOU is not an instrument.

_____ 5. If an accommodation party must pay an instrument, the accommodation party does not have a right to recover the amount paid from the person accommodated.

_____ 6. The rights of parties to a nonnegotiable instrument are governed by general rules of contract law.

_____ 7. If an agent signs an instrument for a principal, disclosing the identity of the principal and the fact that the agent is signing only as an agent, the agent is not personally liable to pay the instrument.

_____ 8. If an agent signs a check drawn on the principal's bank account without stating the agent's representative capacity, then the agent may be personally liable to pay the check.

_____ 9. A term in a note requiring a maker to provide collateral renders the note nonnegotiable.

_____ 10. A term in a note authorizing a holder to accelerate the due date if the maker defaults renders the note nonnegotiable.

Multiple Choice

_____ 1. Pat (as drawer) signed and issued a negotiable instrument ordering Charles (as drawee) to pay $100 on demand to Mike (as payee). Under these facts, this instrument is a:
   a. Negotiable promissory note.
   b. Negotiable draft.
   c. Check.
   d. Certificate of deposit.

_____ 2. Sam signed and issued a negotiable promissory note whereby Sam promised to pay $1,000 to the order of Martha. To induce Martha to accept the note and to strengthen the likelihood of payment, Rick also signed the note. The note was then delivered to Martha. Under these facts:
   a. Sam is a drawer.
   b. Sam is a drawee.
   c. Sam is a payee.
   d. Rick is an accommodation party (secondary obligor).

_____ 3. B&K Inc. wanted to borrow $5,000 from Myra. A promissory note was written out in longhand. The note stated that B&K Inc. promised to pay $5,000 on demand to the order of Myra. Tim Blue, President of B&K Inc., was authorized to sign the note and he signed it:

B&K Inc.

By _____Tim Blue_____

Tim Blue, President of B&K Inc.

a. The note is nonnegotiable because it is handwritten.
b. The note is nonnegotiable because it is only signed by an agent of B&K Inc.
c. The note satisfies the writing and signature requirements and it may be negotiable.
d. Tim Blue is personally liable to pay the note if B&K Inc. fails to pay the note.

_____ 4. Which of the following terms in a promissory note would render the note nonnegotiable?
a. Maria signed a note promising to pay $1,000 to the order of Jasmine. The duty to pay is subject
   to the terms of a separate loan contract made between Maria and Jasmine.
b. Kyle signed a note promising to pay $1,000 and 100 bushels of wheat to the order of Kristen.
c. Pete signed a note promising to pay $1,000 to the order of Yvette. In the note, Pete also promised to pay reasonable collection costs and attorney's fees if he failed to pay the note.
d. a and b.

_____ 5. Which of the following facts or terms would render a promissory note nonnegotiable?
a. Carrie issued a promissory note that would ordinarily be negotiable. However, the note is silent regarding when Carrie is to pay the note.
b. Lou issued a promissory note that would ordinarily be negotiable. However, the note states that the holder of the note may extend time for payment if the holder chooses to do so.
c. April, a student, issued a promissory note that would ordinarily be negotiable. However, payment of the note is required only if April graduates from college.
d. Hin issued a promissory note that would ordinarily be negotiable. However, the note was stated to be "payable to bearer."

Case Problem

Answer the following problem, briefly explaining your answer.
On June 1, 2008, Rex executed a promissory note and he delivered the note to Sam West. The note stated "On June 1, 2011, I promise to pay to the order of Sam West One Thousand Dollars ($1,000), together with annual interest at the rate of ten percent (10%) per year."

1. Classify the parties to the promissory note.
2. Is the note negotiable or nonnegotiable?
3. Is the note order paper or bearer paper?
4. Would the note be negotiable if it instead required Rex to pay interest at the rate of 2 percent over the prime rate charged by Citicorp Bank from time to time?

Internet Exercise

James just started a new dog grooming business called "Pruned Puppies." James has desperately little capital and he is trying to save money anywhere he can. He intends to establish a business checking account, but he is concerned with the price that banks charge for checks. Using the Internet:
1. Locate and identify a company that produces and sells checks for individuals and consumers.
2. What terms must each check state or leave a blank for filling in?
3. What risks, if any, would James encounter in ordering his business' checks over the Internet?

CPA REVIEW

The following questions were given on CPA examinations. The answers for these questions are the unofficial answers prepared by the American Institute of Certified Public Accountants, Inc. (AICPA). All material is reproduced with permission of the AICPA.

____ 1. For which of the following negotiable instruments is a bank not an acceptor?
    a. Cashier's check.
    b. Certified check.
    c. Certificate of deposit.
    d. Bank acceptance.

____ 2. Under the Commercial Paper Article of the UCC, which of the following documents would be considered an order to pay?
    I. Draft
    II. Certificate of deposit

    a. I only.
    b. II only.
    c. Both I and II.
    d. Neither I nor II.

___ 3. Under the Commercial Paper Article of the UCC, which of the following circumstances would prevent a promissory note from being negotiable?
a. An extension clause that allows the maker to elect to extend the time for payment to a date specified in the note.
b. An acceleration clause that allows the holder to move up the maturity date of the note in the event of default.
c. A person having a power of attorney signs the note on behalf of the maker.
d. A clause that allows the maker to satisfy the note by the performance of services or the payment of money.

___ 4. Which of the following negotiable instruments is subject to the UCC Commercial Paper Article?
a. Corporate bearer bond with a maturity date of January 1, 2001.
b. Installment note payable on the first day of each month.
c. Warehouse receipt.
d. Bill of lading payable to order.

$10,000	Ludlow, Vermont	February 1, 2011

I promise to pay to the order of Custer Corp. $10,000 within 10 days after the sale of my two-carat diamond ring. I pledge the sale proceeds to secure my obligation hereunder.

        R. Harris_____

R. Harris

Question 5 is based on the following instrument. An instrument reads as follows:

___ 5. Which of the following statements correctly describes the above instrument?
a. The instrument is nonnegotiable because it is not payable at a definite time.
b. The instrument is nonnegotiable because it is secured by the proceeds of the sale of the ring.
c. The instrument is a negotiable promissory note.
d. The instrument is a negotiable sight draft payable on demand.

___ 6. Which of the following conditions, if present on an otherwise negotiable instrument, would affect the instrument's negotiability?

  a. The instrument is payable six months after the death of the maker.
  b. The instrument is payable at a definite time subject to an accelerated clause in the event of a default.
  c. The instrument is postdated.
  d. The instrument contains a promise to provide additional collateral if there is a decrease in value of the existing collateral.

Question 7 relates to the following instrument:

May 19, 2011
I promise to pay to the order of A.B. Shark $1,000 (One thousand and one hundred
  dollars) with interest thereon at the rate of 12% per annum.
  _____*T.T. Tile*_____
T.T. Tile
              Guaranty
  I personally guaranty payment by T. T. Tile.

  _____*N.A. Abner*_____
N. A. Abner

___ 7. The instrument is
  a. Nonnegotiable even though it is payable on demand.
  b. Nonnegotiable because the numeric amount differs from the written amount.
  c. Negotiable even though a payment date is not specified.
  d. Negotiable because of Abner's guaranty.

CHAPTER 29
TRANSFERS OF NEGOTIABLE INSTRUMENTS AND WARRANTIES OF PARTIES

MAKE THE CONNECTION

SUMMARY

Negotiation is the transferring of a negotiable instrument in such a way as to make the transferee the holder. When a negotiable instrument is transferred by negotiation, the transferee becomes the holder of the instrument. If such a holder becomes a holder in due course, the holder will be immune to certain defenses.

An *order instrument* is negotiated by an indorsement and delivery by the person to whom it is then payable. A bearer instrument is negotiated by delivery alone. The order or bearer character of an instrument is determined by the face of the instrument as long as the instrument is not indorsed. If the instrument has been indorsed, the character is determined by the last indorsement.

A number of different kinds of indorsements can be made on negotiable instruments. When an indorser merely authenticates the instrument, the indorsement is called a *blank indorsement*. If the last indorsement is a blank indorsement, the instrument is bearer paper, which may be negotiated by change of possession alone. A special indorsement consists of the authentication by the indorser and words specifying the person to whom the indorser makes the instrument payable. If the last indorsement is a special indorsement, the instrument is order paper and may be negotiated only by an indorsement and delivery. A qualified indorsement eliminates the liability of the indorser to answer for dishonor of the paper by the maker or the drawee. A restrictive indorsement specifies the purpose of the instrument or its use.

A forged or unauthorized indorsement is no indorsement, and the possessor of the instrument cannot be a holder. The impostor rule makes three exceptions to this rule: dummy payee; employee fraud; and impersonating a payee.

A negotiation is effective even though (1) it is made by a minor, (2) it is an act beyond the powers of a corporation, (3) it is obtained by fraud, or (4) the negotiation is part of an illegal transaction. However, the transferor may be able to set aside the negotiation under general legal principles apart from the UCC. The negotiation cannot be set aside if the instrument is held by a person paying it in good faith and without knowledge of the facts on which the rescission claim is based.

The warranties of the unqualified indorser are as follows: (1) the warrantor is a person entitled to enforce the instrument; (2) all signatures on the instrument are authentic and authorized; (3) the instrument has not been altered; (4) the instrument is not subject to a defense or claim in recoupment of any party that can be asserted against the warrantor; with respect to any item drawn on a consumer account, which does not bear a handwritten signature purporting to be the signature of the drawer, that the purported drawer of the draft has authorized the issuance of the item in the amount for which the item is drawn; and (5) the warrantor has no knowledge of any insolvency proceeding commenced with respect to the maker or acceptor or, in the case of an unaccepted draft, the drawer.

LEARNING OUTCOMES
After studying this chapter, you should be able to

A. TRANSFER OF NEGOTIABLE INSTRUMENTS

B. HOW NEGOTIATION OCCURS: BEARER INSTRUMENTS

C. HOW NEGOTIATION OCCURS: ORDER INSTRUMENTS
LO.1   Explain the difference between negotiation of order paper and negotiation of bearer paper
LO.2   List the types of indorsements and describe their uses

D. PROBLEMS IN NEGOTIATION OF INSTRUMENTS
LO.3   Determine the legal effect of forged and unauthorized indorsements
LO.4   Be familiar with the forged payee impostor exceptions

E. WARRANTIES IN NEGOTIATION
LO.5   List the indorser's warranties and describe their significance

CHAPTER OUTLINE

A. TRANSFER OF NEGOTIABLE INSTRUMENTS

1.   EFFECT OF TRANSFER

▶ Negotiable instruments are transferred by negotiation or assignment. ▶ Effect of negotiation: (1) transferee is a holder and may be a holder in due course; (2) transferee may have a greater right to payment than the transferor; and (3) transferee may take paper free from some defenses. ▶ Effect of assignment: (1) transferee is an assignee and cannot be a holder or holder in due course; (2) transferee has the same right to payment as the transferor; and (3) transferee is subject to all defenses.

2.   DEFINITION OF NEGOTIATION

Negotiation means paper is transferred in such a way that a transferee is a holder.

3.   HOW NEGOTIATION OCCURS: THE ORDER OR BEARER CHARACTER OF AN INSTRUMENT

GENERAL RULES. ▶ Requirements for negotiation are dictated by whether paper is order or bearer paper. ▶ Whether paper is order or bearer paper is determined when it is about to be transferred.
STUDY HINT.   Instruments may change back and forth between being order and bearer paper.
LEARNING OUTCOME EXAMPLE: See *Bumgarner v Wood* on textbook p. 643.

B. HOW NEGOTIATION OCCURS: BEARER INSTRUMENTS

Negotiation of bearer paper requires only a transfer of possession; an indorsement is only required if the transferee insists. A transferor who indorses bearer paper incurs the liability of an indorser.

C. HOW NEGOTIATION OCCURS: ORDER INSTRUMENTS

► Negotiation of order paper requires: (1) a proper indorsement; and (2) authorized delivery of the paper to a transferee. ► Indorsement and delivery may be made by the party to whom paper is then payable, or by that person's authorized agent.

4. BLANK INDORSEMENT

➤ *Description*: Indorser signs an instrument without indicating to whom it is to be paid.

➤ *Example*: Sara Thompson (payee) indorsed a check "Sara Thompson."

➤ *Effect of blank indorsement*: (1) passes ownership; (2) creates bearer paper; (3) creates implied warranties by indorser; and (4) imposes secondary liability on indorser to pay the instrument.

5. SPECIAL INDORSEMENT

➤ *Description*: Signature of indorser coupled with words specifying the person (the indorsee) or account to whom the instrument is payable.

➤ *Example*: Sara Thompson (payee) indorsed a check "Pay to Karen Kay (signed) Sara Thompson."

➤ *Effect of special indorsement*: (1) passes ownership; (2) creates order paper; (3) creates implied warranties by indorser; and (4) imposes secondary liability on indorser to pay the instrument.

6. QUALIFIED INDORSEMENT

➤ *Description*: Blank or special indorsement coupled with "without recourse" or similar words.

➤ *Example*: Sara Thompson (payee) indorsed a check "Without recourse, Sara Thompson."

➤ *Effect of qualified indorsement*: (1) passes ownership; (2) creates certain implied warranties by indorser; and (3) does not impose liability on indorser to pay the instrument.

7. RESTRICTIVE INDORSEMENT

➤ *Description*: Restrictive indorsements condition an indorsee's right to receive payment or restrict disposition of funds.

➤ ➤ *Example*: Ina indorsed a check "For deposit only, Ina Lee." Such a check may still be negotiated.

➤ *Effect of restrictive indorsement*: (1) requires the first party who takes the instrument after a restriction is applied to comply with that restriction; (2) otherwise has same effect as a blank indorsement.

➤ **LEARNING OUTCOME EXAMPLE**: See *Hyatt Corp. v Palm Beach Nat. Bank* on textbook p. 650.

8. CORRECTION OF NAME BY INDORSEMENT

▶ A payee (indorsee) whose name is misspelled can indorse the misspelled name, the correct name, or both. ▶ A person giving value or taking the instrument for collection may require indorsement of both names. ▶ Fictitious or trade names are treated like misspelled names and the same procedures for correction apply.

9. BANK INDORSEMENT

If a customer does not indorse a check when it is deposited, the bank can supply the indorsement.

10. MULTIPLE PAYEES AND INDORSEMENTS

▶ Paper payable to joint payees (indorsees) ("pay to the order of Tom *and* Mae") requires indorsement by both parties. ▶ Paper payable to alternate payees ("pay to order of Tom *or* Mae")

may be indorsed and delivered by either party. ▶ If multiple payees are named but it is not clear whether they are joint or alternate, they are considered to be alternate. ▶ LEARNING OUTCOME EXAMPLE: See *Schulingkamp v Carter* on textbook p. 648.

11. AGENT OR OFFICER INDORSEMENT

Paper payable to a government official or corporate officer can be indorsed and negotiated by either the agent or the government body or corporation they represent.

12. MISSING INDORSEMENT
A transfer of order paper without an indorsement is only an assignment. A transferee who gives value for the paper can require the transferor to indorse the paper.

D. PROBLEMS IN NEGOTIATION OF INSTRUMENTS

13. FORGED AND UNAUTHORIZED INDORSEMENTS

GENERAL RULES. ▶ A forged or unauthorized indorsement is legally not the indorsement of the person whose name is signed. Therefore, order paper is not negotiated if an indorsement required for negotiation is forged or unauthorized. ▶ A bank that negotiates a check bearing a forged or unauthorized indorsement is liable for the amount of the check to the check's true owner.
LIMITATION. A forged (unauthorized) indorsement may be an effective indorsement in some cases if the rightful owner's negligence or other improper conduct contributed to the forgery.
STUDY HINT. In general, there cannot be a holder, holder in due course, or holder through a holder in due course after order paper has been transferred under a forged, required indorsement.
LEARNING OUTCOME EXAMPLE: See Thinking Things Through on textbook p. 651.

14. QUASI FORGERIES: THE IMPOSTOR RULE

➤ *When the impostor rule applies*: A forged indorsement may effectively negotiate order paper if:

▶ *Impersonating payee*: Party pretending to be a payee convinces a drawer (maker) to issue paper owed to the payee. Example: Jim, using a forged license, is issued a check that was owed to Pat.

► *Dummy payee*: Drawer (maker) issues an instrument payable to a payee, but does not intend the payee to have any interest in the instrument. Example: To defraud creditors, Drawer issues a check payable to a payee; Drawer then forges the payee's signature and cashes the check.

► *Dummy payee supplied by employee*: Employee causes employer to issue paper payable to a payee (whether a real or imaginary person) and the employee keeps the paper and forges the indorsement. Example: Ty (bookkeeper) issued a check on behalf of his employer payable to Hank, and Ty kept and cashed the check.

➢ *Effect of impostor rule*: A forged indorsement is treated as a genuine indorsement.

➢ *Limitations on impostor rule*: ► This rule does not apply if an instrument is issued to an actual creditor for the correct amount of a debt and someone (even an employee) steals it and forges the indorsement. ► Also, party must take paper in good faith and for payment/collection.

➢ *Negligence of drawee not required*: The impostor rule applies even if a drawee bank negligently pays an instrument.

➢ **LEARNING OUTCOME EXAMPLE**: See *B.D.G.S., Inc. v Balio* on textbook p. 654.

15. EFFECT OF INCAPACITY OR MISCONDUCT ON NEGOTIATION

► Negotiation is valid even if it is: (1) by a person who lacks capacity; (2) obtained by fraud or mistake; or (3) done in breach of a duty. ► But, a transferor can set aside the negotiation unless the paper is held by one with rights of a holder in due course or one who gave value, without notice of the defense.

16. LOST INSTRUMENTS

➢ *Order instruments*: A finder of lost order paper is not a holder and cannot enforce payment. The original owner of a lost instrument can still enforce it against any party who is liable on it.

➢ *Bearer instruments*: A finder of lost bearer paper is a holder and may enforce payment.

E. WARRANTIES IN NEGOTIATION

17. WARRANTIES OF UNQUALIFIED INDORSER

➢ *Scope of warranties*: An indorser making an unqualified indorsement for consideration warrants:
(1) indorser is entitled to enforce the instrument; (2) all signatures are genuine and authorized; (3) the instrument has not been altered; (4) the instrument is not subject to any defense or claim of any party that can be asserted against the indorser; and (5) the indorser has no knowledge of an insolvency proceeding against a maker, an acceptor, or the drawer of an unaccepted draft. No distinction is made between the warranties of an unqualified blank indorsement and an unqualified special indorsement.

➢ *What is not warranted*: An indorser does not warrant that a maker or drawee will actually pay.

A holder's indorsement of a check does not warrant that the drawer's account has funds to pay the check.

> *Beneficiary of implied warranties*: ▶ Warranties of an unqualified indorser pass to the transferee and any later transferee. ▶ There is no requirement that a later transferee act in good faith or be a holder.

> *Disclaimer of warranties*: Warranties can be disclaimed for all instruments except checks.

> *Notice of breach of warranty*: Notice must be given within 30 days after learning of or having reason to know of the breach and the identity of the indorser to protect rights.

> *Warranties made by party who presents an instrument for payment or is the last party in line before the payor*: This party warrants: (1) that he or she is, or was at the time the party transferred the draft, a person entitled to enforce the draft or authorized to obtain payment or acceptance of the draft on behalf of a person entitled to enforce the draft; (2) the draft has not been altered; and (3) he or she has no knowledge that the signature of the drawer of the draft is unauthorized.

18. WARRANTIES OF OTHER PARTIES

> *Qualified indorser*: Qualified indorsers make the same warranties as unqualified indorsers.

> *Transfer by delivery (no indorsement)*: The transferor makes the same warranties as an unqualified indorser, but only the immediate transferee can enforce them.

CONCEPT REVIEW AND APPLICATIONS

Matching Exercise

Select the term or phrase that best matches a definition or statement stated below. Each term or phrase is the best match for only one statement or definition. Not all terms and phrases will necessarily be used.

alternative payees	holder	negotiation
blank indorsement	holder in due course	qualified indorsement
delivery	impostor rule	restrictive indorsement
forged or unauthorized	indorsee	special indorsement
indorsement	indorsement	

_____ 1. Indorsement that states the person to whom the instrument is to be paid.

_____ 2. Indorsement signed "without recourse," thereby negating the indorser's secondary liability.

_____ 3. Exception to the general rule that order paper cannot be negotiated by a forged indorsement.

_____ 4. Transfer of negotiable instrument in the manner required for a transferee to be a holder.

_____ 5. Indorsement that consists only of the signature of the indorser.

_____ 6. Indorsement that conditions the right of an indorsee to be paid an instrument or that restricts disposition of funds paid in satisfaction of an instrument.

_____ 7. Party to whom a negotiable instrument has been negotiated.

_____ 8. Party to whom an indorsement directs payment to be made.

_____ 9. In general, the signature of the payee on an instrument.

_____ 10. A holder who has given value, taken in good faith without notice of dishonor, defenses, or that instrument is overdue, and who is afforded special rights or status.

True/False

Write **T** if the statement is true, write **F** if it is false.

_____ 1. The requirements for negotiating negotiable instruments depend on whether the paper is order or bearer paper at the time of transfer.

_____ 2. Merely merely delivering the paper to the transferee can negotiate order paper; the indorsement of the transferor is not needed to negotiate order paper.

_____ 3. A transferee who takes an instrument by assignment has only the same right to enforce payment as the transferor (assignor) had, and the transferee takes it subject to all defenses.

_____ 4. If a negotiable promissory note is payable to "Alice Jones or Dick Roberts," the indorsements of both Alice and Dick are needed to negotiate the note.

_____ 5. A check payable to "Ed Fry, President of Bay Co.," can be indorsed and negotiated by only Ed.

_____ 6. In general, an indorser is anyone who signs an instrument in any capacity other than as a maker or drawer.

_____ 7. Employer issued a check to a creditor in payment of an actual debt. Employer's agent then stole the check. In this case, the agent can negotiate the check by forging the creditor's indorsement.

_____ 8. Employer is fraudulently induced by Employer's agent to issue a check to a fictitious (nonexistent) creditor, and Employer gives the check to the agent. In this case, the agent can negotiate the check by indorsing the fictitious creditor's name.

_____ 9. Sue impersonated Ida. Sue convinced Drawer to issue a check payable to Ida, and to give the check to Sue. In this case, Sue cannot negotiate the check by forging Ida's indorsement.

_____ 10. An instrument cannot be negotiated if a minor makes a required indorsement.

Multiple Choice

_____ 1. Tom (as maker) issued and delivered to Sid a note payable to the order of Sid. In this case:
   a. To negotiate the note, Sid must indorse the note and deliver it to the transferee.
   b. Sid can assign the note to Bev merely by delivering it to Bev; Sid's indorsement is not necessary to assign the note to Bev.
   c. If a thief steals the note from Sid, forges Sid's indorsement, and delivers it to a good faith transferee for value, then the note has been negotiated to the transferee.
   d. a and b.

_____ 2. Greg (as drawer) issued and delivered a check to Rose payable to the order of cash. In this case:
   a. To negotiate the check, Rose must indorse the check and deliver it to a transferee.
   b. To negotiate the check, Rose is only required to deliver the check to a transferee.
   c. If a thief steals the check from Rose and transfers it to an innocent transferee, the thief has not negotiated the check to the transferee, and the transferee cannot be a holder.
   d. a and c.

_____ 3. Drawer issued a check payable to the order of Penny Thorpe. Penny indorsed the check "Penny Thorpe" and delivered it to Terry who took it in good faith and for value. Under these facts:
   a. Penny's indorsement is a special indorsement.
   b. The check was order paper both prior to and after its negotiation by Penny to Terry.
   c. The check was order paper when issued and it was bearer paper after Penny indorsed it.
   d. The check was bearer paper both prior to and after its negotiation by Penny to Terry.

_____ 4. Drawer issued a check payable to the order of cash and delivered it to Peter Bryan. Peter indorsed the check "Pay to Carla Wilson, (signed) Peter Bryan" and delivered it to Carla who took it in good faith and for value. Under these facts:
   a. Peter's indorsement is a special indorsement. To further negotiate this check, Carla must indorse the check and deliver it to a subsequent transferee.
   b. The check was bearer paper both prior to and after its negotiation by Peter to Carla.
   c. The check was order paper both prior to and after its negotiation by Peter to Carla.
   d. a and b.

_____ 5. Maker issued and delivered her negotiable promissory note to Perry Mills. Perry negotiated the note to Hans who took it in good faith and for value. Perry indorsed the note "Without recourse, Perry Mills." Under these facts:
   a. Perry's indorsement is an unqualified indorsement.
   b. Perry's indorsement is a qualified indorsement that destroys the negotiable nature of the note.
   c. If Maker fails to pay the note, Perry does not have secondary liability to pay it.
   d. a and c.

Case Problem

Answer the following problem, briefly explaining your answer.

Drawer issued a check for $100 payable to the order of Leslic Fay. Leslie indorsed the check "Leslie Fay," and she delivered it to Bella who paid $100 to Leslie. Bella transferred the check to Henry Baker without indorsing the check, and Henry paid Bella $100 for the check. Henry indorsed the check, "For Deposit Only, Henry Baker," and deposited the check in his account.
1. Was Leslie's indorsement a qualified or unqualified indorsement?
2. Did Leslie negotiate the check to Bella?
3. Did Bella negotiate the check to Henry?
4. Did Henry negotiate the check to his bank?

_____

_____

_____

Internet Exercise

Jill moved to town a few days ago and she has not had time to open a bank account. However, she has a check from her parents for $500 that she needs to cash in order to put a deposit on an apartment. Jill has a laptop computer and she is wondering if there are any services advertised on the Internet that may help her. Under these facts:
1. Locate and identify a company that advertises check cashing.
2. Describe two risks that this type of company faces in cashing checks of strangers, such as Jill.
3. Suggest a strategy that this type of company can use to minimize or avoid the risks described above.

_____

_____

_____

CPA REVIEW

The following questions were given on CPA examinations. The answers for these questions are the unofficial answers prepared by the Institute of Certified Public Accountants, Inc. (AICPA). All material is reproduced with permission of the AICPA.

_____ 1. One of the requirements to qualify as a holder of a negotiable bearer check is that the transferee must
     a. Receive the check that was originally made payable to bearer.
     b. Take the check in good faith.
     c. Give value for the check.
     d. Have possession of the check.

_____ 2. Under the Commercial Paper Article of the UCC, which of the following statements best describes the effect of a person endorsing a check "without recourse"?
     a. The person has no liability to prior endorsers.
     b. The person makes no promise or guarantee of payment on dishonor.
     c. The person gives no warranty protection to later transferees.
     d. The person converts the check into order paper.

Question 3 relates to the instrument below. The following endorsements appear on the back of a negotiable promissory note payable to Lake Corp.

> Pay to John Smith only
> *Frank Parker*, President of Lake Corp.
>
> *John Smith*
>
> Pay to the order of Sharp, Inc., without recourse, but only if Sharp delivers computers purchased by Mary Harris by March 15, 1993
> *Mary Harris*
>
> *Sarah Sharp*, President of Sharp, Inc.

____ 3. Which of the following statements is correct?
   a. The note became nonnegotiable as a result of Parker's endorsement.
   b. Harris' endorsement was a conditional promise to pay and caused the note to be nonnegotiable.
   c. Smith's endorsement effectively prevented further negotiation of the note.
   d. Harris' signature was not required to effectively negotiate the note to Sharp.

____ 4. In order to negotiate bearer paper, one must
   a. Endorse the paper.
   b. Endorse and deliver the paper with consideration.
   c. Deliver the paper.
   d. Deliver and endorse the paper.

Question 5 relates to the instrument below. The following endorsements appear on the back of a negotiable promissory note made payable "to bearer." Clark has possession of the note.

> Pay to Sam North
> *Alice Fox*
>
> *Sam North*
> (without recourse)

____ 5. Which of the following statements is correct?
   a. Clark's unqualified endorsement is required to further negotiate the note.
   b. To negotiate the note, Clark must have given value for it.
   c. Clark is not a holder because North's qualified endorsement makes the note nonnegotiable.
   d. Clark can negotiate the note by delivery alone.

_____ 6. Under the Commercial Paper Article of the UCC, which of the following requirements must be met for a transferee of order paper to become a holder?
  I. Possession
  II. Endorsement of transferor

  a. I only.
  b. II only.
  c. Both I and II.
  d. Neither I nor II.

Question 7 relates to the instrument below.

Pay to John Jacobs
Mary Noah

John Jacobs

(without recourse)

_____ 7. The following indorsements appear on the back of a negotiable promissory note made payable" to bearer." The note is in the possession of James Mix.
Which one of the following statements is correct?
  a. Mix is not a holder because Jacobs' qualified indorsement makes the note non-negotiable.
  b. Mix can negotiate the note by delivery alone.
  c. The unqualified indorsement of Mix is required in order to further negotiate the note.
  d. In order for Mix to negotiate the note Mix must have given value for it.

CHAPTER 30
LIABILITY OF THE PARTIES UNDER NEGOTIABLE INSTRUMENTS

MAKE THE CONNECTION

SUMMARY

A holder of a negotiable instrument can be either an ordinary holder or an HDC. The ordinary holder has the same rights that an assignee would have. Holders in due course and holders through an HDC are protected from certain defenses. To be an HDC, a person must first be a holder—that is, the person must have acquired the instrument by a proper negotiation. The holder must then also take for value, in good faith, without notice that the paper is overdue or dishonored, and without notice of defenses and adverse claims. Those persons who become holders of the instrument after an HDC are given the same protection as the HDC through the shelter provision, provided they are not parties to any fraud or illegality affecting the instrument.

The importance of being an HDC is not being subject to certain defenses when demand for payment is made. These defenses are limited defenses and include ordinary contract defenses, incapacity unless it makes the instrument void, fraud in the inducement, prior payment or cancellation, nondelivery of an instrument, conditional delivery, duress consisting of threats, unauthorized completion, and theft of a bearer instrument. Universal defenses may be asserted against any assignee, an ordinary holder, or HDC. Universal defenses include fraud as to the nature or essential terms of the paper, forgery or lack of authority, duress depriving control, incapacity, illegality that makes the instrument void, and alteration. Alteration is only a partial defense; an HDC may enforce the instrument according to its original terms.

The Federal Trade Commission rule on consumer credit contracts limits the immunity of an HDC from defenses of consumer buyers against their sellers. Immunity is limited in consumer credit transactions if the notice specified by the FTC regulation is included in the sales contract. When a notice preserving consumer defenses is stated in a negotiable instrument, no subsequent person can be an HDC.

Holders and HDCs are required to present instruments for payment to primary parties. Primary parties are makers and drawees. If the primary party refuses to pay, or dishonors, the instrument, it must give notice of dishonor in a timely fashion. The holder can then turn to secondary parties, drawers, and indorsers (secondary obligors) for payment.

LEARNING OUTCOMES
After studying this chapter, you should be able to

A. PARTIES TO NEGOTIABLE INSTRUMENTS: RIGHTS AND LIABILITIES
LO.1 Distinguish between an ordinary holder and a holder in due course
LO.2 List the requirements for becoming a holder in due course

B. DEFENSES TO PAYMENT OF A NEGOTIABLE INSTRUMENT
LO.3 Explain the rights of a holder through a holder in due course
LO.4 List and explain the limited defenses not available against a holder in due course
LO.5 List and explain the universal defenses available against all holders

C. LIABILITY ISSUES: HOW PAYMENT RIGHTS ARISE AND DEFENSES ARE USED

LO.6 Describe how the rights of a holder in due course have been limited by the Federal Trade Commission

CHAPTER OUTLINE

A. PARTIES TO NEGOTIABLE INSTRUMENTS: RIGHTS AND LIABILITIES

1. TYPES OF PARTIES

One claiming a right to be paid paper may be an assignee or a holder. A holder is (1) an ordinary holder or (2) a holder in due course or (holder through a holder in due course).

2. ORDINARY HOLDERS AND ASSIGNEES

GENERAL RULES. ▶ An ordinary holder is a party to whom is transferred (1) a negotiable instrument (2) by negotiation, but (3) who fails for any reason to qualify as a holder in due course. ▶ In general, an ordinary holder can enforce payment of an instrument, but a holder in due course enjoys special protections and rights to collect a negotiable instrument in certain circumstances.

STUDY HINTS. ▶ The fact that a person is only an ordinary holder is irrelevant unless the party from whom payment is demanded has a limited defense that can avoid liability for payment. ▶ A holder can sue anyone who is liable on paper regardless of the order in which they signed the paper.

LEARNING OUTCOME EXAMPLE. See Sections 2 and 3 on textbook p. 666 for examples of distinction.

3. THE HOLDER-IN-DUE-COURSE PROTECTIONS

(a) *Holder in due course*

▶ A holder in due course is a party to whom is transferred: (1) a negotiable instrument; (2) by negotiation; (3) for value; (4) in good faith; (5) without notice that the instrument is overdue or has been dishonored; and (6) without notice of any defense or adverse claim. ▶ Important rules:

➢ *Value*: ▶ Value is (1) *actually* performing an act for which paper is given, or (2) taking paper as security for, or in payment of, an existing debt. ▶ A bank gives value for a check only when it pays cash for a check or when a customer deposits a check into an account and the customer withdraws the money from the account. ▶ An unperformed promise is not value.

➢ *Good faith*: ▶ Good faith: honesty in fact and observance of reasonable standards of fair dealing. ▶ In the close connection doctrine, a transferee cannot be a holder in due course if it is so connected with the payee or transferor that it is deemed to know of troublesome facts. ▶ Bad faith is a transferee's knowledge of facts that indicate a transfer may be improper, such as an inexplicable deep discount for paper. Negligent ignorance of facts is not bad faith.

> *Ignorance of instrument's being overdue or dishonored*: ▶ *Overdue*: (1) a time instrument is overdue the day after payment is due (or after a due date has been accelerated); (2) a demand instrument is overdue when a reasonable time has elapsed after its issuance. ▶ *Dishonored*: a maker or drawee has refused to pay an instrument. ▶ It is not improper to negotiate an instrument that is overdue or that has been dishonored; it simply means that a subsequent party who takes an instrument with notice of such matters cannot be a holder in due course.

> *Ignorance of defenses and adverse claims*: ▶ A transferee is not a holder in due course if, at time of acquisition, he or she had notice that (1) a party who is liable on the paper had a defense to paying, or (2) someone else claimed to own the paper. However, holder in due course status is not affected if notice is received after a transferee acquires the paper.
> ▶ LEARNING OUTCOME EXAMPLE: See *Any Kind Checks Cashed, Inc.* v *Talcott* on textbook p. 670.

(b) *Holder through a holder in due course ("shelter rule")*

> *Defined*: (1) Party to whom a negotiable instrument is negotiated (i.e., a holder) (2) at any time after the instrument was held by anyone who was a holder in due course.

> *Example*: Drawer issued a check to Paul. Paul negotiated it to a holder in due course who then negotiated it to Ann. Ann did not pay value, and she had notice that the check was overdue and that Drawer claimed a defense. Ann is a holder through a holder in due course.

> *Rights*: Holder through a holder in due course has the same rights as holder in due course.

> *Study hints*: ▶ In an action to collect a negotiable instrument, a plaintiff must prove that he
> or she has the rights of a holder in due course only if the defendant asserts a universal defense.
> ▶ Under revised Article 3, the original payee of an instrument is not a holder in due course. ▶ LEARNING OUTCOME EXAMPLE: See *Porter County Development Corp.* v *Citibank* on textbook p. 669.

B. DEFENSES TO PAYMENT OF A NEGOTIABLE INSTRUMENT

4. CLASSIFICATION OF DEFENSES

Parties who have liability to pay an instrument may have a defense that partially or completely avoids their liability to pay. Defenses are either limited defenses or universal defenses.

5. DEFENSES AGAINST ASSIGNEE OR ORDINARY HOLDER

An assignee or ordinary holder takes an instrument subject to all limited and universal defenses.

6. LIMITED DEFENSES NOT AVAILABLE AGAINST A HOLDER IN DUE COURSE

> *Ordinary contract defenses*: Breach of warranty and failure of consideration are limited defenses.

> *Incapacity of defendant*: Lack of capacity (other than that of minority) is a limited defense if it renders a contract voidable. Incapacity that renders a contract void is a universal defense.

> *Fraud in the inducement*: ▶ This type of fraud occurs when a party knowingly executes an instrument, but the party has been fraudulently induced into signing it. ▶ Example: Buyer issued Seller a check in payment for land that Seller misrepresented to Buyer. Seller negotiated the check to Vick, a holder in due course. Seller's fraud is a limited defense, and Buyer must pay Vick the amount of the check.

> *Prior payment or cancellation*: ▶ The fact that a party has paid an instrument or that it has been canceled are limited defenses. ▶ Example: Mel issued a note payable June 1. On March 1, Mel paid the note, but he failed to take it back. On May 1, the note was negotiated to Ray, a holder in due course. Mel's prior payment is a limited defense, and he cannot assert it against Ray.

> *Nondelivery of an instrument*: ▶ The fact that paper is stolen, and then delivered without the original owner's authority is a limited defense. ▶ Example: Dave issued a check payable to cash, and he delivered it to Paul. Thief stole the check and negotiated it to Hal, a holder in due course. The unauthorized delivery to Thief is a limited defense; Paul cannot assert it against Hal.

> *Conditional or specified purpose delivery*: ▶ The fact that an unconditional instrument is actually subject to secret, unfulfilled conditions is a limited defense. ▶ Example: Molly issued a note to Patti, subject to an oral condition that it was not payable until Patti transferred property to Molly. Patti negotiated the note to Hazel, a holder in due course who was unaware of the condition. Molly cannot assert the conditional delivery to Patti as a defense to paying Hazel.

> *Duress (threats)*: Duress is a limited defense if it renders a contract voidable under state law.

> *Unauthorized completion*: ▶ Unauthorized completion of paper is a limited defense. ▶ Example: Dora issued a check, leaving the amount blank. She gave the check to Son and told him not to complete it for $20. Son filled in $200, and negotiated it to Hugh, a holder in due course. Dora cannot assert the unauthorized completion against Hugh; Dora must pay $200.

> *Theft*: The fact that a bearer instrument has been stolen from an owner is a limited defense.

7. **UNIVERSAL DEFENSES AVAILABLE AGAINST ALL HOLDERS**

> *Fraud as to the nature or essential terms of the paper*: ▶ This fraud occurs when a maker, drawer or indorser is defrauded about the legal nature or basic terms of an instrument. ▶ Example: Lois, an elderly person, signs a note because she is defrauded into believing that it is only a request for credit. ▶ This defense cannot be raised if the fraud results from the party's own negligence.

> *Forgery or lack of authority*: ▶ A maker, drawer, or indorser can use against anyone the defense that his or her signature was forged or was made without authority. ▶ Example: Thief stole Dee's checkbook and forged her signature on a check. Dee can assert this defense against anyone.

> *Duress depriving control*: Duress that renders a contract void is a universal defense.

> *Incapacity*: Lack of contractual capacity due to minority is a universal defense. Lack of capacity due to other reasons is a universal defense only if it renders an obligation void under state law.

> *Illegality*: ▶ Illegality is a universal defense if it renders a contract void under state law. ▶ Example: A note is issued in payment for stolen goods. ▶ But, if paper is issued in an illegal transaction that is not void under state law, the defense is merely a limited defense.

> *Alteration*: ▶ An alteration occurs if a party to a paper fraudulently alters terms of the paper changing the obligation of another party to the paper. ▶ A holder in due course and a paying bank or drawee can enforce an altered instrument according to its original terms. ▶ Example: Dan issued a check for $10 to Pete, and Pete changed the amount to $100. Pete negotiated the check to Holly, a holder in due course. Holly can enforce the check for $10.

> LEARNING OUTCOME EXAMPLE: See the Thinking Things Through discussion of the Corner Check Cashing Company on textbook p. 677.

8. DENIAL OF HOLDER-IN-DUE-COURSE PROTECTION

> *Participating transferee*: If a transferee of a negotiable instrument is closely connected or related to either (1) the transaction that gave rise to the instrument or (2) to the transferor of the instrument, then a court may hold that the knowledge of the transferor is imputed to the transferee. This imputed knowledge may negate the transferee's holder in due course status.

> *The Federal Trade Commission (FTC) rule*: ▶ An FTC rule requires that a contract in a consumer credit transaction contain a notice that a buyer may assert all defenses against any person enforcing a negotiable promissory note given in connection with the transaction. ▶ A consumer credit transaction is one for the sale of goods or services for personal, family, or household use. This rule does not apply to commercial transactions. ▶ Example: Kim issued a negotiable note to May Co. to pay for a bed for her home. FTC rules would require this note to contain the foregoing notice and, if this notice was stated, then Kim could use any defense against a subsequent holder in due course who acquired the note. ▶ If a notice preserving consumer defenses is stated in a negotiable instrument, no subsequent person can be a holder in due course. ▶ LEARNING OUTCOME EXAMPLE: See the language of the rule on textbook p. 676.

C. LIABILITY ISSUES: HOW PAYMENT RIGHTS ARISE AND DEFENSES ARE USED

9. THE ROLES OF PARTIES AND LIABILITY

▶ The primary party is the maker of a note or the drawee of a draft that has accepted the draft. ▶ The primary party is the first party from whom payment must first be demanded. ▶ Secondary parties are indorsers of any instrument and the drawer of a draft. ▶ Secondary parties are liable to pay an instrument if the primary party fails to do so.

10. ATTACHING LIABILITY OF THE PRIMARY PARTIES: PRESENTMENT

Presentment occurs when the holder demands payment from the primary party.

11. DISHONOR AND NOTICE OF DISHONOR

▶ Dishonor occurs when a primary party refuses to pay. ▶ Notice of dishonor must be given to hold most secondary parties liable. ▶ Example: banks must give notice by midnight of next business day.

CONCEPT REVIEW AND APPLICATIONS

Matching Exercise

Select the term or phrase that best matches a definition or statement stated below. Each term or phrase is the best match for only one statement or definition. Not all terms and phrases will necessarily be used.

alteration	good faith	maker
assignees	holder in due course	notice of dishonor
close-connection doctrine	holder through a holder in	presentment
dishonor	due course	primary party
drawee	holders	secondary parties
drawers	indorsers	universal defenses
fraud in the inducement	limited defenses	value

_____ 1. Third party to whom contract rights are transferred.

_____ 2. Unauthorized change or completion of a negotiable instrument designed to modify the obligation of a party to the instrument.

_____ 3. Defenses to payment that can be asserted against any party, including a holder in due course.

_____ 4. Misrepresentation that induces a party to knowingly sign a negotiable instrument.

_____ 5. Holder who takes an instrument for value, in good faith, and without notice of certain matters.

_____ 6. Defenses to payment that can be asserted against an assignee or ordinary holder, but cannot be asserted against a holder in due course or a holder through a holder in due course.

_____ 7. Holder who enjoys the same rights as a holder in due course.

_____ 8. Actual performance of an act in exchange for an instrument, or taking an instrument as security or payment for an existing obligation.

_____ 9. Parties to an instrument to whom holders turn when the primary party, for whatever reason, fails to pay the instrument. Parties are also called secondary obligors under Revised Article 3

_____ 10. Formal request for payment on an instrument.

True/False

Write **T** if the statement is true, write **F** if it is false.

_____ 1. An ordinary holder does not have any right to demand or enforce payment of an instrument.

_____ 2. In general, a person entitled to payment may sue any one or more of the parties liable to pay the instrument, regardless of the order in which the parties signed the instrument.

_____ 3. A holder through a holder in due course has the same right to collect and enforce payment of a negotiable instrument as does a holder in due course.

_____ 4. Evidence that a person paid an extremely small price for an instrument may indicate bad faith.

_____ 5. It is illegal to negotiate an instrument that is overdue.

_____ 6. A person has notice of a fact only when the person has actual knowledge of the fact.

_____ 7. Limited defenses can be asserted against anyone, including a holder in due course.

_____ 8. Duress is a universal defense if, under state law, duress would render a contract void.

_____ 9. Ordinary contract defenses are limited defenses that cannot be used against holders in due course.

_____ 10. Maker issued a note due May 1. Maker prepaid the note on March 1, but Maker did not retake the note. On April 1, the payee negotiated the note to Hal, a holder in due course. In this case, Maker's prior payment is a limited defense, and it cannot be asserted against Hal.

Multiple Choice

_____ 1. In which case did Holder give value sufficient to be a holder in due course?
a. Drawer issued a check to Paul. Paul indorsed the check, and delivered it to Holder as a gift.
b. Maker issued a check to Rod. Rod indorsed the check and delivered it to Holder in payment for services Holder promised to perform for Rod. Holder did not perform the services.
c. Maker issued a negotiable note payable to Priscilla. Priscilla indorsed the note and negotiated it to Holder in payment of an existing debt that she owed Holder.
d. b and c.

_____ 2. Mac issued a negotiable note to Peg to pay for goods. Peg negotiated the note to Chris, who negotiated the note to Herb. Herb paid value for the note, and he took it in good faith. Which additional fact would *not* prevent Herb from being a holder in due course?
a. The note was due June 1, and Chris negotiated the note to Herb on July 1.
b. At the time the note was negotiated to Herb, Herb knew that the note had become due and that Mac had refused to pay it.
c. At the time the note was negotiated to Herb, Herb knew that Peg claimed ownership of the note because she had been defrauded into transferring it to Chris.
d. One day after the note was negotiated to Herb, Mac informed Herb that the goods delivered to Mac were defective, and he had a breach of contract defense.

_____ 3. In which case does Denise have a limited defense that cannot be used against a favored holder?
   a. Denise issued a check to Contractor in payment for certain remodeling work. Contractor performed the work improperly, a breach of contract.
   b. Denise issued a check to Payton. Denise issued the check due to wrongful physical abuse by Payton. Under state law, the duress exerted by Payton would render the obligation void.
   c. Denise's checkbook was stolen by Thief. Thief forged Denise's signature to a check.
   d. When Denise was a minor, she issued a check in payment for a magazine subscription.

_____ 4. In which case does Dana have a universal defense that can be asserted against all holders?
   a. While intoxicated, Dana bought a painting and she issued a check in payment. Under state law, Dana's lack of capacity due to intoxication would render the obligation voidable.
   b. Dana issued a check in payment for illegal drugs. Under state law, negotiable instruments issued for illegal drugs are void.
   c. Dana issued a check to Perry as payment for landscaping services that Perry agreed to perform. Perry wrongfully failed to perform the services.
   d. Dana issued a check to Stockbroker. Delivery of the check was conditioned on Stockbroker's delivery of certain stock to Dana. Stockbroker failed to deliver the stock to Dana.

Case Problem

Answer the following problem, briefly explaining your answer.
Manley issued a $20,000 negotiable note to Preston to pay for a parcel of land. Preston misrepresented to Manley that the parcel contained fifty acres, when in fact it contained only forty acres. Preston negotiated the note to Carl. Carl paid Preston $20,000 for the note, and he took it without notice of Preston's fraud. Later, Carl negotiated the note to Ned who knew that Manley claimed that he had been defrauded.

1. Is Carl a holder in due course?
2. Describe Ned's status?
3. Manley's defense of fraud is what type of defense?
4. Can Manley assert this defense against Ned?

_____

_____

_____

Internet Exercise

Mindy issued a negotiable note to P&P Co. to pay for a stove for her home. The note contained all notices required by FTC rules. The stove breached various warranties. P&P negotiated the note to Harry, who took it for value, in good faith, and with no notice of the breach.

1. Using the Internet, locate and identify the FTC regulation that regulates consumer credit transactions.
2. Does this FTC regulation apply in this case? Must Mindy pay the amount of the note to Harry?
3. Would the FTC regulation apply if Mindy had instead paid with a personal check? Would Mindy have to pay the amount of the check to Harry?

_____

_____

_____

CPA REVIEW

The following questions were given on CPA examinations. The answers for these questions are the unofficial answers prepared by the American Institute of Certified Public Accountants, Inc. (AICPA). All material is reproduced with permission of the AICPA.

_____ 1. Jim Bass is in possession of a negotiable promissory note made payable "to bearer." Bass acquired the note from Mary Frank for value. The maker of the note was Fred Jackson. The following indorsements appear on the back of the note:

Sam Peters
Pay to Jim Bass
Mary Frank
Jim Bass
(without recourse)

Bass presented the note to Jackson, who refused to pay it because he was financially unable to do so. Which of the following statements is correct?
   a. Peters is not secondarily liable on the note because his indorsement was unnecessary for negotiation.
   b. Peters is not secondarily liable to Bass.
   c. Frank will probably not be liable to Bass unless Bass gives notice to Frank of Jackson's refusal to pay within a reasonable time.
   d. Bass would have had secondary liability to Peters and Frank if he had not qualified his indorsement.

_____ 2. Hunt has in his possession a negotiable instrument which was originally payable to the order of Carr. It was transferred to Hunt by a mere delivery by Drake, who took it from Carr in good faith in satisfaction of an antecedent debt. The back of the instrument read as follows, "Pay to the order of Drake in satisfaction of my prior purchase of a new video calculator, signed Carr." Which of the following is correct?
   a. Hunt has the right to assert Drake's rights, including his standing as a holder in due course and also has the right to obtain Drake's signature.
   b. Drake's taking the instrument for an antecedent debt prevents him from qualifying as a holder in due course.
   c. Carr's endorsement was a special endorsement; thus Drake's signature was not required in order to negotiate it.
   d. Hunt is a holder in due course.

_____ 3. A person who endorsed a check "without recourse"
   a. Has the same liability as an accommodation endorser.
   b. Only negates his liability insofar as prior parties are concerned.
   c. Gives the same warranty protection to his transferee as does a special or blank endorser.
   d. Does not promise or guarantee payment of the instrument upon dishonor even if there has been a proper presentment and proper notice has been given.

_____ 4. Silver Corp. sold 20 tons of steel to River Corp. with payment to be by River's check. The price of steel was fluctuating daily. Silver requested that the amount of River's check be left blank and Silver would fill in the current market price. River complied with Silver's request. Within two days, Silver received River's check. Although the market price of 20 tons of steel at the time Silver received River's check was $80,000, Silver filled in the check for $100,000 and negotiated it to Hatch Corp. Hatch took the check in good faith, without notice of Silver's act or any other defense, and in payment of an antecedent debt. River will
   a. Not be liable to Hatch, because the check was materially altered by Silver.
   b. Not be liable to Hatch, because Hatch failed to give value when it acquired the check from Silver.
   c. Be liable to Hatch for $100,000.
   d. Be liable to Hatch, but only for $80,000.

_____ 5. Frey paid Holt $2,500 by check pursuant to an agreement between them whereby Holt promised to perform in Frey's theater within the next year. Holt endorsed the check, making it payable to Len Able. Holt's status with regard to the check was one of a(an)
   a. Assignee since a payee may not also be a holder in due course.
   b. Holder since Holt's promise failed to satisfy the value requirement necessary to become a holder in due course.
   c. Holder in due course under the shelter rule since Able's rights as a holder in due course revert to Holt.
   d. Holder in due course since all the requirements have been satisfied.

_____ 6. Under the Commercial Paper Article of the UCC, which of the following circumstances would prevent a person from becoming a holder in due course of an instrument?
   a. The person was notified that payment was refused.
   b. The person was notified that one of the prior endorsers was discharged.
   c. The note was collateral for a loan.
   d. The note was purchased at a discount.

CHAPTER 31
CHECKS AND FUNDS TRANSFERS

MAKE THE CONNECTION

SUMMARY

A *check* is a particular kind of draft; it is drawn on a bank and is payable on demand. A delivery of a check is not an assignment of money on deposit with the bank on which it is drawn. A check does not automatically transfer the rights of the depositor against the bank to the holder of the check, and there is no duty on the part of the drawee bank to the holder to pay the holder the amount of the check.

A check may be an *ordinary check,* a *cashier's check*, or a *teller's check.* The name on the paper is not controlling. Unless otherwise agreed, the delivery of a certified check, a cashier's check, or a teller's check discharges the debt for which it is given, up to the amount of the check.

Certification of a check by the bank is the acceptance of the check—the bank becomes the primary party. Certification may be at the request of the drawee or the holder. Certification by the holder releases all prior indorsers and the drawer from liability.

Notice of nonpayment of a check must be given to the drawer of a check. If no notice is given, the drawer is discharged from liability to the same extent as the drawer of an ordinary draft.

A depositor may stop payment on a check. However, the depositor is liable to a holder in due course unless the stop payment order was for a reason that may be raised against a holder in due course. The stop payment order may be made orally (binding for 14 calendar days) or with a record (effective for six months). The depository bank is the agent of the depositor for the purpose of collecting a deposited item. The bank may become liable when it pays a check contrary to a stop payment order or when there has been a forgery or an alteration. The bank is not liable, however, if the drawer's negligence has substantially contributed to the forgery. A bank that pays on a forged instrument must recredit the drawer's account. A depositor is subject to certain time limitations to enforce liability of the bank. Banks are subject to reporting requirements under the USA Patriot Act.

A customer and a bank may agree that the bank should retain canceled checks and simply provide the customer with a list of paid items. The customer must examine canceled checks (or their electronic images) or paid items to see whether any were improperly paid.

An *electronic funds transfer (EFT)* is a transfer of funds (other than a transaction originated by check, draft, or other commercial paper) that is initiated through an electronic terminal, telephone, computer, or magnetic tape to authorize a financial institution to debit or credit an account. The Electronic Funds Transfer Act requires that a financial institution furnish consumers with specific information containing all the terms and conditions of all EFT services. Under certain conditions, the financial institution will bear the loss for unauthorized transfers. Under other circumstances, the consumer will bear the loss.

Funds transfers regulated by UCC Article 4A are those made between highly sophisticated parties that deal with large sums of money. If any part of the funds transfer is subject to the EFTA, such as consumer transactions, the entire transfer is expressly excluded from the scope of Article 4A. A funds transfer is simply a request or an instruction to pay a specific sum of money to, or to the credit of, a specified person.

LEARNING OUTCOMES
After studying this chapter, you should be able to

A. CHECKS
LO.1 List and explain the duties of the drawee bank
LO.2 Explain the methods for, and legal effect of, stopping payment

B. LIABILITY OF A BANK
LO.3 Describe the liability of a bank for improper payment and collection
LO.4 Discuss the legal effect of forgeries and material alterations
LO.5 Specify the time limitations for reporting forgeries and alterations

C. CONSUMER FUNDS TRANSFERS

D. FUNDS TRANSFERS
LO.6 Describe the electronic transfer of funds and laws governing it

CHAPTER OUTLINE

A. CHECKS

1. NATURE OF A CHECK

GENERAL RULE. ▶ A check is a type of draft that is drawn on a bank. ▶ A drawer has conditional liability to pay a dishonored check. ▶ A drawee bank does not owe a duty to *the payee* to pay a check unless the bank has accepted it.

LIMITATIONS. ▶ A postdated check (a check that is dated later than the date that it is actually issued) is not payable until the date shown. Thus, a postdated check is, in effect, a time instrument. ▶ A bank is not required to honor a postdate provision unless the drawer has filed appropriate papers with the bank pertaining to the postdating.

STUDY HINTS. ▶ Under bad check laws, it may be a crime if a check is not paid due to insufficient funds and it was issued with the intent to defraud. ▶ A check may be an ordinary check, a cashier's check (check drawn by a bank on itself), or a teller's check (check drawn by a bank on another bank in which it has funds deposited). ▶ Revised Article 4 recognizes a "substitute check" which is an electronic image or printout of a paper check and it has the same legal effect as the paper check.

2. CERTIFIED CHECKS

GENERAL RULES. ▶ A certified check is a check that has been accepted by the drawee bank, whereby the bank agrees to have primary liability to pay it regardless of the balance in the drawer's account at the time payment is demanded. ▶ Certification may be obtained by: (1) a holder (discharges all prior indorsers and drawer from conditional liability); or (2) by a drawer (does not discharge any parties).

LIMITATION. A certification must be written on the check and duly signed by a bank officer.

LEARNING OUTCOME EXAMPLES: See Thinking Things Through on textbook p. 691.

3. PRESENTMENT FOR OBTAINING PAYMENT ON A CHECK

▶ A check can ordinarily be presented for payment immediately after it is issued. But, if a check is postdated, it cannot be presented until the date stated on the check. ▶ A check is overdue the day after demand for payment is made or ninety days after the date of the check, whichever is earlier. ▶ In order to charge a secondary party (drawer or indorser) on a check or record, presentment for payment must be made on the drawee within a "reasonable time" after the secondary party signs the paper. To hold a drawer liable, the "reasonable time" for presentment is ordinarily presumed to be 90 days from the date of the check or the date it was issued. To hold an indorser liable, the check should be presented within 30 days after it is indorsed.
▶ LEARNING OUTCOME EXAMPLE: See, *Rovell v American Nat'l Bank* on textbook p. 697.

4. DISHONOR OF A CHECK

GENERAL RULE. ▶ Dishonor occurs if a drawee refuses to accept or pay a check drawn on it by a depositor. ▶ Banks in the chain of collection for a check must give notice of dishonor by midnight of the next banking day. ▶ Others, including the payee or holder of the check, must give notice of dishonor within 30 days after they learn that the instrument has been dishonored.
STUDY HINT.   An overdraft is a check that is paid by a bank even though it exceeds funds on deposit and it is treated as a loan from the bank to the customer.

5. THE CUSTOMER-BANK RELATIONSHIP

➤ *Privacy*: ▶ A bank must maintain the confidentiality of customer information. The USA Patriot Act imposes some reporting requirements on banks including cash transactions over $10,000.

➤ *Payment*: A depositary bank has a duty to pay checks to the extent there are sufficient funds.

➤ *Stale checks*: A bank may pay a stale check (i.e., one presented for payment more than six months after the date issued), but it is not required to do so unless the check is certified.

➤ *Payment after depositor's death*: A bank may continue to pay a customer's checks until the bank actually knows of the customer's death. Even with knowledge of the customer's death, the bank may continue to pay the customer's checks for ten days following his or her death unless told not to do so by an interested party, such as an heir or the government.

➤ **LEARNING OUTCOME EXAMPLE**: See *IBP, Inc. v Mercantile Bank of Topeka* on textbook p. 694.

6. STOPPING PAYMENT OF A CHECK

GENERAL RULES. ▶ A drawer can stop payment by notifying the drawee bank. ▶ An order may be oral or written; if oral, it is binding for 14 days; if written, it is effective for 6 months.
LIMITATION.   A drawer cannot stop payment of a certified check or a cashier's check.
STUDY HINT.   A drawer may be liable on a check even if payment is stopped.

7. WRONGFUL DISHONOR OF A CHECK

GENERAL RULE. ▶ A bank is liable to the drawer for any damages caused by a wrongful dishonor. ▶ A dishonor is wrongful if: (1) a check is properly payable and (2) the account has funds to pay it. A dishonor for lack of funds is also wrongful if a bank has agreed to pay a drawer's overdrafts.

LIMITATION. ► The drawee is NOT liable to a holder for wrongfully dishonoring an uncertified check. ► However, the drawee IS liable to a holder for wrongfully dishonoring a certified check.

8. AGENCY STATUS OF COLLECTING BANK

A collecting bank is typically only a depositor's agent for purposes of collecting a check. Until final settlement, the depositor owns the check and bears the risk of nonpayment.

9. BANK'S DUTY OF CARE

► Banks must use ordinary care in handling checks. Parties in the bank collection process may alter their rights, but liability for bad faith or failure to us ordinary care cannot be disclaimed. ► Ordinarily, banks need not physically inspect checks that are automatically processed. ► Anyone encoding data on an item or transmitting the information electronically warrants that the information is correct (encoding warranty).

B. LIABILITY OF A BANK

10. PREMATURE PAYMENT OF A POSTDATED CHECK

A bank is not liable to a drawer for paying a postdated check prior to the date stated unless the drawer gave the bank prior notice that the check was being issued and should not be paid until the stated date.

11. PAYMENT OVER A STOP PAYMENT ORDER

► A bank that pays a depositor's check contrary to a valid stop payment order is liable to the depositor for any damages caused unless there was a valid limitation of liability. But, a bank must be given a reasonable time within which to act on an order (usually a few hours is sufficient). ► LEARNING OUTCOME EXAMPLE: See *South Central Bank of Daviess County v Lynnville Nat. Bank* on textbook p. 699.

12. PAYMENT ON A FORGED SIGNATURE OF DRAWER

GENERAL RULE. A drawee is liable to a drawer if it pays a check with a forged (i.e., unauthorized and fraudulent) drawer's signature, even if the drawee could not detect the forgery.

LIMITATIONS. ► Preclusion rule: depositor whose negligence substantially contributed to a forgery cannot assert the forgery and cannot make a drawee bank recredit its account if the bank paid the item. ► Preclusion rule also applies if a drawer's negligence contributes to alteration of a check.

STUDY HINT. Ordinarily, a drawee bank bears any loss caused by its payment over a forged drawer's signature. The drawee cannot recover from an innocent drawer or indorser on any theory.

13. PAYMENT ON A FORGED OR MISSING INDORSEMENT

If a bank pays a depositor's check that has a forged required indorsement or a required indorsement is missing, the bank must recredit the depositor's account and the depositor will not bear the loss.

14. ALTERATION OF A CHECK

A drawee bank that pays an altered check can charge a drawer's account for only the original amount of the check, unless the alteration is due to the drawer's negligence.

15. UNAUTHORIZED COLLECTION OF A CHECK

➢ A bank that improperly collects payment of a check for a customer is liable to the true check owner.

➢ A collecting bank is not liable if it is obeying its customer's instructions.

16. TIME LIMITATIONS

➢ *Single forgery or alteration*: Drawee that uses ordinary care is not liable to a drawer for a forged or altered check if: (1) the drawer did not use reasonable care to inspect the checks and notify the bank of unauthorized signatures or alterations; (2) drawer did not give the bank notice of a forged drawer's signature or alteration within one year after receipt of the bank statement; or (3) drawer did not give the bank notice of a forged indorsement within 3 years after receipt of a statement.

➢ *Unauthorized signatures/alterations by same person:* If there is a series of improper items, a customer's failure to notify the bank of the first improperly paid item within 30 days may cause   liability for the remainder of the improperly paid items. LEARNING OUTCOME EXAMPLE: See *Burns v Neiman Marcus* on textbook p. 702.

➢ *Statute of limitations for liability under Article 4*: three years.

C. CONSUMER FUNDS TRANSFERS

17. ELECTRONIC FUNDS TRANSFER ACT (EFTA)

Electronic funds transfer is a transfer of funds (not using check, draft, or other paper instrument) that electronically authorizes institutions to credit or debit funds to or from an account. EFTA governs such transfers made by consumers.

18. TYPES OF ELECTRONIC FUNDS TRANSFER SYSTEMS

▶ EFT systems include: automated teller machine (ATM); pay-by-phone system; direct deposit and withdrawal; point-of-sale terminal; and Internet banking. ▶ Consumers must be informed in advance of all terms for EFT services and must be given periodic statements of account activity. With certain exceptions, financial institutions are liable to consumers for violation of EFT account terms. ▶ Internet banking is a customer's use of a computer to access the bank system to pay bills, transfer funds, and even obtain loans.

19. CONSUMER LIABILITY

▶ Consumer's maximum liability for unauthorized use of EFT card: (1) $50 if issuer is notified within two days after consumer learns of loss of card; or (2) $500 if no notice is given within two days. ▶ A consumer bears a loss caused by a failure to report an improper transfer within sixty days after a statement was sent.

D. FUNDS TRANSFERS

20. WHAT LAW GOVERNS?

UCC Article 4A governs funds transfers if a state adopted 4A or if a Federal Reserve Bank is involved.

21. CHARACTERISTICS OF FUNDS TRANSFERS

Article 4A transfers typically involve large sums of money between sophisticated nonconsumers.

22. PATTERN OF FUNDS TRANSFERS

▶ Funds transfers may involve two or more parties. ▶ Example: A&A buys land for $500,000 and A&A tells its bank to debit its account for $500,000 and to credit the seller's account for this sum.

23. SCOPE OF UCC ARTICLE 4A

Article 4A governs most funds transfers, but does not govern: transfers by consumers regulated by the EFTA, debit transfers, payment by credit card, nonbank transfers of money (e.g., Western Union), or payments made by check.

24. DEFINITIONS

➤ *Funds transfer*: request to pay money to an account or party. ▶ *Originator*: party starting funds   transfer.

➤ *Beneficiary*: party (account) for whose benefit funds are transferred. ▶ *Beneficiary's bank*: final bank in transfer--pays beneficiary. ▶ *Payment order*: request that bank make a funds transfer. ▶ *Acceptance*: beneficiary bank applies or agrees to apply funds for the benefit of a beneficiary.

25. MANNER OF TRANSMITTING PAYMENT ORDER

Article 4A does not regulate the manner of carrying out funds transfers; computers are often used.

26. REGULATION BY AGREEMENT AND FUNDS TRANSFER SYSTEM RULES

Parties' agreement or clearinghouse rules may designate controlling law or change Article 4A rules.

27. REIMBURSEMENT OF THE BANK

Ultimately, an originator is responsible for the cost of funds the originator ordered to be transferred.

28. ERROR IN FUNDS TRANSFER

A bank that prepares an incorrect payment order is liable for any overpayment, duplicate payment, or a payment to the wrong person or account because of an error in the designation.

29. LIABILITY FOR LOSS

Bank is not liable for executing an unauthorized order if a commercially reasonable security procedure is used unless someone unrelated to the originator made the order.

CONCEPT REVIEW AND APPLICATIONS

Matching Exercise

Select the term or phrase that best matches a definition or statement stated below. Each term or phrase is the best match for only one statement or definition. Not all terms and phrases will necessarily be used.

agency	Electronic Funds Transfer Act (EFTA)	postdated
agent	electronic funds transfer (EFT)	presentment
bad check laws	encoding warranty	stale check
beneficiary	funds transfer	stop payment order
beneficiary's bank	intermediary bank	substitute check
cashier's check	money order	teller's check
certified check	originator	time draft
check	overdraft	USA Patriot Act
credit transfer	payment order	Wrongfully dishonored
debit transfer		
demand draft		

_____ 1. Instruction by a drawer to a drawee bank not to pay a check.

_____ 2. Check presented more than six months after the date on which it was issued.

_____ 3. Request to pay money to or for the credit of a party without physically transferring money.

_____ 4. Check that is drawn by a bank upon itself and that is payable to another party.

_____ 5. Party who initiates a funds transfer request.

_____ 6. Check that is accepted by a drawee bank at the request of the drawer or a holder.

_____ 7. Law that governs electronic fund transfers by consumers.

_____ 8. Direction or request made by an originator or subsequent bank to make a funds transfer.

_____ 9. Final bank that makes payment or gives credit to a beneficiary in accordance with payment order.

_____10. Party who ultimately receives funds pursuant to a funds transfer.

True/False

Write **T** if the statement is true, write **F** if it is false.

_____ 1. A drawer may be criminally prosecuted for issuing a bad check if the drawer's account has insufficient funds to pay the check and the check was issued with the intent to defraud a payee.

_____ 2. A postdated check is payable immediately after issuance even though it is dated with a later date.

_____ 3. In general, a drawer can stop payment of a certified or cashier's check.

_____ 4. Certification of a check must be written on the check and must be signed by an agent of the bank.

_____ 5. An indorser's conditional liability is discharged if a check is not presented for payment within three days after the date the indorser signed the check.

_____ 6. A bank cannot be held liable by a drawer for damages caused by a wrongful dishonor of a check.

_____ 7. A drawee bank is liable for a drawer's damages that are caused by the bank's payment of a check in violation of a valid stop payment order unless there was a valid limitation of liability.

_____ 8. Drawer issued a postdated check and informed Drawee Bank of this fact. Nonetheless, Drawee Bank paid the check before the date of the check. In this case, Drawee Bank cannot be held liable for damages that Drawer may suffer due to the early payment the check.

_____ 9. If a drawee bank charges a drawer's account for a check that has a forged required indorsement, the drawee bank must recredit the drawer's account for the amount of the check.

_____10. A drawer may lose the right to assert against a drawee bank a claim that a check had been altered if the drawer's negligence substantially contributed to the alteration.

Multiple Choice

_____ 1. Drawer issued a check to Patty. Patty indorsed the check in blank and negotiated it to Harold. At Harold's request, Bank of Fruita, the drawee bank, certified the check. In this case:
a. Certification discharged Drawer from its conditional liability to pay the check.
b. Certification discharged Patty from her conditional liability to pay the check.
c. When the check is presented for payment, Bank of Fruita must pay the check even if there are insufficient funds in Drawer's account to pay the check.
d. All the above are correct.

_____ 2. Select the correct answer.
a. Kunio has a checking account at City Bank. Kunio is under FBI investigation. In this case, the FBI cannot obtain Kunio's bank records without his consent or a valid search warrant.
b. On January 1, Anna issued a check to Lee. On August 1, Lee presented the check to Anna's bank and the bank refused to cash it. In this case, Anna's bank breached a duty to Anna.
c. Al died on May 1. Al's bank was informed of his death on May 4. A check issued by Al was presented for payment on May 12. In this case, the bank cannot properly pay the check.
d. All of the above are correct.

_____ 3. Oscar issued a check to Juan. Juan negotiated the check to Laura, a holder in due course. On April 2, Oscar gave his bank an oral stop payment order on the check because the check had been issued as payment for goods that breached certain warranties (a limited defense). On April 4, Laura presented the check for payment, and Oscar's bank paid the check. In this case:
a. The stop payment order was not binding. Stop payment orders must be made in writing.
b. The stop payment order was not binding. A bank has three days before it must act in accordance with a stop payment order.
c. The stop payment order was binding, but Oscar is still liable to pay the check to Laura.
d. The stop payment order was binding, and it terminated Oscar's liability to pay the check.

_____ 4. Cody has a checking account with State Bank. Cody has $10,000 in his checking account. Cody issued a check to Paul for $5,000. Paul properly presented the check for payment to State Bank, but the bank dishonored the check. As a result, Cody incurred $100 damages and Paul incurred $50 damages. In this case:
a. State Bank is not liable to Cody or Paul.
b. State Bank is liable to Paul for $50 in damages, but it is not liable to Cody.
c. State Bank is liable to Cody for $100 in damages, but it is not liable to Paul.
d. State Bank is liable to Cody for $100 in damages, and it is liable to Paul for $50 in damages.

_____ 5. Dan's checkbook was stolen by Thief. Thief forged Dan's signature on a check and issued it to Penny, who was unaware of the forgery. Penny presented the check for payment to First Bank, the drawee bank. First Bank paid the check and charged Dan's account for the amount of the check. In this case:
a. First Bank was entitled to charge Dan's account for the check, and it has no obligation to recredit his account.
b. First Bank must recredit Dan's account for the amount of the check.

   c. Between First Bank and Dan, First Bank must bear any loss that may occur due to its payment of the check.
   d. b and c.

Case Problems

Answer the following problems, briefly explaining your answers.

1. Jeff duly issued a check to Ernie for $100. Ernie wrongfully raised the amount to $1,000, and he presented the check to Last Bank, the drawee. Last Bank paid Ernie $1,000 out of Jeff's account. Last Bank exercised reasonable care at all times. One week after receiving his bank statement, Jeff noticed the improper payment, and he informed Last Bank of the alteration.
   (a) Describe Jeff's duty to examine his bank statement and to report alterations to Last Bank. (b) Did Jeff give timely notice of the alteration? (c) For how much, if any, can Last Bank charge Jeff's account?

_____

_____

_____

_____

2. Greg has a bank account with First Federal Bank. First Federal issued Greg an ATM card that allowed him to withdraw funds from his personal bank account through the use of automated teller machines. On Monday Greg's ATM card was stolen by a thief who used it to withdraw $750 from Greg's account. Greg discovered the theft on Thursday, and he immediately informed First Federal of the theft.

   (a) What law governs Greg's rights in this case?
   (b) Describe a consumer's liability for the unauthorized use of a lost or stolen EFT card.
   (c) For how much of the unauthorized transfer is Greg liable?

_____

_____

_____

_____

Internet Exercise

Acme Import and Export Corp. is located in Walla Walla, Washington. It presently focuses on trade with the Far East, but is expanding its operations to place greater emphasis on trade with South America.

Therefore, Acme has contracted to purchase a warehouse in Miami. In order to complete the purchase, however, Acme needs to transfer $5 million from its Walla Walla bank to its bank in Florida, Last Florida Savings and Loan. Under these facts:

1. How can Acme electronically transfer the necessary funds? What law governs this transaction?
2. Using the Internet, locate and identify a financial institution that would facilitate this transaction.
3. Who will be the parties to the proposed funds transfer, and define the nature of the role that each will play.

_____

_____

_____

_____

CPA REVIEW

The following questions were given on CPA examinations. The answers for these questions are the unofficial answers prepared by the American Institute of Certified Public Accountants, Inc. (AICPA). All material is reproduced with permission of the AICPA.

_____ 1. West Corp. received a check that was originally made payable to the order of one of its customers, Ted Burns. The following endorsement was written on the back of the check: Ted Burns, without recourse, for collection only. Which of the following describes the endorsement?

	Special	Restrictive
a.	Yes	Yes
b.	No	No
c.	No	Yes
d.	Yes	No

_____ 2. One of the requirements to qualify as a holder of a negotiable bearer check is that the transferee must
   a. Receive the check that was originally made payable to bearer.
   b. Take the check in good faith.
   c. Give value for the check.
   d. Have possession of the check.

Question 3 relates to a check that has the following endorsements on the back:

Paul Folk, without recourse George Hopkins, payment guaranteed Ann Quarry, collection guaranteed Rachel Ott

_____ 3. Which of the following conditions occurring subsequent to the endorsements would discharge all of the endorsers?
   a. Lack of notice of dishonor.
   b. Late presentment.
   c. Insolvency of the maker.
   d. Certification of the check.

_____ 4. Cobb gave Garson a signed check with the amount payable left blank. Garson was to fill in, as the amount, the price of fuel oil Garson was to deliver to Cobb at a later date. Garson estimated the amount at $700, but told Cobb it would be no more than $900. Garson did not deliver the fuel oil, but filled in the amount of $1,000 on the check. Garson then negotiated the check to Josephs in satisfaction of a $500 debt with the $500 balance paid to Garson in cash. Cobb stopped payment and Josephs is seeking to collect $1,000 from Cobb. Cobb's maximum liability to Josephs will be
   a. $0
   b. $500
   c. $900
   d. $1,000

Question 5 relates to the instrument below. Fred Anchor is the holder of the following check:

Peter Mason	Champaign, Illinois	4/30 1990
Pay to the order of Mary Nix or bearer		$93.00
Ninety-Three ------------------------------------Dollars		
Second Bank 0453-0978		
Peter Mason		

The check is endorsed on the back as follows:
Mary Nix, Pay to John Jacobs
Mark Harris
John Jacobs, (without recourse)

_____ 5. Jacobs gave the check to his son as a gift, who transferred it to Anchor for $78.00.
Which of the following statements is correct?
    a.   The unqualified endorsement of Jacobs was necessary in order to negotiate the
check to his son.
    b.   Nix's endorsement was required to negotiate the check to any subsequent holder.
    c.   Anchor does not qualify as a holder because less than full consideration was
given for the check.
    d.   The check is bearer paper in Jacobs' son's hands.

_____ 6. For which of the following negotiable instruments is a bank not an acceptor?
    a.   Cashier's check.
    b.   Certified check.
    c.   Certificate of deposit.
    d.   Bank acceptance.

CHAPTER 32
NATURE OF THE DEBTOR-CREDITOR RELATIONSHIP

MAKE THE CONNECTION

SUMMARY

Suretyship and guaranty undertakings have the common feature of a promise to answer for the debt or default of another. The terms are used interchangeably, but a guarantor of collection is ordinarily only secondarily liable, which means that the guarantor does not pay until the creditor has exhausted all avenues of recovery. If the guarantor has made an absolute guaranty, then its status is the same as that of a surety, which means that both are liable for the debt in the event the debtor defaults, regardless of what avenues of collection, if any, the creditor has pursued.

Surety and guaranty relationships are based on contract. Sureties have a number of rights to protect them. They are exoneration, subrogation, indemnity, and contribution. In addition to those rights, sureties also have certain defenses. They include ordinary contract defenses as well as some defenses peculiar to the suretyship relationship, such as release of collateral, change in loan terms, substitution of debtor, and fraud by the creditor.

A letter of credit is an agreement that the issuer of the letter will pay drafts drawn on the issuer by the beneficiary of the letter. The issuer of the letter of credit is usually a bank. There are three contracts involved in letter-of-credit transactions: (1) the contract between the issuer and the customer of the issuer, (2) the letter of credit itself, and (3) the underlying agreement between the beneficiary and the customer of the issuer of the letter of credit.

The parties to a letter of credit are the issuer, the customer who makes the arrangement with the issuer, and the beneficiary who will be the drawer of the drafts to be drawn under the letter of credit. The letter of credit continues for any time it specifies. The letter of credit must be in writing and signed by the issuer. Consideration is not required to establish or modify a letter of credit. If the conditions in the letter of credit have been complied with, the issuer is obligated to honor drafts drawn under the letter of credit.

LEARNING OUTCOMES
After studying this chapter, you should be able to

A. CREATION OF THE CREDIT RELATIONSHIP

B. SURETYSHIP AND GUARANTY
LO.1   Distinguish a contract of suretyship from a contract of guaranty
LO.2   Define the parties to a contract of suretyship and a contract of guaranty
LO.3.   List and explain the rights of sureties to protect themselves from loss
LO.4   Explain the defenses available to sureties

C. LETTERS OF CREDIT
LO.5   Explain the nature of a letter of credit and the liabilities of the various parties to a letter of credit

CHAPTER OUTLINE

A. CREATION OF THE CREDIT RELATIONSHIP

A debtor-creditor relationship is created when parties enter into a contract pursuant to which one party (the creditor) loans money to the other party (the debtor) who agrees to repay the loan principal together with a specified rate of interest over a stated period of time.

B. SURETYSHIP AND GUARANTY

1. DEFINITIONS

A person may contractually agree to be responsible for the debt or obligation of another person. These agreements may take several forms including:

➢ *Suretyship*: ► A suretyship is a three-way contract by which a third party (the obligor or surety) agrees to be *primarily liable* to a creditor (the obligee) for the debt of another (the principal; principal debtor; or debtor). ► If the debtor fails to pay, the creditor can demand performance immediately from the surety without first trying to collect from the debtor. ► Example: Pam (principal) borrowed $20,000 from Carl (obligee), and Stuart (surety) agreed to be surety. Payment is due May 1. On May 1, Carl can demand payment from Pam or Stuart.

➢ *Guarantee of collection*: ► A guarantee of collection is a contract whereby a third party (the obligor or guarantor) agrees to be *secondarily liable* for an obligation of the principal debtor if the debtor defaults. ► In this guarantee, a creditor must first try to collect from the debtor before proceeding against the guarantor. ► Example: Paul (principal) bought a plane from Chris on credit, and Gary (guarantor) guaranteed collection of the debt. When payment is due, Chris must try to collect from Paul. If Paul fails to pay, Chris can then demand payment from Gary.

➢ *Absolute guarantee*: ► An absolute guarantee is a special type of guarantee by which a guarantor becomes *primarily liable* for an obligation of the debtor. ► An absolute guarantee creates the same obligations as a suretyship. ► A guarantee of payment is an absolute guarantee.

➢ **LEARNING OUTCOME EXAMPLE**: See the example on corporate officers and their relationship with company debt on textbook p. 718.

2. INDEMNITY CONTRACT DISTINGUISHED

► An indemnity contract is an agreement, supported by consideration, whereby a party agrees to pay for a specified loss of another. ► Example: insurance contract. ► An indemnity contract is not a suretyship or a guarantee.

3. CREATION OF THE RELATIONSHIP

Contract principles that apply include:

➢ *Contract law*: Contract law generally applies to suretyship, guarantee, and indemnity contracts. A creditor must usually notify a guarantor of the creditor's acceptance of a guarantee contract.
➢ *Statute of frauds*: Typically, guarantee and surety contracts must be written to be enforceable, but a writing is not needed for contracts that are intended to primarily benefit the guarantor or surety.

➤ *Consideration*: ► When the original contract and the guarantee contract are made at the same time, the consideration under the original contract supports both contracts. ► If a guarantee contract is made after the original contract, a creditor must give the guarantor new consideration.

4. RIGHTS OF SURETIES

Sureties enjoy rights that help them to avoid losses in certain situations. These rights include:

➤ *Exoneration*: ► A surety may be released from liability that arises due to the creditor's improper action. ► Example: A surety may be released from liability if a creditor cannot collect from a debtor because the creditor inexcusably failed to take timely action to collect from the debtor.

➤ *Subrogation*: ► A surety that makes payment to a creditor acquires the creditor's claim and legal rights against the principal debtor. The surety may then collect the debt from the debtor. ► Example: Dan failed to pay a $5,000 debt to Chris, and Surety paid the debt. Surety is now subrogated to Chris' $5,000 claim, and Surety can sue Dan to collect this sum.

➤ *Indemnity*: ► A surety that has paid a creditor is entitled to reimbursement from the principal debtor for the amount paid. ► Example: Carlos defaulted on a debt and Surety paid the debt. Surety is entitled to be repaid by Carlos.

➤ *Contribution*: ► If more than one surety agrees to be liable for a debt, each surety is liable to the creditor for the entire debt until it has been paid in full. ► But, unless otherwise agreed, cosureties must pay an equal share of a debt. Consequently, a cosurety who pays a debt may seek contribution (reimbursement) from the other sureties to the extent that they failed to pay their share of the debt. ► Example: Bob and Mary are cosureties of a $1,000 debt owed by Dick. When Dick failed to pay, Bob paid the entire debt. Bob can recover $500 from Mary.

➤ **LEARNING OUTCOME EXAMPLE**: See the *Feigenbaum v Guaracini* case on textbook p. 720.

5. DEFENSES OF SURETIES

In certain situations, a surety may be able to avoid liability to a creditor by asserting either ordinary contract defenses or special defenses available to sureties.

(a) *Ordinary contract defenses*

GENERAL RULE. ► A surety may assert against a creditor any contract defense that a contracting party could ordinarily raise. Potential contract defenses include: (1) lack of contractual capacity; (2) failure of consideration; and (3) fraud or concealment of material facts by a creditor. ► Example: Jacqueline bought a TV on credit and Sara, a minor, agreed to be a surety for the debt. Sara can assert her minority in order to avoid paying this debt.
LIMITATION. Fraud that is committed by a debtor without the knowledge or participation of the creditor does not ordinarily release a surety.

(b) *Suretyship defenses*

GENERAL RULE. A surety may avoid liability by raising special defenses that are available to sureties. These defenses include: (1) the original obligation is invalid (for example, the original contract is illegal and void); (2) the debtor has been discharged (for example, the debt has been paid); (3) the creditor allows a third party to take the place of the original debtor; and (4) the creditor has released back to the debtor collateral that secured the debtor's performance.

STUDY HINT. If an original duty is materially modified to a gratuitous surety's detriment (surety not paid to serve as surety) and without their consent, the surety is released from liability.

LEARNING OUTCOME EXAMPLE: See *Security State Bank v Burk* on textbook p. 723.

C. LETTERS OF CREDIT

A letter of credit is an agreement by which one party agrees, in advance, to pay drafts drawn by the beneficiary of the letter. A letter of credit is a (1) financing arrangement that enables a debtor to know how much money will be provided by the issuer of the letter of credit, and (2) a security device that assures a creditor regarding the sum of money it can legally demand from the letter of credit issuer.

6. DEFINITION

GENERAL RULES. ▶ A letter of credit is a legal commitment by the issuer of the letter to pay a stated sum of money to a beneficiary when specific conditions are met. ▶ A letter-of-credit transaction generally involves three contracts: (1) an agreement between the issuer and the issuer's customer to issue the letter of credit; (2) the letter of credit that obligates the issuer to pay a beneficiary; and (3) the underlying agreement between the issuer's customer and the beneficiary that typically gives rise to the obligation that is to be satisfied by payments made by the issuer.

LIMITATION. Consideration is not required to make or modify a letter of credit.

STUDY HINTS. ▶ A letter-of-credit issuer is the principal debtor on the letter of credit, and the letter of credit and its duties are independent of other agreements. Thus, a surety cannot refuse to pay a creditor because the debtor defrauded the surety. ▶ A beneficiary can enforce a letter of credit even if a beneficiary did not rely upon the letter of credit or give the issuer consideration for the letter of credit.

7. PARTIES

Parties to a letter-of-credit transaction include: (1) an issuer (commonly a bank) that is obligated to pay the letter of credit; (2) the issuer's customer who obtained issuance of the letter of credit; (3) a beneficiary who is entitled to receive payment; and (4) an advising bank.

8. DURATION

GENERAL RULE. A letter of credit continues for the time specified in the agreement or until the maximum amount of money to be paid pursuant to the letter of credit is paid by the issuer.

LIMITATION. Unless otherwise stated in a letter of credit, the letter of credit cannot be revoked or modified by the issuer or the issuer's customer without the consent of the beneficiary.

9. FORM

GENERAL RULES. ▶ A letter of credit must (1) be in writing and (2) be signed by the issuer. ▶ An instrument is presumed to be a letter of credit if it is credit issued by: (1) a bank that requires a documentary draft or documentary demand for payment as a condition for payment; or (2) someone other than a bank who requires that documents of title be furnished with a demand for payment.

LIMITATION. If an instrument does not require the foregoing documentary evidence, it is not a letter of credit unless the instrument is conspicuously stated to be a letter of credit.

10. DUTY OF ISSUER

GENERAL RULE. Provided the conditions specified in a letter of credit are met, an issuer must honor drafts properly drawn on the letter or be liable for breaching the contract with its customer.

LIMITATION. An issuer is responsible for assuring that a beneficiary has given the issuer all required documents before paying on the letter of credit, and an issuer cannot obtain reimbursement if it fails to do so. But, an issuer is not required to verify other matters relating to the transaction.

LEARNING OUTCOME EXAMPLE: See *SouthTrust Bank of Alabama, N.A. v Webb-Stiles Co., Inc.,* textbook p. 727.

11. REIMBURSEMENT OF ISSUER

GENERAL RULE. An issuer of a letter of credit may obtain reimbursement from its customer for any proper payments made by the issuer pursuant to the letter of credit.

LIMITATION. An issuer cannot obtain reimbursement for: (1) improper payments; (2) payments that exceed the amount of the letter of credit; or (3) payments made after the letter of credit expired.

CONCEPT REVIEW AND APPLICATIONS

Matching Exercise

Select the term or phrase that best matches a definition or statement stated below. Each term or phrase is the best match for only one statement or definition. Not all terms and phrases will necessarily be used.

advising bank	guaranty of collection
concealment	issuer
contribution	letter of credit
correspondent bank	obligee
co-sureties	pledge
creditor	principal debtor
debtor	standby letter
fraud	

_____ 1. Person who is owed a debt that is subject to a guarantee or suretyship contract.

_____ 2. Obligor of a suretyship, in other words, party who is primarily liable for the debt or obligation of the principal debtor.

_____ 3. Contract by which an issuer agrees to pay drafts issued by a beneficiary if certain specified conditions are met.

_____ 4. Right of a cosurety to seek reimbursement from other sureties for their proportionate share of a debt that was paid by the cosurety.

_____ 5. Form of guaranty in which creditor cannot proceed against guarantor until after proceeding against the debtor.

_____ 6. Absolute promise to pay when a debtor defaults.

_____ 7. Letter of credit for a contractor ensuring he will complete the project as contracted.

_____ 8. Person who incurs the original liability to pay a debt or to perform an obligation.

True/False

____ 1. A surety has primary liability for the obligation of the principal debtor.

____ 2. On a debtor's default, a creditor can collect immediately from the debtor or the debtor's surety.

____ 3. Under a guarantee of collection contract, a creditor must attempt to collect payment from the principal debtor before the creditor can require payment by the guarantor.

____ 4. The general rules of contract law do not apply to suretyship contracts.

____ 5. Guarantee contracts do not need to be in writing.

____ 6. If a guarantee is made after and independent from the original contract, new consideration must be given for the guarantee in order to make the guarantee legally enforceable.

____ 7. A surety who pays a debtor's obligation has a right to be indemnified (reimbursed) by the debtor.

____ 8. Sureties can only assert special suretyship defenses; sureties are not entitled to assert ordinary contract defenses that the surety may have against the creditor.

____ 9. In general, a guarantor's liability for an obligation may be terminated if the obligation is materially modified without the guarantor's consent.

____10. A surety can be held liable for an obligation even if it arises out of an invalid, illegal contract.

Multiple Choice

____ 1. Tasha wanted to buy a Blackberry on credit from Seller. In exchange for Seller's agreement to sell the Blackberry to Tasha, Annette agreed in writing to guarantee Tasha's obligation for the purchase price. Under these facts:
   a. A suretyship contract is created.
   b. An indemnity contract is created.
   c. Annette's agreement to guarantee Tasha's obligation is not enforceable because Seller did not give any consideration to Annette.
   d. Annette's agreement to guarantee Tasha's obligation is enforceable.

_____ 2. Dina bought a car on credit from Creditor for $5,000. This debt is secured by a lien on the car. Samuel is the surety for this debt. Dina stopped paying and she was preparing to sell the car and abscond with the proceeds. Samuel notified Creditor of these facts, but Creditor failed to act for nine months enabling Dina to sell the car. Had Creditor acted, Samuel would have incurred no liability. Creditor sued Samuel as surety. What defense does Samuel have against Creditor?

    a. Defense of contribution.

    b. Defense of subrogation.

    c. Defense of exoneration.

    d. Samuel does not have any defense against Creditor.

_____ 3. Lender agreed to loan $25,000 to Art, and Art's warehouse was collateral for the loan. To induce Jesse to be a surety for this loan, Lender altered documents given to Jesse to hide the fact that the warehouse had been condemned and was to be demolished. Jesse relied on these fraudulent documents and agreed to be surety. Unknown to Lender, Art also misrepresented his financial condition to Jesse. Art failed to repay the loan, the warehouse was demolished, and Lender sued Jesse as surety. What defense does Jesse have *against Lender*?

    a. Suretyships are illegal and unenforceable.

    b. Lender defrauded Jesse.

    c. Art defrauded Jesse.

    d. Jesse does not have any defense against Lender.

_____ 4. Glaxco contracted to buy $1 million of china from Seller on credit. Key S&L issued a letter of credit agreeing to pay Seller $250,000 upon receipt of documents evidencing delivery of the china to Glaxco. Glaxco failed to pay for the china, and Seller demanded payment of the entire price from Key S&L. Under these facts:

    a. Key S&L must pay $1 million to Seller.

    b. Key S&L must pay $250,000 immediately upon demand by Seller.

    c. Key S&L must pay $250,000 to Seller after it receives the required documents.

    d. Key S&L must not pay anything to Seller until Key S&L receives the required documents and Key S&L inspects the china to assure that Seller properly performed the contract.

Case Problem

David, Tom, and Janet formed a corporation. Last Bank loaned $75,000 to the corporation. David, Tom, and Janet agreed to be cosureties for the loan. The corporation has defaulted on the loan, and Last Bank plans to sue Janet for payment of the loan.

1. Must Last Bank attempt to collect payment from the corporation before it can demand payment from the co-sureties?
2. Can Last Bank collect the full amount of the loan from Janet?
3. If Janet pays the loan, does she have a right to contribution from David and Tom? If so, how much can Janet recover from David and Tom?
4. Does Janet have a legal right against the corporation if she pays the loan?

_____

_____

_____

_____

Internet Exercise

Lex is negotiating to sell a $150,000 private airplane to Azure Corp., a Nigeria-based company. Azure representatives have offered to pay with a letter of credit drawn on the Last Bank of Nigeria. This is Lex's first international sale, and he feels insecure about doing this transaction on his own. He has asked you the following:

1. Using the Internet, locate and identify a U.S. financial institution that can assist Lex in this transaction.
2. What major risk does the proposed letter of credit arrangement pose for Lex?
3. What kind of letter of credit should Lex request in order to avoid this risk?

_____

_____

_____

_____

CPA REVIEW

The following questions were given on past CPA examinations. The answers for these questions are the unofficial answers prepared by the American Institute of Certified Public Accountants, Inc. (AICPA). All material is reproduced with permission of the AICPA.

_____ 1. Green was unable to repay a loan from State Bank when due. State refused to renew the loan unless Green provided an acceptable surety. Green asked Royal, a friend, to act as surety on the loan. To induce Royal to agree to become a surety, Green fraudulently represented Green's financial condition and promised Royal discounts on merchandise sold at Green's store. Royal agreed to act as surety and the loan was renewed. Later, Green's obligation to State was discharged in Green's bankruptcy. State wants to hold Royal liable. Royal may avoid liability.
   a. If Royal can show that State was aware of the fraudulent representations.
   b. If Royal was an uncompensated surety.
   c. Because the discharge in bankruptcy will prevent Royal from having a right of reimbursement.
   d. Because the arrangement was void at the inception.

_____ 2. Wright cosigned King's loan from Ace Bank. Which of the following events would release Wright from the obligation to pay the loan?
   a. Ace seeking payment of the loan only from Wright.
   b. King is granted a discharge in bankruptcy.
   c. Ace is paid in full by King's spouse.
   d. King is adjudicated mentally incompetent.

_____ 3. Which of the following defenses would a surety be able to assert successfully to limit the surety's liability to a creditor?
   a. A discharge in bankruptcy of the principal debtor.
   b. A personal defense the principal debtor has against the creditor.
   c. The incapacity of the surety.
   d. The incapacity of the principal debtor.

_____ 4. Which of the following rights does a surety have?

	Right to compel the creditor to proceed against principal debtor	Right to compel the creditor to collect from the principal debtor's collateral
a.	Yes	Yes
b.	Yes	No
c.	No	Yes
d.	No	No

_____ 5. Ingot Corp. lent Flange $50,000. At Ingot's request, Flange entered into an agreement with Quill and West for them to act as compensated co-sureties on the loan in the amount of $100,000 each. Ingot released West without Quill's or Flange's consent, and Flange later defaulted on the loan. Which of the following statements is correct?
   a. Quill will be liable for 50% of the loan balance.
   b. Quill will be liable for the entire loan balance.
   c. Ingot's release of West will have no effect on Flange's and Quill's liability to Ingot.
   d. Flange will be released for 50% of the loan balance.

_____ 6. A party contracts to guarantee the collection of the debts of another. As a result of the guarantee, which of the following statements is correct?
   a. The creditor may proceed against the guarantor without attempting to collect from the debtor.
   b. The guarantee must be in writing.
   c. The guarantor may use any defenses available to the debtor.
   d. The creditor must be notified of the debtor's default by the guarantor.

_____ 7. Which of the following events will release a noncompensated surety from liability?
   a. Release of the principal debtor's obligation by the creditor but with the reservation of the creditor's rights against the surety.
   b. Modification by the principal debtor and creditor of their contract that materially increases the surety's risk of loss.
   c. Filing of an involuntary petition in bankruptcy against the principal debtor.
   d. Insanity of the principal debtor at the time the contract was entered into with the creditor.

_____ 8. Nash, Owen, and Polk are co-sureties with maximum liabilities of $40,000, $60,000 and $80,000, respectively. The amount of the loan on which they have agreed to act as co-sureties is $180,000. The debtor defaulted at a time when the loan balance was $180,000. Nash paid the lender $36,000 in full settlement of all claims against Nash, Owen, and Polk. The total amount that Nash may recover from Owen and Polk is
   a. $0
   b. $ 24,000
   c. $ 28,000
   d. $ 140.000

CHAPTER 33
CONSUMER PROTECTION

MAKE THE CONNECTION

SUMMARY

Modern methods of marketing, packaging, and financing have reduced the ordinary consumer to a subordinate position. To protect the consumer from the hardship, fraud, and oppression that could result from being in such an inferior position, consumer protection laws, at both the state and federal levels, afford rights to consumers and impose requirements on those who deal with consumers.

When a consumer protection statute is violated, an action may sometimes be brought by the consumer against the wrongdoer. More commonly, an action is brought by an administrative agency or by the state attorney general.

Consumer protection laws are directed at false and misleading advertising; misleading or false use of labels; the methods of selling, with specific requirements on the disclosure of terms and the permitting of consumer cancellation of home-solicited sales; and types of credit arrangements. The consumer is protected in a contract agreement by regulation of its form, prohibition of unconscionable terms, and limitation of the credit that can be extended to a consumer. Credit card protections include prohibition of the unauthorized distribution of credit cards and limited liability of the cardholder for the unauthorized use of a credit card. Included in consumer protection laws are the application of payments; the preservation of consumer defenses as against a transferee of the consumer's contract; product safety; the protection of credit standing and reputation; and (to some extent) real estate development sales, franchises, and service contracts. Lemon laws provide special protection to buyers of automobiles for personal, household, or family use.

LEARNING OUTCOMES
After studying this chapter, you should be able to

A. GENERAL PRINCIPLES
LO.1   Explain what consumer protection laws do

B. AREAS OF CONSUMER PROTECTION
LO.2   List the rights and protections consumer debtors have when a collector contacts them
LO.3   Give a summary of the rights of consumers with regard to credit reports
LO.4   Describe the types of protections available for consumers who have credit cards

CHAPTER OUTLINE

A. GENERAL PRINCIPLES

1. EXPANSION OF CONSUMER PROTECTION

GENERAL RULE.   Consumer protection laws (deceptive trade practices laws) protect "consumers," which in many cases includes any person, business, or governmental body that uses goods or services.

335

STUDY HINTS.   ►Consumer protection statutes often expedite consumers' obtaining relief. ► Remedies provided by consumer protection statutes often eliminate the need for a consumer to prove that a tort has been committed or establish actual damages because the statutes typically establish what must be proven in order to recover and a formula for computing damages.

LEARNING OUTCOME EXAMPLE: See the discussion of Jessica Simpson and William Shatner in the Sports &Entertainment Law box on textbook p. 744.

2. WHO IS A CONSUMER?

In a consumer protection action, the consumer must first prove that he or she is a "consumer." Once this is shown, the accused business must prove that consumer protection laws do not apply or establishing an exception or exemption.

3. WHO IS LIABLE UNDER CONSUMER PROTECTION STATUTES?

In general, defendants in a consumer protection lawsuit are (1) persons or businesses (2) who regularly engage in (3) the type of transaction that resulted in the injury to the consumer.

4. WHEN IS THERE LIABILITY UNDER CONSUMER PROTECTION STATUTES?

GENERAL RULES. ► Consumer protection laws typically require some fault, i.e., commission of a prohibited act or omission. ► Intent is not required in that fault can be established by showing reckless or indifferent conduct.

LIMITATION.   Consumer protection does not protect consumers who are unreasonably careless in conducting business, such as consumers who sign contracts without reading or understanding them.

STUDY HINT.   Deceptive advertising is an act that is prohibited by consumer protection statutes that provide remedies for consumers who were deceived or misled by the ads.

5. WHAT REMEDIES DO CONSUMERS HAVE?

GENERAL RULES. ► Depending on the state, consumer laws may be enforced by: (1) the FTC that monitors compliance with federal consumer trade laws; (2) a state attorney general who may file an action on behalf of consumers; or (3) in many cases, individual consumers. ► Some statutes require a refund for or replacement of defective goods that cannot be repaired in a reasonable time. Other statutes void a consumer contract that violates the statute.

LIMITATION.   Some statutes require consumers to first give a defendant notice before suing.

STUDY HINTS.   ► Consumer laws often provide special remedies so that it is financially feasible for consumers to pursue their rights in court. ► In order to make help consumers enforce their rights, consumer laws often provide alternative dispute mechanisms for determining the parties' rights.

LEARNING OUTCOME EXAMPLES: See Ethics & the Law on textbook p. 754; see the *Commonwealth v Welch* case on textbook p. 753.

6. WHAT ARE THE CIVIL AND CRIMINAL PENALTIES UNDER CONSUMER PROTECTION STATUTES?

GENERAL RULE.   General laws, consumer protection statutes, and deceptive trade practices laws may subject a seller or lender to civil and/or criminal penalties for wrongful consumer practices.

STUDY HINT.   Consumers who sue for violation of consumer protection statutes typically may recover compensatory damages to make up for their actual loss and, under certain laws, also punitive damages.

B. AREAS OF CONSUMER PROTECTION

7. ADVERTISING

GENERAL RULES. ► Laws commonly forbid deceptive advertising, and these laws are liberally (broadly) interpreted. ► The Federal Trade Commission (FTC) can issue orders forbidding deceptive ads, and it may require retractive advertising to correct false or deceptive statements. **STUDY HINT.** False advertising laws are intended to prevent misleading (deceptive) ads even if an advertiser is not acting fraudulently. Thus, good faith and lack of intent to deceive are not defenses.

8. LABELING

Exaggerated terms and misleading labels are prohibited by consumer protection regulations.

9. SELLING METHODS

➤ *Home-solicited sales*: ► A sale of goods or services for $25 or more that is made at a buyer's home can be set aside within three business days after the sale. ► There is no requirement that goods are defective or that a seller acted improperly in order to set aside a contract.

➤ *Referral sales*: UCCC forbids reducing a price because a buyer referred customers to the seller.

➤ *Telemarketing fraud*: ► FTC regulations limit the time of telemarketing calls, require a statement of what telemarketers are selling, and prohibit access to bank accounts without authorization. ► Among other things, the federal Telephone Consumer Protection Act generally makes it unlawful for telemarketers to make calls using automatic telephone dialing systems or artificial or prerecorded voices, to use any telephone fax, computer, or other device to send unsolicited ads, or to make calls before 8:00 AM or after 9 PM. ► There are additional state regulations on telephonic marketing. ► The FTC has established a National Do Not Call Registry whereby consumers can permanently register to not be called as part of telephone solicitation campaigns by merchants and service providers. When a consumer registers with the do-not-call list, merchants and service providers cannot contact the consumer by telephone unless the company has done business with the consumer before or the consumer has voluntarily given the company his or her telephone number. Charities are exempt from the rule.

10. THE CONSUMER CONTRACT

➤ *Form of contract*: Contracts must: (1) itemize payments; (2) clearly state finance charges; (3) be printed in a certain type size; and (4) be given to the buyer.

➤ *Contracts printed on two sides*: If a consumer contract is printed on both sides of a page, each side must warn a consumer to read the opposite side, and the consumer must sign the backside of each page.

➤ *Particular sales and leases (Motor Vehicle Information and Cost Savings Act)*: ► This Act requires an automobile dealer to disclose to the buyer various elements in the cost of an automobile. ► A car buyer who is harmed when a dealer fails to disclose that an odometer has been reset can recover the greater of three times the actual loss, or $1,500. ► A seller is liable if he or she knew or should have known an odometer is wrong.

> *Contract terms*: ► The UCCC forbids terms that allow a judgment to be entered against a debtor without giving the debtor a chance to make a defense. ► Some states forbid acceleration clauses that make an entire debt due if a debtor fails to make a payment. ► The federal Warranty Disclosure Act establishes disclosure standards for warranties for consumer goods.

> *Limitations on credit*: ► Laws commonly forbid open-end home mortgages that secure a present debt plus future debts, and terms granting a security interest in all household goods of a debtor. ► A subprime loan is one typically made to high-risk borrowers. Subprime loans sometimes involve predatory lending practices and are subject to increasing federal and state regulation.

> *Unconscionability*: Charging excessive prices for goods sold on credit, and price gouging in abnormal market situations (i.e., high demand-low supply situations) may be unconscionable.

11. CREDIT DISCLOSURES

> *Disclosure of transaction terms*: ► Federal law requires a lender to disclose all (1) interest charges and (2) points or fees for making a loan. ► If a seller advertises that he or she will sell or lease on credit, a seller must disclose: (1) total cash price; (2) down payment required; (3) number, amount, and due dates of payments; and (4) annual percentage rate of credit costs (APR).

> *More-than-four-installments rule*: ► The Truth in Lending Act applies to any consumer contract that is payable in more than four installments, whether a finance charge is expressly stated or not. ► If such a consumer contract does not expressly impose a finance charge, this Act requires that the contract "clearly and conspicuously" state that "the cost of credit is included in the price."

12. CREDIT CARDS

GENERAL RULES. ► Federal regulations forbid the unsolicited distribution of credit cards to persons who have not applied for them. ► The holder of a credit card may be liable for up to $50 of unauthorized use. ► Some laws prohibit sellers from adding any surcharge to the purchase price because the buyer uses a credit card instead of paying with cash or a check. ►Federal law significantly limits solicitation of credit card accounts from persons under the age of 21, charges for late payments, disclosure of information relating to credit card balance transfers.

LIMITATION. Unauthorized purchases by an authorized user (i.e., by someone who is permitted to use a credit card) are deemed authorized use, and the cardholder is liable for all such charges.

LEARNING OUTCOME EXAMPLES: See the discussion of the CARD Act on textbook p. 748; see E-Commerce & Cyberlaw on textbook p. 749.

13. GIFT CARDS

The federal CARD Act now regulates various disadvantageous practices of credit card issuers that acted to the detriment of the card holders, such as fees that may cause the value of a gift card to decline over time.

14. PAYMENTS

Generally, payments on an open charge account must be applied to the earliest (oldest) charges.

15. PRESERVATION OF CONSUMER DEFENSES

FTC regulations require consumer contracts to include a clause that allows a consumer to assert against a third party (an assignee) any defenses that would have been available against the seller.

16. PRODUCT SAFETY

GENERAL RULE. The Consumer Product Safety Act: (1) sets product safety standards; (2) establishes civil and criminal penalties; and (3) authorizes suits for damages and injunctions against violators.
STUDY HINT. Tampering with consumer products is a federal crime.

17. CREDIT, COLLECTION, AND BILLING METHODS

> *Equal Credit Opportunity Act: Credit discrimination*: Under the Equal Credit Opportunity Act, it is illegal to discriminate against an applicant for credit because of race, color, religion, national origin, marital status, sex, age, or because all or a part of the applicant's income is derived from public assistance.

> *Fair Credit Billing Act: Correction of errors*: A creditor or credit card issuer must investigate and respond in writing to written complaints by consumers regarding alleged credit card errors.

> *Improper collection methods*: ► The Fair Debt Collection Practices Act generally forbids unreasonable debt collection practices. This Act only applies to parties who engage in the business of collecting debts for others, such as collection agencies. ► Prohibited acts may include: (1) notifying an employer that an employee is delinquent on a debt; (2) sending bills that appear to be legal process; and (3) sending delinquency notices in a manner easily seen by others.

> *Consumer leases*: Some states give consumer leases the same protection as consumer credit sales.

18. PROTECTION OF CREDIT STANDING AND REPUTATION

> *Scope of law*: ► The Fair Credit Reporting Act (FCRA) regulates "consumer credit" transactions.
> ► The FCRA does not apply to credit given for business purposes. ► It is a crime to obtain or furnish a report for an improper purpose.

> *Privacy*: Credit bureaus must: (1) inform a person who is being investigated of the right to learn the results of the investigation; and (2) on request, state to whom credit reports were given.

> *Protection from false information*: ▶ On request, a credit bureau must disclose to a party certain data in the party's file. ▶ Disputed information must be verified within a reasonable time. ▶ Most legal actions cannot be reported after seven years, and bankruptcies cannot be reported after ten years.

> *LEARNING OUTCOME EXAMPLE*: See the *Phillips v Grendahl* case on textbook p. 756.

18. OTHER CONSUMER PROTECTIONS

> *Real estate development sales*: Sellers of subdivided land may have to file a development statement with HUD and provide a property report to prospective buyers or tenants.

> *Service contracts*: A consumer service contract is subject to UCCC regulations if it is (1) for $25,000 or less and (2) a credit charge is imposed or the contract is paid in installments.

> *Franchises*: Prospective buyers of franchises must be given a detailed disclosure statement.

> *Automobile lemon laws*: All states have lemon laws to protect consumers who buy defective cars.

CONCEPT REVIEW AND APPLICATIONS

Matching Exercise

Select the term or phrase that best matches a definition or statement stated below. Each term or phrase is the best match for only one statement or definition. Not all terms and phrases will necessarily be used.

compensatory damages   franchisors

consumer   hearsay evidence

consumer credit   predatory lending

development statement   property report

franchise   punitive damages

franchisees   subprime lending market

_____ 1. Any buyer afforded special protections by statute or regulation.

_____ 2. Credit that is extended to a person for his or her personal, family, or household uses.

_____ 3. A practice on the part of the subprime lending market whereby lenders take advantage of less sophisticated consumers or those who are desperate for funds by using the lenders' superior bargaining positions to obtain credit terms that go well beyond compensating them for their risk.

_____ 4.   Sum of money that will compensate an injured plaintiff for his or her actual loss.

_____ 5.   A credit market that makes loans to high-risk consumers, such as those who have bankruptcies, no credit history, or a poor credit history.

_____ 6.   In a business context, the right granted by contract or governmental award, to engage in a particular activity or to operate a particular business within a particular geographic area or for a particular number of years.

_____ 7.   Damages, in excess of those required to compensate the plaintiff for the wrong done, that are imposed to punish the defendant because of the particularly wanton or willful character of wrongdoing.

_____ 8.   Condensed version of a property development statement filed with the secretary of HUD and given to a prospective customer at least 48 hours before signing a contract to buy or lease property.

True/False

Write **T** if the statement is true, write **F** if it is false.

_____ 1.   In many states, consumer protection laws protect individual consumers and also certain businesses or governments that purchase goods or services.

_____ 2.   The defendant in a consumer protection lawsuit is usually a party who regularly sells goods or services of the kind involved in the lawsuit.

_____ 3.   Consumer laws do not typically allow a consumer to rescind a contract merely because the consumer misunderstood the contract due to the consumer's negligent failure to read the contract.

_____ 4.   In general, a seller cannot enforce a consumer's obligation if the seller failed to disclose information that was required to be disclosed by consumer protection laws.

_____ 5.   In general, a seller violates deceptive advertising laws only if the seller acts in bad faith or with the intent to deceive consumers.

_____ 6.   A merchant who sells a product with a "seal of approval" may be liable for breach of a guarantee if the product has not in fact been approved by the indicated party.

_____ 7.   A car dealer who sells a car without disclosing that the odometer has been reset violates the Motor Vehicle Information and Cost Savings Act if the seller knows or should know that the odometer was reset.

_____ 8. Federal law does not regulate the disclosure of finance charges in consumer contracts.

_____ 9. It is unlawful to send credit cards to persons who have not applied for them.

_____ 10. Consumer protection laws generally require a creditor to apply payments on open charge accounts to the most recent charges.

Multiple Choice

_____ 1. Mark was delinquent in repaying a loan. The loan was turned over to Assured Collections. Assured sent letters to Mark that appeared to be court orders to pay. It also sent collection letters to Mark's work in envelopes marked "Final Demand for Delinquent Payment," and Assured told Mark's employer of the delinquent loan. Mark's employer concluded Mark was untrustworthy and fired him. In all likelihood, did Assured violate the Fair Debt Collection Practices Act?
   a. No. The Act does not apply to parties who engage in the business of collecting debts for others.
   b. No. The Act does not apply if a debtor is in fact delinquent on an obligation.
   c. No. The Act only applies to collection of business obligations.
   d. Yes.

_____ 2. Nutri-Shop, a health-food store, purchased and offered for sale multi-grain muffins from a new supplier. Nutri-Shop believed that the muffins contained no fat, and it added a "Fat-Free" label to the muffins. It was later determined that each muffin contained 16 grams of fat, and a customer brought suit against Nutri-Shop for misleading labeling. This was the only time Nutri-Shop had been charged with misleading labeling. Under these facts:
   a. Nutri-Shop will probably be held liable for misleading labeling.
   b. Nutri-Shop cannot be held liable because this was a one-time violation, not a pattern of illegal conduct.
   c. Nutri-Shop cannot be held liable because it did not intend to violate the law.
   d. Nutri-Shop has the burden of proving that the person who brought suit is not a consumer under the consumer protection statute under which the charges were brought.

_____ 3. Which of the following is _not_ a remedy under consumer protection legislation?
   a. Refund of the purchase price if defective goods cannot be repaired within a reasonable time.
   b. Voiding a contract so that the consumer can keep the goods without making further payment after the seller violates the statute.
   c. A lawsuit brought by the state attorney general on behalf of injured consumers.
   d. All of the above may be remedies under consumer protection laws.

_____ 4. Hope's Department Store planned its 4th of July advertising brochure and sent it to the printer the second week of June. The brochure was sent to customers the third week of June, and the prices in the ad were to be good July 2-5. One of the featured items was a 3-speed oscillating fan that came in a variety of colors. The regular price of the fan was $29.95 and the sale price was $24.95. On June 10, the inventory of this particular fan was fifty units, but because of unusually hot weather during June, all of Hope's inventory of this 3-speed oscillating fan was sold by July 1. Under these facts:

    a. Hope could not be liable for false advertising because at the time the advertising brochure was
       planned and printed, Hope had the 3-speed oscillating fans in stock.
    b. Hope could not be liable for false advertising because the demand for the fan prior to sale was
       unusually high and Hope could not have known its inventory would be depleted prior to the sale.
    c. Hope is liable for false advertising because the 3-speed fan it advertised at a reduced price was out of stock at the time the sale was to begin.
    d. Hope could not be liable for false advertising because statutes prohibiting false advertising are
       strictly interpreted.

_____ 5. Kay applied for a personal loan from Last Bank. Last Bank requested a credit report from R&R Credit Bureau. R&R conducted an investigation of Kay in order to prepare an investigative consumer report. R&R discovered that Kay had received a discharge in bankruptcy seven years previously, and that six months ago a neighbor stated that Kay was unemployed. In this case:

    a. R&R cannot report the bankruptcy to Last Bank.
    b. R&R cannot report the neighbor's statement to Last Bank without verifying its accuracy.
    c. R&R does not have to inform Kay that she is entitled to discover the results of R&R's investigation of her.
    d. R&R does not have to disclose any information to Kay regarding anything in its files on her.

_____ 6. Swift's advertised a Model 3446 Sony television for 12 monthly payments of $200 each. No finance charges were expressly stated. Under these facts:

    a. The Truth in Lending Act will govern this consumer sale.
    b. The Truth in Lending Act will not govern this sale because payment is to be made in more than four installments.
    c. The Truth in Lending Act will not govern this sale because there is no finance charge expressly imposed.
    d. There are no statutory requirements as to what statements must be made in the advertisement.

_____ 7. Sonya contracted to buy storm windows for her home for $2,000. The contract was negotiated and signed at her home. The next day, Sonya decided she could not afford the windows. What are Sonya's options under federal law?

a. Sonya can rescind (set aside) the sale within three days after signing the contract.

b. Sonya can rescind the sale only if the seller was guilty of misconduct.

c. Sonya can rescind the sale only if she can prove the windows are defective.

d. Sonya cannot rescind the sale once the contract is signed.

_____ 8. A Federal Trade Commission regulation designed to stop telemarketing fraud:

a. Allows access to consumers' bank accounts as long as the telemarketer states truthfully what he or she is selling.

b. Subjects telemarketers to fines if they continue to call persons who have asked not to be called.

c. Subjects telemarketers to fines if they call consumers before 9 a.m. or after 8 p.m.

d. Subjects telemarketers to fines if they do not identify themselves, the company they represent,

and the type and price of product or service they are selling.

_____ 9. Ace Siding Company is preparing a contract to sell Anita new siding for her home. Ace is selling the siding to Anita on credit for $10,000. Under these facts:

a. Under FTC rules, the contract must contain a clause stating that an assignee of the contract will be subject to any defenses that Anita could have asserted against Ace.

b. In many states, Ace cannot take an open-end mortgage that will secure payment of the contract price for the siding and payment of any future debts that Anita may owe Ace.

c. In some states, the contract cannot contain an acceleration clause that would make the entire debt due if Anita fails to make a monthly payment.

d. All of the above.

_____ 10. Jake authorized his girlfriend Jolene to use his credit card in order to buy a birthday gift for Jake's mother. Without his permission, Jolene also used the card to buy an $800 leather coat for herself. Jake refused to pay the credit charge for the coat since Jolene was not authorized to use his card for that purpose. Under these facts:

a. Jake is required to pay for only $50 of the unauthorized charge for the coat.

b. Jake is required to pay for only $500 of the unauthorized charge for the coat.

c. Jake must pay the entire $800 charge for the coat.

d. Jake is not required to pay for any portion of the charge for the coat.

Case Problem

Answer the following problem, briefly explaining your answer.

Farr RV Sales Co. plans to advertise for sale and sell a consumer recreational vehicle. The vehicle will be sold on credit for $24,000, payable in 48 monthly installments. The buyer will be required to pay a down payment and to pay interest on the unpaid portion of the purchase price. Farr intends to use a form of contract that is printed on both sides of a sheet of paper.

1. What federal law generally regulates the disclosure of finance terms in this case?
2. What financial terms must Farr disclose to the buyer?

_____

_____

_____

_____

Internet Exercise

Carla is 50 years old and married, but she is the sole supporter of herself and three minor children. Carla works part-time and earns $500 monthly. She also receives $800 monthly in federal public assistance funds. Carla wants to buy a used car, thereby enabling her to obtain full-time employment. Carla applied for a car loan from Ace Loans, but was refused. Ace turned down the loan because Carla: (1) is over 40; (2) is married; and (3) has inadequate income because Ace refused to count her public assistance as income.

Carla has asked you to use the Internet to answer the following questions:

1. What federal law generally regulates the granting of credit in this case?
2. Is there a federal publication that summarizes federal laws relating to the extension of consumer credit? If so, identify the web site where this publication is located.
3. Did Ace Loans violate federal law in considering the three criteria above? Explain.

_____

_____

_____

_____

CHAPTER 34
SECURED TRANSACTIONS IN PERSONAL PROPERTY

MAKE THE CONNECTION

SUMMARY

A security interest is an interest in personal property or fixtures that secures payment or performance of an obligation. The property that is subject to the interest is called the *collateral,* and the party holding the interest is called the *secured party. Attachment* is the creation of a security interest. To secure protection against third parties' claims to the collateral, the secured party must perfect the security interest. *Tangible collateral* is divided into classes: consumer goods, equipment, inventory, general intangibles, farm products, and fixtures. Under Revised Article 9, intangibles have been expanded to include bank accounts, checks, notes, and health care insurance receivables.

Perfection of a security interest is not required for its validity, but it does provide the creditor certain superior rights and priorities over other types of creditors and creditors with an interest in the same collateral. Perfection can be obtained through possession, filing, automatically (as in the case of a PMSI in consumer goods), by control for accounts under Revised Article 9, or temporarily when statutory protections are provided for creditors for limited periods of time.

Priority among creditors is determined according to their status. Unperfected, unsecured creditors simply wait to see whether there will be sufficient assets remaining after priority creditors are paid. Secured creditors have the right to take the collateral on a priority basis. As between secured creditors, the first creditor's interest to attach takes priority in the event the creditors hold security interests in the same collateral. A perfected secured creditor takes priority over an unperfected secured creditor. Perfected secured creditors with interests in the same collateral take priority generally on a first-to-perfect basis. Exceptions include PMSI inventory creditors who file a financing statement before delivery and notify all existing creditors, and equipment creditors who perfect within 20 days of attachment of their interests.

A buyer in the ordinary course of business always takes priority, even over perfected secured creditors who have knowledge of the creditor's interest. A buyer not in the ordinary course of business loses out to a perfected secured creditor but extinguishes the rights of a secured creditor unless the buyer had knowledge of the security interest. A buyer from a consumer debtor takes free and clear of the debtor's creditor's perfected security interest unless the creditor has filed a financing statement and perfected beyond just the automatic PMSI consumer goods perfection.

Upon default, a secured party may repossess the collateral from the buyer if this can be done without a breach of the peace. If a breach of the peace could occur, the secured party must use court action to regain the collateral. If the buyer has paid 60 percent or more of the cash price of the consumer goods, the seller must resell them within 90 days after repossession unless the buyer, after default, has waived this right in writing. Notice to the debtor of the sale of the collateral is usually required. A debtor may redeem the collateral prior to the time the secured party disposes of it or contracts to resell it.

LEARNING OUTCOMES
After studying this chapter, you should be able to

A. CREATION OF SECURED TRANSACTIONS
LO.1   Explain the requirements for creating a valid security interest

LO.2   List the major types of collateral

B. PERFECTION OF SECURED TRANSACTIONS
LO.3 Define perfection and explain its significance in secured transactions

C. RIGHTS OF PARTIES BEFORE DEFAULT

D. PRIORITIES
LO.4 Discuss the priorities of parties with conflicting interests in collateral when default occurs

E. RIGHTS OF PARTIES AFTER DEFAULT
LO.5 State the rights of the parties on the debtor's default

CHAPTER OUTLINE

A. CREATION OF SECURED TRANSACTIONS

1. DEFINITIONS

▶ A secured transaction is created when a buyer or borrower (debtor) grants a seller or lender (creditor or secured party) a security interest in personal property (collateral). ▶ A security interest allows a creditor to repossess and sell collateral if a debtor fails to pay a secured debt. ▶ The seller or lender is a creditor and does not own the collateral, whereas the buyer or debtor generally does.

2. CREATION OF A SECURITY INTEREST (ATTACHMENT)

GENERAL RULE. A security interest is created ("attaches") when the following requirements are met: (1) there is a security agreement; (2) creditor has given value (lent money to debtor or sold goods to debtor on credit); and (3) debtor has rights in the collateral (debtor owns or leases the collateral).
LIMITATION. Security agreements must be written unless creditors have possession of collateral.
STUDY HINTS. ▶ If the creditor has possession of the collateral, the security agreement may be oral regardless of the amount involved.▶ Field warehousing (discussed in Chapter 22) is possession that would permit an oral security agreement.
LEARNING OUTCOME EXAMPLE: See *ProGrowth Bank, Inc. v Wells Fargo Bank, N.A.* on textbook p. 773.

3. PURCHASE MONEY SECURITY INTEREST

A purchase money security interest: (1) secures payment of the unpaid price for the collateral; or (2) secures repayment of a loan that was both used to buy the collateral.

4. THE NATURE AND CLASSIFICATION OF COLLATERAL

GENERAL RULES. ▶ *Consumer goods*: goods bought for personal, household, or family use. ▶ *Equipment*: goods bought for use in business. ▶ *Inventory*: goods bought for sale or lease; raw materials; work in process; and business supplies. ▶ *Farm products*: crops, livestock, and supplies produced or used in a farming operation. ▶ *Fixtures*: personal property that becomes part of real estate. ▶ "Electronic chattel paper" is a record of a party's right to money or property which is stored in an electronic format. Example: Joe's right to funds in his eBay account.

STUDY HINTS. ► A buyer's primary intended use determines how to collateral is classified. ► A security interest can be granted in property that the debtor may obtain at a later date. This property is called after-acquired property, and the lien granted is called a floating lien. ► In general, a security interest automatically attaches to the proceeds from a sale of collateral. **LEARNING OUTCOME EXAMPLE:** See *In re Lull* on textbook p. 768.

B. PERFECTION OF SECURED TRANSACTIONS

► Once a security interest has been created, it is enforceable against the debtor. Perfection of the interest, however, is necessary for a creditor to gain priority to collateral over other creditors and third parties. ► LEARNING OUTCOME EXAMPLE: See E-Commerce & Cyberlaw, "Engines are from Mars; Priorities are from Financing Statements," textbook p. 774.

5. PERFECTION BY CREDITOR'S POSSESSION

A creditor may perfect a security interest in any tangible collateral by taking possession of it.

6. PERFECTION FOR CONSUMER GOODS

A purchase money security interest in consumer goods is automatically perfected upon attachment

7. PERFECTION FOR HEALTH CARE INSURANCE RECEIVABLES

A new type of collateral is health care insurance receivables. If a consumer gives a creditor a security interest in future health insurance proceeds, then perfection is automatic.

8. AUTOMATIC PERFECTION

A creditor has automatic perfection (i.e., needs to do nothing to perfect) in (1) software that is sold with a computer that is subject to the creditor's purchase money security interest (PMSI) and a PMSI in consumer goods.

9. TEMPORARY PERFECTION

Creditors generally have temporary perfection in collateral in the following situations: (1) four months temporary perfection when collateral is moved to another state; and (2) twenty days temporary perfection in negotiable instruments.

10. PERFECTION BY CONTROL

► Control is a form of possession under Article 9, and it occurs when a creditor is able to require the debtor account holder to clear all transactions in that account with them. The debtor cannot use the funds that have been pledged as collateral without permission from the party holding the control.
► Example: debtor pledges money in its bank account as collateral to the bank and the debtor cannot have access to such funds without the bank's permission.

11. PERFECTION FOR MOTOR VEHICLES

In most states, the only way to perfect a security interest in motor vehicles is by having the security interest properly recorded on the certificate of title.

12. PERFECTION BY FILING A FINANCING STATEMENT

GENERAL RULES. ▶ A financing statement is a written notice of a security interest. ▶ In general, security interests in all types of collateral (except noninventory motor vehicles) may be perfected by filing a financing statement centrally with the secretary of state. ▶ A secured party only must show that a filed document is both "authorized" and an "authenticated record." **LIMITATIONS.** ▶ States may require that filings for fixtures and other real property-related collateral be filed locally. ▶ A financing statement does not give rise to perfection if it is filed in the wrong place, is substantially misleading, or is not authorized by the debtor.

13. LOSS OF PERFECTION

(a) *Possession of collateral*: Perfection by possession is lost if creditor returns collateral to debtor.

(b) *Consumer goods*: Perfection that is automatically obtained in consumer goods is lost by resale of the goods to a subsequent buyer who bought it: (1) without knowledge of the interest; (2) for value; and (3) for personal, family, or household use. a consumer.

(c) *Lapse of time*: Perfection obtained by filing a financing statement expires after five years unless a continuation statement is filed within six months prior to the expiration of a current statement.

(d) *Removal from state*: In most cases, perfection is lost if collateral is removed to another state unless a creditor files a financing statement in the new state within four months after removal.

(e) *Motor vehicles*: Perfection is lost if a new title is issued and the lien is not stated on the title.

C. RIGHTS OF PARTIES BEFORE DEFAULT

14. STATEMENT OF ACCOUNT

A debtor may request a creditor to approve (or correct) a written statement of the debtor's account.

15. TERMINATION STATEMENTS

When the debt is paid, a debtor can request a creditor to furnish a termination statement.

16. CORRECTION STATEMENTS

▶ Debtors may protest a filed financing statement by filing their own correction statement. ▶ A correction statement does not invalidate the financing statement, but it does give public notice of a dispute. ▶ A debtor may file a correction statement if a creditor fails to give a termination statement.

D. PRIORITIES

17. UNSECURED PARTY VERSUS UNSECURED PARTY

▶ Unsecured creditors do not have a right to repossess a debtor's property even when the debtor fails to pay. ▶ Unsecured creditors share equally in remaining assets if a debtor files for bankruptcy.

18. SECURED PARTY VERSUS UNSECURED PARTY

► A secured creditor has the right to repossess a collateral if a debtor fails to pay a secured debt.
► A secured creditor has priority to the collateral over the debtor and unsecured creditors.
► LEARNING OUTCOME EXAMPLE: See *General Motors Acceptance Corp. v Lincoln* on textbook p. 777.

19. SECURED PARTY VERSUS SECURED PARTY

The first unperfected security interest to attach to collateral has priority to collateral over the debtor, unsecured creditors, and later unperfected security interests in the same collateral.

20. PERFECTED SECURED PARTY VERSUS SECURED PARTY

A perfected security interest has priority over both prior and later unperfected security interests.

21. PERFECTED SECURED PARTY VERSUS PERFECTED SECURED PARTY

GENERAL RULE. In general, the first secured party to file a financing statement or otherwise perfect their security interest in collateral has priority to the collateral over all others.
LIMITATIONS. The following are three major exceptions to the above general rule:

➢ *Perfected purchase money security interest in inventory*: A purchase money security interest in inventory has priority over a prior, perfected security interest in the same inventory if: (1) the security interest is perfected when the debtor receives the collateral; and (2) proper notice, if required, is given to parties who hold conflicting security interests.
➢ *Perfected purchase money security interest - noninventory collateral*: A purchase money security interest in collateral other than inventory has priority over a prior, perfected security interest in the same collateral if the security interest is perfected within 20 days after the debtor receives the collateral.
➢ *Status of repair or storage lien*: One who repairs or stores goods has a lien on the goods to secure payment. This lien wins over a perfected security interest in the goods unless the lien is created by a statute that states otherwise.

22. SECURED PARTY VERSUS BUYER OF COLLATERAL FROM DEBTOR

➢ *Unperfected security interest*: Buyer of collateral takes it subject to a prior unperfected security interest unless the buyer (1) paid value and (2) the buyer did not know of the security interest.
➢ *Perfected security interest*: Buyer of collateral takes it subject to prior perfected interest unless a creditor consents to sale or buyer bought inventory from debtor in ordinary course of business.
➢ *Automatically perfected security interest* in consumer goods may lose to later consumer who purchases such goods (see §13(b) above).

E. RIGHTS OF PARTIES AFTER DEFAULT

23. CREDITOR'S POSSESSION AND DISPOSITION OF COLLATERAL

> *Repossession*: ▶ On a debtor's default a creditor can use self-help to repossess collateral. A court order is not needed unless repossession cannot be done without committing a breach of the peace. ▶ LEARNING OUTCOME EXAMPLEs: See *Chrysler Credit v Koontz* on textbook p. 782; see Thinking Things Through, "Breaking, Entering, and Dragging to Repossess," textbook p. 783; see Ethics & the Law, "Women, Children, and the Repo Guys," textbook p. 784.

> *Disposition of collateral*: ▶ Creditor may sell or lease collateral to obtain payment. ▶ Collateral may be sold at private or public sale; time and terms of sale must be commercially reasonable.

24. CREDITOR'S RETENTION OF COLLATERAL

With two exceptions, a creditor can keep collateral as payment in full of a secured debt.

25. DEBTOR'S RIGHT OF REDEMPTION

Debtor may redeem (recover) collateral at any time before a creditor has disposed of or contracted to sell the collateral. To redeem, debtor must pay the entire debt, plus any legal costs or expenses.

26. DISPOSITION OF COLLATERAL

With a few exceptions, reasonable notice of sale (which may be oral) must be given to a debtor.

27. POSTDISPOSITION ACCOUNTING

▶ Proceeds from disposition of collateral are applied in this order: (1) expenses of disposing of collateral; (2) payment of the secured debt owed to the creditor; and (3) payment of debts owed to other parties with security interests in the collateral. ▶ A debtor is liable for any unpaid deficiency.

CONCEPT REVIEW AND APPLICATIONS

Matching Exercise

Select the term or phrase that best matches a definition or statement stated below. Each term or phrase is the best match for only one statement or definition. Not all terms and phrases will necessarily be used.

after-acquired goods
automatic perfection
breach of the peace
collateral
consumer good
creditor
debtor
field warehousing
financing statement
first-in-time provision
first-to-perfect basis
floating lien

perfected security interest
pro rata
purchase money security interest (PMSI)
secured party
secured transaction
security agreement
security interest
self-help repossession
temporary perfection
termination statement
value

_____ 1. Security interest that attaches to after-acquired goods of a debtor.

_____ 2. Security interest that gives a creditor priority to collateral over most creditors who subsequently acquire a security interest in the collateral or buyers who subsequently purchase the collateral.

_____ 3. Good that is used or bought primarily for personal, family, or household purposes.

_____ 4. Property that is subject to a security interest.

_____ 5. Document that is filed with an appropriate government office, thereby giving third parties notice of a security interest and perfecting a security interest in many kinds of collateral.

_____ 6. Agreement signed by debtor that grants a secured party a security interest in described collateral.

_____ 7. Security interest that secures repayment of either the unpaid purchase price for collateral or a loan that was used to purchase the collateral.

_____ 8. Statement filed to give notice of payment of a secured debt and termination of a security interest.

True/False

Write **T** if the statement is true, write **F** if it is false.

_____ 1. Article 9 of the UCC governs secured transactions in personal property.

_____ 2. A security agreement may be oral if the secured party retains possession of the collateral.

_____ 3. Collateral is classified according to the debtor's primary intended use of the collateral.

_____ 4. Only creditors with a perfected security interest can repossess collateral upon a debtor's default.

_____ 5. In general, a perfected security interest gives a secured party a superior right to collateral over most subsequent security interests in the collateral and most buyers of the collateral.

_____ 6. If a security interest is perfected in one state and the collateral is then moved to another state, nothing is required to be filed in the second state to continue perfection of the security interest.

_____ 7. In most states, if a title is issued for a motor vehicle, a creditor can perfect a security interest in motor vehicles only by filing a financing statement.

_____ 8. Article 9 prohibits a creditor from taking a floating lien in after-acquired inventory.

_____ 9. A financing statement must be signed by a debtor, but it need not describe the collateral.

_____10. If a financing statement is filed in the wrong office, it does not perfect a security interest.

Multiple Choice

_____ 1. IKR Finance loaned $1,000 to Debtor. Debtor agreed to repay the $1,000 in one year, and Debtor signed a written security agreement granting IKR a security interest in an item of equipment owned by Debtor to secure this debt. IKR did not perfect the security interest. In this case:
   a. The security interest is attached. If Debtor defaults, IKR can repossess and sell the collateral.
   b. The security interest has not attached because IKR does not have possession of the collateral.
   c. The security interest has not attached because IKR did not give value.
   d. The security interest has not attached because IKR failed to perfect the security interest.

_____ 2. Select the collateral that is consumer goods:
   a. Debtor grants a security interest in an oven Debtor intends to use in Debtor's restaurant.
   b. Debtor grants a security interest in a stereo that Debtor intends to sell in Debtor's store.
   c. Debtor grants a security interest in a table saw that Debtor intends to use at home.
   d. Debtor grants a security interest in Debtor's corn crop that is growing on Debtor's farm.

_____ 3. Spokes Inc. sold a bike to Dee on credit for Dee's personal use. Dee granted Spokes a security interest in the bike to secure payment of the unpaid purchase price. Spokes did not file a financing statement. Under these facts:
   a. Spokes' security interest in the bike is perfected.
   b. If Dee sells the bike to Phil for his personal use, Phil pays value, and Phil does not know of the security interest, then Phil will take the bike free from Spokes' security interest.
   c. If a repair shop obtains a lien on the bike for unpaid repair charges, Spokes' security interest will have priority over the common law lien.
   d. a and b.

_____ 4. Leo lent $10,000 to B&B, a tire dealer. B&B signed a security agreement granting Leo a security interest in B&B's existing tire inventory. Leo did nothing to perfect this security interest, and B&B kept possession of the inventory. Under these facts:
   a. Leo's security interest is perfected; a security interest in inventory is automatically perfected.
   b. Leo's security interest is unperfected; Leo cannot repossess the inventory if B&B defaults.
   c. Leo's security interest is unperfected; Leo's security interest has priority over a subsequent unperfected security interest that another creditor may take in the inventory.
   d. Leo's security interest is unperfected; Leo's security interest has priority over a subsequent perfected security interest that another creditor may take in the inventory.

_____ 5. On May 1, First Bank perfected a security interest in Debtor's inventory. On June 1, Bob bought an item of the secured inventory from Debtor for cash in the ordinary course of business. On July 1, Second Bank acquired a perfected security interest in Debtor's same inventory. In this case:
   a. Bob took the item of inventory subject to First Bank's security interest.
   b. First Bank has a security interest in the proceeds received from the sale of inventory to Bob.
   c. First Bank's security interest has priority over Second Bank's security interest.
   d. b and c.

Case Problem

Answer the following problem, briefly explaining your answer.
Acme Loans has a perfected security interest in Debtor's inventory to secure repayment of a $50,000 loan. Debtor has defaulted on three $1,000 monthly payments, and Acme has accelerated the entire debt.
1. Can Acme repossess the inventory without obtaining a court order to do so?
2. Can Acme commit a breach of the peace if necessary to repossess the inventory?
3. Can Debtor redeem the collateral?
4. How are proceeds from the sale to be applied? Would Debtor be liable for any deficiency?

_____

_____

_____

Internet Exercise

Time to go shopping again, but beware of unknown secured parties!
1. Using the Internet, find and identify two products that are for sale; one new and one used.
2. If you purchased these items, would a party with a perfected security interest in each of these items have priority to these items and, therefore, have the right to retake them from you?

_____

_____

_____

_____

CPA REVIEW

The following questions were given on CPA examinations. The answers for these questions are the unofficial answers prepared by the American Institute of Certified Public Accountants, Inc. (AICPA). All material is reproduced with permission of the AICPA.

____ 1. Under the Secured Transactions Article of the UCC, which of the following requirements is necessary to have a security interest attach?

	Debtor has rights in the collateral	Proper filing of a security agreement	Value given by the creditor
a.	Yes	Yes	Yes
b.	Yes	Yes	No
c.	Yes	No	Yes
d.	No	Yes	Yes

____ 2. Under the Secured Transactions Article of the UCC, which of the following purchasers will own consumer goods free of a perfected security interest in the goods?
   a. A merchant who purchases the goods for resale.
   b. A merchant who purchases the goods for use in its business.
   c. A consumer who purchases the goods from a consumer purchaser who gave the security interest.
   d. A consumer who purchases the goods in the ordinary course of business.

_____ 3. Under the Secured Transactions Article of the UCC, what would be the order of priority for the following security interests in consumer goods?
I.   Financing agreement filed on April 1.
II. Possession of the collateral by a creditor on April 10.
III. Financing agreement perfected on April 15.

    a. I, II, III.
    b. II, I, III.
    c. II, III, I.
    d. III, II, I.

_____ 4. Under the Secured Transactions Article of the UCC, which of the following remedies is available to a secured creditor when a debtor fails to make a payment when due?

	Proceed against the collateral	Obtain a general judgment against the debtor
a.	Yes	Yes
b.	Yes	No
c.	No	Yes
d.	No	No

_____ 5. Roth and Dixon both claim a security interest in the same collateral. Roth's security interest attached on January 1, 1989, and was perfected by filing on March 1, 1989. Dixon's security interest attached on February 1, 1989, and was perfected on April 1, 1989, by taking possession of the collateral. Which statement is correct?
a. Roth's security interest has priority because Roth perfected before Dixon perfected.
b. Dixon's security interest has priority because Dixon' s interest attached before Roth' s interest was perfected.
c. Roth's security interest has priority because Roth' s security interest attached before Dixon' s security interest attached.
d. Dixon's security interest has priority because Dixon is in possession of the collateral.

_____ 6. Winslow Co., which is in the business of selling furniture, borrowed $60,000 from Pine Bank. Winslow executed a promissory note for that amount and used all of its accounts receivable as collateral for the loan. Winslow executed a security agreement that described the collateral. Winslow did not file a financing statement. Which of the following statements best describes this transaction?
a. Perfection of the security interest occurred even though Winslow did not file a financing statement.
b. Perfection of the security interest occurred by Pine having an interest in accounts receivable.
c. Attachment of the security interest did not occur because Winslow failed to file a financing statement.
d. Attachment of the security interest occurred when the loan was made and Winslow executed the security agreement.

___ 7. Drew bought a computer for personal use from Hale Corp. for $3,000. Drew paid $2,000 in cash and signed a security agreement for the balance. Hale properly filed the security agreement. Drew defaulted in paying the balance of the purchase price. Hale asked Drew to pay the balance. When Drew refused, Hale peacefully repossessed the computer. Under the UCC Secured Transactions Article, which of the following remedies will Hale have?

a. Obtain a deficiency judgment against Drew for the amount owed.
b. Sell the computer and retain any surplus over the amount owed.
c. Retain the computer over Drew's objection.
d. Sell the computer without notifying Drew.

CHAPTER 35
BANKRUPTCY

MAKE THE CONNECTION

SUMMARY

Jurisdiction over bankruptcy cases is in U.S. district courts, which may refer all cases and related proceedings to adjunct bankruptcy courts.

Three bankruptcy proceedings are available: liquidation (Chapter 7), reorganization (Chapter 11), and extended-time payment (Chapter 13). A liquidation proceeding under Chapter 7 may be either voluntary or involuntary. A *voluntary case* is commenced by the debtor's filing a petition with the bankruptcy court. A voluntary petition is subject to the means test to determine if the debtor meets the standard for declaring bankruptcy. An involuntary case is commenced by the creditors' filing a petition with the bankruptcy court. If there are 12 or more creditors, at least 3 whose unsecured claims total $13,475 or more must sign the involuntary petition. If there are fewer than 12 creditors, any creditor whose unsecured claim is at least $13,475 may sign the petition. If the debtor contests the bankruptcy petition, it must be shown that the debtor is not paying debts as they become due. Eligibility for Chapters 7 and 11 bankruptcy excludes railroads, municipalities, and Small Business Administration companies. Individual debtors are restricted on Chapter 7 and 11 filings by their ability to repay. If found to have the means to pay, they go into a Chapter 13 proceeding. Chapter 13 eligibility is limited to consumers with $336,900 in unsecured debt and $1,010,650 in secured debt.

An automatic stay prevents creditors from taking legal action against the debtor after a bankruptcy petition is filed. The trustee in bankruptcy is elected by the creditors and is the successor to, and acquires the rights of, the debtor. In certain cases, the trustee can avoid transfers of property to prevent creditors from satisfying their claims. Preferential transfers may be set aside. A transfer for a present consideration, such as a cash sale, is not a preference.

Bankruptcy law regulates the way creditors present their claims and how the debtor are exempt from the bankruptcy estate, such as a portion of the value of the debtor's home.

Secured claims are not affected by the debtor's bankruptcy. Unsecured claims are paid in the following order of priority:

1. Support or maintenance for a spouse, former spouse, or child.

2. Costs and expenses of administration of the bankruptcy case.

3. Claims arising in the ordinary course of a debtor's business or financial affairs after the commencement of the case but before the order of relief (involuntary).

4. Claims for wages, salaries, or commissions, including vacation, severance, or sick leave pay earned within 180 days before the filing of the petition or the date of cessation of the debtor's business, limited to $10,950 for each person.

5. Claims arising for contributions (up to $5,400) to employee benefit plans based on services rendered within 180 days before the filing of the petition or when the debtor ceased doing business.

6. Farm producers (up to $10,950) and fishers against debtors who operate grain storage facilities or fish produce storage or processing facilities, up to $5,400 per claim.

7. Claims by consumer creditors, not to exceed $2,425 for each claimant.

8. Certain taxes and penalties due government units, such as income and property taxes.

9. All other unsecured creditors.

10. Remainder (if any) to debtor.

The decree terminating bankruptcy proceedings is generally a discharge that releases the debtor from most debts. Certain debts, such as income taxes, student loans, loans obtained by use of a false financial statement, alimony, and debts not listed by the debtor, are not discharged.

Under Chapter 11 bankruptcy, individuals, partnerships, and corporations in business may be reorganized so that the business can continue to operate. A plan for reorganization must be approved by the court. Under a Chapter 13 bankruptcy proceeding, individual debtors with a regular income may adopt extended-time payment plans for the payment of debts. A plan for extended-time payment must also be confirmed by the court. Federal, state, and local law may not discriminate against anyone on the basis of a discharge in bankruptcy.

LEARNING OUTCOMES
After studying this chapter, you should be able to

A. BANKRUPTCY LAW

B. HOW BANKRUPTCY IS DECLARED
LO.1   List the requirements for the commencement of a voluntary bankruptcy case and an involuntary bankruptcy case

C. ADMINISTRATION OF THE BANKRUPTCY ESTATE
LO.2   Explain the procedure for the administration of a debtor's estate

D. DEBTOR'S DUTIES AND EXEMPTIONS
LO.3   List a debtor's duties and exemptions

E. DISCHARGE IN BANKRUPTCY
LO.4   Explain the significance of a discharge in bankruptcy

F. REORGANIZATION PLANS UNDER CHAPTER 11.

G. PAYMENT PLANS UNDER CHAPTER 13
LO.5   Explain when a business reorganization plan or an extended-time payment plan might be used

CHAPTER OUTLINE

A. BANKRUPTCY LAW

1.   THE FEDERAL LAW

▶ Bankruptcy law is based upon the Bankruptcy Reform Act, as amended by the Bankruptcy Abuse Prevention and Consumer Protection Act of 2005 (BAPCPA). ▶ Jurisdiction over bankruptcy matters is vested in the federal district courts, which refer bankruptcy matters to federal bankruptcy courts.

2. TYPES OF BANKRUPTCY PROCEEDINGS

➢ *Liquidation or Chapter 7 bankruptcy*: ► Under Chapter 7, all assets the debtor owned at the time of filing for bankruptcy (except for exempt assets) are liquidated and the proceeds distributed to creditors.► Subject to certain limitations for individuals, Chapter 7 bankruptcy is generally available to individuals, partnerships, and corporations, except farmers, railroads, savings and loans, small business investment firms, insurance companies, and municipalities.

➢ *Reorganization or Chapter 11 bankruptcy*: ► Any party who can file for Chapter 7 can file for Chapter 11 bankruptcy, except for railroads and stockbrokers. ► In a reorganization proceeding, a debtor is not liquidated. Instead, a debtor reorganizes its business and finances in order to become a viable business.

➢ *Consumer debt adjustment plans or Chapter 13 bankruptcy*: ► Chapter 13 is available to individuals who have a stable income, have unsecured debts less than $307,675 and secured debts less than $922,975. ► Debtors restructure their finances and develop a plan to pay off their creditors over time.

B. HOW BANKRUPTCY IS DECLARED

3. DECLARATION OF VOLUNTARY BANKRUPTCY

GENERAL RULES. ► A Chapter 7 bankruptcy is commenced by the filing of a petition in the bankruptcy court by the debtor. ► A husband and wife may file jointly for bankruptcy.
LIMITATIONS. ► If an individual debtor fails a certain "means" test, then the BAPCPA empowers a court either to dismiss the debtor's Chapter 7 petition or to convert it into a Chapter 11 or 13 proceeding. This means test determines the debtor's ability to pay his or her debts with the debtor's disposable income. ► The means test is comprised of two steps as follows:

Step 1: If the debtor's family earns less than the average income for a comparable family in the debtor's state then the debtor may file for Chapter 7 bankruptcy.

Step 2: If the debtor's family earns more than the average income for a comparable family in the debtor's state then the following formula determines whether the debtor may file for Chapter 7 bankruptcy:

(a) Compute the debtor's current monthly income less certain allowed monthly expenses (not including any payments for debts) ("disposable income").

(b) Multiply "disposable income" by 60 ("product").

(c) If the "product" is less than either (1) 25% of the debtor's nonpriority unsecured claims or $6,000, whichever is greater or (2) $10,000, then the debtor may file for Chapter 7 bankruptcy.

(d) If the debtor fails the test in (c) above, then the debtor's petition is presumed to be bankruptcy abuse and is subject to being dismissed or changed to a Chapter 11 or 13 proceeding.

LEARNING OUTCOME EXAMPLES: See the Ethics & the Law discussion of recording artists on textbook p. 797; see *In re Jass* on textbook p. 798.

4. DECLARATION OF INVOLUNTARY BANKRUPTCY

▶ Creditors may file a petition for bankruptcy against any debtor who could voluntarily file for Chapter 7 bankruptcy, with the exception of nonprofit corporations. ▶ If a debtor has 12 or more creditors, at least three creditors with unsecured claims totaling $13,475 or more must sign the involuntary bankruptcy petition. If there are fewer than 12 creditors (excluding employees and insiders), any creditor with an unsecured claim of $13,475 or more may sign.

5. AUTOMATIC STAY

▶ The filing of a voluntary or involuntary petition for bankruptcy gives rise to an automatic stay that prevents creditors from beginning or continuing any lawsuits or other legal action to collect debts, except for certain exceptions for child and family support. ▶ The stay continues until either: (1) the case is closed or dismissed; or (2) the debtor is discharged.

6. IF THE CREDITORS ARE WRONG: RIGHTS OF DEBTOR IN INVOLUNTARY BANKRUPTCY

A debtor may get damages, costs, and attorney fees if: (1) an involuntary case is dismissed other than by consent of the debtor and petitioning creditors; or (2) a creditor files a petition in bad faith.

C. ADMINISTRATION OF THE BANKRUPTCY ESTATE

7. THE ORDER OF RELIEF

The order of relief is a procedural step whereby the court takes jurisdiction of the bankruptcy matter.

8. LIST OF CREDITORS

▶ Debtors must file a list of creditors, and the creditors are then notified of an action. ▶ Debts not disclosed are not discharged in bankruptcy.

9. TRUSTEE IN BANKRUPTCY

▶ A trustee in bankruptcy is appointed by the court to manage the debtor's estate and the trustee assumes ownership of all assets of the estate. ▶ A trustee can set aside: (1) voidable transfers of property; (2) preferences and (3) statutory liens that became effective only on the filing of a petition in bankruptcy.

10. THE BANKRUPT'S ESTATE

A debtor's estate generally consists of: (1) the debtor's nonexempt property owned at the time of filing of the petition; (2) property inherited by a debtor within six months after filing for bankruptcy; and (3) any property recovered by the trustee by setting aside improper preferences (see § 11 below).

11. VOIDABLE PREFERENCES

GENERAL RULE. A trustee can set aside: (1) a debtor's transfer of property made within one year of filing that is done with an intent to defraud creditors, or that renders a debtor insolvent or unreasonably reduces a debtor's assets; (2) preferential payment of any past debt that is made by an insolvent debtor within ninety days prior to filing; and (3) preferential payment to an insider (relative, partner, director, or controlling person) that is made by an insolvent debtor within twelve months of filing.

LIMITATION. ▶ *Permitted transfers*: (1) transfers for present consideration (cash sales or purchases); (2) payments in the ordinary course of business and according to industry terms and practices (e.g., payment of current phone bill); and (3) child support or alimony. ▶ Nonconsumer debt payments of less than $5,475 made during the voidable preference period are exempt.

STUDY HINTS. ▶ If a transfer (payment) can be set aside, a trustee can recover property (money) from the transferee. ▶ A debtor is presumed to be insolvent within ninety days prior to filing for bankruptcy. ▶ Balance sheet test: insolvency means fair value of assets is less than liabilities.

12. PROOF OF CLAIM

A creditor must ordinarily file a proof of claim in order to recover from a debtor's bankruptcy estate. It must ordinarily be filed within 90 days after the first meeting of creditors.

13. PRIORITY OF CLAIMS

➢ *First*: Even though a debtor has filed for bankruptcy, secured creditors are eventually allowed to enforce their security interests in the debtor's property prior to payment of other creditors.

➢ *Second*: The remaining assets of the debtor are used to pay unsecured creditors according to the following priority: (1) Allowed claims for debts to a spouse or children that were obligations at the time of the petition; (2) costs and expenses of administration of the bankruptcy action; (3) ordinary business claims incurred after the case is begun and before a trustee is appointed; (4) a maximum of $10,950 per claim for wages or commissions owed to an employee and earned within 180 days of the bankruptcy filing or cessation of the debtor's business; (4) certain contributions up to $5,400 made to employee benefit plans for services rendered within 180 days prior to filing for bankruptcy or cessation of business; (5) certain funds owed to farmers and fishermen; (6) a maximum of $2,425 per claim for undelivered consumer goods or services; (7) allowed alimony and child support claims; and (8) certain federal and state income taxes and property taxes.

➢ *Third*: All claims that are not completely satisfied by the foregoing payments share pro rata in the remaining assets, if any, of the debtor.

D. DEBTOR'S DUTIES AND EXEMPTIONS

14. DEBTOR'S DUTIES

Debtors must file: (1) a list of creditors; (2) a schedule of assets and liabilities; and (3) a statement of financial affairs. Debtors must submit to examination under oath at the first meeting of creditors.

15. DEBTOR'S EXEMPTIONS

► In general, debtors can choose to keep that property which is exempted from creditors' claims by federal law or that property which is exempted by state law. ► Federal exemptions include one car, property used to earn a living, wedding rings, payments under a life insurance contract, and alimony and child support. ► BAPCPA generally requires an individual to have resided 730 days or longer in a particular state in order to use that state's law for determination of exempt property. It also generally limits a homestead exemption under state law to $136,875 unless the debtor acquired the interest more than 1215 days before the bankruptcy petition was filed.

16. DEBTOR'S PROTECTION AGAINST DISCRIMINATION

The government cannot discriminate against persons because they have previously been discharged in bankruptcy.

E. DISCHARGE IN BANKRUPTCY

17. DENIAL OF DISCHARGE

GENERAL RULES. ► A discharge is a court decree that releases a debtor from most debts that are not paid in a bankruptcy proceeding. ► A discharge will be denied if a debtor: (1) fraudulently transferred or concealed property within one year of filing a petition in bankruptcy; (2) failed to keep proper financial records; (3) made a false oath or account; (4) failed to satisfactorily explain a loss of assets; (5) refused to obey a court order or to testify after receiving immunity; (6) obtained a discharge within the past eight years; or (7) effectively waives a discharge.
LIMITATION. A debtor is not discharged from: (1) certain taxes; (2) student loans incurred within the past 7 years (unless payment causes undue hardship); (3) loans dishonestly obtained; (4) unscheduled debts; (5) debts arising from fraud, embezzlement, or larceny; (6) alimony or child support; (7) judgment for willful or malicious injury; (8) judgment for drunk driving; (9) debt to a single creditor for more than $5,550 for luxury goods or services if the debt is incurred within 90 days prior to filing; and (10) cash advances greater than $825 incurred using credits cards within 70 days prior to filing for bankruptcy.
LEARNING OUTCOME EXAMPLE: See *In re Looper* on textbook p. 811.

F. REORGANIZATION PLANS UNDER CHAPTER 11

18. CONTENTS OF THE PLAN

GENERAL RULES. A debtor submits a plan which specifies how creditors will be repaid. If confirmed by the court, the plan binds the debtor and all creditors.
LIMITATION. A plan must treat all creditors within the same class in the same manner.
STUDY HINTS. A plan may provide for assumption, rejection, or assignment of executory contracts.
LEARNING OUTCOME EXAMPLE: See Ethics & the Law, The Skies Are not So friendly on textbook p. 809.

19. CONFIRMATION OF THE PLAN

Typically, the court will confirm a plan if it is proposed in good faith and it is reasonable.

G. PAYMENT PLANS UNDER CHAPTER 13

20. CONTENTS OF THE PLAN

A plan must provide for payment in full of all priority claims.

21. CONFIRMATION OF THE PLAN

The court will confirm a plan if it is proposed in good faith and is in the creditors' best interest.

22. DISCHARGE OF THE DEBTOR

When all payments under a confirmed plan are completed, a debtor is discharged from liability for all debts that are dischargeable in a Chapter 7 liquidation proceeding.

CONCEPT REVIEW AND APPLICATIONS

Matching Exercise

Select the term or phrase that best matches a definition or statement stated below. Each term or phrase is the best match for only one statement or definition. Not all terms and phrases will necessarily be used.

automatic stay	claim	order of relief
balance sheet test	discharge in bankruptcy	preferences
bankruptcy courts	insiders	preferential transfers
bona fide	insolvency	proof of claim
Chapter 7 bankruptcy	involuntary bankruptcy	trustee in bankruptcy
Chapter 11 bankruptcy	liquidated	voluntary bankruptcy
Chapter 13 bankruptcy	means test	

_____ 1. Creditor's written statement that alleges a claim against a debtor and the basis for the claim.

_____ 2. Certain transfers of money or security interests in the time frame just prior to bankruptcy that can be set aside if voidable.

_____ 3. Relatives, business partners, directors, or controlling persons of an insolvent debtor.

_____ 4. Court decree that releases a debtor from unpaid debts upon conclusion of a bankruptcy action.

_____ 5. Bankruptcy proceeding that is commenced by the filing of a petition by a debtor.

_____ 6. Bankruptcy proceeding that is commenced by the filing of a petition by creditors against a debtor.

_____ 7. Automatic prohibition that prevents a creditor from starting or continuing any legal action to collect a debt after a petition for bankruptcy has been filed.

_____ 8. Improper transfers of property by a debtor to a creditor that allows the creditor to recover more than would be paid to the creditor pursuant to a bankruptcy liquidation.

_____ 9. Method to determine whether a debtor is solvent by comparing the fair value of a debtor's assets to the debtor's liabilities.

True/False

Write **T** if the statement is true, write **F** if it is false.

____ 1. Bankruptcy courts are state courts.

____ 2. A debtor cannot contest an involuntary bankruptcy petition that is filed by the debtor's creditors.

____ 3. A creditor whose unsecured claim is $5,000 or more can file an involuntary petition for a Chapter 7 bankruptcy against a debtor if the debtor has fewer than twelve creditors.

____ 4. An individual whose unsecured or secured debts exceed certain limits may not be entitled to file a petition for Chapter 13 bankruptcy.

____ 5. In a Chapter 7 bankruptcy, a trustee generally assumes ownership of all nonexempt property belonging to the debtor at the time of filing of the petition for bankruptcy.

____ 6. A preferential transfer of property made to an insider by an insolvent debtor may be set aside by a trustee if the transfer was made within one year prior to the filing of a bankruptcy petition.

____ 7. In a Chapter 11 bankruptcy, the business of a debtor is discontinued and the assets of the debtor are liquidated in order to pay the creditors.

____ 8. A discharge does not release a debtor from liability for unpaid student loans that came due within seven years prior to filing for bankruptcy unless payment would cause an undue hardship to the debtor.

____ 9. A Chapter 13 debtor cannot be discharged unless all claims entitled to priority are paid in full.

____ 10. In general, a debtor can claim only the exempt property that is permitted by the Bankruptcy Act. States do not have the power to specify property that may be exempt in a bankruptcy action.

Multiple Choice

____ 1. Dollar Bank holds numerous delinquent unsecured loans. Dollar Bank wants to force its delinquent debtors into Chapter 7 liquidation proceedings in order to limit its losses. Against which creditors can Dollar Bank file an involuntary petition for Chapter 7 bankruptcy?

    a. McDonald & McDonald, a law firm doing business as a partnership.

    b. Running Rails Railroad Company.

    c. Farwell Credit Union.

    d. The Rock Insurance Company.

____ 2. B&B Bakery just filed for Chapter 7 bankruptcy. B&B is in default on a loan from Arco Finance. Arco has a perfected security interest in B&B's equipment to secure payment of this debt. Under these facts:

    a. Arco can file a lawsuit against B&B in state court to collect the loan.

    b. Arco can immediately repossess and sell B&B's equipment pursuant to its security interest.

    c. Arco cannot sue B&B in state court and it cannot immediately repossess the equipment due to an automatic stay, but Arco will have priority to the equipment in the bankruptcy action.

    d. Arco no longer has a right to be paid; this right was terminated by the bankruptcy filing.

____ 3. Barbara was unemployed and insolvent. On June 10, Barbara sold her gold watch to a jeweler for $1,500, a fair value. On June 11, Barbara paid: $300 to her landlord for the current month's rent; $1,100 to her grandmother in payment of an old loan that would not have been paid in a Chapter 7 liquidation; and $100 in payment of the minimum monthly amount due on her personal credit card. On August 1, Barbara filed a petition for Chapter 7 bankruptcy. Which transfer or payment can be set aside by the bankruptcy trustee?

    a. Sale of the watch.

    b. Rent payment.

    c. Credit card payment.

    d. Loan payment that was made to Barbara's grandmother.

____ 4. Joyce filed a voluntary petition for Chapter 7 bankruptcy. Which of the following facts would *not* be a sufficient ground to deny Joyce a discharge in bankruptcy?

    a. Joyce was discharged in bankruptcy five years prior to filing the present bankruptcy petition.

    b. One month prior to filing for bankruptcy, Joyce transferred a rare coin collection to her brother with the intent to conceal the coin collection from her creditors.

    c. At the meeting of her creditors, Joyce lied under oath regarding her assets.

    d. Two months prior to filing for bankruptcy, Joyce sold her condo for a fair price.

____ 5. Ramon filed for Chapter 7 bankruptcy, and he received a discharge. Certain debts were not paid in Ramon's bankruptcy. Which of the following unpaid debts was discharged?

    a. $2,000 in child support owed for the support of Ramon's minor children.

    b. $1,500 owed to MasterCard.

    c. $1,000 in federal income taxes owed for the prior year.

    d. $5,000 judgment resulting from Ramon's embezzlement of money from a former employer.

____ 6. ARK Co. has filed a petition for Chapter 11 bankruptcy. ARK is a lessee under a long-term, executory real estate lease. ARK is also indebted to ten unsecured creditors who are included in the same class of creditors. ARK's rehabilitation plan:

    a. Can provide for payment in full of some unsecured creditors and for only partial payment of other unsecured creditors.

b. Must provide for equal treatment of all of the unsecured creditors.

c. Cannot reject the lease.

d. Is not binding on ARK's creditors even if the plan is confirmed by the bankruptcy court.

_____ 7.   Jason submitted a proposed Chapter 13 extended payment plan for confirmation. Under the plan, the trustee in bankruptcy will be paid only 90 percent of the trustee's fees. Unsecured, nonpriority creditors, including Lakewood City which is owed $500 for unpaid water bills, will be paid only 80 percent of their respective claims. Under these facts:

a. The plan can provide for payment of only 90 percent of the bankruptcy trustee's fees.

b. Jason will remain liable for all debts that are not paid in full.

c. Jason generally will be discharged from unsecured, nonpriority debts that are not paid in full.

d. Lakewood City can refuse to register Jason's car if he fails to pay the water bills in full.

Case Problems

Answer the following problems, briefly explaining your answers.

1. Green Oaks Health Club Inc. cannot pay its debts as they become due, and it is has defaulted on all of its
obligations. Green Oaks has ten creditors. Green Oaks' unsecured creditors are Apple Linen Co. which is owed $15,000, and Baker Co. which is owed $4,000.

a. Can Green Oaks file a voluntary petition for Chapter 7 bankruptcy?

b. Who can file an involuntary petition for Chapter 7 bankruptcy against Green Oaks?

c. If an involuntary petition is properly filed, would a court enter an order for relief against Green Oaks?

_____

_____

_____

_____

2. Tarco Inc. filed for Chapter 7 bankruptcy. Tarco's assets are a building and $10,000 cash. Tarco has these creditors: (1) First Bank is owed $50,000. This debt is fully secured by the building. (2) Bud is owed $500 for a deposit he paid Tarco for consumer goods he never received. (3) Mr. Atkins, the bankruptcy trustee, is owed a $6,000 fee. (4) Tina is owed $1,000 for wages she earned thirty days prior to Tarco's filing for bankruptcy. (5) Fuller Co. has a $5,000 unsecured claim for goods it sold to Tarco.
Discuss the rights of Tarco Inc.'s creditors to be paid.

_____

_____

_____

_____

Internet Exercise

Linda has learned that the extent to which a person's primary residence may be exempt property in a Chapter 7 bankruptcy often depends on state laws. She has asked you to use the following questions:
1. Does federal bankruptcy law allow states to grant greater exemptions than are allowed under federal law?
2. Using the Internet, identify three states that have more generous residence or personal property exemptions than are offered under the U.S. Bankruptcy Code. Identify the amount of the state exemptions.

_____

_____

_____

_____

CPA REVIEW

The following questions were given on past CPA examinations. The answers for these questions are the unofficial answers prepared by the American Institute of Certified Public Accountants, Inc. (AICPA). All material is reproduced with permission of the AICPA.

_____ 1. Deft, CPA, is an unsecured creditor of Golf Co. for $6,000. Golf has a total of 10 creditors, all of whom are unsecured. Golf has not paid any of the creditors for three months. Under Chapter 11 of the Federal Bankruptcy Code. which of the following statements is correct?
   a. Golf may not be petitioned involuntarily into bankruptcy because there are less than 12 unsecured creditors.
   b. Golf may not be petitioned involuntarily into bankruptcy under the provisions of Chapter 11.
   c. Three unsecured creditors must join in the involuntary petition in bankruptcy.
   d. Deft may file an involuntary petition in bankruptcy against Golf.

_____ 2. Which of the following transfers by a debtor, within ninety days of filing for bankruptcy, could be set aside as a preferential payment?
   a. Making a gift to charity.
   b. Paying a business utility bill.
   c. Borrowing money from a bank secured by giving a mortgage on business property.
   d. Prepaying an installment loan on inventory.

_____ 3. By signing a reaffirmation agreement on April 15, 1991, a debtor agreed to pay certain debts that would be discharged in bankruptcy. On June 20, 1991, the debtor's attorney filed the reaffirmation agreement and an affidavit with the court indicating that the debtor understood the consequences of the reaffirmation agreement. The debtor obtained a discharge on August 25, 1991. The reaffirmation agreement would be enforceable only if it was
   a. Made after discharge.
   b. Approved by the bankruptcy court.
   c. Not for a household purpose debt.
   d. Not rescinded before discharge.

_____ 4. Larson, an unemployed carpenter, filed for voluntary bankruptcy on August 14,1990. Larson's liabilities are listed below:
   Credit card charges due May 2, 1989 $3,000
   Bank loan incurred June 1990 $5,000
   Medical expenses incurred June 1983 $7,000
   Alimony due during 1988 $1,000

   Under the provisions of Chapter 7 of the Federal Bankruptcy Code, Larson's discharge will not apply to the unpaid
   a. Credit card charges.
   b. Bank loan.
   c. Medical expenses.
   d. Alimony.

_____ 5. Which of the following claims will not be discharged in bankruptcy?
   a. A claim that arises from alimony or maintenance.
   b. A claim that arises out of the debtor's breach of a contract.
   c. A claim brought by a secured creditor that remains unsatisfied after the sale of the collateral.
   d. A claim brought by a judgment creditor whose judgment resulted from the debtor's negligent operation of a motor vehicle.

Questions 6 through 8 are based on the following:

Dart Inc., a closely held corporation, was petitioned involuntarily into bankruptcy under the liquidation provisions of Chapter 7 of the Federal Bankruptcy Code. Dart contested the petition. Dart has not been paying its business debts as they became due, has defaulted on its mortgage loan payments, and owes back taxes to the IRS. The total cash value of Dart's bankruptcy estate after the sale of all assets and payment of administration expenses is $100,000. Dart has the following creditors:

Fracon Bank is owed $75,000 principal and accrued interest on a mortgage loan secured by Dart's real property. The property was valued at and sold, in bankruptcy, for $70,000.

The IRS has a $12,000 recorded judgment for unpaid corporate income tax.
JOG Office Supplies has an unsecured claim of $3,000 that was timely filed.
Nanstar Electric Co. has an unsecured claim of $ 1,200 that was not timely filed.
Decoy Publications has a claim of $14,000, of which $2,000 is secured by Dart's inventory that was valued and sold, in bankruptcy, for $2,000.

_____ 6. What dollar amount would Nanstar Electric Co. receive?
   a. $0
   b. $800
   c. $1,000
   d. $1,200

_____ 7. What total dollar amount would Fracon Bank receive on its secured and unsecured claims?
   a. $70,000
   b. $72,000
   c. $74,000
   d. $75,000

_____ 8. What dollar amount would the IRS receive?
   a. $0
   b. $ 8,000
   c. $10,000
   d. $12,000

CHAPTER 36
INSURANCE

MAKE THE CONNECTION

SUMMARY

Insurance is a contract called a *policy*. Under an insurance policy, the insurer provides in consideration of premium payments, to pay the insured or beneficiary a sum of money if the insured sustains a specified loss or is subjected to a specified liability. These contracts are made through an insurance agent, who is an agent for the insurance company, or through an insurance broker, who is the agent of the insured when obtaining a policy for the latter.

The person purchasing an insurance contract must have an insurable interest in the insured's life or property. An insurable interest in property exists when the damage or destruction of the property will cause a direct monetary loss to the insured. In the case of property insurance, the insured must have an insurable interest at the time of loss. An insurable interest in the life of the insured exists if the purchaser would suffer a financial loss from the insured's death. This interest must exist as of the time the policy is obtained.

Ocean marine policies insure ships and their cargoes against the perils of the sea. Inland marine policies insure goods being transported by land, by air, or on inland and coastal waterways.

For fire insurance to cover a fire loss, there must be an actual hostile fire that is the immediate cause of the loss. The insurer is liable for the actual amount of the loss sustained up to the maximum amount stated in the policy. An exception exists when the policy contains a coinsurance clause requiring the insured to maintain insurance up to a certain percentage of the value of the property. To the extent this is not done, the insured is deemed a coinsurer with the insurer, and the insurer is liable for only its proportional share of the amount of insurance required to be carried. A homeowners insurance policy provides fire, theft, and liability protection in a single contract.

Automobile insurance may provide protection for collision damage to the insured's property and injury to persons. It may also cover liability to third persons for injury and property damage as well as loss by fire or theft.

A life insurance policy requires the insurer to pay a stated sum of money to a named beneficiary upon the death of the insured. It may be a term insurance policy, a whole life policy, or an endowment policy. State law commonly requires the inclusion of an incontestability clause, whereby at the conclusion of the contestability period, the insurer cannot contest the validity of the policy.

LEARNING OUTCOMES
After studying this chapter, you should be able to

A. THE INSURANCE CONTRACT
LO.1 Explain the necessity of having an insurable interest to obtain an insurance policy
LO.2 Recognize that the formation of a contract is governed by the general principles of contract law
LO.3 Explain why courts strictly construe insurance policies against insurance companies

B. KINDS OF INSURANCE

LO.4 List and explain the five major categories of insurance
LO.5 Explain coinsurance and its purpose
LO.6 Explain incontestability clauses

CHAPTER OUTLINE

A. THE INSURANCE CONTRACT

Insurance is a contract by which an insurer, for consideration, promises (1) to pay a party a sum of money if a specified casualty or loss occurs to property or a person in which the party has an insurable interest, or (2) to indemnify a party for a loss or liability to which that party is subjected.

1. THE PARTIES

➤ *Insurer (underwriter)*: Insurance firm or other party who promises to pay for a specified loss.

➤ *Insured (assured; policyholder)*: Person to whom a promise to insure is made.

➤ *Policy*: Written contract stating the terms of the insurer's agreement to pay for a loss.

➤ *Insurance agent*: Agent representing one insurance company in making an insurance contract.

➤ *Insurance broker*: Independent contractor who represents many insurers. Brokers are: (1) agents for insureds regarding obtaining policies; (2) agents for insurers regarding transmitting payments.

2. INSURABLE INTEREST

GENERAL RULES. ▶ An insurance contract cannot be enforced unless *the party obtaining insurance* has an insurable interest which means: (1) an insured who obtains property insurance will suffer a direct monetary loss if the property is destroyed; or (2) the beneficiary who insures another person's life must expect a monetary gain from the continued life of the person insured. ▶ The insurable interest must exist: (1) when loss to insured property occurs; or (2) when life insurance on another person was obtained.
LIMITATION. A person obtaining insurance on his or her own life may name anyone as a beneficiary, and the beneficiary need not have an insurable interest to enforce the insurance contract.
STUDY HINT. A business has an insurable interest in the life of partners or key employees.
LEARNING OUTCOME EXAMPLE: See the Vin Harrington example of insurable interest in property, p. 822.

3. THE CONTRACT

▶ General contract law governs insurance contracts, and insurance contracts must usually be written. ▶ Information stated on an insurance application is part of the contract and binds the applicant. ▶ Rules of interpretation: (1) policy terms that conflict with statutes are void; (2) terms required by law to be in a policy are implied into a policy if not expressly stated; and (3) if laws require a contract to state all terms, then a term not stated in a contract cannot be used to defeat a claim. ▶ The Electronic Signatures in Global and National Commerce Act (E-sign) generally applies to the insurance business. ▶ Insurers cannot cancel health or life insurance by means of electronic notices. ▶ LEARNING OUTCOME EXAMPLE: See the *Long v Time Insurance* case where false answers to material questions on the insurance application made the insurance contract voidable by the insurer, p. 824.

4. ANTILAPSE AND CANCELLATION STATUTES AND PROVISIONS

GENERAL RULE. If premiums for *life insurance* are not paid on time, laws or policies usually allow a thirty or thirty-one-day grace period within which to pay. If an insured fails to pay life insurance premiums on time, laws may make an insurer to: (1) issue a paid-up policy for a lesser amount; (2) issue extended insurance for a stated period; or (3) pay the policy's cash surrender value to the insured.

LIMITATIONS. ▶ An insurance contract may either permit or prohibit a unilateral cancellation by the insurer. ▶ An insurer is often required to give prior written notice of cancellation of a policy.

5. MODIFICATION OF CONTRACT

▶ Typically, both parties must consent to a modification. ▶ Changes are made by (1) endorsement or (2) attaching a rider. ▶ If a policy term and an endorsement conflict, the endorsement controls.

6. INTERPRETATION OF CONTRACT

▶ In general, insurance contracts are interpreted according to ordinary rules of contract interpretation. ▶ Contract terms are given the ordinary meaning that would be understood by the average person. ▶ If a policy term is ambiguous, it is interpreted in favor of the insured.
▶ LEARNING OUTCOME EXAMPLE: See the discussion and examples in which the courts awarded coverage for the insured because the insurers chose the ambiguous language of the policies, p. 827.

7. BURDEN OF PROOF

▶ If a claim is disputed, an insured must prove (1) a loss occurred (2) while a policy was in force and (3) the loss was covered by the policy. ▶ An insurer claiming a policy exception that avoids coverage of a loss must prove that the exception applies. ▶ Exceptions to coverage are interpreted against the insurer.

8. INSURER BAD FAITH

GENERAL RULES. ▶ An insurer has a duty to act in good faith in processing and paying claims.
▶ An insurer's negligent or bad faith refusal to defend an insured or to settle a case against an insured within policy limits may render the insurer liable for: (1) resultant damages; and (2) in some states, the excess judgment entered against the insured. ▶ In some states, an insurer's bad faith failure to pay an insured's claim renders the insurer liable for a statutory penalty or exemplary damages, and attorney fees.

LIMITATION. An insurer is not liable for damages or penalties if there are reasonable grounds for contesting an insured's claim.

STUDY HINT. Bad faith is an unfounded or frivolous refusal to honor the terms of a policy.

9. TIME LIMITATIONS ON INSURED

To recover, an insured must: (1) promptly notify an insurer of a claim; (2) submit proof of loss in the time required by the policy; and (3) start a legal action based on the policy in the time specified.

10. SUBROGATION OF INSURER

An insurer who pays an insured's claim acquires any claim the insured had against a third party who caused the loss. The insurer may sue the wrongdoer to recover any amounts paid by the insurer.

B. KINDS OF INSURANCE

11. BUSINESS LIABILITY INSURANCE

GENERAL RULE. ► A business may buy a commercial general liability (CGL) policy that insures it against liability for damages for bodily injury or property damage due to any occurrence. It covers such things as product liability and liability for cleanup of pollution. ►An insurer generally must defend an insured when it is a "close issue" whether the policy covers the loss in question.
STUDY HINT.   Other types of business insurance: liability insurance for directors and officers; product liability insurance; professional malpractice insurance.

12. MARINE INSURANCE (COVERS LOSSES RELATED TO TRANSPORTATION OF GOODS)

➢ *Ocean marine insurance*: This insurance insures goods being transported in international and coastal waters. ► Kinds of policies: (1) hull insurance covers physical damage to vessel; (2) cargo insurance insures cargo owner for loss to shipped goods; (3) liability insurance insures ship owner against liability for damage the owner's ship causes to other ships or their cargo;   (4) freight insurance insures that a ship owner will be paid for transportation costs. ► An insurer may be required to reimburse an insured for expenses the insured incurred in order to avoid a covered loss. ► All risk policies consolidate all types of ocean marine insurance into one policy.

➢ *Inland marine insurance*: Insures goods shipped by air and on land, rivers, lakes, or coastal waters.

13. FIRE AND HOMEOWNERS INSURANCE

➢ *Fire insurance*: Fire insurance covers property loss that is caused by an actual, hostile fire (a fire that is uncontrollable, burns with excessive heat, or escapes from where it is supposed to be).

➢ *Coinsurance*: ► An insurer is generally liable for the actual amount of loss up to the amount of the policy. This obligation may be limited by coinsurance which requires a policyholder to maintain a minimum amount of insurance, typically 80 percent of the insured property's value. If this required minimum amount of insurance is not carried, a policyholder's recovery is computed: (1) amount of loss multiplied by (2) amount of insurance actually carried divided by required minimum amount of insurance. ► Some states do not permit coinsurance clauses. ► LEARNING OUTCOME EXAMPLE: See the example of the homeowner who underinsured his property, resulting in the insurer paying a claim at a proportionate share of the amount of insurance required, p. 834.

➤ *Assignment*: Unless otherwise agreed, fire insurance cannot be assigned without insurer's consent.

➤ *Occupancy*: Fire policy limits on permitted use and occupancy of property are strictly enforced.

➤ *Homeowners insurance*: ► Homeowners insurance covers: (1) fire losses; (2) liability for injuries suffered by others while on the insured's property; (3) liability for injuries unintentionally caused to others off the insured premises (no coverage for injuries caused by operation of motor vehicles); and (4) losses from theft. ► Policy protects all family members living with the insured.

14. AUTOMOBILE INSURANCE

Most auto insurers use the Personal Auto Policy (PAP) standard form. Important clauses of PAP include the following types of provisions:

➤ *Perils covered*: PAP covers: injuries to person or property of others; medical expenses of covered persons; damages insured is entitled to recover from uninsured motorists; damage to insured auto.

➤ *Covered persons*: Named insured; family members; others persons permitted to drive the car.

➤ *Use and operation*: The PAP policy covers the "use and operation" of a vehicle, which includes loading and unloading a vehicle as well driving the vehicle.

➤ *Notice and cooperation*: Insurer's duty is conditioned on insured's giving notice and cooperating.

➤ *No-fault insurance*: No-fault insurance laws: (1) require an insurer to pay for an insured's loss regardless of who was at fault; and (2) prevent an insured from suing the party at fault unless the insured dies or suffers certain permanent serious injuries, or damages exceed a certain amount.

15. LIFE INSURANCE

➤ *Types of life insurance*: The three major types of life insurance are:

► *Term insurance*: Coverage terminates at the end of a specified period. The face amount of the policy is paid to a beneficiary if the insured dies during the policy period. If the insured lives beyond the policy period, the policy expires. The policy has little or no cash surrender value.

► *Whole life insurance (ordinary life insurance)*: Coverage lasts throughout insured's lifetime, and a portion of each premium is an investment that accumulates as a cash surrender value.

► *Endowment insurance*: Face amount of policy is paid if insured dies within the policy period. Otherwise, the policy amount is paid to the insured at the end of the policy period.

➢ *Additional coverage*: For an extra premium, life insurance may provide: (1) double indemnity that pays double the policy amount if death is caused by an accident; or (2) disability insurance that insures against a person's being unable to engage in any occupation due to injury or disease.

➢ *Exclusions*: Life insurance does not usually insure against death caused by: (1) suicide; (2) drugs; (3) another's intentional act; (4) execution for a crime; (5) war activities; or (6) operation of aircraft.

➢ *Beneficiary*: Most policies provide that a beneficiary may be changed without the beneficiary's consent.

➢ *Incontestability clause*: Laws often require life insurance to include an incontestability clause. If two years have passed since a policy was issued, this clause makes an insurer pay and prevents it from contesting a policy due to an insured's fraud or other misconduct in obtaining the policy.

➢ *Imposter fraud*: This defense may arise when an insured fraudulently arranges to have another person take a physical required by the insurer. Thus far, states are split on whether an insurer may raise this defense after the period for contestability has expired.

CONCEPT REVIEW AND APPLICATIONS

Matching Exercise

Select the term or phrase that best matches a definition or statement stated below. Each term or phrase is the best match for only one statement or definition. Not all terms and phrases will necessarily be used.

beneficiary	policy	marine insurance
cargo insurance	hull insurance	ocean marine
cash surrender value	incontestability clause	policy
coinsurance clause	inland marine	risk
disability	insurance	subrogated
double indemnity	insurance agent	term insurance
endowment insurance	insurance broker	underwriter
fire insurance policy	insured	whole life insurance
freight insurance	insurer	
homeowners insurance	liability insurance	

_____ 1. Party who represents one insurance company in making insurance contracts.

_____ 2. Party who is legally entitled to receive insurance benefits upon the death of an insured.

_____ 3. Life insurance that pays a policy's face amount to a beneficiary if an insured dies within the policy period, or it pays this sum to the insured if the insured is alive at the end of this period.

_____ 4. Insurance that generally covers losses to goods occurring during transportation.

_____ 5. Investment component of a whole life insurance policy that increases in value over time.

_____ 6. Contract term that, after a specified time, prevents an insurer from contesting a life insurance contract due to the insured's fraud or misconduct in obtaining the policy.

_____ 7. Contract term that entitles a beneficiary to recover twice the face amount of life insurance if the insured is killed in an accident.

_____ 8. Life insurance written for a specified number of years; policy has little or no cash surrender value.

_____ 9. Party who is an independent contractor representing numerous insurance companies.

_____ 10. Life insurance for the entire life of an insured that has a cash surrender value.

True/False

Write **T** if the statement is true, write **F** if it is false.

_____ 1. In general, an insurance contract is governed by general rules of contract law, and it is interpreted according to ordinary rules of contract interpretation.

_____ 2. Information on an insurance application may become part of the contract and bind an insured.

_____ 3. Beneficiaries named by a person who is insuring his or her own life must have an insurable interest in order to recover under the policy.

_____ 4. If a term of an insurance contract is unclear, it is interpreted in favor of the insurer.

_____ 5. Under no-fault insurance laws, a person wrongfully injured by another person in an automobile accident cannot sue the wrongdoer unless certain exceptions are applicable.

_____ 6. In order to recover, an insured must prove that a covered loss occurred within the policy period.

_____ 7. An insurer is not in bad faith if it has reasonable grounds to believe that a claim is not valid.

_____ 8. If an insurer pays an insured's claim, the insurer does not have subrogation rights that entitle the insurer to enforce the insured's right to recover from a third party who caused a loss.

_____ 9. Inland marine insurance insures goods during domestic transportation by air; over land; or on rivers, lakes, or coastal waters.

_____ 10. A term life insurance policy generally has little or no cash surrender value.

Multiple Choice

_____ 1. Jocelyn worked exclusively for SafetyFirst Insurance Company. She wrote a general liability policy for Luke, who wanted coverage for his business. Under these facts:
   a. Jocelyn is an insurance broker for SafetyFirst.
   b. Jocelyn is an insurance agent for SafetyFirst.
   c. Jocelyn is the underwriter for the general liability policy.
   d. SafetyFirst is the assured.

_____ 2. Wayne is an independent contractor who writes insurance policies for several insurance firms. He wrote an endowment life insurance policy for Jonathan with GrandLife Insurance Co. Under these facts:
   a. Wayne is an insurance broker, and he acted as an agent for Jonathan when obtaining the policy for him with GrandLife.
   b. Wayne is an insurance broker, and he acted solely as an agent for GrandLife when writing the policy for Jonathan.
   c. Wayne is an insurance agent, and he acted solely as an agent for GrandLife when writing the policy for Jonathan.
   d. Wayne is an insurance agent. He is acting as the agent of Jonathan for the purpose of obtaining his policy and Wayne is also acting as the agent of GrandLife with respect to transmitting Jonathan's payments to GrandLife.

_____ 3. Which of the following is incorrect?
   a. A person has an insurable interest in property whenever the destruction of the property will cause a direct monetary loss to that person.
   b. To collect on property insurance, the insured must have an insurable interest at the time the loss occurs.
   c. To collect on life insurance, the beneficiary who obtained the policy must have had an insurable interest at the time of the insured's death.
   d. To collect on life insurance, the beneficiary who obtained the policy must have had an insurable interest at the time the policy was obtained.

_____ 4. Marvin purchased a standard form of life insurance on Lisa's life, naming himself as beneficiary. The policy contains a clause granting a thirty-day grace period, but the policy is silent regarding the insurer's right to modify the policy. Premiums are due June 1. Under these facts:

    a. Marvin cannot enforce the policy unless he had an insurable interest in Lisa's life at the time   he purchased the policy.

    b. Marvin cannot enforce the policy unless he has an insurable interest in Lisa's life at the time of her death.

    c. If Marvin fails to pay the premium on June 1, the insurer can immediately cancel the policy.

    d. The insurer can unilaterally modify the policy whenever it chooses to do so.

Case Problem

Answer the following problem, briefly explaining your answer.

Mario owned a fire insurance policy on a business building. In the policy, Mario agreed to a coinsurance term that required him to insure the building for 80 percent of its value. The building's value was $100,000. Mario only insured the building for $60,000. A fire broke out in the building causing a $10,000 loss.

1. Who has the burden to prove whether or not the fire was covered by the policy?
2. Must Mario have an insurable interest in the building in order to enforce the policy?
3. If the loss is covered, what effect does Mario's failure to carry the required amount have on his right to recover under the policy?
4. How much can Mario recover?

_____

_____

_____

_____

Internet Exercise

Amber is single, twenty-three years of age, and recently graduated from college. She has also recently started her own florist shop.

In her undergraduate law class, Amber studied insurance, among other things. Now, she is trying to decide what type of personal and/or business insurance she needs to adequately protect herself and her business. Amber has asked for your assistance in answering the following questions:

1. Locate and identify one or more Internet web sites that provide practical information regarding what insurance is most appropriate for an individual or business.
2. Identify two types of personal and two types of business-related insurance that Amber should acquire.

_____

_____

_____

_____

CPA REVIEW

The following questions were given on CPA examinations. The answers for these questions are the unofficial answers prepared by the American Institute of Certified Public Accountants, Inc. (AICPA). All material is reproduced with permission of the AICPA.

___1. Which of the following parties has an insurable interest?
   I. A corporate retailer in its inventory.
   II. A partner in the partnership property.

   a. I only.
   b. II only.
   c. Both I and II.
   d. Neither I nor II.

___2. To recover under a property insurance policy, an insurable interest must exist

	When the policy is issued	At the time of the casualty
a.	Yes	Yes
b.	Yes	No
c.	No	Yes
d.	No	No

___3. Daly tried to collect on a property insurance policy covering a house that was damaged by fire. The insurer denied recovery, alleging that Daly had no insurable interest in the house. In which of the following situations will the insurer prevail?
   a. The house belongs to a corporation of which Daly is a 50% stockholder.
   b. Daly is not the owner of the house but a long-term lessee.
   c. The house is held in trust for Daly's mother and, on her death, will pass to Daly.
   d. Daly gave an unsecured loan to the owner of the house to improve the house.

____4. Hart owned a building with a fair market value of $400,000. The building was covered by a $300,000 fire insurance policy containing an 80% co-insurance clause What amount would Hart recover if a fire totally destroyed the building?
   a. $0
   b. $240,000
   c. $256,000
   d. $300,000

____5. In 1985, Ring purchased a building for $90,000 and insured it with a $90,000 fire insurance policy having a standard 80% coinsurance clause. Ring never increased the amount of the policy. In 1990, the building, worth $120,000, was destroyed by fire. What amount could Ring collect from the insurance company?
   a. $0
   b. $72,000
   c. $90,000
   d. $120,000

____6. Clark Corp. owns a warehouse purchased for $150,000 in 1990. The current market value is $200,000. Clark has the warehouse insured for fire loss with Fair Insurance Corp. and Zone Insurance Co. Fair's policy is for $150,000 and Zone's policy is for $75,000. Both policies contain the standard 80% coinsurance clause. If a fire totally destroyed the warehouse, what total dollar amount would Clark receive from Fair and Zone?
   a. $225,000
   b. $200,000
   c. $160,000
   d. $150,000

____7. One of the primary purposes of including a coinsurance clause in a property insurance policy is to
   a. Encourage the policyholder to insure the property for an amount close to its full value.
   b. Make the policyholder responsible for the entire loss caused by some covered perils.
   c. Cause the policyholder to maintain a minimum amount of liability insurance that will increase with inflation.
   d. Require the policyholder to insure the property with only one insurance company.

____8. Long purchased a life insurance policy with Tempo Life Insurance Co. The policy named Long's daughter as beneficiary. Six months after the policy was issued, Long died of a heart attack. Long had failed to disclose on the insurance application a known pre-existing heart condition that caused the heart attack. Tempo refused to pay the death benefit to Long's daughter. If Long's daughter sues, Tempo will
   a. Win, because Long's daughter is an incidental beneficiary.
   b. Win, because of Long's failure to disclose the pre-existing heart condition.
   c. Lose, because Long's death was from natural causes.
   d. Lose, because Long's daughter is a third-party donee beneficiary.

CHAPTER 37
AGENCY

MAKE THE CONNECTION

SUMMARY

An agency relationship is created by an express or implied agreement by which one person, the agent, is authorized to make contracts with third persons on behalf of, and subject to, the control of another person, the principal. An agent differs from an independent contractor in that the principal, who controls the acts of an agent, does not have control over the details of performance of work by the independent contractor. Likewise, an independent contractor does not have authority to act on behalf of the other contracting party.

A special agent is authorized by the principal to handle a specific business transaction. A general agent is authorized by the principal to transact all business affairs of the principal at a certain place. A universal agent is authorized to perform all acts that can be lawfully delegated to a representative.

The usual method of creating an agency is by express authorization. However, an agency relationship may be found to exist when the principal causes or permits a third person to reasonably believe that an agency relationship exists. In such a case, the "agent" appears to be authorized and is said to have apparent authority.

An unauthorized transaction by an agent for a principal may be ratified by the principal.

An agent acting with authority has the power to bind the principal. The scope of an agent's authority may be determined from the express words of the principal to the agent; this is called express authority. An agent has incidental authority to perform any act reasonably necessary to execute the authority given the agent. An agent's authority may be implied so as to enable the agent to perform any act in accordance with the general customs or usages in a business or an industry. This authority is often referred to as customary authority.

The effect of a proper exercise of authority by an agent is to bind the principal and third person to a contract. The agent, not being a party to the contract, is not liable in any respect under the contract. A third person dealing with a person claiming to be an agent has a duty to ascertain the extent of the agent's authority and a duty to take notice of any acts that are clearly adverse to the principal's interests. The third person cannot claim that apparent authority existed when that person has notice that the agent's conduct is adverse to the interests of the principal. A third person who has knowledge of limitations on an agent's authority is bound by those limitations. A third person is not bound by secret limitations.

While the agency relationship exists, the agent owes the principal the duties of (1) being loyal, (2) obeying all lawful instructions, (3) exercising reasonable care, (4) accounting for all property or money belonging to the principal, and (5) informing the principal of all facts relating to the agency that are relevant to the principal's interests. An agency relationship can be terminated by act of either the principal or the agent. However, the terminating party may be liable for damages to the other if the termination is in violation of the agency contract.

Because a known agent will have the appearance of still being an agent, notice must be given to third persons of the termination, and the agent may have the power to bind the principal and third persons until this notice is given.

An agency is terminated by operation of law upon (1) the death of the principal or agent, (2) insanity of the principal or agent, (3) bankruptcy of the principal or agent, (4) impossibility of performance, caused, for example, by the destruction of the subject matter, or (5) war.

In states that have adopted the Uniform Durable Power of Attorney Act (UDPAA), an agency may be created that is not affected by subsequent disability or incapacity of the principal. In UDPAA states, the agency may also come into existence upon the "disability or incapacity of the principal." The designation of an attorney in fact under the UDPAA must be in writing.

LEARNING OUTCOMES
After studying this chapter, you should be able to

A. NATURE OF THE AGENCY RELATIONSHIP
LO.1   Explain the difference between an agent and an independent contractor

B. CREATING THE AGENCY
LO.2   Explain three methods of creating an agency relationship

C. AGENT'S AUTHORITY
LO.3   Recognize that third persons who deal with an agent are required to take notice of acts contrary to the interests of the principal

D. DUTIES AND LIABILITIES OF PRINCIPAL AND AGENT
LO.4   List and explain the duties an agent owes the principal

E. TERMINATION OF AGENCY
LO.5   Explain how the Uniform Durable Power of Attorney Act changes the common law rule on incapacity of the principal

CHAPTER OUTLINE

A. NATURE OF THE AGENCY RELATIONSHIP

1. DEFINITIONS AND DISTINCTIONS

GENERAL RULES. ▶ An agency is a relationship that is based on an express or implied agreement by which an agent is authorized to negotiate or make contracts for a principal with a third party.
▶ Example: general manager; sales representative. ▶ An agent should be distinguished from:

➢ *Employee*: ▶ An employee is a person who is hired to do a service that does not involve making contracts for the employer. ▶ Example: college professor; machine operator.

➢ *Independent contractor*: ▶ An independent contractor is a person who is hired to perform a task; the employer has the right to dictate the result, but not the method or manner by which the result is obtained. ▶ Example: Homeowner hires a contractor to replace a roof.

STUDY HINTS. ▶ A principal is liable on contracts that are made on its behalf by an agent who has actual or apparent authority to act for the principal. ▶ The authority to make contracts is what distinguishes an agent from an employee. ▶ The right to control the manner or method by which work is to be performed is what distinguishes an employee from an independent contractor. **LEARNING OUTCOME EXAMPLE:** See the Ned and Tracy Seizer example and the "right to control" test, beginning on textbook p. 851.

2. CLASSIFICATION OF AGENTS

➤ *Special agent*: ▶ A special agent is authorized to represent a principal regarding a specific transaction or a specific contract. ▶ Example: attorney authorized to make a lease for a client.

➤ *General agent*: ▶ A general agent is authorized to represent a principal regarding all contracts of a business or all business conducted at a location. ▶ Example: general manager of a shoe store.

➤ *Universal agent*: ▶ A universal agent is authorized to represent a principal regarding all matters that can lawfully be delegated. ▶ Example: unlimited power of attorney to make any contract.

3. AGENCY COUPLED WITH AN INTEREST

▶ *Interest in the authority*: agent paid consideration for right to exercise authority.
▶ *Interest in the subject matter*: agent has an interest in the property in question (e.g., security interest in collateral).

B. CREATING THE AGENCY

4. AUTHORIZATION BY APPOINTMENT

GENERAL RULE. A principal can expressly create an agency either in writing or orally.
LIMITATION. In a majority of states, appointment of agents to buy or sell an interest in land must be written.
STUDY HINT. A written authorization is a power of attorney; the agent is an attorney in fact.

5. AUTHORIZATION BY CONDUCT (APPARENT AUTHORITY)

➤ *Nature of apparent authority*: ▶ Apparent authority arises when, by words or conduct, a principal misleads a third party into reasonably believing that an agent has authority to act for the principal. ▶ Example: Paul, a storeowner, appointed Kim as store manager. Managers can customarily hire employees, but Paul told Kim not to do so. Kim later hired Erik as a new store employee; Erik was unaware of the limit on Kim's authority. Kim had apparent authority to hire Erik.

➤ *Effect of apparent authority*: (1) the principal and third party are bound to the contract; and (2) the agent is liable to the principal for losses suffered by the principal in connection with the contract.

➤ *Limitations on apparent authority*: ▶ (1) apparent authority cannot be based on an agent's words; and (2) an objective standard is used to determine apparent authority.
▶ LEARNING OUTCOME EXAMPLE: See the *Taylor* case where actual authority to perform some tasks created apparent authority to perform other related tasks, textbook p. 854.

6. **AGENCY BY RATIFICATION**

   ➤ *Intention to ratify*: ▶ In general, a principal may ratify any unauthorized action by an agent. ▶ In general, a principal may ratify a contract by express words or by conduct indicating an intent to ratify. Examples: With knowledge of a contract, a principal: (1) performs the contract;
   (2) accepts or keeps contract benefits; (3) enforces the contract; or (4) fails to disavow the contract. a ratification may be written or oral or arise by conduct.

   ➤ *Requirements for ratification*: ▶ (1) Intent to ratify; (2) agent contracted for an identified principal; (3) principal had capacity to contract; and (4) the principal has full knowledge of all facts to the extent desired. ▶ LEARNING OUTCOME EXAMPLE: See the agency by ratification example of James and Calvin Reiner on textbook p. 855.

   ➤ *Effect of ratification*: ▶ A ratified contract is treated as if it were actually authorized. ▶ When a contract is ratified, the principal and third party are bound by the contract, but the agent is not.

7. **PROVING THE AGENCY RELATIONSHIP**

   The party who will benefit from proof that an agency existed must prove such relationship.

C. **AGENT'S AUTHORITY**

8. **SCOPE OF AGENT'S AUTHORITY (AND TYPES OF AUTHORITY)**

   GENERAL RULE. An agent may obligate a principal when the agent has the following authority:

   ➤ *Express authority*: Express authority arises when a principal expressly tells an agent to do an act.

   ➤ *Incidental authority*: ▶ It is implied that an agent has incidental authority to do acts that are reasonably necessary to carry out the agent's express authority. ▶ Example: Principal expressly authorizes Jerry to manage the financial operations of a shopping center. In this case, Jerry has incidental authority to receive rent checks from tenants of the shopping center.

   ➤ *Customary authority*: ▶ It is implied that an agent has customary authority to do any act that is customarily done by this type of agent in the community in question. ▶ Example: Roger is the general manager of a restaurant. If it is customary in Roger's community that restaurant managers can hire necessary cooks, then Roger would have customary authority to hire a cook.

   ➤ *Apparent authority*: ▶ An agent may have apparent authority to bind a principal (see § 7 above).

   STUDY HINT. An agent who acts with no authority cannot obligate a principal to a contract.

9. **EFFECT OF PROPER EXERCISE OF AUTHORITY**

   ▶ If an agent contracts on behalf of a disclosed principal with actual authority to do so: (1) the principal and third party are liable to one another on the contract; and (2) the agent is not a party to, nor liable on, the contract. ▶ Example: Paul authorized Alice to buy a snowmobile on his behalf from Wanda, and Alice did so. If Paul fails to pay, Wanda can sue Paul for breach of contract, but she cannot sue Alice because Alice was not a party to the contract. ▶ An electronic agent is a computer program or other electronic means that is used to automatically start an action or respond to an electronic record or action (e.g., ATM) ▶ Electronic agents have authority to make contracts.

10. DUTY TO ASCERTAIN EXTENT OF AGENT'S AUTHORITY

GENERAL RULES. ▶ Third parties cannot rely on agents' statements regarding the extent of the their authority. ▶ Third parties deal who deal with an agent whose authority is limited to a special purpose can hold the principal liable on a contract only if the agent has actual authority to enter into it.

STUDY HINTS. ▶ Typically, an attorney is retained for a special purpose. Thus, an attorney cannot settle a client's claim without the client's consent. ▶ If a third party observes an agent acting against a principal's interests, the third party deals with the agent at the third party's own risk.

LEARNING OUTCOME EXAMPLE. See the example of the Fire Company that failed to verify with the principal an agent's authority to receive a prepayment check of $55,000 made out in the agent's name, textbook p. 858.

11. LIMITATIONS ON AGENT'S AUTHORITY

GENERAL RULES. ▶ If a third party knows that an agent's authority is subject to certain limits, the third party cannot hold the principal liable for the agent's actions that exceed such limits. ▶ If a third party knows that an agent's authority is based on a writing, the third party is charged with knowledge of limits stated in the writing. ▶ A third party is charged with knowledge of obvious limits on authority that are inherent in certain agencies. Example: Authority of government agents is typically restricted.

LIMITATION. A third party's right to hold a principal liable on a contract is not affected by secret limits that the principal may have placed upon an agent's authority.

D. DUTIES AND LIABILITIES OF PRINCIPAL AND AGENT

12. DUTIES AND LIABILITIES OF AGENT DURING AGENCY

(a) *Loyalty*

GENERAL RULES. ▶ During the agency relationship, an agent owes a duty to be loyal and faithful to a principal. ▶ An agent cannot: (1) make or retain secret profits derived from the agency; (2) buy property from, or sell property to, a principal without disclosing the agent's interest; (3) accept secret benefits from a third party relating to an agency transaction; (4) aid or provide confidential information to a principal's competitors; or (5) represent both a principal and third party without disclosing such representation and obtaining the consent of both parties.

STUDY HINTS. ▶ A principal can avoid a contract that was made by an agent who failed to disclose his or her interest in the matter. ▶ A principal can sue an agent for any secret or improper profits or commissions that the agent made in connection with a transaction that was undertaken with or on behalf of a principal. ▶ A contract is voidable if the principal did not know that the agent also represented the other contracting party.

(b) *Obedience and performance*

▶ An agent must: (1) obey a principal's lawful instructions; and (2) perform all agency duties for the time and in the manner agreed upon. ▶ An agent is liable to a principal for damages caused by a failure to obey orders even if the agent acted in good faith and with the intent to help the principal.

(c) *Reasonable care*

An agent must perform duties with the care that a reasonable person would use. If an agent possesses a special skill, the agent must use such skill.

(d) *Accounting*

An agent must account for, and keep separate, the principal's money and property.

(e) *Information*

An agent must inform a principal of all facts relevant to the agency that may affect the principal's interests, including all facts relating to the desirability of a transaction.

13. DUTIES AND LIABILITIES OF AGENT AFTER TERMINATION OF AGENCY

When an agency ends: (1) an agent's duties continue only as needed to finish prior duties; and (2) an agent can compete against a former principal (unless a covenant not to compete limits this right).

14. DUTIES AND LIABILITIES OF PRINCIPAL TO AGENT

▶ A principal has a duty to perform all duties set forth in any contract of employment with the agent. ▶ Unless otherwise agreed, an agent is generally not entitled to commissions or other compensation with regard to repeat business or other sales that occur after termination of the agency relationship.

E. TERMINATION OF AGENCY

15. TERMINATION BY ACT OF PARTIES

➢ *Expiration of contract*: An agency contract terminates on the date stated in the contract.

➢ *Agreement*: A principal and agent can agree to cancel an agency contract.

➢ *Option of a party*: A contract may give one party the unilateral right to cancel an agency.

➢ *Revocation of principal*: ▶ *Power*: A principal has the power to terminate an agency at any time, even if termination is a breach of contract. ▶ *Legal right*: (1) If an agency contract does not have a fixed duration (agency at will), a principal has the right to terminate the agency whether the agent has acted properly or not. (2) If an agency contract has a fixed duration, a principal has the right to revoke the agency only if the agent is guilty of misconduct; otherwise, a principal is liable for damages. ▶ A termination or revocation must be clear and unequivocal to be effective.

> ➤ *Renunciation by agent*: An agency is terminated if an agent refuses to continue to serve as agent. The rules regarding a principal's power and right to terminate an agency also apply to the agent.

> ➤ *Rescission*: An agency contract can be rescinded to the same extent that other contracts can be.

16. TERMINATION BY OPERATION OF LAW

► An agency terminates *immediately* upon the death of a principal or agent. ► An agency is also terminated by: (1) insanity or bankruptcy (but not mere insolvency) of a principal or agent; (2) destruction of the subject matter, change in law, or other event that makes it impossible to perform the agency; or (3) war between the countries in which the principal and agent reside.

17. DISABILITY OF THE PRINCIPAL UNDER THE UDPAA

GENERAL RULE. The Uniform Durable Power of Attorney Act (UDPAA) allows a principal to create a power of attorney: (1) that is not affected by the principal's disability or incapacity; or (2) that comes into existence only upon the principal's disability or incapacity.
LIMITATION. The UDPAA requires that a power of attorney be (1) written, (2) designate an attorney in fact, and (3) state a principal's intent to create one of these types of powers of attorney.
LEARNING OUTCOME EXAMPLE. See the *Estate of Graham* case on the limits of a durable power of attorney, textbook p. 864.

18. TERMINATION OF AGENCY COUPLED WITH AN INTEREST

A principal cannot terminate an agency coupled with an interest before expiration of the interest.

19. PROTECTION OF AGENT FROM TERMINATION OF AUTHORITY

> ➤ *Exclusive agency*: Agent may be given the exclusive right to sell a product for a principal in which case the agent is entitled to commissions for all sales, regardless of who makes the sale.

> ➤ *Secured transaction*: Security interest in property may secure payment of an agent's commission.

> ➤ *Payment from fund or third person*: An escrow fund, letter of credit, or guarantees by third parties may be used to assure payment of commissions.

20. EFFECT OF TERMINATION OF AUTHORITY

► *Between a principal and agent*, an agent's authority is not terminated until the agent is given notice of termination. ► If a principal voluntarily ends an agency, an agent has *apparent authority* to bind the principal after termination until: (1) actual notice of termination is given to third parties who have dealt with the agent; or (2) constructive notice (newspaper ads) is given to the public.

CONCEPT REVIEW AND APPLICATIONS

Matching Exercise

Select the term or phrase that best matches a definition or statement stated below. Each term or phrase is the best match for only one statement or definition. Not all terms and phrases will necessarily be used.

agency

agent   independent contractor

apparent authority   interest in the authority

attorney in fact   interest in the subject matter

customary authority   power of attorney

express authorization   principal

general agent   special agent

incidental authority   universal agent

_____ 1. Written appointment and authorization of an agent.

_____ 2. Agent who is authorized to perform all acts that can be delegated lawfully to an agent.

_____ 3. Any party authorized to make a contract on behalf of a principal with a third party.

_____ 4. Authority of an agent that arises due to the words or conduct of a principal that reasonably misled a third party into believing that an agent has authority to act on behalf of the principal.

_____ 5. Agent who is appointed and given authorization by a written power of attorney.

_____ 6. Authority created by oral or written instructions given by a principal to an agent.

_____ 7. Person who is hired to do a task and who retains control over the method for completing the task.

_____ 8. Agent who is authorized to represent a principal regarding an entire business.

_____ 9. Party on whose behalf an agent is authorized to negotiate and make a contract.

_____ 10. Agent who is authorized to represent a principal regarding only a specific business transaction.

True/False

Write **T** if the statement is true, write **F** if it is false.

_____ 1. A third party is entitled to rely on an agent's statements regarding the extent of the agent's authority.

_____ 2. An employer generally controls the method used by an independent contractor to perform a task.

_____ 3. An employee is a person who is hired to perform a task that does not involve negotiating or making contracts on behalf of the employer.

_____ 4. An agent who has a special skill must exercise that skill in performing an agency.

_____ 5. The UDPAA prohibits any clause in a power of attorney that states that the power of attorney shall be unaffected by the principal's subsequent disability or incapacity.

_____ 6. In a majority of states, an authorization of an agent must be in writing if it authorizes the agent to buy land for a principal.

_____ 7. An agent is generally entitled to be paid commissions or other compensation with regard to repeat business or other sales that occur after termination of the agency relationship.

_____ 8. An agent has authority to represent a principal only if a principal expressly authorizes an agent to act on his or her behalf.

_____ 9. In general, a third party is not be bound by limitations that a principal places on an agent's authority if the limitations are not obvious and the third party is not informed of such limitations.

_____10. If a principal ratifies a contract, then both the principal and agent are liable on the contract.

Multiple Choice

_____ 1. Yankee Manufacturing Co. hired Roadways Inc. to build a new road at Yankee's plant. Roadways was obligated to build the road in accordance with certain plans. Roadways was to use its own tools, employees, and construction methods; Yankee did not have the right to control the manner or method by which Roadways built the road. In this case, Roadways is Yankee's:
a. Agent.
b. Principal.
c. Employee.
d. Independent contractor.

_____ 2. Perry LLC (limited liability company) in writing authorized Allied Corporation to contract to sell certain land belonging to Perry LLC. Pursuant to this authorization, Allied made a contract on Perry LLC's behalf to sell the land to Zak. Under these facts, the contract between Perry LLC and Zak is:

a. Void. An agent cannot be authorized to sell land on behalf of a principal.

b. Void. A corporation cannot be an agent.

c. Void. An LLC cannot be a principal.

d. Valid. Allied was properly authorized, and Allied had the capacity to contract.

_____ 3. Rozwell Heating Co. hired Dawn as a district sales manager for Rozwell's Midwest division. Dawn was authorized to negotiate and make all contracts to sell Rozwell's heating equipment in Ohio, Michigan, Indiana, and Illinois. Under these facts, Dawn is a:

a. Special agent.

b. General agent.

c. Universal agent.

d. Employee.

_____ 4. In which situation did Paula have authority to make the contract in question on behalf of Rod?

a. Rod signed a written power of attorney that authorized Paula to make a contract to sell his car. On Rod's behalf, Paula signed a contract for the sale of Rod's car.

b. Without Rod's knowledge or consent, Paula contracted on Rod's behalf to sell his sailboat.

c. Paula was authorized to sell goods for Rod. Paula was not expressly authorized to sell goods on credit. However, for several years Paula has repeatedly sold goods on credit, and Rod knew of these sales and never objected. Paula has now made another contract to sell goods on credit.

d. a and c.

_____ 5. Without authority to do so, Avery contracted to buy a printer on behalf of P&P Printing Inc. The printer was delivered to P&P. Avery only told P&P the price and credit terms regarding the purchase; P&P indicated that it was not concerned regarding the other terms of the contract. P&P accepted and kept the printer, and P&P used it in its business. At all relevant times, P&P was capable of contracting and the contract was legal. Under these facts:

a. The contract is binding on P&P because P&P ratified the contract.

b. The contract is not binding on P&P because P&P did not expressly ratify the contract.

c. The contract is not binding on P&P because P&P did not know all of the contract terms.

d. The contract is not binding on P&P because Avery did not initially have authority to make it.

_____ 6. Principal hired Alex as general manager for a fixed two-year term. One year has now passed, and Principal no longer wants Alex to be general manager. However, Alex has properly performed all of his contractual and agency duties. Under these facts:

a. Principal has the legal right and power to terminate Alex as general manager.

b. Principal has the legal right, but not the power, to terminate Alex as general manager.

c. Principal has the power, but not the legal right, to terminate Alex as general manager.

d. Principal does not have the legal right or the power to terminate Alex as general manager.

_____ 7. Pam, a world-famous actress, hired Arnie as her agent to negotiate and make acting contracts on her behalf. The parties' agency relationship would *not* be terminated by operation of law if:
   a. Pam was subsequently killed while making a film.
   b. Pam was subsequently discharged in bankruptcy.
   c. The movie industry subsequently caused Arnie to become permanently insane.
   d. Pam subsequently indicated to Arnie that she thought his services were unsatisfactory and that she was considering hiring a new agent.

_____ 8. Juan was the new car sales manager for Rev Car Sales. Juan was authorized to sell Rev's cars, but he was told not to accept promissory notes as payment. In good faith and with the intent to benefit Rev, Juan sold a car to Buyer in exchange for Buyer's promissory note. Buyer subsequently failed to pay the note, and Rev suffered a $3,000 loss. Under these facts:
   a. Juan is liable to Rev for $3,000 because he breached his duty of obedience when he accepted the promissory note from Buyer.
   b. Juan is not liable to Rev because Juan acted in good faith in accepting the note.
   c. Juan is not liable to Rev because Juan intended to benefit Rev when he accepted the note.
   d. Juan is not liable to Rev because an agent can disobey a principal's instructions if the agent believes that it is in the principal's best interest to do so.

_____ 9. Kyle was sales manager of Mango Co., a fruit wholesaler. Kyle's authority was stated in a written statement of authority, which stated that he could make sales for only $10,000 or less. But it was customary for agents, such as Kyle, to have authority to make sales for up to $50,000. Kyle made a $20,000 sale to Acme. Acme was unaware of the statement of authority and the limit on Kyle's authority. Kyle told Acme that he had authority to make the sale. In this case:
   a. Mango is bound by this sale because it misled Acme into believing that Kyle had authority to make the sale, and Acme is not charged with knowledge of the statement of authority.
   b. Mango is bound by this sale because Acme was entitled to rely on Kyle's statements regarding the extent of his authority.
   c. Mango is not bound by this sale because Acme is charged with knowledge of the limits on Kyle's authority that are stated in the statement of authority.
   d. a and b.

Case Problems

Answer the following problems, briefly explaining your answers.

1. Carl hired Aurora as manager of Carl's auto parts store. Managers of auto parts stores customarily have authority to order inventory. However, Carl told Aurora not to order any inventory without his prior approval. One day, a parts supplier asked Carl if he wanted to buy any inventory. Carl replied: "Go see Aurora, my manager. She will handle this entire matter." Reasonably believing that Aurora had authority to order parts for Carl, the supplier contacted Aurora. Without Carl's consent, Aurora contracted to buy parts from the supplier in violation of Carl's instructions to her.

(a) What type of authority, if any did Aurora have to contract on Carl's behalf with the parts supplier?

(b) Is Carl legally obligated to perform the contract with the parts supplier?

_____

_____

_____

_____

2. Haskins Inc. hired Robin as vice president of purchasing. Robin was authorized to make contracts to buy materials for Haskins and to take delivery of the materials. On many occasions, Robin contracted on behalf of Haskins to buy materials from Sun Co. On June 1, Haskins gave Robin notice that she was terminated. On June 10, Robin contracted on behalf of Haskins to buy materials from Sun Co. Robin took and wrongfully kept the materials. Sun Co. did not know that Haskins had terminated Robin. On June 15, Haskins gave written notice to Sun Co. that Robin had been terminated.

(a) When was Robin's *express authority* to act for Haskins effectively terminated? (b) Did Robin have authority to make the June 10 contract with Sun Co.? If so, what type of authority did she have?

(c) Is Haskins obligated to perform the June 10 contract? (d) What should Haskins have done differently?

_____

_____

_____

_____

Internet Exercise

Bill and Mary are an elderly married couple. Bill and Mary want to be certain that, should either of them become incapacitated, the other spouse can legally act on behalf of the other. Bill and Mary live in your state and they feel fairly certain that the state has enacted a version of the Uniform Durable Power of Attorney Act or a comparable law. However, they have asked you to use the Internet to verify that this is correct. Therefore, using the Internet, verify that your state has adopted the Uniform Durable Power of Attorney Act or a comparable law. If you cannot verify this fact, then locate and identify two states that have enacted this law. Identify the web site where you found the law or laws in question.

_____

_____

_____

_____

CPA REVIEW

The following questions were given on CPA examinations. The answers for these questions are the unofficial answers prepared by the American Institute of Certified Public Accountants, Inc. (AICPA). All material is reproduced with permission of the AICPA.

_____ 1. Thorp was a purchasing agent for Ogden, a sole proprietor, and had the express authority to place purchase orders with Ogden's suppliers. Thorp placed an order with Datz, on Ogden's behalf after Ogden was declared incompetent in a judicial proceeding. Thorp was aware of Ogden's incapacity. Which of the following statements is correct concerning Ogden's liability to Datz?
   a. Ogden will be liable because Datz was not informed of Ogden's incapacity.
   b. Ogden will be liable because Thorp acted with express authority.
   c. Ogden will not be liable because Thorp's agency ended when Ogden was declared incompetent.
   d. Ogden will not be liable because Ogden was a nondisclosed principal.

_____ 2. Bolt Corp. dismissed Ace as its general sales agent and notified all of Ace's known customers by letter. Young Corp., a retail outlet located outside of Ace's previously assigned sales territory, had never dealt with Ace. Young knew of Ace as a result of various business contacts. After his dismissal, Ace sold Young goods, to be delivered by Bolt, and received from Young a cash deposit for 20% of the purchase price. It was not unusual for an agent in Ace's previous position to receive cash deposits. In an action by Young against Bolt on the sales contract, Young will
   a. Lose, because Ace lacked any implied authority to make the contract.
   b. Lose, because Ace lacked any express authority to make the contract.
   c. Win, because Bolt's notice was inadequate to terminate Ace's apparent authority.
   d. Win, because a principal is an insurer of an agent's acts.

_____ 3. Kent, without authority, contracted to buy computer equipment from Fox Corp. for Ace Corp. Kent told Fox that Kent was acting on Ace's behalf. For Ace to ratify the contract with Fox,
   a. Kent must be a general agent of Ace.
   b. Ace must know all material facts relating to the contract at the time it is ratified.
   c. Ace must notify Fox that Ace intends to ratify the contract.
   d. Kent must have acted reasonably and in Ace's best interest.

_____ 4. Starr is an agent of a disclosed principal, Maple. On May 1, Starr entered into an agreement with King Corp. on behalf of Maple that exceeded Starr's authority as Maple's agent. On May 5, King learned of Starr's lack of authority and immediately notified Maple and Starr that it was withdrawing from the May 1 agreement. On May 7 Maple ratified the May 1 agreement in its entirety. If King refuses to honor the agreement and Maple brings an action for breach of contract, Maple will
   a. Prevail since the agreement of May 1 was ratified in its entirety.
   b. Prevail since Maple's capacity as a principal was known to Starr.
   c. Lose since the May 1 agreement is void due to Starr's lack of authority.
   d. Lose since King notified Starr and Maple of its withdrawal prior to Maple's ratification.

_____ 5. When a valid contract is entered into by an agent on the principal's behalf, in a nondisclosed principal situation, which of the following statements concerning the principal's liability is correct?

	The principal may be held liable once disclosed	The principal must ratify the contract to be held liable
a.	Yes	Yes
b.	Yes	No
c.	No	Yes
d.	No	No

_____ 6. Pell is the principal and Astor is the agent in an agency coupled with an interest. In the absence of a contractual provision relating to the duration of the agency, who has the right to terminate the agency before the interest has expired?

	Pell	Astor
a.	Yes	Yes
b.	No	Yes
c.	No	No
d.	Yes	No

_____ 7. Wok Corp. has decided to expand the scope of its business. In this connection, it contemplates engaging several agents. Which of the following agency relationships is within the statute of frauds and thus should be contained in a signed writing?
   a. A sales agency where the agent normally will sell goods which have a value in excess of $500.
   b. An irrevocable agency.
   c. An agency which is of indefinite duration but which is terminable upon one month's notice.
   d. An agency for the forthcoming calendar year which is entered into in December of the prior year.

_____ 8. Red entered into a contract with Maple on behalf of Gem, a disclosed principal. Red exceeded his authority in entering into the contract. In order for Gem to successfully ratify the contract with Maple,
   a. Gem must expressly communicate his intention to be bound.
   b. Gem must have knowledge of the relevant material facts concerning the transaction.
   c. Red must not have been a minor.
   d. Red must have acted reasonably and in Gem's best interest.

_____ 9. Ace engages Butler to manage Ace's retail business. Butler has the implied authority to do all of the following, except
   a. Purchase inventory for Ace's business.
   b. Sell Ace's business fixtures.
   c. Pay Ace's business debts.
   d. Hire or discharge Ace's business employees.

_____ 10. Borg is the vice-president of purchasing for Crater Corp. He has authority to enter into purchase contracts on behalf of Crater provided that the price under a contract does not exceed $2 million. Dent, who is the president of Crater, is required to approve any contract that exceeds $2 million. Borg entered into a $2.5 million purchase contract with Shady Corp. without Dent's approval. Shady was unaware that Borg exceeded his authority. Neither party substantially changed its position in reliance on the contract. What is the most likely result of this transaction?
   a. Crater will be bound because of Borg's apparent authority.
   b. Crater will not be bound because Borg exceeded his authority.
   c. Crater will only be bound up to $2 million, the amount of Borg's authority.
   d. Crater may avoid the contract since Shady has not relied on the contract to its detriment.

_____ 11. Ritz hired West for six months as an assistant sales manager at $4,000 a month plus 3% of sales. Which of the following is correct?
   a. The employment agreement must be in writing and signed by the party to be charged.
   b. The agreement between Ritz and Wes formed an agency coupled with an interest.
   c. West must disclose any interests he has which are adverse to Ritz in matters concerning Ritz's business.
   d. West can be dismissed by Ritz during the six months only for cause.

CHAPTER 38
THIRD PERSONS IN AGENCY

MAKE THE CONNECTION

SUMMARY

An agent of a disclosed principal who makes a contract with a third person within the scope of authority has no personal liability on the contract. It is the principal and the third person who may each sue the other in the event of a breach. A person purporting to act as an agent for a principal warrants by implication that there is an existing principal with legal capacity and that the principal has authorized the agent to act. The person acting as an agent is liable for any loss caused the third person for breach of these warranties. An agent of a partially disclosed or an undisclosed principal is a party to the contract with the third person. The agent may enforce the contract against the third person and is liable for its breach. To avoid problems of interpretation, an agent should execute a contract "Principal, by Agent." Agents are liable for harm caused third persons by their fraudulent, malicious, or negligent acts.

An undisclosed or a partially disclosed principal is liable to a third person on a simple contract made by an authorized agent. When a third person makes payment to an authorized agent, it is deemed paid to the principal.

A principal or an employer is vicariously liable under the doctrine of *respondeat superior* for the torts of an agent or an employee committed within the scope of authority or the course of employment. The principal or the employer may also be liable for some crimes committed in the course of employment. An owner is not liable for torts caused by an independent contractor to third persons or their property unless the work given to the independent contractor is inherently hazardous.

A salesperson is ordinarily an agent whose authority is limited to soliciting offers (orders) from third persons and transmitting them to the principal. The principal is not bound until he or she accepts the order. The customer may withdraw an offer at any time prior to acceptance.

LEARNING OUTCOMES
After studying this chapter, you should be able to

A. LIABILITY OF AGENT TO THIRD PERSON
LO.1   Explain when an agent is and is not liable to a third person as a party to a contract
LO.2   Describe how to execute a contract as an agent on behalf of a principal

B. LIABILITY OF PRINCIPAL TO THIRD PERSON
LO.3 Explain the legal effect of a payment made by a third person to an authorized agent

C. LIABILITY OF PRINCIPAL FOR TORTS AND CRIMES OF AGENT
LO.4 Explain the doctrine of *respondeat superior*

D. TRANSACTIONS WITH SALES PERSONNEL
LO.5 Distinguish between the authority of a soliciting agent and that of a contracting agent

CHAPTER OUTLINE

A. LIABILITY OF AGENT TO THIRD PERSON

1. ACTION OF AUTHORIZED AGENT OF DISCLOSED PRINCIPAL

An agent is not personally liable on a properly executed contract that is made for a disclosed principal if the agent has actual authority or the principal ratifies the contract.

2. UNAUTHORIZED ACTION

GENERAL RULES. ▶ An agent impliedly warrants to a third party that the agent has authority to bind a principal to the contract. ▶ If an agent acts with no authority: (1) the principal is not liable on the contract; and (2) the agent is personally liable to the third party for any loss the third party suffers.

STUDY HINT.   An agent's good faith mistake regarding his or her authority is not a defense.

3. DISCLOSURE OF PRINCIPAL

➢ *Disclosed principal*: ▶ A disclosed principal exists if an agent discloses: (1) the principal's existence and identity; and (2) that the agent is acting for a principal. ▶ Liability: agent is not liable on the contract. ▶ LEARNING OUTCOME EXAMPLE: See the Biefeld Jewelers example in which Margie Biefeld was acting as an agent for a disclosed principal when she signed the contract and was not a party to the contract, textbook p. 876.

➢ *Partially disclosed principal*: ▶ A partially disclosed principal exists if an agent discloses the existence, but not the identity, of the principal. ▶ Liability: agent is liable on the contract to third party.

➢ *Undisclosed principal*: ▶ An undisclosed principal exists if an agent does not disclose: (1) the existence or identity of the principal; or (2) that the agent is acting as an agent. ▶ Liability: agent is liable on the contract.

4. ASSUMPTION OF LIABILITY

An agent may agree to be personally liable on a contract made between a principal and a third party.

5. EXECUTION OF CONTRACT

▶ Between an agent and third party, an agent can avoid liability on a contract made in the agent's name by proving that it was actually intended to be a contract between a principal and the third party. ▶ An agent's signature should (1) state the principal's name, (2) "by" or "per" the agent. When signed in this manner, a principal is disclosed and an agent is not liable on the contract. ▶ LEARNING OUTCOME EXAMPLE: See the "B. G. Gray, by Jane R. Craig" example on textbook p. 878.

6. TORTS AND CRIMES

An agent is liable for any tort or crime committed by the agent, even while acting for a principal.

B. LIABILITY OF PRINCIPAL TO THIRD PERSON

7. AGENT'S CONTRACTS

➢ *Simple contract with principal disclosed*: A disclosed principal is liable if (1) an agent had actual authority or (2) the principal ratified the contract. The agent is not liable on the contract.

➢ *Simple contract with principal partially disclosed*: If a principal is partially disclosed, the principal and agent are liable on the contract, and the third party must elect which one to hold liable.

➢ *Simple contract with principal undisclosed*: ► An undisclosed principal is liable if an agent had actual authority to contract. ► *Election of remedies rule*: In some states, a third party must elect whether to hold the agent or undisclosed principal liable on a contract. (2) *Modern rule*: In some states, a third party can hold the agent and the undisclosed principal jointly and severally liable on a contract.

8. PAYMENT TO AGENT

► Payment to an agent with actual authority to accept payments is deemed payment to a principal, even if the principal does not receive the money. ► Payment to an agent who has no authority to accept money is not valid payment unless the principal receives the money.

9. AGENT'S STATEMENTS

A principal is bound by statements made by an agent while acting within the scope of authority.

10. AGENT'S KNOWLEDGE

A principal is bound by an agent's knowledge of most facts acquired while the agent is acting within the scope of authority, but a principal is not bound by knowledge of facts unrelated to the agency.

C. LIABILITY OF PRINCIPAL FOR TORTS AND CRIMES OF AGENT

11. VICARIOUS LIABILITY FOR TORTS AND CRIMES

GENERAL RULES. ► *Respondeat superior*: Traditionally, an employer has vicarious liability for the negligence of an employee who is acting within the scope of employment. Under the modern rule, an employer is also liable for an employee's intentional tort, fraud, or violation of a government regulation that is committed within the scope of employment. ► The same rules make a principal liable for torts committed by an agent who is acting within the scope of authority.

LIMITATION.   There is no vicarious liability for: (1) a tort if an employee is not acting within the scope of employment; or (2) an intentional tort committed by an employee for a personal reason.

STUDY HINT.   An employee is acting within the scope of employment if the employee's action is intended to further the employer's interests (even if the employee is violating a work rule).

LEARNING OUTCOME EXAMPLE. See the Crane Brothers, Inc. example of employer liability for torts of the employees, textbook p. 883; see the Rev. Joel Thomford example in which Rev. Thomford's employer, the church, was not liable for the pastor's accidental shooting of a parishioner on a hunting trip not sponsored by the church, textbook p. 884.

12. NEGLIGENT HIRING AND RETENTION OF EMPLOYEES

GENERAL RULE.   An employer is liable for an employee's tort (including intentional tort) due to the employer's negligence in hiring or retaining the employee if (1) the employer knew or should have known that the employee posed an undue risk to others (2) regarding the harm that the employee actually caused to a third party.

LIMITATION.   In general, hiring a person with a criminal record does not, by itself, prove negligence on the part of an employer.

13. NEGLIGENT SUPERVISION AND TRAINING

GENERAL RULE.   An employer is directly liable for harm that an employee causes a third party if the employee's conduct was due to the employer's negligent failure to properly supervise or train the employee.

STUDY HINT.   Example: employer negligently fails to train employee and, as a result of the improper training, employee harms a third party.

14. AGENT'S CRIMES

GENERAL RULE.   In general, a principal is liable only for an agent's crimes that the principal authorized or ratified.

LIMITATION.   ▶ Some modern government regulations make an employer criminally liable for employee crimes that are committed within the scope of employment. ▶ Examples: environmental laws; liquor sales laws.

15. OWNER'S LIABILITY FOR ACTS OF AN INDEPENDENT CONTRACTOR

GENERAL RULE.   An owner is generally not liable for an independent contractor's torts.

LIMITATIONS.   ▶ An owner is liable for an independent contractor's tort if: (1) the owner controls the independent contractor's actions; or (2) the fact that a party is an independent contractor is not disclosed. ▶ Trend: An owner is liable for an independent contractor's tort if the assigned work: (1) is inherently dangerous; or (2) involves a heightened risk that a tort may be committed.

16. ENFORCEMENT OF CLAIM BY THIRD PERSON

A person can sue the employer or employee or both parties, but the person can recover only once.

D. TRANSACTIONS WITH SALES PERSONNEL

17. SOLICITING AND CONTRACTING AGENTS

▶ An order given to a soliciting agent is only an offer; it is not a contract until accepted by a principal. ▶ But, an acceptance of an order by a contracting agent forms a contract.

CONCEPT REVIEW AND APPLICATIONS

Matching Exercise

Select the term or phrase that best matches a definition or statement stated below. Each term or phrase is the best match for only one statement or definition. Not all terms and phrases will necessarily be used.

contracting agent   principal

respondeat superior   soliciting agent

disclosed principal   undisclosed principal

partially disclosed   vicarious liability

_____   1.   Principal whose existence and identity are disclosed to the third party at time of contracting.

_____   2.   Liability imposed upon an employer or principal for a wrong committed by an employee or agent.

_____   3.   Doctrine that imposes vicarious liability on an employer for a tort that was committed by an employee while the employee was acting within the scope of employment.

_____   4.   Principal whose existence, but not identity, is disclosed to the third party at time of contracting.

_____   5.   Principal whose existence and identity are not disclosed to the third party at time of contracting.

_____   6.   Sales agent (salesperson) who does not have authority to accept a customer's order.

_____   7.   Agent who has authority to accept a customer's order, thereby forming a contract.

True/False

_____ 1. In general, an agent of a disclosed principal is liable to a third party if the principal fails to perform a contract.

_____ 2. An agent generally can avoid liability for breach of the implied warranty of authority by providing the third party with a copy of the writing that defines the agent's authority.

_____ 3. An agent may agree to be personally bound by a contract that the agent made on behalf of a principal.

_____ 4. If an authorized agent signs the principal's name without indicating the agent's name or identity, then the signature generally operates as the signature of the principal.

_____ 5. In a lawsuit between an agent and a party to a contract, parol evidence may be admitted to prove whether the agent or a principal was intended to be the other party to the contract.

_____ 6. An employee is not personally liable for a tort or crime that the employee commits if the employee was acting within the scope of employment.

_____ 7. Payment by a third party to an authorized agent discharges the party's liability to the principal.

_____ 8. A principal is bound by an agent's knowledge of facts that are within the scope of the agency.

_____ 9. A principal is criminally responsible for all crimes that are committed by an agent.

_____ 10. Placing an order with a soliciting agent creates a contract between the customer and principal.

Multiple Choice

_____ 1. Select the correct answer.
   a. Barry is manager of A&A Clothing Store, and he is authorized to buy inventory for the store. On behalf of a fully disclosed A&A, Barry bought a shipment of shirts from Seller. In this case, Barry is personally liable to Seller if A&A fails to pay for the shirts.
   b. Ali is manager of Bea's Candy Store. With no authority to do so, Ali made a contract on behalf of Bea's to buy a store from Seller. In this case, Bea's is not bound by the contract, but Ali is liable to Seller because Ali breached an implied warranty of authority.
   c. Fred contracted to sell land to Buyer on behalf of Pam, a minor. Buyer was unaware that Pam was a minor. Pam now refuses to perform the contract because she is a minor. In this case, Fred is not liable to Buyer for losses that Buyer may suffer because Pam is a minor.
   d. a and b.

_____ 2. Rosa was an agent for Saxon Inc. On behalf of Saxon and with actual authority to do so, Rosa contracted to buy a business from Seller. Rosa is not personally liable on the contract if:
   a. The existence and identity of Saxon was disclosed to Seller at time of contracting.
   b. The existence and identity of Saxon was disclosed to Seller soon after the contract was made.

c. The existence, but not the identity, of Saxon was disclosed to Seller at time of contracting.

d. Rosa did not intend to be personally bound on the contract. Rosa's disclosure or failure to disclose Saxon's existence and identity would not affect her liability on the contract.

_____ 3. On behalf of May (a disclosed principal), Yen contracted to sell a patent to Ted. Yen had actual authority to sell the patent and to accept payment for the patent. Ted paid the price to Yen, who wrongfully kept the money. Under these facts:

a. Yen is personally bound by the contract.

b. May is not personally bound by the contract.

c. May is bound by the contract, and Ted's payment to Yen discharged his liability to May.

d. May is bound by the contract, and Ted's payment to Yen did not discharge his liability to May.

_____ 4. With actual authority to do so, Susan contracted to lease a town house from Lessor on behalf of Birch. Susan made the contract in her personal name, without disclosing to Lessor the existence or identity of Birch or that Susan was acting only as an agent for Birch. Under these facts:

a. Birch cannot be bound by the contract because Birch was an undisclosed principal.

b. Birch cannot be bound by the contract because Birch was a partially disclosed principal.

c. Birch cannot be bound by the contract because her name and identity were not expressly stated in the contract.

d. Birch is bound by the contract once Lessor learns of her identity. But, under the traditional rule followed in some states, Lessor must elect whether to hold Susan or Birch liable.

_____ 5. Todd is an employee of C&C Car Sales. During working hours, Todd committed the torts described below. Under these facts, C&C may be vicariously liable for which torts?

a. Todd intentionally hit Jim because Jim was dating Todd's girlfriend.

b. While making a delivery for C&C, Todd negligently damaged Kip's car. Todd was speeding at the time of the accident, a violation of a work regulation adopted by C&C.

c. Todd secretly abandoned his work and, while he was driving to see a friend thirty miles away, Todd negligently caused an accident with Helen.

d. All of the above.

Case Problem

Answer the following problem, briefly explaining your answer.

Donna hired Pace Remodeling Co. to remodel her house for $30,000. Pace was required to remodel the house in accordance with certain plans, and Pace was to complete the work by May 1. Pace had the exclusive right to control the manner and method for performing the work, including the right to select the workers and tools to be used. One day, a Pace employee was picking up a bathtub to be installed in Donna's house. While loading the tub into a truck, the employee negligently dropped the tub, injuring Roger, a passer-by.

1. What is the relationship between Donna and Pace?
2. Is Donna vicariously liable for Roger's injury?
3. Is Pace vicariously liable for Roger's injury?

_____

_____

_____

_____

Internet Exercise

Diane is a production worker at Baker Corp. Clay, Diane's immediate supervisor, requested that Diane have sexual relations with him and he threatened to fire her if she refused. Diane always refused Clay's requests, and he finally fired her because of her refusals. Baker executives were unaware of Clay's conduct. Diane is considering filing a sex discrimination claim against Baker Corp. under Title VII of the Civil Rights Act of 1964. However, Diane is uncertain whether Baker Corp., as principal, can be held liable under this law for the misconduct of its agent, Clay. She has turned to you for help.

1. Using the Internet, locate and identify a recent U.S. Supreme Court that addresses Diane's situation.
2. Analyze whether Baker Corp. has vicarious liability for Clay's actions in this case.

_____

_____

_____

_____

CPA REVIEW

The following questions were given on CPA examinations. The answers for these questions are the unofficial answers prepared by the American Institute of Certified Public Accountants, Inc. (AICPA). All material is reproduced with permission of the AICPA.

_____ 1. Easy Corp. is a real estate developer and regularly engages real estate brokers to act on its behalf in acquiring parcels of land. The brokers are authorized to enter into such contracts, but are instructed to do so in their own names without disclosing Easy's identity or relationship to the transaction. If a broker enters into a contract with a seller on Easy's behalf,

   a. The broker will have the same actual authority as if Easy's identity had been disclosed.
   b. Easy will be bound by the contract because of the broker's apparent authority.

    c. Easy will not be liable for any negligent acts committed by the broker while acting on Easy's behalf.

    d. The broker will not be personally bound by the contract because the broker has express authority to act.

_____ 2. Which of the following rights will a third party be entitled to after validly contracting with an agent representing an undisclosed principal?

    a. Disclosure of the principal by the agent.

    b. Ratification of the contract by the principal.

    c. Performance of the contract by the agent.

    d. Election to void the contract after disclosure of the principal.

_____ 3. North, Inc. hired Sutter as a purchasing agent. North gave Sutter written authorization to purchase, without limit, electronic appliances. Later, Sutter was told not to purchase more than 300 of each appliance. Sutter contracted with Orr Corp. to purchase 500 tape recorders. Orr had been shown Sutter's written authorization. Which of the following statements is correct?

    a. Sutter will be liable to Orr because Sutter's actual authority was exceeded.

    b. Sutter will not be liable to reimburse North if North is liable to Orr.

    c. North will be liable to Orr because of Sutter's actual and apparent authority.

    d. North will not be liable to Orr because Sutter's actual authority was exceeded.

_____ 4. When an agent acts for an undisclosed principal, the principal will not be liable to third parties if the

    a. Principal ratifies a contract entered into by the agent.

    b. Agent acts within an implied grant of authority.

    c. Agent acts outside the grant of actual authority.

    d. Principal seeks to conceal the agency relationship.

_____ 5. Able, as agent for Baker, an undisclosed principal, contracted with Safe to purchase an antique car. In payment, Able issued his personal check to Safe. Able could not cover the check but expected Baker to give him cash to deposit before the check was presented for payment. Baker did not do so and the check was dishonored. Baker's identity became known to Safe. Safe may not recover from

    a. Baker individually on the contract.

    b. Able individually on the contract.

    c. Baker individually on the check.

    d. Able individually on the check.

_____ 6. A principal will not be liable to a third party for a tort committed by an agent

    a. Unless the principal instructed the agent to commit the tort.

    b. Unless the tort was committed within the scope of the agency relationship.

    c. If the agency agreement limits the principal's liability for the agent's tort.

    d. If the tort is also regarded as a criminal act.

_____ 7. Neal, an employee of Jordan, was delivering merchandise to a customer. On the way, Neal's negligence caused a traffic accident that resulted in damages to a third party's automobile. Who is liable to the third party?

	Neal	Jordan
a.	No	No
b.	Yes	Yes
c.	Yes	No
d.	No	Yes

_____ 8. If an agent has, within the scope of the agency relationship, committed both negligent and intentional acts resulting in injury to third parties, the principal
   a. May be liable even if the agent's acts were unauthorized.
   b. May effectively limit its liability to those third parties if the agent has signed a disclaimer absolving the principal from liability.
   c. Will be liable under the doctrine of respondeat superior only for the intentional acts.
   d. Will never be criminally liable unless it actively participated in the acts.

_____ 9. An agent will usually be liable under a contract made with a third party when the agent is acting on behalf of a(an)

	Disclosed principal	Undisclosed principal
a.	Yes	Yes
b.	Yes	No
c.	No	Yes
d.	No	No

CHAPTER 39
REGULATION OF EMPLOYMENT

MAKE THE CONNECTION

SUMMARY
The relationship of employer and employee is created by the agreement of the parties and is subject to the principles applicable to contracts. If the employment contract sets forth a specific duration, the employer cannot terminate the contract at an earlier date unless just cause exists. If no definite time period is set forth, the individual is an at-will employee. Under the employment-at-will doctrine, an employer can terminate the contract of an at-will employee at any time for any reason or for no reason. Courts in many jurisdictions, however, have carved out exceptions to this doctrine when the discharge violates public policy or is contrary to good faith and fair dealing in the employment relationship. The Fair Labor Standards Act regulates minimum wages, overtime hours, and child labor.

Under the National Labor Relations Act, employees have the right to form a union to obtain a collective bargaining contract or to refrain from organizational activities. The National Labor Relations Board conducts elections to determine whether employees in an appropriate bargaining unit desire to be represented by a union. The NLRA prohibits employers' and unions' unfair labor practices and authorizes the NLRB to conduct proceedings to stop such practices. Economic strikes have limited reinstatement rights. Federal law sets forth democratic standards for the election of union offices.

The Employees Retirement Income Security Act (ERISA) protects employees' pensions by requiring (1) high standards of those administering the funds, (2) reasonable vesting of benefits, (3) adequate funding, and (4) an insurance program to guarantee payments of earned benefits.

Unemployment compensation benefits are paid to persons for a limited period of time if they are out of work through no fault of their own. Persons receiving unemployment compensation must be available for placement in a job similar in duties and comparable in rate of pay to the job they lost. Twelve-week maternity, paternity, and adoption leaves are available under the Family and Medical Leave Act. Employers and employees pay Social Security taxes to provide retirement benefits, disability benefits, life insurance benefits, and Medicare.

The Occupational Safety and Health Act provides for the (1) establishment of safety and health standards and (2) effective enforcement of these standards. Many states have enacted "right-to-know" laws, which require employers to inform their employees of any hazardous substances present in the workplace.

Workers' compensation laws provide for the prompt payment of compensation and medical benefits to persons injured in the course of employment without regard to fault. An injured employee's remedy is generally limited to the remedy provided by the workers' compensation statute. Most states also provide compensation to workers for occupational diseases.

The Bill of Rights is the source of public-sector employees' privacy rights. Private-sector employees may obtain limited privacy rights from statutes, case law, and collective bargaining agreements. Employers may monitor employee telephone calls, although once it is determined that the call is personal, the employer must stop listening or be in violation of the federal wiretap statute. The ordinary-course-of-business and consent exceptions to the Electronic Communications Privacy Act of 1986 (ECPA) give private employers a great deal of latitude to monitor employee e-mail. Notification to employees of employers' policies on searching lockers, desks, and offices reduces employees' expectations of privacy, and a search conducted in conformity with a known policy is generally not an invasion of privacy. Drug and alcohol testing is generally permissible if it is based on reasonable suspicion; random drug and alcohol testing may also be permissible in safety-sensitive positions.

Immigration laws prohibit the employment of aliens who have illegally entered the United States.

LEARNING OUTCOMES
After studying this chapter, you should be able to

A. THE EMPLOYMENT RELATIONSHIP
LO.1 Explain the contractual nature of the employment relationship

LO.2 Explain how whistleblower protection under Sarbanes-Oxley is limited to conduct in violation of fraud or securities laws

B. LABOR RELATIONS LAWS
LO.3 Explain how the National Labor Relations Act prohibits employers from firing employees attempting to form a union, and requires employers to bargain with unions in good faith over wages, hours, and working conditions

C. PENSION PLANS AND FEDERAL REGULATION
LO.4 Explain how ERISA protects employee pensions and benefits

D. UNEMPLOYMENT BENEFITS, FAMILY LEAVES, AND SOCIAL SECURITY
LO.5 Explain the essentials of unemployment benefits, family and medical leaves, military leaves, and social security benefits

E. EMPLOYEE HEALTH AND SAFETYS
LO.6 Explain how OSHA is designed to ensure workers safe and healthful working conditions

F. COMPENSATION FOR EMPLOYEE INJURIES
LO.7 Explain the three types of benefits provided by Workers' Compensation statutes

G. EMPLOYEE PRIVACY
LO.8 Explain the sources of privacy rights, and applications to telephone, e-mail, text-messaging, and property searches

H. EMPLOYER-RELATED IMMIGRATION LAWS
LO.9 Explain an employer's verification obligations when hiring new employees and discuss special hiring programs allowing aliens to work in the U.S.

CHAPTER OUTLINE

A. THE EMPLOYMENT RELATIONSHIP

1. CHARACTERISTICS OF RELATIONSHIP

An employee is a person who is hired to perform a service subject to the control of an employer. An employee is different from an agent and an independent contractor

2. CREATION OF EMPLOYMENT RELATIONSHIP

► Both the employer and the employee must consent to the creation of an employment relationship. ► Most employment relationships are made pursuant to employment contracts that may be either express or implied (e.g., one accepts services for which there is an expectation of payment).

► Contracts may be: (1) individual contracts negotiated with each employee; or (2) collective bargaining contracts that are negotiated by a representative of all employees.

3. DURATION AND TERMINATION OF EMPLOYMENT CONTRACT

➤ *Employment-at-will doctrine*: under the employment-at-will doctrine, either party may terminate an employment contract that does not state a fixed duration at any time, and for any reason or for no reason. However, a contract that states a fixed term can be terminated only for just cause.

➤ *Developing exceptions to employment-at-will doctrine*: The right to fire an employee at will is limited in most states by: (1) statutes; (2) public policy exceptions that forbid discharging an employee for refusing to do an illegal act, filing a worker's compensation claim, cooperating with a federal criminal prosecution, giving truthful testimony, or reporting illegal activities in the workplace; (3) duty to act in good faith and deal fairly that forbids a discharge if done only to benefit an employer; or (4) employer statements in personnel policies or employee handbooks that are viewed as part of the employment contract thus limiting the power to discharge a worker.

➤ *Justifiable discharge*: A contract that can be terminated for only "just or good cause" may be terminated because of an employee's: (1) nonperformance of duties; (2) fraud in obtaining the employment; (3) disobedience of proper orders; (4) disloyalty; (5) theft or other dishonesty; (6) illegal drug use; (7) misconduct; or (8) incompetency.

➤ **LEARNING OUTCOME EXAMPLE**: See the *FedEx* case in which the employment contract and the employee handbook both preserved the employer's at-will termination powers, textbook p. 900.

4. WHISTLEBLOWER PROTECTION UNDER THE SARBANES-OXLEY ACT

► Title VIII of the Sarbanes-Oxley Act (SOA) forbids a publicly traded company or any of its agents from taking an adverse employment action against an employee who in any manner assists in legal proceedings regarding (1) mail, wire, bank or securities fraud, (2) violation of any federal securities law, or (3) any federal law that protects shareholders from fraud. ► An employee who believes that he or she has been subject to a violation of the above law must file a complaint with OSHA within 90 days. ► Damages, attorney fees, expert witness fees and reinstatement to employment are available remedies.

► LEARNING OUTCOME EXAMPLE: See the example in which David Welch was *not* protected under SOX because he, as CFO, refused to sign an SEC quarterly report due to accounting irregularities that did not amount to fraud or a violation of securities laws, textbook p. 901.

5. DUTIES OF THE EMPLOYEE

GENERAL RULE. An employee must (1) perform his or her contractual duties and (2) not disclose or use an employer's confidential trade secrets (whether this is expressly forbidden or not).

STUDY HINT. Unless otherwise agreed, an employee owns an invention that he makes. But an employment contract can legally state that the employer owns any invention made by the employee.

6. RIGHTS OF THE EMPLOYEE

➢ *Compensation:* ▶ Employees have a right to be paid agreed wages, earned vacation pay, and bonuses. ▶ Unless otherwise agreed, a discharged employee has a right to be paid to the end of the pay period.

➢ *Federal wage and hour law:* ▶ Fair Labor Standards Act provides that most workers cannot be paid less than a set minimum wage and this applies to time spent in job-related training. ▶ Executive, administrative, and professional employees and outside salespersons are exempt minimum wage and overtime provisions of this Act. ▶ Other provisions of this Act relate to (1) subminimum wage, (2) wage deductions, (3) overtime pay and (4) child labor (restrictions for hours of work and assignments for minors under 16).

B. LABOR RELATIONS LAWS

7. THE NATIONAL LABOR RELATIONS ACT (NLRA)

The NLRA established the right of employees to bargain collectively with employers.

8. NATIONAL LABOR RELATIONS BOARD (NLRB)

▶ Important functions of the NLRB include (1) investigating and enforcing unfair labor cases and (2) conducting union representation elections and decertification elections (i.e., elections to remove a union). ▶ The NLRB will certify a union as the exclusive representative of all employees within a given bargaining unit if a majority of the employees vote in favor of union representation.

9. ELECTION CONDUCT

▶ During a pre-election period, the NLRA forbids: (1) employer interference or coercion of employees and threats of reprisals or promises of benefits. ▶ The "24-hour rule" forbids unions and employers from making speeches to captive audiences for 24 hours prior to a union election.

10. UNION ACTIVITY ON PRIVATE PROPERTY

GENERAL RULES. Employers can generally forbid union solicitation during working hours and prohibit all nonemployees, including nonemployee union officials, from soliciting on the employer's premises.

LIMITATION. An employer cannot deny access to nonemployee union officials during nonworking time unless legitimate efficiency or safety concerns exist.

11. FIRING EMPLOYEES FOR UNION ACTIVITY

► An employer cannot punish or fire an employee for lawful union activities or for supporting unionization. Example: it is an unfair labor practice to threaten employees with closing a plant and moving its operations to Mexico if the employees vote in favor of being represented by a union. ► In a "dual-motive" case, an employer fires an employee for violation of a company rule and for union activity. To recover, the employee must prove that the union activity was a motivating factor for the discharge. If this is proven, the employer is liable unless the employer can prove that the employee would have been fired for legitimate reasons without considering the union activity. ► LEARNING OUTCOME EXAMPLE: See the *Sam Santillo* case on wrongful termination of an employee because of his union activity, textbook p. 909.

12. DUTY OF EMPLOYER TO BARGAIN COLLECTIVELY

GENERAL RULE. Once a union is elected and certified, an employer must bargain in good faith with the union regarding all mandatory subjects of bargaining including: (1) working conditions; (2) wages; (3) hours; (4) seniority; (5) promotions; (6) layoff terms; and (7) grievances.
LIMITATION. An employer may, but is not required to, bargain regarding permissive subjects of bargaining, such as internal union affairs and benefits for already retired workers.

13. RIGHT TO WORK

Twenty-one states have adopted right-to-work laws that forbid agreements which deny a person employment because he or she is not a member of a union or does not pay union dues.

14. STRIKE AND PICKETING ACTIVITY

➤ *Rights of strikers*: ► Employees can strike if: (1) an employer fails to agree to a union's demands ("economic strikers"); or (2) an employer engages in unfair labor practices ("unfair labor practice strikers"). ► Once a strike is over, economic strikers can require reinstatement to their former jobs only when positions become available; but employers must immediately reinstate unfair labor practice strikers even if permanent replacements have been hired.

➤ *Picketing*: ► Legal picketing includes: (1) primary picketing, i.e., placing persons outside the site of a labor dispute; and (2) product picketing, i.e., picketing neutral retail stores and asking shoppers not to buy the employer's product. ► Illegal picketing includes: (1) mass picketing, i.e., using picketers to shut down entrance to job site; and (2) secondary picketing, i.e., picketing an employer's customers or suppliers to force them not to do business with the employer.

15. REGULATION OF INTERNAL UNION AFFAIRS

The Labor-Management Reporting and Disclosure Act (LMRDA) imposes many standards in connection with union elections, such as secret ballots in local elections, to assure that union elections are democratic.

C. PENSION PLANS AND FEDERAL REGULATION

16. ERISA

▶ Employees Retirement Income Security Act (ERISA) requires: (1) administrators of pension funds to handle funds so as to protect employees' interests; (2) vesting of pension rights within 5 to 7 years; and (3) actuarially-established employer contributions. ▶ The Pension Benefit Guaranty Corp. which guarantees that pension benefits will be paid if an employer goes out of business. ▶ A benefits claims committee is often formed to make coverage decisions for a pension plan and a court will not disturb its decisions unless the decisions are arbitrary and capricious.

D. UNEMPLOYMENT BENEFITS, FAMILY LEAVES, AND SOCIAL SECURITY

17. UNEMPLOYMENT COMPENSATION

➢ *Benefits*: States provide unemployment benefits for most laid-off employees. However, agricultural, domestic, and state and local government employees are generally not covered.

➢ *Eligibility*: In most states, benefits are denied if an employee: (1) is unavailable for work in a similar job; (2) refuses similar work for comparable pay; (3) quits without cause; or (4) is fired for misconduct.

➢ *Funding*: Employers are taxed for unemployment benefits based on their experience rating.

18. FAMILY AND MEDICAL LEAVES OF ABSENCE

GENERAL RULE.   Family and Medical Leave Act of 1993 entitles male or female employees to twelve weeks of unpaid leave during any twelve-month period: (1) due to birth or adoption of the employee's child; (2) to care for the employee's spouse, child, or parent who has a serious health problem; or (3) due to a serious health problem of the employee that makes the employee unable to perform his or her job.
LIMITATIONS.   ▶ To be eligible for this leave, an employee must (1) be employed by the employer for at least 12 months and (2) have worked at least 1250 hours during the twelve months preceding the leave. ▶ If an employee does not return when the leave expires and is not otherwise legally entitled to additional leave, then the employer may discharge the employee.

19. LEAVES FOR MILITARY SERVICE UNDER USERRA

GENERAL RULES. ▶ The Uniformed Services Employment and Re-Employment Rights Act (USERRA) generally requires reservists who are returning from military service to be "promptly reemployed" by their previous employer to the same or comparable position with the same seniority, status and pay had they not been activated. ▶USERRA also (1) protects against premature discharge, (2) requires reasonable accommodation of disabled individuals, and (3) provides an array of remedies for violations.
LIMITATION.   USSERRA entitles an employer to discharge a reemployed serviceman for cause and exempt an employer from reemploying or continuing employment where changed circumstances make doing so impossible, unreasonable or a hardship.

20. SOCIAL SECURITY

Employers and employees are required to pay social security taxes to provide employees insurance for: (1) retirement benefits; (2) disability benefits; (3) life insurance; and (4) health insurance.

E. EMPLOYEES' HEALTH AND SAFETY

21. STANDARDS (OCCUPATIONAL SAFETY AND HEALTH ACT)

Under OSHA the government may create safety standards to protect employees from "significant" health risks. Standards must be economically feasible and are adopted only after hearings.

22. EMPLOYER DUTIES

▶ Employers have a duty to keep a workplace safe from hazards likely to cause death or serious injury. ▶ OSHA requires employers to keep records of serious occupational illnesses or injuries.

23. ENFORCEMENT

▶ OSHA can inspect workplaces and it may issue a citation for violation of safety or health regulations. ▶ Employers cannot retaliate against employees for refusing to work in dangerous conditions, testifying in OSHA proceedings, or filing complaints. ▶ LEARNING OUTCOME EXAMPLE: See the Thinking Things Through discussion for reasons why taking chances or shortcuts in violation of OSHA standards is bad management, textbook p. 920.

24. STATE "RIGHT-TO-KNOW" LEGISLATION

Many states require employers to notify an employee's doctor, local public and fire officials, and neighborhood residents regarding hazardous substances used or maintained at the workplace.

F. COMPENSATION FOR EMPLOYEES' INJURIES

25. COMMON LAW STATUS OF EMPLOYER

GENERAL RULES. ▶ Workers' compensation laws typically do not apply to certain employers, such as employers of agricultural, domestic, or casual workers. ▶ If workers' compensation laws do not apply, the common law requires an employer: (1) to provide a reasonably safe workplace, safe tools, and sufficient, capable coworkers; and (2) to warn of unusual dangers.
LIMITATION. Under common law, an employer is not liable for an employee's injury if (1) the employee was to any extent negligent, (2) the injury was caused by a fellow employee, or (3) the injury was caused by an ordinary work hazard.

26. STATUTORY CHANGES

GENERAL RULES. ▶ Workers' compensation pays medical benefits, a portion of lost wages for a stated number of weeks, and death benefits if an employee suffers work-related injuries or certain occupational diseases. ▶ Compensation is provided whether the employer or employee is negligent.
LIMITATIONS. ▶ An employee cannot sue an employer under tort law for a work-related injury - workers' compensation is the employee's exclusive remedy. ▶ Typically, no compensation is provided for willful, self-inflicted injuries or injuries received while the employee is intoxicated.

G. EMPLOYEE PRIVACY

27. SOURCE OF PRIVACY RIGHTS

The Constitution is the source of rights for government workers. Statutes, case law, and union contracts provide privacy rights for private workers.

28. MONITORING EMPLOYEE TELEPHONE CONVERSATIONS

Employers can monitor employees' calls in the ordinary course of business and with their consent.

29. E-MAIL MONITORING

► Employers can monitor employees' e-mail in the ordinary course of business and with their consent. ► Employers cannot access an employee's privately owned website under false pretenses.

30. PROPERTY SEARCHES

► Public employees can search employees' lockers and take similar actions. ►Private employers generally may take such actions including installing video surveillance cameras in public areas if notice is given. Video monitoring should not be used in private environments, e.g., restrooms etc.

31. DRUG AND ALCOHOL TESTING

Random drug testing is generally only allowed for jobs with safety or security concerns.

H. EMPLOYER-RELATED IMMIGRATION LAWS
32. EMPLOYER LIABILITY

The Immigration Reform and Control Act (IRCA) establishes civil and criminal penalties for employers who knowingly hire aliens who have illegally entered the United States.

33. EMPLOYER VERIFICATION AND SPECIAL HIRING PROGRAMS

► When an employer hires someone, IRCA requires the employer to verify that the employee is legally entitled to work in the U.S. This is done by confirming that the employee has certain documents. ►LEARNING OUTCOME EXAMPLE: See the Brazilian Quality Stones example of a CEO who did not meet his burden of proof that responsibilities were "primarily managerial," textbook p. 927.

CONCEPT REVIEW AND APPLICATIONS

Matching Exercise

Select the term or phrase that best matches a definition or statement stated below. Each term or phrase is the best match for only one statement or definition. Not all terms and phrases will necessarily be used.

economic strikers

employment-at-will

doctrine

mass picketing

primary picketing

right-to-work laws

secondary picketing

shop right

_____ 1. Employees who are striking because an employer would not agree to a union's economic demands.

_____ 2. Legal presentations in front of a business notifying the public of a labor dispute.

_____ 3. Illegal tactic of employees massing together in great numbers to effectively shut down entrances of the employer's facility.

_____ 4. Picketing an employer with which a union has no dispute to persuade the employer to stop doing business with a party to the dispute; generally illegal under the NLRA.

_____ 5. Legal principle that generally authorizes an employer at any time and for any reason to discharge an employee who is not hired for a fixed term.

_____ 6. Right of an employer to use in business without charge an invention discovered by an employee during working hours and with the employer's material and equipment.

_____ 7. Laws restricting unions and employees from negotiating clauses in their collective bargaining agreements that make union membership compulsory.

True/False

Write **T** if the statement is true, write **F** if it is false.

____ 1. An employment relationship is not created without the consent of both the employer and the employee.

____ 2. The Sarbanes-Oxley Act forbids retaliation against governmental employee whistleblowers but does not protect employee whistleblowers in private industry.

_____ 3. An employment-at-will contract is one that states a fixed term of employment, such as one year.

_____ 4. An employer has "good cause" to fire an employee if the employee committed fraud in obtaining employment or if the employee disobeys proper orders of the employer.

_____ 5. Absent a binding nondisclosure agreement, an employee can disclose an employer's confidential information and trade secrets after termination of employment.

_____ 6. The USERRA generally requires reservists who are returning from military service to be promptly reemployed by their previous employer to the same or comparable position.

_____ 7. Under IRCA, an employer may be subject to civil and criminal penalties for knowingly hiring an alien who is not legally entitled to work in the United States.

_____ 8. The Fair Labor Standards Act requires that all employees, including executive and administrative employees, be paid a specified minimum wage.

_____ 9. The Fair Labor Standards Act restricts the hours of work and work assignments for employees who are under the age of sixteen.

_____10. In most states, an employee is ineligible for unemployment benefits unless the employee is available and willing to take a similar replacement job for comparable pay.

Multiple Choice

_____ 1. Marlene has been a full-time employee of Garland Corp. for two years. Marlene recently became pregnant and gave birth to a son. Garland Corp. is subject to the Family and Medical Leave Act of 1993. Under these facts:
a. Marlene is entitled to receive one year of paid leave so she can care for her son.
b. Marlene is entitled to receive twelve weeks of paid leave so she can care for her son.
c. Marlene is entitled to receive twelve weeks of unpaid leave so she can care for her son.
d. Marlene is not entitled to receive any paid or unpaid leave so she can care for her son.

_____ 2. Ben's employment contract with Employer states that Ben can be terminated only for "good cause." Under these facts, Ben _cannot_ be fired for which of the following reasons?
a. Ben used illegal drugs during working hours.
b. Ben participated in lawful union activities.
c. Ben disclosed his employer's confidential customer list to a competitor.
d. Ben falsely stated on his employment application that he had a required college degree.

_____ 3. In most states, which individual would be eligible to receive unemployment benefits?
a. Mary quit her job because it was boring.
b. Jim was laid off from his job as a carpenter due to a recession in the building industry.
c. Frank cannot find work because he is a full-time student and is unavailable for work.
d. Elizabeth was fired because she was embezzling money from her employer.

_____ 4. Teresa filed a safety complaint with OSHA against her employer, Bayside Industries. Teresa has alleged that there are serious safety hazards at Bayside's plant. OSHA has indicated that it wants to inspect Bayside's plant. Under these facts:

    a. OSHA has the authority to inspect Bayside's plant, and Bayside cannot require OSHA to obtain a warrant prior to inspecting its plant.

    b. OSHA has no authority to inspect Bayside's plant. OSHA has only the power to adopt health
        and safety regulations.

    c. OSHA can issue a citation against Bayside if it finds safety violations at Bayside's plant, but   Bayside can contest the citation if it chooses to do so.

    d. Bayside can discharge Teresa for filing the complaint with OSHA.

_____ 5. Sharon was injured while working for Ajax Corp. Sharon's accident and resultant injuries were the result of her negligence and the negligence of Ajax Corp. Also, Ajax alleges that the accident was due to Sharon's intoxication, which claim she denies. Under these facts:

    a. Sharon cannot recover workers' compensation because her negligence caused the accident.

    b. Sharon can forego workers' compensation, and she can instead elect to sue Ajax under tort law   for all damages caused by Ajax's negligence.

    c. If Sharon was intoxicated, this fact would not affect her right to workers' compensation.

    d. If Sharon was not intoxicated, she can recover workers' compensation for medical benefits and a portion of her lost wages.

Case Problems

Answer the following problems, briefly explaining your answer.

1. Weiss Co. employs 70 nonunion factory workers pursuant to contracts that do not state a fixed period of employment. Weiss also employs 10 management employees pursuant to two-year employment contracts. Weiss Co. has experienced financial difficulties and is considering these actions:

    a. discharge Henry, a factory worker, even though he has properly done his work;

    b. discharge Ellen, a factory worker, because she has filed a claim for workers' compensation; and

    c. discharge Karen, a management employee, even though she has properly performed her work.

Which of the foregoing actions may Weiss Co. legally do?

_____

_____

_____

_____

2. The assembly line employees of Sheridan Corp. are represented by Union Local 482. The company and union are unable to agree upon a wage increase for the employees. Also, the company refuses to bargain with the union regarding internal management policies that do not relate to the employees. The union has called a strike because the company failed to agree to the union's requested wage increase for the employees. Under these facts:

   a. Was the company legally required to negotiate with the union regarding the wage increase and/or internal management policies?

   b. May the union legally call a strike because the company refuses to agree to the wage increase?

   c. Can the union picket the company's work site?

   d. If the company hires replacement workers, must it fire them and rehire striking employees once the strike is over?

   _____

   _____

3. Isabel has been a full-time employee of Pell Corp. for ten years during which time Pell Corp. has had a pension plan for its employees. The plan is subject to all ERISA regulations. Isabel is concerned that she may be discharged, thereby depriving her of her pension benefits. She is also concerned that the pension fund may not have sufficient assets to pay her benefits when she retires, or that Pell Corp. may become insolvent thereby depriving her of her pension benefits.

   a. What federal law regulates this pension fund?

   b. When must Isabel's right to pension benefits vest?

   c. What guarantee does Isabel have that she will receive her benefits if Pell Corp. goes out of business?

   _____

   _____

   _____

Internet Exercise

Tracy owns a cafe and she is having a difficult time finding workers for certain positions. She has the following openings: (1) dishwasher who can work on weekends for three hours each day during lunch hour; and (2) short-order cook who can use an electric grill, meat cutter, deep fryer, and vegetable chopper. Three teenagers have applied for these jobs; their ages are 14, 16, and 18. Tracy has asked you if there are any federal laws that prohibit her from hiring any of these teenagers for the jobs in question. Therefore:

1. Using the Internet, identify the federal statutes and administrative regulations, if any, that apply to this case.
2. Which teenager(s), if any, can Tracy hire for the positions in question?

_____

_____

_____

CPA REVIEW

The following questions were given on CPA examinations. The answers for these questions are the unofficial answers prepared by the American Institute of Certified Public Accountants, Inc. (AICPA). All material is reproduced with permission of the AICPA.

____ 1. Which of the following payments are deducted from an employee's salary?

Unemployment compensation insurance	Worker's compensation insurance
a. Yes	Yes
b. Yes	No
c. No	Yes
d. No	No

____ 2. Which of the following provisions is basic to all workers' compensation systems?
   a. The injured employee must prove the employer's negligence.
   b. The employer may invoke the traditional defense of contributory negligence.
   c. The employer's liability may be ameliorated by a co-employee's negligence under the fellow-servant rule.
   d. The injured employee is allowed to recover on strict liability theory.

____ 3. Under which of the following conditions is an on-site inspection of a workplace by an investigator from the Occupational Safety and Health Administration (OSHA) permissible?
   a. Only if OSHA obtains a search warrant after showing probable cause.
   b. Only if the inspection is conducted after working hours.
   c. At the request of employees.
   d. After OSHA provides the employer with at least 24 hours notice of the prospective inspection.

___ 4. Under the Federal Fair Labor Standards Act, which of the following would be regulated?

	Minimum wage	Overtime	Number of hours in the workweek
a.	Yes	Yes	Yes
b.	Yes	No	Yes
c.	Yes	Yes	No
d.	No	Yes	Yes

___ 5. Kroll, an employee of Acorn, Inc., was injured in the course of employment while operating a forklift manufactured and sold to Acorn by Trell Corp. The forklift was defectively designed by Trell. Under the state's mandatory workers' compensation statute, Kroll will be successful in

	Obtaining workers' compensation benefits	A negligence action against Acorn
a.	Yes	Yes
b.	Yes	No
c.	No	Yes
d.	No	No

___ 6. An unemployed CPA generally would receive unemployment compensation benefits if the CPA
   a. Was fired as a result of the employer's business reversals.
   b. Refused to accept a job as an accountant while receiving extended benefits.
   c. Was fired for embezzling from a client.
   d. Left work voluntarily without good cause.

___ 7. Nix, an employee of Fern, Inc., was injured in the course of employment while operating a drill press manufactured and sold to Fern by Jet Corp. It has been determined that Fern was negligent in supervising the operation of the drill press and that the drill press was defectively designed by Jet. If Fern has complied with the state's mandatory workers' compensation statute, Nix may
   a. Not properly commence a products liability action against Jet.
   b. Not obtain workers' compensation benefits.
   c. Obtain workers' compensation benefits and properly maintain a products liability action against Jet.
   d. Obtain workers' compensation benefits and properly maintain separate causes of action against Jet and Fern for negligence.

___ 8. Farr, an employee of Sand Corp., was involved in an accident with Wohl, an independent contractor. Wohl was making a delivery for Byrd Corp. when Farr negligently passed through a red light resulting in the accident and injuries to Wohl and Farr. The accident occurred during Farr's regular working hours and in the course of Farr's employment. If Sand and Byrd have complied with the state's workers' compensation laws, which of the following is correct?

    a. Farr will either be denied workers' compensation benefits or have his benefits reduced due to his negligence.

    b. Farr will be denied workers' compensation benefits since Sand was free from any wrong-doing.

    c. Wohl will be denied workers' compensation benefits under Sand's or Byrd's workers' compensation policy.

    d. Wohl will be denied workers' compensation benefits due to the fellow-servant rule.

CHAPTER 40
EQUAL EMPLOYMENT OPPORTUNITY LAW

MAKE THE CONNECTION

SUMMARY

Title VII of the Civil Rights Act of 1964, as amended, forbids discrimination on the basis of race, color, religion, sex, or national origin. The EEOC administers the act. Intentional discrimination is unlawful when there is disparate treatment of individuals because of their race, color, religion, gender, or national origin. Also, employment practices that make no reference to race, color, religion, sex, or national origin, but that nevertheless have an adverse or disparate impact on the protected group, are unlawful. In disparate impact cases, the fact that an employer did not intend to discriminate is no defense. The employer must show that there is a job related business necessity for the disparate impact practice in question. Employers have several defenses they may raise in a Title VII case to explain differences in employment conditions: (1) bona fide occupational qualifications reasonably necessary to the normal operation of the business, (2) job-related professionally developed ability tests, and (3) bona fide seniority systems. If a state EEO agency or the EEOC is not able to resolve the case, the EEOC issues a right-to-sue letter that enables the person claiming a Title VII violation to sue in a federal district court. An affirmative action plan is legal under Title VII provided there is a voluntary "plan" justified as a remedial measure and provided it does not unnecessarily trammel the interests of whites.

Under the Equal Pay Act (EPA), employers must not pay employees of one gender a lower wage rate than the rate paid to employees of the other gender for substantially equal work. Workers over 40 years old are protected from discrimination by the Age Discrimination in Employment Act (ADEA). Employment discrimination against persons with disabilities is prohibited by the Americans with Disabilities Act (ADA). Under the ADA, employers must make reasonable accommodations without undue hardship on them to enable individuals with disabilities to work.

LEARNING OUTCOMES
After studying this chapter, you should be able to

A. TITLE VII OF THE CIVIL RIGHTS ACT OF 1964, AS AMENDED
LO.1   Explain the difference between the *disparate treatment* theory of employment discrimination and the *disparate impact* theory of employment discrimination

B. PROTECTED CLASSES AND EXCEPTIONS
LO.2   List and explain the categories of individuals protected against unlawful employment discrimination under Title VII.
LO.3   Recognize, and know the remedies for, sexual harassment in the workplace
LO.4   Explain the antiretaliation provision of Title VII

C. OTHER EQUAL EMPLOYMENT OPPORTUNITY
LO.5   List and explain the laws protecting equal pay for women and men for equal work, as well as the laws forbidding discrimination on the basis of age and against individuals with disabilities

D. EXTRATERRITORIAL EMPLOYMENT
LO.6   Explain how both Title VII of the Civil Rights Act and the ADA protect from discrimination U.S. citizens working in foreign countries for American-owned and American-controlled businesses.

427

CHAPTER OUTLINE

A. TITLE VII OF THE CIVIL RIGHTS ACT OF 1964, AS AMENDED

Title VII seeks to eliminate discrimination against job applicants and employees on the basis of race, color, national origin, religion, and sex.

1. THEORIES OF DISCRIMINATION

A discrimination claim may be based on disparate treatment or disparate impact.

➢ *Disparate treatment*: A disparate treatment claim exists when an employer intentionally treats a job applicant or employee less favorably because of his or her race, color, national origin, religion, or sex.

➢ *Disparate impact*: Disparate impact exists when a neutral employment practice has a significantly different, negative impact on a protected group.

➢ **LEARNING OUTCOME EXAMPLE**: See the discussion of the New Haven Firefighters case in which the city relied on a disparate impact theory and the firefighters asserted disparate treatment, textbook p. 936.

2. THE EQUAL EMPLOYMENT OPPORTUNITY COMMISSION (EEOC)

➢ *Procedure*: ▶ The EEOC administers Title VII and other federal antidiscrimination laws relating to employment. A charging party (job applicant or employee) must first file a claim with a state or local EEO agency if one exists. If there is no such state agency, then the EEOC may attempt to resolve the dispute through conciliation. If this is unsuccessful, the EEOC may file suit or it may give the charging party a "right-to-sue letter," entitling the party to file suit in federal court within ninety days.

➢ *Damages*: Victims of discrimination may recover damages, including back pay.

➢ *The Arbitration Option*: ▶ Employers may legally include in all employment contracts (except for transportation workers) an arbitration provision that requires employees to arbitrate all disputes including discrimination claims under federal law. ▶ Such arbitration provisions must, however, be fundamentally fair and cannot alter employees' substantive rights under federal discrimination laws.

B. PROTECTED CLASSES AND EXCEPTIONS

3. RACE AND COLOR

Discrimination based on a person's race or color is prohibited by Title VII. "Race" applies to all members of the following four racial groups: black, white, Native American, and Asian-Pacific.

4. RELIGION

GENERAL RULES. ▶ Employers cannot discriminate against persons on the basis of their religion or religious beliefs. ▶ Employers must try to reasonably accommodate job applicants' and employees' religious beliefs and practices, which may include an employee's body art.

LIMITATIONS ► Employers are not required to violate a collective bargaining agreement or to go to great expense to hire a replacement to accommodate an employee's religious requirements for days off. ► Religious societies and schools may give preference to members of their religion.

5. SEX

GENERAL RULES. ► It is illegal for employers to discriminate against male or female employees on the basis of their sex. ► The Pregnancy Discrimination Act requires that an employer treat pregnancy and related conditions in the same manner that other disabilities are treated.

LIMITATION. Sex refers only to a person's gender (i.e., male or female). Therefore, Title VII does not prohibit discrimination because of a person's sexual orientation.

STUDY HINT. If a particular employment requirement, such as the height, weight, or physical strength, has a disparate impact on women or another protected group, then the employer must be able to show that the requirement is actually job related.

6. SEXUAL HARASSMENT

There are two types of sexual harassment for which an employer may be held liable under Title VII.

➢ *Tangible employment action*: This type of harassment occurs when a supervisor takes significant negative employment actions against an employee because the employee refused the supervisor's request for sexual favors. An employer is always liable this type of harassment.

➢ *Hostile work environment - supervisors*: ► This type of harassment may result from unwelcome sexual propositions, insults, suggestive pictures, and/or physical contact. This violation occurs although no actual action is taken against the employee by the supervisor, but severe or pervasive wrongful conduct is required. ► When no tangible action is taken against an employee, the employer can avoid liability by proving that the employer used reasonable care to avoid this type of conduct, the employer acted promptly to correct any harassment, and the employee unreasonably failed to use corrective measures offered by the employer.

➢ *Hostile work environment – non-supervisors*: An employer is liable for sexual harassment by non-supervisors or customers only when it fails to take remedial action when it knows or should know of this misconduct.

➢ **LEARNING OUTCOME EXAMPLE**: See Figure 40-2 for a presentation of an employer sexual harassment policy, textbook p. 943.

7. PROTECTION AGAINST RETALIATION

► Title VII forbids retaliation against an employee because he or she filed or otherwise assisted in connection with a claim of discrimination in violation of Title VII. ► Protection is afforded against only retaliation that is "materially adverse," not trivial conduct. ► LEARNING OUTCOME EXAMPLE: See the *White* case, which sets forth the elements of retaliatory discrimination and the remedy provided, textbook p. 944.

8. NATIONAL ORIGIN

GENERAL RULE. Title VII forbids discrimination based on a person's national origin.

STUDY HINTS. ► Physical standards, such as height, must be justified as a "business necessity" if they tend to exclude persons of a particular nationality. ► English language skills can be considered in employment decisions only when it is clearly necessary for successful job performance. ► An employer can consider a person's accent only if it impairs his or her ability to communicate effectively.

9. TITLE VII EXCEPTIONS

> *Bona fide occupational qualification (BFOQ) exception*: ► An employer can hire an employee on the basis of religion, sex, or national origin if this consideration is a BFOQ that is reasonably necessary to the normal operation of a particular enterprise. ► There is no BFOQ for race or color. ► A fetal protection policy that is intended to protect unborn children of women cannot be defended as a BFOQ.
> *Testing and educational requirements*: ► Title VII allows professionally developed ability tests that are not used to discriminate. Employers must prove that these tests and educational requirements are job related. ► The Civil Rights Act of 1991 forbids "race-norming," i.e., adjusting test scores or cutoff points to assure that minorities are considered for employment.
> *Seniority systems*: Title VII allows differences in employment terms and compensation that are the result of a bona fide seniority system, so long as there is no intention to discriminate.

10. AFFIRMATIVE ACTION AND REVERSE DISCRIMINATION

GENERAL RULE. An affirmative action plan (AAP) can undertake special efforts to hire, train, and advance women and minorities and, in appropriate cases, can extend preferences to them.
LIMITATIONS. ► An AAP should: (1) have a plan; (2) be justified as remedial; (3) be voluntary; (4) not unnecessarily limit the interests of whites; and (5) be temporary. ► If an AAP is not justified or unreasonably limits the interests of whites, it is "reverse discrimination" and illegal.

C. OTHER EQUAL EMPLOYMENT OPPORTUNITY (EEO) LAWS

11. EQUAL PAY

GENERAL RULE. The Equal Pay Act requires that employers must pay male and female employees the same wage for jobs that are substantially equal.
LIMITATION. Differences in pay for male and female employees are permissible if they are the result of: (1) a seniority system; (2) a merit system; (3) a pay scale based on quality or quantity of production; or (4) any factor other than the sex of the employees.

12. AGE DISCRIMINATION

> The Age Discrimination in Employment Act (ADEA) prohibits employers, unions, and employment agencies from discriminating against persons over 40 years of age on the basis of their age. Twice the amount of damages can be recovered if age discrimination is willful.

> The Older Workers Benefit Protection Act of 1990 prohibits age discrimination in connection with employee benefits unless the employer can prove that the cost of benefits for older workers is more than for younger workers.

> LEARNING OUTCOME EXAMPLE: See the *Rhodes* case with facts and a remedy applicable to age discrimination on textbook p. 949

13. DISCRIMINATION AGAINST PERSONS WITH DISABILITIES

GENERAL RULES. ▶ The Americans with Disabilities Act (ADA) forbids discrimination against persons with disabilities who are qualified, with or without reasonable accommodation, to perform the essential functions of a job. ▶ Employers must make reasonable accommodations for employees with disabilities including: (1) making existing facilities accessible to and usable by persons with disabilities; and (2) restructuring jobs, modifying schedules, and acquiring or modifying equipment.

LIMITATIONS. ▶ The ADA applies only to employers who have 15 or more employees. ▶ If a job offer is contingent on passing a medical test, the employer can revoke the offer if the job would pose a direct threat to the applicant's health. ▶ Whether an impairment is a qualified disability is evaluated in its corrected state. Example: impaired vision corrected by glasses. ▶ Employers are not required to make accommodations that would cause an "undue hardship." ▶ Disabilities not protected under the ADA include current use of illegal drugs, pedophilia, and kleptomania **STUDY HINTS.** ▶ Persons with AIDS and certain contagious diseases are protected from discrimination. ▶ Employers cannot ask job applicants if they need reasonable accommodations *for the job*, but they can ask if applicants can perform job-related duties.

LEARNING OUTCOME EXAMPLE. See the Patrick Brady example of the attention-getting judgment in a case where the employer failed to recognize its obligation to make a reasonable accommodation, textbook p. 953.

D. EXTRATERRITORIAL EMPLOYMENT

GENERAL RULE. The Civil Rights Act of 1991 provides that U.S. citizens employed by American companies in foreign countries are protected by Title VII and the Americans with Disabilities Act. **LIMITATION.** U.S. employers doing business in other countries are not required to comply with Title VII or the ADA if this action would violate the law of the host country.

CONCEPT REVIEW AND APPLICATIONS

Matching Exercise

Select the term or phrase that best matches a definition or statement stated below. Each term or phrase is the best match for only one statement or definition. Not all terms and phrases will necessarily be used.

a. Affirmative action plan
b. Age Discrimination in Employment Act
c. Americans with Disabilities Act (ADA)
d. Bona fide occupational qualification (BFOQ)
e. Discrimination
f. Disparate impact
g. Disparate treatment
h. EEOC
i. Equal Pay Act
j. Hostile work environment harassment
k. Race
l. Reasonable accommodation
m. Reverse discrimination
n. Seniority system
o. Tangible employment action

_____ 1 Discrimination resulting from neutral employment practice that has different effect on a protected class.

_____ 2. Conduct against a person based on the person's race, color, religion, sex, or national origin.

_____ 3. Defense that allows an employer to hire a person on the basis of sex, religion, or national origin when necessary for normal operations of the business.

_____ 4. Law that forbids paying male and female employees different wages for substantially equal work.

_____ 5. Law that prohibits discrimination against persons over forty years of age.

_____ 6. Sexual harassment resulting from unwelcome sexual conduct that poisons the workplace.

_____ 7. Plan that may allow an employer to provide job preferences for women and minorities.

_____ 8. Law that prohibits discrimination against qualified persons with disabilities.

_____ 9. Federal agency that administers Title VII and other federal antidiscrimination laws.

_____ 10. Protected class that includes blacks, whites, Native Americans, and Asian-Pacific persons.

True/False

Write **T** if the statement is true, write **F** if it is false.

_____ 1. Disparate treatment exists when a neutral employment practice has a disproportionate, negative impact on a protected class.

_____ 2. Title VII prohibits discrimination against males and whites.

_____ 3. An employee's religious practices must always be accommodated, even if accommodation requires violation of a collective bargaining agreement.

_____ 4. A religious society may refuse to hire a person who practices a different religion.

_____ 5. It is not a violation of the Equal Pay Act to pay different wages to male and female employeesif the difference is due to a bona fide seniority system.

_____ 6. The sex (gender) of an employee may constitute a BFOQ in certain situations.

7. An employer is liable for sexual harassment that constitutes a tangible employment action whether the employer knew or did not know about the misconduct.

_____ 8. The ADA generally protects U.S. citizens who are employed by U.S. companies in foreign country unless compliance would violate the law of the foreign country.

_____ 9. An affirmative action plan can legally provide that only women or minorities will be considered for jobs.

_____10. In general, it is a violation of the Equal Pay Act for an employer to pay a male employee more than a female employee for performing the same job.

Multiple Choice

_____ 1. The Johnson Trucking Company is a national trucking firm that is owned by four black women. The company hires only women and minorities because the owners are prejudiced against all other persons. Under these facts, this hiring practice:
a. Violates Title VII.
b. Violates the ADA.
c. Violates the ADEA.
d. Does not violate any laws because it is a valid affirmative action plan.

_____ 2. Todd is a lawyer, and he is blind. Todd applied for a job as associate lawyer with a large, national law firm. Todd met all qualifications of the job. He also could perform all of the duties of the job if the firm occasionally provided a reader to help him with his legal research. The law firm rejected Todd's application, arguing that he is not qualified for the job. Under these facts, did the law firm violate the ADA?
a. No, because Todd is blind, a condition that is not protected by the ADA.
b. No, because Todd is not qualified to perform the job in question.
c. Yes, because the ADA requires employers to hire all persons with a disability, whether they are qualified or not.
d. Yes, because Todd is qualified to perform the job in question, if the law firm provides reasonable accommodation.

_____ 3. Mary was recently hired by XYZ Company to work as a stocker in the warehouse. Mary's male coworkers made a couple of sexual jokes in front of Mary. Mary was highly offended by these jokes and she quit. A reasonable person would not have been offended by these jokes, nor would a reasonable person have found the workplace to be hostile. Under these facts:
a. XYZ would be liable to Mary for quid pro quo sexual harassment.
b. XYZ would be liable to Mary for hostile working environment harassment.
c. XYZ would not be liable to Mary for any type of sexual harassment.
d. a and b.

434

_____ 4. Mega Inc. is a U.S. firm that engages in international business. Nancy, a U.S. citizen, applied for a job as a mechanic at Mega Corporation's Paris plant. Nancy was refused employment because the company has traditionally considered women only for secretarial positions at this plant. Under these facts:
   a. Mega Corporation has violated Title VII.
   b. Mega Corporation has not violated Title VII because Title VII does not apply outside the U.S.
   c. Mega Corporation has not violated Title VII because a U.S. company can discriminate in another country if it has traditionally done so.
   d. Mega Corporation has not violated Title VII because Title VII does not prohibit sex discrimination.

_____ 5. The Christian Academy refused to hire Paul for a teaching position because he is Muslim. Instead, the Academy hired a Christian who had less experience than Paul. Under these facts:
   a. The Academy committed religious discrimination in violation of Title VII.
   b. The Academy committed religious discrimination in violation of the ADA.
   c. The Academy did not violate Title VII or the ADA.
   d. a and b.

_____ 6. Dr. Kathy Payne advertised for an "experienced receptionist, females preferred." Payne is a gynecologist and she believes that her patients feel more comfortable when greeted by a female receptionist than when greeted by a male receptionist. Bill, a highly qualified job applicant applied for the advertised job, but was rejected because of his gender. Under these facts, Payne has:
   a. Violated Title VII.
   b. Violated the ADA.
   c. Violated the ADEA.
   d. Not violated any federal antidiscrimination law.

_____ 7. Julio was born in Mexico and now lives in the United States. Julio is not yet a U.S. citizen. He applied for an analyst position at the Intelligence Research Center (IRC), a private firm that provides intelligence analysis for the government. Analysts must have top-secret security clearance, which is impossible to obtain without U.S. citizenship. IRC refused to hire Julio because he did not have the required clearance. Under these facts IRC has:
   a. Violated Title VII.
   b. Violated the ADA.
   c. Violated the ADEA.
   d. Not violated any federal antidiscrimination law.

_____ 8. Ames Fire Department requires firefighters to lift 250 pounds because, at rare times, a firefighter may have to lift this weight. Chris applied for a job as fire fighter and she was qualified to for the duties of the job. Chris and all other female applicants were rejected, however, because they could not lift this weight. Fifty percent of the qualified applicants were women. Has Ames violated Title VII?

   a. Yes, it has committed a disparate treatment violation.
   b. Yes, it has committed a disparate impact violation.
   c. Yes, it has committed a sexual harassment violation.
   d. No, this requirement is a protected BFOQ.

_____ 9. Joe is the principal at Blinker High School. Joe told Maria, a history teacher at the school, that he would terminate her unless she agreed to have sexual relations with him. When Maria refused, Joe caused her dismissal. The Blinker School District that included Blinker High School had no knowledge of Joe's conduct. Has Blinker School District violated Title VII?

   a. Yes, it has committed a disparate treatment violation.
   b. Yes, it has committed a disparate impact violation.
   c. Yes, it has committed a sexual harassment violation.
   d. No, Blinker School District is not responsible for Joe's conduct.

_____ 10. ABC Sporting Goods International fired John as a salesperson because he is homosexual and is infected with the AIDS virus. Under these facts:

   a. ABC's discrimination against John because he is homosexual violates Title VII.
   b. ABC's discrimination against John because he is infected with the AIDS virus violates the ADA.
   c. ABC's conduct does not violate Title VII or the ADA.
   d. a and b.

Case Problem

Answer the following problem, briefly explaining your answer.

Kim Pak was born in Korea and she recently became a U.S. citizen. Kim speaks fluent English, but she has a slight Korean accent. Her accent does not interfere with her ability to communicate with others. Kim applied for the job of manager at the Jasper Hotel, a large hotel in Minneapolis. However, Kim was not hired for this position.

Explain whether the following reasons are proper for not hiring Kim: (1) Kim speaks with a slight Korean accent; (2) Kim is fifty years old, and she may not work for as many years as someone younger; (3) Kim has a hearing disorder and the hotel would have to spend $250 to purchase a special telephone for her.

_____

_____

_____

_____

Internet Exercise

Sarah was an employee at Cook Corp. for two years. During that time, she was subject to repeated, unwelcomed sexual advances and lewd behavior on the part of her male employees and her supervisor. Also, several male workers tried to kiss her and touch her inappropriately. She complained several times to the company's managers, but they merely said: "Boys will be boys. Just learn to live with it." Finally, it became so intolerable that she quit.

(1) Does Sarah have a valid claim against Cook Corp. for sexual harassment? (2) Using the Internet, identify the location of the EEOC home page and summarize what Sarah must do to file a harassment claim.

_____

_____

_____

_____

CPA REVIEW

The following questions were given on CPA examinations. The answers for these questions are the unofficial answers prepared by the American Institute of Certified Public Accountants, Inc. (AICPA). All material is reproduced with permission of the AICPA.

_____ 1. Under the provisions of the Americans With Disabilities Act of 1990, in which of the following areas is a disabled person protected from discrimination?

	Public transportation	Privately operated public accommodations
a.	Yes	Yes
b.	Yes	No
c.	No	Yes
d.	No	No

_____ 2. Under Title VII of the 1964 Civil Rights Act, which of the following forms of discrimination is not prohibited?
a. Sex
b. Age.
c. Race.
d. Religion.

_____ 3. Under the Federal Age Discrimination in Employment Act, which of the following practices would be prohibited?

	Compulsory retirement of employees below the age of 65	Termination of employees between the ages of 65 and 70 for cause
a.	Yes	Yes
b.	Yes	No
c.	No	Yes
d.	No	No

CHAPTER 41
TYPES OF BUSINESS ORGANIZATIONS

MAKE THE CONNECTION

SUMMARY

The three principal forms of business organizations are sole proprietorships, partnerships, and corporations. A *sole proprietorship* is a form of business organization in which one person owns the business, controls all decisions, receives all profits, and has unlimited liability for all obligations and liabilities. A *partnership* involves the pooling of capital resources and talents of two or more persons whose goal is making a profit; the partners are subject to unlimited personal liability. However, newly created forms of business organizations—the *limited liability company* and the *limited liability partnership*—allow for tax treatment as a partnership with certain limited liability for the owners.

A business *corporation* exists to make a profit. It is created by government grant, and its shareholders elect a board of directors whose members are responsible for managing the business. A shareholder's liability is limited to the capital the shareholder invested in the business or paid for shares. Corporate existence continues without regard to the death of shareholders or the transfer of stock by them.

The selection of the form of organization is determined by the nature of the business, tax considerations, the financial risk involved, the importance of limited liability, and the extent of management control desired.

A *joint venture* exists when two or more persons combine their labor or property for a single business undertaking and share profits and losses as agreed. An unincorporated association is a combination of two or more persons for the pursuit of a common purpose.

A *cooperative* consists of two or more persons or enterprises, such as farmers, who cooperate to achieve a common objective, such as the distribution of farm products.

By a franchise, the owner of a trademark, trade name, or copyright licenses others to use the mark or copyright in selling goods or services. To protect against fraud, the FTC requires that franchisors provide prospective franchisees with a disclosure statement 10 days prior to any transaction. The Automobile Dealers' Day in Court Act and the Petroleum Marketing Practices Act are federal laws that provide covered
franchisees with protection from bad-faith terminations. State laws also protect franchisees in a wide range of businesses. A franchisor is not liable to third persons dealing with its franchisees. Liability of the franchisor may, however, be imposed on the ground of the apparent authority of the franchisee or the latter's control by the franchisor. Liability of the franchisor may also arise in cases of product liability.

LEARNING OUTCOMES
After studying this chapter, you should be able to

A. PRINCIPAL FORMS OF BUSINESS ORGANIZATIONS
LO.1   Explain the advantages and disadvantages of the three principal forms of business organizations

B. SPECIALIZED FORMS OF ORGANIZATIONS

LO.2 Recognize that the rules of law governing the rights and liabilities of joint ventures are substantially the same as those that govern partnerships

C. THE FRANCHISE BUSINESS FORMAT

LO.3 Evaluate whether a business arrangement is a franchise protected under state or federal law
Explain how the rights of the parties to a franchise agreement are determined by their contract

LO.4 Explain why freedom from vicarious liability is a reason for franchisors to use the franchise format

CHAPTER OUTLINE

A. PRINCIPAL FORMS OF BUSINESS ORGANIZATIONS

1. INDIVIDUAL (SOLE) PROPRIETORSHIPS

➢ *Definition*: A proprietorship is a business owned and controlled by one person, the proprietor.

➢ *Advantages*: ▶ *Formation*: There is no expense to form a sole proprietorship, and nothing is generally required to establish this business. ▶ *Control*: The owner controls all business decisions. ▶ *Profits*: The proprietor receives all profits of the business. ▶ *Taxation*: Profits of the business are not subject to corporate tax. Instead, profits are taxed only as personal income.

➢ *Disadvantages*: ▶ *Liability*: A proprietor has unlimited personal liability for debts of the business. ▶ *Capital*: The capital (financial resources) of the business is limited to the owner's personal assets. ▶ *Duration*: A sole proprietorship's business commonly terminates on the owner's death or disability.

2. PARTNERSHIPS, LLPs, AND LLCs

➢ *Definitions*: ▶ A partnership is an association of two or more persons who combine their financial resources and business skills to carry on a business for profit as co-owners. ▶ A limited liability partnership (LLP) is a new form of partnership that shields partners from personal liability for certain types of partnership obligations. ▶ A limited liability company (LLC) is a new form of business that is taxed as a partnership, but shields owners (members) from personal liability for the business' debts.

➢ *Advantages of partnerships*: ▶ *Formation*: A partnership does not require a formal organizational structure. Consequently, little or no expense is required to form a general partnership. ▶ *Capital*: The multiple ownership of a partnership permits individuals to combine their financial resources.

➢ *Disadvantages of partnerships*: ▶ *Liability*: Each partner has unlimited personal liability for partnership debts. ▶ *Duration*: The duration of a partnership is potentially unstable because the death of any partner and numerous other events may cause a partnership to dissolve.

3. CORPORATIONS

➢ *Definition*: ▶ A corporation is an artificial legal entity that may be created by permission of the government. ▶ The shareholders are the owners of a corporation, and they elect a board of directors who manage the corporation's business.

➢ *Advantages*: ▶ *Liability*: A shareholder's liability is limited to the amount of capital invested. ▶ *Capital*: A corporation can obtain investments from many individuals in order to raise significant capital. *Duration*: Corporations may enjoy perpetual (continuous) existence because a shareholder's death does not cause a dissolution of a corporation. ▶ *Transferability of ownership*: Shareholders are free to transfer shares.

> *Disadvantages*: ▶ *Formation*: Creating a corporation requires an expenditure of time and money. ▶ *Taxation*: A corporation pays income tax on its profits and shareholders are taxed on dividends paid to them, creating "double taxation."

B. SPECIALIZED FORMS OF ORGANIZATIONS

4. JOINT VENTURES

> *Definition*: ▶ A joint venture is an association of two or more persons who pool their resources in order to engage in a single business undertaking, with profits and losses being shared equally unless otherwise agreed. ▶ Example: Texas Oil Corp. and Ramon Oil Corp. combine their resources to jointly build and operate an oil pipeline that will serve their respective oil fields.

> *Nature of relationship*: A joint venture is quite similar to a general partnership. The primary distinction is that a joint venture is typically formed to accomplish a single enterprise whereas a partnership is usually intended to operate an ongoing business.

> *Duration*: ▶ A joint venture terminates at the time stated in the joint venture agreement. ▶ If a fixed term is not stated, a joint venture can typically be terminated at any time by any party.

> *Liability to third persons*: A member of a joint venture has unlimited personal liability for obligations of a joint venture, including liability for torts committed by other venturers.

> *Controlling law*: ▶ In general, a joint venture is governed by general partnership law.
▶ LEARNING OUTCOME EXAMPLE: See the *PGI/Rathe* joint venture remedy on textbook p. 966.

5. UNINCORPORATED ASSOCIATIONS

> *Definition*: ▶ An unincorporated association is a group of two or more persons who come together in order to further a common (and typically nonprofit) purpose. ▶ Social clubs and fraternal orders are common types of unincorporated associations. ▶ Example: Mary Jean, Tanya, and Diana agree to perform free singing recitals for residents of local retirement communities.

> *Nature of relationship*: ▶ An unincorporated association is not a separate legal entity, and no formal organization is required. An association may result from any conduct or agreement to work together for a common purpose. ▶ Rights of parties are governed by ordinary contract law. Consequently, members cannot be expelled except for reasons expressly agreed upon.

> *Liability*: ▶ An unincorporated association cannot sue or be sued. ▶ An association member is generally not liable for an obligation of the association unless the member authorized or ratified the contract or action in question. ▶ If a member is liable for an association obligation, the member has unlimited personal liability for the obligation.

6. COOPERATIVES

> *Definition*: ▶ A cooperative is an association of two or more independent parties that cooperate with one another in order to accomplish a common objective. ▶ Examples: farmers collectively sell their crops; consumers collectively own and operate a food cooperative (i.e., grocery store).

> *Nature of relationship*: State laws frequently require that the profits of a cooperative must be shared by cooperative members. These laws commonly require that excess funds or profits be distributed to members in proportion to the volume of business that each member has done with the cooperative.

> *Incorporated cooperatives*: Statutes often provide special rules for incorporation of cooperatives.

> *Antitrust law exemption*: The Capper-Volstead Act of 1922 exempts normal activities of farmers' and dairy farmers' cooperatives from the Sherman Antitrust Act that prohibits price fixing. This exemption applies as long as the subject cooperatives do not conspire to fix prices with outsiders.

C. THE FRANCHISE BUSINESS FORMAT

7. DEFINITION AND TYPES OF FRANCHISES

> *Definition*: A franchise is a business arrangement by which an owner of a trademark, trade name, or copyright (franchisor) licenses a franchisee to sell goods or services using this mark, name, or copyright.

> *Types of franchises*: ► Manufacturing or processing franchise: franchisee is granted right to manufacture and sell products using the franchisor's trademark. ► Service franchise: franchisee renders a service under terms of franchise agreement. ► Distribution franchise: franchisor's products sold to franchisee who then resells them in a certain geographical area. Example: gas stations.

8. THE FRANCHISE AGREEMENT

> *Franchise relationship*: ► A franchise is a business relationship between separate businesses that is governed by a franchise contract. A franchisor and franchisee are independent contractors. ► The word "franchise" does not have to be used in order to create a franchise. A relationship is treated as a franchise if it meets the applicable legal test for a franchise.

> *Duration and termination*: ► The franchise contract determines the duration of a franchise and the reasons for which it can be terminated. ► Contracts often allow termination upon afranchisee's death, bankruptcy, failure to make payments, or failure to meet sales quotas. ► LEARNING OUTCOME EXAMPLE: See the *Burger King* example involving cancellation of franchises, textbook p. 970.

9. SPECIAL PROTECTIONS UNDER FEDERAL LAWS

► In some states, prior notice of termination of a franchise is required. ► The federal Automobile Dealers' Franchise Act forbids termination of auto dealership franchises for failure to comply with unreasonable demands. ► Federal law extends special protection to gas station franchisees. ► LEARNING OUTCOME EXAMPLEs: See the *Girl Scouts of Manitou* case applying a state's fair dealership law, textbook p. 969; see the example where Mr. Arciniaga was allowed to proceed with his federal ADDCA lawsuit against General Motors on textbook p. 970.

10. DISCLOSURE

FTC rules require a franchisor to give a franchisee a disclosure statement ten days before signing a franchise contract or paying for a franchise. A franchisor may be fined for up to $10,000 if a franchisor knows or should know of this duty but fails to comply.

11. VICARIOUS LIABILITY CLAIMS AGAINST FRANCHISORS

GENERAL RULE. ▶ In general, a franchisor is not liable for the contracts or torts of a franchisee; the franchisee is solely liable for contract and tort liabilities arising in connection with the franchise. ▶ Example: Acme Corp. grants Boswell a franchise to sell Acme's equipment. Boswell leases a store for its business. If Boswell defaults on the lease, Boswell is solely liable; Acme Corp. is not liable on the lease.
LIMITATION. A franchisor may be liable to a third party in connection with a franchisee's business if: (1) the franchisor controls (or appears to control) the franchisee's business, and the franchisee is not (or does not appear to be) an independent contractor, but instead the franchisee is (or appears to be) an employee or agent; (2) the third party is injured due to the franchisor's negligence; or (3) the third party is injured by products made or supplied by the franchisor.
STUDY HINT. To avoid liability for a franchisee's acts, franchisors often require franchisees to give public notice that they are independent businesses, distinct from the franchisors.
▶ LEARNING OUTCOME EXAMPLE: See the *McDonald's* case in which only the franchisee was liable for the torts to the minor emanating from the McDonald's restaurant, textbook p. 972.

CONCEPT REVIEW AND APPLICATIONS

Matching Exercise

Select the term or phrase that best matches a definition or statement stated below. Each term or phrase is the best match for only one statement or definition. Not all terms and phrases will necessarily be used.

cooperative	limited liability partnership (LLP)
corporations	partnership
franchise	sole or individual proprietorship
franchise agreement	trade dress
franchisee	trade name
franchisor	trade secrets
joint venture	trademarks
limited liability company (LLC)	unincorporated association

_____ 1. Association of two or more independent persons or businesses who cooperate with one another in order to accomplish a common objective.

_____ 2. Unincorporated group of two or more persons who come together to further a common, and frequently nonprofit, goal.

_____ 3. Person to whom a franchise is granted.

    _____ 4. Association, similar to a general partnership, whereby two or more persons combine their resources in order to accomplish a single business undertaking for profit.

    _____ 5. Business arrangement whereby an owner of a trademark, trade name, or copyright licenses a person or business to sell or distribute goods or services using such mark, name, or copyright.

    _____ 6. Association of two or more persons to carry on a business for profit as co-owners.

    _____ 7. Person who grants a franchise to another person.

    _____ 8. Business that is owned and operated by one person.

True/False

____ 1. The owner (member) of an LLC is personally liable for the debts of an LLC.

____ 2. A disadvantage of a sole proprietorship is that its capital is limited to the owner's personal assets.

____ 3. In general, a franchisor is not liable for the contracts and torts of a franchisee.

____ 4. A franchise contract cannot define a franchise's duration; statutes determine this matter.

____ 5. A franchise contract can legally permit a franchisor to terminate a franchise if a franchisee fails to make required franchise payments or if the franchisee fails to meet reasonable sales quotas.

____ 6. Federal antitrust laws prohibit a franchisor and franchisee from agreeing on the price for which the franchisee will resell the franchisor's products.

____ 7. FTC regulations require that a franchisor make certain disclosures to a franchisee at least ten days prior to signing a franchise contract or accepting money for a franchise.

____ 8. A partnership is typically formed to only accomplish a specific undertaking whereas a joint venture is typically formed to engage in an ongoing business.

____ 9. Unless otherwise agreed, the profits of a joint venture are shared equally by the venturers.

____10. A joint venture is legally treated as a corporation and is governed by corporation law.

Multiple Choice

_____ 1. Alex intends to start a for-profit construction business. Alex wants to control the entire business, he does not wish to pay any expenses in order to create the business organization, and he wants to receive the entire net profits from the business. These are Alex's only considerations. Under these facts, which form of business organization is most appropriate for Alex?
   a. Individual (sole) proprietorship.
   b. Partnership.
   c. Corporation.
   d. Joint venture.

_____ 2. Betty and Dan intend to jointly establish and operate a for-profit catering business. Betty and Dan wish to use a form of business organization that: (1) will permit them to pool their respective personal assets for the purpose of conducting this business; and (2) will not entail any organizational fees to establish the business organization. These are the sole considerations of the parties. Under these facts, which form of business organization is most appropriate?
   a. Individual (sole) proprietorship.
   b. Partnership.
   c. Corporation.
   d. Franchise.

_____ 3. Kelly, Pinky, and Bill are planning to start a for-profit manufacturing firm. It is important to the parties that they not have personal liability for obligations of the business, and that the business will continue even if one of the parties dies. These are the sole considerations of the parties. Under these facts, which form of business organization is most appropriate?
   a. Individual (sole) proprietorship.
   b. Partnership.
   c. Corporation.
   d. Joint venture.

_____ 4. Nexus Co. and Tracer Inc. are competing computer manufacturers. However, Nexus and Tracer pooled their resources for the sole purpose of developing a special type of computer chip. Nexus and Tracer each have an equal right to control the business of this limited undertaking. Under these facts:
   a. Nexus' and Tracer's business is a joint venture.
   b. Nexus and Tracer each have unlimited liability for obligations arising out of this business.
   c. The parties' rights relating to this business are generally governed by partnership law.
   d. All of the above.

_____ 5. Betsy, Peter, and Katie operated a not-for-profit shelter for abandoned cats called "Nine Lives Shelter." The parties did not incorporate. On behalf of the shelter, Betsy bought $500 worth of cat food on credit from Seller. Peter and Katie did not know of or consent to this purchase. Under these facts:
   a. Nine Lives Shelter is an unincorporated association.
   b. Peter and Katie are personally liable for the purchase price of the cat food.
   c. Seller can sue Nine Lives Shelter for the purchase price of the cat food.
   d. All of the above.

446

Case Problem

Answer the following problem, briefly explaining your answer.

Sugarland granted Carlos the right to sell Sugarland's candy products and to use its trademark and trade name in connection with his business. One day, Sue bought a piece of Sugarland candy from Carlos. The candy made Sue ill because it was made with a toxic substance, giving rise to a claim for product liability. Also, the next day Tom slipped while walking in Carlos' store. Tom slipped because Carlos had negligently left a spilled drink on the floor.

1. What is the business relationship between Sugarland and Carlos? Describe the nature of this relationship.
2. Is Sugarland liable to Tom and/or Sue? Why or why not?
3. Is Carlos liable to Tom?

_____

_____

_____

Internet Exercise

Alfred owns a construction firm as an individual proprietorship. Business is good and Alfred needs capital with which to expand his operations. Because his capital resources are limited, however, he is considering applying for financial assistance from the federal Small Business Administration (SBA). He has asked you to:

1. Locate and identify the web site where the SBA publishes its Borrower's Guide for SBA loans.
2. Identify the main SBA loan program and what loan amounts the SBA will guarantee under this program.

_____

_____

_____

CPA REVIEW

The following questions were given on CPA examinations. The answers for these questions are the unofficial answers prepared by the American Institute of Certified Public Accountants, Inc. (AICPA). All material is reproduced with permission of the AICPA.

____ 1. A general partnership must
   a. Pay federal income tax.
   b. Have two or more partners.
   c. Have written articles of partnership.
   d. Provide for apportionment of liability for partnership debts.

____ 2. In a general partnership, the authorization of all partners is required for an individual partner to bind the partnership in a business transaction to
   a. Purchase inventory.
   b. Hire employees.
   c. Sell goodwill.
   d. Sign advertising contracts.

____ 3. Rivers and Lee want to form a partnership. For the partnership agreement to be enforceable, it must be in writing if
   a. Rivers and Lee reside in different states.
   b. The agreement cannot be completed within one year from the date on which it will be entered into.
   c. Either Rivers or Lee is to contribute more than $500 in capital.
   d. The partnership intends to buy and sell real estate.

____ 4. Grey and Carr entered into a written partnership agreement to operate a hardware store. Their agreement was silent as to the duration of the partnership. Grey wishes to dissolve the partnership. Which of the following statements is correct?
   a. Unless Carr consents to a dissolution, Grey must apply to a court and obtain a decree ordering the dissolution.
   b. Grey may not dissolve the partnership unless Carr consents.
   c. Grey may dissolve the partnership only after notice of the proposed dissolution is given to all partnership creditors.
   d. Grey may dissolve the partnership at any time.

____ 5. With respect to the following matters, which is correct if a general partnership agreement is silent?
   a. A partnership will continue indefinitely unless a majority of the partners votes to dissolve the partnership.
   b. Partnership losses are allocated in the same proportion as partnership profits.
   c. A partner may assign his interest in the partnership but only with the consent of the other partners.
   d. A partner may sell the goodwill of the partnership without the consent of the other partners when the sale is in the best interest of the partnership.

___ 6. Noll Corp. and Orr Co. are contemplating entering into an unincorporated joint venture. Such a joint venture
    a. Will be treated as a partnership in most important legal respects.
    b. Must be dissolved upon completion of a single undertaking.
    c. Will be treated as an association for federal income tax purposes and taxed at the prevailing corporate rates.
    d. Must file a certificate of limited partnership with the appropriate state agency.

___ 7. Which of the following is a correct statement concerning the similarities of a limited partnership and a corporation?
    a. Both are recognized for federal income tax purposes as taxable entities.
    b. Both can only be created pursuant to a statute and each must file a copy of its certificate with the proper state authorities.
    c. Both provide insulation from personal liability for all of the owners of the business.
    d. Shareholders and limited partners may both participate in the management of the business and retain limited liability.

CHAPTER 42
PARTNERSHIPS

MAKE THE CONNECTION

SUMMARY

A *partnership* is a relationship created by the voluntary association of two or more persons to carry on as co-owners a business for profit.

A partnership agreement governs the partnership during its existence and may also contain provisions relating to dissolution. The partnership agreement will generally be in writing, and this may be required by the statute of frauds. The existence of a partnership may be found from the existence of shared control in the running of the business and the fact that the parties share profits and losses. The sharing of gross returns, as opposed to profits, is slight evidence of a partnership.

Partners hold title to firm property by tenancy in partnership. A creditor of a partner cannot proceed against any specific item of partnership property but must obtain a charging order to seize the debtor-partner's share of the profits. An assignee of a partner's interest does not become a partner without the consent of the other partners and is entitled only to a share of the profits and the assignor's interest upon dissolution.

When there are more than two partners in a firm, the decisions of the majority prevail on ordinary matters relating to the firm's business unless the decisions are contrary to the partnership agreement. A partner's authority to act for the firm is similar to that of an agent to act for a principal. A partner may not bind the firm by a contract that makes it impossible for the firm to conduct its business.

A partner's duties are the same as those of an agent. If there is no contrary agreement, each partner has the right to take an equal part in the management of the business, to inspect the books, to share in the profits, and after payment of all of the firm's debts and the return of capital, to share in the firm's property or surplus upon dissolution.

Partners have unlimited personal liability for partnership liabilities. Partners are jointly liable on all firm contracts. They are jointly and severally liable for all torts committed by one of the partners or by a firm employee within the scope of the partnership's business. A partner remains liable after dissolution unless expressly released by creditors. An incoming partner is not liable for the existing debts of the partnership unless the new partner expressly assumes those debts.

Dissolution ends the right of the partnership to exist as a going concern. Dissolution is followed by a winding-up period and the distribution of assets. A partnership may be dissolved by the parties themselves in accordance with the terms of the partnership agreement, by the expulsion of a partner, by the withdrawal of a partner, or by the bankruptcy of the firm or one of the partners. A court may order dissolution of a partnership upon the petition of a partner because of the insanity, incapacity, or major misconduct of a partner. Dissolution may be decreed because of lack of success, impracticability, or other circumstances that equitably call for dissolution. Notice of dissolution, except dissolution by operation of law, must be given. Actual notice must be given to those who have dealt with the firm as a partnership.

All partners generally have a right to participate in the winding up of the business. After the firm's liabilities to nonpartners have been paid, the assets are distributed among the partners as follows: (1) refund of advances, (2) return of contributions to capital, and (3) division of remaining assets in accordance with the partnership agreement or, if no agreement is stated, division of net assets equally among the partners.

449

LEARNING OUTCOMES

After studying this chapter, you should be able to

A. NATURE AND CREATION

LO.1 Explain how partnerships are created by agreement, and understand that only when the partners' partnership agreement does not resolve an issue does partnership law apply

LO.2 Understand that no writing is needed to form a partnership, nor a tax ID number, nor a partnership name. All that is needed is clear evidence that the partners carried on as co-owners of a business for profit

B. AUTHORITY OF PARTNERS

LO.3 Distinguish between express authority and customary authority of a partner to act for a partnership

C. DUTIES, RIGHTS, AND LIABILITIES OF PARTNERS

LO.4 List the duties of partners to one another

D. DISSOLUTION AND TERMINATION

LO.5 Describe how a partnership may be dissolved by the acts of partners, by operation of law, and by order of the court

CHAPTER OUTLINE

A. NATURE AND CREATION

1. DEFINITION

▶ A partnership is a voluntary association of two or more persons to carry on as co-owners a business for profit. ▶ A partner is an agent of a partnership. A partner is not an employee even while the partner is performing work for the partnership.

2. CHARACTERISTICS OF A PARTNERSHIP

▶ A partnership is a voluntary relationship that is established to conduct a business for profit.
▶ Partners contribute capital or services, or both, and they are co-owners of partnership assets.
▶ A partnership is not a separate entity under the Uniform Partnership Act (UPA), but it is considered an entity under the UCC and by some courts.

3. RIGHTS OF PARTNERS

Partners' rights are determined by the partnership agreement. If an agreement is silent regarding a matter, the parties' rights may be determined by the UPA.

4. PARTNERSHIP AGREEMENT (ARTICLES OF PARTNERSHIP)

GENERAL RULE. ▶ In general, a partnership agreement may be oral or written. ▶ The partnership agreement establishes many of the rights and duties of the partners. ▶ Any matter not addressed in the partnership agreement is determined by reference to the UPA or RUPA.
LIMITATION. A writing is required if a partnership's term is stated to be more than one year.

LEARNING OUTCOME EXAMPLE. See the example of the dentist who was terminated from the three-person dental partnership without cause by majority vote, where the partnership agreement allowed for such a termination, textbook p. 985.

5. DETERMINING THE EXISTENCE OF A PARTNERSHIP (IMPLIED PARTNERSHIPS)

GENERAL RULES. ► A partnership may be implied. If a business has the characteristics of a partnership, it will be treated as a partnership. ► Important factors: (1) intent to do business as a partnership; (2) each party has a right to control the business; and (3) parties share profits and losses.

LIMITATION. Factors that do *not* establish a partnership: (1) profits are paid as wages or rent, or as payment for a debt; (2) gross income is shared; (3) parties merely co-own property and share the rentals from the property; or (4) a party is paid a fixed sum for his or her services.

STUDY HINTS. ► There may be a partnership even if some partners do not make a financial contribution. ► There may be a partnership even if the parties do not call their business a "partnership," and vice versa.

LEARNING OUTCOME EXAMPLE. See the *Byker* case where one individual who carried on a business for a profit was dumbfounded to find out that he was, by law, a partner, textbook p. 986.

6. PARTNERS AS TO THIRD PERSONS (NOMINAL PARTNERS)

GENERAL RULE. A party (nominal partner or partner by estoppel) is liable to a third person: (1) if the party misleads, or permits others to mislead, the third person into falsely believing the party is a partner; and (2) the third person extends credit to or transact business with the partnership in reliance on this misrepresentation.

LIMITATION. Under the Revised Uniform Partnership Act, a nominal partner is called a "purported partner."

7. PARTNERSHIP PROPERTY

GENERAL RULE. Partnership property generally includes: (1) property contributed by partners; (2) property acquired in the partnership's name; and (3) property acquired with partnership funds.

STUDY HINTS. ► Property that a partner agreed to contribute is partnership property even if title is not held in the partnership's name. ► Property bought with partnership funds is presumed to be partnership property unless a party can prove that it was intended to belong to an individual partner.

8. TENANCY IN PARTNERSHIP

GENERAL RULE. Partners hold title to partnership property by tenancy in partnership. This means: (1) each partner has an equal right to use the firm's property for partnership business; (2) a partner does not own, and cannot sell or mortgage, a divisible interest in specific items; (3) one partner's creditor cannot force a sale of specific properties; and (4) on a partner's death, title vests in the other partners.

LIMITATION. If a partner wishes to retain an interest in property that the partner contributes to the partnership, then this interest must be stated when the property is contributed or must be set forth in the partnership agreement.

STUDY HINT. An individual partner's creditor can obtain a charging order against a partner's interest in a partnership. A charging order entitles the creditor (1) to receive the partner's share of partnership profits when paid and (2) to force a sale of the partner's interest in the partnership.

9. ASSIGNMENT OF A PARTNER'S INTEREST

A partner can assign a partnership interest without the other partners' consent. An assignee does not become a partner; an assignee is entitled only to a partner's share of profits and assets upon dissolution.

B. AUTHORITY OF PARTNERS

10. AUTHORITY OF MAJORITY OF PARTNERS (COLLECTIVE MANAGEMENT)

GENERAL RULES. ▶ The decision of the majority of partners controls regarding ordinary matters arising in the usual course of partnership business. ▶ Transactions properly authorized by a majority of the partners are binding on the partnership and on all partners.
LIMITATION. Unanimous consent is required: (1) to amend a partnership agreement or approve an action that conflicts with the agreement; and (2) to authorize any action that changes the nature of, or makes it impossible to carry on, the partnership business (e.g., a sale of all assets of the partnership).

11. EXPRESS AUTHORITY OF INDIVIDUAL PARTNERS

An individual partner has express authority to contract for a partnership if the contract is authorized by (1) the partnership agreement or (2) the required number of partners.

12. CUSTOMARY AUTHORITY OF INDIVIDUAL PARTNERS

GENERAL RULES. ▶ Unless expressly limited, a partner has customary authority to individually do what is needed to carry out partnership business in the usual way. Examples: (1) make ordinary contracts; (2) buy/sell inventory; (3) hire employees; (4) acquire/cancel insurance; (5) compromise and pay debts; (6) settle and receive payment of accounts; (7) make admissions and receive notice regarding partnership matters. ▶ A contract made by a partner with customary authority binds the partnership and all partners.
LIMITATION. There is no customary authority to do an act that requires unanimous approval.
STUDY HINT. A partner acting with customary authority is acting properly.

13. LIMITATIONS ON AUTHORITY (AUTHORITY DESPITE LIMITATIONS)

GENERAL RULES. ▶ Customary authority may be limited by: (1) the partnership agreement; or (2) a vote of a majority of partners. Such limits are binding on partners and third parties with notice. ▶ If a partner contracts for the partnership in violation of a limit on his or her authority, but the third party is unaware of the limitation: (1) the partnership is bound by the contract and (2) the acting partner is liable for any loss resulting from the contract.
LIMITATIONS. ▶ A third party cannot rely on a partner's statements regarding his or her authority. ▶ A third party may be charged with notice that a partner has no authority due to: (1) the nature of the partnership; (2) the transaction is outside the ordinary scope of partnership business; (3) the partnership's being dissolved; or (4) the act's being contrary to partnership interests.
STUDY HINT. Under the RUPA, a partnership may file a statement of partnership authority that states any restrictions on a general partner's authority.

14. PROHIBITED TRANSACTIONS (ACTS FOR WHICH EXPRESS AUTHORITY IS NEEDED)

GENERAL RULE.   A partner cannot do the following acts without express authority: (1) any act that makes it impossible for a partnership to carry on its business; (2) contracts of surety, guaranty, or indemnity; (3) arbitration agreements; (4) confessions of judgment; (5) assignments of partnership property for the benefit of creditors; (6) contracts to pay personal debts using partnership assets.
STUDY HINT.   A partnership is not bound by such acts unless a partner has express authority.

C. DUTIES, RIGHTS, AND LIABILITIES OF PARTNERS

15. DUTIES OF PARTNERS

➢ *Loyalty and good faith*: ▶ A partner is a fiduciary of the partnership. Thus, a partner cannot: (1) misrepresent or conceal relevant facts; (2) make secret profits; (3) use partnership property for personal use; (4) take a partnership's business opportunity; or (5) compete with the partnership. These duties continue until a partner withdraws or a partnership is terminated (not just dissolved). ▶ Under the RUPA, a partner may pursue his or her own personal interests without automatically violating the duty of loyalty.

➢ *Obedience*: ▶ A partner must perform contract duties and obey restrictions imposed by (1) the partnership agreement or (2) a vote of the required number of partners. ▶ A partner must not make contracts for a partnership unless the partner has express or customary authority to do so.

➢ *Reasonable care*: ▶ A partner must use reasonable care in transacting partnership business. ▶ A partner is not liable for reasonable errors of judgment but is liable for negligent actions.

➢ *Information*: A partner must inform the partnership of all matters relating to partnership affairs.

➢ *Accounting*: A partner must account for all partnership property and keep appropriate records.

16. RIGHTS OF PARTNERS AS OWNERS

➢ *Management*: Equal right to participate in partnership's management, regardless of contributions.

➢ *Inspection of books*: Equal right to inspect the books and records of the partnership.

➢ *Share of profits*: Unless otherwise agreed, each partner is entitled to an equal share of profits, regardless of the partners' contributions or services rendered.

➢ *Compensation*: ▶ A surviving partner is entitled to be paid for services done in winding up a partnership. ▶ There is no right to compensation for other services unless all partners agree.

➢ *Repayment of loans*: Partners have a right to be repaid loans made to a partnership, with interest.

➢ *Payment of interest*: Contributions do not bear interest; advances (loans) by partners do.

➢ *Contribution and indemnity*: ▶ A partner who pays more than his or her proportionate share of a partnership debt has a right to contribution (repayment) from the other partners for their share of such debt. ▶ A partnership must indemnify (reimburse) a partner for payments made on behalf of the partnership, and personal liabilities incurred in conducting partnership business.

▶ There is no duty to indemnify if a partner acted in bad faith or negligently, or agreed to pay.

➢ *Distribution of capital*: After payment of creditors and partner loans, a partner is entitled to repayment of contributions and a share of excess assets in accordance with percentage of profits.

17. LIABILITY OF PARTNERS AND PARTNERSHIP

➢ *Nature and extent of partners' liability*: ▶ Partners are jointly liable for unpaid partnership contracts. ▶ A partnership and all partners have joint and several liability for torts committed by any employee or partner while acting within the scope of the partnership business.

➢ *Liability of new partners*: A new partner has limited liability for partnership debts arising prior to the partner's admission. Unless otherwise agreed, a new partner's liability for preadmission partnership debts is limited to his or her contributions to the partnership.

➢ *Effect of dissolution on partner's liability*: Each partner or partner's estate remains liable for unpaid partnership debts following dissolution of the partnership or death of the partner.

18. ENFORCEMENT AND SATISFACTION OF CREDITOR'S CLAIMS

▶ A partnership may be sued by suing the partners doing business as the partnership. ▶ Creditors of an individual partner must first seek payment from a partner's personal assets. If such assets are insufficient to satisfy the debt, then the creditor may seek a charging order, whereby a court orders the partnership to pay the partner's share of partnership profits to the creditor until the debt is paid.

D. DISSOLUTION AND TERMINATION

19. EFFECT OF DISSOLUTION

GENERAL RULES. ▶ Dissolution is a change in the relationship of the partners caused by any partner becoming dissociated from the partnership. ▶ Upon dissolution, a partner has actual authority to contract only to the extent necessary (1) to wind up partnership affairs and (2) to complete existing contracts.

LIMITATIONS. ▶ Dissolution does not terminate a partnership. Remaining partners may continue the partnership without winding up the partnership business if (1) the partnership agreement so provides or (2) dissolution is caused by a breach of contract. ▶ A partnership continues to exist during the winding-up process and it terminates when its affairs are wound up.

STUDY HINT. Termination of a partnership does not terminate the former partners' liability for partnership obligations.

20. DISSOLUTION BY ACT OF THE PARTIES

GENERAL RULE. A partnership may be dissolved by: (1) *agreement*: expiration of the time or fulfillment of the purpose stated in the agreement, or unanimous consent of partners; (2) *expulsion*: expulsion of a partner by the other partners, whether the expulsion is proper or not; or (3) *withdrawal*: partner's withdrawal, whether withdrawal violates a partnership agreement or not.

LIMITATION. A voluntary or involuntary sale or assignment of a partner's interest does not cause a dissolution.

STUDY HINTS. ▶ If a partnership does not have a fixed duration, a partner may withdraw at any time and for any reason without liability. ▶ If a partner wrongfully withdraws from a partnership, the partner is liable to the other partners for any damages caused by the withdrawal. ▶ Restrictions on future employment after a partner withdraws from a partnership are a common provision in partnership agreements.

LEARNING OUTCOME EXAMPLE. See the example of withdrawal by a partner, Mary Harshman, without liability because the partnership was at-will, textbook p. 1000.

21. DISSOLUTION BY OPERATION OF LAW

GENERAL RULE. These events automatically cause a dissolution: (1) death of any partner; (2) bankruptcy (but not insolvency) of the partnership or any partner; or (3) the partnership business becomes illegal.

STUDY HINT. When the executor of a deceased partner continues the business with a surviving partner, there is legally a new partnership.

22. DISSOLUTION BY DECREE OF COURT

GENERAL RULE. A partner may obtain a judicial dissolution of a partnership if: (1) any partner is judicially declared mentally incompetent or is indefinitely incapable of performing his or her duties; (2) any partner engages in serious misconduct (e.g., repeated violations of the partnership agreement); (3) continuous, serious disagreements among partners make it impractical to continue business; (4) business cannot be continued except at a loss; or (5) other equitable reasons justify dissolution.

LEARNING OUTCOME EXAMPLE. See the *Della Ratta* case involving partnership dissolution by decree of court because of impractability, textbook p. 1001.

23. DISSOCIATION UNDER THE RUPA

GENERAL RULES. ▶ Under the RUPA a partner's withdrawal from the partnership known as a "dissociation" does not affect the partnership's continuation ▶ A partner has to power to dissociate at any time, but if such dissociation is wrongful then the partner is liable for damages caused. ▶ Dissociation terminates the withdrawing partner's (1) right to represent the partnership and (2) fiduciary duties, including the duty not to compete against the partnership.

LIMITATION. A partner's withdrawal from a partnership that causes a dissolution does generally precipitate a winding up and termination of the partnership.

STUDY HINT. If dissociation does not cause a dissolution and the remaining partners continue the partnership, then the partnership must buy out the dissociated partner's interest in the partnership.

24. NOTICE OF DISSOLUTION

➢ *Notice to partners*: A partnership and each partner is liable for contracts made by a partner who was unaware of a dissolution that was caused by the death, bankruptcy, or act of another partner.

➢ *Notice to third persons*: ▶ A dissolved partnership is liable to a third party on a contract made by a partner without actual authority if: (1) dissolution is caused by a partner's act; and (2) the third party has no notice of the dissolution. ▶ Required notice: (1) Actual notice must be given to a third party who has dealt with a partnership. (2) Constructive notice, such as newspaper ad, is sufficient if a third party has not dealt with a partnership. (3) Notice is not required if a partnership dissolves by operation of law.

25. WINDING UP PARTNERSHIP AFFAIRS

GENERAL RULE. Unless otherwise agreed, surviving or remaining partners have the right and obligation to wind up the business of a partnership following a dissolution.

LIMITATIONS. ▶ Winding up only permits partners to take actions and make contracts that are necessary to conclude the partnership's business; partners cannot indefinitely continue the business. ▶ Partners who are winding up must account for the share of a partner who has withdrawn, been expelled, or died. If remaining partners wrongfully continue the business, the former partner (or estate) is entitled to the partner's share of partnership assets, *plus interest or a share of the profits*.

26. DISTRIBUTION OF ASSETS

GENERAL RULE. Partnership assets are distributed in the following order:

(1) payment of debts owing to third party creditors;

(2) payment to partners for loans or advances;

(3) return of capital contributions to partners; and

(4) remaining assets, if any, are divided among partners as profits.

STUDY HINT. If the partnership has a loss, then the partners share the loss equally unless the partnership agreement provides otherwise.

27. CONTINUATION OF PARTNERSHIP BUSINESS

By agreement, a partnership's business is often continued by remaining partners after dissolution.

CONCEPT REVIEW AND APPLICATIONS

Matching Exercise

Select the term or phrase that best matches a definition or statement stated below. Each term or phrase is the best match for only one statement or definition. Not all terms and phrases will necessarily be used.

articles of copartnership	general partners	partnership agreement
charging order	operation of law	tenancy in partnership
express authority	partners	unincorporated association
general partnership	partnership	

_____ 1. Authority of a partner given by the partnership agreement or by the required number of partners.

_____ 2. Partnership that is formed for the purpose of generally conducting an ongoing business.

_____ 3. Ownership rights of a partner in specific items of partnership property.

_____ 4. Agreement between partners that establishes the partners' rights and obligations.

_____ 5. Partners who actively engage in a partnership and who are known to the public as partners.

_____ 6. Court decree directing that a partner's share of profits be paid to the partner's individual creditor.

_____ 7. Attaching of certain consequences to certain facts because of legal principles that operate automatically.

True/False

Write **T** if the statement is true, write **F** if it is false.

____ 1. A partner is treated as an agent of a partnership, not as an employee.

____ 2. To be a partnership, the business must be created by a voluntary, consensual association of two or more persons to carry on as co-owners a business for profit.

____ 3. In many states, a fictitious partnership name must be registered with a designated public office.

____ 4. A partnership cannot be created unless parties specifically call their relationship a partnership.

_____ 5. A partnership agreement cannot be enforced unless it is in writing.

_____ 6. The fact that parties share profits earned by a business is *prima facie* evidence that the parties' business relationship is a partnership.

_____ 7. A nominal partner is liable for all debts of a partnership, including debts owed to creditors who were not aware that the nominal partner had been misrepresented as being a partner.

_____ 8. Property may be partnership property even if title is held in the name of an individual partner.

_____ 9. In general, property that is acquired with partnership funds is presumed to be partnership property.

_____ 10. Upon an assignment of a partner's partnership interest, the assignee automatically becomes a partner in the partnership and is entitled to participate in the management of the partnership.

Multiple Choice

_____ 1. In which situation does a partnership probably exist between Felix and Art?
a. Felix owed $10,000 to Art. Felix agreed to pay 10 percent of his company's profits to Art as partial payment of the $10,000 debt.
b. Felix owns an insurance agency. As compensation, Felix pays Art 5 percent of the gross premiums paid on insurance policies that are sold by Art.
c. Felix and Art co-own a grocery store. Felix and Art jointly control the business and they share the net profits and losses derived from the store.
d. All of the above.

_____ 2. Cal, Oscar, and Len are partners. Cal's creditor has obtained a charging order against Cal's partnership interest. Oscar wants to sell his interest in a truck that is owned by the partnership. Len wants to use the partnership's computer to prepare partnership tax returns. In this case:
a. Cal's creditor can force a sale of Cal's interest in specific items of partnership property.
b. Cal's creditor is entitled to Cal's share of partnership profits when they are distributed.
c. Oscar can sell his interest in the partnership truck.
d. Len cannot use the computer without first obtaining the other partners' approval.

_____ 3. Bruce, Mark, and Erwin are partners in B-MER Partnership. The agreement states that the partnership will continue until January 1, 2012. Which event would *not* cause a dissolution?
a. On May 1, 2010, Bruce assigns his partnership interest to Reginald.
b. On May 1, 2010, Mark is declared bankrupt.
c. On May 1, 2010, Erwin dies.
d. On May 1, 2010, a court orders a dissolution because a partner has become permanently incapacitated.

_____ 4. Lee and Mindy are partners in L&M Partnership. The partnership agreement states that the partnership will continue until June 1, 2010. In which situation can Lee properly request a court to enter a decree dissolving the partnership prior to June 1, 2010?
  a. Mindy made an ordinary contract on behalf of the partnership with authority to do so, but Lee objects to the contract.
  b. Mindy has embezzled partnership funds and she refuses to perform her partnership duties.
  c. The partnership is not quite as profitable as it was in the past.
  d. Lee cannot obtain a decree of dissolution; a court cannot dissolve a partnership.

_____ 5. Jim and Ray were partners in a partnership that sold medical supplies. The partnership was dissolved due to Jim's proper withdrawal, and Ray was appropriately notified. After dissolution, Ray contracted on behalf of the partnership to buy a shipment of supplies from Manufacturer who had previously dealt with the partnership. Manufacturer did not know of the dissolution. Ray intended to sell the supplies to new customers that he hoped to solicit on behalf of the partnership. Under these facts:
  a. Ray acted properly in making the contract on behalf of the partnership.
  b. Ray did not act properly in making the contract on behalf of the partnership.
  c. The partnership is liable on the contract.
  d. b and c.

_____ 6. Kit was a partner in a partnership that sold hospital supplies. In which situation did Kit breach a duty that she owed to the partnership or the other partners?
  a. Prior to dissolution, Kit purchased supplies for the partnership. Kit had express authority to act and she used reasonable judgment, but the partnership lost money due to the purchase.
  b. After the partnership dissolved but before it was terminated, Kit set up a new firm that purchased supplies from the partnership at discounted prices. Kit did not disclose her interest in the new firm, and she secretly profited from the firm's transactions with the partnership.
  c. After termination of the partnership, Kit opened a hospital supply company that competed with a new business that was created by her former partners.
  d. All of the above.

_____ 7. Laura is a partner in a partnership that owns a retail tire store. A partner in this type of partnership typically has customary authority to make warranties regarding tires that are sold. However, all partners agreed that no one would warrant tires without first obtaining the other partners' consent. In violation of this restriction, Laura sold tires to John and she warranted the tires against defects. The tires are defective, and John is demanding a refund that will cause a $300 loss. John was not aware of the limitation on Laura's authority. Under these facts:
  a. The partnership is not bound by the warranties made by Laura.
  b. The partnership is bound by the warranties made by Laura.
  c. Laura is liable to the partnership and the other partners for the $300 loss.
  d. b and c.

_____ 8. Don and Rene are the partners in a partnership that owns a retail paint store. Under these facts, Don does *not* have customary authority to make which contract on behalf of the partnership?
   a. Contract to purchase a case of paint.
   b. Contract to hire a salesclerk who is needed to run the store.
   c. Contract to sell the entire store.
   d. Contract to purchase fire insurance for the store.

_____ 9. Cooper, Tex, and Chien are the partners in CTC Partnership. Cooper contributed $50,000 to the partnership, and Tex and Chien each contributed $25,000. The partnership agreement is silent regarding management rights and allocation of profits. Under these facts:
   a. Cooper has the exclusive right to manage the partnership.
   b. Cooper, Tex, and Chien are each entitled to an equal vote regarding partnership matters.
   c. Cooper is entitled to 100 percent of the partnership profits.
   d. Cooper is entitled to 50 percent of the partnership profits.

Case Problem

Answer the following problem, briefly explaining your answer.

Clay, Bonnie, and Tess were partners in a partnership, and they equally shared partnership profits. The partnership has dissolved due to Clay's death. The partnership has $90,000 cash. The partnership owes $20,000 to Rosco, an outside creditor, and it owes Tess $10,000 for an advance she made to the partnership. Clay contributed $15,000 to the partnership, Bonnie contributed $10,000, and Tess contributed $5,000. The partnership agreement is silent regarding the partners' rights upon the death of a partner.

1. Can Bonnie and Tess indefinitely continue the partnership business or must they wind up the partnership's business?
2. In general, who is entitled to wind up the affairs of a partnership?
3. If the partnership in this case is wound up, to whom and in what order will the partnership assets be distributed?

_____

_____

_____

Internet Exercise

Using the Internet, identify at least four states that have enacted the Revised Uniform Partnership Act.

_____

_____

_____

CPA REVIEW

The following questions were given on CPA examinations. The answers for these questions are the unofficial answers prepared by the American Institute of Certified Public Accountants, Inc. (AICPA). All material is reproduced with permission of the AICPA.

___ 1. Which of the following requirements must be met to have a valid partnership exist?

    I. Co-ownership of all property used in a business.
    II. Co-ownership of a business for profit.

    a. I only.
    b. II only.
    c. Both I and II.
    d. Neither I nor II.

Questions 2 and 3 are based on the following:

Downs, Frey, and Vick formed the DFV general partnership to act as manufacturers' representatives. The partners agreed Downs would receive 40% of any partnership profits and Frey and Vick would each receive 30% of such profits. It was also agreed that the partnership would not terminate for five years. After the fourth year, the partners agreed to terminate the partnership. At that time, the partners' capital accounts were as follows: Downs, $20,000; Frey, $15,000; and Vick, $10,000. There also were undistributed losses of $30.000.

___ 2. Which of the following statements about the form of the DFV partnership agreement
    is correct?
    a. It must be in writing because the partnership was to last for longer than one year.
    b. It must be in writing because partnership profits would not be equally divided.
    c. It could be oral because the partners had explicitly agreed to do business together.
    d. It could be oral because the partnership did not deal in real estate.

___ 3. If Frey died before the partnership terminated
    a. Downs and Vick, as a majority of the partners, would have been able to continue
       the partnership.
    b. The partnership would have continued until the five-year term expired.
    c. The partnership would automatically dissolve.
    d. Downs and Vick would have Frey's interest in the Partnership.

___ 4. Grey and Carr entered into a written partnership agreement to operate a hardware
    store. Their agreement was silent as to the duration of the partnership. Grey wishes to
    dissolve the partnership. Which of the following statements is correct?
    a. Unless Carr consents to a dissolution, Grey must apply to a court and obtain a decree ordering
       the dissolution.
    b. Grey may not dissolve the partnership unless Carr consents.
    c. Grey may dissolve the partnership only after notice of the proposed dissolution is given to
       all partnership creditors.
    d. Grey may dissolve the partnership at any time

___ 5. The partners of College Assoc., a general partnership, decided to dissolve the partnership and agreed that none of the partners would continue to use the partnership name. Under the Uniform Partnership Act, which of the following events will occur on dissolution of the partnership?

	Each partner's existing liability would be discharged	Each partner's apparent authority would continue
a.	Yes	Yes
b.	Yes	No
c.	No	Yes
d.	No	No

___ 6. On dissolution of a general partnership, distributions will be made on account of:
I. Partners' capital accounts
II. Amounts owed partners with respect to profits
III. Amounts owed partners for loans to the partnership in the following order

a. III, I, II.
b. I, II, III.
c. II, III, I.
d. III, II, I.

___ 7. Unless otherwise provided in a general partnership agreement, which of the following statements is correct when a partner dies?

	The deceased partner's executor would automatically become become a partner	The deceased partner's estate would be free from any partnership liabilities	The partnership would be dissolved automatically
a.	Yes	Yes	Yes
b.	Yes	No	No
c.	No	Yes	No
d.	No	No	Yes

___ 8. The apparent authority of a partner to bind the partnership in dealing with third parties
   a. Will be effectively limited by a formal resolution of the partners of which third parties are aware.
   b. Will be effectively limited by a formal resolution of the partners of which third parties are unaware.
   c. Would permit a partner to submit a claim against the partnership to arbitration.
   d. Must be derived from the express powers and purposes contained in the partnership agreement.

_____ 9. Acorn and Bean were general partners in a farm machinery business. Acorn contracted, on behalf of the partnership, to purchase 10 tractors from Cobb Corp. Unknown to Cobb, Acorn was not authorized by the partnership agreement to make such contracts. Bean refused to allow the partnership to accept delivery of the tractors and Cobb sought to enforce the contract. Cobb will
   a. Lose because Acorn's action was beyond the scope of Acorn's implied authority.
   b. Prevail because Acorn had implied authority to bind the partnership.
   c. Prevail because Acorn had apparent authority to bind the partnership.
   d. Lose because Acorn's express authority was restricted, in writing, by the partnership agreement.

_____10. Cass is a general partner in Omega Company general partnership. Which of the following unauthorized acts by Cass will bind Omega?
   a. Submitting a claim against Omega to arbitration.
   b. Confessing a judgment against Omega.
   c. Selling Omega's goodwill.
   d. Leasing office space for Omega.

_____11. Blake, a partner in QVM, a general partnership, wishes to withdraw from the partnership and sell her interest to Nolan. All of the other partners in QVM have agreed to admit Nolan as a partner and to hold Blake harmless for the past, present, and future liabilities of QVM. As a result of Blake's withdrawal and Nolan's admission to the partnership, Nolan
   a. Must contribute cash or property to QVM to be admitted with the same rights as the other partners.
   b. Is personally liable for partnership liabilities arising before and after being admitted as a partner.
   c. Has the right to participate in QVM's management.
   d. Acquired only the right to receive Blake's share of QVM's profits.

_____12. The partnership agreement for Owen Associates, a general partnership, provided that profits be paid to the partners in the ratio of their financial contribution to the partnership. Moore contributed $10,000, Noon contributed $30,000, and Kale contributed $50,000. For the year ended December 31, 1993, Owen had losses of $180,000. What amount of the losses should be allocated to Kale?
   a. $40,000
   b. $60,000
   c. $90,000
   d. $100,000

_____13. Which of the following statements is correct concerning liability when a partner in a general partnership commits a tort while engaged in partnership business?
   a. The partner committing the tort is the only party liable.
   b. The partnership is the only party liable.
   c. Each partner is jointly and severally liable.
   d. Each partner is liable to pay an equal share of any judgment.

CHAPTER 43
LPs, LLCs AND LLPs

MAKE THE CONNECTION

SUMMARY

A limited partnership consists of one or more limited partners who contribute cash, property, or services without liability for losses beyond their investment, and one or more general partners, who manage the business and have unlimited personal liability. A limited partner's protection from unlimited liability may be lost if the partner participates in the control of the business. "Safe harbor" activities for limited partners are set forth in the RULPA. General partners may avoid personal liability by incorporating. A certificate of limited partnership must be filed when the partnership is formed for the law to apply. Otherwise, general partnership law applies.

A limited liability company is a hybrid form of business organization that combines the tax advantages of a partnership with the limited liability feature of the corporation. It must be formed in accordance with state law in order to have effect, and the designation LLC must appear with the company's name. Management of an LLC is vested in its members, and members can delegate authority to run the entity to managers, the terms of which are set forth in the company's operating agreement. Members receive profits and losses according to the operating agreement. A member's interest in an LLC is assignable, but consent of the other members is needed for the assignee to participate in the firm's management.

A limited liability partnership is a new form of business organization that allows existing partnerships to convert to this form without major renegotiation of the underlying partnership agreement. Innocent partners in a limited liability partnership are not personally liable for the torts of other partners beyond their investment in the firm.

LEARNING OUTCOMES
After studying this chapter, you should be able to

A. THE ARRIVAL OF PARTNERSHIP LIMITED LIABILITY
LO.1   Explain the history of making limited liability available to general partnerships

B. LIMITED PARTNERSHIP
LO.2   Explain the extent of a founding general partner's liability for the debts of the firm, and how unlimited liability can be avoided by utilization of a corporate general partner
LO.3   Explain the nature and extent of a limited partner's liability for the debts of the firm

C. LIMITED LIABILITY COMPANIES
LO.4   Explain the advantages of a limited liability company

D. LIMITED LIABILITY PARTNERSHIPS
LO.5   Explain how a limited liability partnership "shields" innocent partners from liability to third parties

CHAPTER OUTLINE

A. THE ARRIVAL OF PARTNERSHIP LIMITED LIABILITY

Three types of business entities, in addition to corporations, offer owners varying degrees of limited liability for the entities' obligations. These three organizations are limited partnerships, limited liability companies, and limited liability partnerships.

B. LIMITED PARNTERSHIPS

1. FORMATION OF LIMITED PARTNERSHIPS

➢ *Law*: All states except Louisiana have enacted a version of the Revised Uniform Limited Partnership Act (RULPA).

➢ *Members of a limited partnership*: A limited partnership is comprised of: (1) limited partners who contribute capital and whose liability is limited to their contributions; and (2) general partners who manage the partnership's business and have unlimited personal liability for partnership obligations.

➢ *Certificate of limited partnership*: ▶ A limited partnership can be created only by complying with applicable state law that requires filing a certificate of limited partnership with the appropriate government office. ▶ If a certificate is not filed, then all partners are treated as general partners. However, technical defects in a certificate do not prevent formation of a limited partnership. ▶ The certificate does not have to disclose the names of limited partners.

➢ *Limited Partnership Agreement*: Limited partnership agreements typically are drafted by the original general partners. Accordingly, ambiguous terms are construed against the drafters and in favor of the limited partners.

2. CHARACTERISTICS OF LIMITED PARTNERSHIPS

➢ *Capital contributions*: Under the RULPA a limited partner may contribute cash, property, or services.

➢ *Firm name*: ▶ In general, a limited partner's name cannot be used in the partnership name.

▶ A limited partnership's name must include the words "limited partnership."

➢ *Management and control of the firm*: ▶ General partners manage and control the partnership business, and limited partners cannot control partnership business. Limited partners forfeit their limited liability by exercising control over partnership business. ▶ Under an RULPA "safe harbor," limited partners can do these acts without losing their limited liability: (1) act as contractor or employee; (2) consult with or advise general partner; (3) act as surety; and (4) vote on extraordinary matters, such as dissolution, winding up the partnership or removing a general partner. ▶ General partners have personal liability for partnership obligations. They may avoid this liability by using a corporation as the general partner. ▶ Limited partners have a right to a share of the profits and to a share of the proceeds upon dissolution.

➢ *Right to sue*: ▶ A limited partner may sue on a partnership's behalf if general partners refuse to sue. ▶ A limited partner also may sue a general partner to protect the limited partner's interest.

- ➤ *Dissolution*: Dissolution and winding up are governed by rules applicable to general partnerships.

- ➤ **LEARNING OUTCOME EXAMPLE.** See the *Gilroy* case in which limited partners (investors) lost their limitation of liability by participating in the control of the business, textbook p. 1016.

C. LIMITED LIABILITY COMPANIES

3. CHARACTERISTICS OF LLCs

- ➤ *Tax treatment*: The IRS now holds that an LLC is treated as a partnership for federal taxation purposes if the LLC elects to be so treated. In this situation, the profits and losses of the LLC flow through to (i.e., are taxed to) the owners of the LLC ("members") in proportion to their respective interests in the LLC.

- ➤ *Liability of members*: Members and managers of an LLC are not personally liable for debts of the LLC, provided that they properly disclose that they are acting on behalf of the LLC.

- ➤ *Formation*: ▶ An LLC is a business formed by filing articles of organization with a secretary of state. ▶ An LLC must use the words "Limited liability company" or "LLC" in its name.

- ➤ *Capital contributions*: A "member" (owner) may buy an interest for cash, services, or property.

- ➤ *Management*: ▶ Management of an LLC is vested in its members who may delegate their authority to managers pursuant to an operating agreement. ▶ Managers are fiduciaries of an LLC. ▶ In a member-managed LLC, each member has an equal right to take part in management. ▶ In many states, members of manager-controlled LLCs have no fiduciary duties unless the members exercise some or all of the authority of managers.

- ➤ *Distributions*: Profits/losses are shared by members in accordance with the operating agreement.

- ➤ *LLC property*: An LLC may own and transfer property in its own name.

- ➤ *Assignment*: Members can assign their interests, but assignees do not become members.

- ➤ *Dissolution*: ▶ Most LLCs dissolve upon the consent of the members, or upon the death, bankruptcy, retirement, resignation, or expulsion of a member. ▶ The LLC business may be continued, however, upon the unanimous consent of all remaining members.

- ➤ *Disregarding the LLC entity*: A court may hold owner of an LLC personally liable for obligations of the LLC in extraordinary circumstances.

4. LLCs AND OTHER ENTITIES (DIFFERENT CHARACTERISTICS)

▶ *LLC*: No limit on number of members or who may be members. ▶ *Subchapter S corporation*: It is taxed like a partnership but it can have only 75 or fewer shareholders, shareholders can be only U.S. citizens or resident aliens, and shareholders cannot be corporations or partnerships. ▶ *LLC*: Members may participate in control of business without losing their limited liability. ▶ *Limited partnership*: Limited partners lose their limited liability if they exercise control of business.

D. LIMITED LIABILITY PARTNERSHIPS (LLPs)

5. EXTENT OF LIMITED LIABILITY

► Partners are not liable for others' torts unless the partner participated or controlled others' conduct. ► In some states, partners are not liable for any obligations of an LLP. ► Partners in an LLP remain personally liable for their own wrongdoing.

6. REGISTRATION AND USAGE

► LLPs must register with the state. ► Professional partnerships are most likely to become LLPs.

CONCEPT REVIEW AND APPLICATIONS

Matching Exercise

Select the term or phrase that best matches a definition or statement stated below. Each term or phrase is the best match for only one statement or definition. Not all terms and phrases will necessarily be used.

Articles of organization	Limited partnership
Certificate of limited partnership	Manager
General partner	Member
Limited liability company	Operating agreement
Limited liability partnership	RULPA
Limited partner	

_____ 1. Person to whom members may delegate their power to manage the business of an LLC.

_____ 2. Partner in a limited partnership who manages and controls the partnership business.

_____ 3. Document that must be filed with the secretary of state in order to form a limited liability company.

_____ 4. Document that must be filed with the secretary of state in order to form a limited partnership.

_____ 5. Owner of a limited liability company.

_____ 6. Partnership which, by properly registering with the state, may shield partners from personal liability for some or all of the liabilities of the partnership.

_____ 7. Partner in a limited partnership whose liability is limited to his or her contributions and who does not control the partnership business.

_____ 8. Document that sets forth the management authority of members and managers of an LLC.

_____ 9. Partnership comprised of both general and limited partners.

_____ 10. Form of business organization in which anyone can be an owner, and owners may exercise control of the organization's business without losing their limited liability for business obligations.

True/False

Write **T** if the statement is true, write **F** if it is false.

____ 1. A limited partnership is comprised of only one class of partners - limited partners.

____ 2. A general partner has unlimited personal liability for the obligations of a limited partnership.

____ 3. An LLC can own and transfer property in its own name.

____ 4. Members of a limited liability company do not have unlimited personal liability for company debts.

____ 5. Under the RULPA a limited partner may contribute cash or property, but not services.

____ 6. A court can never hold a member of an LLC personally liable for obligations of the LLC.

____ 7. A member is not automatically entitled to reasonable compensation for services that he or she performs on behalf of an LLC.

____ 8. If a member withdraws from an LLC, the business of the LLC may be continued without terminating the LLC if all of the remaining members agree to do so.

____ 9. A member may assign his or her interest in an LLC without the consent of the other members, but the person to whom the interest is assigned does not have the right to become a member.

____ 10. Corporations and partnerships can be members of a limited liability company but they cannot be shareholders of a Subchapter S corporation.

Multiple Choice

____ 1. Ethel is the general partner in L&L Limited Partnership. Betty is a limited partner in the partnership. A certificate of limited partnership has been properly recorded, but the certificate has a minor technical error. Also, Betty periodically consults with Ethel regarding partnership business, although Ethel in fact controls the business. Under the RULPA:
a. Betty has personal liability for partnership obligations because she is a limited partner.
b. Betty has personal liability for partnership obligations because of the error in the certificate.
c. Betty has personal liability for partnership obligations because she consulted with Ethel.
d. Betty's liability for partnership obligations is limited to her contributions to the partnership.

_____ 2. Rainer and some friends want to invest in the development of a shopping center. They decide to form a limited partnership for this purpose. Which of the following must they have?
   a. At least one general partner.
   b. Limited partners who personally manage the partnership.
   c. The automatic right to transfer all interests in the partnership.
   d. No more than two limited partners.

_____ 3. LuLu and Beth form a limited liability company, which owns and operates a fabric store. LuLu buys the fabric and notions for the store and Beth manages the shop and does the bookkeeping. The business thrives and the women are quite happy until LuLu meets Dino who sweeps her off her feet. LuLu wants to leave the LLC and sell her entire interest in the LLC, including her right to be the fabric buyer and partner, to Pam. Under these facts:
   a. LuLu can assign her financial rights in the LLC without Beth's consent.
   b. LuLu can assign all rights associated with the LLC without Beth's consent so long as Pam has similar capabilities as LuLu.
   c. LuLu can assign all rights associated with the LLC without Beth's consent so long as Pam accepts personal liability for the partnership's debts.
   d. Lulu cannot assign any right associated with the LLC without Beth's consent.

_____ 4. Emma and Justin are U.S. citizens and Iva is a nonresident Russian citizen. The parties intend to form and operate a construction company. The parties want to use a form of business organization that: (1) will permit them to be the sole owners of the company; (2) have the income of the company taxed to them individually; and (3) will not cause any of the owners to have personal liability for any obligations of the company. These are the sole considerations of the parties. Under these facts, which form of business organization is appropriate?
   a. Limited partnership.
   b. LLC.
   c. Subchapter S corporation.
   d. All of the above.

Case Problem

Answer the following problem, briefly explaining your answer.

Fiona and Derrick are the partners in Burger Ville LLP, a limited liability partnership. Burger Ville owns and operates a fast food restaurant.

Fiona was intoxicated one day when working at the restaurant and due to her intoxication she accidentally used bleach to make the ranch dressing for salads. Caesar purchased and ate a salad with the adulterated dressing and he suffered serious injuries as a result.

Under the foregoing facts, discuss the liabilities of the LLP, Fiona, and Derrick for the harm suffered by Caesar.

_____

_____

_____

_____

_____

Internet Exercise

Your mother is an attorney in a large law partnership. She enjoys the collegial nature of the partnership, but she is concerned about being personally liable for malpractice that might be committed by other partners or associate attorneys in the firm. She has asked for your advise on the following matters:

1. What form of business would allow your mother's law firm to continue as a partnership, but shield your mother from liability for malpractice committed by others in her firm?
2. Is there a proposed or final uniform state act for this type of business organization? If so, what is it called and where is it located on the Internet?

_____

_____

_____

_____

_____

CPA REVIEW

The following questions were given on CPA examinations. The answers for these questions are the unofficial answers prepared by the American Institute of Certified Public Accountants, Inc. (AICPA). All material is reproduced with permission of the AICPA.

____ 1. In general, which of the following statements is correct with respect to a limited Partnership.
   a. A limited partner will be personally liable for partnership debts incurred in the ordinary course of the partnership's business.
   b. A limited partner is unable to participate in the management of the partnership in the same manner as general partners and still retain limited liability.
   c. A limited partner's death or incompetency will cause the partnership to dissolve.
   d. A limited partner is an agent of the partnership and has the authority to bind the partnership to contracts.

CHAPTER 44
CORPORATION FORMATION

MAKE THE CONNECTION

SUMMARY

A *corporation* is an artificial person created by government action. It exists as a separate and distinct entity possessing certain powers. In most states, the corporation comes into existence when the secretary of state issues a certificate of incorporation. The most common forms of corporations are private business corporations whose stock is sold to the public (publicly held) and close corporations, which are business firms whose shares are not traded publicly. Corporations may be formed for purposes other than conducting a business. For example, there are nonprofit corporations, municipal corporations, and public authorities for governmental purposes.

An *ultra vires* act occurs when a corporation acts beyond the scope of the powers given it. Because states now grant broad powers to corporations, it is unlikely that a modern corporation would act beyond the scope of its powers.

A *promoter* is a person who brings together the persons interested in the enterprise and sets in motion all that must be done to form a corporation. A corporation is not liable on contracts made by its promoter for the corporation unless it adopts the contracts. The promoter is personally liable for contracts made for the corporation before its existence. A promoter stands in a fiduciary relation to the corporation and stockholders.

The procedures for incorporation are set forth in the statutes of each state. In most states, the corporation comes into existence on issuance of the certificate of incorporation. When all requirements have been satisfied, the corporation is a corporation de jure. When there has not been full compliance with all requirements for incorporation, a de facto corporation may be found to exist. Or when sufficient compliance for a de facto corporation does not exist, in some jurisdictions a third person may be estopped from denying the legal existence of the "corporation" with which it did business (corporation by estoppel).

A corporation has the power to continue as an entity forever or for a stated period of time regardless of changes in the ownership of the stock or the death of a shareholder. It may make contracts, issue stocks and bonds, borrow money, execute commercial paper, transfer and acquire property, acquire its own stock if it is solvent and the purchase does not impair capital, and make charitable contributions. Subject to limitations, a corporation has the power to do business in other states. A corporation may also participate in a business enterprise to the same extent as an individual; that is, it may be a partner in a partnership, or it may enter a joint venture or other enterprise. Special service corporations, such as banks, insurance companies, and railroads, are subject to separate statutes governing their organization and powers.

Two or more corporations may be combined to form a new enterprise. This combination may be a consolidation, with a new corporation coming into existence, or a merger, in which one corporation absorbs the other.

LEARNING OUTCOMES

After studying this chapter, you should be able to

A. NATURE AND CLASSES

LO.1   Recognize that a corporation is a separate legal entity, distinct and apart from its stockholders

B. CORPORATE POWERS

LO.2   Explain the wide range of power given to corporations under modern corporate codes

C. CREATION AND TERMINATION OF THE CORPORATION

LO.3   Understand that the promoter is personally liable for preincorporation contracts

D. CONSOLIDATIONS, MERGERS, AND CONGLOMERATES

LO.4   Explain a stockholder's option when he or she objects to a proposed consolidation or merger of the corporation

LO.5   Recognize that liabilities of predecessor corporations can be imposed on successor corporations when the transaction is a de facto merger or a continuation of the predecessor

CHAPTER OUTLINE

A. NATURE AND CLASSES

1. THE CORPORATION AS A PERSON

▶ A corporation is a separate legal entity that is given powers and created by government permission. ▶ LEARNING OUTCOME EXAMPLE. See the *Collins* case in which Ms. Collins was not personally liable for a loan to her corporation, p. 1032.

2. CLASSIFICATIONS OF CORPORATIONS

➢ *Relation to public*: ▶ *Public corporation*: created to conduct government affairs. Example: municipal (city) corporation. ▶ *Private corporation*: created by individuals for private purpose. ▶ *Quasi-public corporation*: private corporation providing a basic service to the public. Example: gas company.

➢ *Public authorities*: created by government to accomplish specific purpose.

➢ *State of incorporation*: ▶ *Domestic corporation*: doing business in the state of incorporation. ▶ *Foreign corporation*: doing business in a state other than the state in which it was incorporated.

➢ *Special service corporations*: engage in a specialized commercial activity, such as insurance or banking.

➢ *Special characteristic*: ▶ *Close corporation*: stock is owned by one or a few shareholders. ▶ *Subchapter S corporation*: shareholders elect to be treated as partners for income tax purposes.

➢ *Professional corporation*: engages in a profession, such as law. Every member of a corporation must be a licensed member in the profession. A member remains liable for his own conduct.

➢ *Nonprofit corporation*: engages in charitable, educational, religious, or social activities.

3. CORPORATIONS AND GOVERNMENTS

➢ *Power to create and regulate*: Corporations are created by complying with the law of the state of incorporation. (Most states have adopted a version of the Model Business Corporation Act (MBCA)).

➢ *Constitutional rights*: ► In general, a corporation enjoys the same constitutional rights as natural persons. ► However, the privileges and immunities clause does not apply to corporations.

STUDY HINT. A court will *not* ignore a corporation's separate existence merely because: (1) two corporations have the same shareholders or are closely related (parent-subsidiary); (2) a corporation is formed to take advantage of tax benefits or to obtain limited liability for its owners; (3) a corporation cannot pay its debts; or (4) shareholders participate in a corporation's business.

B. CORPORATE POWERS

A corporation has the powers that are authorized by its articles of incorporation in accordance with applicable law. The RMBCA and many states grant a corporation the same powers as natural persons enjoy in order to do all things that are necessary or convenient to carry out the corporation's business.

4. PARTICULAR POWERS

GENERAL RULE. Common corporate powers include the power to: (1) enjoy perpetual life (continuous existence); (2) adopt bylaws (rules governing internal affairs); (3) issue and repurchase stock; (4) make contracts; (5) borrow money; (6) execute commercial paper and issue bonds; (7) buy, sell, transfer, and mortgage property; (8) do business in another state; (9) be a general or limited partner; (10) establish and fund employee benefit plans; and (11) make charitable gifts.

LIMITATIONS. ► Bylaws cannot conflict with the articles of incorporation or state law. ► Under the RMBCA, authorized but unissued (unsold) shares may be sold for whatever price is set by the board of directors. ► A corporation cannot repurchase its stock if the corporation is insolvent or if the purchase would impair the corporation's capital.

STUDY HINTS. ► In most states, a corporation's name must contain some word indicating the company's corporate nature. ► With a few exceptions, a corporation need not use a corporate seal.

5. *ULTRA VIRES* ACTS

An action that exceeds the powers granted by the articles and applicable law is an *ultra vires* act.

C. CREATION AND TERMINATION OF THE CORPORATION

6. PROMOTERS

GENERAL RULES. ► A promoter is personally liable on a contract that the promoter made on behalf of a corporation to be formed unless: (1) the contract states otherwise; or (2) the promoter and third party intended otherwise. ► A corporation is not liable for a promoter's contract unless it expressly or impliedly adopts the contract. A promoter, but not a corporation, is liable for a promoter's tort.

STUDY HINT. A promoter is a fiduciary of the corporation and of prospective shareholders, and the promoter cannot make secret profits while acting on their behalf.

LEARNING OUTCOME EXAMPLE. See the *Clinton Investors Co.* case in which Watkins, a promoter, was held personally liable for a preincorporation lease, p. 1039.

7. INCORPORATION

In order to create a corporation, incorporators sign appropriate forms and file them with the state.

8. APPLICATION FOR INCORPORATION

The process of forming a corporation is ordinarily begun by filing an application for a certificate of incorporation with the secretary of state. The application typically includes articles of incorporation that must contain certain fundamental information about the corporation.

9. THE CERTIFICATE OF INCORPORATION

▶ In most states, a certificate of incorporation is issued after articles of incorporation are filed. ▶ In most states, corporate existence begins when the certificate is issued; in other states, existence begins when an organizational meeting is held. ▶ The Revised Model Business Corporation Act (RMBCA) has eliminated certificates of incorporation; corporate existence begins when articles of incorporation are filed.

10. PROPER AND DEFECTIVE INCORPORATION

GENERAL RULES. ▶ A corporation legally exists if: (1) incorporation procedures are complied with perfectly or with only minor deviations (a *de jure* corporation); or (2) compliance with incorporation procedures is sufficient to warrant recognizing existence of a corporation despite substantial deviations from required procedures (a *de facto* corporation). ▶ If parties completely fail to comply with incorporation procedures: (1) a corporation is not created; and (2) persons acting for the purported corporation have the same liability for business obligations as partners would have.

LIMITATIONS. ▶ Under the corporation by estoppel doctrine followed by some states, a person who contracts with another party believing that the other party is a corporation cannot later impose personal liability on the other party. ▶ The RMBCA and many states do not deny corporate existence because of errors in following incorporation rules if the articles are filed with the state.

11. INSOLVENCY, BANKRUPTCY, AND REORGANIZATION

A corporation experiencing financial difficulties may seek relief under bankruptcy law.

12. FORFEITURE OF CHARTER

Under the RMBCA, a state may seek to dissolve a corporation if the corporation fails to: (1) pay certain taxes; (2) file required annual reports; or (3) maintain a registered agent or office.

13. JUDICIAL DISSOLUTION

▶ In some states, a corporation may be dissolved by judicial decree if management is deadlocked and the deadlock cannot be broken by the shareholders. ▶ After a corporation has been dissolved, a contract made by a corporate officer on behalf of the corporation cannot be enforced against the other contracting party.

D. CONSOLIDATIONS, MERGERS, AND CONGLOMERATES

14. DEFINITIONS

GENERAL RULE. (1) *Consolidation*: two or more corporations combine, terminating their separate existences and forming a new corporation; (2) *merger*: two or more corporations combine; one corporation continues to exist and the other corporation terminates; (3) *conglomerate*: parent corporation creates or acquires subsidiary corporations that engage in unrelated activities.

LIMITATION. When a shareholder dissents to an authorized consolidation or merger, the shareholder must be paid for his or her stock if the shareholder returns the stock to the corporation.

STUDY HINTS. ► A "two-step merger" is a transaction whereby (1) an outside investor buys control of a target corporation, and (2) this control is used to approve a merger of the target corporation with a second corporation owned by the outside investor. ► Statutes commonly require disclosure of details of a merger or consolidation a certain number of days prior to any action on the combinations. These requirements are intended to make sure stockholders are fully informed about the nature and effect of the combinations.

15. LEGALITY

In some cases, a proposed consolidation, merger, or acquisition of assets may be prohibited by federal antitrust laws because it may substantially lessen competition in interstate commerce.

16. LIABILITY OF SUCCESSOR CORPORATIONS

➤ *Mergers and consolidations*: The new or continuing corporation that exists after a consolidation or merger is liable for obligations of the prior companies.

➤ *Asset sales*: A corporation that buys the assets of another company is not liable for the seller's debts unless the asset purchase is in effect a merger or the successor is a mere continuation of the predecessor company. Example: Company *A* buys all assets of Company *B*, issuing Company *A* stock as payment. This transaction will be treated as a merger.

➤ LEARNING OUTCOME EXAMPLE.See the example of Velocity Power Boats, Inc., which became essentially a "new hat" for Thoroughbred Power Boats, Inc., with liability as a corporate successor for a defective Thoroughbred boat, p. 1047.

CONCEPT REVIEW AND APPLICATIONS

Matching Exercise

Select the term or phrase that best matches a definition or statement stated below. Each term or phrase is the best match for only one statement or definition. Not all terms and phrases will necessarily be used.

articles of incorporation	corporation	merge
authorities	corporation by estoppel	police power
bylaws	corporation de jure	private corporation
certificate of incorporation	domestic corporation	promoters
charter	eleemosynary corporation	public corporation
close corporation	foreign corporation	quasi-public corporation
conglomerate	general corporation code	treasury stock
consolidation	incorporators	ultra vires

_____ 1. Document issued by a secretary of state after appropriate application for incorporation and articles of incorporation are filed.

_____ 2. Corporate document stating rules that govern the internal affairs of a corporation.

_____ 3. Created despite significant noncompliance with incorporation requirements.

_____ 4. Person who brings together others who are interested in an undertaking, and who conceives of the idea of forming a corporation.

_____ 5. Relationship of a parent corporation to subsidiary corporations engaged in diversified fields of activity unrelated to the field of activity of the parent corporation.

_____ 6. Fundamental corporate document that is typically filed with a secretary of state in connection with an application to form a corporation.

_____ 7. Action that exceeds the lawful powers of a corporation.

_____ 8. Corporation owned by one or a few persons.

_____ 9. Stock of a corporation that the corporation has issued and repurchased.

_____10. Corporation formed by the government to carry out governmental affairs.

True/False

_____ 1. A corporation is a legal entity that is separate and distinct from its shareholders.

_____ 2. The profits and losses of a Subchapter S corporation are taxed to the shareholders.

_____ 3. In general, corporations do not enjoy the constitutional rights granted to natural persons.

_____ 4. In general, shareholders and officers are personally liable for the debts of a corporation.

_____ 5. A parent corporation is automatically liable for the debts of a subsidiary corporation due to the close relationship between the corporations.

_____ 6. A promoter is a fiduciary of the corporation to be formed and of prospective shareholders. Therefore, a promoter is prohibited from making secret profits at the expense of such parties.

_____ 7. The RMBCA significantly limits the powers of a corporation, and it does not permit a corporation to exercise many of the powers enjoyed by natural persons.

_____ 8. Under the corporation by estoppel doctrine, a creditor cannot assert personal liability against an individual if the creditor thought that the individual was acting on behalf of a corporation.

_____ 9. Under certain circumstances, a secretary of state may seek to dissolve a corporation.

_____ 10. In general, a corporation cannot repurchase its stock.

Multiple Choice

_____ 1. Phyllis and Rod, who are cousins, are the sole shareholders of Food Inc., which was incorporated in Iowa. Food Inc. sells produce to wholesalers and the general public in Arizona. Food Inc. is a:
   a. Quasi-public corporation.
   b. Domestic corporation with regard to its business activities in Arizona.
   c. Professional corporation.
   d. Close corporation.

_____ 2. Lin planned to form a corporation to own and operate a shoe store. Prior to incorporation, Lin leased a store, signing the contract in her individual capacity and on behalf of the corporation to be formed. The corporation has now been incorporated. In most states:
   a. The corporation is liable on the contract even if it does not adopt the contract.
   b. The corporation is liable on the contract only if it adopts the contract.
   c. Lin was automatically released from liability on the contract when the corporation formed.
   d. Lin is automatically released from liability on the contract if the corporation adopts the contract.

_____ 3. Polly is incorporating Polly's Pets Inc. When will corporate existence for this corporation begin?
   a. The corporation will exist as soon as Polly files corporate bylaws with the Secretary of State.
   b. The corporation will exist as soon as Polly commences doing business as a corporation.
   c. Under the RMBCA, the corporation will not exist until Polly files articles of incorporation with the Secretary of State and the state issues a certificate of incorporation.
   d. In some states, the corporation will not exist until Polly files an appropriate application (with articles of incorporation) and the state issues a certificate of incorporation.

_____ 4. The shareholders and board of directors of Acme Inc. and Belco Inc. have voted in favor of combining their respective corporations. Pursuant to this combination, Acme Inc. will terminate and Belco Inc. will continue. This combination is known as a:

    a. Limited liability company.

    b. Merger.

    c. Proprietorship.

    d. Franchise.

Case Problem

Answer the following problem, briefly explaining your answer.

Ted and Alice intend to form a corporation and they are trying to determine what powers the corporation may have. Ted and Alice have asked you the following questions:

1. If the articles of incorporation are silent regarding corporate powers, the RMBCA (and many states) will grant a corporation the right to exercise what general powers?
2. Must the corporate name indicate that the enterprise is a corporation?
3. Can the corporation be formed to have perpetual life?
4. Can the corporation be empowered to buy, sell, and mortgage real and personal property?
5. Must the corporation have a corporate seal?

_____

_____

_____

_____

Internet Exercise

Using the Internet, state the name and briefly describe the purpose of three federal public corporations, quasi-public corporations, and/or public authorities.

_____

_____

_____

_____

CPA REVIEW

The following questions were given on CPA examinations. The answers for these questions are the unofficial answers prepared by the American Institute of Certified Public Accountants, Inc. (AICPA). All material is reproduced with permission of the AICPA.

____ 1. Under the Revised Model Business Corporation Act, which of the following must be contained in a corporation's articles of incorporation?
   a. Quorum voting requirements.
   b. Names of stockholders.
   c. Provisions for issuance of par and non-par shares.
   d. The number of shares the corporation is authorized to issue.

____ 2. Under the Revised Model Business Corporation Act, a merger of two public corporations usually requires all of the following except
   a. A formal plan of merger.
   b. Affirmative vote by the holders of a majority of each corporation's voting shares.
   c. Receipt of voting stock by all stockholders of the original corporations.
   d. Approval by the board of directors of each corporation.

____ 3. Assuming all other requirements are met, a corporation may elect to be treated as an S corporation under the Internal Revenue Code if it has
   a. Both common and preferred stockholders.
   b. A partnership as a stockholder.
   c. (Seventy-five) or fewer stockholders.
   d. The consent of a majority of the stockholders.

____ 4. Which of the following must take place for a corporation to be voluntarily dissolved?
   a. Passage by the board of directors of a resolution to dissolve.
   b. Approval by the officers of a resolution to dissolve.
   c. Amendment of the certificate of incorporation.
   d. Unanimous vote of the stockholders.

____ 5. Generally, a merger of two corporations requires
   a. That a special meeting notice and a copy of the merger plan be given to all stockholders of both corporations.
   a. Unanimous approval of the merger plan by the stockholders of both corporations.
   b. Unanimous approval of the merger plan by the boards of both corporations.
   c. That all liabilities owed by the absorbed corporation be paid before the merger.

CHAPTER 45
SHAREHOLDER RIGHTS IN CORPORATIONS

MAKE THE CONNECTION

SUMMARY

The ownership of a corporation is evidenced by a holder's shares of stock that have been issued by the corporation. Common stock is ordinary stock that has no preferences but entitles the holder to (1) participate in the control of the corporation by exercising one vote per share of record, (2) share in the profits in the form of dividends, and (3) participate, upon dissolution, in the distribution of net assets after the satisfaction of all creditors (including bondholders). Other classes of stock exist, such as preferred stock, that have priority over common stock with regard to distribution of dividends and/or assets upon liquidation. Shares may be acquired by subscription of an original issue or by transfer of existing shares.

Bonds are debt securities, and a bondholder is a creditor rather than an owner of the corporation. Bondholders' interests are represented by an indenture trustee who is responsible for ensuring that the corporation complies with the terms of the bond indenture.

Shareholders control the corporation, but this control is indirect. Through their voting rights, they elect directors, and by this means, they can control the corporation. *Preemptive rights*, if they exist, allow shareholders to maintain their voting percentages when the corporation issues additional shares of stock. Shareholders have the right to inspect the books of the corporation unless it would be harmful to the corporation. Shareholders also have the right to receive dividends when declared at the discretion of the directors. Shareholders may bring a derivative action on behalf of the corporation for damages to the corporation. Shareholders are ordinarily protected from liability for the acts of the corporation.

Ordinarily, each corporation is treated as a separate person, and the law does not look beyond the corporate identity merely because the corporation was formed to obtain tax savings or limited liability. The fact that two corporations have the same shareholders does not justify disregarding the separate corporate entities. However, when a corporation is formed to perpetrate a fraud, a court ignores the corporate form, or "pierces the corporate veil." The corporate form is also ignored to prevent injustice or because of the functional reality that the two corporations in question are one.

LEARNING OUTCOMES
After studying this chapter, you should be able to

A. CORPORATE STOCKS AND BONDS
LO.1 Explain how to calculate the book value of a share of stock
LO.2 Distinguish between stocks and bonds

B. ACQUISITION OF SHARES
LO.3 Distinguish between subscriptions for and transfers of stock

C. RIGHTS OF SHAREHOLDERS
LO.4 Explain the rights of shareholders
LO.5 Explain the nature of a shareholder derivative lawsuit

D. LIABILITY OF SHAREHOLDERS
LO.6 Explain the exceptions to the limited liability of shareholders

CHAPTER OUTLINE

A. CORPORATE STOCKS AND BONDS

1. NATURE OF STOCK

GENERAL RULE.   Stock (shares) represents a fractional ownership of a corporation and its assets. **LIMITATIONS.**   ▶ A shareholder does not own an interest in specific corporate assets. ▶ The Revised Model Business Code (RMBCA) eliminates the concept of no par value, so stock in all states following the RMBCA is no par value. **STUDY HINTS.**   ▶ Stock is issued with a par value or with no par value. ▶ *Book value*: value of net assets divided by outstanding shares. ▶ *Market value*: price for which stock is sold on open market. **LEARNING OUTCOME EXAMPLE.** See the example in which Roger Eggett was awarded the book value of his stock, textbook p. 1056.

2. CERTIFICATES OF STOCK AND UNCERTIFICATED SHARES

Ownership of stock is typically represented by a certificate of stock (share certificate). In some states, uncertificated shares (shares not represented by a stock certificate) may be sold.

3. KINDS OF STOCK

▶ A corporation typically issues common stock and it may also issue preferred stock. ▶ Corporate stock ordinarily exists for the duration of the corporation. ▶ Types of stock include:

➢ *Common stock*: right to vote on certain matters; no preference to dividends or distributions.

➢ *Preferred stock*: nonvoting; preference to dividends and/or distributions on dissolution.

➢ *Cumulative preferred*: dividends accrue for each year that dividends are not paid. Unless otherwise stated, it is frequently presumed that dividends for preferred stock accumulate if a surplus was available for payment of dividends but they were not declared.

➢ *Participating preferred*: preferred stock shares equally with common stock in extra dividends/distributions that are paid after all shareholders first receive equal dividends/distributions.

4. CHARACTERISTICS OF BONDS

▶ A bond is an instrument, secured by corporate assets, promising to repay a loan to a corporation.   ▶ The relation between a bondholder and corporation is that of creditor-debtor. ▶ Principal is paid on the maturity date, and interest is paid periodically. ▶ Bondholders have no right to vote.

5. TERMS AND CONTROL

Rights are stated in the loan contract (bond indenture/deed); indenture trustee represents bondholders.

B. ACQUISITION OF SHARES

6. NATURE OF ACQUISITION

Shares may be acquired from a corporation or from a shareholder of the corporation.

7. STATUTE OF FRAUDS

► Under an earlier version of the UCC, a contract to sell stock must be evidenced by a signed writing that describes the stock and states the number of shares sold and the price. ► The 1994 version of UCC Article 8 dispenses with the writing requirement for sales of securities.

8. SUBSCRIPTION

➤ *Definition*: A stock subscription is a contract to buy an amount of shares when they are issued.

➤ *Preincorporation subscription*: ► In many states, a preincorporation subscription is merely an offer to buy stock; a contract is not formed until the corporation accepts the offer. ► Under the RMBCA, a preincorporation subscription is irrevocable for 6 months unless otherwise stated.

➤ *Subscription after incorporation*: A subscription is an offer; an acceptance is needed to form a contract. Typically, a subscriber is a shareholder as soon as a subscription is accepted.

9. TRANSFER OF SHARES

GENERAL RULE. In general, a shareholder can transfer stock to anyone the shareholder chooses. LIMITATION. Shareholders may agree to reasonable restrictions on stock transfers. (Restrictions are not binding on transferees unless they are stated on a certificate or transferees know about them.)

10. MECHANICS OF TRANSFER

When stock is represented by a certificate, it is transferred by an owner's indorsing the certificate and delivering it to a transferee. But, a transfer of a certificate to a transferee without an indorsement is still effective between the parties.

11. EFFECT OF TRANSFER

GENERAL RULE. UCC Article 8: A good faith buyer of stock for value (1) receives the seller's title to the stock and (2) takes it free from many defenses that could be asserted against the seller. STUDY HINTS. ► A corporation views the owner of stock as being the shareholder of record (person who is registered as the owner on corporate books). ► A corporation may refuse to register a transfer if: (1) the transfer was wrongful; or (2) the outstanding certificate is not surrendered.

12. LOST, DESTROYED, AND STOLEN SHARE CERTIFICATES

► The owner of a lost, destroyed, or stolen certificate can request a new certificate if the owner posts an appropriate bond. ► In certain cases, an owner's rights to lost or stolen stock may be inferior to the rights of a good faith purchaser who purchased the lost or stolen stock for value.

C. RIGHTS OF SHAREHOLDERS

13. OWNERSHIP RIGHTS

► In general, shareholders may sell shares to whomever they wish and for any price they can obtain. ► A shareholder, even a director or officer, may sell shares at a premium, i.e., more than market price.

14. RIGHT TO VOTE

➢ *Who may vote*: Common stockholders who are shareholders of record are usually entitled to vote.

➢ *Number of votes*: Unless otherwise agreed, each shareholder has one vote per share.

➢ *Matters entitled to vote upon*: (1) Election of board of directors; (2) extraordinary matters requiring shareholder approval, such as changing a corporation's capital, mergers, or a sale of all corporate assets; and (3) matters submitted by the board of directors for shareholder approval.

➢ *Straight voting*: Shareholders may cast one vote per share on each matter that is voted upon.

➢ *Cumulative voting*: ► Type of voting that may be used for electing directors. It is mandatory in approximately one-half of all states; it is optional in the other states. ► A shareholder has a number of votes equal to the number of shares owned multiplied by the number of directors being elected. Votes may be cast for one candidate or they may be allocated among several candidates.

➢ *Voting by proxy*: By written proxy, a shareholder may authorize anyone to vote his or her shares.

➢ *Voting agreements and trusts*: Shareholders may agree how they will vote their shares as a group.

15. PREEMPTIVE OFFER OF SHARES

GENERAL RULE.   If a corporation increases the authorized amount of common stock that it may sell, a preemptive right gives existing shareholders a right to buy a pro rata share of the new stock. LIMITATION.   RMBCA: There are no preemptive rights unless this right is stated in the articles.

16. INSPECTION OF BOOKS

► In most states, a shareholder can inspect corporate books if it is done in good faith and for a proper purpose. Proper purposes include: (1) determining the value of stock; (2) investigating management's conduct; and (3) determining a corporation's financial condition. Improper purposes are: (1) harassment; (2) idle curiosity; (3) to obtain information to aid competitors. ► RMBCA requires a corporation to furnish an annual financial statement to shareholders. ► A shareholder may employ an expert to audit the books of the corporation if done for a proper purpose.

17. DIVIDENDS

> *Funds available for declaration of dividends*: ▶ Dividends can ordinarily be declared only to the extent a corporation has earned surplus (retained earnings). ▶ Exception: Wasting asset corporations can pay dividends out of current net profits and, in a few states, so can other types of corporations.

> *Discretion of directors*: The board of directors has broad discretion to determine whether to declare a dividend; it need not declare a dividend even if there are funds available to pay a dividend.

> *Form of dividends*: Dividends may be paid in cash, property, or in shares of the corporation.

> *Effect of transfer of shares*: ▶ Cash dividend: Unless otherwise agreed, if stock is transferred, the owner on the record date (date fixed by board) receives a cash dividend, regardless when it is paid. ▶ Stock dividend: Owner on the date the dividend is distributed is entitled to the dividend.

18. CAPITAL DISTRIBUTION

▶ Upon dissolution, shareholders are entitled to corporate assets that remain after payment of creditors. ▶ Preferred shareholders typically have a limited preference to distributions of these assets.

19. SHAREHOLDERS' ACTIONS

▶ A shareholder may bring a derivative lawsuit on behalf of a corporation if the corporation improperly refuses to sue. In a derivative action, any monetary recovery is paid to the corporation.

▶ Shareholders bringing a derivative suit must show that they "fairly and adequately" represent the interests of other "similarly situated" shareholders. ▶ **LEARNING OUTCOME EXAMPLE**. See the *AIG* case, where stockholder plaintiffs were excused from making a demand on the full board, textbook p. 1070.

D. LIABILITY OF SHAREHOLDERS

20. LIMITED LIABILITY

A shareholder's liability for corporate obligations is generally limited to the capital contributed by the shareholder. Ordinarily, a shareholder does not have personal liability for corporate debts.

21. IGNORING THE CORPORATE ENTITY

GENERAL RULE. Shareholders, directors, and officers are not liable for corporate obligations. **LIMITATIONS.** ▶ A court may "pierce the corporate veil" and hold shareholders liable for corporate obligations if needed to avoid a fraud or injustice. Factors that may justify this action: (1) failure to keep corporate records and commingling of corporate and personal assets; (2) grossly inadequate capitalization; (3) diversion of corporate assets; (4) using a corporation to avoid existing debts; (5) using a corporation to engage in fraud or illegal conduct; and (6) using a corporation to obtain an unjust benefit. ▶ Some courts also disregard a corporation when it is merely the "alter ego" of a person who uses it for wrongful purpose.

STUDY HINT. A court will *not* ignore a corporation's separate existence merely because: (1) two corporations have the same shareholders or are closely related (parent-subsidiary); (2) a corporation is formed to take advantage of tax benefits or to obtain limited liability for its owners; (3) a corporation cannot pay its debts; or (4) shareholders actively participate in a corporation's business.

LEARNING OUTCOME EXAMPLE. See the *Boles* case where Engle diverted assets and, as a result, the corporate entity was disregarded to accomplish justice, textbook p. 1072.

22. OTHER EXCEPTIONS TO LIMITED LIABILITY

➤ *Wage claims*: In some states, shareholders may be liable for wages owed to corporate employees.

➤ *Unpaid subscriptions*: If a corporation is insolvent and money is needed to pay creditors, a shareholder is liable to the corporation and/or creditors for the amount owed for stock. Liability may exist if the par value for stock was not paid or if stock was paid for with overvalued property.

➤ *Unauthorized dividends*: Subject to certain limitations in some states, if a dividend is improperly paid from capital, shareholders are liable to creditors for the amount of the improper dividend.

23. THE PROFESSIONAL CORPORATION

▶ A shareholder in a professional corporation is liable for his or her own torts committed while acting for the corporation. ▶ Depending on state law, a shareholder may or may not be personally liable for torts, such as malpractice, committed by other shareholders while acting for a corporation.

CONCEPT REVIEW AND APPLICATIONS

Matching Exercise

Select the term or phrase that best matches a definition or statement stated below. Each term or phrase is the best match for only one statement or definition. Not all terms and phrases will necessarily be used.

acceptance	deed	proxy
bond	derivative (secondary) action	registered bonds
bond indenture	indenture trustee	sinking fund
book value	market value	stock subscription
capital stock	maturity date	voting by proxy
certificate of stock	outstanding	voting trust
common stock	par value	wasting assets corporations
cumulative voting	preemptive right	
debenture	preferred stock	

_____ 1. Minimum price for which certain designated stock may be initially sold by a corporation.

_____ 2. Instrument promising to repay a loan to a corporation, which is often secured by corporate assets.

_____ 3. Class of stock that generally has voting rights, but no preferences to dividends or distributions.

_____ 4. Class of stock which typically is nonvoting, but which has a preference to dividends and/or distributions upon dissolution of a corporation.

_____ 5. Stock valuation computed by dividing value of corporate assets by number of outstanding shares.

_____ 6. Lawsuit filed by shareholders on behalf of a corporation.

_____ 7. Written offer to purchase a corporation's stock when the stock is issued by the corporation.

_____ 8. Document evidencing a shareholder's ownership of stock.

_____ 9. Writing that authorizes another person to vote one's stock.

_____ 10. Agreement whereby shareholders transfer stock to a trustee who votes the shares in accordance with the parties' agreement.

True/False

Write **T** if the statement is true, write **F** if it is false.

____ 1. Shares of stock cannot be issued without a par value.

____ 2. In general, a purchaser of stock is not a shareholder until a certificate of stock has been issued.

____ 3. Preferred stock is often presumed to be cumulative unless otherwise stated.

____ 4. In general, a contract for the sale of stock must be evidenced by a writing to be enforceable.

____ 5. In virtually all states, a preincorporation subscription agreement is deemed to be automatically binding on the subscriber and the corporation as soon as the corporation is incorporated.

____ 6. In general, ownership of stock that is represented by a certificate is transferred by the delivery of a properly indorsed certificate to a buyer or other transferee.

_____ 7. A good faith buyer who purchases stock for value may take the stock free from certain defenses that could have been asserted by a third party against the seller.

_____ 8. A secured party perfects a security interest in stock by taking possession of the stock certificate.

_____ 9. Cumulative voting enables a minority shareholder to elect a majority of the board of directors.

_____10. A shareholder cannot authorize another person to vote his or her shares.

Multiple Choice

_____ 1. Axco Inc. has two classes of stock: common stock and cumulative preferred stock. In 2008, the board of directors of Axco did not declare a dividend even though there was a surplus sufficient to do so. In 2009, the directors intend to declare a dividend. Under these facts:
   a. Preferred stock must be paid a dividend for 2008 before common stock is paid a dividend.
   b. Preferred stock must be paid a dividend for 2009 before common stock is paid a dividend.
   c. Common stock must be paid a dividend before preferred stock is paid any dividends.
   d. a and b.

_____ 2. Ed was a majority shareholder of MED Inc. In a shareholder agreement, Ed and the other shareholders agreed not to sell their stock to anyone else without first offering it to each other. This restriction was not stated on the stock certificates. In violation of this agreement, Ed sold and transferred his stock to Hank who bought it in good faith and without knowledge of the restriction. Hank paid Ed a premium for his interest in the corporation. Under these facts:
   a. Ed was legally entitled to sell his stock to Hank because it is illegal to restrict stock transfers.
   b. Ed was not legally entitled to sell his stock to Hank, and the transfer to Hank can be set aside.
   c. Ed was not legally entitled to sell his stock to Hank, but the transfer to Hank cannot be set aside.
   d. The sale of stock to Hank was illegal because Hank paid Ed a premium for his stock.

_____ 3. Roger is a minority shareholder in Neco Inc. Roger has demanded to inspect the records of the corporation. *In most states*, is Roger entitled to inspect the corporation's records?
   a. No. Shareholders have no right to inspect corporate records.
   b. Yes, if Roger intends to inspect financial records in order to compute the value of his stock.
   c. Yes, if Roger intends to obtain confidential corporate data in order to aid a competitor.
   d. Yes. Roger is entitled to inspect the records for any purpose; shareholders have an absolute right to inspect corporate records.

_____ 4. KLZ Corp. had a $2 million earned surplus, and its board of directors declared a $1 million cash dividend. The record date for the dividend was March 1, and the payment date was May 1. On April 1, Todd sold and transferred shares of KLZ Corp. stock to Bob. In this case:
   a. The dividend was illegal. Only shareholders can declare a dividend.
   b. The board of directors was legally required to declare the dividend. A board of directors must declare a dividend if a corporation has earned surplus sufficient to pay the dividend.
   c. Todd was legally entitled to the dividend that was paid on the shares he sold to Bob.
   d. Bob was legally entitled to the dividend that was paid on the shares he bought from Todd.

_____ 5. Benito is a shareholder in Wren Corp. Benito purchased 10,000 shares of $10 par-value common stock from Wren Corp. for $10 per share. Benito paid the corporation $50,000 for the stock. Wren Corp. subsequently paid Benito a $5,000 dividend out of capital at a time when it was insolvent and it owed $200,000 to Ace Finance Co. The corporation never paid Ace Finance Co. Under these facts, Benito has personal liability to the corporation and/or Ace Finance Co. for:
   a. $0
   b. $5,000
   c. $55,000
   d. $200,000

_____ 6. Jim and Todd are the shareholders of J&T Inc. In which situation would a court be justified in piercing the corporate veil and imposing liability on Jim and Todd for obligations of J&T Inc.?
   a. Jim and Todd form J&T Inc. in order to obtain substantial tax benefits.
   b. Jim and Todd form J&T Inc. in order to avoid personal liability for future corporate debts.
   c. Jim and Todd form J&T Inc. in order to engage in illegal, fraudulent stock sales that would otherwise cause them significant personal liability.
   d. All of the above situations would justify piercing the corporate veil of J&T Inc.

Case Problem

Answer the following problem, briefly explaining your answer.

ABC Inc. issued common and preferred stock. Earl owns 60,000 shares of ABC common stock and Antonio owns the remaining 40,000 shares of common stock. Trisha owns 200,000 shares of ABC preferred stock, which has typical rights and preferences. At its annual meeting, the shareholders are to elect a board of directors comprised of three directors. The articles of incorporation require cumulative voting for electing the board of directors. Each shareholder has three candidates that he or she would like to be elected to the board.

1. Who is entitled to vote?
2. How many directors can Earl, Antonio, and Trisha elect?
3. Could Earl authorize Ann, a third party, to vote his shares? If so, how would he do this?

_____

_____

_____

_____

Internet Exercise

1. Using the Internet, locate and identify the web site for UCC Article 8.
2. Identify and summarize the section(s) of Article 8 that explain how uncertificated shares of corporate stock are transferred.

_____

_____

_____

CPA REVIEW

The following questions were given on CPA examinations. The answers for these questions are the unofficial answers prepared by the American Institute of Certified Public Accountants, Inc. (AICPA). All material is reproduced with permission of the AICPA.

____ 1. Which of the following actions may a corporation take without its stockholders' consent?
   a. Consolidate with one or more corporations.
   b. Merge with one or more corporations.
   c. Dissolve voluntarily.
   d. Purchase 55% of another corporation's stock.

____ 2. Which of the following rights is a holder of a public corporation's cumulative preferred stock always entitled to?
   a. Conversion of the preferred stock into common stock.
   b. Voting rights.
   c. Dividend carryovers from years in which dividends were not paid, to future years.
   d. Guaranteed dividends.

____ 3. A corporate stockholder is entitled to which of the following rights?
   a. Elect officers.
   b. Receive annual dividends.
   c. Approve dissolution.
   d. Prevent corporate borrowing.

____ 4. Opal Corp. declared a 9% stock dividend on its common stock. The dividend
   a. Requires a vote of Opal's stockholders.
   b. Has no effect on Opal's earnings and profits for federal income tax purposes.
   c. Is includable in the gross income of the recipient taxpayers in the year of receipt.
   d. Must be registered with the SEC pursuant to the Securities Act of 1933.

____ 5. The corporate veil is most likely to be pierced and the shareholders held personally liable if
   a. The corporation has elected S corporation status under the Internal Revenue Code.
   b. The shareholders have commingled their personal funds with those of the corporation.
   c. An ultra vires act has been committed.
   d. A partnership incorporates its business solely to limit the liability of its partners.

____ 6. Which of the following securities are corporate debt securities?

	Convertible bonds	Debenture bonds	Warrants
a.	Yes	Yes	Yes
b.	Yes	No	Yes
c.	Yes	Yes	No
d.	No	Yes	Yes

CHAPTER 46
SECURITIES REGULATION

MAKE THE CONNECTION

SUMMARY

State blue sky laws, which apply only to intrastate transactions, protect the public from the sale of fraudulent securities. The term *security* is defined sufficiently broadly to encompass not only stocks and bonds but also any conceivable type of corporate interest that has investment characteristics.

Two principal laws provide the basic framework for federal regulation of the sale of securities in interstate commerce. The Securities Act of 1933 deals with the issue or original distribution of securities by issuing corporations. The Securities Exchange Act of 1934 regulates the secondary distribution or sale of securities on exchanges. These acts are administered by the Securities and Exchange Commission. Except for certain private and limited offerings, the 1933 act requires that a registration statement be filed with the SEC and that a prospectus be provided to each potential purchaser. Criminal and civil penalties exist for fraudulent statements made in this process. The 1934 act provides reporting requirements for companies whose securities are listed on a national exchange and unlisted companies that have assets in excess of $10 million and 500 or more shareholders.

Rule 10b-5 is the principal antifraud rule under the 1934 act. Trading on "inside information" is unlawful and may subject those involved to a civil penalty of three times the profit made on the improperly disclosed information. Cash tender offers are regulated by the SEC under authority of the Williams Act. The securities industry provides arbitration procedures to resolve disputes between customers and firms.

LEARNING OUTCOMES
After studying this chapter, you should be able to

A. STATE REGULATION
LO.1   Explain the meaning of state "blue sky laws"

B. FEDERAL REGULATION
LO.2   Define "security"
LO.3   Compare and distinguish between the Securities Act of 1933 and the Securities Exchange Act of 1934
LO.4   Explain the factors that subject an individual to liability for insider trading
LO.5   Explain how securities firms regulate themselves and provide a process to resolve controversies relating to the sale of securities

CHAPTER OUTLINE

A. STATE REGULATION

1. STATE BLUE SKY LAWS

▶ Every state has adopted "blue sky laws" to regulate intrastate sales of securities. Regulations include: (1) antifraud rules; (2) broker-dealer licensing; and (3) registration of securities.

► LEARNING OUTCOME EXAMPLE: See the discussion of the common-content features of state securities laws such as antifraud provisions, licensing provisions, and regulation of securities on textbook p. 1084.

2. NATIONAL SECURITIES MARKETS IMPROVEMENT ACT

► This Act exempts from state review and registration requirements securities offered by mutual funds and stocks listed on major U.S. stock exchanges. ► States may still investigate and prosecute fraudulent activities and unlawful conduct by brokers or dealers in securities transactions.

B. FEDERAL REGULATION

3. FEDERAL LAWS REGULATING THE SECURITIES INDUSTRY

➢ *Securities Enforcement Remedies and Penny Stock Reform Act*: gives the SEC new remedial powers to prevent anyone from violating federal securities laws, including the power to issue cease and desist orders and to seek injunctions and monetary penalties.

➢ *Securities Acts Amendments of 1990*: authorizes sanctions against SEC-regulated persons for violating foreign laws.

➢ *Market Reform Act of 1990*: gives the SEC new powers to deal with instability in the securities markets.

➢ *Private Securities Litigation Reform Act of 1995*: Addresses abuses in securities litigation.

➢ *Sarbanes-Oxley Act of 2002*: Addresses abuses dealing with publicly traded companies.

4. DEFINITION OF SECURITY

GENERAL RULES. ► Federal securities laws apply only to interstate transactions involving a security. ► The term "security" is interpreted broadly, and it generally includes any financial instrument that is sold as an investment. ► Examples: stocks, bonds, notes, and "investment contracts," which include certain investments in oil, cattle, and other enterprises. ► The Supreme Court defines an investment contract as: (1) an investment of money (2) in a common enterprise (3) with an expectation of future profits (4) to be derived primarily from the efforts of others.
STUDY HINT. Under the "family resemblance" test, factors that may indicate an instrument is a security include: (1) a party's reason for entering into the transaction (buyer wants to earn a profit); (2) plan of distribution (instrument is commonly sold to the public for investment purposes);
(3) reasonable expectations of the investing public (the public regards the instrument as an investment); and (4) absence of other factors that would reduce the potential risk of the investment.
LEARNING OUTCOME EXAMPLE. See the *Edwards* case as an example of the broad definition of *security* sufficient to encompass virtually any instrument that might be sold as an investment, textbook p. 1087.

5. SECURITIES ACT OF 1933

➢ *Applicability*: ► Regulates initial sale of any security in interstate commerce by an issuing company. ►Primary purpose is to assure full disclosure of information to investors.

> *General requirements*: Prior to sale, an issuer must: (1) file a registration statement with the SEC; and (2) provide a prospectus to each potential purchaser of offered securities.

> *The registration process*: ▶ *Prefiling period*: Prior to filing a registration statement with the SEC, an issuer cannot offer for sale or sell any securities. ▶ *Waiting period*: During the period following the filing of a registration statement but prior to its becoming effective, securities may

be advertised and preliminary prospectuses may be distributed. ▶ *Posteffective period*: After a registration statement has become effective, sales of securities may be completed.

> *Regulation A offerings*: This regulation has a simplified "mini registration" process for securities sales of up to $5 million within a one-year period, and allows an issuer to "test the waters."

> *Registration exemptions*:

(1) *Intrastate offering*: Securities are offered only to residents of the state in which the issuing firm is incorporated and does business.

(2) *Regulation D - Rule 504*: sales of $1 million or less that are sold in a one-year period to any number of accredited or unaccredited investors. No special information is required to be provided to purchasers, general solicitations are forbidden, and resale may be restricted.

(3) *Regulation D - Rule 505*: sales of $5 million or less that are sold in a one-year period to any number of accredited buyers and less than 35 nonaccredited investors. A public offering of securities is prohibited, and certain information must be disclosed if any offeree is nonaccredited.

(4) *Regulation D - Rule 506*: sales of any amount of securities that are sold to any number of accredited investors and less than 35 nonaccredited investors *who must have sufficient business or financial experience to adequately evaluate the investment.*

> *Liability for violations*: ▶ §11 imposes civil liability on an issuer for making materially false or misleading statements in a registration statement, or for omitting required facts. ▶ §12 imposes liability on parties who fraudulently sell a security. ▶ Willful violations may be a crime.

6. SECURITIES EXCHANGE ACT OF 1934

> *Registration and reporting requirements*: ▶ Brokers, dealers, and exchanges dealing in securities in interstate commerce or on national exchanges must register with the SEC. ▶ The 1934 act imposes reporting requirements on (1) firms whose securities are traded on a national stock exchange, and (2) other companies with both assets greater than $10 million and 500 or more shareholders. ▶ The Sarbanes-Oxly Act of 2002 requires written certification of the 10-K and 10-Q reports by each company's CEO and CFO. A knowing misrepresentation is punishable by fines up to $1 million and imprisonment up to 10 years. A willful misrepresentation is punishable by fines up to $5 million and imprisonment up to 20 years.

> *Antifraud provisions*: ▶ Section 10(b) of the 1934 act and SEC Rule 10(b)-5 generally prohibit the use of any manipulative, deceptive, or fraudulent scheme or device in connection with the initial issuance or resale of securities in interstate commerce. Important concepts include:

▶ *Scope of application*: The 1934 act's antifraud provisions apply to an offer to sell or sale of any security (registered or not) involving the use of the mail, interstate commerce, or a national stock exchange. The 1934 act applies to both sellers and buyers of securities. The SEC, but not private investors, can sue aiders and abettors under Section 10(b).

▶ *Rule 10(b)-5 violation*: Important elements needed to prove a Rule 10b-5 violation include: (1) an untrue statement of or a failure to state a "material" fact that is needed to make a statement not misleading; (2) reliance; and (3) a resultant injury. ▶ "Material" means substantial likelihood that a reasonable investor would consider the matter important in making an investment decision. Materiality is determined on a case-by-case basis. ▶ Whether preliminary merger talks are material and must be disclosed depends on (1) the probability that a merger will occur and (2) the importance that the merger will have to the issuer of the security.

▶ The Private Securities Litigation Reform Act recognizes certain "safe harbors" (defenses) to 10(b) liability. This Act also provides for proportionate liability instead of joint and several liability for defendants who did not knowingly commit a violation of federal security laws.

▶ Rules of Professional Conduct for lawyers now permit lawyers to disclose if a client uses a lawyer's advise to commit a crime. A lawyer also may now inform senior corporate officials if the lawyer knows that a corporate officer or employee will likely harm the corporation.

7. TRADING ON INSIDER INFORMATION

➤ *Insider trading overview*: ▶ Section 10(b) and Rule 10b-5 form the basis for punishing insider trading. The Insider Trading and Securities Fraud Enforce Act of 1988 gives the SEC the power to bring actions against persons engaging in insider trading. ▶ This Act authorizes a civil penalty of up to 3 times the profit gained from illegal trading and persons who aid and abet the illegal trading also are subject to fines. Controlling persons whose inadequate supervision enables employees to engage in insider trading are subject to fines under the Act if the supervisors are found to have acted knowingly or recklessly.

➤ *General duty*: ▶ Insiders and other persons identified below have a duty to either (1) disclose material nonpublic information before trading in a security, or (2) abstain from trading in the security. ▶ This duty applies to the purchase or sale of any security in interstate commerce.

➤ *Parties subject to duty*: ▶ *Insiders*: directors, officers, and other corporate employees.

▶ *Temporary insiders*: outside attorneys, accountants, or other professionals who have access to material nonpublic information due to their employment by a company. ▶ *Tippees*: persons who receive material nonpublic information from (1) an insider or temporary insider (2) who breaches a fiduciary duty by improperly disclosing the information to the tippee (3) if the tippee knows or should know that disclosure is a breach of duty. ▶ *Misappropriators*: persons who steal data or wrongfully take information in breach of a fiduciary duty to their employer. ▶ LEARNING OUTCOME EXAMPLE: See the *O'Hagan* case regarding outsiders who have access to confidential information that will affect a company's stock price, textbook p. 1100.

➤ *Disclosure to tippee*: ▶ Disclosure of information to a tippee is a breach of duty if an insider derives a personal or financial gain as a result of the disclosure. ▶ A tippee may act on information if disclosure of the information to the tippee did not breach an insider's duty. ▶ LEARNING OUTCOME EXAMPLE: See the Dirks case that illustrates the rule that when the insider does not breach a fiduciary duty, a tippee does not violate securities laws, textbook p. 1099.

> *Regulation FD*: Issuers of securities cannot selectively disclose important nonpublic information to selected investors before publicly disclosing the information.

> *Remedy*: Investors who bought or sold stock during a time that wrongful insider trading was occurring may recover damages from any insider who traded on the undisclosed information.

> *Other federal law*: The Insider Trading Sanctions Act of 1984 authorizes the SEC to bring an action against a person trading on material nonpublic information and authorizes persons suing for insider trading to recover a penalty for up to three times the wrongful gain.

8. DISCLOSURE OF OWNERSHIP AND SHORT-SWING PROFITS

> *Section 16(a)*: Directors or officers who own securities in a company, and shareholders who own more than 10 percent of a class of stock, must file a statement disclosing their stock ownership.

> *Section 16(b)*: The parties described above must pay to the corporation any short-swing profits (profits made by buying and selling securities in the company within a six-month period). This duty does not require proof of fraud.

9. TENDER OFFERS

> *Defined*: A cash tender offer is an offer made to all shareholders of a corporation to buy their shares at a specified price provided that a minimum number of shares are tendered for sale.

> *Williams Act - disclosure requirement*: Any person making a tender offer must file documents with the SEC disclosing certain information regarding the tender offer and related matters.

> *Williams Act - antifraud provision*: ► Fraudulent, deceptive, or manipulative conduct is prohibited in relation to tender offers. ► Tender offers must remain open for at least twenty business days. ► A violation requires proof of an actionable misrepresentation or other misconduct.

10. REGULATION OF ACCOUNTANTS AND ATTORNEYS BY THE SEC

► Accountants are subject to liability under many provisions of the 1933 act relating to registration statements and prospectuses, and may have liability under Section 10(b) of the 1934 act. ► SEC Rule 2(e) regulates accountants practicing before the SEC. An accountant practicing before the SEC may be disciplined if the accountant is unqualified, unethical, or violates federal law. ► As required by the Sarbanes-Oxley Act of 2002, the SEC has established minimum standards of professional conduct for attorneys practicing before the SEC.

C. INDUSTRY SELF-REGULATION

11. ARBITRATION OF SECURITIES DISPUTES

Many firms that sell securities include an arbitration clause in customer contracts. This clause makes it mandatory that the firm and customer arbitrate a dispute instead of suing in court. A court will set aside an arbitrator's award only if (1) the arbitrator exceeded his or her power or (2) the arbitration process was seriously flawed.

CONCEPT REVIEW AND APPLICATIONS

Matching Exercise

Select the term or phrase that best matches a definition or statement stated below. Each term or phrase is the best match for only one statement or definition. Not all terms and phrases will necessarily be used.

blue sky laws	registration requirements
cash tender offer	registration statement
fraud-on-the-market	security
insider	short-swing profit
insider information	temporary insider
prospectus	tippee

_____ 1. Director, officer, or other corporate employee who has access to material nonpublic information.

_____ 2. Profit made by officers, directors, and certain shareholders by buying and selling securities in their company within a six-month period.

_____ 3. Disclosure document required by the 1933 act to be provided to prospective buyers of securities.

_____ 4. Stock, bond, or other passive form of investment that is subject to federal securities laws.

_____ 5. State laws that regulate the intrastate sale of securities.

_____ 6. Disclosure document required by the 1933 act to be filed with the SEC.

_____ 7. Person to whom an insider discloses material nonpublic information.

_____ 8. Privileged knowledge regarding company business only known to employees.

_____ 9. Person hired by a company to render professional services on an as-needed basis.

_____ 10. General offer to all shareholders of a target corporation to purchase their shares for cash at a specified price.

True/False

Write **T** if the statement is true, write **F** if it is false.

_____ 1. State blue sky laws generally regulate both the intrastate and interstate sale of securities.

_____ 2. If a contract between a securities firm and customer contains an arbitration clause, then the firm and customer must arbitrate a dispute instead of suing in court.

_____ 3. In general, federal securities laws only apply if a transaction involves a security.

_____ 4. The term "security" generally includes any instrument that is bought as a financial investment.

_____ 5. An issuer's compliance with the registration requirements of the 1933 Act does not necessarily mean that a security is a good investment.

_____ 6. During the waiting period, a preliminary prospectus ("red herring" prospectus) may be distributed to prospective investors, and "tombstone" ads may be published.

_____ 7. A sale of stock made solely to residents of the state in which the issuing company is incorporated and primarily does business may be exempt from the 1933 act registration requirements.

_____ 8. Accountants cannot be held liable for misstatements or omissions that were made in registration statements that they helped prepare.

_____ 9. The 1933 act may impose both civil and criminal penalties for its violation.

_____ 10. The 1934 act imposes reporting requirements on all companies that issue securities.

Multiple Choice

_____ 1. Mayfield Corp. is selling a variety of instruments and property in order to raise capital. Which instrument or property would *not* be a security within the meaning of federal securities laws?
a. A share of common stock in Mayfield Corp.
b. A ten-year corporate bond issued by Mayfield Corp. that pays 15 percent annual interest and that is sold to the general public as an investment.
c. A 100 acre parcel of land.
d. Investment interests in a shrimp farm operated by Mayfield Corp., with investors sharing in the profits made by the farming enterprise.

_____ 2. R&V Limited Partnership is planning to issue limited partner interests and to publicly offer these securities for sale in interstate commerce. What must R&V do to comply with the 1933 act?
a. R&V has no duties under the 1933 act. R&V is only required to comply with blue sky laws in the states in which the securities are offered.
b. R&V is only required to file a registration statement with the SEC.
c. R&V is only required to provide a prospectus to prospective investors.
d. Unless it fits within an exemption, R&V is required to both file a registration statement with the SEC and provide a prospectus to prospective investors.

_____ 3. Nassau Inc. plans to issue and sell $10 million worth of preferred stock. The stock will be sold to (1) forty-five banks, investment companies, and other accredited investors; and (2) fifteen nonaccredited investors who have sufficient financial and business experience to evaluate the merits and risks of the investment. There will be no general solicitation or public offering of the stock. Is this offering likely exempt from the registration requirements of the 1933 act?

    a. Yes. Rule 504 of Regulation D exempts this offering.

    b. Yes. Rule 505 of Regulation D exempts this offering.

    c. Yes. Rule 506 of Regulation D exempts this offering.

    d. No. This offering is not exempt from the registration requirements of the 1933 act.

_____ 4. Pepco Inc. just received a secret report conclusively proving that Pepco's only product causes cancer. As a result, the company may be liable to thousands who contracted cancer due to their use of this product. Under these facts, which party is engaging in insider trading in violation of Rule 10b-5?

    a. Tom, a Pepco director, sells his Pepco stock without disclosing the report.

    b. Bonnie, an outside financial analyst who was retained by Pepco to assess the financial impact of this report, sells all of her Pepco stock without disclosing the report.

    c. Faye, a janitor, steals the report and sells her Pepco stock without disclosing the report.

    d. All of the above.

_____ 5. Frye Co. is subject to all provisions of the 1934 Act. Dick is a director of Frye Co., and he owns 5 percent of the company's common stock. Bonnie owns 15 percent of the company's common stock. Sally owns 4 percent of the company's common stock. Under Rule 16 of the 1934 act:

    a. If Dick buys and sells stock in Frye Co. within a six-month period, thereby earning a profit, Dick must pay the profit to the company even if he did not trade on inside information.

    b. Dick, Bonnie, and Sally must each file disclosure statements with the SEC.

    c. Dick, Bonnie, and Sally are each exempt from filing disclosure statements with the SEC.

    d. a and b.

Case Problem

Answer the following problem, briefly explaining your answer.

Midas Inc. owns several gold mines. Unknown to the public, Midas engineers just discovered a massive new gold deposit. After this discovery, the Midas board of directors made several public announcements denying that there were any new discoveries. Without knowledge of the secret discovery, Tom sold his Midas stock for $10 a share. One week later, Midas stock went to $20 per share when the board announced the new discovery.

1. What federal securities act governs this case?
2. What elements must Tom prove to establish a Rule 10b-5 violation by the Midas board of directors?
3. In all likelihood, did the board violate Rule 10b-5?

_____

_____

_____

_____

Internet Exercise

Precious Metals, Inc. (PMI) is a publicly-held corporation and its stock is traded on NASDAQ. The PMI board of directors has authorized the public offering of 1 million shares of the corporation's common stock for an aggregate price of $100 million. Under these facts:

1. Is this stock offering subject to the registration and prospectus requirements of the Securities Act of 1933?
2. Using the Internet, locate and identify the citation for the National Securities Markets Improvement Act.
   Does this Act exempt this stock offering from having to comply with state blue sky laws?

_____

_____

_____

_____

CPA REVIEW

The following questions were given on CPA examinations. The answers for these questions are the unofficial answers prepared by the American Institute of Certified Public Accountants, Inc. (AICPA). All material is reproduced with permission of the AICPA.

___ 1.　Which of the following are exempt from the registration requirements of the Securities Act of 1933?
   a. All industrial development bonds issued by municipalities .
   b. Stock of a corporation offered and sold only to residents of the state in which the issuer was incorporated and doing all of its business.
   c. Bankers' acceptances with maturities at the time of issue ranging from one to two years.
   d. Participation interests in a money market fund that consists wholly of short-term commercial paper.

___ 2.　Acme Corp. intends to make a public offering in several states of 250,000 shares of its common stock. Under the Securities Act of 1933,
   a. Acme must sell the common stock through licensed securities dealers.
   b. Acme must, in all events, file a registration statement with the SEC because the offering will be made in several states.
   c. Acme's use of any prospectus delivered to an unsophisticated investor must be accompanied by a simplified explanation of the offering.
   d. Acme may make an oral offer to sell the common stock to a prospective investor after a registration statement has been filed but before it becomes effective.

___ 3.　While conducting an audit, Larson Associates, CPAs, failed to detect material misstatements included in its client's financial statements. Larson's unqualified opinion was included with the financial statements in a registration statement and prospectus for a public offering of securities made by the client. Larson knew that its opinion and the financial statements would be used for this purpose.
   Which of the following statements is correct with regard to a suit against Larson and the client by a purchaser of the securities under Section 11 of the Securities Act of 1933?
   a. The purchaser must prove that Larson was negligent in conducting the audit.
   b. The purchaser must prove that Larson knew of the material misstatements.
   c. Larson will not be liable if it had reasonable grounds to believe the financial statements were accurate.
   d. Larson will be liable unless the purchaser did not rely on the financial statements.

___ 4.　In order to raise $375,000, Penn Corp. is offering its securities under Rule 504 of Regulation D of the Securities Act of 1933. Under Rule 504, the offering
   a. Must be sold to accredited investors.
   b. Can not be sold to more than 35 non-accredited investors.
   c. Can be sold to an unlimited number of accredited and non-accredited investors.
   d. Will not subject the issuer to the antifraud provisions of the Securities Act of 1933.

___ 5. Dart Corp. engaged Jay Associates, CPAs, to assist in a public stock offering. Jay audited Dart's financial statements and gave an unqualified opinion, despite knowing that the financial statements contained misstatements. Jay's opinion was included in Dart's registration statement. Larson purchased shares in the offering and suffered a loss when the stock declined in value after the misstatements became known. If Larson succeeds in the Section 11 suit against Dart, Larson would be entitled to
   a. Damages of three times the original public offering price.
   b. Rescind the transaction.
   c. Monetary damages only.
   d. Damages, but only if the shares were resold before the suit was started.

___ 6. Rice, Inc. is a reporting company under the Securities Exchange Act of 1934. The only security it has issued is its voting common stock. Which one of the following statements are correct?
   a. Any person who owns more than 5% of Rice's common stock must file a report with the SEC.
   b. Rice need not file its proxy statements with the SEC because it has only one class of stock outstanding.
   c. It is unnecessary for the required annual report (Form 10-K) to include audited financial statements.
   d. Because Rice is a reporting company, it is not required to file a registration statement under the Securities Act of 1933 for any future offerings of its common stock.

___ 7. Which of the following statements is correct with respect to the Securities Exchange Act of 1934?
   a. Issuers whose securities are registered under the Act are required to comply its reporting requirements.
   b. The Act applies only to issuers whose securities are traded on a national securities exchange
   c. The Act subjects all issuers of securities to its registration requirements if the issuer has more than $2.5 million of assets or more than 250 shareholders.
   d. The antifraud provisions of the Act do not apply to issuers of securities that are exempt from the Act's registration requirements.

___ 8. Under the provisions of Section 10(b) and Rule 10b-5 of the Securities Exchange Act of 1934, which of the following activities must be proven by a stock purchaser in a suit against a CPA?
   I. Intentional conduct by the CPA designed to deceive investors.
   II. Negligence by the CPA.

   a. I only.
   b. II only.
   c. Both I and II.
   d. Neither I nor II.

CHAPTER 47
ACCOUNTANTS' LIABILITY AND MALPRACTICE

MAKE THE CONNECTION

SUMMARY

Professionals who agree to perform services for others must perform those services according to the standards of the profession. Accountants, as professionals, must perform their audit work at the levels and standards of competency and thoroughness established for their profession. If an accountant negligently fails to observe those standards, both a breach of contract and a tort occur. This tort of negligent breach of contract constitutes malpractice, and the other party to the contract can sue the wrongdoer either for breach of contract or for the negligence involved.

In some circumstances, not only is the accountant liable to its client, but it may also be liable for malpractice to certain categories of third parties who have used or relied on the financial statement. States and courts differ as to when an accountant is liable to third parties. Some courts do not recognize accountant liability to third parties; these courts require privity between the parties. Most courts hold accountants liable to some third parties but differ as to which third parties and how far to extend the accountant's liability. The various rules that determine accountant liability to third parties are the contact rule, which requires that the third party must have had some contact with the accountant before there can be liability; the known user rule in which the accountant is aware of the third party who will use the accountant's information; the foreseeability rule in which the accountant is held liable if it was possible to foresee that the third party would use the accountant's information; the intended user rule in which the client tells the accountant of the intended use of the audit work; the unknown user rule in which the accountant is not liable to third parties it could not have known would use the information or audit work; and the flexible rule that decides on a case-by-case basis.

Accountants guilty of fraud have liability to all third parties, even those not in privity of contract with the accountant.

To a limited degree, an accountant is protected from malpractice liability by a disclaimer of liability or by the contributory negligence of the plaintiff.

Sarbanes-Oxley(SOX) increases the penalties for accountants who destroy documents when civil or criminal investigations are pending. The act also prohibits conduct by accountants that creates a conflict of interest and requires audit firms to register for authorization to do audit work on public companies. Audit committees of boards are now required to work closely with auditors to make sure that the financial systems in the company and its reports are sound. A federal oversight board reviews the work of audit firms and is authorized to discipline audit firms and accountants for their failure to honor standards or comply with the law.

LEARNING OUTCOMES
After studying this chapter, you should be able to

A. GENERAL PRINCIPLES OF ACCOUNTANTS' LIABILITY
LO.1   Define *malpractice*
LO.2   Distinguish malpractice liability from breach of contract liability

B. ACCOUNTANTS' LIABILITY TO THIRD PARTIES: BEYOND PRIVITY

LO.3   List which third parties may recover for the malpractice liability of accountants and when they may do so.

LO.4   Discuss the difference between accounting malpractice and fraud

C. SARBANES-OXLEY AUDITOR AND ACCOUNTING-RELATED PROVISIONS

LO.5   Explain how Sarbanes-Oxley has affected the accounting profession and accountants' liability

CHAPTER OUTLINE

A. GENERAL PRINCIPLES OF ACCOUNTANTS' LIABILITY

1.   WHAT CONSTITUTES MALPRACTICE?

► Malpractice is a failure by an accountant or other professional to use the care and skill that other members of their profession would use under similar circumstances. ► Malpractice is professional negligence and is a tort. ► An accountant's malpractice may be an actual act, such as making a material miscalculation of a firm's profits, or a failure to do something, such as warning a client of an important problem that the client could have avoided.

2.   CHOICE OF REMEDY

➢ *Breach of contract*: A breach of contract can occur because an accountant fails to fully or completely perform a contract for accounting services.

➢ *Tort liability*: ► In many situations, a client or third party can sue an accountant on the basis of negligence, gross negligence, or fraud if the accountant improperly performs professional services.   ► Malpractice frequently is both the tort of negligence and a breach of a contract to render professional services. ► An injured patient or client has the right to decide whether to sue for the tort or for the breach of contract. For several reasons, plaintiffs in most cases elect to sue for the tort ► In general, a third party (i.e., a person who did not contract directly with the professional) can sue a professional for malpractice only on the basis of tort law; a breach of contract action is generally not available to a third party. ►LEARNING OUTCOME EXAMPLE: See *Ellis v Grant Thornton LLP* on textbook p. 1120.

3.   THE ENVIRONMENT OF ACCOUNTANTS' MALPRACTICE LIABILITY

Many factors have caused the scope of accountants' malpractice liability to expand in this century.

4.   LIMITATION OF LIABILITY

GENERAL RULE.   An accountant can disclaim liability for negligence malpractice if a disclaimer is: (1) clear and unambiguous; and (2) conspicuous (a reasonable person would notice the disclaimer).

LIMITATIONS.   ► Disclaimers do not protect an accountant from liability: (1) if the accountant knows or has reason to know that statements are false; or (2) statements are intentionally misstated.   ► When a malpractice claim against an accountant is based on intentional falsification of data, a limitation of liability is binding because it is against public policy to permit such a limitation when an intentional tort is committed. ► In some states, disclaimers cannot be enforced against a third party who is suing for malpractice.

STUDY HINT. A disclaimer is valid if an accountant must rely on data supplied by others or the data cannot be verified, no opinion is expressed regarding the data, and these facts are disclosed.

B. ACCOUNTANTS' LIABILITY TO THIRD PARTIES: BEYOND PRIVITY

5. STATUS OF THE ACCOUNTANT

▶ An accountant may be a full-time employee of a company, or an independent accountant or auditor. ▶ What constitutes negligence is the same for all of these accountants. ▶ When a third party sues an accountant, privity of contract is not required. In this situation, the accountant's liability to the third party, when recognized, is based on the third party's reliance on the accountant's work. ▶ LEARNING OUTCOME EXAMPLE: See *AUSA Life Insurance Co. v Ernst &* Young on textbook p. 1118.

6. CONFLICTING THEORIES OF ACCOUNTANTS' THIRD-PARTY LIABILITY

There are a number of conflicting theories to determine whether a third party can sue an accountant for negligence due to malpractice. These theories are as follows:

➢ *The privity rule*: ▶ Only an accountant's client (who is in privity of contract with the accountant) can sue for malpractice. A third party cannot sue for malpractice based on negligence. ▶ Example: Third Party Bank cannot recover against Accountant if the bank suffered a loss when it loaned money to Client based on materials negligently prepared by Accountant for Client.

➢ *The contact rule*: ▶ An accountant is liable to a third party if: (1) the accountant met or communicated with the third party; and (2) the accountant knew the purpose for which the third party intended to use the accountant's work and foresaw the other party's reliance. ▶ Example: Accountant prepared statements for Client, and Accountant took the materials to Third Party Bank to negotiate a loan for Client.

➢ *The known user rule*: ▶ An accountant is liable only if the accountant actually knew that a *specific* third party or a member of a specific, identified group would rely on the work. ▶ Example: Client tells Accountant that statements will be given to Third Party Bank in order to obtain a loan. (Note: The fact that it is foreseeable that someone may rely on the work is not sufficient.)

➢ *The foreseeable user rule*: ▶ An accountant is liable to a third party who is a member of a class that the accountant should reasonably foresee may rely on the work. ▶ Example: Third Party Bank may sue Accountant for malpractice if Client tells Accountant that Client intends to use statements prepared by Accountant to obtain a loan from someone. (The *Restatement of Torts* adopts this approach.)

➢ *The intended user rule*: An accountant is liable only to third parties who were expected or intended to rely on the work. Example: Accountant gives financial statements to Third Party, or Accountant gives financial statements to Client knowing that Client will give them to Third Party.

➢ *The flexible rule*: Privity not required; no fixed test; courts decide each case on its own facts.

➢ *Unknown user*: An accountant has no liability to a third party that the accountant has no knowledge of and has no reason to know that the third party is using the accountant's work.

7. NONLIABILITY PARTIES

Accountants do not have liability to the following third parties:

➤ *Interlopers:* An accountant is not liable to a person who is not related to the transaction in question and who unforeseeably relies on statements without being authorized to do so, i.e., an interloper.

➤ *Persons affected by the decision of accountant's client*: ► Most courts hold that a person cannot sue an accountant for malpractice merely because the accountant's client made an unfavorable decision with regard to that person based on incorrect financial materials furnished by the accountant. ► Example: client does not contract with a third party because of incorrect financial report. Third party cannot sue accountant because of the incorrect report.

8. DEFENSES TO ACCOUNTANTS' LIABILITY: CONTRIBUTORY AND COMPARATIVE NEGLIGENCE OF THE CLIENT OR THIRD PARTY

➤ *Contributory negligence*: ► When an accountant is negligent, the client's contributory negligence may negate the liability of the accountant to the client. In some states, this rule applies only if (1) the client interfered with the accountant's audit or (2) the client's negligence contributed to the accountant's error. ► When a third party sues for malpractice, the accountant may raise the third party's contributory negligence as a defense. If the third party acted negligently in relying on a the accountant's work, the third party cannot recover anything from the accountant. ► A client's failure to keep accurate records does not bar an accountant's liability to the client for failing to discover the true facts.

➤ *Comparative negligence*: Some states apply the rule of comparative negligence to accountants' liability cases. Under this theory, accountants' liability is reduced by the percentage of responsibility that clients or third parties bear for their own losses.

9. ACCOUNTANTS' FRAUD MALPRACTICE LIABILITY TO THIRD PARTIES

➤ *What constitutes fraud by accountants*: An accountant commits fraud by knowingly or recklessly making a false statement with the intent that another party relies on the statement, and the other party relies on the statement causing the party a loss.

➤ *Accountant's fraud liability to intended victims*: An accountant is liable to anyone: (1) who is intended by the accountant to rely on a fraudulent statement; or (2) who is a member of a group that is expected to rely on the statement. Privity of contract is not required for liability for fraud.

➤ **LEARNING OUTCOME EXAMPLE**: See *Carlson v Xerox Corp* on textbook p. 1124.

C. SARBANES-OXLEY AUDITOR AND ACCOUNTING-RELATED PROVISIONS

10. AUDITOR INDEPENDENCE

The Sarbanes-Oxley Act mandates a number of steps to ensure greater independence of auditors when conducting audits of their clients. Some of the important provisions include:

➤ *Public Company Accounting Oversight Board*: The PCAOB is established to promote high professional standards for auditors. Among other things, the PCAOB is to develop a registration system for certain accounting firms, establish rules for audit quality, and accountants' ethics, and independence, conduct inspections of public accounting firms and investigate violations.

> ➤ *Registration with the PCAOB*: Any public accounting firm that conducts audits for firms that issue securities must register with the PCAOB.

> ➤ *Maintaining auditor independence*: The Act forbids a number of types of activities by accountants in order to better assure their independence from clients that they audit.

> ➤ **LEARNING OUTCOME EXAMPLE**: See E-Commerce & Cyberlaw on textbook p. 1129.

11. AUDIT COMMITTEES

The Sarbanes-Oxley Act requires that the audit committees of companies being audited must be independent and be allowed to interact with auditors without company management being present.

12. RECORDS RETENTION

The Sarbanes-Oxley Act regulates the retention of records by auditors and accountants and increases the penalties for obstruction of justice by such professionals.

CONCEPT REVIEW AND APPLICATIONS

Matching Exercise

Select the term or phrase that best matches a definition or statement stated below. Each term or phrase is the best match for only one statement or definition. Not all terms and phrases will necessarily be used.

comparative negligence	malpractice
contributory negligence	misrepresentation
exculpatory clause	privity rule
limitation-of-liability	

_____ 1. Defense to negligence that allows plaintiff to recover reduced damages based on his or her degree of fault.

_____ 2. Contractual term stating that one of the contracting parties is not liable for damages in case the party commits a breach of the contract..

_____ 3. Failure to use the care and skill used by other members of the same profession in the community.

_____ 4. Plaintiff's negligence that contributes to injury and at common law bars recovery from the defendant although the defendant may have been more negligent than the plaintiff.

True/False

Write **T** if the statement is true, write **F** if it is false.

_____ 1. In general, a client may sue an accountant who has committed malpractice for either the tort or the breach of contract that results from the malpractice.

_____ 2. In general, a third party can sue an accountant for malpractice only on the basis of tort law.

_____ 3. According to many courts, if an accountant negligently prepared an incorrect profit and loss statement for a company and a manager for the company was denied a promotion because of this incorrect statement, the manager could not sue the accountant for malpractice.

_____ 4. An accountant is liable for all losses suffered by a third party who relied on negligently prepared materials even if the third party was negligent in relying on such materials.

_____ 5. Under the Sarbanes-Oxley Act, a public accounting firm that audits a particular company cannot also perform bookkeeping or other services related to the accounting records or financial statements of the audit client.

_____ 6. Under the *contact rule*, an accountant is not liable to a third party who relied on materials that the accountant negligently prepared unless the accountant met with or had contact with the third party.

_____ 7. Under the *flexible rule*, an accountant's liability to third parties is determined on a case-by-case basis.

_____ 8. Under the *privity rule*, a professional is not liable for malpractice to a third party with whom the professional did not directly contract.

_____ 9. Accountants have a legal duty to exercise the same degree of care, skill, and competence that other accountants in the community exercise; violation of this duty constitutes malpractice.

_____ 10. An interloper can sue an accountant for losses caused by the accountant's malpractice.

Multiple Choice

_____ 1. Carol is a CPA who agreed to prepare a financial statement for Q&R Inc. The contract contains a clear, unambiguous, and conspicuous disclaimer of liability for any incorrect matters stated in the financial statement. If the statement is partly incorrect, in most states the disclaimer would:
    a. Avoid liability for incorrect matters regarding facts relating to Q&R's foreign operations that Carol could not verify, if this limitation is clearly stated in the financial statement.
    b. Avoid liability for incorrectly stated matters that Carol intentionally misstated.
    c. Avoid liability for incorrectly stated matters that Carol had reason to know were inaccurate.
    d. Not avoid liability for any incorrect matters because accountants' disclaimers are prohibited.

_____ 2. Carl is a CPA and, pursuant to a contract with Draco Inc., Carl prepared financial statements for Draco. Carl negligently prepared the statements. Carl knew Draco might use the statements to obtain a loan from an unnamed lender. In fact, Lucky Bank lent money to Draco on the basis of these statements. As a result of Carl's malpractice, both Draco and Lucky Bank suffered a loss. If the *privity of contract rule* is applied in this case, who can sue Carl for malpractice?

    a. Only Draco Inc.

    b. Only Lucky Bank.

    c. Draco Inc. and Lucky Bank.

    d. Neither Draco Inc. nor Lucky Bank.

_____ 3. Stu is a CPA and, pursuant to a contract with Hit Co., Stu prepared financial statements for Hit Co. Stu negligently prepared the statements. Stu knew Hit Co. planned to use the statements in order to obtain a contract from the State of New York and he knew that the State would rely on the statements. Based on these statements, the State did contract with Hit Co., and the State suffered a loss as a result of Stu's malpractice. Select the correct answer if the *contact rule* is used in this case.

    a. The State of New York can sue Stu for malpractice even if Stu never met, communicated with, or had any contact with New York officials.

    b. The State of New York can sue Stu for malpractice if Stu met with New York officials regarding the financial statements of Hit Co.

    c. The State of New York cannot sue Stu for malpractice even if Stu had contact with New York officials regarding the financial statements of Hit Co.

    d. The State of New York could sue Stu for malpractice only if they were in privity of contract.

_____ 4. Kim is a CPA and, pursuant to a contract with ABC Inc., Kim prepared financial statements for ABC. Kim negligently prepared the statements. Kim knew ABC planned to use the statements to obtain a loan from Bucks Bank. Based on these statements, Bucks lent ABC money and Bucks suffered a loss as a result of Kim's malpractice. Select the correct answer under the *known user rule*.

    a. Bucks cannot sue Kim for malpractice. Under this rule, third parties cannot sue an accountant.

    b. Bucks can sue Kim for malpractice only if she actually met with officials of Bucks.

    c. Bucks can sue Kim for malpractice even if she never had any contact with officials of Bucks.

    d. Bucks could sue Kim for malpractice only if they were in privity of contract.

_____ 5. Dan is a CPA and, pursuant to a contract with A&A, Dan prepared financial statements for A&A. Dan negligently prepared the statements. Dan knew A&A planned to use the statements to buy inventory on credit. Based on these statements, Acme sold inventory to A&A and Acme suffered a loss due to Dan's malpractice. Select the right answer if the *foreseeable user rule* is applied.

    a. Acme cannot under any circumstance sue Dan for malpractice.

    b. Acme can sue Dan for malpractice even if Dan did not know A&A was buying from Acme.

    c. Acme can sue Dan for malpractice only if Dan knew that A&A intended to buy from Acme.

    d. Acme can sue Dan for malpractice only if Dan actually met with Acme officials.

Case Problem

Briefly discuss the topics as they relate to the Regarding the Sarbanes-Oxley Act:

1. What events motivated Congress to enact the Act?
2. What are some of the broad subjects addressed by the Act?

_____

_____

_____

_____

Internet Exercise

Tara, a CPA, prepared federal tax returns for Ajax Co. for the years 2004-2007. The tax returns were inaccurate due to Tara's negligence and her failure to apply new IRS regulations. As a result, in 2011 the IRS audited Ajax's returns and assessed significant interest and penalties. Ajax sued Tara for malpractice. Tara defended that the statute of limitations had run and, therefore, Ajax was barred from suing Tara. The applicable statute of limitations in this case is three years.

1. Using the Internet, find and read the New York Court of Appeals decision in *Ackerman v. Price Waterhouse*.
2. Applying the *Ackerman* decision, is Ajax's malpractice claim barred by the statute of limitations? Explain.
3. Do other states apply a different rule? What is it? Under this different rule, would Ajax's claim be barred?

_____

_____

_____

_____

CPA REVIEW

The following questions were given on CPA examinations. The answers for these questions are the unofficial answers prepared by the American Institute of Certified Public Accountants, Inc. (AICPA). All material is reproduced with permission of the AICPA.

_____ 1. Under common law, which of the following statements most accurately reflects the liability of a CPA who fraudulently gives an opinion on an audit of a client's financial statements?
   a. The CPA is liable only to third parties in privity of contract with the CPA.
   b. The CPA is liable only to known users of the financial statements.
   c. The CPA probably is liable to any person who suffered a loss as a result of the fraud.
   d. The CPA probably is liable to the client even if the client was aware of the fraud and did not rely on the opinion.

_____ 2. Which of the following statements best describes whether a CPA has met the required standard of care in conducting an audit of a client's financial statements?
   a. The client's expectations with regard to the accuracy of audited financial statements.
   b. The accuracy of the financial statements and whether the statements conform to generally accepted accounting principles.
   c. Whether the CPA conducted the audit with the same skill and care expected of an ordinarily prudent CPA under the circumstances.
   d. Whether the audit was conducted to investigate and discover all acts of fraud.

_____ 3. Which of the following is the best defense a CPA firm can assert in defense to a suit for common law fraud based on their unqualified opinion on materially false financial statements?
   a. Lack of privity.
   b. Lack of scienter.
   c. Contributory negligence on the part of the client.
   d. A disclaimer contained in the engagement letter.

_____ 4. Sun Corp. approved a merger plan with Cord Corp. One of the determining factors in approving the merger was the financial statements of Cord that were audited by Frank & Co., CPAs. Sun had engaged Frank to audit Cord's financial statements. While performing the audit, Frank failed to discover certain irregularities that later caused Sun to suffer substantial losses. For Frank to be liable under common law negligence, Sun at a minimum must prove that Frank
   a. Knew of the irregularities.
   b. Failed to exercise due care.
   c. Was grossly negligent.
   d. Acted with scienter.

_____ 5. Krim, President and CEO of United Co., engaged Smith, CPA, to audit United's financial statements so that United could secure a loan from First Bank. Smith issued an unqualified opinion on May 20, 1988, but the loan was delayed. On August 5, 1988, on inquiry to Smith by First Bank, Smith, relying on Krim's representation, made assurances that there was no material change in United's financial status. Krim's representation was untrue because of a material change which took place after May 20, 1988. First relied on Smith's assurances of no change. Shortly thereafter, United became insolvent. If First sues Smith for negligent misrepresentation, Smith will be found

   a. Not liable, because Krim misled Smith, and a CPA is not responsible for a client's untrue representations.
   b. Liable, because Smith should have undertaken sufficient auditing procedures to verify the status of United.
   c. Not liable, because Smith's opinion only covers the period up to May 20.
   d. Liable, because Smith should have contacted the chief financial officer rather than the chief executive officer.

_____ 6. If a stockholder sues a CPA for common law fraud based on false statements contained in the financial statements audited by the CPA, which of the following if present, would be the CPA's best defense?

   a. The stockholder lacks privity to sue.
   b. The false statements were immaterial.
   c. The CPA did not financially benefit from the alleged fraud.
   d. The contributory negligence of the client.

_____ 7. When CPAs fail in their duty to carry out their contracts for services, liability to clients may be based on

	Breach of contract	Strict liability
a.	Yes	Yes
b.	Yes	No
c.	No	No
d.	No	Yes

CHAPTER 48
MANAGEMENT OF CORPORATIONS

MAKE THE CONNECTION

SUMMARY

Ordinarily, stockholder action is taken at a regular or special meeting of the stockholders. The presence of a quorum of the voting shareholders is required.

Management of a corporation is under the control of a board of directors elected by the shareholders. Courts will not interfere with the board's judgment in the absence of unusual conduct such as fraud. A director is disqualified from taking part in corporate action when the director has a conflict of interest. Action by directors is usually taken at a properly called meeting of the board. Directors act in a fiduciary capacity in dealing with the corporation. Directors who act in good faith and have exercised reasonable care are not liable for losses resulting from their management decisions. Ordinarily, directors are removed by shareholders.

Officers of a corporation, including a CEO, president, vice president, secretary, and treasurer, are usually selected and removed by the board of directors. Officers are agents of the corporation, and their powers are governed by the law of agency. Their relations with the corporation are fiduciary in nature, and they are liable for any secret profits and for diverting corporate opportunities to their own advantage.

Directors and officers, as in the case of agents generally, are personally responsible for any torts or crimes they commit even if they act on behalf of the corporation. The corporation itself may be prosecuted for crimes and is subject to fines if convicted. The ordinary rules of agency law determine the extent to which a corporation is liable for a contract made or tort committed by a director, officer, corporate agent, or employee.

LEARNING OUTCOMES
After studying this chapter, you should be able to:

A. SHAREHOLDERS
LO.1 Explain how shareholders, as owners of the corporation, exercise limited control over management by voting at shareholders' meetings to elect directors

B. DIRECTORS
LO.2 Explain the qualifications and powers of directors
LO.3 Explain the liability of directors and the meaning of the business judgment rule (BJR)

C. OFFICERS, AGENTS, AND EMPLOYEES
LO.4 Explain the obligation of officers—who have access to corporate information and agency powers—to not violate their fiduciary duties to the corporation

D. LIABILITY
LO.5 Explain how directors, officers, and the corporation itself may be criminally liable for regulatory offenses

CHAPTER OUTLINE

A. SHAREHOLDERS

1. EXTENT OF MANAGEMENT CONTROL BY SHAREHOLDERS

GENERAL RULE. Shareholders have a right to vote regarding: (1) amendments of articles or bylaws; (2) elections of directors; (3) shareholder resolutions; and (4) extraordinary matters, including a merger, dissolution, or sale of all corporate assets not in the regular course of business.
LIMITATION. Shareholders do not directly manage the business of a corporation.

2. MEETINGS OF SHAREHOLDERS

➤ *Requirement*: In general, shareholder action is effective only if taken at a valid meeting.

➤ *Regular meetings*: Time and place is stated in articles or bylaws; notice is generally not required.

➤ *Special meetings*: Meetings are called by directors or sometimes, by holders of sufficient shares of stock. For special meetings, notice that states proposed business must be given to shareholders.

➤ *Quorum*: A valid shareholder meeting requires the presence of a minimum number of shareholders.

➤ *Required approval*: Unless otherwise required by statute or by the articles or bylaws, an affirmative vote of a majority of shares present at a meeting is sufficient to authorize a matter.

3. ACTION WITHOUT MEETING

The RMBCA and numerous states permit an action to be taken by shareholders without holding a meeting if a written consent to the action is signed by all shareholders who were entitled to vote.

B. DIRECTORS

4. QUALIFICATIONS (AND REQUIRED NUMBER)

➤ *Qualification*: Unless otherwise required, anyone (minor or nonshareholder) may be a director.

➤ *Minimum required number of directors*: ► Most states: number fixed by bylaws. ► Many states require at least three directors. ► Some states allow a corporation to have one or more directors. ► In some states, professional corporations may have one or two directors.

5. POWERS OF DIRECTORS

GENERAL RULES. ► The board of directors manages the business of a corporation. ► A board can: (1) authorize any transaction necessary to carry out the corporation's business; (2) appoint or remove officers; and (3) appoint directors to an executive committee to act for the board between meetings.

LIMITATIONS. ▶ A board cannot: (1) authorize extraordinary corporate matters; or (2) delegate to an officer or executive committee total control of a corporation or the power to make unusual contracts. ▶ A court may interfere with a board's management of a corporation if the board approves illegal or fraudulent actions.

6. CONFLICT OF INTEREST

GENERAL RULES. ▶ A director cannot vote on a matter in which he has an undisclosed personal interest. ▶ A corporation may avoid an action if a director is later disqualified due to a conflict. ▶ The federal Sarbanes-Oxley Act of 2002 generally forbids all loans to directors and executive officers by their corporations (except for corporations that engage in consumer credit business). **LIMITATIONS.** ▶ In some states a transaction is proper and cannot be avoided if a director discloses his interest in the transaction and the transaction is fair and reasonable to the corporation.
▶ Some states merely require a director to disclose his or her interest and to abstain from voting.

7. MEETINGS OF DIRECTORS

▶ In most states, a board can act either (1) at a duly called meeting or (2) without a meeting, if a written consent to an action is signed by all directors. ▶ In general, a director cannot vote by proxy.

8. LIABILITY OF DIRECTORS

(a) *The business judgment rule--liability of director*
GENERAL RULES. ▶ A director is a fiduciary of a corporation, and a director owes a high duty of trust and loyalty to a corporation. ▶ *Business judgment rule*: Directors are not personally liable for unprofitable or erroneous decisions if such decisions were made: (1) on an informed basis (i.e., a director did not act with gross negligence); (2) in good faith; and (3) with an honest belief that the action was in the best interest of the corporation. ▶ Directors are protected from personal liability if in good faith they rely upon the opinion of corporate counsel or upon financial reports prepared by independent accountants.
LIMITATION. Traditionally, a director's decision is presumed to be made on an informed basis, in good faith, and with a belief that it is in a corporation's best interest. A party claiming that a director is liable due to a corporate decision must prove one of these elements is missing.
STUDY HINT. State laws often permit stockholders to approve indemnification of directors against liability for their gross negligence if directors did not: (1) act in bad faith; (2) breach their duty of loyalty to the corporation; or (3) obtain improper personal benefits from their acts.
LEARNING OUTCOME EXAMPLES. See the *Walt Disney* case in which an unsuccessful action taken by directors was protected by the BJR, textbook p. 1143; see the *Van Gorkom* case in which directors were not protected by the BJR, because they were grossly negligent in their judgment, textbook p. 1144.

(b) *Removal of director*
GENERAL RULE. Shareholders can typically remove directors. The RMBCA allows removal with or without cause by a majority vote of the shareholders unless the articles state otherwise.
STUDY HINT. In some states, a board may remove and replace one of its own members.

C. OFFICERS, AGENTS, AND EMPLOYEES

► A corporation typically has officers consisting of a president, at least one vice president, a secretary, a treasurer, and a chief executive officer (CEO). Officers are appointed by the board of directors and their duties are stated in the bylaws. ► Officers ordinarily hire employees and agents of a corporation.

9. POWERS OF OFFICERS

➢ *Officers as agents*: ► Officers are agents of a corporation and their authority is generally determined by agency law. ► An officer's implied authority to act for a corporation is not increased simply because the officer is a major shareholder. ► Third parties are charged with knowledge of limits on officers' authority that are stated in recorded articles of incorporation.

➢ *President*: ► According to some authorities, a president has the implied authority to act for a corporation regarding any matter in the normal course of the corporation's business (especially if the president is also general manager). ► A president does not have implied authority to: (1) do acts requiring board authorization; (2) authorize out-of-the-ordinary contracts; (3) execute guarantees or commercial paper; (4) release claims; or (5) obligate the corporation to repurchase its own stock. If a corporation has both a president and CEO, the CEO typically has broad decision-making authority and the president has the power to implement corporate decisions.

10. LIABILITY RELATING TO FIDUCIARY DUTIES

► An officer is liable to a corporation for: (1) secret profits made in connection with any corporate transaction; and (2) profits obtained by personally taking a business (corporate) opportunity in which the corporation may have had an interest. ► An officer who breaches his or her fiduciary duty to a corporation may also forfeit the right to be paid salary and other compensation by the corporation. ► LEARNING OUTCOME EXAMPLES: See the *Demoulas Super Markets* case regarding diverting corporate opportunities, textbook p. 1148; see the *SecurityTitle v Pope* case regarding a manager's duty of loyalty, textbook p. 1149.

11. AGENTS AND EMPLOYEES

The authority, rights, and duties of corporate agents and employees are governed by agency law.

D. LIABILITY

12. LIABILITY OF MANAGEMENT TO THIRD PERSONS

Officers, directors, and executive employees are typically not liable to third parties for any indirect effect that their good faith management decisions may have had on such parties.

13. CRIMINAL LIABILITY

► Officers, directors, and agents are personally liable for their crimes, even if they were acting for a corporation. ► Officers and directors may be guilty of some federal or state crimes if they fail to prevent commission of the crimes and they are a "responsible corporate officer." ► A corporation may be convicted of a crime committed by an officer or agent who was acting within the scope of authority. ► A corporation and its officers may be criminally liable under the

Foreign Corrupt Practices Act for bribing foreign officials. ► Under federal law, corporations that have effective programs to detect and prevent corporate crimes and that voluntarily disclose those crimes to the government are subject to lower fines than corporations without such programs. . ► LEARNING OUTCOME EXAMPLE: See the Gary Lundgren example in which, as a "responsible corporate officer," Gary was held personally liable for environmental law violations, textbook p. 1152.

14. INDEMNIFICATION OF OFFICERS, DIRECTORS, EMPLOYEES, AND AGENTS

► The RMBCA allows a corporation to indemnify persons who acted on its behalf if: (1) they acted in good faith; (2) with a reasonable belief that they acted in the firm's interest; and (3) they had no reason to believe that their conduct was unlawful. ► Some states require indemnification of officers and directors for expenses incurred in defending against unfounded suits brought by shareholders.

15. LIABILITY FOR CORPORATE DEBTS

GENERAL RULE. Officers, directors, and agents are not liable for corporate obligations, even though their acts created the debts.
LIMITATION. In some states, if the corporation improperly does business, the officers and directors can be held liable.

16. PROTECTION OF SHAREHOLDERS

Shareholders who disapprove of board actions may: (1) remove directors; (2) elect new directors at the next annual meeting; or (3) bring a derivative action (when appropriate).

17. CIVIL LIABILITY OF THE CORPORATION

A corporation is liable for contracts made or torts committed by officers/agents acting within the scope of authority.

CONCEPT REVIEW AND APPLICATIONS

Matching Exercise

Select the term or phrase that best matches a definition or statement stated below. Each term or phrase is the best match for only one statement or definition. Not all terms and phrases will necessarily be used.

Business judgment rule
Directors
Executive committee
Extraordinary corporate matters

Foreign Corrupt Practices Act
Officers
Quorum

_____ 1. Directors who are appointed by the board to act on its behalf regarding certain limited matters.

_____ 2. Persons appointed by a board of directors to manage the day-to-day affairs of a corporation.

_____ 3. Persons who have the legal right to collectively manage the business of the corporation.

_____ 4. Transactions that require shareholder approval, such as a merger, dissolution, or sale of all assets of a corporation not in the regular course of business.

_____ 5. Minimum number of shares or shareholders required to be represented at a shareholder meeting in order to have a valid meeting.

_____ 6. Federal law that holds a corporation and its officers liable for illegally bribing a foreign official.

_____ 7. Principle that directors are not liable for business decisions made while acting on an informed basis, in good faith, and with an honest belief that their acts are in the corporation's best interest.

True/False

Write **T** if the statement is true, write **F** if it is false.

_____ 1. The board of directors of a corporation is generally elected by the shareholders.

_____ 2. In general, an officer is not liable for harm that a third party may indirectly suffer as a result of a good faith decision that the officer made on behalf of a corporation.

_____ 3. Some states permit shareholders to act without holding a meeting if a written consent to an action is signed by all shareholders who are entitled to vote regarding that action.

_____ 4. Many states require that a corporation have a board comprised of at least three directors.

_____ 5. The board of directors can delegate total control of a corporation to an individual officer or to an executive committee.

_____ 6. A director does not have personal liability for an erroneous corporate decision he or she makes if the director made the decision in good faith and in reliance upon the opinion of corporate counsel or upon a financial report prepared by an independent accountant.

_____ 7. Directors, but not officers, are fiduciaries of the corporation.

_____ 8. Typically, the board of directors appoints officers of a corporation.

_____ 9. The federal Sarbanes-Oxley Act of 2002 generally permits corporations to make loans to their directors and executive officers if the directors and officers promise to repay the loans within five years.

_____ 10. An officer of a corporation is personally liable to a corporation if the officer personally takes a corporate opportunity without first offering it to the corporation.

Multiple Choice

_____ 1. Hee Haw Inc. owns and operates a fun house. Which transaction can be authorized by the Hee Haw Inc. board of directors without obtaining shareholder approval?
   a. A merger of Hee Haw Inc. with Fun Inc., a separate corporation.
   b. An extraordinary sale of the fun house and all other assets of Hee Haw Inc.
   c. Purchase of a new building for the fun house and the granting of a mortgage on the building.
   d. The board cannot authorize any of the foregoing transactions without shareholder approval.

_____ 2. A special meeting of the shareholders of Camco Inc. was called to vote on a proposed amendment of the corporation's bylaws. Notice of the meeting and the proposed business was given. The corporation has 100,000 shares of outstanding common stock. At the meeting, owners of 70,000 shares are represented. The articles state that a meeting requires the presence of at least a majority of all shares entitled to vote. The articles and state law do not expressly state what percentage of shares must vote in favor of an amendment of a corporation's bylaws. In this case:
   a. Notice of the meeting was not required. Notice is only required for regular meetings.
   b. A quorum is not present at the meeting because all shareholders are not present.
   c. Assuming that the meeting is valid, an affirmative vote by shareholders owning 35,001 or more shares would typically be required to approve the amendment of the bylaws.
   d. Assuming that the meeting is valid, an affirmative vote by shareholders owning 50,001 or more shares would typically be required to approve the amendment of the bylaws.

_____ 3. Terra Inc. is considering buying land from Piedmont Co. Unknown to the Terra board of directors, Piedmont is owned by Roger, a director of Terra. In a number of states:
   a. Roger can vote on the proposed purchase as a director of Terra without disclosing his interest in the transaction.
   b. Terra cannot under any circumstance purchase the property. A corporation cannot agree to a transaction that may involve a conflict of interest with a director of the corporation.
   c. A contract to buy the land from Piedmont is valid and cannot be set aside if it is approved by the Terra board, even if the board is not informed of Roger's interest in the transaction.
   d. A contract to buy the land from Piedmont is valid and cannot be set aside if Roger first discloses his interest in the transaction, and the transaction is fair and reasonable to Terra.

_____ 4. Carmen is president of Acme Corp., a manufacturing firm with assets worth $2 million. Carmen is expressly authorized to manage the day-to-day business affairs of Acme Corp., and she enjoys the customary and incidental authority normally associated with this position. Under these facts, Carmen has authority to take which action on behalf of Acme Corp.?
   a. Employ A&A Accounting Service to prepare the corporation's tax returns.
   b. Agree to repurchase $500,000 worth of the corporation's outstanding stock.
   c. Execute a guarantee by the corporation, guaranteeing payment of another company's debt.
   d. Remove and replace the board of directors of Acme Corp.

_____ 5. Jay is president of Hawk Co., and he did the acts described below on behalf of the corporation. Jay was authorized by the corporation to do these acts. Select the correct answer.
   a. Jay contracted to buy a truck on behalf of the corporation, but the corporation failed to pay for the truck. In this case, Jay is liable for the contract price.
   b. Jay refused to buy goods for the corporation from Winn Co. As a result, Winn Co. suffered a loss. In this case, Jay is liable to Winn Co. for its loss.
   c. Jay bribed a city official in order to obtain a contract for the corporation. Bribery is a crime. In this case, Jay is guilty of the crime even though he acted on behalf of the corporation.
   d. All of the above.

Case Problem

The board of directors of Ameri Finance Inc. approved a $ million loan to L&K. The loan was secured by collateral. Prior to approving the loan, the Ameri board reviewed (1) a credit report that showed L&K was solvent and (2) an appraisal valuing the collateral at $2 million. Later, L&K defaulted on the loan and the collateral was sold for $600,000, causing a $400,000 loss. Ameri shareholders filed a derivative suit, suing the Ameri directors for making this loan.

1. Who has the burden to prove whether the Ameri board acted properly?
2. What test is used to determine the directors' liability?
3. Are the directors personally liable for the loss?

_____

_____

_____

_____

Internet Exercise

Carl Tart Inc. (CTI), a U.S. firm, was bidding on a large government project in Kuwait. CTI submitted a competitive bid, but low-level Kuwait officials were slow in processing it. Ahmad, the Kuwait official who was to award the contract, seemed to favor other companies with whom he had previously done business. In order to improve CTI's chances, Carl personally paid $500 to a low-level official to expedite processing of CTI's bid, and he also gave $100,000 to Ahmad in order to sway him in favor of CTI. Under these facts:

1. What federal law governs the legality of Carl's conduct? What is the citation for this Act?
2. Did either of the payments made by Carl violate this Act? Can Carl be punished for violating this Act?

_____

_____

_____

_____

CPA REVIEW

The following questions were given on CPA examinations. The answers for these questions are the unofficial answers prepared by the American Institute of Certified Public Accountants, Inc. (AICPA). All material is reproduced with permission of the AICPA.

___1. Which of the following actions may a corporation take without its stockholders' consent?
    a. Consolidate with one or more corporations.
    b. Merge with one or more corporations.
    c. Dissolve voluntarily.
    d. Purchase 55% of another corporation's stock.

___2. Generally, a merger of two corporations requires
    a. That a special meeting notice and a copy of the merger plan be given to all stockholders of both corporations.
    b. Unanimous approval of the merger plan by the stockholders of both corporations.
    c. Unanimous approval of the merger plan by the boards of both corporations.
    d. That all liabilities owed by the absorbed corporation be paid before the merger.

___3. Under the Revised Model Business Corporation Act, which of the following statements is correct regarding corporate officers of a public corporation?
    a. An officer may not simultaneously serve as a director.
    b. A corporation may be authorized to indemnify its officers for liability incurred in a suit by stockholders.
    c. Stockholders always have the right to elect a corporation's officers.
    d. An officer of a corporation is required to own at least one share of the corporation's stock.

___ 4. Generally, officers of a corporation
   a. Are elected by the shareholders.
   b. Are agents and fiduciaries of the corporation, having actual and apparent authority to manage the business.
   c. May be removed by the board of directors without cause only if the removal is approved by a majority vote of the shareholders.
   d. May declare dividends or other distributions to shareholders as they deem appropriate.

___ 5. Knox, president of Quick Corp., contracted with Tine Office Supplies, Inc. to supply Quick's stationery on customary terms and at a cost less than that charged by any other supplier. Knox later informed Quick's board of directors that Knox was a majority stockholder in Tine. Quick's contract with Tine is
   a. Void because of Knox's self-dealing.
   b. Void because the disclosure was made after execution of the contract.
   c. Valid because of Knox's full disclosure.
   d. Valid because the contract is fair to Quick.

CHAPTER 49
REAL PROPERTY

MAKE THE CONNECTION

SUMMARY

Real property includes land, buildings, fixtures, and rights in the land of another. Some land interests include the right to use the land, such as easements. Easements can be granted or arise by implication or prescription.

The interest held by a person in real property may be defined in terms of the period of time for which the person will remain the owner. The interest may be a fee simple estate, which lasts forever, or a life estate, which lasts for the life of a person. These estates are known as *freehold estates*. If the ownership interest exists for a specified number of days, months, or years, the interest is a leasehold estate.

Personal property may be attached to, or associated with, real property in such a way that it becomes real property. In such a case, it is called a *fixture*. To determine whether property has in fact become a fixture, the courts look to the method of attachment, to how the property is adapted to the realty, and to the intent of the person originally owning the personal property.

Under common law, the liability of a land owner for injury to third persons on the premises depends on the status of the third persons as trespassers, licensees, or invitees. Many jurisdictions, however, are ignoring these common law distinctions in favor of an ordinary negligence standard or are giving licensees the same protection as invitees.

Real property may be the subject of multiple ownership. The forms of multiple ownership are the same as those for personal property. In addition, there are special forms of co-ownership for real property, such as condominiums and cooperatives.

A *deed* is an instrument by which a grantor transfers an interest in land to a grantee. A deed can be a quitclaim deed or a warranty deed. To be effective, a deed must be signed or sealed by the grantor and delivered to the grantee. Recording the deed is not required to make the deed effective to pass title, but recording provides notice to the public that the grantee is the present owner. The warranties of the grantor relate to the title transferred by the grantor and to the fitness of the property for use. In the absence of any express warranty in the deed, no warranty of fitness arises under the common law in the sale or the conveyance of real estate. Most states today hold that when a builder or real estate developer sells a new home to a buyer, an implied warranty of habitability arises. Title to real estate may also be acquired by eminent domain and adverse possession.

An agreement that creates an interest in real property as security for an obligation and that ends upon the performance of the obligation is a mortgage. A mortgage must be in writing under the statute of frauds. If the mortgage is unrecorded, it is valid between the parties. The mortgage should be recorded to put good-faith purchasers on notice of the mortgage. A purchaser of the mortgaged property does not become liable for the mortgage debt unless the purchaser assumes the mortgage. The mortgagor still remains liable unless the mortgagee agrees to a substitution of parties. If the mortgagor defaults, the mortgagee may enforce the mortgage by foreclosure. Such foreclosure may be delayed because of undue hardship.

LEARNING OUTCOMES

After studying this chapter, you should be able to

A. NATURE OF REAL PROPERTY

LO.1   List the types of real property interests, the rights of the parties and their liabilities

LO.2   Distinguish between liens, licenses, and easements

B. NATURE AND FORM OF REAL PROPERTY OWNERSHIP

LO.3   Discuss the nature and form of real property ownership

C. LIABILITY TO THIRD PERSONS FOR CONDITION OF REAL PROPERTY

LO.4   Explain the liability of landowners for injury to others on their property.

D. CO-OWNERSHIP OF REAL PROPERTY

LO.5   Discuss the forms of co-ownership and parties' rights.

E. TRANSFER OF REAL PROPERTY BY DEED

LO.6   Describe how deeds convey title to land

F. OTHER METHODS OF TRANSFERRING REAL PROPERTY

G. MORTGAGES

LO.7   Describe the characteristics and effect of a mortgage

CHAPTER OUTLINE

A. NATURE OF REAL PROPERTY

1. LAND

Land includes soil, all permanent things attached to it, water on it, minerals, oil, gas, and airspace above.

2. EASEMENTS

> *Definitions*: ► *Easement*: right to use another's land for limited purpose. ► *Dominant tenement*: land benefited by (entitled to use) easement. ► *Servient tenement*: land subject to an easement.

> *Creation*: ► An easement is an interest in land that is created by: (1) deed; (2) implication (implied in connection with a conveyance of land) (called a "way of necessity"); (3) estoppel (unfair conduct gives rise to an easement); or (4) prescription (adverse use of land). ► Oral easements are not binding. ► LEARNING OUTCOME EXAMPLE: See *Frierson v Watson* on textbook p. 1165.

> *Termination*: ► An easement is terminated if it is not used and there is intent to abandon the easement. ► An easement cannot be revoked without the consent of the owner of the easement.

3. **PROFITS**

Profits are the right to take a part of the soil (minerals) or produce of land belonging to someone else.

4. **LICENSES**

▶ A license is a personal, revocable privilege to do an act on another's land. Example: right to camp overnight. ▶ A license may be terminated at any time by the licensor. It continues only as long as the licensor is the owner of the land.

5. **LIENS**

▶ A lien is a security interest in realty. ▶ Examples: mortgages, tax liens, and mechanics' liens.

6. **FIXTURES**

➢ *Definition*: A fixture is personal property that is attached to land or a building in such a manner that it is viewed as being part of the real property. Example: furnace is made a permanent part of a house.

➢ *Tests of a fixture*: Unless otherwise agreed, tests used to decide if property is a fixture include:

(1) *Annexation test*: ▶ Property is a fixture if its removal would materially damage the real property. ▶ Example: lumber that is used to construct a building.

(2) *Adaptation test*: Property is a fixture if specially made for realty. Example: custom-made door.

(3) *Intent test*: Property is a fixture if, at time of affixing, the property owner intended it to be a fixture.

➢ *Movable machinery and equipment*: Movable machinery and equipment is personal property.

➢ *Trade fixtures*: Tenants can usually remove trade fixtures (tenants' equipment used to do business).

B. **NATURE AND FORM OF REAL PROPERTY OWNERSHIP**

7. **FEE SIMPLE ESTATE**

▶ A fee simple estate: (1) lasts forever; (2) is transferable during life; (3) alienable by will; (4) passes to heirs if not willed by a decedent; (5) is subject to rights of surviving spouse; and (6) can be attached by creditors. ▶ LEARNING OUTCOME EXAMPLE: See For Example on Ralph Watkins on textbook p. 1170

8. **LIFE ESTATE**

A life estate lasts only during the life of the person whose life is used to measure its duration.

9. **FUTURE INTERESTS**

Parties may acquire a vested or contingent future interest in property. Example: remainderman interest.

C. LIABILITY TO THIRD PERSONS FOR CONDITION OF REAL PROPERTY

10. COMMON LAW RULE

Under common law, an occupier of land owed the following duties to persons coming upon the land:

> *Trespassers*: Duty not to intentionally harm known trespassers, but no duty to warn or to protect.

> *Attractive nuisance doctrine*: Under an exception to the rule for trespassers, an occupier of land is liable if an injured trespasser is a child who was attracted onto the land by a dangerous condition.

> *Licensees*: ▶ A licensee is a person who is on premises with the occupier's permission. ▶ Duty to warn a licensee of nonobvious dangers known to occupier, but no duty to discover unknown dangers.

> *Invitees*: ▶ An invitee is a person on premises at the invitation of the occupier or for the occupier's benefit. ▶ Duty to reasonably discover and to warn an invitee about or correct dangerous conditions. ▶ LEARNING OUTCOME EXAMPLE: See *Winchell v Guy* on textbook p. 1172.

> **LEARNING OUTCOME EXAMPLE**: See the slip-and-fall example on textbook p. 1171

D. CO-OWNERSHIP OF REAL PROPERTY

11. MULTIPLE OWNERSHIP

Several persons may simultaneously own interests in the same real property. If jointly owned property is sold, the proceeds are held in the same tenancy as the parties held the property.

12. CONDOMINIUMS

> *Ownership*: Common areas are co-owned; separate condominium units are individually owned.

> *Control and expense*: State laws allocate management, control, and expenses among owners in various ways.

> *Collection of expenses from unit owner*: A lien may be placed against a unit for delinquent payments.

> *Tort liability*: A few states allow one injured in common areas to sue only the condo association.

> *Cooperatives distinguished*: A cooperative is usually a corporation that owns a building and stockholders rent units in the building, whereas condominium owners actually own their units.

> **LEARNING OUTCOME EXAMPLE**: See the example on textbook p. 1172 of the rights of condominium owners

E. TRANSFER OF REAL PROPERTY BY DEED

13. DEFINITIONS

► A deed is an instrument or writing by which an owner (grantor) conveys an interest in land to a new owner (grantee or transferee). ► A deed is required to convey real property, whether the conveyance is made in connection with a sale or gift. ► Consideration is not required for a deed to be valid. ► **LEARNING OUTCOME EXAMPLE**: See *Fletcher v Minton* on textbook p. 1177.

14. CLASSIFICATION OF DEEDS

► *Quitclaim deed*: does not state interest being conveyed; transfers only what interest, if any, grantor has. ► *Warranty deed*: transfers specified interest and guarantees the interest is conveyed.

15. EXECUTION OF DEEDS

► A deed must be signed or sealed by the grantor. ► A grantor must have capacity. ► A deed may be set aside for a grantee's fraud. ► To record a deed, laws often require that two or more witnesses sign a deed, and that it be acknowledged by a grantor before a notary public. ► A deed is binding between a grantor and a grantee even if it is not acknowledged or recorded.

16. DELIVERY AND ACCEPTANCE OF DEEDS

► A deed is not effective and title does not pass until the deed is delivered to a grantee with an intent to transfer ownership. ► Delivery includes mailing a deed to a grantee. ► If a deed is given to a third party to give to a grantee only after conditions are met (a delivery in escrow), title passes only when the conditions are met. ► Delivery may be symbolic. Example: Grantor gives Grantee a key to a locked box containing the deed, with the intent to make a present transfer of title.

17. RECORDING OF DEEDS

GENERAL RULES. ► Recording is not needed to make a deed effective, but it provides notice to the public. ► A buyer takes land: (1) subject to valid previously recorded deeds; but (2) free from unrecorded deeds or claims if the buyer was unaware of such deeds or claims when acquiring title. **LIMITATION.**   A grantee who holds title under a recorded deed may lose to another party who claims ownership if: (1) the other party has superior title; (2) the grantee had notice of the other party's claim when title was acquired; (3) a party claiming land by adverse possession occupies the land; (4) the grantee took the land only as a gift; or (5) the grantee acquired the land by fraud.

18. ADDITIONAL PROTECTION OF BUYERS

Buyers may protect themselves by purchasing title insurance, which insures good title, or an abstract of title, which reports all recorded transfers of title and recorded claims against the property.

19. GRANTOR'S WARRANTIES

➢ *Warranties of title*: ▶ *Common law deed*: a grantor may expressly warrant various matters. ▶ *Statutory deed*: laws typically provide that a grantor under a statutory (short form) deed makes certain warranties that include: (1) grantor owns land conveyed (covenant of seisin); (2) grantor has the right to convey the land (covenant of right to convey); (3) land is not encumbered by third party rights, such as liens (covenant against encumbrances); (4) grantor will not disturb grantee's possession (covenant of quiet enjoyment); and (5) grantor will execute additional necessary documents (covenant of further assurances).

➢ *Fitness for use*: In most states, courts hold that a warranty of fitness for use (habitability) is implied in a sale of a new house by a builder or real estate developer.

20. GRANTEE'S COVENANTS

▶ A grantee's promise in a deed that directly relates to the land "runs with the land," i.e., it binds future owners who acquire the grantee's land, and it can be enforced by future owners of the grantor's land. ▶ Restrictive covenants forbid acts by a grantee. Examples: building restrictions.

F. OTHER METHODS OF TRANSFERRING REAL PROPERTY

21. EMINENT DOMAIN

▶ By eminent domain, the government may take (buy) property from private parties for a public use. ▶ It is a sufficient public purpose to take land for public use or to increase public tax revenues. ▶ LEARNING OUTCOME EXAMPLE: See *Kelo v City of New London* on textbook p. 1179.

22. ADVERSE POSSESSION

One may acquire title to land by taking possession of the land if possession is (1) actual, (2) visible and notorious, (3) exclusive, (4) hostile, and (5) continuous for the period required by statute.

G. MORTGAGES

23. CHARACTERISTICS OF A MORTGAGE

▶ A mortgage is a security interest in real property that is given by a mortgagor to a mortgagee. ▶ A mortgagee can enforce a mortgage by foreclosure. ▶ A mortgagor may redeem (recover) property after foreclosure. ▶ A mortgagee's interest ends when the secured debt is paid.

24. PROPERTY SUBJECT TO MORTGAGE

Any interest in real property can be mortgaged.

25. FORM OF MORTGAGE

In general, no particular language is required to create a mortgage. However, a mortgage must be written, and it must express the parties' intent to create a mortgage.

26. CREATIVE FORMS OF FINANCING

► *Adjustable rate mortgage (ARM)*: low initial rate of interest increases over time with market rates. ► *Reverse mortgage*: take out mortgage on free-and-clear property; money is paid to owner over time.

27. RECORDING OR FILING OF MORTGAGE

An unrecorded mortgage binds the parties and their heirs and donees; it does not bind a good faith land buyer or creditor who acquires an interest for value and without knowledge of the mortgage.

28. RESPONSIBILITIES OF THE PARTIES

➢ *Repairs and improvements*: ► Unless otherwise agreed, a mortgagor has no duty to make improvements or to repair premises that are damaged without the mortgagor's fault. ► A mortgagee in possession must make reasonable, necessary repairs but is entitled to reimbursement for such expenses.

➢ *Taxes, assessments, and insurance*: ► The mortgagor must pay taxes and assessments. ► Unless otherwise agreed, neither party is required to insure the property.

➢ *Impairment of security*: A mortgagor may be liable to the mortgagee if the mortgagor damages the mortgaged property, thereby impairing the value of the property.

29. TRANSFER OF INTEREST

► Typically, a mortgagor may transfer property without a mortgagee's consent. But, a mortgagor remains liable for the debt unless the mortgagee agrees otherwise. ► If a transferee "assumes" the mortgage, then the transferee is also liable to pay the mortgage. If a transferee takes the property "subject to" the mortgage, then the transferee is not personally liable to pay the mortgage but the mortgage upon the property may be foreclosed if the mortgage is not paid. ► A mortgagee can assign a mortgage. ► LEARNING OUTCOME EXAMPLE: See the **For Example** discussion of Bob and Jane on textbook p. 1183.

30. RIGHTS OF MORTGAGEE AFTER DEFAULT

If a mortgagor defaults, a mortgagee may (1) declare the entire debt due (even if only a part is in default), and foreclose on and sell the land. Foreclosure eliminates a mortgage and a buyer is not subject to the mortgage. But foreclosure does not end the debt, and a mortgagor is liable for any deficiency.

31. RIGHTS OF MORTGAGOR AFTER DEFAULT

► In certain cases, a mortgagor may obtain a stay of a foreclosure to prevent undue hardship. ► In many states, a mortgagor has a right of redemption after a foreclosure sale, which entitles the mortgagor to recover the property by paying a required sum within a specified time.

CONCEPT REVIEW AND APPLICATIONS

Matching Exercise

Select the term or phrase that best matches a definition or statement stated below. Each term or phrase is the best match for only one statement or definition. Not all terms and phrases will necessarily be used.

abstract of title	estate in fee	prescription
acceptance	fee simple defeasibles	profits
adjustable rate mortgage	fee simple estate	quitclaim deeds
(ARM)	fixture	race statutes
adverse possession	foreclosure	race-notice statutes
assumption	grantee	real property
attractive nuisance doctrine	grantor	recorder
condominium	invitee	redemption
cooperative	judgment liens	remainder interest
covenant against encumbrances	land	reverse mortgage
covenant of further assurances	leasehold estate	runs with the land
covenant of quiet enjoyment	license	servient tenement
covenant of right to convey	licensee	stay (or delay) of foreclosure
covenant of seisin	liens	tax liens
covenants (or warranties) of	life estate	transferee
title	limited covenant	trespasser
deed	mechanic's liens	warranties of title
dominant tenement	mortgage	warranty deeds
easement	notice statutes	way of necessity
easement by implication	notice-race	
eminent domain	possibility of reverter	

_____ 1. Property that is affixed to land or buildings and is legally considered part of real property.

_____ 2. Writing or instrument used to convey real property.

_____ 3. Revocable privilege to perform an act or acts on land belonging to another.

_____ 4. Deeds that only transfer whatever interest, if any, that grantors hold in the property.

_____ 5. Irrevocable right to use land belonging to another.

_____ 6. Land that is benefited by an easement.

_____ 7. Lien that is voluntarily given by a property owner to secure performance of an obligation.

_____ 8. Right to take a part of the soil or produce from land belonging to another.

_____ 9.   Land that is subject to an easement.

_____ 10.   Deeds that convey a specified interest in property and guarantee that such interests are transferred.

True/False

Write **T** if the statement is true, write **F** if it is false.

____ 1.   A landowner's ownership of airspace is subject to reasonable use by aircraft flying overhead.

____ 2.   An oral easement is legally enforceable.

____ 3.   In general, a license can be revoked by the person granting the license.

____ 4.   Whether property is a fixture or not largely depends on the intent of the party affixing the property to the land or building.

____ 5.   In general, movable machinery and equipment are fixtures.

____ 6.   Under common law, an occupier of land must protect trespassers from known dangers.

____ 7.   By statute in most states, a landowner has no duty to warn or protect persons who are permitted to use his or her land for recreational purposes without charge.

____ 8.   A condominium and a cooperative are the same thing.

____ 9.   In a condominium project, individual owners own their respective condominium units and all of the unit owners co-own the common areas.

____ 10.   A deed is not valid unless consideration is given for the deed.

Multiple Choice

____ 1.   Joseph owns a farm. In a signed writing, Joseph granted Fran the irrevocable right to use a road on his farm so that Fran could more easily reach her own property. What kind of interest in land did Joseph grant to Fran?
a. License.
b. Easement.
c. Lien.
d. Profit.

____ 2.   Shanti leased a building. She installed a stove and boiler in the building. When the lease expires, she intends to remove the stove, but not the boiler. The stove can be removed easily without causing harm. Removal of the boiler will seriously damage the building and boiler. Are the stove/boiler fixtures?
a. The stove and boiler are both fixtures.
b. The stove is not a fixture, but the boiler is a fixture.

c. The stove is a fixture, but the boiler is not a fixture.

d. Neither the stove nor the boiler is a fixture.

_____ 3. Jean owns a unit in Essex Condominiums. This condo complex is managed by the Essex Condo Association, which is comprised of Jean and owners of the other condo units. A swimming pool is located in the condo common area. Disputes have arisen regarding this pool. In many states:

a. Jean does not have a right to use the swimming pool.

b. Jean does not have any right to participate in the management of the association.

c. Jean cannot sell her unit without the approval of the association.

d. Jean is obligated to pay a share of the taxes and other expenses of the complex, and she can take a tax deduction for property taxes and mortgage interest that she pays.

_____ 4. May contracted to sell a cottage to Lex. May executed a deed to convey title to Lex, three witnesses signed the deed, and it was acknowledged. Per the contract, May delivered the deed to an escrow firm, with instructions to deliver the deed to Lex when he paid the price to the escrow firm. Under these facts:

a. Title passed to Lex when May signed the deed.

b. Title passed to Lex when May delivered the deed to the escrow firm.

c. Title will pass to Lex when he pays makes the price and the escrow firm delivers the deed to him.

d. Title will not pass to Lex until he records the deed.

_____ 5. Sheena borrowed money from Ace Finance and she executed a written mortgage on her home as security for the loan. Ace Finance inadvertently neglected to record the mortgage. Subsequently, the home was damaged by hail, and property taxes for the home came due. The mortgage is silent regarding duties to repair and taxes. Under these facts:

a. The mortgage is enforceable against Sheena even though it was not recorded.

b. As mortgagor, Sheena has a general obligation to Ace Finance to repair the hail damage.

c. As mortgagee, Ace Finance is obligated to pay the property taxes.

d. None of the above is correct.

Case Problems

Answer the following problems, briefly explaining your answers.

1. Dee purchased a meal at a cafe owned by Maxwell. While Dee was eating her meal, the stool she was sitting on collapsed, injuring her. The stool collapsed due to a defective stand. The defect could have been discovered easily by a simple inspection. However, Maxwell did not know that the stool was defective because he never inspected the premises. Dee sued Maxwell for her injuries. Under the common law:
   a. What is Dee's status?
   b. What duty did Maxwell owe to Dee?
   c. Is Maxwell liable to Dee for her injuries?

_____

_____

_____

2. Martha sold her home to Dylan for $50,000. Martha executed and delivered a statutory warranty deed to Dylan, but Dylan failed to record the deed. Later, Martha sold the same property for value to Sandra. Sandra purchased the property in good faith and she was unaware of the prior conveyance to Dylan. Martha executed and delivered a warranty deed to Sandra, and Sandra recorded the deed.
   a. Who has superior title to the home?
   b. Did Martha breach any warranties to Dylan?

_____

_____

_____

3. Helen obtained a loan from Bank to help finance her daughter's education. Helen granted Bank a mortgage on her home as security for the loan, and the mortgage was duly recorded. The loan agreement and mortgage are silent regarding Helen's right to sell the home. Helen subsequently sold the home to Bryson. Bryson agreed to assume the loan. Bank did not expressly approve or disapprove of the sale, nor did it expressly agree to release Helen from liability for the loan.
   a. Was Helen entitled to sell the home even though it was subject to the mortgage?
   b. Is Helen still liable for the loan?
   c. Is Bryson personally obligated to pay the loan?

_____

_____

_____

Internet Exercise

1. Using the Internet, find and identify three different types of mortgages. Compare the terms of these mortgages, and contrast the major pros and cons for each type of mortgage.
2. What must mortgagees under the foregoing mortgages do in order to assure that their mortgages have priority to the collateral?

_____

_____

_____

_____

CPA REVIEW

The following questions were given on CPA examinations. The answers for these questions are the unofficial answers prepared by the American Institute of Certified Public Accountants, Inc. (AICPA). All material is reproduced with permission of the AICPA.

____1. Which of the following warranties is (are) contained in a general warranty deed?
   I. The grantor has the right to convey the property.
   II. The grantee will not be disturbed in possession of the property by the grantor or some third party's lawful claim of ownership.
   a. I only.
   b. II only.
   c. I and II.
   d. Neither I nor II.

____2. Which of the following is a defect in marketable title to real property?
   a. Recorded zoning restrictions.
   b. Recorded easements referred to in the contract of sale.
   c. Unrecorded lawsuit for negligence against the seller.
   d. Unrecorded easement.

____3. For a deed to be effective between a purchaser and seller of real estate, one of the conditions is that the deed must
   a. Be recorded within the permissible statutory time limits.
   b. Be delivered by the seller with an intent to transfer title.
   c. Contain the actual sales price.
   d. Contain the signatures of the seller and purchaser.

____4. On May 1, 1991, Chance bought a piece of property by taking subject to an existing unrecorded mortgage held by Hay Bank. On April 1, 1992, Chance borrowed money from Link Finance and gave Link a mortgage on the property. Link did not know about the Hay mortgage and did not record its mortgage until July 1, 1992. On June 1, 1992, Chance borrowed money from Zone Bank and gave Zone a mortgage on the same property. Zone knew about the Link mortgage but did not know about the Hay mortgage. Zone recorded its mortgage on June 15, 1992. Which mortgage would have priority if these transactions took place in a notice-race jurisdiction?

    a. The Hay mortgage because it was first in time.

    b. The Link mortgage because Zone had notice of the Link mortgage.

    c. The Zone mortgage because it was the first recorded mortgage.

    d. The Zone and Link mortgages share priority because neither had notice of the Hay mortgage.

____5. Wilk bought an apartment building from Dix Corp. There was a mortgage on the building securing Dix's promissory note to Xeon Finance Co. Wilk took title subject to Xeon's mortgage. Wilk did not make the payments on the note due Xeon and the building was sold at a foreclosure sale. If the proceeds of the foreclosure sale are less than the balance due on the note, which of the following statements is correct regarding the deficiency?

    a. Xeon must attempt to collect the deficiency from Wilk before suing Dix.

    b. Dix will not be liable for any of the deficiency because Wilk assumed the note and mortgage.

    c. Xeon may collect the deficiency from either Dix or Wilk.

    d. Dix will be liable for the entire deficiency.

Questions 6 through 8 are based on the following:

On February 1, Frost bought a building from Elgin, Inc. for $250,000. To complete the purchase, Frost borrowed $200,000 from Independent Bank and gave Independent a mortgage for that amount; gave Elgin a second mortgage for $25,000; and paid $25,000 in cash. Independent recorded its mortgage on February 2 and Elgin recorded its mortgage on March 12. The following transaction also took place:

- On March 1, Frost gave Scott a $20,000 mortgage on the building to secure a personal loan Scott had previously made to Frost.

- On March 10, Scott recorded this mortgage.

- On March 15, Scott learned about both prior mortgages.

- On June 1, Frost stopped making payments on all the mortgages.

- On August 1, the mortgages were foreclosed. Frost, on that date, owed Independent, $195,000; Elgin, $24,000; and Scott, $19,000.

A judicial sale of the building resulted in proceeds of $220,000 after expenses were deducted. The above transactions took place in a notice-race jurisdiction.

____6. What amount of the proceeds will Scott receive?

    a. $0

    b. $1,000

    c. $12,500

    d. $19,000

___ 7. Why would Scott receive this amount?
   a. Scott knew of the Elgin mortgage.
   b. Scott's mortgage was recorded before Elgin's and before Scott knew of Elgin's mortgage.
   c. Elgin's mortgage was first in time.
   d. After Independent is fully paid, Elgin and Scott share the remaining proceeds equally.

___ 8. Frost may redeem the property before the judicial sale only if
   a. There is a statutory right of redemption.
   b. It is probable that the sale price will result in a deficiency.
   c. All mortgages are paid in full.
   d. All mortgagees are paid a penalty fee.

CHAPTER 50
ENVIRONMENTAL LAW AND LAND USE CONTROLS

MAKE THE CONNECTION

SUMMARY

Public and private regulations apply to land use. The public regulations consist of environmental laws and zoning. Environmental laws exist at both the state and the federal levels. At the federal level, regulations govern air pollution through limits on emissions and permits for discharges; water pollution with permit requirements, discharge prohibitions, and treatment standards; solid waste disposal with limitations on dumping and liability for cleanup when hazardous materials are found on property; and environmental quality through the use of advance studies on projects and their impact on the environment. Other federal regulations on the environment protect endangered species, set standards for drinking water, and impose liability for oil spills as well as safety standards for oil tankers.

Environmental laws are primarily enforced at the federal level by the Environmental Protection Agency (EPA), but other federal agencies as well as state agencies work together to enforce these laws, using criminal and civil penalties and injunctions to halt pollution. Private citizens also have the right to bring suit under federal statutes to enforce the requirements imposed.

A *nuisance* is a public or private interference with the use and enjoyment of land, and individuals can bring suit to halt nuisances. Courts perform a balancing test in deciding how to handle concerns about nuisances. They seek to balance the use and enjoyment of land with the economic interests of all involved parties.

Restrictive covenants in deeds are valid land use restrictions that pass from owner to owner and are enforceable as long as they do not violate any constitutional rights. *Zoning* is a public means of regulating land use. Zoning laws are part of an overall plan for development adopted by a governmental entity. Some landowners can obtain variances from zoning laws, and some preexisting uses are permitted to continue with the protection of a nonconforming use.

LEARNING OUTCOMES
After studying this chapter, you should be able to

A. STATUTORY ENVIRONMENTAL LAW
LO.1   List and describe the federal statutes that regulate various aspects of the environment

B. ENFORCEMENT OF ENVIRONMENTAL LAWS
LO.2   Explain how environmental laws are enforced and describe the criminal penalties for violation of environmental laws
LO.3   Define *nuisance* and list the remedies available

C. LAND USE CONTROLS
LO.4   Explain the role and application of covenants and zoning laws

CHAPTER OUTLINE

A. STATUTORY ENVIRONMENTAL LAW

1. AIR POLLUTION REGULATION

GENERAL RULES. ▶ The Clean Air Act (CAA), as amended, is intended to prevent harmful air pollution. ▶ Under the CAA, the Environmental Protection Agency (EPA) develops mandatory standards for acceptable levels of air pollution. Each state is then required to develop a plan to control local pollution in order to achieve the required standard. ▶ The United Nations Framework Convention for Climate Change (UNFCCC) had adopted the Kyoto Protocol, which is a plan for reducing six greenhouse gases. The plan requires the United States and other countries to reduce their carbon dioxide levels to 1990 levels. The United States has not yet adopted the Kyoto Protocol as a treaty.

LIMITATIONS. ▶ Areas that do not meet required standards are called "nonattainment areas" and plans to bring these areas into compliance are strictly reviewed. The EPA's "emissions offset policy" limits the construction of new plants in these areas. ▶ Construction of new plants in nonattainment areas is restricted pursuant to an emissions offset policy developed by the EPA.

STUDY HINTS. Several recent U.S. Supreme Court decisions relate to EPA enforcement of federal air quality regulations. In one case, the Court held that the EPA could increase its permit requirements for plant modifications to now require the use of maximum achievable control technology (MACT), not just best available technology (BAT). In another case, the Court confirmed that the Clean Air Act mandates the EPA to act on greenhouse gases and global warming.

LEARNING OUTCOME EXAMPLE. See *Massachusetts v EPA* on textbook p. 1192.

2. WATER POLLUTION REGULATION

GENERAL RULES ▶ The Federal Water Pollution Control Act, as amended, is commonly known as the Clean Water Act (CWA). ▶ The EPA controls water pollution by establishing effluent guidelines that dictate what may be discharged into waters, how much may be discharged, and by whom.

STUDY HINT. A company must have a permit for discharging waters that are used by the company.

LIMITATION The EPA may use a cost-benefit analysis to determine standards for the quality of the water that is released into waterways. Thus, while companies must generally use the best technology available, the EPA may grant variances from those standards because of the cost involved.

3. SOLID WASTE DISPOSAL REGULATION

Federal laws regulating solid waste include:

➢ *Toxic Substances Control Act (TOSCA)*: This Act controls the manufacture, use and disposal of toxic substances.

➢ *Resource Conservation and Recovery Act (RCRA)*: This Act regulates the disposal of potentially harmful substances through a permit system.

> *Comprehensive Environmental Response, Compensation and Liability Act of 1980 (CERCLA)*:

▶ This Act establishes (1) a national list of inactive hazardous waste sites and (2) a Hazardous Waste Fund (Superfund) to help pay for cleaning up such sites. ▶ The EPA is authorized to sue responsible persons to recover the cost for cleanup operations. ▶ Persons who may be liable for the costs of cleanup include (1) owners and operators of plants that caused contamination and (2) transporters who improperly disposed of hazardous waste, as well as others. ▶ CERCLA has inadvertently resulted in hundreds of thousands of undeveloped lands in the U.S. called "brownfields" contributing to urban blight. The Federal Partnership Action Agenda may now enable a firm to buy a brownfield to clean-up and develop without incurring CERCLA liability.

4. ENVIRONMENTAL QUALITY REGULATION

GENERAL RULES. ▶ The National Environmental Policy Act (NEPA) requires that an environmental impact statement (EIS) be prepared for any major federal action (including passage of new laws) that may significantly affect the quality of the human environment. ▶ An EIS analyzes: (1) the impact of a proposed action; and (2) practical and feasible alternatives to such action.
LIMITATION. NEPA only applies to actions by federal agencies.

5. OTHER ENVIRONMENTAL REGULATIONS

> *Noise Control Act*: sets noise standards for low-flying aircraft.

> *Endangered Species Act*: requires the secretary of the interior to identify and protect endangered species.

> *Safe Drinking Water Act*: establishes national standards for drinking water.

> *Oil Pollution Act*: holds firms financially responsible for oil spills near U.S. coasts. Failure to report a spill may subject a violator to penalties of up to 5 years imprisonment and/or $250,000 per individual and $500,000 for corporations. In addition, civil penalties for the failure to clean up an oil spill can cost a firm up to $50 million in penalties.

6. STATE ENVIRONMENTAL REGULATION

> States regulate the environment and many have adopted laws similar to federal laws.

> State laws cannot conflict with federal law or unduly burden interstate commerce.

B. ENFORCEMENT OF ENVIRONMENTAL LAWS

7. PARTIES RESPONSIBLE FOR ENFORCEMENT

▶ The EPA is primarily responsible for enforcing federal environmental laws. ▶ The Council on Environmental Quality establishes a national policy on the environment.

8. CRIMINAL PENALTIES

Most environmental laws provide for fines, and some authorize criminal prosecution.

9. CIVIL REMEDIES

▶ The EPA can request injunctions to stop wrongful activities by companies. ▶ Private individuals can sue companies that are in violation of federal law or not in compliance with statutory procedures. ▶ LEARNING OUTCOME EXAMPLE: See the list of penalties in Figure 50.1

10. PRIVATE REMEDIES: NUISANCE

GENERAL RULES. ▶ A nuisance is conduct that unreasonably interferes with the enjoyment or use of land. ▶ Examples: noise and dust from a mine that unreasonably impairs the ability of persons to live on adjoining property; emissions from a plant that damages nearby buildings. ▶ Persons affected by a nuisance may sue for (1) damages and (2) an injunction to stop the offending conduct. ▶ A nuisance may be classified according to: (1) who is harmed; or (2) the nature of the offending activity. Types of nuisances include:

➢ *Public nuisance*: Nuisance that affects the community or public at large.

➢ *Private nuisance*: Substantial, unreasonable interference with use of individual's property.

➢ *Permanent and continuing nuisances*: ▶ A permanent nuisance is a single act causing permanent harm to a plaintiff. ▶ A continuing nuisance is a series of related acts or continuing activity.

LIMITATIONS. ▶ A minor interference with the enjoyment of land by others is not a nuisance. ▶ Mere inconvenience or annoyance with another's use of property is not a nuisance.
STUDY HINTS. ▶ An activity or business that is conducted in accordance with applicable laws may nonetheless be a nuisance, depending on the effect that the activity or business has on others. ▶ To determine whether an activity is a nuisance, courts balance the social utility of the plaintiff's interest and the severity of the harm to the plaintiff, with the social utility of the defendant's activity. ▶ The fact that a defendant did not intentionally or negligently create a nuisance is not a defense. ▶ Real property law and the law of nuisance continue to change in order to keep in step with new technologies.
LEARNING OUTCOME EXAMPLE. See *Spur Industries v Del Webb* on textbook p.1202.

11. PRIVATE REMEDIES: DUE DILIGENCE

Prospective land buyers can exercise "due diligence," meaning reasonable investigation, by checking out the history and prior uses of the property, and by having appropriate environmental tests conducted.

C. LAND USE CONTROLS

12. RESTRICTIVE COVENANTS IN PRIVATE CONTRACTS

GENERAL RULES. ▶ A real estate developer who subdivides and sells land may undertake private community planning by including restrictive covenants (restrictions and duties regarding the use of land) in deeds. Such covenants are binding on a buyer. Any subsequent owner is also bound by a valid restrictive covenant that: (1) is stated in a recorded deed; or (2) is known to the buyer. ▶ Example: Seller conveyed land to Buyer. Seller duly recorded a deed that prohibited any buildings more than fifty feet in height. This covenant is binding on Buyer and all future owners. ▶ An owner of land in a development that is subject to restrictive covenants may sue any other owner in the development who is violating the development's restrictive covenants.

LIMITATIONS. ► Restrictive covenants are interpreted narrowly to allow the greatest use of land. ► A restrictive covenant that violates a law or public policy is invalid and unenforceable.

STUDY HINT. Restrictive covenants are interpreted using standard rules of contract interpretation, and words are given their ordinary meaning.

13. PUBLIC ZONING

GENERAL RULES. ► Zoning is government-imposed restrictions on the use that may be made of land. ► Example: Cedar City adopted a zoning ordinance that permitted the construction of only single-family houses in a designated portion of the city. ► Zoning is used to plan future community growth and to ensure reasonable, orderly development. ► A governmental body, such as a city, can adopt zoning ordinances to promote public health, welfare, and safety, or to control population density. ► Ordinarily, a person does not have a right to use property in a manner prohibited by a valid zoning ordinance. ► LEARNING OUTCOME EXAMPLE: See *Hold Fast Tattoo, LLC v City of North Chicago* on textbook p. 1206.

LIMITATIONS. ► A zoning ordinance is invalid if it violates a person's constitutional rights. ► In certain cases, a property use that conflicts with a zoning ordinance may be permitted due to:

➢ *Nonconforming use*: ► A nonconforming use is an existing use of property that conflicts with a newly adopted zoning ordinance. ► In general, a nonconforming use has a constitutional right to continue. ► However, if an owner discontinues a nonconforming use, the owner loses the right to this use through abandonment, and the nonconforming use cannot be resumed at a later time.

➢ *Variance*: ► A variance is an exception granted by an administrative agency that permits a use of property that is inconsistent with an existing zoning ordinance. ► An agency may grant a variance if the desired use for the property is harmonious with the character of surrounding areas. ► Variances are not frequently granted because they defeat the purpose of zoning. Variances are not granted if: (1) doing so would be condemned by the courts; (2) a variance is requested to avoid a hardship that the owner created (e.g., an owner bought land for a purpose that was not permitted by an existing zoning ordinance); or (3) a variance is requested solely to produce more income for the owner.

CONCEPT REVIEW AND APPLICATIONS

Matching Exercise

Select the term or phrase that best matches a definition or statement stated below. Each term or phrase is the best match for only one statement or definition. Not all terms and phrases will necessarily be used.

best technology available
brownfields
bubble concept
Clean Air Act
Clean Water Act
Comprehensive Environmental
   Response, Compensation, and
   Liability Act (CERCLA)
Council on Environmental
   Quality (CEQ)
due diligence
effluent guidelines
emissions offset policy

Endangered Species Act (ESA)
environmental impact
   statement (EIS)
injunction
National Environmental Policy
   Act (NEPA)
Noise Control Act
nonattainment areas
nonconforming use
nuisance
Oil Pollution Act
private nuisance
public nuisance

Resource Conservation and
   Recovery Act (RCRA)
Resource Recovery Act
restrictive covenants
Safe Drinking Water Act
spot zoning
Superfund Amendment and
   Reauthorization Act
Superfund sites
Toxic Substances Control Act
   (TOSCA)
variance
zoning

_____ 1. Study that examines the effect that a proposed action may have on the environment and the practical alternatives to such action that may exist.

_____ 2. First significant federal environmental law, adopted in 1969.

_____ 3. Zoning ordinance exception that is granted by an administrative agency and that permits a property use inconsistent with existing zoning laws.

_____ 4. Major hazardous waste law that created the Superfund to clean up inactive hazardous waste sites.

_____ 5. Government restrictions on land use that are used to plan community growth and development.

_____ 6. Privately created land use restrictions that are stated in recorded deeds.

_____ 7. Federal law that authorizes the EPA to establish standards for air-borne pollution.

_____ 8. Property use that is constitutionally protected even though it conflicts with a newly adopted zoning ordinance.

_____ 9. Conduct that unreasonably interferes with another's enjoyment or use of land.

True/False

Write **T** if the statement is true, write **F** if it is false.

_____ 1. In general, a state can adopt a water pollution law that conflicts with a federal clean water statute.

_____ 2. The federal Superfund is designed to aid in cleaning up inactive hazardous waste sites.

_____ 3. TOSCA is a federal act that controls the manufacture, use and disposal of toxic substances.

_____ 4. An EIS must consider all alternatives to a project, whether the alternatives are feasible or not.

_____ 5. Environmental protection laws are primarily adopted and enforced by administrative agencies.

_____ 6. Companies must first obtain a permit before discharging effluents into navigable waterways.

_____ 7. In general, a party may be criminally prosecuted for violating an environmental law even if the party did not intend to violate the law.

_____ 8. An owner of a home in a development that has restrictive covenants can sue another homeowner in the development for violating one of the development's restrictive covenants.

_____ 9. A party may discontinue a nonconforming use for up to five years without abandoning the right to resume the nonconforming use.

_____ 10. A zoning variance may be granted if the intended use is in harmony with surrounding property.

Multiple Choice

_____ 1. The U.S. Army Corps of Engineers (a federal agency) proposes building a large dam. The dam will affect the environment, and it will require abandonment of several towns. In this case:
   a. The U.S. Army Corps of Engineers must prepare an EIS before it builds the dam.
   b. An EIS must consider the impact that the dam may have on residents and businesses in the towns that must be abandoned if the dam is built.
   c. An EIS must consider feasible, practical alternatives to the dam.
   d. All of the above.

_____ 2. Fairmont Company leased 20 acres of land to Diller Refining Corp. Diller operated a battery manufacturing factory where hazardous chemicals are used in the manufacturing process. The chemicals leaked onto the property in violation of CERCLA. Under these facts, who can be held liable under CERCLA:
   a. No one.
   b. Only Fairmont Company.
   c. Only Diller Refining Corp.
   d. Both Fairmont Company and Diller Refining Corp.

_____ 3.   Richard bought an existing home from Kim. The home is located in a planned development that is governed by restrictive covenants. The covenants are publicly recorded and they were noted on all deeds. In violation of a covenant, Richard built a fence around the home. In this case:
a. Richard's neighbor can sue him for violation of the restrictive covenant.
b. Richard is not bound by the covenants because restrictive covenants are unconstitutional.
c. Richard is not bound by the covenants because he did not buy the home directly from the developer who imposed the restrictive covenants.
d. Richard is not bound by the covenants because a person's use of property can only be restricted by zoning laws.

_____ 4.   Azores Co. held a permit to operate a gravel pit within Pine City, and it had operated a gravel pit within the city for five continuous years. Then Pine City adopted a new zoning ordinance which prohibited gravel pit operations within the city limits. Under these facts:
a. Azores must stop its gravel pit operation on the date the zoning ordinance becomes effective.
b. Azores' gravel pit operation is a nonconforming use, and Azores can continue such use.
c. Azores may stop its gravel pit operation without losing the right to renew such use at a later date.
d. b and c.

Case Problem

Answer the following problem, briefly explaining your answer.

Hank owns and operates a factory that employs 100 people. Hank built the factory next to a quiet residential neighborhood. There are no restrictive covenants or zoning ordinances that prohibit or restrict the factory's operations. However, two neighbors have sued him, asserting that the factory is a nuisance because the noise and traffic generated by the factory interferes with their enjoyment of their property.

1. What will a court consider in determining whether the factory is a nuisance?
2. Is it possible for a lawful activity, such as Hank's factory, to be a nuisance?

_____

_____

_____

_____

Internet Exercise

Chemical Corp. manufactures several products using heavy metals and other chemical substances. Recently, a government agent requested access to Chemical's plant and its manufacturing records in order to verify that Chemical was complying with the Toxic Substances Control Act. Also, subpoenas were served on several Chemical officials, requiring them to testify at a forthcoming administrative hearing regarding Chemical's compliance with the Act. Chemical management has asked you to determine the following:

1. Was the agent entitled to conduct the inspection in question? What was the agent required to present?
2. Does the Act authorize the government to subpoena persons to testify about a firm's compliance with the law?

_____

_____

_____

_____

CHAPTER 51
LEASES

MAKE THE CONNECTION

SUMMARY

The agreement between a lessor and a lessee by which the latter holds possession of real property owned by the former is a lease. Statutes in many states prohibit discrimination by an owner who rents property. Statutes in some states require that the lease not be unconscionable. Tenancies are classified according to duration as tenancies for years, from year to year, at will, and at sufferance.

A lease is generally not terminated by the death, insanity, or bankruptcy of either party except for a tenancy at will. Leases are usually terminated by the expiration of the specified term, notice, surrender, forfeiture, or destruction of the property or because of fraud. A tenant has the right to acquire possession at the beginning of the lease and has the right to retain possession until the lease is ended. Evictions may be either actual or constructive. The tenant is under a duty to pay rent as compensation to the landlord.

An assignment of a lease by the tenant is a transfer of the tenant's entire interest in the property to a third person; a sublease is a transfer of less than an entire interest—in either space or time. A lease may prohibit both an assignment and a sublease. If the lease is assigned, the assignee is liable to the landlord for the rent.

Such an assignment, however, does not discharge the tenant from the duty to pay rent. In a sublease, the sublessee is not liable to the original lessor for rent unless that liability has been assumed or is imposed by statute.

The tenant need not make repairs to the premises, absent an agreement to the contrary. A warranty of habitability was not implied at common law, but most states now reject this view and imply in residential leases a warranty that the premises are fit for habitation.

A landlord is usually liable to the tenant only for injuries caused by latent defects or by defects that are not apparent but of which the landlord had knowledge. The landlord is not liable to the tenant for crimes of third persons unless they are reasonably foreseeable.

LEARNING OUTCOMES
After studying this chapter, you should be able to

A. CREATION AND TERMINATION
LO.1 List the ways in which a lease may be terminated

B. RIGHTS AND DUTIES OF PARTIES
LO.2 List and explain the rights and duties of the parties to a lease

C. LIABILITY FOR INJURY ON PREMISES
LO.3 Describe a landlord's liability for a tenant's and a third person's injuries sustained on the premises

D. TRANSFER OF RIGHTS
LO.4 Define *sublease* and *assignment of a lease* and distinguish between them

CHAPTER OUTLINE

A. CREATION AND TERMINATION

1. DEFINITION AND NATURE

▶ A lease is a relationship and agreement whereby one party (a lessee) is permitted to possess real property belonging to another (a lessor or landlord). ▶ Modern law focuses on the contractual nature of the lease relationship. Consequently, contract concepts, such as warranties, often apply to leases.

2. CREATION OF THE LEASE RELATIONSHIP

GENERAL RULES. ▶ A lease is created by an express or implied contract. ▶ Under common law, an oral lease is valid. ▶ In many states today, leases for more than three years must be in writing. In other states, leases for more than one year must be written.
LIMITATIONS. ▶ The federal Fair Housing Act and laws in many states forbid lessors from discriminating on the basis of race, religion, national origin, or color. ▶ Some states prohibit unconscionable terms in leases.

3. CLASSIFICATION OF TENANCIES

➢ *Tenancy for years*: lease is for definite duration (not necessarily a year).

➢ *Tenancy from year to year (periodic tenancy)*: lease is for indefinite duration; rent is paid periodically; proper notice is required to terminate.

➢ *Tenancy at will*: lease is for indefinite duration, and it may be terminated at any time by either party.

➢ *Tenancy by sufferance*: If a tenant holds over without permission, the tenant is a tenant by sufferance until the landlord decides whether to treat the party as a tenant or as a trespasser.

4. TERMINATION OF LEASE

GENERAL RULE. Leases are terminated by: (1) proper notice (either notice required by lease or notice required by statutes if lease is a tenancy from year to year); (2) expiration of lease term in a tenancy for years (notice not required); (3) landlord's acceptance of tenant's surrender of premises; (4) forfeiture of tenant's interest due to tenant's breach (if termination is allowed by lease); (5) destruction of premises; (6) fraud; or (7) tenant being transferred (if termination allowed by lease).
LIMITATION. A lease is generally not terminated by the death, insanity, or bankruptcy of either party unless (1) the lease is a tenancy at will or (2) the lease provides otherwise.

5. NOTICE OF TERMINATION

▶ If a party's intention to terminate is clear, no special words must be used in order to give notice of termination. ▶ Unless statutes require otherwise, an oral notice is sufficient to terminate a lease.

6. RENEWAL OF LEASE

▶ Parties may renew an expired lease. ▶ If a lease requires notice to renew, renewal cannot occur without notice. ▶ A lease may provide that it automatically renews unless a party states otherwise.

B. RIGHTS AND DUTIES OF PARTIES

7. POSSESSION

GENERAL RULES. ▶ A tenant has a right to possess leased premises on the date the lease begins. ▶ A tenant has the right to exclusive possession of leased premises, and may exclude a landlord from the premises unless otherwise agreed. ▶ A tenant can sue a landlord for a wrongful eviction.
▶ Evictions may be: (1) actual; (2) constructive (landlord acts or fails to act to keep premises in habitable condition thereby compelling a tenant to vacate the premises); or (3) partial.
LIMITATION. A lessee cannot remain in leased premises and claim a constructive eviction.
STUDY HINT. Most written leases have a covenant of quiet enjoyment. This clause expressly protects the tenant from interference by the landlord (but not from interference by third parties).

8. USE OF PREMISES

▶ A lease may state permissible uses of property; any different use may create a right to terminate a lease. ▶ If no particular use is specified, any lawful use contemplated by the parties is permitted. ▶ A lease may allow a landlord to make reasonable, binding regulations. ▶ A lease may forbid pets.

9. RENT

GENERAL RULES. ▶ A tenant must pay the agreed rent. ▶ If a tenant assigns a lease, the original tenant and assignee are both liable for rent. ▶ If premises are sublet, the original tenant is liable for rent; a sublessee is not liable to a lessor for rent unless liability is imposed by the sublease or by law. ▶ Rent must be paid (1) at the time stated in a lease or (2) if not stated, at the end of the lease term.
LIMITATION. Government regulations (e.g., rent controls) may limit rent that may be charged.
STUDY HINT. Leases may include escalation clauses that automatically increase rent.

10. REPAIRS AND CONDITION OF PREMISES

GENERAL RULES. ▶ Unless otherwise agreed, a tenant has no duty to make repairs (although a tenant is liable for willful or negligent damage). ▶ Housing laws may require a landlord to maintain premises in a habitable condition. ▶ At common law, a landlord did not warrant the habitability of a residence. But in most states today, a landlord is held to impliedly warrant the habitability of residences. Moreover, if premises are unfit, a tenant may sometimes withhold rent or pay rent into an escrow account, or the rent may be reduced to reflect the actual rental value of the premises. ▶ Landlords must comply with the Americans with Disabilities Act (ADA), which forbids discrimination on the basis of disability in deciding whether to rent to a person and requires landlords to make reasonable modifications to accommodate tenants with disabilities.
STUDY HINT. A landlord cannot enter and inspect premises unless given this right by a lease.
LEARNING OUTCOME EXAMPLE. See *Bender v Green* on textbook p. 1221.

11. IMPROVEMENTS

► Unless otherwise agreed, neither a tenant nor a landlord is required to make improvements.
► If a lease requires either party to make improvements, failure to comply is an actionable breach.

12. TAXES AND ASSESSMENTS

► Unless otherwise agreed, a landlord pays taxes and assessments. ► Tax increases resulting from a tenant's improvements are paid: (1) by the landlord if the improvements remain with the property; or (2) by the tenant if the improvements can be removed by the tenant.

13. TENANT'S DEPOSIT

► A landlord may require a tenant to pay a deposit to protect against the tenant's default. ► Some states treat a deposit as a trust fund, requiring a landlord: (1) to tell the tenant where the money is deposited; and (2) to pay a penalty if the deposit is used prior to a breach of the lease by the tenant.

14. PROTECTION FROM RETALIATION

The URLTA and most state laws prohibit a landlord from evicting a tenant or otherwise retaliating because a tenant (1) exercises a legal right or (2) reports the landlord for violating housing codes.

15. REMEDIES OF LANDLORD

➢ *Landlord's lien*: Lessor has no lien for unpaid rent unless lien is given by a lease or statute.

➢ *Suit for rent*: If a tenant fails to pay rent, a landlord may sue for the rent that is due.

➢ *Recovery of possession*: ► Leases often allow a landlord to recover possession of premises if a tenant defaults. ► At common law and in many states, a landlord has a right of re-entry (right to retake premises without legal proceedings). ► Modern cases do not permit a lessor to lock out a tenant for nonpayment of rent, and legal proceedings are needed to regain possession.

➢ *Mitigation of damages*: A majority of states do not make a landlord mitigate (avoid) damages by seeking a new tenant if a tenant abandons premises. A modern trend requires mitigation.

C. LIABILITY FOR INJURY ON PREMISES

16. LANDLORD'S LIABILITY TO TENANT

► Absent a duty to make repairs, a landlord is not liable for a tenant's injuries caused by defects in premises that are under the tenant's control or that are known to the tenant. ► Landlords are not liable for unforeseeable crimes committed by others. But, when criminal acts of third persons are reasonably foreseeable, the landlord may be held liable for the harm caused a tenant. ► Commercial leases can excuse landlords from liability for tenants' losses; some states restrict this right in connection with residential leases. ► A term in a residential lease that excuses a landlord from liability for damage caused by water, snow, or ice is void. ► Learning outcome example: See *Yu Fang Tan v Arnel Management Co.* on textbook p. 1225.

17. LANDLORD'S LIABILITY TO THIRD PERSONS

► In general, a landlord is not liable to a third party who is injured due to the condition of premises that are under a tenant's control. ► A landlord is liable for injuries caused: (1) by defective premises under the landlord's control; or (2) by a condition the landlord had a contractual duty to correct.

18. TENANT'S LIABILITY TO THIRD PERSONS

Regardless of whether a landlord is obligated to repair, a tenant in possession of property is liable for injuries to licensees and invitees that are caused by the tenant's failure to use due care.

D. TRANSFER OF RIGHTS

19. TENANT'S ASSIGNMENT OF LEASE AND SUBLEASE

► An assignment of a lease is a transfer of a tenant's entire interest to another. An assignee is bound by (and liable under) the original lease. ► A sublease transfers only a portion of a tenant's interest. Unless otherwise agreed, a sublessee is not liable to the lessor.

CONCEPT REVIEW AND APPLICATIONS

<u>Matching Exercise</u>

Select the term or phrase that best matches a definition or statement stated below. Each term or phrase is the best match for only one statement or definition. Not all terms and phrases will necessarily be used

Assignment (of lease)	landlord
constructive eviction	lease
covenant of quiet enjoyment	lessee
escalation clause	lessor
forcible entry and detainer	periodic tenancy

_____ 1. Eviction that results from an act or omission by a landlord that substantially deprives a tenant of the enjoyment and use of leased premises.

_____ 2. Lease term that provides for automatic rent increases under certain conditions.

_____ 3. Party who owns real property and permits occupation of the property by another.

_____ 4. Relationship or agreement by which one party lawfully occupies the property of another.

_____ 5. Promise by landlord not to interfere with a tenant's enjoyment and use of leased premises.

_____ 6. Party who lawfully occupies (leases) real property that is owned by another.

_____ 7. Transfer of a tenant's entire interest in a lease.

True/False

Write **T** if the statement is true, write **F** if it is false.

_____ 1. Most states make a landlord mitigate damages by re-renting premises after a tenant abandons a lease.

_____ 2. One required element of a landlord-tenant relationship is that the landlord has a reversionary interest in the premises, i.e., the premises revert back to the landlord once the lease terminates.

_____ 3. A tenant who holds over without permission may be treated as a trespasser by the landlord.

_____ 4. A tenancy for years is automatically terminated by the bankruptcy of the tenant.

_____ 5. Unless otherwise agreed, a tenant is generally entitled to exclude a landlord from leased premises during the term of a lease.

_____ 6. Modern leases commonly provide that a landlord may terminate a lease if a lessee uses premises in a manner that is different from the use permitted by the lease.

_____ 7. Leases can include escalation clauses, and an escalation clause may be enforceable even if it requires payment of more rent than the tenant anticipated that he or she would have to pay.

_____ 8. Unless otherwise agreed, a tenant generally has a duty to make all repairs to leased premises.

_____ 9. In some states, a tenant may withhold payment of rent if the premises are unfit to live in.

_____ 10. A landlord is entitled to evict a tenant for reporting housing code violations to the government.

Multiple Choice

_____ 1. Isako leased a home for an indefinite time. The lease requires Isako to pay rent on a monthly basis, on the first day of each month. Sixty days' prior written notice is required to terminate the lease. Under these facts, Isako's tenancy is classified as a:
a. Tenancy for years.
b. Tenancy from year to year.
c. Tenancy at will.
d. Tenancy at sufferance.

_____ 2. Sara leased an apartment from Landlord. Subsequently, Landlord intentionally shut off all utilities to Sara's apartment in order to do major remodeling at the apartment complex. Landlord kept the utilities shut off for an indefinite time. As a result of Landlord's conduct, Sara had no practical choice but to move out. Landlord's conduct is best described as being:
a. An actual eviction of Sara.
b. A partial eviction of Sara.
c. A constructive eviction of Sara.
d. Permissible conduct.

_____ 3. Landlord leased a home to Jack for a two-year term. Annual property taxes at that time were $1,000. Shortly after making the lease, Landlord built a garage at the home, and Jack built a movable, aboveground swimming pool at the home. Jack has the right to remove the pool when the lease expires. The annual property taxes increased $300 due to the garage, and $200 due to the pool. The lease is silent regarding taxes. How much of the property taxes must Jack pay?
   a. $0
   b. $200
   c. $500
   d. $1,500

_____ 4. Lee rented a house to Kirk. Kirk failed to pay the rent, and Lee terminated the lease. The lease is silent regarding landlord liens, and the state in question does not have any statutes on point. The state recognizes the common law right of re-entry. In this case:
   a. Lee cannot sue Kirk for the unpaid rent.
   b. Lee can sue Kirk for the unpaid rent.
   c. Lee can re-enter the apartment and evict Kirk without first utilizing legal proceedings.
   d. b and c.

_____ 5. Sam leased a warehouse from Landlord. Landlord is obligated to maintain the warehouse parking lot, and Sam has exclusive control over and responsibility for the warehouse. Landlord is liable for which of the following losses?
   a. Sam's inventory was destroyed when an unknown arsonist burned down the warehouse.
   b. A third party slipped on oil that Sam negligently spilled on the warehouse floor.
   c. A third party fell in a pothole that was negligently allowed to exist in the parking lot.
   d. b and c.

Case Problem

Answer the following problem, briefly explaining your answer.

Jackie leased several offices from Landlord pursuant to a three-year lease. Later, Jackie agreed to lease one of the offices to Kate for one year. The agreement between Jackie and Kate did not state whether it was an assignment or a sublease, and it did not address the parties' responsibility for performance of the original lease. Subsequently, Kate did not pay the rent for the office she leased from Jackie, and Landlord was not paid the rent for this office. Landlord sued Jackie and Kate for the unpaid rent for the office.

1. Is the agreement between Jackie and Kate an assignment or a sublease?
2. Is Jackie liable to Landlord for the unpaid rent?
3. Is Kate liable to Landlord for the unpaid rent?

_____

_____

_____

_____

Internet Exercise

Georgia Petroleum Corp. has decided to expand its domestic oil exploration activities. It has determined that there are some excellent prospects on certain federal lands, and it has requested you to find some preliminary information on leasing federal lands for oil and gas exploration.

1. Using the Internet, locate and identify federal regulations regarding leasing federal lands for oil and gas exploration.
2. Identify some matters that these regulations address.

_____

_____

_____

_____

CPA REVIEW

The following questions were given on CPA examinations. The answers for these questions are the unofficial answers prepared by the American Institute of Certified Public Accountants, Inc. (AICPA). All material is reproduced with permission of the AICPA.

___ 1. Which of the following forms of tenancy will be created if a tenant stays in possession of the leased premises without the landlord's consent, after the tenant's one-year written lease expires?
   a. Tenancy at will.
   b. Tenancy for years.
   c. Tenancy from period to period.
   d. Tenancy at sufferance.

___ 2. A tenant renting an apartment under a three-year written lease that does not contain any specific restrictions may be evicted for
   a. Counterfeiting money in the apartment.
   b. Keeping a dog in the apartment.
   c. Failing to maintain a liability insurance policy on the apartment.
   d. Making structural repairs to the apartment.

___ 3. Delta Corp. leased 60,000 square feet in an office building from Tanner under a written 25-year lease. Which of the following statements is correct?
   a. Tanner's death will terminate the lease and Delta will be able to recover any resulting damages from Tanner's estate.
   b. Tanner's sale of the office building will terminate the lease unless both Delta and the buyer consented to the assumption of the lease by the buyer.
   c. In the absence of a provision in the lease to the contrary, Delta does not need Tanner's consent to assign the lease to another party.
   d. In the absence of a provision in the lease to the contrary, Delta would need Tanner's consent to enter into a sublease with another party.

___ 4. Lusk borrowed $20,000 from Marco Finance. The loan was secured by a mortgage on a four-unit apartment building owned by Lusk. The proceeds of the loan were used by Lusk to purchase a business. The mortgage was duly recorded 60 days after Marco loaned the money to Lusk. Six months after borrowing the money from Marco, Lusk leased one of the apartments to Rudd for $800 per month. Neither Rudd nor Lusk notified Marco of the lease. Subsequently, Lusk defaulted on the note to Marco and Marco has commenced foreclosure proceedings. Under the circumstances,

   a. Marco's mortgage is junior to Rudd's lease because the mortgage was not a purchase money mortgage.

   b. Marco's mortgage is junior to Rudd's lease because Marco failed to record the mortgage for 60 days after the closing.

   c. Rudd's lease is subject to Marco's mortgage because Marco recorded its mortgage prior to the time Rudd's leasehold interest arose.

   d. Rudd's lease is subject to Marco's mortgage because of the failure to notify Marco of the lease.

___ 5. Mack & Watts, CPAs, wishes to relocate its office. Its existing lease is for four years, with one year remaining. Its landlord is not agreeable to canceling the lease. The lease also prohibits a sublease without the landlord's consent but is silent as to anassignment. Mack & Watts has found a financially responsible and respectable prospective subtenant but is convinced that the landlord will not consent to a sublease. Which of the following statements is correct?

   a. A sublease without the landlord's consent would not be a breach of the lease.

   b. An assignment by Mack & Watts would be a breach of the lease.

   c. An assignment by Mack & Watts would not relieve it of liability under the lease.

   d. A sublease with the landlord's consent would relieve Mack & Watts of liability under the lease.

___ 6. Mini, Inc., entered into a five-year lease with Rein Realtors. The lease was signed by both parties and immediately recorded. The leased building was to be used by Mini in connection with its business operations. To make it suitable for that purpose, Mini attached a piece of equipment to the wall of the building.
Which of the following statements is correct regarding Mini's rights and liabilities?

   a. Mini is prohibited from assigning the lease if it is silent in this regard.

   b. Mini has a possessory interest in the building.

   c. Mini is strictly liable for all injuries sustained by any person in the building during the term of the lease.

   d. Mini's rights under the lease are automatically terminated by Rein's sale of the building to a third party.

CHAPTER 52
DECEDENTS' ESTATES AND TRUSTS

MAKE THE CONNECTION

SUMMARY

A *will* is a writing that provides for a disposition of property to take effect upon death. A man who makes a will is called a *testator;* a woman, a *testatrix*. The person to whom property is left by will is a *beneficiary*. A *legacy* is a gift of personal property by will; a gift of real property by will is a *devise*. A testator must have testamentary capacity to make a will and must manifest some intention that the will is to be effective only upon death. The will must be signed by the testator and be witnessed.

A will may be modified by a codicil or revoked either by the act of the testator or by operation of law. *Probate* is the process by which a proper court official accepts a will. Probate may be refused or set aside on grounds that the will is not the free expression of the testator.

A *holographic* will is an unwitnessed will written entirely in the handwriting of the testator. A *self-proved will* may be admitted to probate without the testimony of subscribing witnesses. A *living will* allows a person to make wishes known regarding life-sustaining medical treatment.

If there is a valid will, the last phase of administration of the estate is the distribution of property after the payment of all debts and taxes. *General legacies* are bequests of money, whereas *specific legacies* or *specific devises* are gifts of identified personal or real property. Legacies abate in the following order: residuary, general, and specific. If a beneficiary named in the will has died before the testator and no alternate provision has been made for that beneficiary, antilapse statutes provide that the gift will not lapse. In that event, the children or heirs of the beneficiary may take the legacy in the place of the deceased beneficiary.

If the decedent does not dispose of all property by will or does not have a will, the property will be distributed according to state intestacy statutes. A surviving spouse may generally elect to take the statutory allocation instead of that provided in the will.

The estate of the testator will be administered by the person appointed in the will (the *executor*) or, if there is no will, by a person appointed by the court (an *administrator*). Creditors who have claims against the estate are required to give notice of their claims to the personal representative; otherwise, the claims will be barred.

A *trust* is a legal device by which property is held by one person for the benefit of another. The settlor creates the trust, and the person for whose benefit the trustee holds the property is the beneficiary. Property held in trust is called the *trust corpus, trust fund, trust estate*, or *trust res*.

A trust is usually created by a trust agreement or deed of trust. No particular form or language is required. A trust is not created unless an active duty is placed on the trustee to manage the property in some manner. A trustee's acceptance of duties is presumed.

Legal title to trust property is given to the trustee, and the beneficiary holds equitable title. A beneficiary may transfer an interest in the trust except in the case of a spendthrift trust.

The trustee can exercise only those powers that are given by law or the trust instrument. The trustee must administer the trust and carry out the trust in a proper manner. A trustee is liable for breach of the terms of the trust agreement. A trust comes to an end when its terms so provide or when it becomes impossible to attain the object of the trust.

LEARNING OUTCOMES
After studying this chapter, you should be able to

A. WILLS
LO.1   Define *testamentary capacity* and *testamentary intent*
LO.2   Discuss how a valid will is created
LO.3   Explain how a will may be modified or revoked

B. ADMINISTRATION OF DECEDENTS' ESTATES
LO.4   Describe briefly the probate and contest of a will
LO.5   Describe the ordinary pattern of distribution by intestacy

C. TRUSTS
LO.6   Explain the nature of a trust

CHAPTER OUTLINE

A. WILLS

1. DEFINITIONS

▶ *Will*: writing that determines the distribution of a person's property upon his or her death. ▶ *Testator (testatrix)*: person who makes a will. ▶ *Beneficiary*: person to whom property is left by a will. ▶ *Legacy (bequest)*: gift of personal property under a will. ▶ *Devise*: gift of real property under a will.

2. PARTIES TO WILL

➢ ▶ *Testator*: In general, a person (testator or testatrix) can make a valid will only if he or she: (1) is eighteen years of age or older; and (2) possesses testamentary capacity. ▶ LEARNING OUTCOME EXAMPLE: See *Maimonides School v Coles* on textbook p. 1235.

➢ *Beneficiary*: ▶ There are no special requirements for beneficiaries. ▶ A guardian may need to be appointed to administer property left to a minor unless: (1) a will directs a trustee to hold the property; or (2) property is not significant and it is paid to the minor or to the person maintaining the minor.

3. TESTAMENTARY INTENT

▶ A valid will requires that a testator have testamentary intent (intent that action is effective only on death). This intent is present if a will: (1) transfers property on death; or (2) an executor is named. ▶ LEARNING OUTCOME EXAMPLE: See *Ramsey v Taylor* on textbook p. 1242.

4. FORM

▶ If a will does not comply with statutory requirements, the will is invalid and a decedent's property is distributed as if no will existed. ▶ Ordinarily, a will must be written and must be signed by the testator, but it need not be dated. ▶ Most states require attestation (witnessing testator's execution of will) by two witnesses; some states require publication (testator verifies that a will is his will). ▶ A self-proved will eliminates some formalities of proof, and they are valid if executed in accordance with a statute.

5. MODIFICATION OF WILL

▶ A separate writing (codicil) may amend a will. A codicil must satisfy the requirements for making a will. ▶ A will cannot be changed by crossing out terms and writing in new ones (an "interineation").

6. REVOCATION OF WILL

▶ A testator revokes a will (or a part of it) if the testator, with intent to revoke, tears or destroys the will or crosses out a part of it. ▶ In some cases, a will is revoked in whole or in part if a testator marries, divorces with a property settlement, or has a child after making the will. ▶ LEARNING OUTCOME EXAMPLE: See *In re Estate of Speers* on textbook p. 1238.

7. ELECTION TO TAKE AGAINST THE WILL

A surviving spouse may ignore a will and elect to take the share he or she would have received had there been no will. Misconduct (e.g., desertion, nonsupport) may bar a right to make this election.

8. DISINHERITANCE

With two exceptions, anyone may be disinherited or excluded from sharing in an estate.

9. SPECIAL TYPES OF WILLS

▶ *Holographic will*: unwitnessed will, entirely in a testator's handwriting. ▶ *Living will*: document allowing a person to state whether life-sustaining medical treatments should be used during an incurable, irreversible medical condition.

B. ADMINISTRATION OF DECEDENTS' ESTATES

10. DEFINITIONS

▶ *Executor (executrix)*: party named in will to administer estate. ▶ *Administrator (administratrix)*: party appointed by court to administer estate. ▶ *Personal representative*: executor or administrator.

11. PROBATE OF WILL

▶ Probate is a determination by an appropriate court or official that a will meets the statutory requirements for being a decedent's will. ▶ In general, a will has no legal effect until it is probated.

12. WILL CONTEST

▶ Probate of a will may be refused or set aside if: (1) a testator lacked testamentary capacity; (2) a will was made as a result of undue influence, duress, fraud, or mistake; or (3) the will is a forgery. ▶ LEARNING OUTCOME EXAMPLE: See Ethics & Law discussion of Brooke Astor on textbook p. 1243

13. WHEN ADMINISTRATION IS NOT NECESSARY

Administration is not required if: (1) the decedent owned no property at death; or (2) all property was owned jointly with another person who takes the property by right of survivorship.

14. APPOINTMENT OF PERSONAL REPRESENTATIVE

▶ To represent an estate, personal representatives must first be appointed by a court or appropriate official. Appointment is made by letters testamentary for executors, and letters of administration for administrators. ▶ An administrator is appointed only if an executor is not named or appointed.

15. PROOF OF CLAIMS AGAINST THE ESTATE

Most states provide that a creditor's claim is barred unless filed with an estate within a certain time.

16. CONSTRUCTION OF A WILL

A will is interpreted according to its ordinary meaning, and courts try to carry out all terms of a will.

17. TESTATE DISTRIBUTION OF AN ESTATE

➢ *Definitions*: When a testator dies leaving a valid will, property is generally distributed in the manner directed. Conveyances include: ▶ *General legacy*: bequest of sum of money. ▶ *Specific legacy (devise)*: bequest of specific item of personal (real) property. ▶ *Residuary bequest*: bequest of all property of a decedent that remains after general and specific legacies are satisfied.

➢ *Abatement and ademption*: ▶ If assets are insufficient to satisfy all bequests, bequests abate (are reduced) in the following order (bequests in the same class abate proportionately): (1) residuary; (2) general; (3) specific. ▶ If property given by a specific legacy is disposed of before a testator dies, the legacy is adeemed (canceled); the beneficiary gets nothing.

➢ *Antilapse statute*: Unless a testator directs otherwise, a beneficiary's children or heirs take a gift that was bequeathed to the beneficiary if the beneficiary dies before the testator dies.

18. INTESTATE DISTRIBUTION OF AN ESTATE

▶ State laws commonly provide that property of a decedent who dies without a valid will (intestate) is distributed in the following manner after debts are paid: (1) surviving spouse takes all unless there are surviving children, in which case the spouse takes a one-third or one-half share and children take the remainder; (2) lineal (blood) descendants (children; grandchildren; etc.) take all if there is no spouse; (3) parents of a decedent take all if there is no spouse or lineal descendants; (4) collateral heirs (brothers; sisters; their descendants) take all if none of the foregoing persons survive. ► Property not distributed under these rules passes to the state by escheat. ► Distributions to two or more heirs who have equal rights to property are distributed per capita (equal shares). ► Persons entitled to distribution are determined as of date of death. If a distributee dies *after* a testator, the person's share goes to his/her estate. ► Statutes often provide that an heir who murders the decedent cannot inherit by intestacy. ► LEARNING OUTCOME EXAMPLE: See Figure 52.2 on textbook p. 1246; see *In re Estate of Morris P. Van Der Veen* on textbook p. 1247.

C. TRUSTS

19. DEFINITIONS

> *Trust*: legal device by which one person (trustee) holds property (trust corpus or res) in trust for another (beneficiary or cestui que trust).

> *Settlor*: person who creates a trust.

> *Inter vivos (living) trust*: trust that takes effect during a settlor's lifetime.

> *Testamentary trust*: trust created by a will, and the trust is effective upon the death of the settlor.

> *Trust agreement*: writing creating a trust.

20. CREATION OF TRUSTS

GENERAL RULE. Typical requirements to create a trust: (1) any lawful purpose; (2) in writing if the trust relates to land, is created by will, or takes effect on death; (3) designation of a beneficiary, the trust purpose, and the trust property; and (4) the trust intends to and does give the trustee an active duty to manage the trust.
LIMITATION. A trust does not require consideration, and capacity of a beneficiary is irrelevant.

21. NATURE OF BENEFICIARY'S INTEREST

► A trustee holds legal title to trust property; a beneficiary holds equitable title. ► With the exception of a spendthrift trust, a beneficiary's creditors may reach trust property to satisfy claims.

22. POWERS OF TRUSTEE

A trustee can exercise only powers that are conferred by the trust or by law or that are judicially implied.

23. DUTIES OF TRUSTEE

► A trustee must (1) try to protect a trust from losses; (2) manage it to yield income; (3) administer it according to the terms of the trust; and (4) make periodic accountings of trust affairs. ► A trustee cannot delegate personal duties. ► A trustee must use reasonable skill and care, and a trustee is liable for losses caused by the trustee's failure to do so. ► A trustee cannot personally profit from being trustee, except for allowable compensation.

24. REMEDIES FOR BREACH OF TRUST

A trustee's breach of a trust may result in: (1) a money judgment and/or injunction against a trustee; (2) criminal prosecution of a trustee; (3) removal of a trustee; (4) suit against a surety on a trustee's bond; (5) suit against third parties who participated in the breach of trust; and (6) recovery of trust property from a transferee unless the party paid value and took property without notice of a breach.

25. TERMINATION OF TRUST

A trust may terminate: (1) according to its terms; (2) if a trust's stated object is impossible to obtain;
(3) if a settlor properly revokes the trust; (4) if all interests merge in the same person; or
(5) if all beneficiaries request termination and there is no express purpose that requires continuation.

CONCEPT REVIEW AND APPLICATIONS

Matching Exercise

Select the term or phrase that best matches a definition or statement stated below. Each term or phrase is the best match for only one statement or definition. Not all terms and phrases will necessarily be used.

abate	holographic will	specific legacies
acknowledgment	income	spendthrift trust
adeemed	interlineation	stirpes
administrator	intestate	testamentary capacity
administratrix	intestate succession	testamentary intent
affidavits	legacy	testamentary trust
antilapse statutes	legal title	testate
attestation clause	legatee	testate distribution
beneficiary	letters of administration	testator
bequest	letters testamentary	testatrix
cestui que trust	lineals	trust
claims	living trust	trust agreement
decedent	living wills	trust corpus
devise	per capita	trustee
devisee	per stirpes	trustor
disinherited	personal representatives	Uniform Probate Code (UPC)
distribution per stirpes	probate	Uniform Simultaneous Death
donor	revoke	Act
equitable title	right of escheat	
executor	self-proved wills	
general legacies	settler	

_____ 1. Laws that state beneficiaries' children take a legacy if the beneficiaries die before a testator and the testator did not state an alternative disposition in the event that the beneficiaries died first.

_____ 2. Document(s) by which a person indicates whether life-sustaining medical treatment should be used in the event the person suffers an irreversible, incurable illness.

_____ 3. Blood descendants of a person (i.e., children, grandchildren, and their descendants).

_____ 4. Act by which a court or official accepts a will and determines that it meets the requirements for being the will of a testator or testatrix.

_____ 5. Loss of all or a portion of something, such as loss or reduction of a bequest if an estate has insufficient property to fulfill the bequest.

_____ 6. Male person who makes a will.

_____ 7. Executors or administrators who administer a decedent's estate.

_____ 8. Cancellation of a specific legacy if the bequeathed property is disposed of before the testator dies.

_____ 9. Bequest of real property made in a will.

_____ 10. Distribution of property of a person who dies without a valid will.

True/False

Write **T** if the statement is true, write **F** if it is false.

_____ 1. Property of a person who dies without a will is distributed according to intestate succession.

_____ 2. Attestation is the act of having a will witnessed by a required number of witnesses, whereas publication is the act of a testator or testatrix acknowledging that a will is his or her will.

_____ 3. Most states do not require attestation of a will.

_____ 4. In general, a will is not required to be in writing to be enforceable.

_____ 5. A will is revoked if a testator burns or destroys the will with the intent to revoke the will.

_____ 6. In some states, a will is automatically revoked, in whole or in part, if the testator marries, or has additional children (by birth or adoption) after making the will.

_____ 7. Probate of a will is typically an optional procedure; a will is generally effective without probate.

____ 8. In general, a spouse can elect to forego what is bequeathed by a will, thereby electing to take what the spouse would have received had there been no will.

____ 9. Under the intestate succession laws in most states, a surviving spouse takes all of a decedent's estate even if there are surviving children.

____10. If a distributee is entitled to receive property from a decedent's estate by intestate distribution and the distributee dies *after* the decedent, the distributee's right to receive a share of the decedent's estate is forfeited; the right to receive the property does not pass to the distributee's estate.

Multiple Choice

____ 1. Sabrina made a will leaving everything to her daughter. Two years later, Sabrina decided she wanted to change her will in order to leave some jewelry to her best friends. Under these facts:
a. Sabrina can change her will only by first destroying the will and then making a new one.
b. Sabrina can change her will by crossing out undesired bequests and writing in new bequests.
c. Sabrina can change her will by signing a codicil that is properly attested and published.
d. Sabrina cannot change her will; a person is legally prohibited from changing an executed will.

____ 2. Harvey drank heavily for years. Due to his drinking, Harvey suffered permanent mental impairment, and he could not recall to whom he was related or what he owned. Nonetheless, Harvey executed a properly attested and published will. The will left everything to Bob, a recent acquaintance; nothing was left to Harvey's son whom Harvey had forgotten about. In this case:
a. The will is invalid because a testator cannot disinherit a child.
b. The will is invalid because Harvey did not have testamentary capacity.
c. The will is valid.
d. a and b.

____ 3. Sue died, leaving her property to her nieces and nephews. She bequeathed a stamp collection to Rich; $5,000 each to Sue and John; and her residuary estate to Marty. But after payment of debts and expenses, the remaining assets of Sue's estate were only the stamps and $5,000. Under these facts:
a. The stamp collection will be sold for cash. Then, Rich, Sue, John, and Marty will each receive one-fourth of the assets of the estate.
b. Rich will receive the stamp collection, and Marty will receive the $5,000.
c. Rich will receive the stamp collection, and Sue and John will each receive $2,500.
d. Rich will receive the stamp collection; Sue, John, and Marty will equally divide the $5,000.

____ 4. Ladd died without a will. He is survived by his wife, two children, and his mother and father. Under typical intestate succession rules, how will Ladd's property be distributed?
a. Ladd's wife will receive all of the property.
b. Ladd's wife will receive one-third or one-half of the property, and his children will each receive equal portions of the remaining property.
c. Ladd's children will equally share all of the property.
d. Ladd's wife, children, and parents will each receive one-fifth of his property.

_____ 5. Hector is trustee of a trust. The trust beneficiaries are Hector's nephews. The trust has $50,000 cash. In most states, what would Hector be permitted to do as trustee?
   a. Hector can invest the cash in U.S. Treasury bonds and corporate stocks.
   b. Hector can make an interest-free loan of the trust's cash to his business.
   c. Hector can delegate all of his duties under the trust to his wife.
   d. a and c.

Case Problem

Answer the following problem, briefly explaining your answer.

Settlor validly created a charitable trust. The trust designated Mona as trustee, and the trust agreement stated that Settlor reserved the right to terminate the trust at any time. Mona never formally accepted her appointment as trustee, but she did serve as trustee for one year. During this time, she irresponsibly invested the trust assets in speculative investments, causing significant losses of the trust corpus.
1. Is Mona the trustee even though she never formally accepted her appointment?
2. Can Settlor revoke the trust?
3. Did Mona breach any duty?
4. What remedies may be available in light of Mona's conduct?

_____

_____

_____

_____

Internet Exercise

1. Using the Internet, locate and identify a uniform state act that deals with the allocation of trust funds between principal and interest.
2. Under this act, when does the right of the income beneficiary begin and end?

_____

_____

_____

_____

CHAPTER 1
THE NATURE AND SOURCES OF LAW

Matching Exercise	
1. Procedural law	6. Precedent
2. Administrative regulations	7. Case law
3. Substantive law	8. *Stare decisis*
4. Duty	9. Right of privacy
5. Statutory law	

True/False			Multiple Choice		
1. F	4. F	7. F	1. c	3. d	5. b
2. T	5. T	8. T	2. d	4. d	6. c
3. T	6. F				

Case Problem

1. Principles of equity will determine whether Janis can obtain the remedy sought. Specific performance is an equitable remedy.

2. Among other things, Janis needs to prove that her legal remedy, i.e., money damages, is not adequate. She can establish this by proving that the painting is unique.

Internet Exercise

1. The U.S. Constitution can be found at http://www.law.cornell.edu/constitution/constitution.table.html.

2. The right to privacy is not expressly stated by any of the Amendments to the U.S. Constitution.

3. The right to privacy is said to emanate from a penumbra of the Amendments, including the First, Fifth, and Fourteenth Amendments.

CHAPTER 2
THE COURT SYSTEM AND DISPUTE RESOLUTION

Matching Exercise	
1. Answer	6. Complaint
2. Original jurisdiction	7. Appellate jurisdiction
3. Process	8. Garnishment
4. Counterclaim	9. Limited jurisdiction
5. Plaintiff	10. Reverse

True/False			Multiple Choice	
1. T	5. T	9. T	1. c	6. a
2. F	6. F	10. T	2. a	7. b
3. T	7. T		3. b	8. b
4. T	8. T		4. b	9. c
			5. d	10. d

Case Problem

1. Roger cannot file his lawsuit in any court he chooses. Each court has jurisdiction, i.e., the legal power, to decide only certain types of cases. A party must file a lawsuit in a court that has jurisdiction in that case.

2. A court may have original or appellate jurisdiction, or both. A court with original jurisdiction has the power to decide a case for the first time. Moreover, courts with original jurisdiction may have general jurisdiction to try all cases, or they may have limited jurisdiction to decide only a particular type of action. In this case, the State District Court has the original jurisdiction to hear and decide this case for the first time.

3. Roger will file his lawsuit in a civil court because civil courts have the power to decide lawsuits involving private wrongs.

Internet Exercise

The National Center for State Courts' web site can be found at http://www.ncsconline.org/.

1. At time of publication, the most current data available on this website was for 2006. For this year, the number of civil cases reported as being filed in state courts of general jurisdiction was 5,296,706. See http://www.ncsconline.org/D_Research/csp/2007_files/State%20Court%20Caseload%20Tables%20-%20Trial%20Courts.pdf, then select Table 1.

2. At time of publication, all states maintained some sort of state court web site. Using the http://www.ncsconline.org/, click on Information & Resources, then click on Browse by state, and then select the state of interest.

3. Some may argue that providing information on how to file a lawsuit, which is provided by some state and local court web sites, only serves to increase the number of frivolous lawsuits filed each year. Others may counter, however, that such information makes the legal system more accessible to everyone, one of the fundamental goals of our legal system.

CHAPTER 3
BUSINESS ETHICS, SOCIAL FORCES, AND THE LAW

Matching Exercise

1. Ethics
2. Integrity
3. Stakeholders
4. Conflict of interest
5. Positive law

6. Business ethics
7. Civil disobedience
8. Situational ethics
9. Natural law

True/False		Multiple Choice

1. T	6. T	1. c
2. T	7. F	2. b
3. T	8. F	3. a
4. F	9. T	4. d
5. T	10. T	5. c

CPA Review

1. c	3. a	5. b	7. b
2. b	4. a	6. c	8. a

Case Problem

1. (a) Adoption of the law that restricts an employer's right to fire an employee at will furthers these social forces: (i) protection of the person (protecting employment relationship); (ii) protection from exploitation, fraud, and oppression (protects against unfair discharges of employees); and (iii) flexibility (law changes to reflect evolving social values). (b) Not adopting this law furthers these social forces: (i) freedom of personal action (employers may discharge employees when they wish); and (ii) stability (law remains same).

2. (a) Adoption of law permitting limited gambling furthers these social forces: (i) protection of the state (increased tax revenues); (ii) freedom of personal action (people are free to gamble); (iii) freedom of use of property (people may use their money for gambling if they choose) and (iv) flexibility (law changes to meet society's evolving values). (b) Not adopting this law furthers these social forces: (i) protection of public health, safety, and morals (increased crime is avoided); (ii) protection from exploitation, fraud, and oppression (exploitation of people with gambling problems is avoided); and (iii) stability (law stays same).

Internet Exercise

Many companies have enacted a code of ethics, and each code is unique. On their face, many corporate codes are adopted to provide guidance for employees and to instill certain basic values. Many codes seek to encourage utilitarian values of good and/or recognition of principles of natural law.

CHAPTER 4
THE CONSTITUTION AS THE FOUNDATION OF THE
LEGAL ENVIRONMENT

Matching Exercise

1. Bedrock view
2. Constitution
3. Living-document view
4. Privileges and immunities clause
5. Commerce clause

6. Due process clause
7. Federal system
8. Police power
9. Preemption
10. *Ex post facto* laws

True/False

1. F	5. T	9. F
2. F	6. F	10. T
3. T	7. T	
4. T	8. T	

Multiple Choice

1. c	5. c	9. d
2. a	6. a	10. c
3. d	7. c	
4. a	8. c	

Case Problem

1. Yes, Amax is engaging in interstate commerce. Interstate commerce is interpreted broadly. As interpreted, it includes any commerce going between states, and it also includes most business and labor activities.

2. Yes, the Constitution authorizes the federal government to regulate interstate commerce. Consequently, the federal government may regulate the business that Amax Corp. conducts in interstate commerce.

3. In general, Colorado may constitutionally regulate the business that Amax Corp. conducts within Colorado. Subject to certain limitations, states have the police power to regulate activities within their boundaries in order to protect the health, safety, welfare, and morals of people.

4. In regulating Amax's business activities, Colorado cannot: (a) regulate matters that have been preempted by the federal government; (b) adopt laws that conflict with federal laws; (c) discriminate against Amax Corp.'s interstate activities; or (d) impose an unreasonable burden on Amax Corp.'s interstate activities.

Internet Exercise

1. A recent Supreme Court case addressing the scope of "interstate commerce" is *United States v. Lopez*.

2. Applying the reasoning of this case, Congress has the authority to forbid the 3Dchemical because it involves business activities and, therefore, interstate commerce. Congress does not have the authority to make it a crime to say profane words in public. Under the reasoning in *Lopez*, this activity is completely unrelated to business and, therefore, it is not interstate commerce.

CHAPTER 5
GOVERNMENT REGULATION OF COMPETITION AND PRICES

Matching Exercise

1. Tying
2. Clayton Act
3. Market power
4. Robinson-Patman Act
5. Sherman Antitrust Act

6. Divestiture order
7. Treble damages
8. Takeover laws
9. Price discrimination

True/False

1. T
2. F
3. F
4. T
5. T

6. T
7. T
8. T
9. F
10. F

Multiple Choice

1. d
2. d
3. a
4. c

5. d
6. b
7. c
8. a

9. d
10. a

Case Problem

1. Plan A would be illegal price discrimination in violation of federal antitrust law. The Clayton Act generally prohibits a party (typically a manufacturer) from charging different customers different prices for the same goods.

2. Plan B would be legal under federal antitrust law. A company can charge a different (lower) price in one market for a product if this lower price is necessary to meet the competition in that market, i.e., competitors sell competitive products in that market for a lower price.

Internet Exercise

1. The U.S. Supreme Court's decision in *FTC v. Superior Court Trial Lawyers Assn.* is located at http://supreme.justia.com/us/493/411/case.html.

2. Applying the reasoning in the foregoing case, the physicians are engaging in an illegal boycott that was intended to promote a conspiracy to fix prices for their services. Furthermore, horizontal price-fixing is per se illegal whether or not the participants in the boycott possess market power.

CHAPTER 6
ADMINISTRATIVE AGENCIES

Matching Exercise

1. Cease-and-desist order	6. Exhaustion of administrative remedies
2. Freedom of Information Act	7. Administrative law
3. Administrative agency	8. Administrative Procedure Act
4. Consent decree	9. Open meeting law
5. *Federal Register*	

True/False

1. F	5. F	9. F
2. F	6. T	10. F
3. F	7. F	
4. T	8. F	

Multiple Choice

1. c	4. a	7. a	10. d
2. a	5. d	8. b	
3. d	6. d	9. b	

Case Problem

1. (a) The EPA can adopt a new policy regarding storm water runoff. (b) Under the modern view, an administrative agency possesses all of the powers necessary to carry out its duties. Under this view, the EPA would be able to adopt the storm water regulation.

2. (a) Due process requires notice and a hearing before the FDA imposes a fine. (b) Preliminary steps include: parties may file written, informal complaints with the FDA regarding Medco; the FDA may determine whether it has jurisdiction; and the FDA may determine whether it should take further action. (c) Medco has no right to a jury trial. (d) Informal procedures may include a consent decree or voluntary settlement agreement.

3. (a) No, Sue cannot appeal the decision to a court until she exhausts the internal agency appeals procedure. (b) Yes, Sue can appeal a final decision to court. However, Beauty Co. could not do so because it is not directly affected by the decision. (c) To the extent authorized by law, the State Health Agency can enforce its decision by issuing or seeking a cease and desist order against Sue, and by assessing or seeking a fine against Sue.

Internet Exercise

1. 15 U.S.C. § 1391(c) defines "motor vehicle" for purposes of NHTSA regulations. The NHTSA has, in turn, interpreted a motor vehicle to exclude low-speed vehicles, such as golf carts, that cannot exceed 25 m.p.h. *See* 49 CFR 571 @ http://www4.law.cornell.edu/cfr/49p571.htm - /start.

2. On-the-Move Co.'s present carts would not be subject to NHTSA regulations.

3. Because of their increased speed, On-the-Move Co.'s new carts may be subject to NHTSA regulations.

CHAPTER 7
THE LEGAL ENVIRONMENT OF INTERNATIONAL TRADE

Matching Exercise

1. Act-of-state doctrine	6. Blocking laws
2. Most-favored-nation clause	7. Export sale
3. Effects doctrine	8. Dumping
4. Secrecy laws	9. Intellectual property rights
5. Sovereign immunity doctrine	10. Sovereign compliance doctrine

True/False

1. T	6. F
2. T	7. T
3. T	8. T
4. T	9. F
5. F	10. F

Multiple Choice

1. d	6. d
2. b	7. c
3. c	8. b
4. d	9. d
5. a	10. c

Case Problem

1. The Export Administration Act will primarily regulate BYTE Corp.'s export operations.

2. BYTE Corp. needs to check the Commerce Control List (CCL) to see if the computer parts are listed. If they are not listed, no export license is needed. If they are listed, they will have an Export Control Classification Number, which shows the reason for control of the export. BYTE should then check the Commerce Country Chart to see if a license is needed to send the computer parts and technology to the firm in Mongolia.

3. Criminal and civil sanctions could be imposed if BYTE falsifies information on a license application.

Internet Exercise

1. The North American Free Trade Agreement (NAFTA) applies to Thread-Bare's proposed international operations in Mexico. This agreement regulates trade between the United States, Mexico, and Canada. A copy of NAFTA may be found at http://www-tech.mit.edu/Bulletins/nafta.html.

2. Pursuant to NAFTA, Mexico agreed that companies from other member countries, such as Thread-Bare, would not be required to employ only Mexican workers. Foreign companies also have the right to import necessary materials.

CHAPTER 8
CRIMES

Matching Exercise

1. Misdemeanors
2. White-collar crime
3. Uttering
4. Foreign Corrupt Practices Act
5. Economic Espionage

6. Search warrant
7. Conspiracy
8. Embezzlement
9. Racketeer Influenced and Corrupt Organizations Act (RICO)Act
10. Felonies

True/False

1. T
2. T
3. F
4. F
5. F

6. T
7. T.
8. F
9. T
10. T

Multiple Choice

1. d
2. d
3. c
4. d
5. a

6. c
7. d
8. d
9. d
10. c

Case Problem

1. Drake committed numerous white collar crimes including: (a) *use of mails to defraud* as a result of his transmission of fraudulent information in interstate commerce; (b) *racketeering* in violation of Federal Racketeering Influenced Corrupt Organizations Act (RICO) as a result of his repeated fraudulent and criminal activities; (c) *bribery* due to his payments to government officials in order to wrongfully obtain their approval of these land sales; and (d) *swindle* as a result of his obtaining money by fraud from Mrs. Hinton and other unsuspecting buyers.

2. Drake may be subject to the following criminal penalties: criminal fines; order of restitution to return money paid by the land purchasers; forfeiture of property that was used to commit these crimes or property that was obtained as a result of these crimes; and imprisonment.

3. Under federal RICO laws, Mrs. Hinton may be able to sue for treble (triple) damages.

Internet Exercise

1. The Economic Espionage Act of 1996 is 18 U.S.C. 1831 and may be found via http://www.tscm.com/USC18_90.html.

2. Yes, Leo violated the act by unlawfully stealing the trade secrets with the intent to aid a foreign agent. Leo may be fined for up to $500,000 and/or imprisoned for up to 15 years.

3. Yes, White Corp. violated the Act and may be fined for up to $5 million.

CHAPTER 9
TORTS

Matching Exercise	
1. Contract interference	6. Slander of title
2. Slander	7. Absolute privilege
3. False imprisonment	8. Product disparagement
4. Malpractice	9. Tort
5. Libel	10. Negligence

True/False				Multiple Choice			
1.	T	6.	T	1.	d	6.	d
2.	T	7.	F	2.	c	7.	a
3.	F	8.	T	3.	b	8.	c
4.	F	9.	T	4.	d	9.	d
5.	F	10.	F	5.	c		

Case Problems

1. (a) Lily owed Paul a duty to drive in the manner that a reasonable person would drive under similar circumstances. Thus, Lily had a duty to drive 30 m.p.h. (b) Yes, Lily was negligent because she breached her duty to Paul by driving too fast, and her excessive speed caused injuries to Paul. The fact that others were driving as fast as she was driving is not a defense. (c) Under common law contributory negligence, Paul could recover nothing because his negligence was a partial cause of his damages. (d) Under comparative negligence, Paul may recover $4,000, which represents that percent of his damages that were caused by Lily's negligence.

2. (a) Maxco's sale of the kangaroo meat constitutes the tort of fraud because Maxco intentionally misrepresented a material fact thereby misleading the buyer. (b) The intentional misstatements regarding the quality of the food sold by Juan's Cafe is the tort of disparagement of goods. (c) Maxco's conduct that caused Queen's Cafes to breach its contract with a competitor is the tort of malicious interference with contract. Competition does not entitle Maxco to maliciously induce a breach of contract.

Internet Exercise

1. "Veggie libel laws" are state statutes that, to a varying degree, enable food producers to sue critics of their products for product disparagement. One website providing some information dealing with "veggie libel laws" may be found at http://en.wikipedia.org/wiki/Food_libel_laws.

2. A major argument in favor of veggie laws is that they protect producers and various industries from malicious, untrue statements that may wrongfully injure sales of their products. On the other hand, detractors of such laws maintain that they constitute an unconstitutional limitation on individuals' freedom of speech.

CHAPTER 10
INTELLECTUAL PROPERTY RIGHTS AND THE INTERNET

Matching Exercise

1. Trade secret
2. Prior art
3. Distinctiveness
4. Mask work
5. Trade dress

6. Semiconductor chip
7. Service mark
8. Copyright
9. Secondary meaning
10. Trademark

True/False

1. T
2. T
3. T
4. F
5. T

6. T
7. F
8. T
9. T
10. T

Multiple Choice

1. d
2. b
3. c
4. d

5. c
6. d
7. c

8. c
9. c
10. b

Case Problem

1. Baxco can register the mark "Xeri-fun" for its candy product. A person is entitled to register a fanciful or arbitrary mark that distinguishes a product or service from the products or services of competitors. Baxco can also register the mark "Appalachian Whiskey." One can register a geographical mark if it has acquired a secondary meaning. Baxco cannot register the mark "soft-serve ice cream" because it is merely a generic mark.

2. If a party intentionally infringes on its registered mark, Baxco can obtain an injunction to prevent the party's wrongful use of the mark, and it can also recover its lost profits and other actual damages. The court also has the discretion to triple the damages awarded because the infringement was intentional. In exceptional cases the court may also award Baxco its attorney fees.

Internet Exercise

1. Yes, Beth is entitled to copyright her story because it is an original work.

2. Beth must file an application form "PTO Form 1478" with the U.S. Patent and Trademark Office. Together with this form, she must also submit a drawing page of the mark and three specimens of the mark in use, and pay the appropriate fee.

CHAPTER 11
CYBERLAW

Matching Exercise
1. E-sign
2. Defamation
3. Identity theft
4. Warrant
5. Fair use
6. Invasion of privacy
7. Cyberlaw
8. Appropriation

True/False		Multiple Choice	
1. T	6. T	1. d	6. c
2. F	7. T	2. b	7. b
3. T	8. F	3. c	
4. F	9. T	4. d	
5. F	10. F	5. d	
	11. F		

Case Problem

Cara has committed fraud (misrepresentation) and she also has violated federal securities law.

Internet Exercise

1. The electronic system for receiving and processing digital applications and digital deposits of copyrighted works for electronic registration via the Internet is known as the Copyright Office Electronic Registration, Recordation, and Deposit System (CORDS).

2. http://www.loc.gov/copyright/cords/

CHAPTER 12
NATURE AND CLASSES OF CONTRACTS: CONTRACTING ON THE INTERNET

Matching Exercise

1. Bilateral contract
2. Implied contract
3. Voidable contract
4. Quasi contract
5. Offeror

6. Void agreement
7. Express contract
8. Valid agreement
9. Unilateral contract
10. Privity of contract

True/False

1. T
2. T
3. F
4. T
5. T

6. T
7. F
8. T
9. F
10. T

Multiple Choice

1. a
2. d
3. b
4. b

5. c
6. a
7. a

8. b
9. c
10. c

Case Problem

1. Dan is required by quasi contract to pay for the value derived from the engine overhaul. Quasi contract is a contract implied in law that requires a person to pay for a benefit if payment is necessary to avoid an unjust enrichment. It would be unjust not to make Dan pay since he could have avoided the mistake by Ty's if he had told them not to work on the engine when he overheard the mechanic.

2. Under quasi contract, Dan must pay $500, which is the reasonable value of the engine overhaul. Dan is not obligated to pay for any lost profits or other damages that Ty's may have suffered. Note that

Internet Exercise

1. The federal Electronic Signatures in Global and National Commerce Act (E-Sign) can be located at http://frwebgate.access.gpo.gov/cgi-bin/getdoc.cgi?dbname=106_cong_bills&docid=f:s761enr.txt.pdf.

2. Section 101 of E-Sign generally validates the use of electronic signatures and contracts in interstate and foreign commerce, both by consumers and businesses. Section 101 (c), however, generally requires that consumers be given described disclosures and that they consent to their electronic communication if any other statute or rule of law requires that written disclosure of information be given consumers under the circumstances.

CHAPTER 13
FORMATION OF CONTRACTS: OFFER AND ACCEPTAN.

Matching Exercise

1. Firm offer
2. Counteroffer
3. Requirements contract
4. Acceptance
5. Output contract
6. Divisible contract
7. Offer

True/False			Multiple Choice	
1. T	6. F		1. b	6. c
2. T	7. F		2. a	7. b
3. F	8. T		3. d	
4. T	9. T		4. b	
5. T	10. T		5. b	

CPA Review

1. b	3. d	5. c	7. b
2. c	4. a	6. d	

Case Problem

1. (a) Seller's advertisement was not an offer. In general, advertisements to sell do not manifest the necessary contractual intent to be an offer. (b) Yes, Bart objectively (outwardly) manifested the necessary intent to be bound by his offer. Bart's subjective or secret intentions are not controlling. (c) Seller's acceptance formed a legally enforceable contract.

2. (a) Missy must communicate an acceptance to Fawn in order to accept. Silence is not a valid acceptance. (b) The modern rule is that an offeree can communicate an acceptance in any reasonable manner. In this case, it appears reasonable for Missy to use the same method of communication that Fawn used. (c) If not accepted by Missy, the offer will lapse (expire) a reasonable time after it was made. (d) If Missy mails her acceptance, the acceptance will be effective when it is properly posted and deposited in the mail.

3. (a) Henry's invitation for bids was only an invitation to others to make offers; it was not an offer that can form a contract. Felix's bid was an offer to buy, and Henry's acceptance formed a contract. (b) No, Henry did not have to accept Rene's bid. An auctioneer is not required to accept a bid unless the auction is conducted "without reserve." Thus, Henry was entitled to withdraw the chair from bidding and to refuse to sell it to Rene.

Internet Exercise

Typically, general advertisements for goods or services are merely invitations to others to make an offer. A few ads, however, may be sufficiently detailed and manifest a sufficient intent to be construed as offers. The amount of detail and objective intent are determinative. Evaluate your advertisement accordingly.

Matching Exercise

1. Contractual capacity
2. Status quo ante
3. Confidential relationship
4. Necessaries
5. Economic
6. Physical duress
7. Duress
8. Reform (contract)
9. Fraud
10. Undue influence

True/False

1. F	6. F		
2. T	7. T		
3. F	8. F		
4. T	9. T		
5. T	10. T		

Multiple Choice

1. c	5. b
2. c	6. c
3. d	7. d
4. c	

CPA Review

1. d	3. b	5. b	7. c
2. b	4. b	6. b	

Case Problem

1. (a) No, Nancy did not ratify the contract. A minor cannot ratify a contract until the minor attains majority. (b) Yes, Nancy can avoid this contract because she was a minor at the time of contracting. Upon disaffirmance, Nancy must return the dog. The seller must repay all money paid by Nancy, even though the dog is ill. (c) No, Nancy could not avoid the contract one year after she turned 18. This would be an unreasonable time to wait.

2. (a) Traditionally, *caveat emptor* was the rule and a party did not have a duty to voluntarily disclose information to the other party. Thus, Lon would not have a duty to volunteer information regarding the foundation. (b) If Lon plastered over the damaged foundation in order to hide the damage, this conduct would be fraud and it would render the contract voidable. (c) Under modern rules, Lon must disclose the asbestos because it is an important, latent defect that buyers would not be able to discover upon a reasonable inspection.

3. (a) Seller committed fraud. Seller intentionally misrepresented a material fact, with the intent that Buyer rely on the misrepresentation, and Buyer was induced into contracting. (b) The contract is voidable at Buyer's option.

Internet Exercise

1. Innumerable companies have order forms posted on the Internet. These forms, when completed by a buyer, constitute an offer. Most of these forms fail to mention the buyer's capacity.

2. It is wise to include a representation to the effect that the buyer is an adult. This representation, if false, (a misrepresentation of age) may help a merchant to recover his or her actual losses if a minor signs the form and later disaffirms the contract.

CHAPTER 15
CONSIDERATION

Matching Exercise

1. Cancellation provision
2. Past consideration
3. Consideration
4. Promissory estoppel
5. Forbearance
6. Composition of creditors
7. Illusory promise

True/False				Multiple Choice		
1.	T	6.	T	1.	c	6. d
2.	T	7.	F	2.	d	7. b
3.	F	8.	T	3.	d	
4.	F	9.	F	4.	c	
5.	F	10.	F	5.	a	

CPA Review

1. a		3. d		5. a		7. d	
2. a		4. a		6. a		8. b	

Case Problems

1. (a) No, the agreement with Randy is not legally binding because Randy's services are past consideration. Randy's services are not valid consideration because when the services were rendered, they were not done as the price demanded for the bonus. (b) No, the agreement with Fred is not legally binding because Fred did not give consideration. Fred's promise not to breach his contract is a promise to perform a preexisting duty. (c) No, Aries cannot refuse to perform the contract with Hill for the reason that Hill's consideration was inadequate. Courts will not examine the adequacy of the considerations exchanged.

2. Yes, Ratco's promise is enforceable under the doctrine of promissory estoppel even though Lad did not give consideration for the promise to hire him. Ratco should have expected Lad to rely on its promise, Lad did rely on the promise, and injustice can be avoided only by enforcing Ratco's promise to hire Lad.

Internet Exercise

1. UCC §§ 2-205 & 2-209 govern this case. *See* UCC @ http://www.law.cornell.edu/ucc/2/

2. Tom's offer was not a firm offer because it was not written. Thus, Tom was entitled to revoke. *See* § 2-205.

3. The parties' agreement to modify the contract is enforceable. Consideration is not required. *See* § 2-209.

CHAPTER 16
LEGALITY AND PUBLIC POLICY

Matching Exercise		
1. Lottery		7.
2. Public policy		
3. Contract of adhesion		
4. Good faith		
5. *In pari delicto*		
6. Usury		

True/False	
1. F	6. T
2. F	7. T
3. T	8. T
4. T	9. F
5. F	10. F

Multiple Choice	
1. a	3. b
2. b	4 a

CPA Review			
1. d	3. d	5. d	7. a
2. b	4. a	6. a	

Case Problem

1. The required license is a protective license. The license is required in order to assure the competency of general contractors to engage in this profession and to protect the public from improperly performed work. This purpose is indicated by the experience and examination requirements.

2. The agreement is void. An agreement that requires violation of a protective licensing statute is generally void.

3. No, Mara cannot enforce the agreement, and she cannot recover the agreed price. These remedies are not available because the contract is void.

Internet Exercise

1. Pursuant to 18 U.S.C. 201 (b)(c), Kim's acceptance of the $5,000 "thank you" that was given to her is a federal crime. See http://www4.law.cornell.edu/uscode/18/201.html. This conduct renders the contract illegal and void. While Kim's awarding of the government contract to Farris Inc., which is owned by her best friend, does not appear to violate 18 U.S.C. 201, it nonetheless clearly involves a conflict of interest. Depending on other facts, this conflict of interest may jeopardize the enforceability of this contract.

2. Kim should have refused the $5,000 and excused herself from consideration of the contract with Farris Inc.

CHAPTER 17
WRITING, ELECTRONIC FORMS, AND INTERPRETATION OF CONTRACTS

Matching Exercise

1. Statute of frauds	4. Ambiguous term
2. Parol evidence rule	5. Incorporation by reference
3. Suretyship	6. Personal representative

True/False

1. F	6. T
2. T	7. F
3. T	8. F
4. T	9. T
5. T	10. T

Multiple Choice

1. a	5. d
2. d	6. d
3. b	7. d
4. a	8. c

CPA Review

1. a	3. c	5. c
2. b	4. d	6. b

Case Problem

1. Yes, Sid can use parol evidence to explain the meaning of "serious defects." Parol evidence can be used to explain ambiguous contract terms.

2. No, Sid cannot use parol evidence to prove that the parties had previously agreed to a payment date that contradicts a clear term of the contract. Parol evidence cannot be used to contradict or change terms of a final written contract.

3. Yes, Sid may prove the subsequent price modification. The parol evidence rule does not apply to subsequent contract modifications.

Internet Exercise

1. In *Zaitsev v. Salomon Brothers, Inc.*, 60 F.3d 1001 (2nd Cir. 1995), the U.S. Court of Appeals correctly concluded that the employment contract was required to be evidenced by a sufficient writing because it could not be performed within one year. It was also correct in finding that the writing in question was insufficient. The writing did not state that Mr. Zaitsev was to receive a guaranteed annual bonus of $400,000 or five years employment, terms that are material.

2. As a matter of business strategy, Mr. Zaitsev should have made certain that all of the alleged terms of his employment agreement were evidenced by a sufficient writing.

CHAPTER 18
THIRD PERSONS AND CONTRACTS

Matching Exercise

1. Assignee
2. Third-party beneficiary
3. Assignment
4. Delegation of duties
5. Intended beneficiary

6. Obligor
7. Duty
8. Obligee
9. Assignor

True/False

1. T
2. F
3. T
4. T
5. F

6. T
7. F
8. T
9. T
10. F

Multiple Choice

1. d
2. b
3. d

4. a
5. c

CPA Review

1. a
2. d

3. b
4. a

5. d
6. c

7. a

Case Problem

1. Yes, Erecto was legally entitled to delegate the excavation work to Gopher Inc. without first obtaining Owner's consent. In general, a party can delegate a duty to perform standardized, nonpersonal services that do not involve a special skill.

2. Yes, Erecto is liable to Owner for the improperly performed work. A delegating party remains responsible for the proper performance of delegated work.

Internet Exercise

There are many types of insurance offered over the Internet. In this case, three forms of insurance, among others, that the partnership should acquire and the appropriate third-party beneficiary (if any) under each type of insurance is as follows:

1. Partnership should purchase life insurance on each partner: third-party beneficiary is the other partner.

2. Partnership should purchase automobile insurance on the company vehicle: no third-party beneficiary.

3. Partnership should purchase renter's insurance to insure partnership property located at the leased building: no third-party beneficiary.

CHAPTER 19
DISCHARGE OF CONTRACTS

Matching Exercise

1. Statute of limitations
2. Condition
3. Accord and satisfaction
4. Substantial performance
5. Condition precedent

6. Tender
7. Recission
8. Waiver
9. Substitution

True/False

1. F
2. F
3. T
4. T
5. T

6. F
7. T
8. T
9. T
10. T

Multiple Choice

1. a
2. b
3. c

4. b
5. a
6. a

7. d
8. d
9. b

10. b

CPA Review

1. c
2. d

3. d
4. a

5. a
6. b

7. a
8. d

Case Problem

1. According to some modern courts, a contract may be discharged by supervening (commercial) impracticability if an unforeseen event makes it unreasonably expensive or burdensome for a party to perform.

2. According to some modern courts, a contract may be discharged by economic frustration if an unforeseen event destroys the purpose or value of the contract.

3. No, Roger's contract to buy the mining company is not discharged by either of these doctrines because the fall in the price of silver was foreseeable. The doctrines of supervening impracticability and economic frustration apply only to unforeseeable events. In addition, the contract is not discharged under these doctrines because Roger assumed the risk that the price of silver would fall and thereby hurt the profitability of the company.

Internet Exercise

1. The termination clause in the contract between Janice and the U.S. Department of Wildlife gave the federal agency the unilateral right to terminate the contract for the convenience of the government.

2. The federal regulations at 49 CFR 48 et. seq. set out a procedure whereby Janice and the agency may enter into a settlement agreement regarding the amount of compensation, if any, that she is entitled to receive.

Matching Exercise

1. Direct damages	6. Penalty
2. Punitive damages	7. Consequential damages
3. Injunction	8. Waiver
4. Liquidated damages	9. Compensatory damages
5. Exculpatory clause	10. Specific performance

True/False

1.	T	6.	F
2.	F	7.	T
3.	F	8.	T
4.	T	9.	F
5.	T	10.	T

Multiple Choice

1.	c	4.	b
2.	b	5.	d
3.	c		

CPA Review

1.	a	3.	b	5.	b
2.	c	4.	d	6.	a

Case Problem

1.   The liquidated damage amount is valid because: (a) it was difficult to foresee the precise damage that might be caused if Mica Co. failed to complete the building on time; and (b) the liquidated amount was a reasonable estimate of the probable damages.

2.   Pack Rat Storage can recover $2,000 liquidated damages. A party who is entitled to damages recovers the amount of liquidated damages even if the actual loss is larger or smaller than the liquidated amount.

Internet Exercise

1.   *BMW of North America, Inc. v. Gore* may be found via http://www.law.cornell.edu/supct/search/display.html?terms=damages&url=/supct/html/94-896.ZD1.html.

2.   In this case, punitive damages were awarded because of BMW's fraudulent conduct, not for breach of contract.

3.   The U.S. Supreme Court stated that whether a punitive damage award is constitutional or not is determined by examining (a) the degree of reprehensibility of the defendant's conduct, (b) the ratio between the compensatory damages awarded and the amount of the punitive damages, and (c) the difference between the punitive damages and the civil or criminal sanctions that the government could impose due to the defendant's conduct.

CHAPTER 21
PERSONAL PROPERTY
AND BAILMENTS

Matching Exercise

1. Gift causa mortis	6. Tenancy in common
2. Escheat	7. Personal property
3. Community property	8. Joint tenancy
4. Inter vivos gift	9. Lost property
5. Real property	

True/False

1. F	6. F
2. T	7. F
3. T	8. T
4. F	9. F
5. T	10. F

Multiple Choice

1. b	4. a
2. c	5. c
3. d	6. a

CPA Review

1. d	2. d

Case Problem

Jethro's estate is entitled to the car. At the time that Jethro thought that he was dying from brain cancer, he attempted to make a gift causa mortis of the vehicle to Sally Mae, his girlfriend. However, one required element for this type of gift is that the donor die as anticipated. In this case, Jethro recovered fully and did not die of brain cancer, as feared. His subsequent, later death from some other cause does not suffice.

Internet Exercise

There are numerous firms that advertise services that may create a bailment. These firms include storage companies, moving companies, and automobile rental companies. The foregoing three types of services would create mutual-benefit bailments since both parties to such agreements would be benefited. Under the modern rule of *bailment law*, each bailor would owe a duty of reasonable care.

CHAPTER 22
LEGAL ASPECTS OF SUPPLY CHAIN MANAGEMENT

Matching Exercise

1. Field warehousing	6. Special bailments
2. Airbill	7. Factor
3. Guest	8. Negotiable bill of lading
4. Public warehouse	9. Nonnegotiable (straight) bill of lading
5. Common carrier	10. Contract carrier

True/False

1. F	6. F
2. T	7. T
3. T	8. T
4. F	9. T
5. T	10. F

Multiple Choice

1. b	6. c
2. b	7. d
3. c	8. d
4. a	9. b
5. a	

CPA Review

1. a	2. b	3. c	4. a

Case Problem

1. A hotelkeeper has a lien on the baggage of a guest to secure payment of room charges. Thus, the Essex Motel has a lien on Sam's baggage. The Essex may sell Sam's baggage at a public sale if this is necessary to obtain payment for Sam's room charges.

2. A lien is lost if a hotelkeeper returns baggage to a guest. Consequently, the Essex lost its lien on Joe's baggage when it unconditionally returned the baggage to Joe.

3. Yes, the Essex must return Bob's baggage. A hotelkeeper must return baggage once room charges are paid.

Internet Exercise

1. The federal regulation that governs limitations of liability for baggage by interstate common carriers is 49 CFR 374.41, which is located at http://ecfr.gpoaccess.gov/cgi/t/text/text-idx?c=ecfr&sid=7312334cd7b54ee3ed4228230c67d3e9&rgn=div8&view=text&node=49:5.1.1.2.17.4.1.1&idno=49.

2. Pursuant to the foregoing regulation, Lawrence properly limited his liability to $250.

CHAPTER 23
NATURE AND FORM OF SALES

Matching Exercise

1. Bill of sale
2. Existing goods
3. Future goods
4. Gift
5. Contracts for the International Sale of Goods (CISG)
6. Firm offer
7. Consumer lease
8. Lease
9. Goods
10. Finance lease

True/False		Multiple Choice	
1. F	6. F	1. a	6. c
2. F	7. F	2. b	7. d
3. F	8. F	3. c	8. d
4. T	9. T	4. b	9. b
5. T	10. T	5. d	10. d

CPA Review

1. a	3. d	5. c	7. a
2. d	4. d	6. c	

Case Problem

1. Tonko's acceptance formed a contract. Under Article 2, a definite unconditional acceptance may form a contract even if it proposes an additional term.

2. The additional term did not become part of the contract. If either party is not a merchant, then an additional term is not part of the contract unless the offeror agrees to it.

Internet Exercise

1. The CISG can be found at http://fletcher.tufts.edu/multi/texts/BH775.txt.

2. The CISG governs the contract with Dover Co. The CISG does not govern the contract with Felipe because it does not apply to contracts for goods that are intended for personal use. The CISG also does not apply to the contract with Kiev Inc. because the CISG does not apply if a party is from a country that has not adopted this convention.

3. Yes, the contract is enforceable. The CISG does not require that a contract be evidenced by a writing in order to be enforceable.

CHAPTER 24
TITLE AND RISK OF LOSS

Matching Exercise

1.	Sale on approval	6.	Future goods
2.	Consignor	7.	Voidable title
3.	Fungible goods	8.	Consignment
4.	Warehouse receipt	9.	Bill of lading
5.	Sale or return	10.	Consignee

True/False

1.	T	6.	T
2.	F	7.	F
3.	F	8.	T
4.	F	9.	F
5.	T	10.	T

Multiple Choice

1. d
2. c
3. d
4. b

CPA Review

1.	d	5.	a
2.	c	6.	d
3.	d	7.	b
4.	a		

Case Problem

1. Buyer received Owner's title to the lawn mower. If an owner entrusts a good to a merchant who regularly buys and sells goods of that kind, then the merchant has the power to transfer the owner's title to a buyer in the ordinary course of business.

2. Buyer did not receive Owner's title to the car. The car was not entrusted to a merchant who regularly bought and sold cars. Thus, Buyer only received Wet N' Wild's title to the car, which was no title at all.

Internet Exercise

1. The federal regulation that governs limitations of liability for baggage by interstate common carriers is 49 CFR 374.401, which is located at http://www.access.gpo.gov/nara/cfr/waisidx_03/49cfr374_03.html.

2. Pursuant to the foregoing regulation, Lawrence properly limited his liability to $250.

CHAPTER 25
PRODUCT LIABILITY: WARRANTIES AND TORTS

Matching Exercise

1. Implied warranty
2. Implied warranty of merchantability
3. Express warranty
4. Strict tort liability
5. Full warranty
6. Warranty of title
7. Privity of contract
8. Warranty against encumbrances
9. Warranty of fitness for a particular purpose
10. Limited Warranty

True/False		Multiple Choice	
1. T	6. F	1. d	6. b
2. F	7. T	2. b	7. a
3. T	8. F	3. b	
4. F	9. F	4. a	
5. T	10. T	5. c	

CPA Review

1. d   2. d   3. a   4. c   5. a   6. d   7. c

Case Problem

1. (a) Gary and his wife can sue Crest for breach of warranty. In most states, a buyer and a member of the buyer's family can sue for injuries suffered due to a breach of warranty. (b) Yes, Gary and his wife can both sue for strict tort liability. Under the modern trend, any person who is harmed by a defective, unreasonably dangerous product can sue. (c) Yes, Aqua and Crest both have strict tort liability for the harm. The seller and the manufacturer of a defective product may both be liable. (d) Gary and his wife can sue for their personal injuries and lost personal property, and Gary can sue for the loss of the boat.

2. (a) In general, Vision can disclaim all implied warranties. Disclaimers made in accordance with Article 2 are not unconscionable. (b) No, Vision cannot disclaim the warranty of merchantability by including an inconspicuous disclaimer in its contracts. To exclude this warranty, a disclaimer must be conspicuous and mention "merchantability." (c) A disclaimer stating that goods are sold "AS IS" excludes warranties of merchantability and fitness for a particular purpose.

Internet Exercise

1. Many products are offered for sale on the Internet, either with or without an express warranty or extended warranty (which typically takes the place of a seller's express warranty that is part of the sales contract).

2. Whether it is a sound strategy to pay more in order to obtain additional warranty protection depends on the manufacturer, the reliability of the product, and the price for this extra protection.

CHAPTER 26
OBLIGATIONS AND PERFORMANCE

Matching Exercise

1. Anticipatory repudiation   6. Good faith

2. Repudiation   7. Commercial impracticability

3. Acceptance   8. Right to cure

4. Seasonable

5. Commercial units

True/False

1.	T	6.	T
2.	T	7.	T
3.	F	8.	F
4.	F	9.	F
5.	T	10.	T

Multiple Choice

1.	a	3.	c
2.	b	4.	d

CPA Review

1.	b	3.	c	5.	c	7.	b
2.	d	4.	a	6.	d		

Case Problem

Grace can revoke her acceptance of the piano. She accepted the piano when she kept it despite its nonconformity. However, she kept it only because of Mistro's assurance that it would cure the nonconformity. When Mistro failed to cure, Grace is entitled to revoke her acceptance because the use of the wrong wood in making the piano is a substantial impairment.

Internet Exercise

The answers to Art's questions may be resolved by reference to UCC Article 2, which may be found at http://www.law.cornell.edu/ucc/2/. You should have determined the following:

a. Art must pay at the time he takes delivery of the sofa. See UCC § 2-511.

b. Art may offer to pay by check if this is a normal method of payment. But, Seller can demand cash if Art is given a reasonable extension of time within which to obtain the cash. See UCC § 2-511.

CHAPTER 27
REMEDIES FOR BREACH OF SALES CONTRACTS

Matching Exercise

1. Incidental damages
2. Liquidated damages
3. Statute of limitations
4. Secured transaction
5. Consequential damages
6. Breach

True/False

1.	F	6.	T
2.	F	7.	F
3.	F	8.	F
4.	T	9.	T
5.	T	10.	T

Multiple Choice

1.	c	3.	d
2.	d	4.	a

CPA Review

1.	b	3.	a	5.	a	7.	d
2.	d	4.	b	6.	b		

Case Problem

1. Yes, Alicia must give Seller notice of the breach within a reasonable time after learning of the defective transmission.

2. If Alicia fails to give notice of the breach, she cannot sue Seller for the breach.

3. If Seller refuses to cure the nonconformity, Alicia can recover $2,200 damages. For breach of warranty, a buyer can recover damages equal to the value that goods would have had if they were as warranted ($11,000), minus their actual value ($9,000), plus incidental damages ($200).

4. No, Alicia cannot cancel the contract. A buyer cannot cancel if the buyer accepts and keeps the goods.

Internet Exercise

When shopping for goods over the Internet or in person, it is important for a buyer to analyze the proposed contract for terms that may limit the buyer's remedies. These limitations, such as "Buyer's only remedy in the event that Seller breaches this contract is to request Seller to repair the product or replace it, at Seller's discretion." This limitation, which is generally enforceable, poses the risk that a buyer may wind up with a problem vehicle that the Seller is not obligated to take back or replace.

CHAPTER 28
KINDS OF INSTRUMENTS, PARTIES, AND NEGOTIABILITY

Matching Exercise

1. Negotiable draft		6. Drawee	
2. Check		7. Accommodation party	
3. Money order		8. Order paper	
4. Acceptor		9. Drawer	
5. Negotiable promissory note		10. Bearer paper	

True/False

1. T	5. F	9. F
2. F	6. T	10. F
3. F	7. T	
4. T	8. F	

Multiple Choice

1. b	2. d	3. c	4. d	5. c

CPA Review

1. d	3. d	5. a	7. c
2. a	4. b	6. a	

Case Problem

1. Rex is the maker of the promissory note, and Sam West is the payee.

2. The promissory note is negotiable. It is written and signed by Rex, the maker. The note states an unconditional promise to pay a sum certain in money ($1,000, plus annual interest of 10 percent), at a definite time (June 1, 2009), and it is payable to the order of Sam.

3. The note is order paper because it is originally drawn "to the order" of a named person, Sam West.

4. The note would be negotiable even if it requires Rex to pay a variable rate of interest.

Internet Exercise

1. There are numerous companies that advertise the sale of blank checks for individuals and consumers, as well as for businesses.

2. The checks must provide for all terms of negotiability that are required to create a negotiable instrument.

3. While most firms that sell blank checks go to great pains to provide secure channels for a person to transmit information, there is an inevitable risk that such information may be intercepted, enabling someone to create and cash bogus checks that are drawn on another's account. James' company, as drawer, would not liable for such forged checks. Nevertheless, significant inconvenience would undoubtedly result. Thus, James should make certain that the best method of confidential communication is used when he places his order.

CHAPTER 29
TRANSFERS OF NEGOTIABLE INSTRUMENTS AND WARRANTIES OF PARTIES

Matching Exercise

1. Special indorsement
2. Qualified indorsement
3. Imposter rule
4. Negotiation
5. Blank indorsement

6. Restrictive indorsement
7. Holder
8. Indorsee
9. Indorsement
10. Holder in due course

True/False

1. T	6. T
2. F	7. F
3. T	8. T
4. F	9. F
5. F	10. F

Multiple Choice

1. d 2. b 3. c 4. a 5. c

CPA Review

1. d	3. d	5. d	7. b
2. b	4. c	6. c	

Case Problem

1. Leslie's indorsement was an unqualified indorsement because it did not purport to eliminate her secondary liability to pay the check.

2. Leslie negotiated the check to Bella. At the time it was transferred by Leslie, the check was order paper. Thus, her indorsement and delivery of the check was a negotiation.

3. Bella negotiated the check to Henry. At the time it was transferred by Bella, the check was bearer paper. Thus, her delivery of the check was an effective negotiation.

4. Yes, Henry negotiated the check to his bank. His indorsement, although restrictive in nature, did not affect his negotiation of the check.

Internet Exercise

1. Check cashing has become big business, and many companies advertise this service in various cities.

2. Two risks that this type of company faces are forged drawers' signatures and altered amounts.

3. One strategy that this type of company can use to minimize or avoid the foregoing risks is to call the drawer and confirm that the check is authorized and the amount is correct.

CHAPTER 30
LIABILITY OF THE PARTIES UNDER NEGOTIABLE INSTRUMENTS

Matching Exercise

1. Assignee
2. Alteration
3. Universal defenses
4. Fraud in the inducement
5. Holder in due course

6. Limited defenses
7. Holder through a holder in due course
8. Value
9. Secondary parties
10. Presentment

True/False

1. F
2. T
3. T
4. T
5. F

6. F
7. F
8. T
9. T
10. T

Multiple Choice

1. c
2. d

3. a
4. b

CPA Review

1. c
2. a

3. d
4. c

5. b
6. a

Case Problem

1. Yes, Carl is a holder in due course (HDC). Carl is a holder, he paid value for the note, he acted in good faith, and he did not have notice of Preston's fraud at the time the note was negotiated to him.

2. Yes, Ned is a favored holder. Ned is not a HDC because he took the note with notice of Manley's defense. But, Ned is a holder through a holder in due course because he is a holder (he took a negotiable instrument by negotiation) and he took the note after it was held by a HDC (Carl).

3. Manley's defense is fraud in the inducement, a limited defense.

4. No, Manley cannot assert his defense of fraud against Ned because Ned has all the rights of a HDC, and limited defenses cannot be asserted against a HDC. Therefore, Manley must pay the note to Ned.

Internet Exercise

1. 16 CFR 433.2 governs consumer credit transactions in relation to preservation of consumers' claims and defenses. This regulation may be found via http://www.gpoaccess.gov/cfr/retrieve.html.

2. The FTC regulation applies in this case since it is a consumer credit transaction. Mindy, therefore, does not have to pay the note to Harry because she can assert her defense against him.

3. The FTC regulation would not apply if Mindy had paid with a personal check. Therefore, Mindy would have had to pay the amount of the check to Harry since he is a HDC.

CHAPTER 31
CHECKS AND FUNDS TRANSFERS

Matching Exercise

1. Stop payment order
2. Stale check
3. Funds transfer
4. Cashier's check
5. Originator
6. Certified check
7. Electronic Fund Transfers Act (EFTA)
8. Payment order
9. Beneficiary's bank
10. Beneficiary

True/False		Multiple Choice
1. T	6. F	1. d
2. F	7. T	2. a
3. F	8. F	3. c
4. T	9. T	4. c
5. F	10. T	5. d

CPA Review

1. c	3. d	5. d
2. d	4. d	6. c

Case Problem

1. (a) Jeff has a duty to use reasonable care in promptly examining his bank statement (and canceled checks if they are returned) to discover any alterations and to notify Last Bank of any alteration. (b) Yes, Jeff gave timely notice. He acted with reasonable promptness; he gave notice within one year after he received his statement, as required by law. (c) Last Bank can charge Jeff's account for only $100; it must recredit the account for $900.

2. (a) Electronic Fund Transfers Act (EFTA) governs this case because it is a consumer electronic fund transfer. (b) A consumer's liability is: a maximum of $50 if notice is given to the issuer within two days after the consumer learns of a loss or theft; a maximum of $500 if notice is not given within this two-day period. A consumer bears a loss caused by a failure to report an unauthorized transfer within sixty days after receiving a statement of the account. (c) Greg is liable for $50 since he reported the theft of his card within two days.

Internet Exercise

1. Acme can transfer the funds using an electronic funds transfer. UCC Article 4A governs this case since it involves a funds transfer that utilizes a Federal Reserve bank.

2. There are numerous financial institutions that advertise their services in facilitating funds transfers.

3. Acme is both the originator and beneficiary, and Last Florida Savings and Loan is the beneficiary's bank.

CHAPTER 32
NATURE OF THE DEBTOR-CREDITOR RELATIONSHIP

Matching Exercise	
1. Creditor	6. Guaranty of payment
2. Surety	7. Standby letter
3. Letter of credit	8. Principal debtor
4. Contribution	
5. Guaranty of collection	

True/False	
1. T	6. T
2. T	7. T
3. T	8. F
4. F	9. T
5. F	10. F

Multiple Choice	
1. d	3. b
2. c	4. c

CPA Review			
1. a	3. c	5. a	7. b
2. c	4. d	6. b	8. c

Case Problem

1. No, Last Bank does not have to first try to collect from the corporation, because the cosureties have primary liability for the debt.

2. Yes, Last Bank can collect the full amount from Janet. Each surety is liable to a creditor for the full amount of the debt.

3. Yes, if Janet pays the entire loan, she has a right of contribution against both David and Tom because, unless otherwise agreed, cosureties are liable for an equal share of a debt. Consequently, Janet would be entitled to recover $25,000 from both David and Tom.

4. Yes, if Janet pays the loan, she would have a right of subrogation, and she has the right to recover from the corporation any amounts that she pays.

Internet Exercise

1. There are a number of financial institutions that advertise their assistance in connection with international letter-of-credit transactions.

2. One major risk for Lex is that the letter of credit issued by the Last Bank of Nigeria may not be paid.

3. Lex should request a letter of credit that is confirmed by his bank, thereby making his bank also liable for payment of the letter of credit.

CHAPTER 33
CONSUMER PROTECTION

Matching Exercise	
1. Consumer	5. Subprime lending market
2. Consumer credit	6. Franchise
3. Predatory lending	7. Punitive damages
4. Compensatory damages	8. Property report

True/False

1. T	6. T
2. T	7. T
3. T	8. F
4. T	9. T
5. F	10. F

Multiple Choice

1. d	6. a
2. a	7. a
3. d	8. b
4. c	9. d
5. b	10. c

Case Problem

1. The Truth in Lending Act will generally regulate the disclosure of finance terms in this case. This Act applies to any consumer contract that is payable in more than four installments.

2. Farr must disclose (a) the total cash price; (b) the amount of down payment required; (c) the number, amount, and due dates of payments; and (d) the annual percentage rate of credit charges (APR).

Internet Exercise

1. The federal Consumer Credit Protection Act (CCPA) generally regulates creditors' conduct in connection with extending credit to consumers.

2. A helpful site regarding consumer credit may be found at http://www.dol.gov/compliance/laws/comp-ccpa.htm.

3. Under the CCPA, it is illegal for a creditor to discriminate against an applicant for credit on the basis of the person's marital status, age, or because all or a part of the applicant's income is derived from public assistance. As a consequence, Ace Loans violated federal law in this case.

CHAPTER 34
SECURED TRANSACTIONS IN PERSONAL PROPERTY

Matching Exercise	
1. Floating lien	6. Security agreement
2. Perfected security interest	7. Purchase money security interest (PMSI)
3. Consumer good	8. Termination statement
4. Collateral	
5. Financing statement	

True/False	
1. T	6. F
2. T	7. F
3. T	8. F
4. F	9. F
5. T	10. T

Multiple Choice				
1. a	2. c	3. d	4. c	5. d

CPA Review			
1. c	3. a	5. a	7. a
2. d	4. a	6. d	

Case Problem

1. Acme can use self-help to repossess the collateral on Debtor's default, and a court order is not required.

2. Acme cannot commit a breach of the peace in repossessing the collateral. If a breach may occur, a court order must be obtained.

3. Prior to sale, Debtor may redeem by paying the entire debt and all of Acme's attorney's fees and costs..

4. Proceeds from sale are applied first to the expenses incurred in connection with the repossession and sale of the collateral; secondly, to Acme's secured debt; any excess is paid to other secured parties with interests in the collateral; and any remaining surplus is paid to Debtor. Debtor is liable for any deficiency.

Internet Exercise

1. Innumerable goods, both new and used, are offered for sale over the Internet.

2. If you purchase inventory from a merchant and the purchased item is subject to a perfected purchase money security interest, then you have priority to the item. But, if you buy other items, such as equipment, that are subject to a perfected security interest, then the secured party may have priority to the collateral.

CHAPTER 35
BANKRUPTCY

Matching Exercise

1. Proof of claim
2. Preferential transfers
3. Insider
4. Discharge in bankruptcy
5. Voluntary bankruptcy
6. Involuntary bankruptcy
7. Automatic stay
8. Preferences
9. Balance sheet test

True/False		Multiple Choice	
1. F	6. T	1. a	6. b
2. F	7. F	2. c	7. c
3. F	8. T	3. d	
4. T	9. T	4. d	
5. T	10. F	5. b	

CPA Review			
1. d	3. d	5. a	7. c
2. d	4. d	6. a	8. d

Case Problem

1. (a) Yes, Green Oaks may file a petition. (b) If a debtor has less than twelve creditors, any unsecured creditor with a claim of $13,475 or more may file an involuntary petition. Thus, Apple Linen Co. may file an involuntary petition against Green Oaks. (c) Yes, a court would enter an order for relief in this case.

2. First Bank is a secured creditor and, therefore, has priority to enforce its security interest in the building. After secured creditors have enforced their rights, certain unsecured creditors enjoy a priority. In this case, creditors have priority in the following order: Mr. Atkins will be paid his $6,000 trustee fee as a cost of administration; then Tina will be paid her $1,000 in wages because they were earned within 90 days of the filing; then Bud will be repaid his $500 deposit because it was given for consumer goods. Remaining assets are paid to unsecured creditors who have no priority. Thus, Fuller Co. gets the remaining $2,500.

Internet Exercise

1. States may grant exemptions that are more generous than those allowed by the U.S. Bankruptcy Code.

2. Three states with more generous homestead exemptions than are allowed under federal law are: (a) Minnesota ($200,000 for non-agricultural), (b) Florida (no dollar limit), and (c) Oregon ($25,000).

CHAPTER 36
INSURANCE

Matching Exercise

---

1. Insurance agent
2. Beneficiary
3. Endowment insurance
4. Marine insurance
5. Cash surrender value

6. Incontestability clause
7. Double indemnity
8. Term insurance
9. Insurance broker
10. Whole life insurance

True/False

---

1. T
2. T
3. F
4. F
5. T

6. T
7. T
8. F
9. T
10. T

Multiple Choice

---

1. b
2. a

3. c
4. a

CPA Review

| 1. c | 3. d | 5. c | 7. a |
| 2. c | 4. d | 6. b | 8. b |

Case Problem

1. Mario has the burden to prove that the loss was covered by the policy.

2. Yes, in order to enforce the policy, Mario must have had an insurable interest in the building at the time the loss occurred.

3. Mario's failure to carry the minimum amount of insurance required by the policy's coinsurance clause will reduce, but not eliminate, his right to recover for the loss.

4. Mario can recover $7,500. The amount of recovery is the covered loss of $10,000 multiplied by: the actual insurance carried ($60,000) divided by the required minimum insurance ($80,000), i.e., three-fourths.

Internet Exercise

1. Numerous sites offer practical information regarding what insurance is appropriate for an individual or a business.

2. Amber should get health and disability insurance to protect herself. For her business, she should obtain fire insurance and public liability insurance.

CHAPTER 37
AGENCY

Matching Exercise

1. Power of attorney
2. Universal agent
3. Agent
4. Apparent authority
5. Attorney in fact
6. Express authority
7. Independent contractor
8. General agent
9. Principal
10. Special agent

True/False			Multiple Choice	
1. F	6. T		1. d	6. c
2. F	7. F		2. c	7. d
3. T	8. F		3. b	8. a
4. T	9. T		4. d	9. a
5. F	10. F		5. a	

CPA Review

1. c	4. d	7. d	10. a
2. c	5. b	8. b	11. c
3. b	6. b	9. b	

Case Problem

1. (a) Aurora had apparent authority. Aurora did not have express authority because Carl told her not to make such contracts. But, Carl's conduct in appointing Aurora as manager and in referring the supplier to her misled the supplier into believing that she had authority to represent Carl. (b) Yes, Carl is obligated to perform the contract. A principal is bound by a contract made by an agent with apparent authority.

2. (a) Robin's express (actual) authority terminated on June 8 when she received notice of her termination. (b) Robin had apparent authority to make the June 10 contract on behalf of Haskins. Because Robin had previously dealt with Sun Co., she had apparent authority to bind Haskins to a contract with Sun Co. until Sun Co. was given actual notice of her termination. (c) Because Robin had apparent authority, Haskins is obligated to perform the contract. (d) Upon terminating Robin, Haskins should have immediately given notice of her termination to Sun Co. and all other parties with whom Robin had previously dealt.

Internet Exercise

1. Information regarding states that have enacted the Uniform Durable Power of Attorney Act may be found via http://www.nccusl.org/nccusl/uniformact_factsheets/uniformacts-fs-udpaa.asp.

2. Forty-three states, the District of Columbia and the U.S. Virgin Islands have enacted this uniform act or a version of it.

CHAPTER 38
THIRD PERSONS IN AGENCY

Matching Exercise	
1. Disclosed principal	6. Soliciting agent
2. Vicarious liability	7. Contracting agent
3. *Respondeat superior*	
4. Partially disclosed	
5. Undisclosed principal	

True/False	
1. F	6. F
2. T	7. T
3. T	8. T
4. T	9. F
5. T	10. F

Multiple Choice	
1. b	4. d
2. a	5. b
3. c	

CPA Review				
1. a	3. c	5. c	7. b	9. c
2. c	4. c	6. b	8. a	

Case Problem

1. The relationship between Donna and Pace is that of owner-independent contractor. Donna had only the right to control the final result to be produced by Pace. Donna did not have the right to control the manner or method by which the work was to be performed.

2. No, Donna is not liable for Roger's injury. An owner is generally not liable for a tort committed by an independent contractor or by an independent contractor's employee.

3. Under the doctrine of *respondeat superior*, Pace is liable to Roger for his injuries because Roger was injured due to the negligence of the Pace employee who was acting within the scope of employment.

Internet Exercise

1. *Burlington Industries, Inc. v. Ellerth*, 524 U.S. 742 (1998), addresses the issues raised in this case.

2. Under the reasoning in *Burlington Industries*, Baker Corp. has vicarious liability for Clay's actions. The Supreme Court stated that an employer is liable for a supervisor's conduct if the supervisor actually took adverse actions against an employee because the employee refused the supervisor's unwelcomed sexual requests. Moreover, the employer in this situation is liable even if the employer does not know about the supervisor's wrongful conduct.

CHAPTER 39
REGULATION OF EMPLOYMENT

Matching Exercise	True/False		Multiple Choice
1. Economic strikers	1. T	6. T	1. c
2. Primary picketing	2. F	7. T	2. b
3. Mass picketing	3. F	8. F	3. b
4. Secondary picketing	4. T	9. T	4. c
5. Employment-at-will	5. F	10. T	5. d
6. Shop right			
7. Right-to-work laws			

CPA Review

1. d	3. c	5. b	7. c
2. d	4. a	6. a	8. c

Case Problems

1. (a) Weiss Co. can legally discharge Henry. Henry is an employee at will because his employment contract does not state a fixed duration of employment. Thus, Weiss Co. is entitled to discharge Henry at any time and for no reason, even though he has properly performed his job. (b) Weiss Co. cannot legally discharge Ellen because public policy typically forbids discharging an employee for filing a workers' compensation claim. (c) Weiss Co. cannot legally discharge Karen. Karen can be prematurely discharged only for good cause because she was employed for a fixed term. Weiss Co. does not have good cause to discharge Karen since she has properly performed her job.

2. (a) The company was required to negotiate the wage increase with the union because this is a mandatory subject of bargaining. The company was not required to negotiate internal management policies that are unrelated to the employees. (b) The union is legally entitled to call a strike because the company refused the union's economic demands. (c) Yes, the union is entitled to engage in primary picketing, i.e., placing persons around the company's place of business. (d) Because the employees are "economic strikers" (i.e., they are striking for economic reasons), the company would not be required to fire replacement workers in order to give the strikers their former jobs.

3. (a) Employee Retirement Income Security Act regulates employee pension funds, such as Pell Corp.'s plan. (b) Isabel's rights to pension benefits must vest within 5 or 7 years. (c) The Pension Benefit Guaranty Corporation essentially guarantees that employees will be paid their benefits even if an employer goes out of business.

Internet Exercise

1. The Fair Labor Standards Act governs this case. Regulations interpreting this Act are set forth in 29 CFR 570, which may be found at http://www.gpoaccess.gov/cfr/index.html.

2. Tracy may hire any of the three teenagers for the dishwasher position (*see* 29 CFR 570.34). However, she can hire only the 16- or 18-year-old for the short order cook position. (*see* 29 CFR 570.120).

CHAPTER 40
EQUAL EMPLOYMENT OPPORTUNITY LAW

Matching Exercise

1. Disparate impact
2. Discrimination
3. Bona fide occupational qualification
4. Equal Pay Act
5. Age Discrimination in Employment Act

6. Hostile work environment
7. Affirmative action plan
8. Americans with Disabilities Act (ADA)
9. EEOC
10. Race

True/False

1. F
2. T
3. F
4. T
5. T

6. T
7. T
8. T
9. F
10. T

Multiple Choice

1. a
2. d
3. c
4. a
5. c

6. a
7. d
8. b
9. c
10. b

CPA Review

1. a

2. b

3. b

Case Problem

1. It is wrong for the hotel to refuse to hire Kim because she has a slight accent. Refusing to hire Kim for this reason is discrimination on the basis of her national origin and constitutes a violation of Title VII.

2. It is improper to refuse Kim employment because she is fifty years old. Doing so constitutes intentional discrimination on the basis of age and violates the Age Discrimination in Employment Act.

3. Refusal to hire Kim because she has a hearing impairment violates the Americans with Disabilities Act. An employer cannot refuse to hire a person if the person is qualified to perform the essential functions of the job with a reasonable accommodation. In this case, it would be reasonable to require a large hotel to expend $250 to accommodate Kim's disability.

Internet Exercise

1. Yes, Sarah has a claim against Cook Corp. for sexual harassment.

2. The EEOC home page is located at http://www.eeoc.gov/. To file a sexual harassment claim, Sarah must file a charge with the EEOC by mail or phone. She must file the charge within 180 days of the discriminatory conduct, provided that different time requirements apply if the charge must first be filed with the state.

CHAPTER 41
TYPES OF BUSINESS ORGANIZATIONS

Matching Exercise

1. Cooperative
2. Unincorporated association
3. Franchisee
4. Joint venture
5. Franchise

6. Partnership
7. Franchisor
8. Sole or individual proprietorship

True/False

1. F
2. T
3. T
4. F
5. T

6. T
7. T
8. F
9. T
10. F

Multiple Choice

1. a
2. b
3. c

4. d
5. a

CPA Review

1. b	3. b	5. b	7. b
2. c	4. d	6. a	

Case Problem

1. The business relationship between Sugarland and Carlos is a franchise. Sugarland and Carlos are independent contractors.

2. Pursuant to the foregoing rule, Sugarland is not liable to Tom. However, Sugarland is liable to Sue because Sugarland's own action, the manufacture of the defective candy, gives rise to product liability on the part of Sugarland.

3. Yes, a franchisee is liable for his or her own contracts and torts. Therefore, Carlos is liable to Tom because Carlos was negligent.

Internet Exercise

1. The *Borrower's Guide for SBA Loans* may be found at www.sba.gov./gopher/Financial-Assistance/General-Information-And-Publications/gen4.txt.

2. The SBA's primary domestic loan program is the 7(a) Guaranty Program. Pursuant to this program, the SBA will guarantee up to 80 percent of loans for $100,000 or less, and up to 75 percent of loans between $100,000 and $750,000.

CHAPTER 42
PARTNERSHIPS

Matching Exercise

1. Express authority
2. General partnership
3. Tenancy in partnership
4. Articles of partnership
5. General partners
6. Charging order
7. Operation of law

True/False

1.	T	6.	T
2.	T	7.	F
3.	T	8.	T
4.	F	9.	T
5.	F	10.	F

Multiple Choice

1.	c	4.	b	7.	d
2.	b	5.	d	8.	c
3.	a	6.	b	9.	b

CPA Review

1.	b	5.	c	9.	c	13.	c
2.	a	6.	a	10.	d		
3.	c	7.	d	11.	c		
4.	d	8.	a	12.	d		

Case Problem

1. Bonnie and Tess cannot indefinitely continue the partnership business. Unless otherwise agreed, a partnership business must be wound up following a dissolution.

2. In general, all surviving or remaining partners have a right to participate in the winding up of a partnership. Consequently, Bonnie and Tess will wind up the partnership.

4. Partnership assets will be distributed in the following order: (1) Rosco, the outside creditor, will be paid $20,000; (2) Tess will be repaid her $10,000 advance; (3) Clay's estate will be paid $15,000 on account of Clay's contribution to the partnership, Bonnie will be repaid her $10,000 contribution, and Tess will be repaid her $5,000 contribution; and (4) the remaining $30,000 will be distributed to Clay's estate, Bonnie, and Tess according to the ratio for sharing profits, so each party will receive $10,000.

Internet Exercise

Some of the states that have enacted a version of the Revised Uniform Partnership Act are Wyoming, Montana, North Dakota, Florida, and West Virginia.

CHAPTER 43
LPs, LLCs AND LLPs

Matching Exercise

1. Manager
2. General partner
3. Articles of organization
4. Certificate of limited partnership
5. Member

6. Limited liability partnership
7. Limited partner
8. Operating agreement
9. Limited partnership
10. Limited liability company

True/False

1. F
2. T
3. T
4. T
5. F

6. F
7. T
8. T
9. T
10. T

Multiple Choice

1. d
2. a

3. a
4. b

CPA Review

1. b

Case Problem

1. An LLP is liable for the acts of its authorized agents under rules of agency law and for the conduct of employees and partners who are acting within the scope of employment under the doctrine of *respondeat superior*. Thus, the LLP in this case is liable for Fiona's negligence.

2. In an LLP, a partner is personally liable for wrongs that he or she personally commits or for wrongs committed by persons whom the partner is supervising. Thus, Fiona is liable for her own negligence.

3. A partner in an LLP does not have personal liability for torts committed by others who are acting on behalf of the partnership provided that the partner is not also participating in or supervising this activity. Derrick therefore is not personally liable for Fiona's negligence.

Internet Exercise

1. A limited liability partnership would allow your mother's law firm to continue as a partnership but shield her from liability for malpractice committed by others in her firm.

2. At time of publication, the National Conference of Commissioners on Uniform State Laws has prepared a Uniform Limited Liability Partnership Act. This draft may be found *via* http://www.law.cornell.edu/uniform/vol7.html - partn.

CHAPTER 44
CORPORATION FORMATION

Matching Exercise	
1. Certificate of incorporation	6. Articles of incorporation
2. Bylaws	7. Ultra vires
3. De facto	8. Close corporation
4. Promoter	9. Treasury stock
5. Conglomerate	10. Public corporation

True/False

1. T	6. T
2. T	7. F
3. F	8. T
4. F	9. T
5. F	10. F

Multiple Choice

1. d	4. a
2. b	
3. d	

CPA Review

1. d	3. c	5. a
2. c	4. a	

Case Problem

1. If the articles are silent, the RMBCA and many states automatically grant a corporation the same powers as individuals to do what is necessary or convenient to carry out the corporation's business.

2. In most states, the corporation's name must indicate that the enterprise is a corporation.

3. Yes, the corporation can be granted perpetual life, i.e., it may have continuous existence unaffected by the death of a shareholder.

4. Yes, a corporation can be empowered to buy, sell, and mortgage real and personal property.

5. The corporation need not have a seal unless it is required by statute or a seal would be required of an individual.

Internet Exercise

Three federal public corporations or quasi-public corporations include the Federal Deposit Insurance Corporation (insures deposits in federally chartered banks), the National Railroad Passenger Corporation (provides national passenger transportation by rail), and the Pension Benefit Guaranty Corporation (insures private pension funds).

CHAPTER 45
SHAREHOLDER RIGHTS IN CORPORATIONS

<table>
<tr><td colspan="2">Matching Exercise</td></tr>
<tr>
<td>
1. Par value
2. Bond
3. Common stock
4. Preferred stock
5. Book value
</td>
<td>
6. Derivative (secondary) action
7. Stock subscription
8. Certificate of stock
9. Proxy
10. Voting trust
</td>
</tr>
<tr><td colspan="2">True/False</td></tr>
<tr>
<td>
1. F
2. F
3. T
4. T
5. F
</td>
<td>
6. T
7. T
8. T
9. F
10. F
</td>
</tr>
<tr><td colspan="2">Multiple Choice</td></tr>
<tr>
<td>
1. d
2. c
3. b
</td>
<td>
4. c
5. c
6. c
</td>
</tr>
<tr><td colspan="2">CPA Review</td></tr>
<tr>
<td>
1. d
2. c
</td>
<td>
3. c   5. b
4. b   6. c
</td>
</tr>
</table>

Case Problem

1. Only Earl and Antonio are entitled to vote. In general, preferred stockholders are not entitled to vote.

2. Earl will elect two directors, and Antonio will elect one director. Under cumulative voting, a party may cast a number of votes equal to the number of shares owned multiplied by the number of directors being elected. Therefore, Earl will have 180,000 votes and Antonio will have 120,000 votes. By concentrating all of his votes for one candidate, Antonio will be able to elect one director, and Earl will elect the remaining two directors.

3. Yes, Earl may authorize Ann, a third party, to vote his share by giving her a written proxy.

Internet Exercise

1. UCC Article 8 may be found at www.law.cornell.edu/ucc/8/overview.html.

2. UCC §§ 8-407 & 8-408 explain how uncertificated shares of corporate stock are transferred. The owner of uncertificated shares must give to the corporation an appropriate instruction requesting the transfer of shares to another party. The corporation then records the transfer on its books. Within two days, the corporation must send to the new owner an "initial transaction statement," which confirms the transfer of shares.

CHAPTER 46
SECURITIES REGULATION

Matching Exercise

1. Insider	6. Registration statement
2. Short-swing profit	7. Tippee
3. Prospectus	8. Insider information
4. Security	9. Temporary insider
5. Blue sky laws	10. Cash tender offer

True/False

1. F		6. T	
2. T		7. T	
3. T		8. F	
4. T		9. T	
5. T		10. F	

Multiple Choice

1. c	3. b	5. a
2. d	4. a	

CPA Review

1. b	3. c	5. c	7. a
2. d	4. c	6. a	8. a

Case Problem

1. The Securities Exchange Act of 1934 would govern this case because it involves a secondary sale (resale) of securities in interstate commerce.

2. To establish a 10(b)-5 violation, Tom must prove: (a) that the Midas board of directors made an untrue statement of a material fact; (b) that he relied on the board's misrepresentation; and (c) he was injured due to the misrepresentation.

3. In this case, Tom can establish a 10(b)-5 violation by the Midas board of directors. The untrue statements by the board were clearly material, Tom's reliance on the misstatements by the board is presumed, and he suffered an injury because he sold his stock for $10 a share when it was actually worth $20 a share.

Internet Exercise

1. The proposed stock offering by PMI is subject to the registration and prospectus requirements of the Securities Act of 1933. It is an interstate public offering of securities and is not exempt from the 33 Act.

2. The citation for the National Securities Markets Improvement Act is 15 U.S.C. 77r, and it may be found via http://uscode.house.gov/search/criteria.shtml. Pursuant to this Act, the proposed offering in this case is exempt from state blue-sky laws because the securities are traded on NASDAQ.

CHAPTER 47
ACCOUNTANTS' LIABILITY AND MALPRACTICE

Matching Exercise	
1. Comparative negligence	3. Malpractice
2. Exculpatory clause	4. Contributory negligence

True/False	
1. T	6. T
2. T	7. T
3. T	8. T
4. F	9. T
5. T	10. F

Multiple Choice	
1.	4.
2.	5.
3. Malpractice	

CPA Review			
1. c	3. b	5. b	7. b
2. c	4. b	6. b	

Case Problem

1. The financial collapses of Enron and WorldCom during 2001-2002 prompted Congress to undertake reforms of the accounting and auditing professions that are embodied in the Sarbanes-Oxley Act.

2. Some of the broad purposes of the Act include: (a) establishing an accounting oversight board; (b) regulating the independence of auditors; (c) setting rules for corporate responsibility and governance including regulations for company audit committees; and (d) regulating the professional responsibility rules for attorneys who work with companies on certification of financial statements.

Internet Exercise

1. *Ackerman v. Price Waterhouse*, 84 N.Y.2d 535 (1994), may be found at http://www.law.cornell.edu/nyctap/I94_0198.htm.

2. The New York Court of Appeals in *Ackerman* held that the statute of limitations for an accountant's malpractice started to run on the date that the work product was delivered to the client. Applying this rule, Ajax's malpractice claim is barred by the statute of limitations.

3. Other states hold that the statute of limitations for an accountant's negligence in preparing tax returns does not begin until the IRS assesses a penalty. Under this rule, Ajax's claim would not have been barred.

CHAPTER 48
MANAGEMENT OF CORPORATIONS

Matching Exercise

1. Executive committee

2.. Officers

3. Directors

4. Extraordinary corporate matters

5. Quorum

6. Foreign Corrupt Practices Act

7. Business judgment rule

True/False

1. T
2. T
3. T
4. T
5. F

6. T
7. F
8. T
9. F
10. T

Multiple Choice

1. c
2. c
3. d

4. a
5. c

CPA Review

1. d
2. a

3. b
4. b

5. d

Case Problem

1. The party who challenges a board of directors' decision has the burden to prove that the directors acted improperly. Thus, the minority shareholders bear the burden of proof in this case.

2. The business judgment rule determines whether directors are personally liable for losses that a corporation suffers due to their decision.

3. Under this rule, directors are not liable for losses caused by their decision if the decision was made on an informed basis, in good faith, and in the honest belief that it was in the corporation's best interest. Also, this rule creates a presumption that directors acted in accordance with these requirements. In this case, this presumption shields the Ameri directors from liability because they acted on an informed basis and they met the other requirements of this rule.

Internet Exercise

1. The federal Foreign Corrupt Practices Act, 15 U.S.C. 78dd-2, governs the legality of Carl's conduct.

2. The payment to Ahmad, the high-level Kuwait official violated this Act, but the payment to the low-level official did not. CTI may be subject to a fine, and Carl may be subject to a fine not to exceed $100,000 and/or imprisonment for not longer than five years.

CHAPTER 49
REAL PROPERTY

Matching Exercise			
1. Fixture	4. Quitclaim deeds	7. Mortgage	10. Warranty deeds
2. Deed	5. Easement	8. Profits	
3. License	6. Dominant tenement	9. Servient tenement	

True/False		Multiple Choice
1. T	6. F	1. b
2. F	7. T	2. b
3. T	8. F	3. d
4. T	9. T	4. c
5. F	10. F	5. a

CPA Review			
1. c	3. b	5. d	7. b
2. d	4. b	6. d	8. c

Case Problem

1. (a) Under common law, Dee is an invitee because it is implied that she was invited into Maxwell's cafe and her presence was of benefit to Maxwell. (b) Under common law, Maxwell owed Dee a duty to take reasonable steps to discover any danger, and to warn or to eliminate these dangers. (c) Yes, Maxwell is liable to Dee. Maxwell failed to reasonably inspect the premises, which would have revealed the danger.

2. (a) Sandra has superior title. In general, a grantee that is conveyed title to property by valid recorded deed takes the property free from a prior unrecorded deed if the grantee acted in good faith, paid value, and did not have notice of the prior deed. (b) Statutes usually provide that a grantor under a statutory warranty deed makes warranties to a grantee. In this case, Martha breached at least one of these warranties. She breached the warranty that she would do nothing to interfere with Dylan's possession of the home.

3. (a) Yes, unless otherwise agreed, a mortgagor is entitled to sell or transfer mortgaged property. Therefore, Helen was legally entitled to convey the home to Bryson. (b) Yes, Helen is still personally liable to pay the loan. Transfer of mortgaged property does not release a mortgagor from liability unless the mortgagee agrees. (c) Yes, Bryson assumed the loan thereby becoming personally obligated to pay it. .

Internet Exercise

1. Three types of mortgages advertised on the Internet include 30-year mortgages, 15-year mortgages, and adjustable-rate mortgages. The pros and cons of mortgages often depends on the stability of interest rates.

2. In most states, a mortgagee must be first to record its mortgage. In some states, it is also required that the mortgagee have no knowledge of any prior unrecorded mortgages at the time of filing.

CHAPTER 50
ENVIRONMENTAL LAW AND LAND USE CONTROLS

Matching Exercise

1. Environmental impact statement (EIS)
2. National Environmental Policy Act (NEPA)
3. Variance
4. Comprehensive Environmental Response, Compensation, and Liability Act (CERCLA)
5. Zoning

6. Restrictive covenants
7. Clean Air Act
8. Nonconforming use
9. Nuisance

True/False

1. F
2. T
3. T
4. F
5. T

6. T
7. T
8. T
9. F
10. T

Multiple Choice

1. d
2. a

3. a
4. d

Case Problem

1. To determine whether Hank's factory is a nuisance, a court will weigh the seriousness of the harm that the factory causes to the neighbors and the social utility of limiting the noise and traffic in the residential neighborhood, against the social utility of the factory, e.g., it employs 100 people.

2. Yes. An otherwise lawful activity, such as the factory, may constitute a nuisance if it substantially and unreasonably interferes with others' enjoyment and use of their property.

Internet Exercise

1. Pursuant to the Toxic Substances Control Act, 15 U.S.C. 2601 et. seq., the federal agent was entitled to conduct the inspection in question, provided that the agent presented appropriate credentials and a written notice to Chemical Corp. that the inspection was to take place.

2. The Act authorizes the federal government to subpoena persons, such as Chemical's officials, to testify about a firm's compliance with the law.

CHAPTER 51
LEASES

Matching Exercise	
1. Constructive eviction	6. Lessee
2. Escalation clause	7. Assignment (of lease)
3. Lessor	
4. Lease	
5. Covenant of quiet enjoyment	

True/False

1. F	6. T
2. T	7. T
3. T	8. F
4. F	9. T
5. T	10. F

Multiple Choice

1. b	4. c
2. c	5. c
3. b	

CPA Review

1. d	3. c	5. c
2. a	4. c	6. b

Case Problem

1. The agreement between Jackie and Kate is a sublease. Jackie transferred to Kate only a portion of her right to the leased premises.

2. Yes, Jackie is liable to Landlord for the unpaid rent. A sublease does not terminate the original tenant's obligations under a lease.

3. No, Kate is not liable to Landlord for the unpaid rent. Absent an express agreement to the contrary, a sublessee is not bound by the terms of the original lease, and a sublessee does not have an obligation to perform the original lease. Consequently, Landlord cannot hold Kate liable for payment of rent under the original lease.

Internet Exercise

1. Numerous federal regulations govern leasing of federal lands for oil and gas exploration. Many of these regulations are set forth in 43 CFR 3100.

2. Among other things, these regulations dictate who may obtain leases, matters related to surface use rights, and obligations of lessees in using federal property.

CHAPTER 52
DECEDENTS' ESTATES AND TRUSTS

Matching Exercise

1. Antilapse statutes	6. Testator
2. Living wills	7. Personal representatives
3. Lineals	8. Adeemed
4. Probate	9. Devise
5. Abate	10. Intestate succession

True/False

1. T	6. T
2. T	7. F
3. F	8. T
4. F	9. F
5. T	10. F

Multiple Choice

1. c	4. b
2. b	5. a
3. c	

Case Problem

1. Yes, Mona is the trustee. A person who knows that he or she is designated as a trustee is presumed to accept such appointment unless the person states otherwise.

2. Yes, settlor can terminate the trust. A settlor may terminate a trust if the right to do so is stated in the trust agreement.

3. Mona breached her duty to exercise reasonable skill, prudence, and diligence in acting on behalf of the trust. The risky speculative investments violated this standard of conduct.

4. Remedies may include: recovering a judgment against Mona for losses caused by her misconduct; an injunction to prevent further wrongful conduct; and removal of Mona as trustee.

Internet Exercise

1. The Uniform Principal and Income Act (1997) deals with the allocation of trust funds between principal and interest. This uniform law is found at http://www.law.upenn.edu/bll/archives/ulc/upaia/upaia97.htm.

2. Pursuant to § 301 of the Act, the right of the income beneficiary to receive income begins on the date stated in the trust, or if no date is stated, on the date that an asset becomes subject to the trust. The right to income ends the day before the beneficiary dies or another terminating event occurs.